INSIDERS' GUIDE

SANTA FE

by

Anne Hillerman

&

Tamar Stieber

The Insiders' Guide®
An imprint of Falcon® Publishing, Inc.
A Landmark Communications company
P.O. Box 1718
Helena, MT 59624
(800) 582-2665
www.insiders.com

•

Sales and Marketing: Falcon Publishing, Inc.
P.O. Box 1718
Helena, MT 59624
(800) 582-2665
www.falcon.com

•

SECOND EDITION
1st printing

•

•

Printed in the United States of America

•

Front cover photo: Hotel Loretto; Back photo: Apache dancer, Don Strel;
Banner photos: Puye Cliffs, Don Strel; Loretto in winter, Don Strel; Chili ristras, Chris
Corrie; Indian dancer, Chris Corrie; Hot-air balloons, Terry Moore, courtesy of Albuquerque
Convention and Visitors Bureau; Spine photo: Katchina doll, Don Strel

•

Publications from *The Insiders' Guide®* series are available at special discounts for
bulk purchases for sales promotions, premiums, or fundraisings. Special editions,
including personalized covers, can be created in large quantities for special needs.
For more information, please contact Falcon Publishing.

ISBN 1-57380-122-4

Preface

Santa Fe is a jewel of a city. And like a jewel, either in the rough or finely cut, it has many facets, not all of which present themselves at first glance—or even after 36 years, the combined length of time the authors of the *Insiders' Guide to Santa Fe* have lived in this beautiful and complex town. As journalists, we've probed the city from the outside in. As residents, we've explored it from the inside out. We come to this project with different experiences and differing perspectives but with a shared affection and abiding respect for the city we call home. We've tried to impart our knowledge and enjoyment of Santa Fe in an illustrative, entertaining, and thoroughly candid fashion.

This is not meant to be an exhaustive account of what Santa Fe has to offer. That's why we have telephone books. The purpose of the *Insiders' Guide to Santa Fe* is to give you a taste of this extraordinary city, including its natural and cultural history, its physical and spiritual beauty, and, of course, suggestions about where to eat and sleep and what to see and do while you're here. Whether you're staying a couple of days, a couple of weeks, or the rest of your life, we're confident you'll find information in these pages you won't see in other travel guides. Even locals, who will probably look upon this book as more of a curiosity than a guide, may learn a thing or two, just as we did in the course of our research.

As you can see just from the size of this book, Santa Fe has an enormous variety of attractions—its natural beauty and clean, crisp mountain air being high on the list—and distractions, ranging from the down-home to the urbane. For many visitors to the capital of New Mexico, a "backwater" state that even many Americans don't realize is one of our 50, this is a surprising revelation. But keep in mind that, despite its sophisticated trappings, Santa Fe is really just a small town in size and at heart. You're not going to find the same level of service and efficiency here that you would in, say, San Francisco or Miami. What you will find is a beautiful little city with friendly people and a fascinating history that predates Plymouth Rock. You'll also find a city and county deeply in touch with their cultural roots, perhaps more so than most places in the United States. And you'll find ageless mystery here—a magic that has drawn humankind to this very spot for literally thousands of years.

Please keep in mind as you read the *Insiders' Guide to Santa Fe* that people and places change, especially in an area undergoing as much metamorphosis as Santa Fe has in recent years and probably will continue doing far into the new millenium. We can't guarantee that the quality—or even the places—we've discovered in our travels will be the same during yours. Please let us know if you've had either a bad experience or a good one. We care. We update the guide periodically, so if you have comments, suggestions, or recommendations, visit our website at www.insiders.com and send them to us from there. Or write to us in care of:

The Insiders' Guide to Santa Fe
Falcon Publishing, Inc.
P.O. Box 1718
Helena, Montana, 59624

About the Authors

Tamar Stieber

For Tamar Stieber, Santa Fe was merely a stopover on the way to Texas rather than a final destination point. It was the spring of 1988 and she was driving from her home in Berkeley, California, to Austin to visit her sister. With a few weeks to burn, she had mapped out a long, scenic route that would take her through Nevada, Utah, Colorado, and New Mexico before winding up in Texas. Santa Fe was her next-to-last port-of-call.

It took less than two days for the high-desert city to seduce her. Like countless others who have passed beneath the shadow of the Sangre de Cristo Mountains, she was astounded by the region's natural beauty and intrigued by its unique blend of cultures.

Despite her abiding love for Northern California, where she had lived for nine years, Tamar was unable to shake her attraction to New Mexico. In 1989, she left her job at the *Vallejo Times Herald*, where she had arrived only six months earlier after a year and a half at *Sonoma Index-Tribune*. She drove to Santa Fe, where she'd landed a job covering northern New Mexico for one of the local papers. A year later, she won a Pulitzer Prize for a series of stories connecting an over-the-counter-food supplement with a disabling blood disorder she uncovered first in New Mexico.

Now freelancing, Tamar has written for such publications as *The Nation*, *Glamour*, *American Archaeology,* and *New Mexico Magazine* and has been a regular contributor to *The Denver Post*. Her stories have also appeared in the *San Francisco Examiner* and *The Sacramento Bee*. She has won writing awards from the Associated Press Managing Editors, the New Mexico Press Association, and the Albuquerque Press Club. She was also a finalist in 1990 for the prestigious Livingston Award.

Originally from New York—she was born in Brooklyn, raised in the suburbs, and lived in Manhattan for five years—Tamar spent three years in London in the early 1970s, using that city as a base from which to travel throughout Europe. In 1980, she moved to San Francisco, where she got her start in journalism a year later as a secretary for the Associated Press. She quit in 1983 to go back to school, graduating in 1985 from the University of California, Berkeley with a degree in film, a Phi Beta Kappa key, and high honors. She also graduated with high honors in 1988 from the Police Reserve Academy at Napa Valley College in California's wine country.

An avid film fan, Tamar still gets a thrill when the lights go down in a darkened theater and the screen comes alive with moving images. She is also a voracious reader and a tireless, if not particularly gifted, athlete.

Anne Hillerman

Anne Hillerman arrived in Santa Fe (from her birth state of Oklahoma) as a frisky three-year-old and has lived there most of her life. As a girl, she attended Loretto Academy and rode her bike through the open fields from her home in Casa Alegre to the swimming pool at Perez Park.

The oldest of author Tony Hillerman's six children, Anne began writing as a teenager and became a journalist despite good advice to get into a profession where she could make money. After attending the University of Massachusetts and graduating from the University of New Mexico, she got a job as a reporter covering the state legislature in Santa Fe. She met her husband through her next job, education and arts reporter for The (Santa Fe) *New Mexican.* Anne spent many years as editorial page editor for the Albuquerque *Journal North,* the edition of the state-wide newspaper that serves Santa Fe. She now works as a financial writer on the Internet for a venture capital company and as a freelance writer.

Anne is the author of three books for children and a nonfiction adventure, *Ride the Wind USA to Africa.* Her writing has appeared in *New Mexico Magazine, Southwest Art, Santa Fe Woman, New Mexico Almanac, Spirit* (Southwest Airlines) and other airline magazines, the *Los Angeles Times,* and the *Peak Ski Guide.* Among her memorable projects are creating an interactive video to teach managers to improve their communications skills, developing a morning television newscast, writing travel articles on Hawaii, Alaska's Glacier Bay, and, of course, working on the *Insiders' Guide to Santa Fe.* She recently finished her newest book, a collection of stories that feature children from different cultures as heroes.

Anne has won awards for her articles from the National Federation of Press Women, New Mexico Press Association, New Mexico Associated Press Managing Editors, and New Mexico Press Women. In addition to honoring as a writer, New Mexico Press Women also named her "Woman of Achievement."

When she's not working, Anne likes to ski, read, do volunteer projects with children, and travel. She, her photographer husband, and their son live in the Santa Fe foothills where they enjoy the sunsets and not having a lawn to mow.

Deep blue skies, towering clouds, and sandstone formations provide the visitor with stunning landscapes.

Photo: Don Strel

About the Photos . . .

Don Strel of Southwest Assignments Ltd. gathered the photographs for the *Insiders' Guide to Santa Fe,* and many of the images used are his own. Strel has been photographing Santa Fe and the Southwest for the last 30 years. His work has been featured in national and international magazines and newspapers including *Ski, Skiing, Los Angeles Times, Detroit Free Press, Atlanta Journal Constitution,* and the *Albuquerque Journal.* His photographs were also included in two recent books—*Ride the Wind, USA to Africa* and *Christmas Celebration, Santa Fe Traditions, Foods and Crafts.* If you would like to contact Strel regarding his work, write to him at Southwest Assignments, 304 Calle Oso, Santa Fe, NM 87501, call (505) 983-5615 or e-mail to swassign@ix.netcom.com

Acknowledgments

Anne

Introducing your beloved home town to strangers, even interested strangers, is a tremendous responsibility. I find Santa Fe endearing, and I hope the city will shine brightly in your eyes too.

Santa Fe is a beautiful town filled with interesting, original people. It's a place justly proud of its history and its multicultural richness, which are reflected in the arts, architecture, the names of the streets and on the faces of the people you'll meet here.

I was honored to work on the first *Insiders' Guide to Santa Fe* and grateful to have been asked to help write this second edition. Despite having been a Santa Fe resident for more than 25 years, I learned a lot about my home town through my work on Insiders'. Luckily, Santa Fe is filled with eager teachers. I visited museums and galleries I hadn't seen, ate in restaurants I'd always meant to get to, and attended events that, somehow, had missed my attention.

I'd like to thank all the people who helped me with this project, beginning with my husband, Don Strel, who was always available to brainstorm ideas, to read rough drafts, and to offer encouragement and constructive criticism. I'm grateful to my friend, writer Sharon Lloyd Spence, for her loan of Santa Fe materials for the first edition and for her willingness to listen to me complain when the job seemed overwhelming.

I owe historian Stanley Hordes more than just thanks for the time, effort, and energy he spent reviewing the History chapter and trying to steer me on the right path. Thanks to his good advice, I was able to update that section with little difficulty. Special thanks to Joyce Ice of the Museum of International Folk Art for her tremendous assistance on the Regional Arts chapter. Barbara Bellomy of the Museum of New Mexico and Alexis Sabin of *New Mexico Kids* generously shared their professional Insider advice. Jill May of the Santa Fe Ski Area and Joyce Idema of the Santa Fe Opera both went out of their way to make sure I had what I needed for the book.

Thanks to the many cheerful and gracious public relations staff members, secretaries, restaurant managers, and other people who answered questions and provided information for me to work with. Pattie Freeman, Cindy Bellinger, and Carrie Reinecke helped with phone calls and faxing for fact checking. I couldn't have done this job without these smart, well-organized women who, thank goodness, are also blessed with a good sense of humor.

Finally, thanks to editor Erin Turner for her understanding when the death of a dear friend and the Cerro Grande Fire caused me to miss some deadlines. I had more fun than I thought I would doing something called "work."

Tamar

In memory of Mildred West, John West, and my beloved dogs Boyo and Seamus. I'm deeply greateful to the friends and family who helped this project flow, including writer and film historian Joseph Dispenza for his friendship, encouragement and finely honed wit; Camille Flores for her inner and outer beauty, and her loyal and steadfast friendship; new friends Sally and Alan Greenall for their selflessness and moral support; historian Stan Hordes for his enthusiasm, historical acumen, and cultural sensitivity; friend and librarian Judy Klinger for her dogged, detailed, and reliable research at the drop of a hat and her compassion, both personal and professional; Marco Macchione for providing a temporary office, a timely haven and welcome laughter; Irene, Michael and Shane Mayer-Feldberg for opening their home and their hearts and for unhesitatingly coming to the rescue; Carl Miller, Sandra Thomas, and the rest of the gang at Carl & Sandra's for keeping body, mind and spirit intact; Orlando Romero, director of the Fray Angélico Chávez History Library, for his interest, his keen local perspective, and for sharing some of the myths behind the stories and vice versa; Florence and Fred Stieber for more than they'll ever know; Jerry West for his eagerness to share information, for entrusting me with much-loved books, and especially for his friendship; Letta Wofford, for providing a constant source of inspiration and information, for her bottomless resilience and internal fortitude, and for her indefatigable sense of humor.

Special thanks go to my co-author, Anne Hillerman, for her professionalism, camaraderie, and never-ending supply of clippings, books and suggestions; and our editor, Erin Turner, for her unceasing patience, flexibility, encouragement, and good cheer despite an overwhelming workload.

Thanks, too, to the many others who went the extra mile to provide vital information, share a personal perspective or, in some cases, offer a shoulder: Kim Alderwick, the Rev. Talitha Arnold of United Church of Santa Fe; Richard Atkinson, manager of the Public Lands Information Center; Liz Stefanics, director of Open Hands; Baptist Church historian Betty Danielson; Don Jones; Shane Miller; Terry Nefos, former director of Santa Fe Transit Services and Aviation; Mike Pitel, retired state tourism spokesman; Chrissy Salazar of Presbyterian Medical Services, Albuquerque International Sunport spokeswoman Maggie Santiago; Jean Schaumberg; Ron Shirley, the City of Santa Fe's Parks Division director; State Historian Robert Torrez; Ingrid Vollnhofer and Norma McCallan from the State Library's Southwest Room; Pueblo historian Dave Warren; Santa Fe Economic Development Planner Steve Whitman; Arbitron's Dave Willinski; and Danielle and Lee Wilson.

And a very special note of appreciation to the late Fray Angélico Chávez, whose books on northern New Mexico—in particular, *My Penitente Land*—proved invaluable in helping to unravel some of the misconceptions about my chosen home without diminishing one iota from its myriad and wonderful mysteries.

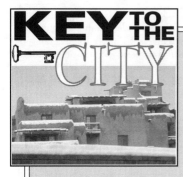

KEY TO THE CITY

Vital Statistics

Mayor:
Larry Delgado

Governor:
Gov. Gary Johnson

Capital of New Mexico:
Santa Fe

Other major cities:
Albuquerque, Las Cruces, Los Alamos, Taos, Roswell

Population:
Santa Fe 67,879; Santa Fe County 123,386; New Mexico 1,736,931

Area of Santa Fe:
37.3 square miles

Santa Fe's Nickname:
The City Different

Santa Fe's Average Temperatures:
July: High 91, Low 57
January: High 40, Low 19

Average rainfall:
14 inches

Average snowfall:
32 inches

Average number of sunny days per year:
300

Santa Fe founded: 1608
New Mexico achieved statehood: 1912

Major universities:
College of Santa Fe, St. John's College, Santa Fe Community College

Major area employers:
Santa Fe Public Schools, U.S. Government, St. Vincent Hospital, City of Santa Fe

Major airports:
Albuquerque International about 60 miles to the south

Major interstates:
Interstate 25 north-south

Public transportation:
Santa Fe Trails bus system serves the city of Santa Fe

Driving laws:
Seat belts and child restraints are mandatory.
If you are taking up residency in New Mexico, you must surrender your license from any other state and apply for a New Mexico license within 30 days of moving to New Mexico. All first-time licensees in New Mexico, ages 18 to 24, inclusive (not required for persons 25 years and older) are required to take the "None for the Road" DWI awareness class. The fee is $16 for a four-year license or $32 for an eight-year license. Drivers who are 75 years old or older must renew their licenses yearly, but they are not charged renewal fees.

Alcohol laws:
You must be 21 to drink in New Mexico, and you can buy alcohol of all sorts after 12 noon in supermarkets and elsewhere. The bars may remain open until 2 AM. In New Mexico the legal limit for blood-alcohol content is 0.08 for drivers. Administrative license suspension for the first offense is 90 days, with the possibility of restored driving privileges after 30 days of the suspension. There is no mandatory jail time or community service for the first DWI offence.

Daily newspapers:
The *Santa Fe New Mexican*, *Journal North Edition of the Albuquerque Journal*

Sales tax:
Gross receipts tax is 6.437 percent on all goods and services including food inside the city limits.

Room tax:
11.25 percent

The Chamber of Commerce:
510 N. Guadalupe St., Suite N., (505) 988-3279

Visitor Center and Convention Bureau: 201 W. Marcy at Sweeney Center, (505) 995-6200, (800) 777-2489

Time and Temperature:
(505) 473-2211

Important phone numbers:
911 emergency
(505) 983-3361 St. Vincent Hospital

Towering clouds and expansive vistas are among Santa Fe's attractions.

Photo: Don Strel

Table of Contents

Directory of Maps

Santa Fe and Surrounding Area

NAVAJO LAKE

84

CARSON NATIONAL FOREST

522

CARSON NATIONAL FOREST

CARSON NATIONAL FOREST

64
84

SAN JUAN MTNS.

64

64

Jicarilla Apache Indian Reservation

84

Taos

N

68

SANTA FE NATIONAL FOREST

TURKEY MTNS.

25

CORNUDO HILLS

Los Alamos

Santa Fe

CIBOLA NATIONAL FOREST

NACIMENTO MTNS.

Santa Fe Municipal Airport

84

Las Vegas

SAN MATEO MTNS.

RIO SALADO

14
(Turquoise Trail)

Albuquerque

40

40

Laguna Indian Reservation

25

RIO GRANDE

60

54

Alamo Navajo Indian Reservation

60

Metropolitan Santa Fe

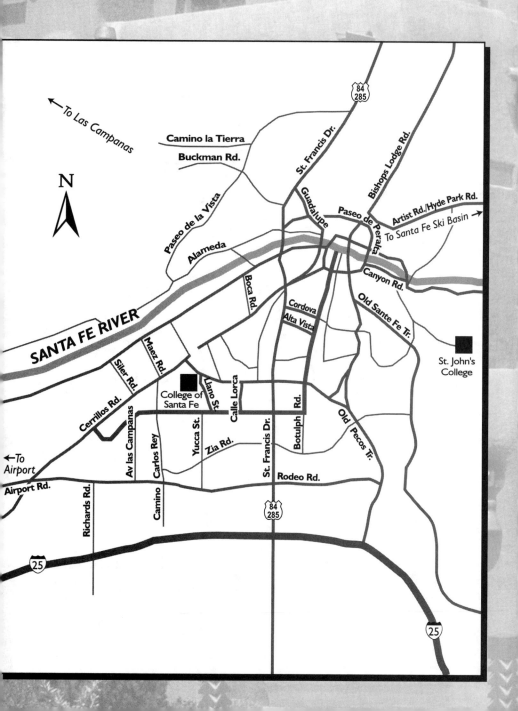

Downtown Santa Fe

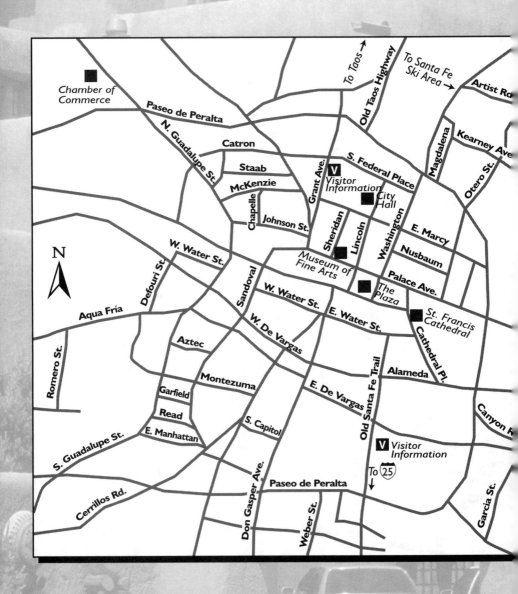

How to Use This Book

Where you start reading the *Insiders' Guide to Santa Fe* depends on your needs. One of the things we've liked about writing this book, and one of the things we hope you'll appreciate as you read it, is that each chapter is packed with useful information designed to be accessible and, we hope, entertaining. In this our second edition, we've added new "Close-ups," stories that give you insights into some of the people, places, and events that make our area special. Throughout the text you'll find tips that provide an Insider's look into our beautiful city.

If you're on the plane heading for New Mexico, you'll probably want to look at the Getting Around chapter to help you figure out the best way to get from the Albuquerque airport to Santa Fe. If you're using the book to plan a vacation, our extensive accommodations chapters offer valuable information for finding a motel, bed and breakfast, deluxe resort, or vacation rental. Use the Annual Events chapter to discover if a festival or something special is going on when you plan to be in town. The maps will help you find Santa Fe's sights and attractions.

We've got it covered in terms of what to do and where to go when you get here, too. The Attractions chapter, for example, gives you a comprehensive overview of Santa Fe's historic buildings, museums, and other places of interest. Kidstuff offers an overview of what to do to keep the little ones happy. Add the Parks and Recreation, Nightlife, and Arts chapters, and you have a cornucopia of ideas, from galleries to golf, from hikes in the mountains to evenings with Mozart, from pottery classes to poetry readings.

To help visitors gain a greater appreciation for our town, the book includes a readable thumbnail history of the city from its prehistoric days as an Indian hunting camp to the present, post-atomic age. You'll find a layman's explanation of the American Indian and Hispanic cultures as reflected in the city's contemporary life and some suggestions on shopping for the handmade arts and crafts famous in both these traditions. Unlike most guidebooks, we include a close look at the diversity of religions and spiritual practices available here, and information on education, mainstream and alternative health services, and childcare. If you're considering a move to Santa Fe, be sure to read our Neighborhoods and Real Estate chapter for a comprehensive overview.

We've attempted, above all else, to give you information you can use to enrich your visit here or to help you decide if Santa Fe would be an appropriate place for you to live. If you've used other books in the Insiders' Guide series (and if you haven't, we hope you will), you'll find this book similar in terms of content. This edition's fresh design makes the information more accessible.

Finally, we beg your indulgence if you encounter phone numbers or addresses that have changed since publication. For example, at the time our guide went to press, the area code for all of New Mexico was 505, but

Taking a tour of Santa Fe will give the visitor a feel for the old and new.

plans were afoot to make some changes. We verified addresses and websites—but the currents of change run strongly here. Shops come and go; restaurants change owners, chefs, and focus; hotels move from private ownership to corporate properties; galleries get new artists. This ever-changing scene—against the city's historic backdrop—keeps Santa Fe fresh and interesting.

If you'd like to share your own Insiders' tips with us, we'd love to hear from you. You can write in care of Insiders' Guides, Falcon Publishing, P.O. Box 1718, Helena, Mt. 59624 or visit www.insiders.com and drop us an e-mail from there.

Area Overview

July 17, 1997, marked yet another scorching day in New Mexico's capital city. The heat spell that started nearly a month earlier was beginning to take its toll on this high desert community unaccustomed to prolonged temperatures in the 90s. Located in the north-central mountains of the state—just 60 miles north of Albuquerque but a full 2,000 feet higher—Santa Fe's 7,000-foot elevation normally precludes more than a handful of such blistering hot days each year. Soaring mercury notwithstanding, it felt like just another weekday in the bustling, quaintly beautiful downtown as locals and tourists alike lounged in the Plaza, seeking shelter from the unforgiving sun under trees or with the cool comfort of an ice cream cone from the busiest Häagen Dazs in the country.

But this particular Thursday was no ordinary day, not even for a town where the peculiar and the remarkable are often perceived as banal—hence Santa Fe's moniker, "The City Different." On Johnson Street, just a few blocks northwest of the Plaza, some 5,000 people were lining up in a queue that overflowed into neighboring Grant, Griffin, and McKenzie Streets. Many would wait up to an hour and a half to be among the first to cross the threshold of the sparkling, 13,000-square-foot Georgia O'Keeffe Museum on opening day.

LOOK FOR:
• Tricultural Harmony
• Growing Pains
• Quality of Life
• Things To Do
• Local Color—Santa Fe Style
• Politics Food
• Language
• Tolerance
• Bievenidos

As Oscar-winning actor Gene Hackman—one of Santa Fe's many celebrated residents and a board member of the new museum—gave the keynote speech, the staff at nearby Woolworth's was reeling from a different sort of news. In just a few months, the five-and-dime would close its doors forever, never to sell another handkerchief, hair net, or one of its famous original Frito pies. For more than 60 years, Woolworth's stubbornly remained a stalwart Plaza landmark, one of the last vestiges of old Santa Fe in a downtown overflowing with upscale galleries, restaurants, and trinket shops.

It was a striking juxtaposition of events, and completely serendipitous. Woolworth's corporate offices in New York surely had no idea that their announcement to close every Woolworth's in the nation would coincide with the grand opening of a Santa Fe museum dedicated to artist Georgia O'Keeffe—an East Coast émigrée whose paintings of red

INSIDERS' TIP

New Mexico's official state symbol is the Zia, an ancient sun sign taken from a design seen on a late-19th-century water jar from Zia Pueblo. The New Mexico flag—designed in 1923 by Reba Mera and officially recognized two years later, features a Zia symbol in red on a field of bright gold. Those were the colors of Queen Isabel of Castilla, which the Spanish conquistadores brought with them to the New World.

hills, bleached bones, and cerulean skies would, for millions around the world, become synonymous with New Mexico and the American Southwest.

Here was a perfect metaphor for what Santa Fe had become, perhaps what it has always been—a confluence of contradictions where the old and the new, the practical and the luxurious, the working stiffs and the well-to-do live side-by-side in a constant state of often creative, occasionally troublesome tension known as "tricultural harmony."

History

For those of you who still believe the Pilgrims were the first Europeans to settle in what would become the United States of America, throw away your old Anglo-centric textbooks and ideas and take note: Santa Fe was founded around 1608. That's 12 years before the Pilgrim's landed on Plymouth Rock, making Santa Fe America's oldest state capital and its second-oldest city. Only St. Augustine, Florida, founded in 1563, is older.

You can almost feel the history buzz beneath your feet as you walk the narrow, winding streets of downtown Santa Fe toward the Plaza—the social, commercial, and historical heart of the city. The Plaza is the site of the original settlement of Santa Fe. It's also where the Santa Fe Trail—the 19th century trade route that originated in Independence, Missouri—ended and el Camino Real, the 16th century "Royal Road" or "King's Highway" from Mexico City, began.

A few structures, such as the Palace of the Governors on the Plaza's north side, actually date back to the 17th century. But most downtown buildings have been renovated or newly built with facades of adobe-colored stucco designed to blend in with the early 20th century Spanish-Pueblo revival architecture whose earth tones, flat roofs, small, deeply set windows, and protruding vigas (log beams) and canales

INSIDERS' TIP

Don't assume that because you're out of the big city, you're out of the woods when it comes to crime. Santa Fe has a high rate of thefts, especially from automobile break-ins, which accounted for nearly 40 percent of all property crimes in 1996. Lock your car at all times and avoid leaving tempting items in plain view. Try to park in well-trafficked areas or at least well-lighted ones.

(rectangular overhead drainage pipes) imitate construction methods used for centuries by the Pueblo Indians. You'll also see examples of the Territorial style, a relative of Greek revival architecture that first came to Santa Fe in 1846 with the U.S. occupation. These buildings, both old and new, are characterized by red brick facades, slender exterior columns, dentiled cornices, and larger windows and doors than in classical Spanish-Pueblo revival buildings like the Museum of Fine Arts and La Fonda Hotel on the Plaza. Whatever and wherever the architecture, you're likely to find a pendulous red chile ristra hanging welcomingly from a viga or portal (porch).

Despite its facelift and a proliferation of tourist-oriented businesses, the Plaza remains the soul of Santa Fe—a meeting place for old-timers and newcomers, for lunch breaks and lovers' trysts, for political rallies and historical festivals, or just to put your feet up and sleep.

Tricultural Harmony

Though many ethnic groups coexist in Santa Fe, the three that dominate are Hispanics, Native Americans and "Anglos"—a category that refers to anyone who's not Hispanic or Native American, including such distinctly non-Anglo ethnicities as Italians, Jews, and Poles, and sometimes even Asians and African Americans! Together, they create a fascinating mosaic of cultures and values that overlap and occasionally conflict. Voices are sometimes raised, as are fists—the latter only figuratively as a rule. Much of the of the tension stems from ethnic and economic reapportionment.

Only 30 years ago, Santa Fe was a relatively poor, primarily Hispanic town where Anglos comprised a mere 35 percent of the population. Today, Hispanics are in the minority for the first time in recent history—48 percent to Anglos' 49 percent. Though the margin is tiny, it is hugely symbolic of a growing sense among Hispanics that wealthy Anglos have invaded what was once a tranquil little town and, however unwittingly, overshadowed the traditional culture. To a lesser—or at least less vocal—extent, Santa Fe's Native American community shares many of these sentiments. Though only 2.1 percent of the city's population, Indians exert a far greater influence than their numbers imply.

Santa Fe's changing population and complexion leads to an occasional outbreak of resentment directed not only at "newcomers"—a euphemism for even longtime Anglo residents—but toward Santa Fe's bread and butter: tourists. Certainly, there's nothing new about tourist towns biting the hand that feeds them. But in Santa Fe, tourism has supplanted even government as the state capital's chief employer, bringing with it waves of change and a city unsure how to deal with it. Because tourists come with cash—lots of it, in many cases—they unintentionally highlight the growing gap between Santa Fe's haves and have-nots. Sadly, this disparity tends to break down along ethnic lines, creating what the city has termed an "Us versus Them" society. Consequently, in a city renowned for its friendliness, visitors sometimes encounter, a reluctant welcome from overzealous Santa Feans who want to avoid the "Californication" of their home town, as a popular bumper sticker proclaims. Locals are understandably worried that their beautiful little city will turn into a mini-Los Angeles or Phoenix, both of them prototypes of unbounded growth and insidious urban sprawl. And without official intervention, it surely would. But the city and county are striving to safeguard the region's special blend of traditions, cultures and natural beauty—assets that paradoxically draw more newcomers—while at the same time developing economies and housing that will meet the needs of present and future residents.

Growing Pains

Like an adolescent whose emotions can't keep up with his or her physical development, Santa Fe is facing an identity crisis. It's asking itself what it wants to be when it grows up. And growth is definitely a burning issue—perhaps the greatest single issue the city and county face. Santa Fe's beauty, its reputation for tolerance of most lifestyles and, in recent years, it's trendiness have attracted so many new residents that the county's population has tripled over the past 50 years to about 120,000 residents. Of those, 65,000 live within the city limits. That's up nearly a third from the 49,299 who called Santa Fe home in 1980.

Unfortunately, income and housing and especially water haven't kept up with the influx of new bodies. In other words, welcome to Santa Fe, but don't count on a job that will leave much spending money after you've paid your rent or mortgage and your water bill. Although the average weekly wage for 1996 in Santa Fe – $420.52 – was comparable to the national average of $410.72, housing costs on average were 25 percent higher than the rest of the country. For example, one-bedroom apartments rented for an average of $522.16 per month. A two-bedroom apartment cost another $131.85. Meanwhile, the median cost of a house that same year ranged from $139,500 in the most affordable area—the southwest quadrant—to $378,500 in the chi-chi northeast corner of the city.

The question is not only how people manage, but why? In a phrase: quality of life.

Quality of Life

Whatever their differences, Santa Feans agree on at least one thing—they live in a very special place that ranks high on the quality-of-life scale. It's why people come here; it's why they stay.

Quality of life means different things to different people. In Santa Fe, it almost universally refers to the unique combination of small town atmosphere in a centrally located, urban setting with access to a wide variety of cultural activities that range from the urbane to the rustic—all this against a backdrop of extraordinary natural beauty and a healthy climate with crisp, clean mountain air.

Undoubtedly, the most striking thing about Santa Fe is the loveliness and grandeur of the landscape and its brilliant skies. Artists, particularly painters, have been attracted to northern

New Mexico since time immemorial, lured by natural light that is like no other in the world. It's both dazzling and subtle and eternally difficult to capture on canvas. Many have tried, few have succeeded. Even those who have managed to lasso some of the luminescence of a New Mexico sky will tell you their work doesn't approach the real thing.

Of course, this is all part of the mythology of Santa Fe and the American West. And it's why artists migrated en masse to Santa Fe, Taos, and elsewhere in northern New Mexico beginning in the late 19th century. They found themselves enthralled not only by the colorful combination of cultures they found here, but also by the austere beauty of the physical surroundings. For many, it was the most exotic place they'd ever experienced. Their enthusiasm drew other artists and intellectuals who attracted still more of their ilk and, voilá, Santa Fe and its northern neighbor, Taos, turned into artist's colonies.

An hour's drive in any direction will quickly tell you why. The vistas are as fascinating as they are beautiful, changing from minute-to-minute, mile-to-mile. A bend or two in the road can take you from gently rolling hills pocked with piñon, juniper, and scrub brush to flat-topped mesas standing dark and aloof against streaky, iridescent blue skies. Another few miles and you're in the forest among white-barked aspen, ponderosa pine, and depending on the season, snow.

Snow? Seasons? In the desert? Indeed, many visitors come to Santa Fe with the misconception that because it's desert, northern New Mexico is always hot. Wrong! This is high desert; mountain country. That means four distinct seasons, including winters that get an average of 30 to 34 inches of snow each year and attract in the neighborhood of 250,000 skiers from around the world. Santa Fe sits in the foothills of the Sangre de Cristo mountain range at an elevation of 7,000 feet. While the mountains are rugged—Santa Fe Baldy reaches over 12,600 feet, while Wheeler Peak in Taos measures in at 13,161 feet—they also protect the region below from the elements, affording Santa Fe relatively mild weather conditions.

Still, Mother Nature likes to flex her muscles every once in a while with dry, scorching hot spells or brutally cold winters. So be prepared for all possibilities. Generally, however, the seasons are predictable, each arriving with its distinct brand of beauty—perhaps none more vibrantly than autumn.

In fall, the hillsides explode with reds and orange, pinks and purples, and the shimmering gold of aspen groves that streak through the mountains. The colors compel even the most jaded locals to stare in awe at nature's artistry. Many join the tourists at the Santa Fe Ski Area to take a lift up the mountain and get a birds-eye view of the autumn leaves.

Springtime in Santa Fe County is also a sight to behold. The high desert virtually comes alive with wildflowers, the winter-barren earth bursting forth in colorful blooms and—hay fever sufferers beware—pollen. Do bring plenty of extra-strength Allerest but, whatever else you do, don't hide indoors.

Things to Do

If you insist on staying indoors, you can choose from a host of activities: world-class museums for art, history, and native culture; historic buildings and churches; and more than 250 art galleries in a city reputed to be the third-largest art market in the country. Classical music lovers can enjoy the Santa Fe Opera, Santa Fe Chamber Music Festival, and Santa Fe Desert Chorale in summer; Santa Fe Pro Musica from September to May; and the Santa Fe Symphony Orchestra and Chorus year-round.

Santa Fe also offers a nightly assortment of live music and dancing from piano bars and cabaret to salsa, jazz, blues, rock, and much, much more. Flamenco fans look forward to summer when the dazzling María Benítez Teatro Flamenco returns. It's also the season for St. John College's annual Shakespeare in Santa Fe, an outdoor festival where even those who couldn't possibly sit through another performance of The Tempest or The Merchant of Venice can indulge in other diversions, including dining al fresco on gourmet fare. July and August bring Spanish Market and Indian Market which, combined, attract up to 150,000 visitors each year. Equally popular is September's Fiestas de Santa Fe commemorating Don Diego De Vargas' reconquest of New Mexico 12 years after the 1680 Pueblo Revolt. Several days of pageantry and parades culminate in the burning of "Zozobra"—a 40-foot-plus effigy of "Old Man Gloom." (See our Arts and Annual Events chapters for more about these events.)

Then, of course, there's the real outdoors—camping, hiking, bicycling, swimming, tennis, golf, rock-climbing, and horseback riding all within a few miles of town; hunting and fishing, rafting, and hot-air ballooning will require a bit of travel. But few will complain about the scenery along the way. Winter sports include downhill skiing, snowboarding, and even inner tubing down the slopes of the Santa Fe National Forest. Cross-country skiers and snow-shoers can blaze their own trails through the trees.

When all else fails, there's shopping, of course. Whether you're in the market for jewelry, pottery, clothing, or kitsch, you'll be overwhelmed by the number and variety of places to explore.

Local Color—Santa Fe Style

Santa Fe has a unique style that's instantly recognizable. Whether it's art or architecture, food or clothing, home décor or entertainment, it's always colorful, casual, and downright earthy. Architecturally, for example, it doesn't get much earthier than adobe, which after all is mud brick. Even faux adobe buildings are earth-toned and, like the real thing, often trimmed with turquoise window panes and doorways, rough-hewn vigas (log ceiling beams); and bright red chile ristras. Inside you're likely to find terracotta saltillo tile on the floor; hand-painted ceramic tile in the kitchen or bathroom; colorful, geometric-designed Navajo rugs on the walls and/or floors; perhaps a wooden *santo* (religious sculpture) or an Indian pot in a *nicho* (niche) built right into the wall; maybe even a *banco* (earthen bench) on either side of a corner *kiva* fireplace. Some homes will feature handcrafted, rustic and usually very expensive Santa Fe style furniture. The price reflects the intricate, hand-carved details whose irregularities and imperfections lend it a rough beauty. Staining or etching in turquoise or other colors can add another few dollar signs to the cost.

Santa Fe also has a distinctive clothing style, conspicuous not only for its color and flair, but for its casualness. You'll rarely see anyone wearing a business suit here—except lawyers, and then only when they're in court, or state legislators, many of whom are lawyers, and only when they're in session. Cynics might suggest that's because lawyers are among the few in New Mexico who can afford to buy business suits. While there's an element of truth in that, the fact

The Santa Fe River Park walk offers a chance to stroll peacefully under a canopy of cottonwoods.

Photo: Chris Corrie

is that Santa Fe men would rather wear Dockers or denims and bolo ties than business suits and silk ties, while women seem to be more comfortable in prairie skirts and boots than dresses and heels, though you'll see plenty of those, too. Even in Santa Fe's most expensive restaurants, diners are as likely to be dressed in jeans and fancy cowboy boots as Armanis and Donna Karans. Day or night, it's a sure bet you'll see lots of jewelry on both men and women—heavy silver bracelets, watchbands, and rings trimmed with turquoise, onyx, and other stones; concho or silver-buckled leather belts; bolo ties; squash blossom necklaces; big, dangly earrings with crystals and gems on women; men with a small stud or hoop in their ear, even at City Hall. You'll see a variety of cowboy hats, too, but probably not as many as you expected.

As you'll notice in real life and in parody, Santa Fe style is easy to overdo. In your travels around the Plaza, be sure to look for a now-famous cartoon poster entitled "Another Victim of Santa Fe Style." It shows a woman dressed head-to-toe in haute Santa Fe fashion—cowboy boots, broomstick skirt, concho belt, squash blossom necklace, big earrings, etc.—lying lifelessly on a flawlessly tiled, Navajo-rug-covered floor as one of the brightly colored wooden snakes that previously lived on her wall slithers across the floor toward an open door.

Politics

Stop half a dozen Santa Feans on the street and ask what the favorite local pastime is. They may hesitate for a millisecond before answering, "politics." While this may be less than shocking in a state capital—especially one in which nearly every third worker has a government job—the tremendous interest residents take in local issues is still striking. Santa Feans discuss politics over breakfast, lunch, and dinner; at work and at play; on street corners; in the malls; at the library; and via e-mail. In fact, local government garners so much interest that Channel 6, the cable public access station, televises meetings of local government bodies for those who can't attend in person.

In addition to the ever contentious subjects of development and water rights, one of the major issues stirring up Santa Feans is the prospect of having truckloads of nuclear waste pass through their fair city en route to the Waste Isolation Pilot Plant (WIPP), an underground nuclear dump near Carlsbad, New Mexico. The DOE plans to bury mixed radioactive waste 2,150 feet below the ground in 225-million-year-old rock salt deposits.

Food

Eating is another favorite pastime in Santa Fe, especially when it comes to local cuisine. While the ingredients might be the same ones used in other Hispanic cultures—Mexican, Tex-Mex, Spanish, etc.—the food here is a culinary blend of Indian and Mexican influences that's as distinct as the local dialect. This is largely due to the ubiquitous chile pepper. Whether you like it hot or mild, whether you prefer green or red or even "Christmas" (some of each), you're going to encounter New Mexican chile in many different forms, usually in traditional native foods such as enchiladas, tamales, carne adovada (marinated and baked pork), or posole (stewed hominy), but also in hamburgers, on pizza, and even in apple pie. Regardless of nationality, most of Santa Fe's more than 200 restaurants use locally grown chile in at least one of their dishes whether it's a five-star restaurant—and Santa Fe boasts many—or McDonald's. Don't be shy about using a sopaipilla—a hollow, deep-fried yeast bread eaten with honey—to wipe up that last drop of chile from your plate. Celebrated not only for its fine New Mexican fare, Santa Fe is deservedly famous for the variety and quality of its many other restaurants, from nouvelle cuisine with a Southwestern twist to Chinese, French, Greek, Indian (from India), fine Italian, Japanese, Middle Eastern, Native American, Thai, Tibetan, vegetarian . . . the list goes on.

Language

Spanish is the second official language of Santa Fe—the first language for an estimated 10,000 residents. Some are old-timers who live in isolated villages in the north. Others are Mexican and Central American immigrants who surprisingly often face similar prejudices in

New Mexico, among both Hispanics and Anglos, as they do in other states that share a common border with Mexico. Locals pepper their conversations with colorful Spanish words and phrases that are unique to New Mexico and have no adequate translation in English. Newspapers throughout the state contain liberal sprinklings of Spanish with tildes (~) and accent marks (´) appearing as a matter of course. Many also feature Spanish-language sections.

But don't come to Santa Fe planning to speak Spanish with the natives. While a huge portion of the population speaks Spanish at home—around 35,000, according to the last census—English tends to be the language of choice here. Remember, New Mexico is one of the 50 United States—the 47th, to be precise. Though, apparently enough Americans are unaware of that fact to warrant an anecdotal column in *New Mexico Magazine* called "One of Our Fifty is Missing."

Among the most infamous anecdotes—it appeared in *Time* magazine and other national publications as well as on national television and radio—recounts how a Santa Fe man called Atlanta to order volleyball tickets for the 1996 Olympics. When he gave the agent his New Mexico address, she told him she could only sell tickets in the United States; that he'd have to call his country's national committee for tickets. He tried to explain, first to the agent and then to her supervisor, that New Mexico joined the Union in 1912 and is as American as Georgia peaches, but to no avail. It wasn't until he offered an address in Phoenix that they agreed to send him his tickets.

Tolerance

By the late 19th Century, Santa Fe had already earned a reputation for tolerance, primarily because of the artists who "discovered" it and lived quietly among the natives. The area was still enough off the beaten path to attract some of society's outcasts and eccentrics—artists, healers, spiritualists, or simply individualists. Today, however, the beaten path leads directly to Santa Fe's door, where everyone is welcome provided they "don't move the furniture," as a colorful and controversial former mayor once put it. She was referring to what a North Carolinian acquaintance of ours calls RAREs—Recent Arrivals Rearranging Everything. These are the people who move to Santa Fe for its unique beauty and relaxed, small-town charm, then immediately want to change things once they get here. It understandably causes resentment.

RAREs are a relatively recent phenomenon—and a rather conventional one at that. Long before RAREs appeared on the scene, Santa Fe served as a beacon for alternative lifestyles and ideologies, attracting more than its share of Aquarian Age adherents. It began in the 1960s with the hippie movement which found, if not open arms, at least passive ones in northern New Mexico. Today, Santa Fe is filled with old and young flower children as well as aura readers, channelers, Iron Johns, non-native shamans, white Rastafarians, and women who run with wolves. Once merely the state capital of New Mexico, Santa Fe is now the New Age capital of the United States.

Santa Fe's more traditional spiritual community offers options as diverse as they are plentiful from Assembly of God to Zen Buddhism as well as Baha'i, Hinduism, Islam, Mormonism, Sikh, Sufism, and Unitarian, to name just a few. There's never a moment's doubt, however, as to which religion dominates. One need only look up at the mountain range that reigns regally and protectively over the region—the Sangre de Cristo, or "Blood of Christ," Mountains—to be reminded that Catholicism runs deeply in the veins and the hearts of northern New Mexicans.

Running just as deeply is an abiding respect for the traditional herbal medicine of Hispanic healers called *curanderas* or Indian medicine men. Perhaps for that reason, Santa Fe has long been a mecca for alternative health care. Even a brief glance in the Yellow Pages offers a mind-boggling array of therapies including acupuncture, chiropractors, hypnotism, massage therapy, homeopathy, energy healing, biofeedback, herbs, and spiritual healing.

Bienvenidos

New Agers, old-timers, and trust funders; Hispanics, Native Americans, and Anglos—they're all part of the fabric of Santa Fe, a cloth tightly woven from a variety of belief systems, traditions and lifestyles. The only way to know it is to experience it—and even then it could take a lifetime.

So *¡Bienvenidos á Santa Fe!* And remember, don't move the furniture.

Getting Here, Getting Around

Four hundred years ago, there was only one way into Santa Fe—el Camino Real (the "Royal Road" or "King's Highway"), an arduous and, for some, fatal network of roads and trails that began in Mexico City. This *camino de tierra adentro*, or "road to the interior," started out as Indian trails and slowly extended northward, segment-by-segment, throughout the 16th century, as *conquistadores* and settlers; missionaries and merchants; and seekers of fame, fortune, and adventure all made their way to New Mexico.

More than two centuries later, on September 1, 1821, William Becknell left Franklin, Missouri, with a wagon load of goods to trade with Indians. He never got farther than Santa Fe where, despite Spain's restrictions against Anglo Americans and trade with the eastern United States, colonists eagerly bought all his goods, which were scarce and highly coveted in the territory. This was in November. The following month—on Dec. 26, 1821—word reached Santa Fe that Mexico, and therefore New Mexico, had won independence from Spain. With that news, the frontier opened and, with it, so did the Santa Fe Trail. For the next six decades, until the first locomotive steamed through northeastern New Mexico, the 900-mile stretch from Independence, Missouri, to Santa Fe, New Mexico, remained a bustling, if hazardous, trade route that represented profits to businessmen, adventure to mountain men, and converts for Protestant missionaries—all of them willing to risk death by disease, starvation, or hostile Indians to achieve their goals.

Only traces of the original Santa Fe Trail remain in the city, most notably behind the Museum of Indian Arts and Culture three miles southwest of the Plaza, where some claim you can still see the indentation of wagon wheels in the hard, dry dirt. Much of the original trail is now beneath the pavement and dirt of the well-traveled Old Santa Fe Trail—a scenic, narrow road wending its way from County Road 67 south of the city to its terminus at the Santa Fe Plaza. El Camino Real, however, is still a vital Santa Fe thoroughfare—at least the part now called Agua Fría ("Cold Water") Street, which begins in the Guadalupe District west of the Plaza and meanders parallel to the Santa Fe River through the west side barrio and the Historic Village of Agua Fría

Today, of course, there are a number of ways to get into and out of Santa Fe, as well as around and through it—though never enough for some people and far too many for others. Additional roads naturally translate into more traffic and all its accouterments: congestion, noise, and the threat of polluting our pristine skies. So far, however, a population painfully aware of this particular downside of growth, as well as city and county governments that for the most part are sympathetic to their constituents' concerns, are trying to find a happy medium that allows for expanding our highways and byways without destroying the aesthetic, cultural, and historic integrity of Santa Fe. Here's what we've got thus far:

By Air

Santa Fe is the only state capitol in the country that doesn't have its own commercial airport—another reason it deserves its reputation as "The City Different." The city has a municipal airport for commuter and private jets. But if you're traveling by commercial jet, you must fly into Albuquerque and use ground transportation to Santa Fe. The drive will take between 1 and 1½ hours, depending on the mode of travel and the weight of your foot on the gas pedal.

Albuquerque International Sunport

Located 60 miles south of Santa Fe, the Albuquerque International Sunport is the only airport in New Mexico with jet airline service. Regardless of your specific destination in the state, if you plan to get there via a commercial flight, your visit to the Land of Enchantment will begin in Albuquerque, the state's largest city. The airport, which the city shares with Kirtland Air Force Base, lies at the southern end of Albuquerque, approximately four miles south of the central business district.

Albuquerque International Sunport
2200 Sunport Blvd. SE, Albuquerque
• (502) 842-4366

From the moment you set foot inside the Albuquerque International Sunport's cool, pink and turquoise, adobe-style interior, you know you're in the Southwest. The terminal's ornate, carved beamed ceilings are part of the original building in the current location. Albuquerque architect William Emmett Burk, Jr., (1909–1988) designed the twenty laminated beams, each about 84 feet long and carved with decorative motifs used by Pueblo and Navajo Indians. The airport's art collection comprises original paintings, weavings, sculpture, photography, and other media—all by New Mexico artists, many of them with national and international reputations. The terminal houses twelve eateries ranging from a full-service restaurant and lounge to delis and snack bars; a microbrewery; and a smoke-free sports bar; three gift and news shops; five cart vendors selling tee-shirts, balloons, key chains and other tchotchkies; a bank and ATM; a barber shop; and a shoeshine stand.

The airport's 574,000-square-foot terminal has come a long way from 1928, when the entire airport was little more than a small adobe building and a dirt runway a few miles southwest of its present location. The first aircraft to land there was a Stearman piloted by Ross Hadley, who was chauffeuring "air tourists" from Hollywood to New Mexico. Other cross-country pilots quickly followed suit, including Charles Lindbergh; Arthur S. Goebel, the 1927 Dole Prizewinner for the first flight to Honolulu from the mainland; and air speedster Frank Hawk. The little Albuquerque airport saw its first commercial flights in 1929, when Western Air Express operated one eastbound and one westbound flight per day with radio equipment installed by the U.S. president's son, Herbert Hoover, Jr. Two months later, Trans-Continental Air Transport began operating a fleet of 10 Ford tri-motored transports, each accommodating up to 18 passengers.

The airport grew quickly to accommodate newer, faster planes as well as the public's demand for more flights. When wind severely damaged the airport in 1938, the city decided to build a new, larger one on 53 acres nearby. Using Works Progress Administration (WPA) and military funds, it completed construction in 1939, with Kirtland Field and Air Force base occupying the east end of the airport. By 1945, the property had grown to 223 acres. Five years later, the federal government took possession of the airport. Over the next decade it would expand Kirtland and build what is now Sandia National Laboratories. In 1962, the federal government returned much of the airport to the city, retaining title to the facilities on the air base, paying Albuquerque for continued use of the airfield and providing crash, fire, and rescue services for civilian aircraft. Nine years later, the airport began international service. It underwent a major remodeling in 1986, added a new traffic control tower in 1994 and, in 1996, underwent a small-scale expansion.

Today, Albuquerque International Sunport has 23 gates in two concourses. Twelve commercial carriers offer non-stop service to 28 cities including Atlanta; Chicago; Dallas; Denver; Houston; Las Vegas, Nevada; Los Angeles; Minneapolis; Oakland; Orlando; Phoenix; Pittsburgh; St. Louis; Salt Lake City; San Diego; San Francisco; Seattle; Tampa; and Tucson. A four-level parking structure and adjacent surface lot accommodate 3,700 vehicles. Short-term parking rates start at $1 per half-hour with a maximum of $7 per day for the first 72 hours, $10 per day thereafter.

AIS is home to two fixed base operators—Cutter Flying Service, (505) 842-4184 or (800) 627-2887and Seven Bar Aviation, (505) 842-4990 or (800) 593-4990. Other companies that provide services to business and private fliers include Four Seasons Aviation, (505) 842-4955; RBR Aircraft, (505) 842-6015; Robertson Aircraft, (505) 842-4999; Seven Bar Flying Service, (505) 842-4949; and South Aero, (505) 842-4337.

Commercial Airline Phone Reservation Numbers:

America West	• (800) 235-9292
American Airlines	• (800) 433-7300
Continental Airlines	• (800) 525-0280
Delta Airlines	• (800) 221-1212
Frontier Airlines	• (800) 432-1359
Northwest Airlines	• (800) 225-2525
Southwest Airlines	• (800) 435-9792
TWA	• (800) 221-2000
United Airlines	• (800) 241-6522

Commuter Airline Phone Reservation Numbers:

Mesa Airlines	• (800) 637-2247
Rio Grande Air	• (505) 764-3041
Skywest Airlines	• (800) 453-9417

Bus Service from AIS to Santa Fe

Greyhound/TNM&O
• **(505) 242-4998**

Greyhound and TNM&O coaches provide bus service between the Albuquerque airport and the Santa Fe Bus Depot on St. Michael's Drive. Call for times and prices.

Renting a Car at the Albuquerque International Sunport

To get from AIS to Santa Fe, follow the signs to exit the airport, which will put you westbound on Sunport Blvd. Follow the blue interstate signs for U.S. 25 North for approximately one mile and turn right at the on-ramp for exit 221. Continue on U.S. 25 northbound

for about 60 miles and get off at the St. Francis Drive exit for downtown Santa Fe.

Car Rentals

Advantage Rent a Car • (505) 842-6566
Alamo Rent-A-Car • (505) 842-4057
Avis Rent-A-Car
   • (505) 842-4080, (800) 331-1212
Budget Car Rental • (505) 842-4021
Dollar Rent-A-Car • (505) 842-4224
Hertz Rent-A-Car • (505) 842-4235
National Car Rental
   • (505) 842-4222, (800) 227-7368
Thrifty Car Rental • (505) 842-8733

Shuttle Service:

Several companies operate non-stop shuttles between Albuquerque International Sunport and Santa Fe. Fares range from $20 to $25 each way with pickups and dropoffs at various hotels, motels, and bed and breakfast inns throughout Santa Fe. Some carriers also stop at the College of Santa Fe and St. John's College (see our "Education" chapter). Be sure to confirm the exact location before buying your ticket. Under normal circumstances, you can figure on a 70-minute commute to or from the airport. However, normal circumstances won't apply after the summer of 2000, when the "Big I"—as the intersection of U.S. 40 and U.S. 25 in Albuquerque is fondly known—will be undergoing a major facelift. Allow for an additional half-hour on the road–more during rush hour—while construction is in progress. Be sure to ask the carrier about the delay when you make your reservations. Although reservations are not required, we strongly advise that you guarantee your seat or you could find yourself left in the dust with your baggage in hand and a useless plane ticket in your pocket. Most shuttles accept traveler's checks and credit cards, though you can only charge your ticket at the time you make your reservations.

Coach USA Express Shuttle
8401A Jefferson NE, Albuquerque
• **(505) 242-3880, (800) 256-8991**

Coach USA provides non-stop service between the Albuquerque International Sunport and Santa Fe with nine shuttles operating between 6 AM and 11 PM. The first bus leaves the airport at 8 AM; the last departs at 11 PM. The first and last shuttles out of Santa Fe leave at 6 AM and 8 PM respectively with passenger pickups and drop-offs at selected hotels in the Plaza area and on Cerrillos Road as well as St. John's and College of Santa Fe. Tickets cost $25 each way.

Sandia Shuttle Express
3600 Cerrillos Rd.,
Ste.207C
• (505) 243-3244
(Albuquerque),
(505) 474-5696 (Santa
Fe), (888) 775-5696
Sandia Shuttle Express makes 10 runs daily to and from the Albuquerque airport for $20 each way. The first run of the day is at 6:45 AM out of Santa; the last van leaves the Capital City at 6 PM. From the airport, you can catch the first shuttle to Santa Fe at 8:45 AM and the last at 8:20 PM. Sandia Shuttle Express picks up and drops off passengers at all Santa Fe hotels, motels, bed and breakfast inns and a number of other locations in and around the capital city including retirement homes, the College of Santa Fe, Fort Marcy Compound, and St. John's College.

Santa Fe Shuttle
3113 Yale SE, Albuquerque
• (505) 243-2300, (888) 833-2300
Have an early morning flight? Santa Fe Shuttle sends its first bus out of Santa Fe at 5:05 AM. Its seventh, and last, bus to the airport leaves Santa Fe at 8:25 PM. From the airport you can catch a ride to Santa Fe as early as 7:20 AM or as late as 10:45 PM. Each one-way ticket runs $21. Santa Fe Shuttle will stop at any hotel, motel, or bed and breakfast in Santa Fe, but only to pick up or drop off registered guests. For all other passengers, the buses stop at Water and Sandoval streets or College of Santa Fe. The company will also go to St. John's College by special arrangement.

Twin Hearts Express and Transportation
102 Demus Lane, Taos
• (505) 751-1201, (800) 654-9456
Twin Hearts will take you from the Albuquerque airport all the way to south central Colorado, if you want, with stops at Santa Fe, Taos, and other points in between. The $20

fare buys you a ticket from the airport to Santa Fe starting at 11:30 AM and ending at 3:30 PM. From Santa Fe, the first pickup is at 8:30 AM, the last at 12:30 PM. Twin Hearts will stop at all Santa Fe hotels, motels, and bed and breakfasts.

INSIDERS' TIP
Perhaps the most important piece of advice to anyone visiting Santa Fe's downtown is to leave your car at home or in the hotel parking lot. Not only is downtown parking hard to come by, but the streets, some of which are 400 years old, are narrow and winding and often congested with cars and sightseers. So put on your walking shoes and stretch those muscles. It's the best way to see the downtown anyway.

By Air to Santa Fe

Santa Fe Municipal Airport
443 Airport Rd.
• (505) 955-2908 (information);
(505) 955-2900 (manager)
Santa Fe's own municipal airport, at the southwest corner of the city, provides commuter service between Santa Fe and Denver and handles all types of private aircraft. The 2,100-acre airport was established in 1941 as a military airfield during World War II. It became a "commercial" airport—technically a "non-hub primary" airport—in the 1950s when it replaced its tiny terminal with the larger one you see today. Inside, you'll find the Santa Fe Airport Grill, (505) 471-5227 open 6:30 AM to 2 PM.

Airport parking is in an outdoor lot and costs $2 per day. The airport handles about 230 takeoffs and landings a day, most of them private corporate aircraft. Commercial commuter airlines, limited to planes with 30 seats or fewer, comprise about 10 percent of all flights. As a result, you'll rarely have to wait for a flight unless it has been delayed in Denver. Only one commuter line operates out of SFMA. United Express, (505) 473-4118 or (800) 241-6522, has 11 arrivals and departures daily. The air traffic control tower, (505) 471-3810, is open between 7 AM and 9 PM, though flights can take off and land 24 hours a day. Both the New Mexico State Police and Army National Guard keep aircraft at the SFMA. The airport has two fixed base operators that fuel and service private, government and commuter aircraft: Santa Fe Jet Center, (505) 471-2525, and Executive Aviation, (505) 471-2700. Zia also provides air taxi and charter service.

For ground transportation, you have a number of choices. Avis, (505) 471-5892, and Hertz, (505) 471-7189, have rental cars at the airport.

GETTING HERE, GETTING AROUND

To get to the downtown area, head east on Airport Road for about three miles. Turn left on Cerrillos Road for approximately five miles. It will turn into Galisteo Road as you near downtown and dead-end at San Francisco Street exactly one block west of the Plaza. The drive will take about 20 minutes. Or you can take the Road Runner Shuttle, (505) 424-3367, to or from any hotel in town for $11. Road Runner also shuttles passengers to casinos and Los Alamos and operates charter buses to the Santa Fe Opera (see "The Arts"), the ski area ("Winter Sports"), and other local and regional destinations.

By Land

Maybe things in Santa Fe haven't changed all that much after all since the days of el Camino Real and the Santa Fe Trail. Here we are, 400 years and 250 years later, respectively, and there still are only two direct overland routes to the state capital—U.S. 25 northbound from Las Cruces, near New Mexico's southern border, and southbound from Buffalo in north central Wyoming; N.M. 84/285 south from Taos and Chama. The closest east-west route is U.S. 40, which intersects U.S. 25 in Albuquerque at what's popularly called "The Big I."

Getting to Santa Fe is the easy part. It's getting around that's hard, especially in an old downtown filled with narrow, winding, one-way streets that seem to lead everywhere but where you want to go or continually lead you right back from where you came. Even if you manage to navigate the downtown area, at some point you're going to have to find a place to leave your car. And you thought parking was difficult in Manhattan! It's also at a premium in Santa Fe, especially in summer—so much so that a former municipal judge decided it just wasn't cricket to fine locals who parked illegally when legal parking spots were so hard to find. Every year at Thanksgiving, he offered amnesty to parking scofflaws who donated a turkey or two to one of the local homeless shelters in lieu of paying their fines. This wound up costing the city tens of thousands of dollars in lost revenue and eventually cost the judge his robes.

All this is to suggest that if your digs are within walking distance of downtown use shank's pony to get there. Not only will you work off that extra sopaipilla you had for lunch, but you'll also see a lot more of Santa Fe. Beware, however, that Santa Fe is not particularly pedestrian friendly once you leave downtown. Sidewalks are rare; traffic lights on main drags often don't allow enough time to cross the street without making a run for it; and in wider, more heavily trafficked roads where the

The trains from Chicago and Los Angeles stop only in Lamy, 18 miles to the south of Santa Fe. However, the Santa Fe Southern Railway will take you on a pleasure ride to Lamy.

Photo: Chris Corrie

speed limits are higher, drivers may not be as aware of pedestrians as they might be in areas with more foot traffic.

If you're too far from the Plaza or just too tired to walk, the downtown has nine municipal parking lots, including one parking garage and eight surface lots, several of which will accommodate RVs. They charge either 50 cents or 60 cents per half hour with a maximum of $5 and $6 respectively per day (more for RVs). There are also six reasonably priced private lots within walking distance of the Plaza that charge between $1 and $1.50 per hour and up to $9 all day. Street parking downtown comes in two forms: metered at 25 cents for 20 minutes (30 minutes at some older meters) Monday through Saturday (Sundays are free); and permit parking for residents. While you may get away with a free half-hour on the meter (but don't count on it), residents jealously guard the parking rights they fought so hard to get, so please respect the residential parking signs. When all else fails, try the meters in front of the main post office on South Federal Place, behind City Hall and just two blocks from the Plaza. You may have to drive around the block a few times, but with a little persistence, your chances of landing a spot there are pretty good. On weekends—except during Indian Market, Spanish Market, and Fiestas (see "Annual Events"), you're almost guaranteed a spot in front of the state capitol building, affectionately called the Roundhouse for reasons that will become obvious once you've seen it.

Of course, you can avoid both walking and parking by using public transportation (see entries below) or cycling (see "Recreation and Sports").

Bus and Shuttle Service:

Greyhound/TNM&O
858 St. Michael's Drive
• (505) 471-0008, (800) 231-2222

Greyhound and TNM&O coaches provide bus service between the Albuquerque airport

and the Santa Fe bus station on St. Michael's Drive with coaches leaving for the airport and Albuquerque bus station at 7:30 AM, 3:50 PM and 8:05 PM. There's an additional 1:45 AM coach to the Albuquerque bus station. Buses also run between Santa Fe and Alamogordo, Carlsbad, Clovis, Gallup, Grants, Las Cruces, Las Vegas (N.M.), Roswell, and Taos in New Mexico; Alamosa, Colorado Springs, Denver, and Pueblo in Colorado; Amarillo, Dallas, and El Paso, Texas; Flagstaff and Phoenix in Arizona; and New Orleans. Call the bus station for times and fares. The depot is open Monday through Friday from 7 AM to 5:30 PM and 7:30 PM to 9:45 PM and on weekends when buses arrive and depart.

Lamy Shuttle and Tours
1476 N. Miracerros Loop
• (505) 982-8829

The Lamy shuttle takes reservations to meet the Amtrak trains that arrive once a day at the Lamy Depot from Chicago and Los Angeles. For $14 per person—which works out to under $1 a mile—the shuttle provides door-to-door service from the depot to your hotel or residence and vice versa. As its name implies, the company also offers custom tours. Call for details and prices.

Santa Fe Trails Transit System
2931 Rufina Street
• (505) 438-1464

Not even 12 years old, the city bus system—Santa Fe Trails—can take you nearly anywhere you want to go within the city limits on any of 10 different routes. Buses run Monday through Friday from 6 AM to 10:30 PM and Saturdays from 8 AM to 8 PM. (Times may vary depending on the route.) There's no bus service on Sundays or major holidays. You can pick up a bus schedule and information book on board any Santa Fe Trails bus and at more than 75 locations throughout the city including most public buildings and many stores. At 50 cents per ride for adults, including free transfers, Santa Fe Trails is one of the best buys in town. Seniors 60 and older and students from 6 to 17 years pay only 25 cents per ride, including trans-

> ## INSIDERS' TIP
>
> Santa Feans seem to be allergic to their turn signals. If you stay here long enough, you, too, will find you use your directionals less and less often, though whether it's from spite or assimilation is hard to determine. The reverse, of course, is that you'll often run into (sometimes literally) a car whose turn signal is flashing although the driver has no intention of turning. Maybe it's because drivers here are so unaccustomed to using their signals that they forget to turn them off. In any case, drive defensively.

fers. Children under 6 ride free when accompanied with an adult. Santa Fe Trails also offers one day passes for $1 and monthly passes for only $10. You can't beat it. The buses even have bike racks for cyclists who get caught in the rain or just can't bear to ride out that last stretch. For help planning a trip or for answers to any questions, call the customer assistance center, (505) 438-1464 between 7 AM and 7 PM.

Sandia Shuttle Express
3600 Cerrillos Rd., Ste.207C
• **(505) 474-5696 (Santa Fe),**
(505) 243-3244 (Albuquerque),
(888) 775-5696
Sandia Shuttle Express provides nonstop service between Santa Fe and the Albuquerque airport (see listing under Albuquerque International Sunport),

Train Service

Amtrak
County Road 33, Lamy
• **(505) 466-4511, (800) 872-7245**
Amtrak's Southwest Chief trains, which run eastbound from Los Angeles and westbound from Chicago, meet each afternoon at the train depot in Lamy, located approximately 18 miles southwest of Santa Fe. Call Lamy Shuttle and Tours, (505)982-8829 (see entry above) to arrange transportation to or from the downtown area. To get to the Lamy Depot from Santa Fe, take U.S. 25 North to exit 290 (N.M. 285). Go

south on N.M. 285 approximately 6 miles to the Lamy turnoff on the left. Drive a short ways to the center of the village. You'll easily spot the railroad station on your right.

Santa Fe Southern Railway
410 S. Guadalupe St.
• **(505) 989-8600, (888) 989-8600**
Santa Fe Southern Railway runs on tracks originally laid by the Atchison, Topeka & Santa Fe Railway in 1880. ATSF ended passenger service to its namesake city in 1960. When the line itself became threatened in 1992, Santa Fe Southern came into existence to preserve the historic piece of railroad. Today, SFSR delivers freight to Santa Fe and once again offers passenger service, however limited. The train travels only between Santa Fe and Lamy, some 18 miles away. The ride is a delightful one in which passengers can watch the high desert scenery through the windows of a restored 1920s coach. The train leaves the Santa Fe Depot 10:30 AM and returns by 4 PM. Passengers can bring a picnic lunch or buy one from a caterer at the depot (except for Sundays in winter). Snacks and drinks are available on board. Fares for passengers 14 and older range from $20 to $40, depending on the class of service. Seniors 60 and over pay up to $35 per ticket while fares for children 3 to 13 cost between $13 and $28. Except in "The Dome"—a silver vintage club car with 16 seats encased in glass—two-year-olds ride free with a limit of two toddlers per adult. Friday nights from April through Octo-

Santa Fe Trails, the local bus system, is inexpensive and covers the major arteries in Santa Fe.

Photo: Don Strel

ber, the Santa Fe Southern Railway runs the popular "High Desert Highball" featuring hors d'oeuvres and a cash bar on board. Fares range from $25 to $30. On Saturday nights a savory barbecue supper awaits you in Lamy complete with campfire and live music. Tickets run $45 to $65 for adults, not including booze; $30 to $50 for children 13 and under. Call Santa Fe Southern to arrange special events or private parties. Depot hours are 9 AM to 5 PM Monday through Saturday, 11 AM to 5 PM on Sunday.

Charter Vans and Tours

Custom Tours by Clarice
3201 Calle de Molina
• **(505) 438-7116**

Grayline Tours of Santa Fe
1330 Hickox St.
• **(505) 983-9491**

Santa Fe Transportation
1201 Cerrillos Rd.
• **(505) 982-3504**

Limousines

Limotion VIP Limousine Service
1443 St. Francis Dr.
• **(505) 820-0816, (800) 882-9480**

Carey Limousine Worldwide Chauffeur Services
820 Coal Ave. SE, Albuquerque
• **(888) 644-4514**

Rental Car Companies

Advantage Rent-A-Car
309 W. San Francisco St.
• **(505) 995-4535, (800) 777-5500**
1907 St. Michael's Dr. Unit F
• **(505) 983-9470, (800) 777-5500**

Avis Rent-A-Car
234 Don Gaspar Ave
• **(505) 982-4362**
Garrett's Desert Inn,
311 Old Santa Fe Trail
• **(505) 982-4361,**
(800) 831-2847, or (800) 331-1212
Santa Fe Municipal Airport,
443 Airport Rd.
• **(505) 471-5892, (800) 831-2847, or (800) 331-1212**

Budget/Sears Rent A Car
• **(800) 527-0700**

Enterprise Rent-A-Car
2641A Cerrillos Rd.
• **(505) 473-3600, (800) RENTCAR (736-8227)**
4450 Cerrillos Rd.
• **(505) 474-3234, (800) RENTCAR (736-8227)**

Hilton of Santa Fe
100 Sandoval St.
• **(505) 989-8859, (800) RENTCAR (736-8227)**

Hertz Rent A Car
Santa Fe Municipal Airport,
443 Airport Rd., Suite 6
• **(505) 471-7189, (800) 654-3131**

Thrifty Car Rental
2865 Cerrillos Rd.
• **(505) 474-3365, (800) 367-2277**

Taxi Service

Capital City Cab Co.
2875 Industrial Rd.
• **(505) 438-0000**

History

One of the things that differentiates Santa Fe from other cities in the United States is its long, rich history. Although some date the city's history to 1608, the date Governor Peralta and the Spanish colonists settled here, the area had seen centuries of human habitation before that. The story of Santa Fe stretches from the nomadic natives who camped here around 10,000 B.C. to modern trailblazers working using Santa Fe as a base for their work in human gene research or to develop practical uses for the technology born of the atomic bomb at nearby Los Alamos.

Early Indian Days

It's difficult to re-create the history of Santa Fe's earliest residents because they left no written records save their carved petroglyphs. From archaeological evidence, though, we know that Indians camped in the Santa Fe area on hunting trips for bison and other animals as long ago as 10,000 B.C. You could consider them the area's first tourists.

By about 5,500 B.C.. the hunters had established permanent annual camps in the area. Recent work on a new highway northwest of Santa Fe uncovered some of the old camping sites to which Indian bands returned year after year. From the few clues that remain about these early residents, we know they hunted deer and antelope with obsidian points on primitive spears or atatls and ate piñon nuts and seeds as part of their diet.

As the seasons rolled on, the Santa Fe area attracted permanent residents. Archaeologists have found pit houses, cave-like homes built partly underground, along the Santa Fe River and its tributaries. For about eight centuries, Indians lived in what is now known as Santa Fe, first in the dark pit houses and later in organized pueblos, some with hundreds of rooms and community plazas. A suspected 13th-century eastward migration of the ancestors of today's Pueblo people, also known as Anasazi, from such places as Mesa Verde on the Colorado plateau temporarily swelled the area's population. What brought them here? While no one knows for sure, water probably attracted these first settlers to what was to become Santa Fe and elsewhere throughout the arid Southwest.

While no one knows the exact figures, the combined population of the pueblos near the current site of Santa Fe may have been several thousand. At least seven major pueblos existed within a 20-minute drive of the spot where the Plaza now stands. Archaeologists gave the pottery made by these communities its own distinctive names, among them Santa Fe Black on White, Agua Fría Glaze on Red and Cienegilla Polychrome.

The Tano Indians occupied a number of large villages south of Santa Fe for centuries. Archaeologists have discovered evidence of pueblo communities beneath Agua Fría Village on the west side of Santa Fe, in Arroyo Hondo and Galisteo to the south, Cerrillos to the southwest and near the current Fort Marcy park, a few blocks from the Plaza. Another pueblo may have occupied the very site on which the Plaza now stands. Archaeologists speculate that sometime after A.D. 900 Indians built the Pueblo of Ogapoge, as it is called by tradition, on or near the site of Santa Fe's Plaza and spreading south. By the time the first Spanish arrived in the 16th century, however, Ogapoge had been abandoned for more than a century.

The Arroyo Hondo Pueblo had 1,000 rooms built around 10 plazas by 1330. The pueblo's population fluctuated, and at one point the Indians moved out, probably because of lack of rainfall, but later reoccupied it. Then the rain stopped again, and the population began to decline. Archaeological evidence shows that in 1410 a fire destroyed the pueblo, and the Indians left Arroyo Hondo for the last time. After many generations of life in and near the present site of Santa Fe, the Pueblo Indians moved away between the years of 1400 and 1425, possibly settling at the villages of Tesuque, Pecos, and Cienegilla in the Galisteo Basin and along the Rio Grande. The clues these people left behind point to drought as the prime motivator for the move. Skeletons of children and young adults buried in the ruins at Arroyo Hondo Pueblo, for example, exhibit evidence of extreme malnutrition. Tree-ring data indicate that this period saw the worst drought in 1,000 years. Nearby settlements of Tesuque, Nambe, and San Juan remained and continue to be occupied to this day.

The Spanish Arrive

Historians tracing the story of the early Spanish presence in Santa Fe face a major challenge. An Indian revolt—the only successful native uprising against European settlement in the United States—destroyed the city's official records dating from the early Spanish explorations until 1680. Nonetheless, using copies of some of the documents that survived in the Vatican, in Mexico City, and in Spain, along with archaeological evidence and the journals and letters of explorers who came later, we have a fairly good idea of what life was like here in the 17th century.

When wealthy and well-placed Juan de Oñate became the first person to receive permission to establish a colony in New Spain—at his own expense—he was one of many who expected to enjoy some of the riches of the region. For years, rumors of cities of gold had spawned Spanish exploration. Wealth, however, only provided part of the motivation. The Spanish explorers and colonists also wanted land of their own, sought to convert more souls to Catholicism, and viewed the new territory as a much-needed buffer against the rival Europeans who had settled elsewhere in the vast new world. Oñate, accompanied by 129 soldiers and their families and a small group of friars, arrived near San Juan Pueblo in 1598, approximately 25 miles north of the ruins of Ogapoge. They called their encampment San Juan de los Caballeros. The colonists found life difficult here, but Gov. Oñate spent most of his time exploring. By 1600, the Spaniards had moved their capital across the Rio Grande, the area's largest river, to the confluence of the Rio Chama and the Rio Grande. The fledgling colony, which they called San Gabriel, struggled to survive and sent no riches back to Spain. Ever optimistic, Oñate and his men rode through much of the rest of New Mexico hunting for gold and demanding submission of the Indians to the Spanish crown and their conversion to the Christian God.

At Acoma Pueblo, Indians attacked and killed 13 Spanish who visited the pueblo in search of provisions. One of those killed was Oñate's nephew. In retaliation, the Spanish military declared a "holy war" on the pueblo based on the assumption that there could be no peace in New Mexico until the Indians either submitted to Spanish dominance or died. At the governor's command (and with the approval of the friars), 70 Spanish soldiers vowed revenge on the Acoma. Another Oñate nephew, the brother of the killed leader, took Spanish troops to the pueblo. They demanded the surrender of the Indians responsible for the deaths and the Acomas' acquiescence to the king. The Indians resisted, but the better-armed Spanish defeated them after three days of battle and hundreds of deaths. The conquerors destroyed the pueblo and brought those whom they held responsible for the earlier Spanish deaths to Santo Domingo Pueblo for trial. Oñate meet the party there and dealt with the Acoma prisoners.

The Acoma and people from other pueblos who may have watched the trial probably didn't comprehend the formality of Spanish law, but they understood the results. The governor sentenced some 20 Acoma males age 25 and older to have one foot hacked off. They, along with the captured Acoma women and young boys, had to serve 20 years as slaves to the Spanish. Two

A Santa Fe Timeline

1150–1400 - Pueblo Indian villages thrive along the Santa Fe River.

Early 15th century - Indians abandon the villages closest to Santa Fe such as Pindi, Ogapoge, and Arroyo Hondo pueblos.

1598 - Juan de Oñate claims New Mexico for the Spanish and establishes the first Spanish settlement in New Spain near San Juan Pueblo northwest of Santa Fe.

1608–10 - Pedro de Peralta establishes the city of Santa Fe as New Mexico's capital. The Palace of the Governors is built. El Camino Real runs from Mexico City to Santa Fe as a supply route for the Spanish missions and colony.

1680 - The Pueblo Indians drive the Spanish out of Santa Fe and New Mexico. The Indians burn Spanish records and remodel the Palace of the Governors to serve their needs.

1692 - Diego de Vargas brings a Spanish military expedition back to Santa Fe and reclaims Santa Fe for the King of Spain.

1693–1696 - Vargas returns to Santa Fe with a band of settlers. After a fierce battle, the Indians give up the Palace of the Governors. Vargas spends the next few years reconquering the outlying pueblos.

1712 - Santa Fe celebrates its first official Fiesta in thanksgiving for the reconquest.

1777 - The first known map of Santa Fe is drawn.

1778 - Juan Bautista de Anza arrives in Santa Fe as governor and begins making peace with the Comanches.

1792 - Pedro Vial blazes a trail from Santa Fe to St. Louis and returns the following year, making the first complete journey over what was to be known as the Santa Fe Trail.

1807 - American explorer Zebulon Pike and his party are arrested as intruders in Spanish New Mexico. The Spanish government institutes protective trade measures to restrict American influence in New Spain, including Santa Fe.

1821 - Mexico wins independence from Spain. Trader William Becknell arrives in Santa Fe to do business.

1822 - The first wagons roll into the Santa Fe Plaza over the Santa Fe Trail, leading the way for millions of dollars of trade goods and new ideas and cultural influences in Santa Fe.

1833 - The first gold mines west of the Mississippi open in the Ortiz Mountains between Santa Fe and Albuquerque.

1834 - New Mexico's first newspaper, *El Crepúsculo de la Libertad*—the *Dawn of Liberty* is published in Santa Fe.

1837 - A group of northern New Mexican farmers and Indians band together to protest new taxes imposed by the Mexican government. Gov. Albino Pérez is killed. Manuel Armijo resumes his post as governor.

1846 - The United States declares war on Mexico. U.S. General Stephen W. Kearny occupies Santa Fe without firing a shot after Mexican governor Armijo flees.

1847 - Territorial Gov. Charles Bent is assassinated in Taos. U.S. forces quell the rebellion in an attack that seriously damages the mission church at Taos Pueblo.

1848 - The Treaty of Guadalupe Hidalgo is signed. Mexico cedes New Mexico to the United States.

1850 - New Mexico becomes an U.S. territory.

1851 - The first English language school is founded in Santa Fe by Bishop Jean Lamy.

1851 - A territorial library in founded in Santa Fe.

1861–62 - Confederate soldiers from Texas invade Santa Fe and occupy the Palace of the Governors. The Battle of Glorieta, near Santa Fe, ends Confederate control in New Mexico and squelches their plan to capture the West.

1869 - Construction of St. Francis Cathedral begins.

1870 - The territorial governor disposes of many of the official records of New Mexico. Only about one-fourth are recovered.

1874 - Workers lay the foundations for Loretto Chapel.

1879 - Governor Lew Wallace writes a portion of Ben Hur in the Palace of the Governors.

1880 - The Atchison, Topeka & Santa Fe Railroad arrives in Santa Fe over a spur line from the main station in Lamy. Travel along the Santa Fe Trail dies off.

1881 - Santa Fe installs its first water and telegraph systems.

1891 - The City of Santa Fe is officially incorporated.

1892 - New Mexico's new territorial capitol building burns in Santa Fe. Arson by Albuquerque boosters who want the seat of government moved south is suspected but never proven.

1907 - The Palace of the Governors, saved from demolition, becomes a museum.

1909 - The joint Museum of New Mexico-School of American Archaeology, under the influence of Edgar Lee Hewitt, establish the criteria for Santa Fe Style.

1912 - New Mexico becomes the 47th state.

1913 - The Palace of the Governors is remodeled with a Pueblo-Revival-style portal. Soon many other buildings receive similar treatment, and new architecture also adopts this look.

1917 - The Museum of Fine Arts, another example of Santa Fe style, is dedicated.

1922 - The Southwestern Association on Indian Affairs establishes the annual Indian market, a show and sale that remains part of modern Santa Fe's cultural life.

1926 - The Old Santa Fe Association is formed to help preserve city landmarks.

Pedro de Peralta, who replaced Don Juan de Oñate as New Mexico's Spanish governor, is depicted in a statue on Grant Avenue.

Photo: Don Strel

1926 - Artist Will Shuster founds a "revolutionary protest fiesta" that includes the burning of Zozobra. Zozobra quickly become a mainstay of the Santa Fe Fiesta.

1927 - The Daughters of the American Revolution offer to Santa Fe the *Madonna of the Trail* statue, which depicts a white Madonna pioneer. Writers Frank Applegate and Mary Austin speak out against the statue, noting it does not represent the real pioneers of the region at all...the Spanish people. The city ultimately refuses the gift.

1942 - The federal government selects Los Alamos Boys School site for a secret project to develop an atomic bomb. Scientists and their families begin coming to Santa Fe on their way to the research site.

1945 - Scientists working in Los Alamos produce the world's first atomic bomb.

1948 - Indians receive the right to vote.

(Continued on next page)

HISTORY

1957 - Santa Fe adopts its Historic District Ordinance to help protect landmark buildings.

1957 - John Crosby founds the Santa Fe Opera.

1961 - Architect John Gaw Meem and other concerned residents establish The Historic Santa Fe Foundation in response to the demolition of an historic house for a parking lot. The foundation continues to work to promote the preservation of the city's unique architectural character.

1964 - St. John's College of Annapolis establishes a second campus in Santa Fe.

1966 - New Mexico's present state capitol building, the Roundhouse, is dedicated in Santa Fe.

1975 - Extensive archaeological work begins at the Palace of the Governors.

1975 - Democrat Jerry Apodaca becomes New Mexico's first Hispanic governor since 1918.

1975 - The Santa Fe Chamber Music Festival is established.

1980s - Celebrities "discover" Santa Fe. The city begins to become trendy; real estate prices start to climb. New Age seekers begin to come to Santa Fe as a spiritual center.

1983 - Santa Fe Community College is created.

1987 - The Santa Fe City Council adopts an archaeological review ordinance protecting artifacts older than 75 years.

1989 - Santa Fe Children's Museum is founded.

1994 - Debbie Jaramillo becomes Santa Fe's first woman mayor.

1995 - Landscaping crews remove the last of the trees which Archbishop Jean Baptiste Lamy planted in the St. Francis Cathedral Rectory Garden. The parish replaced the pine, apple, almond, and apricot trees—some dead, some diseased—with new trees and donated the wood to local wood workers.

2000 - Santa Fe peacefully welcomes the new millennium.

Hopi Indians caught at Acoma had their right hands cut off and were set free, "in order that they may convey the news of this punishment," Oñate commanded.

Life in the colony resumed, with Oñate continuing his search for the riches that would repay his personal investment in the settlement and bring honor to Spain. The governor headed west to the Colorado River and then south to the Gulf of California, taking possession of more new land for his king. His efforts left him exhausted and used up his family fortune. Meanwhile, rather than living the easy life as they'd envisioned, the colonists had to work hard to survive in this demanding land. They resented the chronic lack of food and the failure to find gold. The poverty and desolation, the suffering of the women and children, the bugs in summer, cold of the winter, and the sullen looks of the Indians, who resented the Spanish intrusion, disheartened the settlers.

Historian John Kessell in his book, *Kiva, Cross, and Crown*, reported that the colonists had a saying about New Mexico: *"Ocho meses de invierno y cuatro de infierno!"* which translates as "Eight months of winter and four months of hell!"

So it was no wonder that when the governor left once again to search for wealth, accompanied by half of the colony's armed men and a couple of friars, those left behind made tracks, too. Most of the colonists and all but one of the friars seized the opportunity, deserted their wretched settlement and headed back to Mexico. Only two dozen settlers and one Franciscan remained. When Oñate and his party returned, the governor ordered the fleeing colonists pursued, but they had too much of a lead to be captured. When the defectors reached Mexico, they reported the expedition's dismal lack of success in converting the

HISTORY

INSIDERS' TIP

In *Down the Santa Fe Trail and into Mexico*, Susan Shelby Magoffin tells of her experience as the first white American woman to come to Santa Fe. She traveled in a private carriage heavy with books and included two servant boys in her entourage. Less than a dozen American women crossed the trail in its first 25 years of existence.

Indians or finding gold. The Viceroy of Mexico, with the concurrence of the King of Spain, decided to abandon the New Mexico experiment.

And it would have been, except for a plea for fairness toward the Christianized Indians. (While estimates of the number of converts differed considerably, all agreed that some Indians had become Christians.) Rather than abandon these new converts or force them to leave New Mexico, secular and religious authorities decided to keep the new areas as mission territory. The viceroy named a new governor, Pedro de Peralta, but ordered Oñate to remain until Peralta arrived. Embarrassed and disgraced, Oñate resigned in 1607.

When Peralta arrived, Oñate and his son, Cristóbal, left for Mexico City, but on the journey Cristóbal died. The courts charged Oñate with failure to obey royal decrees, lack of respect for the friars, and mistreatment of the Indians, especially of the Acomas. He was fined, banned perpetually from New Mexico, and returned to Spain in disgrace.

Conventional history places the establishment of Santa Fe, where Peralta moved the capital, at 1608. Some historians say Oñate or his son founded Santa Fe as early as 1605. But even the 1608 date makes Santa Fe the oldest capital city in the United States, predating the establishment of New England's more famous Plymouth colony by more than 10 years. Governor Peralta and settlers from San Gabriel selected a site on the southern end of the Sangre de Cristo Mountains. The new site had a higher elevation, which meant cooler summers, and offered better protection against the attacks of the Apache, Navajo, and Comanche tribes. The Spanish laid out the town, which they called Santa Fe (meaning "Holy Faith"), according to instructions from Spain; modern Santa Fe retains this basic design in its oldest neighborhoods.

The city grew from the mud with small, one-story adobe buildings situated around a rectangular plaza. Most historians believe the original Plaza was at least an additional block larger than today's Plaza. Land for farming lay just beyond this town square and the city spread along the Santa Fe River—a decision the settlers came to regret. The most important building was the Casas Reales, which later became know by its English name, the Palace of the Governors. The governors and their families lived in this adobe compound, with adjoining rooms for municipal offices, meetings of the town council, storage, and a jail. Many settlers moved from San Gabriel to the new city, attracted by the promise of land of their own with water rights if they could

Santa Fe is a base for exploring the rest of Northern New Mexico, including scenic Truchas, pictured here.

Photo: Don Strel

survive for 10 years. Other newcomers trickled in over el Camino Real, an important trail into the territory from Mexico. All roads in the province—and there weren't many—led to Santa Fe.

In the early 1600s, Santa Fe had approximately 1,000 residents, including Mexican Indians who came to Santa Fe as servants of the Spanish and who lived separately in Barrio Analco across the Santa Fe River. The population included settlers of pure Spanish blood, many mestizos—or people of mixed race—and people from France and Portugal. Some were black, and at least one came from Flanders. Santa Fe's early settlers were uniformly Catholic, including some Spanish of Judaic heritage whose ancestors chose baptism rather than deportation or death from the Inquisition.

Santa Fe and New Mexico grew slowly as more colonists arrived and babies were born. The statue of *La Conquistadora*, which ultimately became the city's most revered religious object, arrived in 1625. The economy ran largely on the barter system; by and large, people helped their neighbors. While in some ways life was hard on the frontier, in other ways the settlers were freer than they may have been in Spain or Mexico. People made their own fun, and gambling flourished in the new settlement as it did in most frontier towns.

The arrival of the supply caravan from Mexico City over el Camino Real every three years brought village-wide celebration. Although the central purpose of the caravans was to bring supplies for the missions and official correspondence from government headquarters in Mexico, the wagons also delivered a few precious luxury items such as silver, silk, lace, tobacco, saddles, writing desks, and chocolate. And the visitors had news and gossip from the world outside dusty Santa Fe.

By 1680, three generations of Santa Fe residents had been born, some of whom had Indian mothers. Ninety percent of the city's population was native to the province. As it grew, the village's two major areas of conflict continued to fester. First, ever-present friction between the church and state over who ruled not only the Indians but also the colony as a whole sometimes required settlers to choose between the governor and the friars. Meanwhile, the Pueblo Indians were growing increasingly unhappy with the Spanish for their economic exploitation and periodic attempts to undermine the Indians' spiritual, political, and social way of life. The colony established the *encomienda* system, which granted certain settlers the right to collect tributes from Indians who lived on designed parcels of land.

As historian Kessell explains it, the encomienda system was born of the 1573 colonization laws, which stated that Indians should be persuaded to pay moderate amounts of tribute in local products. "In no legal sense did a grant of Indians in encomienda ("in trust") imply that the recipient had use of native land or labor, but rather only the collection of tribute—usually maize (corn) and mantas (woven material) and animal skins—in kind as personal income." In exchange, the Spanish *encomiendero*, or the man who received the tribute, was supposed to protect the colony—including the Pueblo Indians—by answering the governor's call to arms whenever the need arose. And the Indians, whether they liked it or not, received the "benefits" of Christianity and becoming subjects of the king of Spain.

Spanish law made it clear that Indians had to be paid at least minimum wage if they worked for the colonists. But New Mexico was a long way from Spain and the territory was poor. Pueblo Indians were often forced to labor against their will by the encomienderos. Adding to the uproar, raiding Comanche and other non-farming Indians frequently stole the crops and livestock of both the Pueblo Indians and the Spanish settlers.

But Indian-Spanish relationships weren't exclusively antagonistic. In the worldview of the Franciscans, Indian souls deserved God's salvation, the same as those of the Spanish. In the years since Oñate's arrival, the friars had married many Pueblo Indians and Spanish. The families served as godparents for each other's children and had established friendships based on mutual respect and the need to cooperate. This wasn't enough, however, to stay the building forces of revolution.

INSIDERS' TIP

Agua Fría Village, a historic area that has been encompassed by the city's growth, was built on the site of Pindi Pueblo. Indians occupied the pueblo's several hundred rooms between 1250 and 1350. The Laboratory of Anthropology organized its excavation in 1932 and 1933. The ruins of another major pueblo, Arroyo Hondo, lie 8 miles south of Santa Fe and were the focus of extensive archaeological and ecological research by the School of American Research between 1970 and 1974.

HISTORY

Ancient symbols carved or scratched into rocks tell only part of the story of the "Ancient Ones".

Photo: Don Strel

In 1675, Spanish officials flogged a large group of Pueblo religious leaders, including Popé from San Juan Pueblo, for practicing witchcraft—a common mischaracterization of Native religion. This public humiliation, which followed an earlier incident in which 1,600 ceremonial masks, prayer sticks, and fetishes had been burned, brought ramifications for New Mexico for many years to come.

The Pueblo Revolt

After his flogging, Popé fled to Taos where he began to work with other Pueblo Indian leaders and in the Hopi country to organize a sophisticated rebellion. The cautious conspiracy went on for five years, hampered by the fact that the Pueblo Indians did not share a common language. (See our Local Cultures chapter). The Indians agreed to join forces to drive the Spanish invaders out of Santa Fe and the rest of what had been their territory. They timed the rebellion for the year before the supply train arrived so the settlers would be low on food and ammunition. On August 9, 1680, runners with knotted ropes signifying the exact day of the revolt went from pueblo to pueblo, telling the Indian warriors that the time had come. Popé originally planned the uprising to coincide with the Feast of San Lorenzo but changed the date when he realized that the Spanish were on to the plan.

Despite Popé's switch, Santa Fe's Governor Antonio de Otermín discovered the plot two days before the date of the rebellion. Even with the knowledge, the governor failed to marshal any organized defense. The Indians' split the scattered Spanish settlements in New Mexico into two groups, one centered Santa Fe and one in Isleta. They tried to convince each group of settlers that the other had been killed and that their situation was hopeless. The Pueblo warriors rode through the territory, burning and sacking missions, killing priests, attacking settlers, and stealing or stampeding livestock.

When word of the uprising arrived in Santa Fe, Governor Otermín sent messengers to warn all settlers in the outlying districts to defend themselves. Those who lived between Taos and Cochití Pueblo literally ran for their lives to the walled city of Santa Fe. Settlers between Cochití and Socorro sought safety at Isleta Pueblo, (near what is now Albuquerque) which remained friendly to the Spanish. Settlers living on the western side of the province, from Ziá and Jémez Pueblos across to Zuni and Oraibi, had to fend for themselves. Most were killed.

At the Palace of the Governors, Otermín distributed weapons to the male colonists, and they prepared for a siege. Each new group of refugees brought grim reports of how the murder and rebellion had spread. Otermín sent soldiers to assist settlers who had held out in Los Cerrillos and La Cañada, helping them reach Santa Fe. The Spanish made sure that *La Conquistadora*, the 3-foot image of the Virgin, was safe inside the thick adobe walls.

By August 13 the Indians arrived in Santa Fe, and a nine-day siege began. Some 1,000 men, women, and children, along with a few of their animals, waited inside the Palace. The Indians cut off the acequia, a stream that supplied water to the Palace. To preserve precious food and water, the colonists let their animals die. The Indians burned Santa Fe, and the besieged band watched the glow of flames from their homes and crops in the evening sky. The Pueblo leader sent a delegate to the settlers with a red flag and a white flag. The Spanish could pick the white flag, surrender, and leave. If they picked red and chose to fight, they should prepare to die. Otermín scolded the emissary and gruffly instructed him to tell the Indians to abandon the revolt and ask God to forgive them. The Indians scoffed at the message.

Finally, Otermín had to make a decision. Rather than perish of thirst and starvation, the Spanish decided to attempt to fight their way out of the Palace at dawn. Otermín advanced with a small force of handpicked soldiers and caught the Indians by surprise. Although the rebels numbered about 1,500 warriors, the Spanish claimed to have slain 300, captured 47, and temporarily driven away the rest.

During that lull in the battle, the Spanish left their fortification for water and led the weakened livestock out to the ruined fields to scrounge for food. They saw the extent of the devastation the Indians had wrought. With their possessions destroyed, homes burned, and crops ravaged, they knew they could not survive the winter in Santa Fe. On August 21, 1680, Otermín signed an affidavit that he and the remaining Santa Fe settlers would abandon the villa. The party divided all clothing, food, and livestock among the sorrowful families and, in military formation, marched southward down el Camino Real, the route their optimistic ancestors had taken into New Mexico 82 years earlier.

The Spanish had lost 21 clergymen and between 380 and 400 settlers—a devastating blow to the new colony. At least 20 more were missing, either left behind as captives or in hiding from the

Religious art played an important role in keeping the faith alive for New Mexico's isolated Spanish Catholics.

Photo: Don Strel

Indians. Many, including Otermín himself, were wounded. The disheartened band headed down river toward El Paso, joined on the way by other terrified settlers and Indians who had befriended the Spanish and feared for their lives. Otermín, stunned by the defeat, vowed to reconquer the territory and led two unsuccessful expeditions. In 1683, his term as governor ended.

After Otermín, other Spanish conquistadors attempted to reclaim New Mexico, but the Indians rebuffed them all. Spain viewed the loss of the territory as an embarrassment. The Indians ruled New Mexico for 12 years, during which time they attempted, with wide success, to obliterate all traces of the European settlers and their religion. They destroyed most of the Spanish buildings and replaced them with cornfields, saving only the Casas Reales. (The walls and foundation of San Miguel Mission—New Mexico's oldest church—also remained.) Indians burned the Spanish records, crosses, and other traces of the foreigners. Some moved into the Casas Reales, modifying it to suit their needs. Some historians believe that they also built a pueblo on the Plaza.

When things settled down, many of the Indians left Santa Fe and returned to their home pueblos. The Indian coalition dissolved, despite the efforts of some leaders to keep it together. In 1690, the king of Spain appointed Diego de Vargas to be New Spain's new governor. Vargas agreed to reclaim the territory for Spain at his own expense. Vargas traced his family back to a famous senator of imperial Rome and believed he had the necessary military and organizational skills, along with the requisite courage, to face the Indians and succeed. He planned a two-stage reconquest: first a military presence and then the return of the settlers.

INSIDERS' TIP

By late 1941, 2,000 New Mexican soldiers were stationed in the Philippines. They had received the WWII assignment because they spoke Spanish. Many of these New Mexicans were killed after the Japanese occupied the Philippines; others died later in prisoner of war camps. Only 900 returned home from the war; half of those didn't survive their first year of freedom.

The Spanish Return

On September 13, 1692, at 4 AM, Vargas and a band of 40 Spanish soldiers and 50 Indian allies arrived at the pueblo that had once been Santa Fe. Vargas had given the order: No one was to fire a shot unless and until he himself so signaled. The Spanish approached the Palace in the early morning darkness, crying in unison, "Glory to the Blessed Sacrament of the Altar!" With the help of Spanish soldiers who spoke the language of the pueblo, Vargas told the Indians that he had come in peace to pardon them and accept their obedience to God and the king of Spain. The Indians initially refused to acquiesce. Vargas instructed his men to encircle the stronghold, positioning himself in front of the main gate. Taking his cue from Otermín's experience, he ordered his men to shut off the acequia that allowed water to flow into the fortification. The Spanish then brought forward the cannon they'd hauled all the way from El Paso, and pointed it at the pueblo wall. The Indians began to surrender.

As the native leaders tentatively appeared, Vargas climbed down from his horse to embrace them. They invited Vargas and his men inside the Palace. The Franciscans celebrated mass, absolved the Indians of their sins and baptized the children born since 1680. This is the peaceful reconquest that the historic Santa Fe Fiesta celebrates, a credit to Vargas' faith in God and in himself. However, the story was far from over.

Vargas and his men returned to Mexico and came back with 70 families of settlers, about 800 people. They left El Paso in mid-October of 1693 and got to Santa Fe on December 16 after camping in snow and bitter cold for two weeks. With them, they brought the statue of the Virgin, *La Conquistadora*, home to Santa Fe to stay. This time the Indians declined to abandon their home and its food supplies, and a fierce battle ensued. Vargas and his men succeeded in seizing the Casas Reales. Vargas ordered the execution of 70 of the Indian defenders he had captured. Some 400 others became slaves to the Spanish for 10 years. It took the Spanish years of battle to subdue the rest of New Mexico, but 1696 they had reconquered all the pueblos. The longest and most successful uprising of Native Americans against foreign colonists had ended and Spanish rule reestablished. Twenty-six Spanish governors followed Vargas. Some represented Spain with honor, wisdom and integrity; others were ignorant and corrupt. All faced hardships in managing a poor isolated colony besieged by raids from Apache, Navajo, and other Indians and requiring almost constant support from the mother country.

HISTORY

18th-Century Santa Fe

Although New Mexico's reinstated Spanish government and settlers faced many of the same problems as before, the encomienda system never functioned again. The Spanish abandoned attempts to integrate the Pueblo Indians into Spanish society, probably with relief on both sides. The Indians and the friars made peace; as long as the Indians officially professed to be Christians, the friars generally ignored their ceremonial dances and other non-Christian rituals.

In 1712 the residents of Santa Fe established a fiesta to celebrate Vargas' initial entry into the city. Santa Fe's defensive walls came down, and some settlers moved to homes along the Santa Fe River to protect their fields from animals and marauding neighbors. Like most villages in New Spain, Santa Fe struggled to survive during the 18th century, with the settlers fighting poverty, disease and the whims of the weather. But life wasn't all hard work, even on the frontier. People loved the *fandangos*, or social dances. Utilitarian folk arts of many kinds flourished, in part because of the colony's isolation from manufactured products. Spain discouraged foreign trade, and as a result, many New Mexicans learned crafts such as folk painting, weaving, and wood carving, which they refined over generations.

Santa Fe remained Spain's capital in the northern provinces for the next 125 years. Visitors from Spain and Mexico often noted their impressions of Santa Fe in their journals. Fray Francisco Atanasio Domínguez, who came in 1776, described the town as "a rough stone set in fine metal"—a reference to the city's lovely environment—and noted, "it lacks in everything."

The first known map of Santa Fe, drawn by army officer Joseph de Urrútia in 1768, includes "Camino de Galisteo" and "Camino de Pecos," which seem to be near the routes of present Galisteo Street and Old Pecos Trail. The Santa Fe depicted by Urrútia was made totally of adobe with a garrison of soldiers to protect it.

Almost continuous raids by the Comanches, Apaches, Navajos, and Utes against both the Pueblos Indians and the Spanish settlements marked life in 18th-century Santa Fe. The Spanish launched frequent campaigns of reprisal and retaliation; their attacks in turn prompted the Indians to seek revenge, and the cycle continued. Frontiersman Juan Bautista de Anza, governor of New Mexico from 1778 to 1787, made peace with the Comanches, a happy condition that continued through 1794.

Santa Fe, along with Taos, Pecos, and Abiquiú, hosted annual trade fairs to allow the Spanish and the nomadic Indians to exchange goods. The barter system still ran strong, but by the end of the century money had begun to circulate in New Mexico, and Santa Fe, as the capital, led the trend.

INSIDERS' TIP

The Spanish established the Inquisition in New Mexico in 1626. Historians praise its first agent, Fray Alonso de Benavides, as a model of reason and moderation. Benavides' chronicles of New Mexico provide vivid and interesting information about Santa Fe in its early days

Santa Fe's population grew slowly. The 1790 census shows farming as the main occupation of the 2,542 residents. The survey also found adobe makers, carpenters, blacksmiths, barrelmakers, muleskinners, shoemakers, weavers, and tailors. Although only one teacher is specifically identified in the old document, many historians are impressed with the high quality of the written records that describe life and all its wrinkles in 18th-century Santa Fe.

The Louisiana Purchase in 1803 signaled the beginning of the end of Spanish control over New Mexico. The purchase inspired U.S. residents to move westward. American trappers had trespassed in the territory for decades, but in 1805 Zebulon Pike led a group of explorers westward into New Spain under direct orders from President Thomas Jefferson. The Spanish arrested Pike and jailed him in Santa Fe. The governor treated Pike to dinner, outfitted him in new clothes, and sent him down to Durango, Mexico, where he was further questioned and released. He later wrote about his adventures, fueling curiosity about New Mexico and Santa Fe.

For almost 300 years, el Camino Real was the major thoroughfare for missionaries, colonists, soldiers, and commercial caravans into New Mexico. But that was about to change.

The longest of America's trails, el Camino Real ran 1,200 miles from Santa Fe to Mexico City. Until the opening of the Santa Fe Trail, it was virtually Santa Fe's only link to the outside world. The passage from Mexico to Santa Fe took months and put the travelers in danger; in addition to severe natural forces, the fear of attack by Indians was ever present. Once they arrived in Santa Fe, the Mexican caravans would pause several weeks or months, buying local products with which to return south. Beginning about 1709, the caravans became annual events from Chihuahua, and the northern part of el Camino Real became known as the Camino de Chihuahua. When the initial profitability of trading in Santa Fe began to wane for merchants who took the Santa Fe Trail from Independence, Missouri, some U.S. wagons used the Camino de Chihuahua to continue into Mexico.

The Mexican Period

In the late 18th century, Spain, preoccupied with the Napoleonic War, lost its grip on its New World colonies. Mexico gained its independence from Spain, and New Mexico, then part of Mexico, came along with it. Although Mexican independence had little initial effect, the winds of change again swept over Santa Fe with hurricane force.

Santa Fe remained the provincial capital during Mexican rule, as it had during centuries of Spanish authority. With a population of almost 5,100 at the turn of the century, Santa Fe was the official seat of government for a territory that stretched to Arizona and included parts of Colorado and Utah. Conflict with Indians and lack of adequate finances continued, and the understaffed and underfunded Mexican government provided even less to New Mexico than had Spain.

Albuquerque-born Manuel Armijo, who served as New Mexico's governor during most of the Mexican period, became one of the most colorful and controversial figures in the state's history. Some scholars regard him as a cowardly scoundrel; others characterize him as a pragmatic leader and successful administrator.

Armijo acted notoriously independently of the Mexican government, often refusing to enforce Mexican laws he considered inappropriate for the colony. Armijo declined to collect taxes, for example, saying that service in the militia was enough of a burden for New Mexico's poor residents.

In 1835 the Mexican government replaced Armijo with Albino Peréz, a Mexican nobleman with a taste for luxury. In 1837, the residents of New Mexico rebelled against the Mexican rules and Peréz, who personified their resentment. A mob savagely murdered the governor and 16 other civil servants and elected Jose Gonzales, a Taos Indian, to rule them. Gonzales appointed Armijo as part of a delegation to go to Mexico and reassure the Mexican officials that all was under control. But, sensing an opportunity, Armijo instead gathered a small army and marched into Santa Fe to officially "reclaim" the city for Mexico. Gonzales resigned. In 1838 the Mexican government confirmed Armijo as governor once again. In 1844 Armijo resigned and was replaced with a governor from Mexico who re-instigated war with the Utes. The Mexicans removed him from office in 1845, re-installing Manuel Armijo.

Unlike the Spanish governors who preceded him, Armijo welcomed Anglo-American traders, seeing tremendous economic advantage to Santa Fe—and himself—from the caravans. He also realized the United States could pose a threat to Mexican rule and repeatedly pleaded with Mexico for more trained soldiers, weapons, and supplies. Mexico, overwhelmed with its own problems, ignored his requests.

The same year Mexico won its independence, William Becknell, the man who became known as "The Father of the Old Santa Fe Trail," arrived in Santa Fe on an exploratory mission with pack mules loaded with items for trade. The Mexican governor, Facundo Melgares, encouraged Becknell to tell other Anglo-Americans that Santa Fe would welcome them. By 1822, caravans were on the move down the Santa Fe Trail. (Although Becknell gets the credit for "founding" the trail, Spanish explorer Pedro Vial originally blazed the route in 1792.)

For decades, the arrival of the caravans brought buyers, sellers, animals, and goods of all sorts to the territory. The wagons made a 900-mile trip from central Missouri on the edge of the American frontier to Santa Fe's Plaza. The trail entered and left the Plaza at its southeast corner, near the present intersection of San Francisco and Shelby Streets. The traders and their merchandise came down what's now Shelby Street with a jog east at the present Water Street, then followed the modern Santa Fe street named Old Santa Fe Trail south to near the intersection of Old Pecos Trail. Even today, homeowners who live slightly out of town along the Old Santa Fe Trail can find the ruts in their yards made by the heavy wagons.

By 1866—just as the transcontinental railroad reached Kansas—the trail had seen 5,000 wagons. In keeping with the Spanish custom of hospitality, boisterous parties welcomed the

An early (circa 1920's) photo showing local Indians selling their pottery in front of the Museum of Fine Art.

HISTORY

caravans, especially the early ones. For Santa Fe residents, the trail meant a less-expensive supply of manufactured goods and a link to the outside world. Previously, the residents acquired anything they needed and couldn't make themselves from Chihuahua on El Camino Real or at the Indian trade fairs. The goods from Mexico were less diverse and more expensive than the assortment of things now available from the Santa Fe Trail.

In the early years of the Santa Fe Trail, the travelers did not pass a single permanent settlement between the western boundaries of Missouri and San Miguel del Vado, about 50 miles east of Santa Fe. The trip put them to the test as they faced water and food shortages, Indian attacks, disease, freezing storms, floods, and starvation. The wagons seldom covered more than 15 miles a day. Santa Fe looked good to these weary travelers, but they were quick to note how different the city was from the places they'd come from.

For most, Santa Fe was the first foreign city they'd ever visited. The locals dressed differently, ate different food, and spoke different languages. Most of those who arrived in Santa Fe had never encountered Spanish culture but had heard the "Black Legend." This common Anglo-American misperception maintained that the Spanish conquerors and settlers were unusually cruel to the Indians. The image was frequently reinforced in England and the Protestant countries of Europe with publications that illustrated Spanish mistreatment of natives with scenes of torture, maimings, and hangings. Since much of Europe was at war with Spain, this material could be considered anti-Spanish propaganda. While some individual Spanish were cruel and tyrannical, on the whole there is no evidence to demonstrate that the Spanish treated Indians any more or less cruelly than did other conquerors.

INSIDERS' TIP

During World War II, the first Japanese detainees arrived in Santa Fe on March 14, 1942, and went to a former Civilian Conservation Corps camp in an area now known as Casa Solana. At peak population, Camp Santa Fe held as many as 2,000 prisoners.

Santa Fe's adobe look was strange to the newcomers; many didn't even recognize the small, brown, box-like buildings as houses at first. Some travelers compared Santa Fe to a prairie dog town, perhaps not realizing that the mud bricks were ideal material for keeping out the day's heat and, once warmed by the fires from wood stoves in the winter, they retained heat far better than a log home. Inside, the homes lacked the furnishings common to the United States. Instead of formal beds, for instance, Santa Fe's practical residents folded their sleeping mattresses to double as couches during the day.

And the differences were more than just superficial. Blacks and Indians living in New Mexico and other Mexican territories had full rights of citizenship, unlike their counterparts in the United States. Also, as specified in the Mexican Constitution, all residents had the right of free speech. The Mexicans abolished the old Spanish caste system which established rigid social rankings based on a person's degree of Spanish blood. At the Governor's Ball in 1839, for example, an American visitor noted that the poor and rich alike attended and even danced together.

INSIDERS' TIP

A projectile found in northeastern New Mexico, in Folsom, served as a turning point in American archaeology. Radiocarbon dating at the Folsom site showed that people had been in the region beginning 10,900 years ago—near the end of the last ice age. Identical versions of the Folsom point have been found as far east as Iowa, as far west as the Great Basin, and from southern Canada all the way down to northern Mexico.

Another strong difference between Mexican Santa Fe and the United States was the status of women. Santa Fe women enjoyed much more freedom than their counterparts in the U.S. They retained their maiden names after marriage. They smoked, danced, and enjoyed gambling as much as the men. The women dressed less formally and in styles considerably less confining than those worn by women in the early 19th-century United States. Not only were they were not considered their husbands' property, women in Santa Fe had property rights and legal rights denied their U.S. counterparts. They worked for wages in jobs such as bakers, weavers, card dealers, and, of course, prostitutes. Women could own rental property and flocks and were not legally required to share their money with their husbands. Both wives and husbands could take spouses to court for legal redress of their grievances.

The U.S. travelers also entered a territory that was largely on its own in terms of religion. The Mexican government had offered no financial support to the Catholic Church—the only religion in the territory other than that of the American Indians—and priests were included in Mexico's orders for all Spanish-born citizens to leave the country. Afterwards, historians report, only five to eight priests remained to minister to the far-flung population. As a result of the lack of clergy, lay Catholic orders developed in rural communities to keep the faith alive. These brotherhoods became known as the Penitentes for their severe penance during Holy Week. As another result of the scarcity of priests and the high fee on marriage, more than half of the couples in Santa Fe lived together without the church's blessing.

Commerce and information flowed both ways along the Santa Fe Trail. In addition to selling the American products they brought by the wagonload, caravans returned to the United States with hides, pelts, and Indian weavings from New Mexico. Some Santa Fe merchants journeyed to the United States themselves to make purchases and return with goods that could be sold at a substantial profit. One of Santa Fe's best-known merchants was Gertrudes Barcelo, or "La Tules." La Tules made her money gambling and invested it in American goods, which she had shipped to Santa Fe to sell at a profit. Another trader who profited from the wagons was Governor Manuel Armijo himself. In addition to the benefit of their trade goods, the U.S. merchants paid customs duties on their cargoes, money that supported New Mexico's government, and paid the Santa Fe soldiers' salaries. Some travelers from the United States became citizens and lifelong residents of Santa Fe, holding office and helping the territory in many ways, including fighting Indian raiders as members of the citizen militia. Others were arrogant and lawless, trapping animals illegally, cheating their customers, demeaning the territory's Spanish-speaking people and their culture, and selling guns to hostile Indians.

Besides bringing merchandise, the trail brought massive cultural change. In June 1846, New Mexico's governor received word that the United States had declared war on Mexico. The war put Armijo in a terrible position. His duty as governor would be to fight the Americans in what was sure to be a doomed effort. After assembling several thousand disheveled troops for battle in

HISTORY

The Palace of the Governor's houses a vast collection of early artifacts and memorabilia.

Photo: Blair Clark, courtesy of Museum of New Mexico

Apache Canyon outside of Santa Fe, Armijo decided not fight and fled to Mexico. He was tried and acquitted of treason in Mexico City and returned to New Mexico, where he died under U.S. rule. Questions remain about Armijo's motivation: Was he bribed to leave or did he decide that avoiding bloodshed was in the best interests of New Mexico?

U.S. Gen. Stephen Watts Kearny and his staff rode into Santa Fe unobstructed to meet with New Mexico's acting governor, who greeted them politely and served them dinner complete with wine imported from El Paso over el Camino Real. The next day, Kearny made a speech to Santa Fe residents, attempting to alleviate their fears. He promised that their religion and language would be protected, that all provisions needed by the U.S. soldiers would be purchased, not stolen. He assured Santa Fe residents that they would have a voice in the new government and a role in the area's future. Three years later, in 1850, New Mexico became a U.S. territory and remained as such for more than 60 years before finally achieving statehood.

Santa Fe, U.S.A.

Kearny and his forces had taken Santa Fe without firing a shot, and the Stars and Stripes now flew over the Plaza. Five days after his arrival, the general instructed the soldiers with him to begin building the garrison of Fort Marcy on a hill overlooking the city. For the next 10 years, until New Mexico became involved in the Civil War, soldiers stationed here spent their time fighting off Apache and other Indian raids and protecting new immigrants along the Santa Fe Trail.

In 1847, however, the soldiers left their Santa Fe base and headed north to quell a revolution after hearing some startling news: the state's first U.S. territorial governor, Charles Bent, had been assassinated in Taos. The conspirators planned to attack and kill all Anglo Americans in northern New Mexico as well as all New Mexico natives who had accepted positions in the new government. On the night of January 18, conspirators had murdered Bent and five others and paraded Bent's scalp through the town. They continued the rampage, attacking and killing seven other men a few miles north of Taos; more were shot in Mora.

The U.S. forces responded with troops from Albuquerque joining the Santa Fe army. After defeating the rebels in a battle at Embudo, the U.S. forces continued on to Taos. They discovered that the unhappy New Mexicans had fortified themselves in the church at Taos Pueblo. Army artillery broke down the church walls, and after 150 rebels died in the fight, the others fled or surrendered. U.S courts tried the prisoners and hanged six of the leaders for their role in the bloody attempt at revolution.

The Taos rebellion was the last organized revolt against American authority in New Mexico, but raids and uprisings continued through 1847. Meanwhile, the English-speaking soldiers protected the Santa Fe settlers, new and old, from Indian raids. The U.S. government began work on a new State Capitol, intended to replace the Spanish Casas Reales. Construction began in 1850, but the money ran out before crews finished the work.

Native Santa Fe residents slowly adjusted to the U.S. presence and the slow but steady influx of Americans. They didn't complain about the establishment of twice-a-month mail service beginning in 1857. Stage coaches added Santa Fe to their line, and the city enjoyed a temporary economic boom in the 1850s, a period described by historian Marc Simmons as the heyday of the Santa Fe Trail.

As a concession to the ethnic realities of the area, territorial government was conducted in both English and Spanish, and the legislature itself was primarily Hispanic until 1886. Hispanics outnumbered non-Hispanics by about 50 to 1.

Among the travelers the trail brought was Santa Fe's first bishop, Frenchman Jean Baptiste Lamy. Lamy recruited adventurous priests, nuns, and brothers from Europe to help establish schools, hospitals, and orphanages in New Mexico and to care for the territory's sprawling population of Catholics. Lamy began construction of St. Francis Cathedral and Loretto Chapel. He introduced reform into New Mexico's long-neglected Catholic Church but declined to show what many residents believed was sufficient respect for New Mexico's indigenous religious traditions.

Lamy's imposition of northern European cultural values on New Mexico's Catholics, who had been largely independent of church authority for many decades, led to resentment. His clashes with native clergy and what many considered his disrespect for northern New Mexico's indigenous arts and culture—much of which had been created for the glory of God and the saints—brought conflict that continued throughout his long tenure as bishop and archbishop.

Other settlers of the 19th century came to Santa Fe as traders who wished to establish businesses or as sheep raisers, ranchers, and homesteaders looking for a fresh start. The people of Santa Fe called them "Anglo"—a word used to mean people who were not Spanish or American Indian.

The influx of Anglo settlers was prompted by cheap land and the rumor that the New Mexico climate was good for one's health. Health seekers and artists, who also appreciated Santa Fe's brilliantly clear air and high-country climate, continued to visit and move to Santa Fe off and on throughout the city's history. Many Spanish women married Anglos, but whether they did or not, women lost many of the freedoms they'd enjoyed prior to U.S. occupation.

Reflective of the changes that overtook the territory, Santa Fe received its first Protestant church—the first in New Mexico—built by the Baptists at the corner of Grant and Griffin Streets in 1854. The Presbyterians acquired the property in 1857 and remodeled it several times, ending with the Pueblo-Revival style building that exists today.

Despite the area's geographic isolation, the Civil War found New Mexico. In February 1862, a Confederate general leading troops from Texas invaded, won several crucial battles, and took control of Santa Fe. But Confederate rule didn't last long. On March 26, Union and Confederate forces met about 15 miles from Santa Fe. The Union troops destroyed Confederate supplies in the Battle of Glorieta and the Texans went south, abandoning their dreams of capturing the West.

The end of the Civil War brought no peace to the Santa Fe area because the major battles, conflicts with the Plains Indians, increased during U.S. rule. Unlike the Mexicans and Spanish governors, who had recognized Indian rights and lands, the new territorial government took a radically different approach. Reflecting the cultural values of the day, the U.S. government openly suppressed Indian rights and worked to destroy Native American culture. One of the most effective methods was forcing Indian children to leave their homes and go to boarding schools where they could not speak their native languages, practice their traditional religion, or stay in close touch with their families. As more settlers moved in, the problems worsened.

Conflict between the territorial government and the Spanish citizenry also continued. One governor, William Pile, angered Santa Fe residents when he ordered workers to dispose of all historic documents in a room at the Palace of the Governors, as the Casas Reales was now called. Outraged Hispanic and Anglo residents attempted to recover the priceless papers. Some were found as waste paper or meat wrappers; many were lost forever.

Once the Anglos gained political power in Santa Fe, an ugly anti-Hispanic prejudice took its toll on the area. Although the treaty of Guadalupe Hidalgo specified that Spanish and Mexican land grants in the territories acquired by the United States after the Mexican War would be respected, this was not to be. Differences in the systems of law made it difficult for many land-grant owners to substantiate their land titles. Although some of Santa Fe's prominent longtime families managed to keep their land and their power, most fared badly. Not speaking English or understanding the American legal system, they were easy prey for unscrupulous lawyers and politicians. The Spanish and Mexican judicial system required only that alcaldes, or judges, know how to read and write; the U.S. system called for trained lawyers. Anglo lawyers soon concentrated in Santa Fe, and many grew rich on their clients' misfortune.

INSIDERS' TIP

New Mexico Governor Manuel Armijo rented rooms in the Palace of the Governors to travelers who arrived in Santa Fe along the Santa Fe Trail.

One of Santa Fe's most powerful men during this period was Thomas Catron. Catron moved to Santa Fe from Missouri, learned to speak and write Spanish, and amassed more than a million and a half acres of land-grant property. A lawyer, Catron involved himself in local politics, ruled the powerful Republican Party, then worked as an advocate for statehood. He became one of New Mexico's first two senators. During his day and afterward, many accused him of unethical practices; his defenders say he accumulated his fortune and power legally and died bankrupt.

Accusations of fraud, political corruption, and malfeasance flowed freely for years in territorial New Mexico. Finally, the U.S. Secretary of the Interior suspended New Mexico's Gov. Samuel Axtell and named Lew Wallace in his place. Wallace is the best known of the state's territorial rulers, not so much for his politics, but because he worked on his famous novel, *Ben Hur*, while living at the Palace of the Governors.

In addition to the problems of Spanish families, who felt they were being unjustly deprived of their land, Wallace had to deal with Indian uprisings, raids by Billy the Kid in southeastern New Mexico, and growing conflict between cattle and sheep ranchers. He coined the often-repeated expression: "Every calculation based on experience elsewhere fails in New Mexico." During Wallace's administration the first successful effort was made to preserve and catalog priceless documents from Santa Fe's Mexican and Spanish periods.

Just as the Santa Fe Trail brought tremendous change to Santa Fe, so did another transportation innovation, the railroad. In 1880 the train made its presence felt and change followed rapidly. Even though it was named Atchison, Topeka & Santa Fe, the company planned to bypass Santa Fe because of engineering problems. A group of city boosters prevailed on the railroad to run an 18-mile spur to serve Santa Fe. Without rail service, they feared that Santa Fe would lose its prominence to rail towns such as Las Vegas and Albuquerque. The locomotives quickly brought the end to the Santa Fe Trail and delivered curious tourists to the city's doorstep. The spur line cut through the western part of town; railyards and depots went up using not adobe but red bricks brought by the trains.

The look of Santa Fe began to change. The railroad delivered building materials not previously available, among them wood for shingles and siding and glass for windows. Santa Fe residents enjoyed these new options; some wished to duplicate the homes they'd known in the East or Midwest; some long-time residents liked the idea of a more modern-looking house.

As Santa Fe's look began to become more like other cities in the United States, preservationists and the city promoters worried that the town would sacrifice its architectural distinctiveness and that the popularity of the new materials would mean the end of adobe and of Santa Fe's unique look. If the city lost its charm, they believed, it would also lose the tourist dollars that had begun to flow into its economy.

Historical sites, like the Nambé Mission, remind visitors of the colorful past of Santa Fe.

Photo: Don Strel

These city boosters, among them artists, archaeologists, civic leaders, and merchants, began to develop a plan for Santa Fe's future that included a unique architectural vision. The Pueblo-Revival style, also known as Spanish Pueblo style, combined modern convenience with the city's traditional look and ultimately came to be known as "Santa Fe Style."

In the 1880s, however, Santa Fe's style was not so tightly defined. A new State Capitol building and a governor's mansion—both not "Santa Fe style"—were constructed on vacant land south of the Santa Fe River. The capitol burned under mysterious circumstances five years later. Some blamed arson by Albuquerque partisans who wanted their town to become the state capital. Another new capitol, complete with pillars and a dome rather than Santa Fe–style vigas and a portal, was built in 1900.

But the proponents of Santa Fe's architectural heritage won a larger battle. The city persuaded the Territorial Legislature to renovate the Palace of the Governors and transform it into a museum instead of demolishing the old building. The Palace and the Fine Arts Museum constructed in the new "Santa Fe" style set the tone for later construction. La Fonda Hotel, the School of American Research, and the old Post Office building across from the Cathedral Place all testify to the early popularity of this look, which was to become an enduring trademark of modern Santa Fe.

Santa Fe's allure began to spread. Governor Lew Wallace wrote enthusiastically about his new home, one of many 19th-century writers and artists who raved about Santa Fe's attractions. Although the territory had its problems, no one wanted to know about that; the city's romanticization had begun. The railroad made it easier to come West, and visitors did.

With wonderful foresight, the territory of New Mexico established the Bureau of Immigration, a precursor to the modern Department of Economic Development, in Santa Fe in 1880. The department offered information to outsiders who hoped to make money here, but also received inquiries from artists, writers, and anthropologists drawn by Santa Fe's physical beauty and Hispanic and Indian cultures. Santa Fe's business community came together in 1882 as the Santa Fe Board of Trade, spearheading the movement that led to the incorporation of the city in

INSIDERS' TIP

South of Santa Fe on Cochití Pueblo land, seven sites have been excavated, showing that hunter/gatherer bands roamed the upper Rio Grande Valley as far back as 11,000 years ago.

1891. By the end of the 19th century, many community leaders recognized that Santa Fe's economic future hinged on two factors: tourism and government employment. In the decades that followed, their insight continued to ring true.

Statehood and Beyond

When Gen. Kearny first brought U.S. rule to Santa Fe, the city's population was estimated at between 2,000 and 4,000. By 1910, that figure was 5,600, with an additional 9,200 people living outside the city proper. Santa Fe and New Mexico marked the early years of the 20th century with ongoing cries for the rights of statehood. Three attempts at admission to the Union had failed, at least partly because of continuing anti-Catholic, anti-Spanish sentiment in Congress. New Mexico suggested joint statehood with Arizona in 1906, but Arizona rejected the idea. Finally, on January 6, 1912, President William Howard Taft signed the bill making New Mexico the 47th state.

Although it has been amended several times, the state constitution has never been rewritten—but the idea arises frequently. Generally a conservative document, the constitution specified that Spanish was equal to English in both public education and legal discourse, and included a bill of rights that again stressed that the rights provided in the Treaty of Guadalupe Hidalgo must be upheld. William C. MacDonald was New Mexico's first U.S. governor, living and working from Santa Fe, which continued to be the state capital.

In 1916, the old Fort Marcy headquarters were demolished to make way for the construction of the new Fine Arts Museum. A few years later, a group of artists and newcomers resurrected the Santa Fe Fiesta, including secular events and more parties to give the festival additional appeal. The custom of honoring *La Conquistadora* had survived, but when Santa Fe became a Mexican city the community began to celebrate Mexican independence rather than the exploits of Vargas—who became known in Santa Fe as "DeVargas."

In the 1920s, Santa Fe's art colony thrived, and visitors returned to the city seeking to become permanent residents. Painters captured the city's beauty on canvas and spread the word with their work. Before World War I, Sheldon Parsons, Victor Higgins, Gerald Cassidy, William Penhallow Henderson, B.J.O Nordfeldt, and many more artists enriched the city in many ways. Will Shuster—now best known for creating Zozobra—and four other Santa Fe painters became known as Los Cinco Pintores and spread the glory of Santa Fe's scenery and people with their art. John Sloan, George Bellows, and Leon Kroll—important names in 20th-century American art—spent time visiting and painting in Santa Fe. Edward Hopper and Marsden Hartley lived here in the 1920s and '30s, as did Robert Herni and Andrew Dausburg. In 1925 author Mary Austin and group of artists and collectors founded the Spanish Colonial Arts Society to encourage Hispanic artists to continue working in the traditions of the 18th century and to sell and promote their work. The 1920s also saw Santa Fe's first Indian Market, which became a long-standing community event. Leading southwestern anthropologist Clyde Kluckhohn arrived in Santa Fe in 1925. In addition to "real" art, Santa Fe of this era also was filled with curio shops for tourists, including travelers who came on the Indian Detours circuit, a popular Southwestern touring business based in Santa Fe.

In the 1930s Santa Fe architect John Gaw Meem accelerated the trend to re-create Santa Fe's traditional look. The National Park Service Headquarters, built during the New Deal era, is a beautiful example of Pueblo-Revival style. In the 1930s, due partly to the pressure applied to the federal government by some of the city's well-placed Anglo residents and changing cultural views, the repression of Indian culture eased. The U.S. Indian School, a boarding school that brought Indian students to Santa Fe, was allowed to open an art department. The result renewed interest in Indian art among both American Indians themselves and in the broader culture.

INSIDERS' TIP

The pen used by President William Howard Taft to sign the document authorizing New Mexico's statehood is on display at the Palace of the Governors, 107 W. Palace Avenue. New Mexico became the 47th state in 1912.

HISTORY

From birth to death, the Catholic Church was a crucial influence on early New Mexico's Spanish settlers.

Photo: Chris Corrie

Toward the Millennium

In the 1940s New Mexico assumed growing national importance due to its crucial role in the development of the atomic bomb. The U.S. government took over Los Alamos Ranch School in 1943, transforming the site into a secret center for nuclear research. The project brought a steady stream of scientists and their families through Santa Fe for the clandestine work. By 1945 more than 3,000 civilian and military personnel were living there. Atomic bombs built in Los Alamos were dropped in Nagasaki and Hiroshima, Japan. Los Alamos National Laboratory (LANL), operated by the United States Department of Energy through a contract with the University of

California, continues as a major contributor to Santa Fe and northern New Mexico's economy. The lab conducts a variety of scientific and technological research, including work on nuclear weapons. With approximately 7,000 on staff and millions of dollars worth of contracts with northern New Mexico businesses, LANL's presence is seen by some as a blessing. Others believe that weapons research should have no place in the modern world, much less in northern New Mexico.

Despite the pressures of contemporary society, Native Americans have held on to their culture and traditions.

Photo: Don Strel

Through the 1950s, Santa Fe continued to grow, spreading southwest. However, during the 1960s and '70s urban renewal, highway construction, State Capitol expansion projects, and the construction of large office buildings for state workers changed the city's urban pattern. The project caused realignment of roads and division of neighborhoods. Shopping centers, which offered lower rents and convenient parking, drew local customers away from downtown; Plaza businesses began to cater more to tourists and art buyers.

The construction of the Santa Fe Opera and its subsequent rise to national prominence helped keep Santa Fe's arts community in the spotlight. Established in 1957, the Opera successfully involved Santa Fe and New Mexico residents and businesses in its fund-raising. The Opera also attracted major corporate and out-of-state donors and now draws an international audience. The establishment of the Santa Fe Chamber Music Festival in 1975 added to Santa Fe's stature as an arts center. (See our Arts chapter.)

In 1957, the city created a historic district encompassing the Plaza and the eastern part of town. After the construction of two large buildings downtown in the 1970s and '80s, the city again tightened its protection for historic properties. Since then the designations have been expanded, and the rules and regulations for protecting historic properties in other neighborhoods clarified. Excavation at the Palace of the Governors in 1975 uncovered evidence from all periods of the history of the building. Visitors to the Palace today can see storage bins from 1693 in a glass-covered pit beneath the floorboards.

The establishment of St. John's College in 1964 enhanced Santa Fe's status as an educational center. The creation of Santa Fe Community College in 1983 made it possible for the first time for Santa Fe students to continue their learning at a public college without leaving home. (See our Education chapter.) Beginning in the early 1980s, Hollywood and music celebrities "discovered" Santa Fe, many buying homes in the area and others vacationing here regularly. Their presence and the resulting media attention added to Santa Fe's growing attraction as a place for millionaires to build second homes. This led to more gourmet restaurants, first-rate art galleries, and luxury shops. It also led to accelerating rents and real estate prices, higher property taxes, and the dislocation of some longtime residents. Santa Fe also attracted many "New Agers" and has become a center for the study and practice of alternative medicine.

INSIDERS' TIP

A excavation behind the former Woolworth's building just off the Plaza in 1999 uncovered almost 30 boxes of historic debris. The crews found numerous artifacts from the Old Santa Fe Trail days. People who work downtown, visitors, and school groups had an opportunity to watch the urban archaeologists on the job and ask them questions about

HISTORY

By the late 1990s, the city's population reflected the influx of non-Hispanic residents; Hispanics became a minority here for the first time in the city's history.

Modern Santa Fe contends with issues that face many cities in the United States: traffic, the need for affordable housing, problems with the public school system, crime, and growing demand for city services. In 1994, Santa Fe elected its first woman mayor, former city councilor Debbie Jaramillo. Jaramillo's anti-tourism comments and the hiring of her brother and brother-in-law in major city jobs led to considerable controversy and brought negative national attention to Santa Fe. But the Jaramillo administration also inaugurated a successful affordable-housing program, purchased the railyard property, and initiated new services for children and teenagers. The voters replaced Jaramillo with a more moderate mayor and also approved a city charter allowing "home rule" which, among other changes, gives Santa Fe voters the right to recall public officials.

INSIDERS' TIP

Santa Fe residents had no idea what was going on in the Jémez Mountains at the secret research site that became Los Alamos. As work on the atomic bomb continued, one rumor had it that the crews were building windshield wipers for submarines.

The city's reputation as an intellectual center was boosted with the opening of the Santa Fe Institute, a high-tech think tank which draws scientists, computer experts, writers, and intellectuals from around the world. In the 1990s Santa Fe was also home to more than 50 publishing companies. As the city grows in the new millennium, Santa Fe's economic base remains tourism and government, with a recent influx of small entrepreneurial companies including spin-offs of technology developed by Los Alamos National Laboratory.

Modern Santa Fe's population reflects the city's deep roots. You'll find American Indian families, the descendents of the founding Spanish immigrants, great grandchildren of merchants who arrived over the Santa Fe Trail, and new residents from California, Texas, and elsewhere, who find the city's culture, history, and natural environment irresistible. Readers of the upscale Condé Nast travel publications consistently rank Santa Fe among their top 10 national and international destinations. The city's visitors bureau estimates that 3 million tourists spend time here over the course of a year—with more than half of them arriving in the three months of summer.

If you want to learn more about Santa Fe's rich and long history, wonderful books await you. Check the shop at the Palace of the Governors or any of the city's bookstores. Now that you know a little about the forces that shaped modern Santa Fe, please use this guide to get the most out of your visit.

HISTORY

Local Cultures

LOOK FOR:
- **Hispanic Culture**
- **Pueblo Culture**
- **A Footnote on Anglos**

Northern New Mexico is a land of conquest and reconquest, sometimes accomplished by forceful means, other times without a drop of blood spilled. The region has changed hands and complexions many times, starting with the Pueblo Indians, whose agrarian, cliff-dwelling forebears settled the region as far back as the 1st century B.C.

Pueblo culture as we know it today took root at the beginning of the 14th century and flourished for 300 years—until its first encounter in 1540 with Europeans, who brought guns as well as a new world of diseases against which the natives had no natural defenses. Through force in some cases and friendly but firm persuasion in others, Spanish conquistadores, priests, and settlers claimed the region in the name of the motherland and the Catholic Church, only to lose it in 1680 in the Pueblo Revolt (see our History chapter). Spain reconquered the New Mexico territory in 1692 and held onto it until 1821, when Mexico won independence from Spain and claimed the territory as its own. But the Mexican flag flew over New Mexico only 27 years, to be replaced by the Stars and Stripes after Mexico lost a two-year war with the United States. It ceded the territory in 1848 to its young northern neighbor in accordance with the terms of the Treaty of Guadalupe Hidalgo.

Hispanic Culture

The result of this checkered history is a checkerboard of cultures, with Anglo-Americans among the last to arrive. "Anglo" culture is a category that today in New Mexico encompasses everything from white-bred Middle Americans to African Americans, Arabs, Asians, East Indians, Irish, Italians, Jews, Poles, Russians, and anyone else not of Hispanic or Native American origin. Despite the subtle and not-so-subtle encroachment of Anglo culture over the past 150 years, the dominant flavor of northern New Mexico is without a doubt Hispanic. What that means, however, has been an ongoing—and often heated—debate in which many hispanos have shunned their Mexican roots in favor of their Spanish heritage, while a few have taken the opposite stance.

Today, however, most people agree that local Hispanic culture has its roots in both Spain and Mexico as well as in Native America. Whatever the precise definition, it's a combination unique to New Mexico—one you'll see, hear, and feel the moment you emerge from the airplane into the Albuquerque International Sunport and make your way toward Santa Fe or other points north. It's all around you—in the art and the architecture, the music and the clothing, the food, and the language . . . especially the language.

Here we live in flat-roofed adobe homes on *caminos* and *calles*. Outside, our *portales* (porches) are decorated with bright red chile *ristras*. Inside, our *casas* have corner *kiva* fireplaces and log *vigas* that hold up

INSIDERS' TIP

Low-riders are sleek, customized cars that sit low to the ground—in some cases low enough to be grounded by a speed bump. Many are fitted with hydraulics that raise and lower the vehicle at the flick of a switch. Chrome is often a prominent feature on low-riders, as are eye-catching, incredibly intricate paint jobs. Some are literally works of art, including one from New Mexico that's in the Smithsonian Institution in Washington, D.C. To catch a glimpse of low-riders in Santa Fe, head on over to Alameda Street on a Saturday night. If you're driving, don't plan to be anywhere in a hurry because the low-riders are cruisin'. Española , just a half-hour north of Santa Fe, is the "Low Rider Capital of the World," according to MTV.

latilla ceilings. Our walls are decorated with built-in *nichos* displaying handcrafted santos—religious images carved by *santeros*—that glorify *Díos*. We wear bolo ties and concho belts. We dance to ranchero music, mariachi, or salsa, which is also something we eat with tortilla chips and guacamole before digging into plates filled with enchiladas or burritos with red or green chile and perhaps a side of posole or chicos. Chicos are also children, whom parents affectionately call *mi hijo* or *mi hijita*—elided to *m'ijo* or *m'ijita*—sending them off to *la escuela* (school) where they recite the Pledge of Allegiance first in English, then in Spanish.

That's a far cry from the time between the 19th century and the mid-20th century, when New Mexican children were punished for speaking Español in school. Today, students learn early on that the Spanish arrived in New Mexico years before the real Anglos—the English Puritans—landed at Plymouth Rock. They're fully aware that Santa Fe is the oldest state capital and the second-oldest city in the nation.

In schools and elsewhere throughout New Mexico, there's a pride in *la raza*, which literally means "the race" but has become synonymous with a Hispanic heritage that locally has produced artists and artisans whose work is recognized throughout the United States and abroad. Traditional or folk artists utilize native materials—wood, tin, silver, straw, etc.—and techniques that in many cases their families have been using for generations. While the Spanish and Mexican influences are apparent in their work, the styles are uniquely New Mexican—and often unique to a particular family. Like their brethren around the world, contemporary hispano artists, work in every imaginable medium. Sculpture, painting, photography, jewelry, and, yes, those elegant, traffic-stopping labors of love called low riders (see our tip in this chapter) all play an integral role in the northern New Mexico art scene. So do Hispanic literature, film, theater, dance, music, and lore.

The area reflects a lively traditon of Spanish arts.

Photo: Don Strel

Of course, Hispanics—who represent nearly half the population of Santa Fe—play major roles in all walks of life, not just the arts. They're accomplished doctors, dentists, lawyers, teachers, priests, and politicians, to name just a few professions. In fact, the two most powerful men in the State Legislature are Hispanic and have each been in their respective positions—speaker of the House of Representatives and Senate president pro tem—for a decade and a half.

But la cultura hispana is far more than what people do for a living, the clothes they wear, the food they eat or even the language they speak, though the latter is closer to the crux of the matter. Here in northern New Mexico, Hispanic culture is *la gente* (the people), whose first priority generally is *la familia* followed by *la comunidad*. Sometimes they're one and the same.

Embedded in the local Hispanic culture is a deep-rooted sense of *hidalguismo*—an aristocratic lineage that hearkens back to the founding of Santa Fe in 1608 by the nobility (*los hidalgos*) in concert with the Catholic Church. While *el hidalguismo* and the entitlement that came with it is today merely a vestige, the Catholic Church has survived intact. Indeed, *el catolicismo* touches all aspects of *la vida* in northern New

A marker gives some history of the church at Las Trampas, a small village north of Santa Fe. El Catolicismo (the Catholic Church) has influenced the area since the 17th century.

Photo: Don Strel

Mexico, regardless of one's faith. From the *Sangre de Cristo* (Blood of Christ) Mountains that loom over the northern Rio Grande Valley to the myriad churches, missions, and *moradas* (see the close-up on Penitentes in our Worship chapter) dotting the landscape; from invocations at government functions and school sporting events to Las Fiestas de Santa Fe which, despite its secular trappings, is Catholic at its core; from the festive farolitos that light rooftops and driveways throughout the Christmas season to the annual Easter pilgrimage to the Santuario de Chimayó—there's no question that northern New Mexico, and particularly La Villa Real de Santa Fe (Royal City of the Holy Faith), was founded as a far reaching bastion of the Spanish Catholic Church. It remains tied to those roots at its deepest levels.

Spain's influence in New Mexico goes beyond religion and art. Spanish colonizers who survived the perilous six-month trek along el Camino Real—the 2,000-mile "Royal Road" or "King's Highway" from Mexico City to Santa Fe—brought with them mining and forging equipment and techniques. They showed the Native Americans how to use metals for weapons, tools, and art. They brought the wheel, introduced horses to the continent, and taught pueblos how to raise cattle and sheep. They engineered the efficient and esthetic acequia irrigation system still used throughout New Mexico today.

Despite armed conflicts between the two cultures, the settlers in time found they had more in common with their native neighbors than they did with distant Spain, if only because they shared a common enemy in the hostile Plains Indians. Years of commingling among the Spanish, Mexicans, and Indians eventually gave rise in New Mexico to a unique mestizo culture of its own—one rich with tradition, much of it oral. *La curandera* (healer) cures body and mind with unwritten methods passed down to her, and which she will pass on to the next generation; *el mayordomo* consults no manual to direct the annual cleaning of the *acequias* (irrigation ditches); *la cuentista* (storyteller) needs no script to relate *los cuentos* (tales) and *las leyendas* (legends) that hundreds of years of telling and retelling have refined and embellished.

What we've described thus far is a colorful portrait of Hispanic life in northern New Mexico. But this multifaceted culture that has flourished here since the 16th century has of late been confronted with a dark side. In Santa Fe, where until recently hispanos were in the majority, the unemployment and poverty rates among Hispanics are disproportionately high. Consequently, so are the dropout rate, homicide rate, and incidents of domestic violence. The powers that be attribute this largely to a movement away from what was once primarily a land-based culture to a free-market, wage-dependent economy where traditional skills such as farming and ranching are no longer marketable. Add to this volatility an invasion of visitors and new, moneyed residents and perhaps you can understand why many in the Hispanic community feel disenfranchised. They sense they're losing their land, their voice, and ultimately their culture to the highest bidder.

For the survival of their rich heritage and a legacy to pass on to future generations, it's vital that Santa Fe cling to its roots. The answer lies not in isolationism, but rather in preserving the cultural vitality of the region without exploiting it.

Pueblo Culture

Centuries before Europeans reached the Americas, New Mexico was home to a thriving native population we call Anasazi—"the ancient ones," according to the most familiar translation from the Navajo, though the term literally means "the enemy of my ancestors." At the height of its civilization (approximately A.D. 900 to 1350), the Anasazi lived in a territory that stretched from central Utah and southern Colorado south to Mexico and from western Arizona into the Texas panhandle. Their abandoned cities of cliff dwellings, pit houses, underground ceremonial kivas, and petroglyphs etched in rock are silent testament to the richness and resourcefulness of their culture. Many of New Mexico's 19 existing Indian pueblos—nine of them within 65 miles from Santa Fe—trace their origins directly to the Anasazi. The Navajo and Jicarilla Apache tribes, located in or near the remote Four Corners region in northeastern New Mexico, and the Mescalero Apaches in south central New Mexico descended from the nomadic Athapascan tribe that arrived later. With some notable exceptions—among them the 1680 Pueblo Revolt (see our History chapter) and the current controversy over tribal casinos—Native Americans in the Southwest have kept a low profile, both politically and socially. Yet their artistic, architectural, and culinary influence on the region is unmistakable. Native culture permeates all aspects of life here to some degree.

It was the Pueblo Indians that Spanish explorers first encountered when they arrived in New Mexico in the mid-1600s. They found a flourishing, agrarian, and relatively peaceful population living in compact, apartment-like dwellings made of stone or adobe. The explorers christened them "pueblo" Indians from the Spanish word for "village"—a term that refers to the entire culture rather than a specific tribe. Spanish settlers adopted the native architecture and adapted the Indians' sophisticated method of underground irrigation to their own acequia system. At the time of the first encounter, close to 50,000 Indians lived on more than 100 pueblos. By 1857, they numbered only 7,000. Their civilization had been decimated by disease, starvation, and execution while their culture was dying from assimilation—both forced and voluntary—and intermarriage. Still, the tribes managed to preserve many traditions by externally adopting the ways of the various paternalistic governments that occupied their native lands while secretly continuing to practice their own pantheistic religions and customs. Many of the new ways stuck, most notably Catholicism, which is widely practiced on the pueblos, though it has been adapted to native practices. This is particularly evident on feast days, which combine elements of the native religion with commemoration of Catholic saints.

Modern Pueblo Life

Today, New Mexico's 19 pueblos count an estimated 30,000 members, many of whom live away from their tribal lands. The pueblos share many characteristics, including similar customs and native languages—Tewa, Tiwa, Towa, and Keresan. (Zuni Indians speak Zunian, which is unrelated to the other four languages.) But each pueblo is a unique, sovereign entity with individual governmental, religious, and social structure. Every tribe also has a distinctive style in jewelry, weaving, basketry, carving, and especially pottery; pueblo pottery is considered among the finest of all North American tribes. The black-on-black pottery made famous by María Martínez, for example, is recognized internationally as being from San Ildefonso Pueblo, while geometric black and white pots are clearly from Ácoma Pueblo, "The City in the Sky" west of Albuquerque.

Pueblo Annual Events

New Mexico's pueblos hold numerous feasts, dances and other celebrations throughout the year that are open to non-Indians. We've included below a tentative schedule. Please call the pueblo before attending any event as schedules can—and often do—change with little advance notice. Feast days remain the same from year-to-year. So do the celebrations for the Transfer of Canes and All King's Day celebrations, which fall respectively on New Years Day and January 6, as do the dances on Christmas Eve and Christmas Day. Be sure to check with the individual pueblo, however, to ascertain that the celebrations are open to the public. Please refer to our close-up on pueblo etiquette before your visit.

January
January 1: Transfer of canes (inauguration of new tribal officials). Various dances. Most pueblos.
January 6: All King's Day celebration in honor of new tribal officials. Most northern pueblos.
January 22-23: Feast day celebrations. Various dances. San Idelfonso Pueblo.
January 25: St. Paul feast day. Various dances. Picurís Pueblo.

February
February 2: Candelaria Day celebrations. Various dances. Picurís Pueblo.
Late February: Deer dance. San Juan Pueblo.

March/April
Ester weekend: Easter dances. Most pueblos.

May
Corn dances. Tesque Pueblo.
May 3: Santa Cruz feast day. Various dances. Cochití. Taos Pueblo.
May 4: Corn dances, footraces. Taos Pueblo.

Feast day celebrations and dances attract visitors to the pueblos.

Photo: Don Strel

June
First Saturday: Blessing of the Fields. Various dances. Tesuque Pueblo.
June 13: San Antonio feast day. Various dances. Santa Clara and Taos Pueblos.
June 24: Feast day. Various dances. Corn dances. San Juan and Taos Pueblos.

July
First weekend: Weekend High Country Arts & Crafts Festival. Picurís Pueblo.
July 4: Nambé Falls celebration. Various dances. Nambé Pueblo.
Second weekend: Annual Pow-Wow. Taos Pueblo.
Mid-July: Annual Northern Pueblo Artist & Craftsman Show. San Ildefonso.
July 25: Santiago Feast day. Corn Dances. Taos Pueblo.

August
August 9-10: San Lorenzo feast day. Various dances. Picurís Pueblo.
August 12: Santa Clara feast day. Various dances. Santa Clara Pueblo.
Late August/Early September: Corn dances. San Idelfonso Pueblo.

September
TBA: Harvest dance. San Juan Pueblo.
September 28-29: San Geronimo feast day. Various dances. Nambé, Picurís, San Juan, and Taos Pueblos.

October
October 3-4: St. Francis of Assisi feast day. Various dances Nambé Pueblo.

November
San Diego feast day. Various dances. Tesuque Pueblo.

December
December 12: Guadalupe feast day celebrations. Pojoaque Pueblo.
December 24: Christmas celebrations. Various dances. Most pueblos.
December 26: Turtle dance. San Juan Pueblo.
December 28: Holy Innocents Day. Children's dances. Picurís, Santa Clara pueblos.

Please call each pueblo for schedule and/or event changes.

Pueblo Etiquette

Remember that old adage, "When in Rome, do as the Romans do?" It applies doubly when visiting Indian reservations. Please don't be lulled into a sense of complacency because people on the reservations speak English. The pueblos are sovereign lands with their own culture and a different code of etiquette than the one with which you're most likely familiar. The language may be the same, but it's a completely different culture. Please take to heart the following suggestions for courteous behavior so as not to offend your hosts or make future guests unwelcome. Please take special note of the rules at the end of this section for taking photographs.

General Etiquette:
• Every pueblo has its own government and its own set of rules for visitors. Please learn the rules and regulations of each pueblo before entering and obey them during your visit.

(Continued on next page)

• While the pueblos are open to the public during the day, private homes are not. Do not enter anyone's house without permission.

• If you are invited into someone's house on a feast day, don't linger at the table after you've finished eating. Your host will want to serve many guests throughout the day.

• By all means, thank your host, but it is inappropriate to offer any payment or tip.

• Pueblo dances are religious ceremonies, not staged performances. Observe them with the respect and quiet attention you would maintain in a house of worship. Please don't talk or wave or otherwise disturb nondancers. It's considered impolite to ask questions about dances or make comments about their meaning. Applause is inappropriate.

• Refrain from talking to dancers and don't approach them as they are entering, leaving, or resting near the *kiva*.

• *Kivas* and graveyards are sacred places and not to be entered by any non-pueblo person.

• Don't wander beyond areas open to tourists.

• Don't climb walls or other structures. Some are hundreds of years old and fragile.

• Do not take or even pick up artifacts such as broken pottery or other objects.

• Obey all parking and traffic signs, especially speed limits, to keep the pueblo safe for children and the elderly.

• Do not bring in pets.

• Alcohol, weapons, and drugs are strictly forbidden.

Photography:

• Permits, fees, and restrictions vary from pueblo to pueblo.

• Any photographs you take must be for private use only and may not be reproduced or used for commercial purposes without written permission.

• Please do not photograph any individuals without their express permission.

• Do not attempt to take a photo or make sketches or recordings if you are forbidden to do so.

• A photo permit does not give anyone license to disrupt dances by getting in front of the dancers or spectators.

Visitors enjoy a Rain Dance performed at San Ildefonso Pueblo.

Photo: Don Strel

LOCAL CULTURES

The Indian Pueblo Cultural Center in Albuquerque offers dances from a number of pueblos in New Mexico and elsewhere.

Photo: Ron Benrmann/Albuquerque Convention and Visitors Bureau

Underlying the art and the very culture of the Pueblo Indians is a deeply personal and religious connection to the earth. Sometimes this is literal, as in the earth-toned, close-to-the-ground, mud and clay pueblo architecture that inspired the Spanish Colonial construction universally recognized as "Santa Fe style." Other times it's symbolic, as in dances or other religious ceremonies. In either case, Native culture embraces the notion that one doesn't own the land, one belongs to it. As such, land is not a resource to be exploited but rather one to be respected. The land defines your origins as it defines your destiny. It also provides shelter and food and is the source of native art.

Until recently, land was the basis of the pueblos' economy—through agriculture, livestock, and the sale of pottery, jewelry, baskets, and other crafts. Today, however, a land-based economy is rapidly being supplanted by casinos as the main source of income for many pueblos. This has stirred a tremendous debate both within and outside the Indian community. Casinos have brought jobs and dollars to communities where unemployment has been as high as 45 percent and where staggering poverty and its associated ills—malnutrition, alcoholism, poor education, domestic violence, and an alarming increase in violent crimes—have over the years become the norm.

With revenue from their casinos, however, many tribes for the first time can afford to build sorely needed infrastructure and social programs. Fewer young men and women are leaving the pueblos, while many who took off for urban centers are returning home. As a result, tribes are gaining the human and material resources necessary to compete with their non-Indian neighbors on a more level playing field. And, indeed, they're taking a more active role in local, state, and federal policy-making. But many say it's a Faustian bargain that comes with its own set of problems, among them gambling addictions, increased substance abuse, the potential for corruption, and especially a clash of values. In trying to balance culture and tradition with political and economic pragmatism, the pueblos are taking steps to diversify their economies in ways

LOCAL CULTURES

that are both lucrative and in harmony with traditional values. But they're not likely to supplant the casinos, at least not any time soon. That genie has long left the bottle, leaving behind it a colossal political, cultural, social, and economic hot potato with still unimagined implications.

Dances and Feast Days

There's no doubt that the pueblos are undergoing dramatic change. Through it all, they continue to practice their old and largely secret ways. These include ceremonial dances, which link the pueblo people to their physical and spiritual ancestors and to nature. Although some dances are open to the public, they are not entertainment. Dances are religious ceremonies, most of which are tied to seasonal or life-cycle events such as hunting, sowing, harvesting, initiations, rites of passage, etc. The pueblos perform dances to sanctify an event, to give thanks or to influence nature—for bountiful crops, for example, or a successful hunt. Non-Indians are privileged to watch selected dances on the pueblos at various times during the year, typically on Christmas Eve, Christmas Day, New Year's Day, Easter, and selected days throughout the year, most in summer. The rest are closed to outsiders—a result, in part, of centuries of persecution by non-Indians who have misunderstood and misinterpreted native rituals. The tribes believe that secrecy has helped their religion survive. For that

Pueblo youth are immersed in Pueblo cultural activites starting at a very early age.

Photo: Chris Corrie

reason, you're likely to be met with a stony silence if you ask questions about dances or volunteer comments on their symbolic or spiritual meaning. Please refer to this chapter's close-up on pueblo etiquette.

Feast days, on the other hand, are a remnant of the pueblos' encounters with Europeans. Yet they're a uniquely Indian event. When the Spanish arrived in New Mexico in the late 16th century, missionaries assigned a patron saint to each pueblo in an effort to convert the Indians to Catholicism. In time, the saints' days became aligned with the pueblos' native religion because they coincided with tribal rituals. Today, feast days are a time when friends and family gather to eat together and participate in native ceremonies. They're also a time when tribal members invite complete strangers into their homes for a meal of green or red chile, posole (stewed hominy), fry bread, cookies, or any of a number of other dishes. Forget the diet when you visit a pueblo on a feast day. It's considered impolite to refuse an invitation to eat. By doing so, you will have spurned your host's hospitality and generosity. Once again, we implore you to read the close-up in this chapter on etiquette.

Feast days are held the same day every year. Dances take place at various times and may be scheduled a year or maybe just a few days ahead of time. We recommend calling the pueblo before visiting to confirm any dates listed here or elsewhere, even in pueblo literature. Schedule changes are common. The pueblo can also provide you with information about taking photographs or making recordings or drawings, any or all of which may be prohibited or for which there may be a charge.

Following are individual descriptions of what collectively are called the Eight Northern Indian Pueblos, all within an hour and a half's drive north of Santa Fe. Each entry includes a brief history as well as the date of the pueblo's annual feast day. You'll find a complete, tentative schedule of dances and other events at the end of this chapter. Most ceremonies begin mid-morning and last until shortly after dusk. Again, please be sure to call the pueblo before attending an event to make sure the date and times haven't changed.

Eight Northern Indian Pueblos Council
San Juan Pueblo, S.R. 74
• (505) 852-4265, (800) 793-4955

The Eight Northern Indian Pueblos Council is a cooperative group that works to promote joint projects and improve the economy, education, and ceremonial efforts of the eight pueblos located due north of Santa Fe. The council, a consortium of the eight pueblos' governors, sponsors the Eight Northern Indian Arts and Crafts Show, which takes place in July at Pojoaque Pueblo. The show features Native American arts and crafts, dancing, and traditional food. Unlike Indian Market (see our Attractions chapter), the Eight Northern Indian Arts and Crafts Show is an Indian-run enterprise.

Nambé Pueblo
Rt. 1, Box 117BB, Nambé
• (505) 455-2036

Patron saint: San Francisco de Asís (St. Francis). Feast day: October 4 with pre-feast celebrations and dances on October 3.

Pronounced Nahm-BEH, the name of this pueblo is Tewa for "Mound of Earth in the Corner"—a poetic and apt description for the 19,076 acres that are home to an estimated 600 tribal members. It is one of the smaller of the northern pueblos. Occupied since A.D. 1300, Nambé was a religious and cultural center for Pueblo Indians throughout the region long before the Spanish arrived. As such, it became a target for conquistadores and priests whose mission included converting the natives to Catholicism. The tribe took an active role in the Pueblo Revolt of 1680, when their priest was killed and their church destroyed.

Today, the tribe is highly assimilated with the surrounding community, which is primarily Hispanic. Over the past decade, however, members have taken an active interest in reviving traditional arts and crafts—a mainstay of the tribe's economy. You'll find many resi-

INSIDERS' TIP

In case you missed our reminder elsewhere in this chapter, don't forget to read our close-up on pueblo etiquette before you visit. It will save you from embarrassing yourself or offending others.

The pueblos welcome visitors to attend some of their dances during the year. Please check with the tribal office before taking photos.

Photo: Chris Corrie

LOCAL CULTURES

dents selling pottery, jewelry, and other crafts out of their homes. The pueblo also houses a sculpture gallery and studio displaying both traditional and contemporary art at the pueblo. Nambé Pueblo offers recreational opportunities galore, including camping, fishing, and boating at Nambé Falls Recreation Area. As the name implies, the recreation area affords a close look at three natural waterfalls as well as a lake and stunning views of the Sangre de Cristo Mountains. You might catch a glimpse of the tribe's buffalo herd, which at last count had 21 animals. The pueblo holds its annual Nambé Falls Celebration on July 4th with a variety of traditional dances, food vendors, and arts and crafts. The pueblo recently formed an economic development corporation that oversees a 150-acre industrial park, a 410-unit mobile home park, a recycling center, and a number of other enterprises. Directions from Santa Fe: Take U.S. Highway 84/285 N. 16 miles to the junction with N.M. Highway 503 north of Pojoaque; then head east 2 miles on N.M. 503.

Picurís Pueblo
Off N.M. Hwy. 75, 13 miles east of Dixon
• (505) 587-2519

Patron saint: San Lorenzo (St. Lawrence). Feast day: August 10 with pre-feast celebrations and dances on August 9.

Once one of the largest of the northern pueblos, today Picurís [pee-kuh-REES]—or Welai, which means "Those Who Paint" in Tiwa—is among the smallest with 345 members living in a secluded valley of the Sangre de Cristo Mountains about an hour north of Santa Fe. The Picurís ancestors arrived in the region around A.D. 750, settling first in a larger pueblo called Pot Creek before moving in or around the year 1250 to its current location some 20 miles south of Taos. The Picurís historically were more aggressive than other pueblos, perhaps because of greater contact with the aggressive Plains Indians. Picurís Indians were deeply involved in the 1680 Pueblo Revolt (see our History chapter), killing their priest and many of the area's Spanish settlers on August 10, 1680, which also happens to be the saint's day for San Lorenzo, for whom the pueblo was named. The Picurís paid a heavy price for their rebellion when the Spanish returned in 1692 and literally taxed them into starvation.

Picurís was 3,000 members strong when the

Spanish arrived. By the end of the 17th century, only 500 were left, and they abandoned their pueblo. They reclaimed their ancestral

Family and community are primary aspects of Indian pueblo life.

Photo: Don Strel

land in 1706—14,947 acres that today boasts a number of excavated ruins and an above-ground ceremonial kiva that's at least 700 years old.

The pueblo's centerpiece remains the San Lorenzo de Picurís mission, an old adobe church that took 12 years to restore by hand. The tribe operates an on-site museum, gift shop, and restaurant and is the majority owner of the Hotel Santa Fe in the capital city. The pueblo has a small buffalo herd and two well-stocked trout-fishing ponds. Tours are available for Anasazi pueblo and church ruins. In addition to the Feast of San Lorenzo in August, the pueblo hosts a feast day for St. Paul (San Pablo) on January 25 and another for St. Anthony (San Antonio) in June. On Father's Day weekend, the tribe hosts a Tri-Cultural Arts & Crafts Fair featuring the work of Native Americans, Hispanics, and "Anglos." The pueblo expects to have opened its new Holistic Healing Center in the summer of 2000. Directions from Santa Fe: Take U.S. Highway 84/285 N. 24.3 miles to the junction with N.M. 68 in Española. Go 20 miles north

INSIDERS' TIP
Most Pueblo people speak their native language, English, and often some Spanish as well.

LOCAL CULTURES

on N.M. 68 to the junction with N.M. 75 in the vicinity of Dixon, and go 13 miles east on N.M. 75.

Pojoaque Pueblo
Rt. 11, Box 21GS, Pojoaque
• (505) 455-3460

Patron saint: Our Lady of Guadalupe. Feast day: December 12.

With an estimated 280 members, Pojoaque (po-WAH-keh) is the smallest of all the northern pueblos. Its name is a Spanish derivative of P'o-Suwae-Geh, which is Tewa for "Water Drinking Place." Because of its abundance of water, Pojoaque was a major gathering place for Pueblo Indians of the Rio Grande prior to the Pueblo Revolt of 1680. The 11,063-acre pueblo sits between Nambé and Tesuque (Teh-SOO-keh) pueblos along U.S. Highway 84/285, the northbound highway out of Santa Fe. Pojoaque is the site of the first Spanish mission in New Mexico, San Francisco de Pojoaque, founded in the early 1600s. The pueblo is notable for twice rising from near extinction. The first occurrence was in 1706 when five families resettled on tribal lands that had been ravaged during and after the Pueblo

Revolt and were completely deserted by the time the Spanish returned in 1692. They rose again in 1934 when 14 individuals returned from nearby pueblos and states to which the Pojoaque tribe had scattered after a turn-of-the-century smallpox epidemic nearly wiped out all its members. A drought and encroachment by non-Indians added to the pueblo's demise. But like the Phoenix, the pueblo quite literally rose from its ashes, with survivors rebuilding it physically and culturally. Its church, built in 1706, is still used today. Among the pueblo's newer buildings is its Poeh Cultural Center and Museum, (505) 455-3334, built in the style of the Anasazi. In addition to showcasing arts and crafts of Tewa-speaking people, the cultural center also offers classes in pottery, sculpture, textiles, and art business management to tribal members and other Indians. The tribe manages a shopping center and a tourist information office that sells artwork from a variety of Tewa-speaking pueblos. But the pueblo's pride and joy without a doubt is its Cities of Gold Casino (505) 455-3313, (800) 455-3313, a 40,000-square-foot gambling hall that employs about 700 people and whose revenue helped finance

> ## INSIDERS' TIP
> In New Mexico, you will more often hear indigenous people refer to themselves as "Indians" than "Native Americans," though the latter is perfectly acceptable.

A Native American Pueblo woman is shown here tending a "horno" which is used for baking bread.

Photo: Chris Corrie

LOCAL CULTURES

the tribe's 124-room Cities of Gold Hotel, (505) 455-0515, (800) 455-0515; Cities of Gold Sports Bar, (505) 455-2072, (800) 455-3313; a brand new wellness center, (505) 455-9355; and even a public library, (505) 455-7411. The tribe also operates a mobile home park, a gas station and convenience store, and a nearby industrial park. A hotel/golf course resort was still under construction when this book went to press. Directions from Santa Fe: Take U.S. 84/285 north 15 miles.

San Ildefonso Pueblo
Rt. 5, Box 315A
• **(505) 455-3549**

Patron saint: San Ildefonso (St. Ildefonse). Feast day: January 23. Pre-feast ceremonies are held on January 22.

Named for a 7th-century archbishop from Toledo, San Ildefonso's Tewa name is Po-Woh-Ge-Oweenge, or "Where the Water Cuts Down Through." A small pueblo, San Ildefonso is also one of the most beautiful with 26,198 acres that run from the Rio Grande to the upper elevations of the Jémez Mountains near Los Alamos. Cottonwood (*alamo*) trees line the riverbanks, deer and elk roam the land, and from all directions you can see Black Mesa—a dark, lonely hill sacred to the pueblo because it's the site where San Ildefonso and other pueblos valiantly but unsuccessfully defended their lands against the Spanish in 1694.

The San Ildefonso Indians are believed to have migrated from the Mesa Verde Anasazi colony in southwestern Colorado, whose ancient cliff dwellings dating back to the 1st century are now a national park. They settled first in what is now Bandelier National Monument near Los Alamos. A drought sent them to lower ground at the end of the 13th century, when they settled in their current location 22 miles northwest of Santa Fe.

San Ildefonso is perhaps best known for its striking black-on-black pottery, especially that of the late María Martínez, whose pots today fetch high prices. Martínez and her husband, Julian, are largely responsible for the resurgence in the 1920s of traditional arts and crafts on San Ildefonso and other pueblos.

Tewa is still spoken by many of the tribe's 300 members, who strive to preserve their cultural identity by observing ancient traditions and preserving or reconstructing original pueblo architecture. The enclosed central plaza, for example, looks much as it did centuries ago right down to the kiva, which the tribe still uses for ceremonial purposes. The pueblo has also taken pains to preserve more recent history, including rebuilding a 17th-century Catholic church originally erected during the Spanish occupation.

Directions from Santa Fe: Take U.S. Highway 84/285 15 miles to the junction with N.M. 502 in Pojoaque; go 6 miles west on N.M. 502.

San Juan Pueblo
S.R. 74
• **(505) 842-4400**

Patron saint: San Juan (St. John the Baptist). Feast day: June 24.

Located some 25 miles north of Santa Fe along the Rio Grande, San Juan is the largest of all the northern pueblos with 2,500 members and a total population of about 5,300 people. Tribe members share complex and closely guarded social and belief systems based on their traditional clan system.

The tribe's 12,238-acre pueblo sits across the Rio Grande from the original San Juan Pueblo, the site of the first Spanish settlement in New Mexico in 1598 and the first capital of the territory. San Juan was also the birthplace of Popé, the man credited with organizing the Pueblo Revolt of 1680 that succeeded in banishing the Spanish from the region for 12 years. San Juan has retained a reputation for leadership among Tewa-speaking people, hence its name, Oke Owingeh, "Place of the Strong People." The pueblo is home to the offices of the Eight Northern Indian Pueblos Council (see earlier entry) and the Bureau of Indian Affairs, Northern Pueblos Agency.

San Juan's two central plazas feature rectangular kivas. To the west of the plaza area stands St. John the Baptist Catholic Church, a 19th-century red brick building facing Our Lady of Lourdes Chapel, which was built from volcanic rock. Among the pueblo's natural attractions are tribal lakes, a recreation area, and a herd of buffalo that may be viewed by reservation only. The tribe's Tsay Corporation recently reopened the Ohkay Casino-Resort, which now features the largest casino floor in New Mexico and 100 hotel rooms. Those who prefer sleeping a little closer to the great outdoors can stay in the pueblo's top-rated RV park. Tsay Corporation also operates the Tewa Indian Restaurant; the Oke Oweenge Crafts cooperative, which displays and sells the pueblo's distinctive red pottery along with wood and stone carvings, weavings, paintings, and jewelry; the Ohkay T'owa Gardens Cooperative, which grows and processes traditional native food products; a construction company; and a cabinet shop. Directions from Santa Fe: Take U.S. Highway 84/285 north 24.3 miles to the junc-

Visitors to Santa Clara's Puyé Cliff Dwellings are offered the opportunity to explore cliff dwellings more than 800 years old.

Photo: Don Strel

tion with N.M. 68 in Española ; head 4 miles north on N.M. 68 to the junction with N.M. 74. Go 1 mile west on N.M. 74.

Santa Clara Pueblo
1 Kee St., Española
• (505) 753-7326

Patron saint: Santa Clara (St. Claire). Feast day: August 12.

With an estimated 1,200 tribal members and 46,000 acres, Santa Clara is the second largest in both population and land of the Eight Northern Indian Pueblos. Located west of the Rio Grande and adjacent to San Ildefonso Pueblo, Santa Clara offers majestic landscapes and stunning views. The Santa Clara people trace their ancestors to the ancient Pueblo Indians who occupied the Puyé Cliff Dwellings along and beneath the mesa tops that loom above the pueblo. They're believed to have arrived in the 12th century, when they carved cave-like "apartments" into the soft volcanic rock along the Pajarito (pa-ha-REE-to, Spanish for "little bird") Plateau leading into the Jémez Mountains. They later moved to the top of the mesa, where they built adobe structures whose remains extend for more than a mile. A drought forced these ancestral Indians to abandon Puyé about 600 years ago. They settled in the what is now the Santa Clara Pueblo, or *Kha p'o,* which is Tewa for "Valley of the Wild Roses." The

Puyé ruins are accessible year-round on foot for the hale and hardy or by driving to the top of the mesa. The pueblo also offers guided tours by reservation only.

Another of the pueblo's great attractions is Santa Clara Canyon, a beautiful recreation area that offers trout fishing in several well-stocked lakes and 86 campsites with tables, lean-tos, RV parking, and picnicking. The canyon is open to visitors from April through October.

Santa Clara Pueblo is justly famous for its lustrous, hand-coiled blackware and redware, both made of clay molded from individual coils and refined by hand, then decorated with carved or painted designs, hand-polished with a smooth stone and finally finished on an open wood fire. You can buy pottery and other arts and crafts in a number of shops on the pueblo. In addition to its patron saint, Santa Clara commemorates St. Anthony with a feast day on June 13.

Directions from Santa Fe: Take U.S. Highway 84/285 N. 24 miles to the junction with N.M. 201 in Española; go 1 mile southwest on N.M. 30.

Taos Pueblo
P.O. Box 1846, Taos 87571
• (505) 758-1028(tourism office),
(505) 758-9593 (governor's office)

Patron saint: San Geronimo (St. Jerome).

Feast day: September 30 with pre-feast ceremonies on September 29.

The oldest and most well-known of all the existing northern pueblos, Taos (rhymes with "house") is also the most striking primarily because of its multistoried, tiered adobe buildings with jutting log vigas and rough-hewn wooden ladders residents still use to reach the upper floors. Taos has inspired countless artists to capture the drama of the pueblo at dusk, when it sometimes appears golden. In winter, its graceful, snow-lined walls, rooftops, and *hornos* (round, outdoor mud ovens pronounced "OR-nose") provide a striking contrast to the deep purple of the Sangre de Cristo Mountains that watch over it.

Taos Pueblo—*Tu-tah* ("Our Village") in the tribe's native Tiwa—sits on 95,343 acres in the foothills of the northern Sangre de Cristos. Except for some scattered modern housing, the pueblo probably looks much as it did 450 years ago, when Spain made its first foray into what would become New Mexico. This may be due in part to the northern location, which historically rendered Taos more inaccessible than other pueblos in the territory. It's surely a result of the Taos people's independence and fierce determination to preserve their ancient traditions and culture. The pueblo maintains a strict taboo on intermarriage and forbids plumbing and electricity in some of the oldest structures. These and other restrictions help maintain an air of serenity that belies a turbulent history whose chapters include the Pueblo Revolt of 1680 and the Taos Rebellion against the United States in 1847, when 150 tribal members died.

Although the Taos people have lived in the same location for more than a thousand years, much of their history and culture remains a mystery to the outside world largely because the pueblo bans excavations. Anthropologists believe the estimated 1,175 Taos Indians who live on the pueblo could be related either to the Anasazi or Chaco cultures, both now extinct. They also suspect that the nearby Plains Indians—in particular the Kiowa and Apache with whom the tribe traded—influenced the pueblo to the extent that it added leather craft to an economy once based primarily on farming, raising cattle and horses, and hunting bear, buffalo, deer, elk, and birds. Today, the pueblo's boots, moccasins, clothing, and drums

are justly famous. These days, however, the pueblo's primary source of income is Taos Mountain Casino.

Although Taos Pueblo shrouds itself in secrecy, visitors are welcome to enjoy the archi-

Award-winning Katchinas are featured at the Eight Northern Indian Pueblos Arts and Crafts Show held every year at a Northern Pueblo the 3rd weekend in July.

Photo: Don Strel

tecture on almost any day and to observe some of the pueblo's ceremonies and rituals on selected dates. These include traditional foot races in May and the Taos Pueblo Pow-Wow the second weekend in July. The pueblo closes to non-Indians for about six weeks starting in February or March for religious activities. Directions from Santa Fe: Take U.S. Highway 84/285 N. 24.3 miles to the junction with N.M. 68 in Española; go 48 miles north on N.M. 68 to the junction with U.S. 64 in Taos; 1 mile north on U.S. 64.

INSIDERS' TIP

Santa Fe Indian Market, which takes place each August, is the world's largest American Indian art market.

Apache dancer at the annual Eight Northern Indian Pueblos Arts and Crafts Show.

Photo: Don Strel

A variety of dances are performed annually at the pueblos including Basket Dance, Harvest Dance, Rain Dance, Deer Dance, and more.

Photo: Don Strel

Tesuque Pueblo
Rt. 5, Box 360-T
• (505) 983-2667, (800) 483-1040

Patron saint: San Diego (St. James). Feast day: November 12.

Tesuque (teh-SOO-keh) Pueblo—*Te-tsu-geh*, or "The Narrow Place of Cottonwood Trees" in Tiwa—encompasses approximately 17,200 acres in the lush foothills of the Sangre de Cristo Mountains, including forest land adjacent to the Santa Fe National Forest and farmland near the Rio Grande. The Tesuque people settled in this area, located just nine miles north of Santa Fe, 14

INSIDERS' TIP
Pojoaque was the first pueblo to elect a woman as governor, which occurred in 1973.

years after the 1680 Pueblo Revolt in which Tesuque Indians literally struck the first blows against the Spanish and suffered the first casualties. Two members of the pueblo also served as messengers to the other tribes, spreading word of the revolt. An earlier pueblo existed before the 12th century but was abandoned after the revolt.

A relatively small pueblo of about 400 tribal members, Tesuque today is nonetheless among the most traditional of the Tewa speaking people. Only a very few of its celebrations are open to the public, and the pueblo sometimes closes to outsiders with little or no notice. The pueblo owns and operates Camel Rock Casino, (505) 984-8414, (800) GO-CAMEL, named for the centuries-old, distinctive sandstone formation near the entrance to the pueblo. It also recently opened Camel Rock Suites, (877) 989-3600, off U.S. 25 at the St. Francis exit (see Hotels and Motels) and took over the famous—and upscale—outdoor flea market on the west side of N.M. 84/285 next to the Santa Fe Opera. On the pueblo itself, visitors may buy permits for fishing and primitive camping at Tesuque's Aspen Ranch. The pueblo also operates Tesuque Natural Farms, an organic produce company that sells at local farmers' markets and to some of Santa Fe's better restaurants. The tribe also sells native arts and crafts including the brightly colored pottery for which the pueblo has become known, figurines, sculpture, painting, jewelry, and traditional clothing. The Tesuque people speak English and their native Tewa.

Directions from Santa Fe: Take U.S. Highway 84/285 N. 9 miles.

A Footnote on "Anglos"

Anglo culture? What's that? If you've seen Woody Allen's 1986 film, Hannah and Her Sisters, you might think it's turkey sandwiches on white bread with mayonnaise. In much of the country, it's the short form for "WASP"—White Anglo Saxon Protestant. In Santa Fe, however, "Anglo" takes on a variety of shades, from African-American to Asian, Arab to Jew. As we've mentioned elsewhere in this guide, the term as generally used in New Mexico refers to anyone who's not Hispanic or Native American, regardless of race or heritage.

Because that embraces so many cultures, it's difficult to define. But it's fun exploring the stereotypes. They include wealthy retirees or celebrities, perhaps buying their second or third home; trust-fund babies (age is unimportant) who come here to "find themselves;" New Age adherents in search of a mystical experience and hoping to find one by sheer proximity to Native Americans; hippies who arrived in the '60s and never left—some of them still hippies, others successful professionals or entrepreneurs; artists and writers looking for their muse; ski bums who work three seasons a year to play on the slopes all winter. We're sure everyone in Santa Fe could come up with a few stereotypes of their own.

Outside the cultural cliches are the "Anglos" who have lived here all their lives, some with roots going back 150 years to the Santa Fe Trail. Others are regular working stiffs who personally, or whose parents, chose Santa Fe as their home because of its physical beauty and fascinating blend of cultures. In the mix are pockets of ethnic communities including Tibetans, who have strong political support here in their fight to reclaim their homeland from China; Chinese, many of whom arrived here in the 19th century with the railroad; African Americans, who account for 0.6 percent of the population; Ashkenazy Jews, whose ancestors helped blaze the Santa Fe Trail; scientists of all backgrounds who work at Los Alamos National Laboratory; and people of literally dozens of other ancestries from Afghanistan to Zimbabwe. Santa Fe is its own melting pot and becoming more so every year as people from one end of the country to the other, one end of the world to the other, discover all it has to offer.

INSIDERS' TIP

You can get a copy of the Eight Northern Pueblos Visitors Guide at the Santa Fe Convention and Visitors Bureau, Sweeney Center, 201 W. Marcy St., (505) 955-6200 or (800) 777-2489 Mexico Tourism Department in Santa Fe at the Lamy Building, 491 Old Santa Fe Trail, (505) 827-7400, (800) 545-2040. The booklet includes descriptions and histories of each pueblo and a tentative calendar of events for the year.

Hotels and Motels

LOOK FOR:
- In or Near
  Downtown
- Cerrillos Road and
  Environs
- County

Price Code

Our legend is based on the lowest rate per night for double occupancy during peak season. Price ratings don't reflect taxes or other surcharges and are subject to change.

$	less than $55
$$	$55–$89
$$$	$90–$139
$$$$	$140–$199
$$$$$	$200 and up

Santa Fe has an amazing number and variety of lodgings ranging from ultra luxurious and very expensive to basic and cheap. In this chapter we've presented a cross-section of the area's hotels and motels in three geographic categories; Downtown, which is usually most desirable because of its proximity to the historic districts and the Plaza; Cerrillos Road and environs, which encompass a 6-mile-long commercial strip that runs south from downtown Santa Fe directly into the beautiful Turquoise Trail; and the county, which takes in rural areas both north and south of town. For other types of accommodations, see our Bed and Breakfast Inns and Vacation Rentals chapters.

Perhaps the single most important warning for visitors to Santa Fe is this: Make your reservations well in advance if you plan to be here during peak times—primarily in summertime and throughout the ski season—when rooms, especially on weekends, are at or near capacity. Lodgings often are booked up to a year in advance for Indian Market (see our Annual Events chapter) in late August and during Christmas—a very special time in Santa Fe, when the nights literally glow from thousands of *farolitos* burning on balconies and rooftops, driveways and pathways, throughout the city. These times can, and usually do, command higher prices than the rest of the year—especially Indian Market, when many establishments add a surcharge to their peak season prices. Some hotels divide the year up into as many as a half-dozen seasons, when prices on single rooms can fluctuate by as much as $50.

While pricing can be tricky in Santa Fe—rooms range anywhere from $34 a night (for a hotel not included in this chapter) to $1,500 for the Presidential Suite at Hotel Loretto—the general rule of thumb is, the closer you are to the Plaza, the more you'll pay. There are a few exceptions, however, which we've noted in this chapter. You'll find that most lodgings fall in the $80 to $180 range; many offer discounts for extended stays. Keep in mind that prices quoted here or elsewhere do not include taxes. Within the city limits, be prepared to pay 6.4375 percent in gross receipts taxes as well as a 5 percent lodgers tax, a special levy whose proceeds are used in part to promote Santa Fe. You'll save money by staying in the county, where lodgers tax is only 4 percent and the gross receipts tax ranges from 5.75 to 6.3125 percent.

Unless otherwise indicated, all lodgings listed below have non-smoking and handicapped- accessible rooms, the latter to a lesser extent in some places than others. If you or a traveling companion use a wheelchair, be sure to confirm specifics—i.e., whether the bathroom doors are wide enough—before you make your reservation. You're probably safe if you simply ask whether the facilities are ADA (Americans with Disabilities Act) approved. People with physical disabilities can obtain a special guide called *Access Santa Fe* by stopping by or writing the State of New Mexico's Welcome Center at (505) 827-7336 or the Governor's Committee on Concerns for the Handicapped, (505) 827-6465, both at 491 Old Santa Fe Trail.

Amenities vary from place to place, but you can generally assume that all but the cheapest lodgings have telephones in the room, many with free local calls. If you're bringing your laptop and plan to spend time sending or receiving e-mail or surfing the Internet, confirm that the phones have dataports or are modem-friendly. You can also expect to find remote-control color cable televisions, though the channel selection may differ from place to place. Many also have VCRs—especially suites, where both VCRs and CD players seem to be standard issue. Even the meanest lodgings, however, pay tribute to Santa Fe Style, even if only by the pattern and colors of the bedspread. For descriptions of the Santa Fe Style embellishments you're likely to encounter in our lodgings—*kivas, vigas, latillas,* and *nichos,* for example—refer to our Santa Fe Style close-up in our Real Estate chapter. With very few exceptions—and they're all noted—establishments listed in this section accept most major credit cards. Even if you loathe using plastic, you'd be well-advised to guarantee your reservation with a credit card during peak season. Also be sure to check on cancellation policies, minimum stays, and surcharges, especially for heavily trafficked weekends like the Indian and Spanish markets or the opening week of the Santa Fe Opera.

One last caveat before you make your reservations: Most lodgings do not allow pets. Some may be willing to break their own rules depending on the animal or the circumstances. Do be sure to check in advance before you plan on taking Duke the dog, Fluffy the cat, or Alisssss, your pet boa constrictor, with you on your Santa Fe vacation.

In or Near Downtown

Eldorado Hotel
**$$$$$ • 309 W. San Francisco St.
• (505) 988-4455, (800) 955-4455**

A favorite for visiting celebrities, the Eldorado is an enormous luxury hotel in the heart of downtown Santa Fe, just two blocks from the Plaza. The hotel boasts 219 elegant

rooms and suites, many featuring *kiva* fireplaces and balconies or terraces with views of the Sangre de Cristo Mountains. The Eldorado pampers guests with plush terrycloth robes, nightly turndown services, extended room service, and valet parking. It even provides private, English-style butler service with deluxe rooms and suites. Guests have access to a rooftop swimming pool and whirlpool along with a fully equipped fitness center, saunas, and professional masseuses.

The Eldorado's award-winning Old House Restaurant—the only AAA, four-diamond

The Hilton Hotel (left) and the Eldorado Hotel to the right offer visitors a central location from which to visit the heart of Santa Fe.

Photo: Don Strel

restaurant in the state—offers fine dining seven nights a week featuring creative gourmet dishes with a Southwestern touch. Less formal dining is available for breakfast and lunch in the Eldorado Court, which on Sunday serves a lavish *prix fixe* champagne brunch, buffet style, with prime rib and other meats carved to your liking; bottomless bowls of fresh shrimp; smoked meats and fish; gourmet salads; omelet and waffle stations; and a decadent dessert table. For live nightly entertainment, guests need go no further than the adjoining lobby lounge.

The Eldorado offers a number of packages, including a one-day "Ski Escape" with continental breakfast and complimentary lift tickets for the Santa Fe or Taos slopes. The hotel's three-night "New Mexico Romance" package welcomes guests with a bottle of chilled champagne in the room, a candlelight dinner at the Old House (you pay for the booze), breakfast in bed each morning, a massage or other spa treatment, and monogrammed robes to take home with you. The "Weekday Bargain" package offers discounted rates for two-day minimum stays from Sunday through Thursday night and includes a continental breakfast.

The Eldorado also manages three bed and breakfast inns, which you can book through the hotel. Ask for the Inns of Santa Fe.

Fort Marcy Hotel Suites
$$$ • 320 Artist Rd.
• (505) 982-6636, (800) 745-9910
Named for an 1846 military outpost, Fort Marcy Hotel Suites opened in 1983 as an alternative to hotel rooms in downtown Santa Fe. On 10 landscaped acres in a quiet residential neighborhood only four blocks from the Santa Fe Plaza—and directly on the road that leads to the Santa Fe Ski Basin—the hotel features 100 one-, two-, and three-bedroom suites with fireplaces, full kitchens, air-conditioning, VCRs, and cable color television with Showtime and the Disney Channel. Guests have access to a hot tub and coin laundry facilities. Rooms come with a complimentary continental breakfast.

Garrett's Desert Inn
$$$ • 311 Old Santa Fe Tr.
• (505) 982-1851, (800) 888-2145
Although making reservations by phone at Garrett's Desert Inn can be a frustrating experience—you may have to let the line ring a good long time before someone finally answers—persistence pays off. Garrett's offers the most affordable rates in downtown Santa Fe. You won't find *vigas*, *kiva* fireplaces, or *saltillo*

tile at Garrett's. What you will get are basic-but-pleasant rooms and location, location, location. If you're looking for luxury, you can walk across the street to the Hotel Loretto, but be prepared to pay from 3 to 10 times as much, depending on the room. Either way, you're two blocks from the Plaza and just footsteps from some of the city's historic landmarks. Garrett's has both a restaurant and lounge on the premises and a seasonal outdoor heated swimming pool. It offers 76 standard rooms and six suites with small living rooms and kitchenettes furnished with microwaves and small refrigerators. The motel has limited wheelchair access.

Hilton of Santa Fe
$$$$ • 100 Sandoval St.
• (505) 988-2811, (800) 336-3676
Although it looks rather ordinary from the outside, the 27-year-old Hilton of Santa Fe [1973] is in fact quite extraordinary in that it was built around a 380-year-old *hacienda* that belonged to one of Santa Fe's early prominent families. Casa de Ortiz now encompasses the hotel's dining room, as well as three luxurious *casitas* built into and around what used to be Nicholas Ortiz III's coach houses. Two of the spacious *casitas* are one-bedroom suites and a third has two bedrooms; each has a "window" from which guests can view the original thick adobe walls that have stood for nearly four centuries. The decor is modern Southwestern with traditional touches like *kiva* fireplaces, *viga* ceilings, and four-poster beds. One *casita* has a heart-shaped tub.

Just a few blocks from the Plaza, the hotel has a total of 157 rooms and suites, including the Casa Ortiz. It boasts Santa Fe's largest outdoor pool, which has a six-foot tile bear fetish on the bottom. Other amenities include an outdoor Jacuzzi, a new health club, and three restaurants. The award-winning Piñon Grill was built on the site of the Ortiz bedroom. The hotel's 6,000-square-foot meeting space was the Ortiz's private sanctuary.

Hotel Loretto
$$$$$ • 211 Old Santa Fe Tr.
• (505) 988-5531, (800) 727-5531
Named for the nearby historic Loretto Chapel whose "miraculous" spiral staircase has no central support, Hotel Loretto—formerly Inn at Loretto—is located near the end of Old Santa Fe Trail, just one block from the Plaza. Its faux-adobe, Pueblo–style architecture is complemented by furniture, doors, windows, corbels, and light fixtures that are 13th century replicas hand crafted by local artisans. Even

The Hotel Loretto is another hotel, designed in the pueblo style, that is centrally located.

Photo: Don Strel

the interior wall mural incorporates designs and symbols found in New Mexico's Pueblo and Spanish artistry, as well as in ancient petroglyphs and weavings. Hotel Loretto is among the most photographed buildings in Santa Fe during the winter months, when its rooftops and balconies light up with faux *farolitos*—a permanent version of the traditional candle-in-a-paper-bag Christmas decoration that has become an internationally recognized symbol of Santa Fe.

Hotel Loretto's 140 recently renovated guest rooms and suites feature individual climate control, refrigerators, in-room coffee service, speaker phones with data jacks, and semi-private balconies with spectacular sunset and mountain views. The 2,800-square-foot Presidential Suite, which goes for $1,500 a night, has wrap-around balconies providing a panoramic view of the city and the Sangre de Cristos, a library, fireplace, and even a custom billiard table. All guests have access to the hotel's heated outdoor pool. The hotel restaurant, Nellie's, features primarily Southwestern-American haute cuisine, though guests with a yen for Asian food may find what they're looking for on Nellie's creative menu. The concierge can direct guests to other fine restaurants as well as arrange for golf, rafting, fly-fishing, skiing, horseback riding, or any number of other activities.

Hotel St. Francis
$$$ • 210 Don Gaspar Ave.
• (505) 983-5700, (800) 529-5700

Built in 1923, the Hotel Saint Francis hearkens back to the old world elegance of 1920s Europe. Renovations in the lobby and rooms, each of which is unique, include refurbished antique and period reproduction furnishings which add to the genteel ambiance of this historic hotel. In keeping with European tradition, the St. Francis offers a locally popular high tea which features an array of pastries, scones, finger sandwiches, and, of course, plenty of fine, freshly brewed tea. The hotel restaurant is open daily and offers seasonal outdoor dining as well as room service. The front verandah, with its old-fashioned but comfortable iron tables and chairs, is a favorite spot for people-watching. Just a block from the Plaza, the hotel is included on the National Register of Historic Places.

Hotel Santa Fe
$$$$ • 1501 Paseo de Peralta
• (505) 982-1200, (800) 825-9876

Unique is a word used so often in Santa Fe that it seems to lose its meaning. But Hotel Santa Fe is indeed unique in that it's the city's only Native American-owned hotel. The Picurís Pueblo is the majority owner, with a 51 percent share, an arrangement that's reflected in more than just finances. The influence of the Picurís (pronounced pick-ku-REES) is captured throughout the hotel—in the Pueblo revival architecture; the decor; the artwork, which includes three garden sculptures by renowned Native American artist Allan Houser; native foods; and hospitality from a staff that is 25 percent Indian.

Hotel guests and the public enjoy entertainment that includes Indian dancers, Hispanic and Indian musicians, lectures by local historians, and native storytellers who weave tales in front of the lobby's majestic *kiva* fireplace. There's also an outdoor heated pool and Jacuzzi and an on-site masseuse. Although there are no sports facilities on the premises, guests can get complimentary passes to the Santa Fe Spa, located a few miles away.

Built in 1991, the 131-room hotel takes up a full block at the corner of Cerrillos Road and Paseo de Peralta—just a few blocks from the heart of the historic Guadalupe district and a 10-minute stroll to the Santa Fe Plaza. If you prefer, you can take the complimentary hotel shuttle to the Plaza, which operates daily until 10 PM. Hotel Santa Fe is located near a variety of fine restaurants, though you needn't leave the premises to eat well. The in-house Corn Dance Café offers *nouvelle* Native American cuisine that features a creative blending of traditional Indian foods and spices. Ask about hotel packages for skiing or romance and for Native Americans and senior citizens.

Inn of the Anasazi
$$$$$ • 113 Washington Ave.
• (505) 988-3030, (800) 688-8100

Just steps from the Plaza stands Inn of the Anasazi, an intimate, elegant luxury hotel named for the ancestors of today's Pueblo Indians. These ancient settlers of the Four Corners Region inhabited the cliff dwellings of Chaco Canyon and Mesa Verde, which served as inspiration for the hotel's architecture and design. The Inn's fifty one guestrooms and eight suites have gas-lit *kiva* fireplaces, four-poster beds, and traditional ceilings with *vigas* and *latillas*. Authentic regional artwork graces the floors and walls. Sheets and towels are pure cotton; organic toiletries are local creations made with native cedar extract. Every room has a coffeemaker, stereo, and VCR. Guests may borrow videotapes from the hotel's extensive collection.

The inn's award-winning, world-class restaurant serves gourmet Native American, northern New Mexican, and American cowboy cuisine using locally grown organic produce, whenever possible. Guests who want a more intimate setting can reserve the wine cellar for a meal for up to 12 people. The hotel also rents out its library/board room for private dinners of up to 40 guests as well as for corporate retreats and board meetings. When it's not rented out, the library is open to guests, who may peruse the library's shelves of books on regional indigenous cultures. Those who want a closer look can request an escort to the Anasazi ruins at Chaco Canyon or Bandelier National Monument or to any of the eight Northern Indian Pueblos.

Inn of the Governors
$$$$ • 101 W. Alameda St.
• (505) 982-4333, (800) 234-4534

Inn of the Governors is a midsized, deluxe hotel just two blocks from the Santa Fe Plaza. Its 94 rooms and six suites are decorated in a light, airy Southwestern style with hand-made furniture, local art work, and special touches—such as hand-painted tin mirrors, turquoise-washed writing desks, wrought iron wall lamps, and carved headboards with Mexican *trasteros* (cupboards). Some rooms also have wood-burning *kiva* fireplaces and/or private balconies overlooking the mountains or downtown.

Amenities include a heated outdoor swimming pool, open year-round, complimentary newspaper and coffee in the morning, and tea and sherry at 4 PM, cable television with in-room movies, and a restaurant/piano bar where guests can eat indoors or on the hotel's private patio.

Inn on the Alameda
$$$$ • 303 E. Alameda St.
• (505) 984-2121, (800) 289-2122

Just a five-minute walk from the Plaza, this small luxury hotel is located near the foot of Canyon Road, a historic and artistic center filled with galleries, boutiques, and fine restaurants. Each of its 69 rooms and suites is individually designed to reflect classic Southwest design including Spanish tile, *vigas,* and native woods; hand-crafted armoires, chairs, beds, and lamps; and unique wall hangings and fixtures. The inn's 10 suites offer private patios or balconies, open courtyards, and *kiva* fireplaces.

Although the hotel has no restaurant on the premises, it does provide a complimentary "Breakfast of Enchantment"—a continental breakfast of fresh fruit and juices, pastries and other baked goods, granolas, cereals, Kona coffee, and more—all served buffet style in the hotel's lounge or delivered to your room. Other amenities include an exercise room, on-call massage, two open-air whirlpool spas, same-day dry cleaning, and coin-operated laundry, cable, and HBO. All rooms come with luxurious robes and fresh flowers; some also have wet bars and refrigerators.

La Fonda Hotel
$$$$$ • 100 E. San Francisco St.
• (505) 982-5511, (800) 523-5002

When Santa Fe was founded in 1610, the town already had a *fonda*, or inn, to accommo-date travelers. More than two hundred years later, La Fonda—literally at the end of the trail—welcomed the first successful trading expedition that created the Santa Fe Trail. Located on the southeast corner of the Plaza, the current structure was built in 1923 on the site of previous inns. Its award-winning Spanish Pueblo-style architecture make it a beacon not only for tourists, but also for locals who meet in the summer at the rooftop Bell Tower bar to watch incredible sunsets over margaritas or

Santa Fe style is a trademark of Santa Fe's luxury hotels.

who gather in La Fiesta Lounge to two-step to the country tunes of now-famous Bill and Bonnie Hearne or to listen to other popular local musicians who perform nightly.

This vibrant, historic landmark is filled with unique paintings; colorful, hand-painted and hand-carved wooden furniture, *vigas,* and corbels, as well as unique paintings and other original artwork. Many of its 167 rooms and suites, each uniquely decorated, have balconies and fireplaces. La Fonda also has a heated outdoor pool, hot tubs, massage service, and a multi-lingual concierge. La Plazuela is an enclosed courtyard restaurant that's open daily.

La Posada de Santa Fe Resort & Spa
$$$$$ • 330 E. Palace Ave.
• (505) 986-0000,
(800) 727-5276

La Posada is Santa Fe's only hotel with a resident ghost. Employees and guests alike swear they've seen, or at least felt, the presence of the long-deceased Julia Schuster Staab, who died on May 15, 1896. Most encounters have occurred in what was Julia's upstairs bedroom, formerly known simply as Room 256, now called the Victorian Suite and renumbered as room 100. Originally from Germany, Julia married wealthy Santa Fe merchant Abraham Staab, who in 1882 built his young wife the Victorian mansion that is now the main building of La Posada. Although Julia is not the only ghost in Santa Fe, she's certainly the most famous. But her presence, at least in principle, doesn't seem to scare away either tourists or locals, who come in droves to this lovely, serene hotel set among 6 acres of lawns, trees, and flowers.

Completely restored and expanded in 1999, La Posada is just two blocks from the Plaza. Many of its 159 faux and real adobe rooms and suites come with *kiva* fireplaces and patios overlooking the rambling grounds that are a favorite setting for weddings. The hotel's romantic Victorian bar, the Staab House Lounge, is popular among locals, as is Fuego Restaurant, which offers fine dining with a Southwestern accent

and the ambiance of a Spanish hacienda. Guests may dine *al fresco* on the restaurant's seasonal terrace. Between gallery hopping and dinner, you might consider indulging in a massage, fa-

Santa Fe's climate makes for lovely outdoor dining in the summer.

cial, or an adobe mud wrap treatment at La Posada's Avanyu Spa.

Plaza Real Hotel
$$$$$ • 125 Washington Ave.
• (505) 988-4900

The Plaza Real is a charming, territorial-style hotel whose 56 rooms feature hand-crafted furnishings, fireplaces, original artwork, and private patios overlooking a very pretty courtyard. The Santa Fe Plaza is literally just steps away and visible from the hotel's sidewalk café, La Piazza, which offers pastries, cappuccino, sandwiches, homemade desserts, spirits, and great people-watching. For more substantial fare, the Santa Fe Salsa Company Fajita Grill on the back patio is open for lunch only. Or you can mingle among the masses on one of the concierge's complimentary city walking tours. The concierge will also make your restaurant reservations and suggest other outside activities. Rooms come with a complimentary continental breakfast served in the Santa Clara Room, on the patio, or delivered to your room.

Radisson Santa Fe Hotel
$$$$
• 750 N. St. Francis Dr.
• (505) 992-5800, (800) 333-3333

While not exactly downtown, this hotel is close enough—a five minute drive to the Plaza in the hotel's free shuttle—to warrant a listing here. On a hilltop immediately north of Paseo de Peralta, which forms a U around the downtown area, the Radisson offers views of the mountains, including legendary Picacho Peak, and breathtaking sunsets from its rooms as well as its restaurant and bar, El Sevilla. The hotel features 145 nicely appointed guest rooms and suites as well as condominium units with fireplaces and either microwaves and refrigerators or full kitchens Guests may work out for free in the 20,000-square-foot Santa Fe Spa next door or relax pool-side in the hotel's landscaped courtyard.

Rio Vista Suites
$$$ • 527 E. Alameda St.
• (505) 982-6636, (800) 745-9910

Located along the Santa Fe River in a quiet residential neighborhood on the city's east side, Rio Vista Suites are the closest accommodations in Santa Fe to gallery- and boutique-lined Canyon Road. Only six blocks from the Plaza, the 12 one-bedroom suites are decorated with southwestern furniture, Mexican *saltillo* tile and brick sidewalks, and include such amenities as fully furnished kitchens, color cable television with free premium channels, and VCRs, CD players, and free parking outside your door. Suites come with a complimentary continental breakfast.

Santa Fe Budget Inn
$$ • 725 Cerrillos Rd.
• (505) 982-5952, (800) 288-7600

Santa Fe Budget Inn is your basic, no-frills motel whose primary assets are location and price. Situated at the corner of Cerrillos Road

INSIDERS' TIP
Like commercial strips everywhere, Cerrillos Road attracts a fair share of burglaries and robberies. Please take all common-sense precautions, such as bringing your belongings from your car into your room at night and locking your vehicle at all times.

and Guadalupe Street—the beginning of Santa Fe's commercial strip—the motel is just six blocks from the Santa Fe Plaza and a short walk to the Guadalupe district, which is filled with restaurants and stores. Budget Inn offers clean, generic rooms with phones, color satellite television, a heated, outdoor swimming pool open during the spring and summer, and plenty of on-site parking. For those without a car, or who can't walk another step, a Santa Fe Trails city bus stops in front of the motel to take you to areas hither and yon. Immediately adjacent is a family-style New Mexican restaurant with a McDonald's the next building over.

Santa Fe Motel
$$$ • 510 Cerrillos Rd.
• (505) 982-1039, (800) 999-1039

The closest motel to the Plaza, the Santa Fe Motel has 22 moderately priced, recently remodeled rooms with color televisions and HBO and direct-dial telephones. Five standard rooms have kitchenettes equipped with dishes and utensils. Eight rooms are in two renovated adobe houses with *viga* ceilings and patio entrances. One of these rooms has a fireplace, another a skylight. The motel serves a complimentary continental breakfast and keeps a pot of hot coffee at the ready all day long.

Santa Fe Plaza Travelodge
$$ • 646 Cerrillos
• (505) 982-3551, (800) 578-7878

The rooms here are basic with a few Southwestern touches, but what you're paying for is convenience, not ambiance. Just five blocks from the Plaza, you'll get a clean, pleasant chamber with cable television, a coffeemaker, a small refrigerator stocked with coffee and tea, a complimentary morning newspaper, and free local calls. These rooms go fast so be sure to book long in advance of your trip, especially during peak season.

Seret's 1001 Nights
$$$ Your 145 E. DeVargas St.
• (505) 982-6636, (800) 745-9910

Just two blocks from the Plaza and across the street from a church reputed to be the oldest in the United States, Seret's 1001 Nights is located amidst some of Santa Fe's most celebrated restaurants and the narrow, rambling, historic streets for which Santa Fe is famous. The hotel's 21 suites, which date back to the 19th century, have restored wooden floors and hand-trowelled, diamond-finished walls. Each has been fitted with centuries-old Spanish colonial handcrafted doors and shutters and furnished by Ira Seret, an internationally-known importer, with custom-made furniture and vintage weavings. All the suites have fireplaces, full kitchens, cable television with free premium channels and VCRs, CD players, and access to a private central courtyard, they also come with a complimentary continental breakfast.

Cerrillos Road and Environs

Best Western Lamplighter Inn
$$ • 2405 Cerrillos Rd.
• (505) 471-8000, (800) 767-5267

The popular Lamplighter Inn is centrally located a just few blocks from one of the busiest intersections in Santa Fe—Cerrillos Road and St. Michael's Drive. In the heart of the commercial district, the Lamplighter is surrounded by dozens of restaurants, from fast food to fine dining in a variety of ethnicities, and literally hundreds of businesses offering just about anything a body or soul could need or desire. You can hop in your vehicle and be downtown in 10 or 15 minutes, depending on traffic, or catch a Santa Fe Trails bus (see our Getting Here, Getting Around chapter), which stops one block from the hotel.

The Lamplighter Inn bows to Santa Fe style with a large *portal*, complete with wooden pillars, beams, and corbels, while several of its 80 units—all recently remodeled—have high, beamed ceilings. Most rooms, however, are generic but pleasant. Sixteen have kitchenettes; the rest come equipped with a refrigerator and coffeemaker. Suites each have a VCR and a foldout couch, in addition to one or two beds. The Lamplighter Inn serves its guests a complimentary hot breakfast from 7 to 11 AM in Andrea's Mexican Restaurant next door. Andrea's, which is part of the inn, specializes in local cuisine and stays open to 9 PM. Among the most popular features of the Lamplighter is its canopied, 25-yard heated indoor/outdoor lap pool.

Comfort Inn
$$ • 4312 Cerrillos Rd.
• (505) 474-7330, (800) 221-2222

Open since 1994, the 83-room Comfort Inn is a relatively new neighbor on the Cerrillos Road strip but has earned a reputation for comfort (as its name implies) and good service at a good price. Located south of the intersection at Cerrillos and Rodeo Roads—approximately six miles from the Plaza—the hotel is within walking distance of Villa Linda Mall, Santa Fe's largest indoor shopping center. And while there's no restaurant in the hotel, there are a number of eateries nearby, including several chains and a privately owned, down-home New Mexican restaurant called the Horseman's Haven. For breakfast, however, guests needn't leave the inn because an expanded continental breakfast comes with their rooms. The hotel serves a buffet of hot and cold cereals, fruit, juice, hot beverages, danish, or muffins in a small dining room adjacent to its high-ceilinged lobby, which has a large *kiva* style fireplace, tiled floor, and a variety of attractive Southwestern decorations. The inn features a heated indoor pool and hot tub, coin-operated laundry, and free local calls in the rooms. Some rooms have whirlpool baths, microwaves, and/or refrigerators. All have hair dryers and coffeemakers.

Comfort Suites
$$$ • 1435 Avenida de Las Americas (off Cerrillos Rd.)
• (505) 473-9004, (800) 228-5150

Built in 1996, the Comfort Suites offers many of the same features and amenities as its (barely) older sister, Comfort Inn (see entry above). The primary difference between the two establishments is the size of the rooms, which is reflected in the price, and the distance to downtown Santa Fe. Located three miles north of the inn—and three miles closer to the Plaza—Comfort Suites offers larger rooms with a divider separating the bedroom from a sitting area that comes furnished with a sleeper sofa, small refrigerator, microwave and, in some rooms, a dining table. Comfort Suites has a heated indoor pool and two hot tubs, one indoors, the other outside. It serves a complimentary continental breakfast buffet and offers views of the city from its top floor. The lobby has a *kiva* style fireplace, tall ceilings, bleached pine furniture, and Native American details like pottery, rugs, and Kokopelli, the fun-loving flute-player.

Courtyard by Marriott, Santa Fe
$$$ • 3347 Cerrillos Rd.
• (505) 473-2800, (800) 222-8733

Although it's located toward the far end of Santa Fe's commercial strip, the Courtyard by Marriott has a distinctly "downtown" feel with its pueblo-style architecture and handsome Southwestern interiors, especially after a recent $3.5 million renovation. Its spacious, meandering lobby offers a number of attractive and comfortable sitting areas, including one with a large *kiva* fireplace graced on both sides by neat stacks of logs. The hotel's 213 rooms and suites feature such Southwestern touches

Christmas is a time when Santa Fe really sparkles, as shown here in the lobby of the Hotel St. Francis.

Photo: Courtesy of Hotel St. Francis

as natural pine furniture and earth-toned colors. All rooms have refrigerators, coffeemakers, hair dryers, irons and ironing boards, two telephones with high-speed Internet access, data ports and voice mail, and cable color television with free and pay-per-view movie channels. Guests also have access to coin-operated laundry facilities. The three-story hotel has an attractive outdoor courtyard, interior and exterior corridors, a heated indoor pool, two indoor hot tubs, and an exercise room. Guests can ride downtown on he hotel's free shuttle, which runs from 8 AM to 9 PM. The hotel restaurant, Café Santa Fe, is open for breakfast and dinner.

El Rey Inn
$$ • 1862 Cerrillos Rd.
• (505) 982-1931, (800) 521-1349

Don't be fooled by its location. El Rey Inn is one of Santa Fe's best kept secrets. Tucked into a busy street about 10 minutes by car from the Plaza, El Rey (The King) offers comfort, surprising tranquillity, and Santa Fe style at affordable rates. Each of its 86 rooms, including 10 suites, is unique and blends traditional Southwestern decor—historic Spanish, Pueblo

Indian or Victorian—with modern comforts, including cable television with HBO and direct-dial phones with voice mail. Rooms open onto spacious gardens, patios, tiled walkways, fountains, and tall elms that cover much of the 5-acre property. A heated pool for seasonal use and two year-round hot tubs—one indoors, the other outside—occupy one corner of the grounds while a playground occupies another

El Rey's overall motif is traditional New Mexican Spanish architecture with wrought iron and whitewashed adobe and stucco. Rooms contain any combination of decorative touches that might include *latillas* held up by rough-hewn *vigas*, *kiva* fireplace, *nichos,* and murals as well as tile, wood, and polished brass accents. A number of rooms also have complete kitchens. Rooms come with a complimentary continental breakfast of coffee and rolls or sweet breads in the inn's spacious, European-style breakfast room, and guests can help themselves to coffee throughout the day. El Rey also has laundry facilities for guests.

Fairfield Inn-Marriott
$$ • 4150 Cerrillos Rd.
• (505) 474-4442, (800) 758-1128

Part of Marriott's economy line, the Fairfield Inn provides guests with reasonable prices and a little Santa Fe style. The lobby and entrance have *vigas, saltillo* tile, and a *kiva* fireplace. Its 55 rooms have southwestern touches and come with a continental breakfast as well as use of the year-round heated indoor pool. They also have data ports for laptop users and cable color television with free HBO. Valet laundry is available for a fee.

Located at the south end of town, about 6 miles from the Plaza, the inn is contiguous with the Villa Linda Mall—the largest indoor shopping center in Santa Fe—and across the street from an upscale new strip mall. While there's no restaurant on premises, the inn is within walking distance of several eateries in and around both malls or a 15-minute drive to downtown Santa Fe, where the choices are greater.

Hostel International de Santa Fe
$ (no credit cards) • 1412 Cerrillos Rd.
• (505) 988-1153

"If they talk funny and have a backpack, they're ours." That's the overriding philosophy of the Hostel International de Santa Fe. The 80-bed hostel was founded in 1983 to make Santa Fe financially viable primarily for students or young workers who have saved for years to see the world. But there's no restriction on age at the hostel, just on attitude. If you feel like you're being sized up when you walk through the door, you're right. Staff members look for any indications that the person in front of them can live communally with strangers.

The hostel caters primarily to people traveling for personal development and self education. A member of the American Association of International Youth Hostels, it naturally leans toward members of youth hosteling associations, though any brand of international youth travel card almost guarantees admission. Still, the management reserves the right to refuse anyone and is not shy about doing it.

The hostel has five single-sex dorms with enough bunk beds to sleep eight people. There are also 15 private rooms for individuals, couples, or families. And there's a fully-equipped cook's kitchen that rivals those in many restaurants with bread, cereals, pasta, rice, beans, coffee, tea, sugar, spices, and other staples for use by lodgers. And, indeed, they are lodgers and not guests. This is a traditional hostel. That means no maid service. Hostelers not only clean up after themselves, but must complete a 15-minute chore they choose themselves every morning. The earlier you get up, the better your choices.

If you call to make reservations, don't be put off if no one answers the phone immediately. In this case, persistence pays off. The hostel offers many amenities you won't find in other places—guitars and other musical instruments; games; pleasant, non-institutional rooms; and lots of information about Santa Fe and its environs. The population tends to be primarily French in August and British in September. The rest of the year, you're likely to bump into anyone from anywhere.

La Quinta Inn
$$$ • 4298 Cerrillos Rd.
• (505) 471-1142, (800) 531-5900

People like La Quinta Inns because they know exactly what to expect. Santa Fe's won't disappoint, unless you're hoping for a touch of Santa Fe in the rooms. The only thing Southwestern about La Quinta is its name. But the 130-room hotel offers the same quality here as in its other hotels across the country including "Gold Medal" rooms featuring floor-length draperies, built-in closets and vanities, ceiling moldings, bigger-than-a-breadbox bathrooms, and color cable television with free pay-per-view movies. Some rooms also have refrigerators. All come with a continental breakfast with cereal, fresh fruit, pastries, bagels, muffin tops, juice, milk, coffee, and tea. Other amenities include a heated outdoor swimming pool, same-day laundry and dry-cleaning, fax service, free local calls, and a coin-operated laundry.

Luxury Inn
$$ • 3752 Cerrillos Rd.
• (505) 473-0567, (800) 647-1346

Despite its name, this privately owned hotel prides itself on providing a homey atmosphere and reasonable rates rather than Santa Fe style, which tends to cost more. Its 51 rooms come with color cable television and free movies; some also have refrigerators and microwaves. Still, there's a bit of luxury here in the seasonal outdoor heated pool and hot tub. The hotel is near dozens of restaurants, some within walking distance, many a short distance by car.

Pecos Trail Inn
$$ • 2239 Old Pecos Trail
• (505) 982-1943, (800) 304-4187

A former speakeasy many decades ago, the Pecos Trail Inn is a family-friendly hotel on Santa Fe's southeast side at the crossroads of two historic trade routes—the Old Santa Fe Trail and the Old Pecos Trail—and near the scenic Old Las Vegas Highway. Situated on 5 acres of piñon trees, the hotel maintains a touch of the rustic despite fast-moving traffic. Guests can visit the park next door, which has a playground, jogging path, and exercise equipment, or enjoy the inn's outdoor heated pool, open from May through September. They also have workout privileges at a local health club for $2.50 a visit.

INSIDERS' TIP

The double "L" in Spanish is pronounced like "Y" in English. So Cerrillos Road is pronounced Seh-REE-yose Road, and villa (as in Villa Linda Mall) is pronounced VEE-yah.

Whether your goal is to explore or relax, Santa Fe provides the opportunity for both.

Just 10 to 15 minutes by car to the Santa Fe Plaza, the Old Pecos Inn is the only hotel in the area, which consists mostly of off-street residential developments rather than strip malls and gas stations. Of the inn's 22 rooms, four are two-bedroom suites with living rooms and fully equipped kitchens, while four units have kitchenettes. It's unlikely that many guests will want to bother cooking breakfast when they can eat anything on the hotel restaurant's breakfast menu for half price. Pepper's Restaurant and Cantina is a family-style restaurant open for breakfast, lunch, and dinner with eclectic offerings ranging from traditional New Mexican and American cuisine to calamari and a decent selection of low-fat, fat-free, and vegetarian dishes.

Santa Fe style has been copied worldwide but finds its natural home in Santa Fe.

Photo: Courtesy of Hotel at Loretto

Santa Fe Lodge Complex
$ • 6800 Cerrillos Rd.
• (505) 471-2727

Built 68 years ago as the Turf Club, the Santa Fe Lodge Complex is one of the oldest of the small motels on the outskirts of the city. In fact, it's the very last inn as you're heading south of town toward the interstate or the Turquoise Trail, a.k.a. N.M. 14. This part of Santa Fe feels like another world, but it's only eight miles—or a 15-minute drive—to the Plaza. Still, it proves you don't have to be downtown to sleep in a room with Mexican tile inlaid on the headboards and *vigas* on the ceiling. Of the motel's 17 rooms, 15 have kitchens. There's even a gas station/convenience store on the premises where you can buy groceries and other supplies, if you plan to do your own cooking. But do take the opportunity to sample the food at the nearby Horseman's Haven. This blink-and-you'll-miss-it truck stop attached to a Texaco station serves up enormous portions of home cooked carne adovada, enchiladas, and other New Mexican dishes at very reasonable prices.

Silver Saddle Motel
$$ • 2810 Cerrillos Rd.
• (505) 471-7663

Independent film fans may already be fa-miliar with the Silver Saddle from a 1988 German documentary called *Motel*. Filmmaker Christian Blackwood accurately portrayed the motel as an old-fashioned, authentically funky, cowboy-style inn, with a western motif provided primarily by the color scheme and the pictures on the wall. As the owner puts it, "We try to keep it simple and rustic." That may mean a few rough edges on this decidedly different "Cerrillos Road joint." But that's all part of the charm. That's not to say the Silver Saddle has no amenities. Guests get a complimentary continental breakfast that has been known to include biscuits and gravy in the winter. Ten of the motel's 25 rooms have kitchenettes, all have queen beds, color cable television with HBO, air conditioning, and free local calls. Only three miles from the Plaza, the Silver Saddle has great shopping right next door at Jackalope (see our "Shopping" section). You can call for reservations or just ride up on your horse.

Stage Coach Motor Inn
$$ • 3360 Cerrillos Rd.
• (505) 471-0707

A brothel in the 1940s, the newly renovated Stage Coach Motor Inn attracts a different sort of clientele these days—many of them low budget but sophisticated travelers looking for what's different in The City Different. All the rooms are done up in Santa Fe style, some of them with *vigas*, many with *saltillo* tile, most with lots of woodwork, and there is a fireplace in one of the two suites. The hotel is proud of its gardens, to which the new resident owners have been paying plenty of attention. They've designated the entire motel as no-smoking and don't as yet have an official handicapped-accessible room.

County

The Bishop's Lodge
$$$$$ • Bishop's Lodge Rd.
• (505) 983-6377, (800) 860-9257

Once the private retreat of frontier Bishop Jean Baptiste Lamy, The Bishop's Lodge has been operating as a resort since 1918, when the family of James R. Thorpe bought the property from the Pulitzer publishing family of St. Louis. Recently purchased by an Australian corporation, the hotel property has changed little. The Bishop's own chapel, which is listed on the National Register of Historic Places, still sits in his original garden among fruit trees planted by 16th century Franciscan priests.

The lodge itself sits in the lush foothills of the Sangre de Cristo Mountains, and, though only three miles from the Santa Fe Plaza, feels like another world entirely. That's because the resort is secluded in a private valley covering nearly 1,000 acres of landscaped property and natural piñon-juniper forest.

The hotel's 101 rooms and 20 suites are divided among 15 distinctive "lodges." The North and South lodges are the oldest and were once grand summer homes before World War I. Among the newest is the Chamisa Lodge, which contains 14 deluxe accommodations above the banks of the little Tesuque Creek. Bishop's Lodge expects to add another 36 deluxe rooms with fireplaces as well as a 3,500-square-foot conference center and a full service Spa and Wellness Center, all to be completed by the summer of 2001

Hotel accommodations include voice-mail telephone with modem jacks; cable color television with HBO; private heat and air-conditioning controls; morning local paper delivery; plush bathrobes; hair-dryers; evening turndown service; and in-room safes. Deluxe rooms and suites also have a *kiva* fireplace, refrigerator, iron and ironing board, and a private balcony or patio. Guests can choose between the "European Plan," which includes only the room, or the "Modified American Plan" which includes a full breakfast and a choice of either lunch or dinner at The Bishop's Lodge Restaurant. The restaurant serves a *prix fixe* Sunday brunch that's popular among locals as well as hotel guests.

The American plan also features a summer-

The Bishop's Lodge offers a variety of amenities on beautiful grounds just a few miles from the Plaza.

Visitors to Santa Fe will find the local heritage reflected in their suroundings, like the Spanish decor of this La Fonda suite.

Photo: Don Strel

time program for children under 12. The hotel offers other special family packages throughout the year such as "Winter Firesides" and "Springtime Splendor." Additional activities include horseback riding, hiking, nature walks, tennis, skeet-shooting, an outdoor pool, indoor Jacuzzi, and an exercise area. Off-site, but still nearby, are golf, rafting, fishing, and skiing.

Pueblo Encantado
$$$$ • 198 NM 592, Tesuque
• (505) 982-3537, (800) 722-9339

Under the new management of Rancho Encantado, which is temporarily closed for renovations, Pueblo Encantado is among the newest deluxe accommodations in the Santa Fe area. Tucked into the foothills of the Sangre de Cristo Mountains, the hotel offers spacious Southwestern accommodations in a relaxing, secluded setting just 10 minutes from downtown Santa Fe. Lodgings range from luxurious double occupancy rooms with king beds and *kiva* fireplaces to one- and two-bedroom villas with dining areas, fully equipped kitchens, living rooms with fireplaces, full baths, and private patios. Pueblo

Encantado is the closest lodging site to the Santa Fe Opera, which is only 5 minutes away. On-site amenities include horseback riding, heated outdoor swimming pool, hiking trails, barbecue area, table tennis, concierge, grocery delivery service, and massage by appointment. Prices include a continental breakfast

Ten Thousand Waves
$$$$ • 3451 Hyde Park Rd.
• (505) 982-9304

Ten Thousand Waves is a Japanese–style health spa built directly into the Sangre de Cristo Mountains. It recently added lodgings called Houses of the Moon to its list of offerings, which includes chlorine-free hot tubs with saunas and cold plunges; numerous styles of professional massage; herbal wraps; salt glows; water therapy; aromatherapy; the list goes on—all in a magnificent alpine setting.

The Houses of the Moon are the closest luxury accommodations to the Santa Fe Ski Area. They consist of seven guest suites—Crescent Moon, Full Moon, Rising Moon, Blue Moon, New Moon, Luna, and Moonlit—located at the end of a path

INSIDERS' TIP

If you have friends who live in Santa Fe, ask them to make your reservations. Locals can often get better prices than out-of-town callers.

The Hotel Loretto is a showcase for pueblo style.

Photo: Don Strel

through a grove of piñon trees. The suites range in size from a 1,000-square-foot space with a Japanese courtyard garden, a fireplace and woodburning stove, a full kitchen and separate bedroom, living room, and dining room to a cozy, rustic studio *casita* with a *kiva* fireplace and a small private courtyard. All have private phones with voice messaging, mini-refrigerators or full kitchens, coffee makers with a supply of gourmet coffees and teas, and access to laundry facilities. Rooms are all non-smoking.

Lodging guests receive complimentary access to the communal, clothing-optional co-ed and women's tubs and to the saunas, as well as preferential treatment for private tubs, which often are booked a week in advance.

INSIDERS' TIP

Most hotels offer discounts for AAA, AARP, and other organizations. They often don't volunteer this information, so make a point of asking.

Bed and Breakfasts

LOOK FOR:
• Santa Fe
• Santa Fe County

Unlike hotels, which are fairly predictable in their offerings, bed and breakfasts, inns, and guest houses tend to be as individual—and often as idiosyncratic—as their owners. That's certainly not a bad thing. In fact it's usually downright pleasant, and it's why guests choose to stay in these more personal lodgings than at larger, generally more homogeneous hotels. But it also means guests should confirm beforehand the rules of each house. For example, a number of Santa Fe inns have resident dogs and/or cats. People with allergies or who share W.C. Fields' philosophy—"Anyone who hates children and dogs can't be all bad"—should make a point of asking about pets on the premises and to which areas they have access. If the innkeepers' pets are particularly territorial, it may mean you can't bring little Fifi with you.

As for W.C.'s other bane—children—most bed and breakfast inns prefer an adult-only clientele to ensure a peaceful stay for their guests. Some, however, will allow children above a certain age—usually 10 years old. Check with the individual establishment for its policies regarding children and additional charges if you bring them. Most inns add $15 or $20 per night for an extra person in the room. Also, beware that some bed and breakfasts require a two-night stay on weekends, though that rule is usually bendable during the off season. Unless we note otherwise, all inns in this chapter accept major credit cards.

The majority of Santa Fe inns boast smoke-free environments, though a rare few may offer a smoking room or two. Be sure to check with your hosts in advance, if you absolutely cannot be within 100 yards of cigarette smoke or, to the other extreme, if you've got to have that last puff 30 seconds before hopping into bed. While your hosts will go out of their way to accommodate you on most things, the no-smoking rule is generally one to which they firmly adhere.

Price Code

Prices shown are based on the lowest rate per night for double occupancy in peak season. Price ratings don't reflect lodgers tax (5 percent in the city or 3 percent in the county) or other surcharges.

$	less than $55
$$	$55–89
$$$	$90–139
$$$$	$140–199
$$$$$	$200 and more

Adobe Abode Bed and Breakfast
$$$ • 202 Chapelle St.
• (505) 983-3133

In a residential neighborhood just a few blocks from the Santa Fe Plaza sits Adobe Abode, an early 19th century mud-brick home-turned-inn with an eclectic charm. Details include antiques from France and England, a mahogany planter's chair from the Philippines, Spanish Colonial turn-of-the-century pieces, handmade aspen pole beds, puppets from Java, and folk-art animals from Oaxaca. You'll find such amenities as custom soaps and shampoos, fine designer linens, thick terrycloth robes, private phones in each room, and cable television. The inn also offers fax service, off-street parking and sherry and cookies all day long. Breakfasts are hearty and imaginative and feature a different Southwestern-style entree every day.

Like the breakfasts, no two rooms at Adobe Inn are the same. Bloomsbury, for example, is done in rose and celadon with an *Out of Africa* feeling while Cabin-in-the-Woods was recently redecorated in a woodsy Adirondack-lodge style. Looking exactly as it sounds is Bronco, a rustic, western-style room with cowboy hats on the wall, a saddle and *riatas* (lassos) on the bedposts, a private covered porch, and a brick patio with twig furniture. Cactus has a distinctly south-of-the-border flavor with hand-loomed fabrics from Oaxaca, whitewashed *vigas*, and a *kiva* fireplace, while *Casita de Corazon*, or "Little House of the Heart," features Santa Fe-style decor, including custom-designed twin beds finished with aspen poles lashed together. Provence Suite contains a full living room and separate bedroom with a queen-sized, whitewashed lodgepole bed and French designer linens that highlight the blue and yellow color scheme so reminiscent of southern France.

Alexander's Inn
$$$ • 529 East Palace Ave.
• (505) 986-1431, (888) 321-5123

This 1903 Craftsman-style home has been lovingly decorated with hand stenciling, dried flowers, and family antiques to create a warm, relaxing, and nurturing atmosphere. The country cottage feel is enhanced by dormer windows and other carefully restored architectural details. Sunlight streams through stained glass windows or lace curtains onto gleaming hardwood floors. Fresh flowers grace every room in the house.

Accommodations include seven guest rooms—five named for flowers and a couple of two-storied units called the Casita and the Cottage, most furnished with four-poster or brass and iron beds. The Peony and Wildflower rooms share a bathroom, the remaining rooms have private baths though the one belonging to the Lavender Room is across the hall. The Rose Room comes equipped with a porch while the Lilac Room features a fireplace and stained glass. The *Casita* ("little house") and the Cottage both have upstairs bedrooms; the living rooms with kiva fireplaces are downstairs, as are the baths. The Casita has a refrigerator and microwave; the Cottage has a private Jacuzzi.

Rooms at the Alexander Inn are spacious and furnished with television and telephone as well as a luxuriously soft bathrobe. At the end of the day you'll find a little basket of chocolates hanging on the doorknob of your room, a sweet good-night before you snuggle in bed under a down comforter. Mornings greet you with the aroma of freshly brewed gourmet coffee and homemade muffins. Other breakfast choices include homemade granola, whole grain breads, yogurt, and seasonal fruit salad. Winter breakfasts are served in a cozy kitchen

warmed by a roaring wood stove. In warmer weather, guests can eat breakfast on the verandah, which overlooks a grassy lawn shaded by lilacs, wisteria, and apricot trees in spring; roses, peonies, lavender, and cosmos in summer. You can while away hours on the front porch's old-fashioned swing, sipping lemonade or iced tea, and munching from the ever-present plate of homemade cookies and brownies, or soak under the stars in a backyard hot tub.

Alexander Inn has three off-site casitas for short- and long-term stays, Just a short walk away, the Primrose is a historic little adobe house with quintessential Santa Fe charm including troweled plaster walls, *saltillo* tile floors, a *kiva* fireplace, and a patio. On a hilltop lot two blocks away, the inn's other two casitas—Juniper and Piñon—offer city and sunset views and a taste of the real Santa Fe. Located in a diverse neighborhood where Hispanic and Anglo, rich and poor, live side-by-side, both houses are decorated in a style best described as Southwest meets Provence. All Alexander Inn guests enjoy full privileges at upscale El Gancho Health Club (see our Parks and Recreation chapter).

Camas de Santa Fe
$$ • 323 E. Palace Ave.
• (505) 984-1337, (800) 632-2627

Close to the heart of historic Santa Fe Plaza, Camas de Santa Fe offers the charm and intimacy of a small European inn, yet has both the convenience and accessibility of a downtown hotel. Designed in the territorial style popular at the turn of the century, most of Camas' guest rooms feature *viga* (beamed) ceilings, hardwood floors, and private baths tiled in a Mexican motif. Some rooms have private entrances, *kiva* or gas fireplaces, refrigerators, even a Jacuzzi. All have air-conditioning, telephones, and cable television. An interesting note: Camas de Santa Fe used to be the office of artist Georgia O'Keeffe's eye surgeon, Dr. John Gundzik, who converted it to a B&B. Guests in rooms No. 2 and No. 6 might even feel her presence. Those are the ones O'Keeffe used.

The inn offers a buffet of juices, fresh brewed teas and coffee, and breads and cereals every morning between 8:00 AM and 10:00 AM This is a good time to trade experiences with other guests or to ask staff for suggestions.

Casa de la Cuma Bed & Breakfast
$$ • 105 Paseo de la Cuma
• (505) 983-1717, (888) 366-1717

Located at the bottom of a narrow, winding street just north of Paseo de Peralta—near the original Cross of the Martyrs (see "Attractions") and its magnificent sunset views—Casa de la Cuma is a pleasant stroll to downtown Santa Fe and the Plaza. This Southwestern-style inn offers three rooms and a suite that share an outdoor patio with a Jacuzzi and mountain views. The largest room contains a hand-crafted king-sized bed; an Indian rug on the wall; an enamel, open-faced woodburning stove; and a private entrance to the patio. Rooms No. 2 and 3 share a bath as well as views both of the Sangre de Cristo Mountains and the inn's lovely garden, which is redolent with lilac bushes and shaded by a peach tree. The suite has its own living room with a queen sleeper couch and a wet bar. Mexican tiles adorn the bathroom. All rooms have air conditioning and televisions. The common room has a cozy fireplace in front of which guests can browse through books and magazines scattered on several coffee tables or simply sit back and enjoy the 1940s Chinle rug on the wall. There's off-street parking for guests, a blessing on the narrow street. An expanded continental breakfast includes breads and pastries baked on premises or from one of Santa Fe's fine bakeries, homemade jam, cereals, a selection of seasonal fruit, juice, freshly brewed coffee, and a variety of teas.

Casa del Toro
$$$ • 229 McKenzie St.
• (505) 995-9689, (888) 995-9689

One of Santa Fe's newest bed and breakfasts, Casa del Toro, sits at the corner of two of downtown Santa Fe's quietest streets—Chapelle and McKenzie—and right around the corner from the new Georgia O'Keeffe Museum. The adobe style house features *viga* ceilings, *kiva* fireplaces, Mexican tile, skylights, and Southwestern art and knickknacks throughout. Each of the inn's seven rooms—four in the main house, three a half block away at 321 McKenzie—has its own bathroom and come furnished with down pillows and comforters and thick terrycloth robes. The largest room has a Jacuzzi as well as a fireplace and a walk-in closet. The smallest is connected by a foyer to another small room suitable for a child—available at no additional charge—with a private bathroom that also connects to the foyer. These rooms share a private entrance from a communal garden patio and are closest to the kitchen for midnight snacking on home-baked goodies available 24 hours a day. The common room conveniently abuts the counter with the snacks. Guests may also help themselves to tea, coffee, hot cider, lemonade, and juices.

Guests rave about the Casa del Toro's gourmet breakfasts, which always include a hot entrée such as a quiche or soufflé with artichoke hearts, spinach, and white chiles; posole (hominy) with a purée made from white chile, cream, butter, and crushed hot peppers. Sometimes there's more traditional fare—breakfast burritos, huevos rancheros, waffles, or pancakes —but always with a gourmet touch such as homemade chorizo or fresh organic fruit from

The Preston House (recently renamed "The Madeleine") is a 1886 Queen Anne-style house and the first bed and breakfast in Santa Fe.

the local farmers market. Breakfast also includes fresh fruit and juice, homemade breads and muffins (chile cheese corn muffins are a favorite), fresh coffee, and a variety of dark and herbal teas. The host will accommodate special diets.

Castillo Inn
$$$ • 622 Castillo Pl.
• (505) 982-1212

Located just two blocks from the Santa Fe Plaza, the charming Castillo Inn offers five rooms that give guests a taste of the various cultures that make Santa Fe unique. The Kachina room, named for the Indian statues that represent friendly messengers from the spirit world, has earth-toned textured walls on which hang dreamcatchers, peace pipes, and other Native American decorations; the Santa Fe room features a hand-carved bed and furniture with soothing, muted peach-colored walls; the Western room has teak floors and paneling; the Mexican room has wrought iron bed, authentic sombreros and bold, fanciful colors; while the English Rose room, with its walls with roses and lace, antique furniture, and claw-foot bathtub, is reminiscent of the Victorian era. Each room has its own private entrance, patio, bath with glycerin soap made on the premises, and a telephone. The inn serves a sit-down breakfast from 8 to 10 AM that includes homemade granola and a variety of sweet breads, fruit plates, juice, freshly ground coffees, and tea. For an additional $5 per person, your hosts will prepare an afternoon tea with homemade scones, creme fraiche, and jam, all on English bone china.

Chapelle Street Casitas
$$ • 209 and 211 Chapelle St.
• (505) 988-2883, (888) 340-2883

Located downtown, in a tranquil, tree-lined residential neighborhood a few blocks northwest of the Plaza—and right around the corner from the new Georgia O'Keeffe Museum—Chapelle Street Casitas offers four attached guest houses in two buildings, each with a fully equipped kitchen that includes a coffemaker and diswasher. The *casitas* are decorated in Southwestern style with antiques and Navajo rugs; authentic Mexican *sombreros*, *serapes*, and saddles; and, in one *casita*, an enamel woodburning stove that opens up like a fireplace. All include an expanded continental breakfast. The building at 209 Chapelle, located at the intersection with Staab Street, is a turn-of-the-century structure with wooden floors, tall windows, and high ceilings with ceiling fans. Innkeepers are long-time New Mexico residents

and avid skiers, hikers, and mountain bikers who are happy to share their knowledge of local trails.

Dancing Ground of the Sun
$$$ • 711 Paseo de Peralta
• (505) 986-9797, (800) 645-5673

Long ago the Pueblo Indians christened this region of northern New Mexico the "Dancing Ground of the Sun." This delightful downtown inn has taken this vision as its namesake. Only two blocks from the historic Santa Fe Plaza, Dancing Ground of the Sun's five casitas and 15 bedrooms are a celebration of light, tradition, color, and design. The theme of Native American spirit dancers plays throughout the suites and is reflected in murals by Taos artist Katherine Henry.

Each suite is named for a colorful figure from Native American lore—Buffalo Dancer, Clown Dancer; Corn Dancer; Deer Dancer; Rainbow Dancer; Spirit Dancer; and Kokopelli, the oft-recognized mythical flute player who represents good fortune and abundance—and features a kiva fireplace, vigas, Southwestern style furniture made by local craftspeople, hand-painted tiles, and numerous other special touches. All casitas have fully equipped kitchens, dining rooms, living rooms, bedrooms, and private baths; some also have, patios and/or washers and dryers. Rooms come with a continental breakfast that includes muffins or bread, fresh fruit, juice, coffee, and tea.

Don Gaspar Compound
$$$ • 623 Don Gaspar Ave.
• (505) 986-8664, (888) 986-8664

Located in the lovely and peaceful South Capital section of Santa Fe, Don Gaspar Compound welcomes you with the spreading arms of an old peach tree and a tranquil, adobe-walled garden courtyard where heirloom flowers and the trickle of water from a central fountain soothe the soul. The 90-year-old inn is a classic example of mission and adobe architecture with brick paths and distressed wooden gates.

Don Gaspar Compound offers six private suites for long- or short-terms stays, including the Main House—a sunny, beautifully appointed bungalow overlooking the gardens that features two woodburning fireplaces, two bedrooms, two baths, a small room with a double futon, and a fully-equipped kitchen. Also containing fireplaces and fully-equipped kitchens are the one-bedroom, one-bath Fountain Casita, named for the courtyard fountain visible through the living room's French doors, and the Courtyard Casita, which has its own private courtyard and garden, stained glass windows above a king-sized bed, and a whirlpool bath.

The Southwest Suite's decor is true to its name with an adobe wood-burning fireplace and fine Southwestern furnishings; the Aspen Suite takes its name from the trees in the garden, which are in full view from the kitchenette and the window seat in the bedroom; and the western style Colorado Room, with French doors opening onto its own patio, could easily be called "home on the range" with its cowboy motif. In addition, the owners make available a charming home located in a quiet residential neighborhood about two miles southwest of Don Gaspar Compound. San Juan House is small two-bedroom, one-bath adobe with French doors in each bedroom that open onto a deck.

All accommodations have private bathrooms, televisions, and private phones. Those without fully equipped kitchens have kitchenettes with refrigerators, microwaves, coffeemakers, toasters, and some utensils. The refrigerators are stocked with fresh coffee beans, spring water, and Blue Sky natural sodas. Guests, including those at San Juan House, generally take their morning meal in Don Gaspar Compound's breakfast room, where they can choose from a variety of gourmet coffees and teas, fresh-squeezed orange juice, pastries, cereals, fresh fruit, and a different regional specialty daily.

Dos Casas Viejas
$$$$ • 610 Agua Fria St.
• (505) 983-1636

Situated in the heart of the historic Guadalupe District, near Sanbusco Market and the Railyard and only 10 minutes by foot to the Plaza, Dos Casas Viejas (Two Old Houses) provides guests with the quintessential Southwestern B&B experience. Housed within a walled and gated adobe compound on a half-acre of land stands and intimate and sophisticated collection of adobe buildings that offer the character, charm, and tradition found in Santa Fe during the 1860s.

Each *casita* provides the utmost in privacy with individual entry gates leading to bricked, landscaped patios, complete custom-built willow furniture, behind adobe walls. French doors lead into the *casitas*, which are decorated with period furnishings as well as state of the art amenities. All have *kiva* fireplaces, *vigas*, cable television, CD players, private telephones, answering machines, and bar refrigerators with complementary beverages and snacks. The inn

provides custom soaps, shampoos, and lotions; luxurious personal robes; and hair dryers.

Guests can breakfast in the dining room, located in the main building adjacent to a lobby/library, take their food back to their quarters or, if they prefer, dine al fresco on the patio of the compound's 40-foot heated lap pool. Dos Casas Viejas can accommodate up to 30 people for weddings, private parties, banquets, or meetings.

Dunshee's
$$$ • 986 Acequia Madre
• (505) 982-0988

With only two units—a large suite in the main house and a two-bedroom guest house next door—Dunshee's is among Santa Fe's smallest inns. However, that's not a reflection on the size of the rooms, which are quite spacious. Traditional New Mexican-style furniture, *kiva* fireplaces, Mexican tile, folk art, and well-placed antiques along with the owner's personal touches—fresh flowers, home-baked cookies, good books, and quiet breakfasts (in the main house only)—create an intimate, homey, old-fashioned atmosphere without sacrificing the convenience and pleasure of modern amenities like phones and televisions.

The main house is a restored adobe that hosts only one party at a time. Accommodations include a private entrance; large living room with a cozy sitting area and a *kiva* fireplace; queen-sized bed in the bedroom, which also has a *kiva* fireplace; a sheltered, flower-filled patio; a *portal* (roofed porch) overlooking a large backyard; an eclectic library; and a refrigerator and microwave. The innkeeper lives on the premises and serves breakfast on the patio or portal in summer or by the fire during crisper weather. Breakfast includes fresh-squeezed juice, freshly ground coffee, home-baked goods, seasonal fruit, and various entrees such as omelets with herbs from the garden, sour cream pancakes, or green chile stew.

The casita next door is a two-bedroom, one-bath pueblo-style adobe guesthouse with a private patio, a living room supplied with books and a stereo system, and a full kitchen complete with a dishwasher. You'll arrive to a full cookie jar and a refrigerator stocked for your first breakfast: gourmet coffee, fresh juice, seasonal fruit, and homemade muffins. Guests can help themselves to herbs and tomatoes from the garden. The casita is available for long-term rentals. Ask for prices.

Located in a historic and charming neighborhood named for the *Acequia Madre* ("mother ditch") that runs through it, Dunshee's is a

Home-cooked breakfasts are the fare at some of Santa Fe's bed and breakfast establishments.

pleasant mile from the Plaza and only three blocks from the galleries and shops, cafes, and restaurants of elegant Canyon Road.

El Farolito Bed & Breakfast Inn
$$$$ • 514 Galisteo St.
• (505) 988-1631, (888) 634-8782

A few short blocks from the Plaza and around the corner from the state capitol building, El Farolito welcomes guests to its off-street compound in the city's historic district. The award-winning inn features five guest rooms and a suite in three buildings, two private casitas and a main house with a dining room and lounge/library. A number of the buildings are adobe and all have been decorated in traditional Southwestern style, ranging from Native American to Mexican folk art. The owners have displayed paintings, pottery, kachinas, weavings, and other items their private art collection throughout the inn.

Each room has its own private entrances and outdoor patio as well as a private, hand-tiled bath, brick or tile floors, wood-beamed ceiling, hand-carved furniture, and a *kiva* fireplaces as well as color cable television and a private phone. Some rooms also have wet bars with small refrigerators. Each room unique, the inn reflects Santa Fe's tri-cultural heritage of Pueblo Indian, Spanish Colonial, and Pioneer Anglo settlers.

The breakfast room is a sunny, brightly colored affair with a fireplace and tables for two, four, and eight, so guests can eat in privacy or company, according to their mood. El Farolito serves an "expanded" Continental breakfast that includes a fresh fruit plate, a variety of home-baked goods, yogurt, cereals, bagels, toast, English muffins, gourmet coffees, teas, and fresh-squeezed juices. Those craving a hot breakfast can try the retro-1960s Café Oasis next door (but not until 9 AM) or to any number of more traditional restaurants downtown.

El Paradero Bed & Breakfast Inn
$$ • 220 West Manhattan Ave.
• (505) 988-1177

Built between 1800 and 1820, El Paradero was originally a Spanish farmhouse to which Territorial touches such as pillars were added in the late 19th century. In 1912, the main house underwent a complete remodeling that included Victorian doors and windows. The current innkeepers bought the house in 1980 and turned it into a bed and breakfast inn—Santa Fe's second. They have since remodeled, adding some modern architectural touches while maintaining the eccentric, rambling character of the old farmhouse—from its thick adobe walls to its high ceilings, *kiva* fireplaces, *vigas*, *bancos* (benches built into the walls), and *nichos* (small niches in the wall to place religious icons or decorations).

El Paradero has fourteen rooms: nine around the courtyard, three upstairs, and two suites in an adjacent 1912 brick coachman's house—a plaqued New Mexico historic structure. Twelve of the rooms have private baths; two less expensive rooms share a pair of bathrooms along a short hallway. Each room is furnished with Southwestern-style furniture, hand-woven textiles, and folk art; many have fireplaces and skylights or mountain-view balconies. Breakfasts are hearty. They include a gourmet entree, home-baked bread, fresh fruit, and juice. Sundays bring lighter-than-air pancakes, a tradition of the innkeepers, who will meet special dietary needs. They serve tea—either hot or iced, hot cider, and homemade baked goods and chips and salsa every afternoon. A warning for those with allergies: A cat and dog live on the premises.

The Spencer House, 222 McKenzie, is among Santa Fe's bed and breakfasts.

Photo: Don Strel

Four Kachinas Inn
$$$$ • 512 Webber St.
• (505) 982-2550, (800) 397-2564

Four Kachinas Inn borrows its name from the ancestral spirits of the Pueblo Indians, who take three forms: pure spirit; a masked dancer believed to embody a particular spirit during a religious ceremony; or a carved doll in the costume of the spirit. It is the latter that you'll notice in various forms at the Four Kachinas, most notably in the Zia and Kachina rooms, which also feature fine Navajo weavings and pottery from the owners' personal collection as well as hand-carved head- and footboards. Of the remaining three rooms, two have a distinctly Hispanic flavor, The colorful San Miguel Room gives a feeling of old world Mexico while the Chimayó Room is filled with Spanish Colonial art—weavings, *retablos*, and a hand-carved king-size bed. In the main house, a landmark Victorian-style cottage, the Digneo Room pays homage to the man who built the house in the early 1900s—a stonemason who worked on St., Francis Cathedral. The room is decorated with period furniture, both antiques and reproductions, including a new, wooden queen-sized bed with a pressed tin headboard and footboard. All rooms come with a private telephone and cable television. Four Kachinas sits on a quiet residential street in view of the state capitol building and just a few short blocks up the Old Santa Fe Trail to the Plaza. The heart of the inn is its sunny, bricked courtyard built alongside the historic *Acequia Madre*—the "Mother Ditch" irrigation channel that meanders through Santa Fe—and the adobe breakfast room/lounge. Built of adobe bricks made on the property years ago, the lounge is a mixture of Native American and Mexican décor and displays fine original work by native artists. Guests may breakfast here or across the courtyard on a variety of home-baked breads and pastries, fresh-squeezed and gourmet bottled juices, high quality coffees and teas, milk, yogurt, and fresh fruit. They're invited to peruse their hosts' personal art and travel library, which includes Santa Fe guidebooks and maps, while enjoying complimentary beverages and snacks all day long.

Grant Corner Inn
$$$ • 122 Grant Ave.
• (505) 983-6678, (800) 964-9003

Surrounded by graceful weeping willow trees and a trim white picket fence, Grant Corner Inn, a 1905 colonial manor home, maintains a country elegance in the heart of downtown Santa Fe. Located just two blocks from the Santa Fe Plaza, the inn offers both comfort and convenience as well as justly famous breakfasts that feature entrées such as creative breakfast burritos, cinnamon raisin French toast, blue corn blueberry pancakes, fruit blintzes, and a variety of freshly baked breads, pastries, coffee cakes, muffins, and cookies from the inn's bakery. Breakfasts come with homemade jams, fresh fruit frappes, freshly squeezed juice, and seasonal fruit. The inn is open to the public Monday through Saturday for breakfast and Sundays for brunch.

The Inn has 10 charming guest rooms—eight on the main premises and two in a hacienda located six blocks away, all with private baths. Rooms are beautifully appointed with antiques, handmade quilts, vintage photographs, and rabbits in every medium—and every corner—imaginable from the collection of the innkeeper, who is also a decorator.

INSIDERS' TIP

Prices in Santa Fe's hotels, motels, and inns are often negotiable, especially during the off-season, which may vary from one establishment to another. Be prepared, however, to meet with some surprise, if not downright indignation, in some quarters if you try to bargain. After all this isn't Mexico. Still it doesn't hurt to ask, and you might just score a good-natured success.

Guadalupe Inn
$$$ • 604 Agua Fria St.
• (505) 989-7422

Located on the historic Camino Real, an ancient route used first by Indians and then by Hispanic traders to get from Mexico to northern New Mexico, the Guadalupe Inn is owned and operated by three members of the Quintana family, who built the bed and breakfast in 1991 on the site of their grand-father's small grocery store— a half mile from the Plaza on Santa Fe's west side. The inn's 11 guest rooms and two-bedroom suite are uniquely decorated in Southwestern style with furniture and fixtures hand-crafted by members of the Quintana family and other artisans. All rooms contain private baths, queen-sized beds, televisions, telephones, and air conditioning. Seven rooms have fireplaces, four feature whirlpool baths, while the Celebration Room has a large porcelain tub with brass claw feet. The suite offers a private balcony with views of the Jémez Mountains to the west and the Sangre de Cristos to the east. Guests share an indoor tiled hot tub surrounded by plants, planked walls, and plenty of windows.

Guadalupe Inn serves a hearty breakfast with an entrée that includes a choice of huevos rancheros, breakfast burritos, or pancakes. Breakfasts always come with homemade pastries or turnovers, cereal, fruit, juice, and coffee or tea.

Inn of the Turquoise Bear
$$$ • 342 E. Buena Vista St.
• (505) 983-0798, (800) 396-4104

This award-winning historic bed and breakfast on the Old Santa Fe Trail occupies the home of poet Witter Bynner (1881–1968), for decades a prominent citizen of Santa Fe who in recent years has slipped into obscurity. During his day, Bynner was a leading figure of Santa Fe's flourishing writer's colony—a noted poet, translator, and essayist who staunchly advocated human rights for women, Native Americans, gays, and other minorities. Bynner also loved a good party, hosting with Robert Hunt, his companion of more than 30 years, many a "Bynner's bash," as photographer Ansel Adams described their riotous soirées. Their home was a gathering place for the literati and glitterati; Santa Fe's answer to Mabel Dodge Luhan's home in Taos. Among Bynner's and Hunt's guests were D. H. Lawrence, who spent his first night in an American home here and eventually settled near Taos; Willa Cather, whose classic novel, *Death Comes for the Archbishop*, has been for many readers their first introduction to Santa Fe; Aldous Huxley; Christopher Isherwood; Thornton Wilder; Mary Hunter Austin; Ansel Adams; composer Igor Stravinsky; poets Edna St. Vincent Millay, Robert Frost, W.H. Auden, and Stephen Spender; Hollywood stars Clara Bow, Errol Flynn, and Rita Hayworth; music critic Carl Van Vechten; dancer and choreographer Martha Graham; Georgia O'Keeffe; and even Robert Oppenheimer, under whose leadership Los Alamos Scientific Laboratory built the world's first atomic bomb.

The new owners of the Bynner estate, Ralph Bolton and Robert Frost (no relation to the other Robert Frost), live on the property and are dedicated to rekindling the spirit of excitement and creativity that thrived there under its last owner as well as restoring and even extending his legacy. To that end they give readings of Bynner's work and, in the process, provide their guests with a unique setting that captures the essence of traditional and literary Santa Fe. Since 1999, the inn has received two prestigious Heritage Preservation awards, first from the City of Santa Fe and, in 2000, from the state. Bynner's rambling adobe is built in the Spanish Pueblo Revival style around a core of rooms that date to the mid-1800s. The grounds are truly magnificent with soaring ponderosa pines, rock terraces, stone benches, and fountains, meandering flagstone paths and gardens filled with lilac, wild roses, and other flowers—all enclosed by adobe walls and coyote fences. The interior contains 11 Southwestern guest rooms, 10 of them with *kiva* fireplaces, *viga* ceilings, *saltillo* tile, private entrances, and brick or wooden floors. Most have private baths and sitting areas; all have phones, cable televisions, and VCRs. The inn has an impressive video library and, as you might expect, an extensive book collection. Among the little luxuries that make Inn of the Turquoise Bear so special are the robes, flowers, and fruit in the rooms. The hosts also serve refreshments at sunset and an expanded continental breakfast that includes fresh squeezed orange juice, cereals, seasonal fruit, a variety of home-baked pastries and breads, and coffee from a roaster down the street. The inn is six blocks from the Plaza and a pleasant stroll to Canyon Road. There are also a number of galleries, shops, and restaurants in the immediate vicinity.

Inn on the Paseo
$$ • 630 Paseo de Peralta
• (505) 984-8200, (800) 457-9045

Two historic homes joined by a central wing comprise Inn on the Paseo, a relatively large B&B with 16 rooms and two suites renovated in 1991 in contemporary Southwestern style. Each room has a private bath, a down comforter and, in most cases, a patchwork quilt handmade by the former innkeeper, a third generation quiltmaker. The decor is country style with washed pine furniture and pastel-colored walls, though no two rooms are alike. One might include a four-poster bed while another a fireplace, a sloped ceiling or, in the Honeymoon suite, a whirlpool bath. Some have hardwood floors, others carpeting. Many feature original works of art which, like the quilts, are for sale. All have private heat and air conditioning controls, telephones, and cable color television with HBO.

Breakfast is made on premises and usually consists of at least one hot entrée—fritatta, French toast, calabacitas, or breakfast burritos, for example—along with homemade breads, fresh fruit, yogurt, hot and cold cereals, juice, and gourmet coffee. Guests can eat indoors or on the back deck. The inn serves homemade cookies and cakes every afternoon along with hot or cold drinks in a living room with a large fireplace, a skylight, and lots of windows overlooking a sunken patio and gardens.

Just a few blocks northeast of the Plaza, Inn on the Paseo is across the street from Cross of the Martyrs (see our "Attractions" chapter) and a short stroll to nearby Canyon Road. The inn offers free parking to guests

La Tienda Inn
$$$ • 445-447 W. San Francisco St.
• (505) 989-8259, (800) 889-7611

This out-of-the-way B&B and its resident cat, Adolfo, are both named to honor the history of one of its buildings—a small adobe built in the 1930s by Adolfo Montoya, who operated a little neighborhood store (*tienda*) behind its thick mud walls and beneath the unpeeled log *vigas* that support its earthen roof. The market remained open under a number of shopkeepers until the 1960s. Now, it's the Old Store Common Room, which has been renovated without sacrificing the traditional architecture or ambiance.

La Tienda has seven individual guest rooms, each with a private bath and entrance and all named for neighbors past and present. The owners discuss the namesakes in their newsletter, which comes out several times a year. Three rooms—Romero, Montoya, and Mascarell—are in the air-conditioned Territorial House, which is nearly 100 years old and is listed in the state Historical Register. The Romero Room features a sun porch and its own picket-fenced garden while the Montoya and Mascarell rooms overlook the front garden and fountain. The remaining rooms are in the "old store adobe," whose thick mud walls keep the rooms cool in summer and warm in winter, though a swamp cooler adds to the comfort in summer. The wheelchair-accessible Trujillo Room has a fireplace, as do the Ortiz and Duran rooms. Duran also has a *viga* ceiling while the Conklin Room opens on to a quiet courtyard. All rooms have telephones and color cable television. They include a generous continental breakfast of warm breads, fresh fruit, and juices served in the room or in the garden when the weather allows. Guests can take afternoon tea in the Common Room where a large *kiva* fireplace beckons when there's a chill in the air.

Las Palomas
$$$$ • 119 Park Ave. and
450 W. San Francisco St.
• (505) 988-4455, ext. 600;
(800) 955-4455, ext., 600

Only six blocks from the Plaza, in two tree-covered compounds with rambling courtyards, Las Palomas offers the charm, elegance, and ambiance of a country inn in the heart of the city. And because of its affiliation with the elegant Eldorado Hotel two blocks away, Las Palomas can provide its guests with the best of both worlds—the intimacy of a small bed and breakfast and the amenities of a world-class resort.

Las Palomas was built sometime around the turn of the century. In restoring these 35 casitas, the owners strove to keep the style and feel of the adobe structures while adding the comforts of modern life. The odd size doorways, uneven adobe walls, and individual *kiva* fireplaces combine with air-conditioning, cable television, VCRs, stereos with CD players, and modern kitchens to strike this aesthetic balance. Each of the fully restored adobe *casitas* has a living room, dining area, kitchen, private bath, and *kiva* fireplace. The inn serves a full continental breakfast each morning.

The Madeleine
$$ • 106 Faithway St.
• (505) 982-3465

Formerly the Preston House—Santa Fe's first bed and breakfast inn—the Madeleine sits tucked at the end of a street that even many Santa Feans don't know exists. Obscured by ancient elms in summer and open to the sun in winter, this lovely 1886 Queen Anne–style house now bears a historical plaque. A charming garden winds its way throughout the property, offering guests a colorful display of seasonal blooms and an inviting patio on which to enjoy reading and afternoon tea and pastries.

The Victorian style guest rooms are fantasies in linen and lace, stained glass, antique armoires, delicate floral wall coverings, and ornately carved fireplaces. All rooms have a telephone and cable television. All but two have private baths. Guests breakfast in a big country kitchen where there's always a hot entrée—fritatta, perhaps, or pancakes or quiche—accompanied by freshly squeezed orange juice, coffee or tea, and breads and pastries baked daily on the premises.

Pueblo Bonito
$$$ • 138 W. Manhattan St.
• (505) 984-8001, (800) 461-4599

Secluded behind thick adobe walls, Pueblo Bonito Bed & Breakfast Inn occupies an old adobe built around the turn of the century. The newly renovated inn is located in the midst of Santa Fe's historic district and a five-minute walk from the Plaza. The compound was once a private estate with its own stable and landscaped grounds. Today it still boasts beautiful private courtyards, narrow brick paths, adobe archways to the street, and shady gardens sheltered by huge trees. The second floor balcony overlooks Santa Fe's winding streets and the Sangre de Cristo Mountains to the east.

Fifteen cozy guest rooms, each with its own corner fireplace and private bath, provide intimacy, hospitality, and traditional Santa Fe ambiance. They're named for area Indian tribes and furnished with Navajo rugs, baskets, and sand paintings; Pueblo and Mexican pottery; antiques; and other work by local artisans. The inn offers many modern conveniences, such as on-site laundry facilities, color cable television, and ample private parking within the compound.

Continental breakfast is served buffet style with a variety of fresh fruits, juices, danish, muffins, and cereals served along with fresh brewed coffee and an assortment of different teas. Guests can eat on the outside patio or in the newly renovated communal dining room. The innkeepers also serve an afternoon tea.

Territorial Inn
$$$ • 215 Washington Ave.
• (505) 989-7737, (800) 745-9910

In the heart of downtown Santa Fe, just two blocks north of the Plaza, Territorial Inn is the last of the private homes along tree-lined Washington Ave. The inn, built in 1896, is a charming blend of New Mexico's various architectural styles, mixing stone and adobe with a pitched roof and Territorial style pillars. The interior is furnished in a turn-of-the-century Victorian/Territorial style with rooms that range in size from large and luxurious to cozy and quaint. Two of the 10 rooms have fireplaces, eight have private baths and all are elegantly decorated. Behind the century-old main

building is a newer structure the inn recently acquired and turned into an additional 10 guest rooms, all with private baths and decorated in the same style as the older rooms.

The grounds feature lawns—a rarity in Santa Fe—as well as large cottonwood trees and a private rose garden. The inn serves a generous complimentary continental breakfast that includes a selection of freshly baked breads from an excellent local bakery, cereals, fruit, juice, coffee, and tea. Guests may dine in their rooms, on the patio, or in the lounge. The inn hosts a social hour in the late afternoon that includes brandy, tea, and other beverages and homemade cookies.

Water Street Inn
$$$ • 427 W. Water St.
• (505) 984-1193

An award-winning adobe restoration has earned Water Street Inn a rightful place among Santa Fe's more luxurious bed and breakfasts. Its eight spacious rooms and four suites all have private baths, *kiva* and/or antique fireplaces (yes, some of the rooms have more than one), and/or wood stoves. The decor is refined Southwestern and varies from room to room with details such as brick floors, beamed ceilings, and built-in sleeping bancos in addition to beds of varying styles, including New Mexico pine, four-posters, pediment, or sleigh. One room boasts a spiral staircase and a private deck, another features a private patio with a portal. A number of rooms open onto a fountained courtyard. One room is handicapped accessible. The four suites are located in a separate building. Three of them feature private, partially enclosed patios, including two with their own fountains. The largest suite, Tesuque, is large enough to sleep five in two separate rooms

Breakfast at the Territorial Inn includes fresh pastries, cereals, fruit, juices, coffees, and a morning paper. The inn also hosts an evening "happy hour" when it serves New Mexican wines and hot hors d'oeuvres. Many fine restaurants are nearby and the Plaza is just two blocks away.

Santa Fe County

Crystal Mesa Farm Bed and Breakfast
$$ • 3547 State Road, No. 14, Building B
• (505) 474-5224

Unlike many bed and breakfasts, Crystal Mesa Farm welcomes children with a collec-

The Territorial Inn is just one-and-a-half blocks from the Plaza.

Photo: Don Strel

tion of miniature critters—pot-bellied pigs, African pygmy hedgehogs, pygmy goats, and a very stubborn miniature donkey called "Duke." Newborns are a constant occurrence, so be sure to ask about any new arrivals. The inn also provides such child-friendly amenities as cribs, room-to-room intercoms, and easy trails peppered with rocks that draw children like magnets. You and your kids can explore *arroyos* (natural rain ditches) and *mesas*, stare endlessly at hawks and falcons, and watch for prairie dogs and coyotes. Crystal Mesa Farm is also an exotic bird rescue station with an aviary/sun room that is home to a number of permanent feathered residents and a few visitors taking temporary refuge. You can even have one of the birds "room" with you during your stay.

Built on the ancient site of the San Marcos Pueblo on the historic Turquoise Trail, this charming bed & breakfast inn offers a lovely alternative to staying in town. Each guest room has a private bath and entrance, cable television, a VCR, and a phone. The San Marcos Suite features a king-size bed flanked by antique columns from an Indian palace, a woodburning stove, and private access to the inn's library and hot tub. The Sunset Room has a west-facing terrace and queen-size bed. An Apache ladder leads to a meditation loft with breathtaking views of the sunset and starry night skies. The Lookout Room boasts a bed designed by famous Santa Fe "cowboy artist" L.D. Burke, a kitchen, and a private deck with its own panoramic view. The more adventurous can follow the Tipi Trail to the inn's Sioux tipi, which contains a platform futon, flagstone floor, sheepskins, and central fire pit which makes for cozy nights in winter.

The Farm's decor is an eclectic blend of Southwestern, cowboy, and Far Eastern antiques along with many contemporary pieces. The inn is filled with stained glass windows, including one called the "star of summer," which focuses the light of sunset during the summer solstice through a central prism onto a nicho across the room, bathing it and the statue it holds in a rainbow of light.

The inn serves a gourmet continental breakfast and hosts a cocktail hour in "The Great Room"—a common area that features a cozy conversation pit with a kiva fireplace and antique wood burning cook stove. Guests are welcome to peruse the extensive library for information on local wildlife, history, ancient and modern Indian sites, and the magic that draws so many to this area. There's also a collection of videotapes on the wildlife, plants, indigenous peoples, history, and lore of the land.

Galisteo Inn
$$$ • HC 75, Box 4
(# 9 La Vega), Galisteo
• (505) 466-4000

Located about 20 miles southeast of Santa Fe, Galisteo was once a Spanish colonial outpost built on the ruins of an ancient Indian pueblo. Today, it's home to artists, writers,

healers, and a native community that retains a strong sense of its Indian and Spanish traditions. It's also home to Galisteo Inn, a 255-year-old hacienda that belonged to one of the area's original Spanish settlers.

The inn itself is an 8,000-square-foot Territorial-style adobe building on eight secluded acres. It features large, missionary-style carved wooden doors; wood-planked floors covered with antique rugs; whitewashed walls and fireplaces with built-in *bancos*; beamed and *latilla*-ed ceilings; hand-crafted period furniture and fixtures; a lounge filled with sofas and books; and an ambiance of genteel country antiquity.

Each of the inn's 12 rooms is named for a native tree—in descending order by price: cottonwood, spruce, birch, piñon, poplar, juniper, ponderosa, elm, chamisa, willow, aspen, and sycamore. Most of the rooms have private baths; some have fireplaces and televisions. All include a full, and fully imaginative, buffet breakfast with a main dish that could be chile fritatta one morning or breakfast burritos the next, along with such standards as home-baked breads, fruit salad, yogurt, smoothies, and freshly brewed coffee and tea.

Among the amenities at Galisteo Inn are a 50-foot, outdoor heated lap pool, open May through October; an outdoor hot tub guests can use all year long; an indoor sauna; and mountain bikes. For additional charges, guests can also enjoy massages, horseback riding, picnic lunches, and the inn's famous nouvelle Southwestern dinners.

Heart Seed B&B and Spa
$$$ • 63 Corazon de Oro (C. R. 55),
Cerrillos
• (505) 471-7026

Heart Seed is both an inn and a spa located 25 miles south of Santa Fe on the scenic Turquoise Trail. The inn's six guest rooms are situated on 80 spectacular acres in the Ortiz Mountains with breathtaking views that let you see for 80 miles. Also on the grounds is a day spa offering a variety of massage, facials, salt glows, and cellulite wraps. Treatments range in price from $60 to $85 an hour. The spa offers discount packages by the day or by the week.

Rooms at the Heart Seed are spacious and attractive with private baths; two rooms have fully equipped kitchenettes. The Desert Hearts Room is decorated in a 1950s cowboy/cowgirl motif with two queen-sized beds, a camp kitchen with a hot plate and cooking supplies, rustic antique furnishings, and a small patio with great mountain views. One of two separate "retreat" buildings houses the Piñon and Juniper rooms—studio apartment–style suites with a fully equipped kitchenette (refrigerator, cooking facilities, table, and chairs), a queen-sized bed and futon couch. The Sage and Chamisa rooms in the second retreat house offer similar accommodations except for their minimal cooking facilities—coffeemaker, toaster oven, and refrigerator. All afford fine views of the Sangre de Cristo and Ortiz Mountains and include a full breakfast—gourmet entrées, homemade breads, and freshly ground coffee—at the main house as well as unlimited use of all facilities except the spa, which is charged separately. The property features a large shaded deck, hot tub, meditation garden, labyrinth, common room/library, hiking trails, a telescope for stargazing, and plenty of bird watching.

Open Sky Bed and Breakfast
$$ • 134 Turquoise Trail
• (505) 471-3475, (800) 244-3475

This is a true country B&B located 20 minutes south of Santa Fe off the historic Turquoise Trail. The inn offers spectacular 360-degree views and Southwest elegance from its adobe architecture to its brick floors and high viga ceilings. Guests can choose from three rooms. The largest is 350 square feet with a private entrance, king-sized bed, shower and bath, fireplace, sitting area, patio, and privacy. The next largest is half the size with a king bed and a full private bath that has both a tub and a shower as well as double sinks. The smallest room has a queen bed and a large private bath next door with a shower and an antique tub. All rooms offer northern views that show the Santa Fe skyline to advantage at night.

Open Sky serves a continental breakfast of fresh breads, cereals, fruit, juice, and a hot beverage of your choice at private tables facing a garden courtyard. The inn also has an outdoor Jacuzzi, a large lounge with a fireplace, and a number of private patios.

The Triangle Inn–Santa Fe
$$ • 14 Arroyo Cuyamungue
• (505) 455-3375

The Triangle Inn is a beautifully rustic country bed and breakfast that caters to the lesbian and gay community. Located on an old adobe compound surrounded by Tesuque, Nambé, and Pojoaque Pueblos, the inn is just 15 minutes north of downtown Santa Fe and convenient to all that northern New Mexico has to offer. Guests stay in their own private *casitas*, which range in size from a cozy studio to a large, two-bedroom house. Each is unique and features Southwestern decor and an attention to detail complemented by Mexican and other handcrafted furnishings, fireplaces, *viga* ceilings, and private courtyards. All have kitchenettes and either king or queen-sized beds with down bedding. Additional amenities include stereos with CD players, color televisions and VCRs, telephones, hair dryers, and gourmet coffees and teas in the room. The hosts even provide you with terry robes and spa towels for use in the bath or the 24-hour hot tub in the main courtyard, which also has a large deck and sunbathing area. The Hacienda Courtyard has extensive gardens, an orchard, and a large freestanding *portal* with an outdoor fireplace. Your hosts serve refreshments here in warmer months. All rooms include a hearty continental breakfast of muffins, a fruit platter, yogurt, oatmeal, juice, coffee, and tea.

INSIDERS' TIP
If you're counting your pennies, staying in the county could save you some money—up to 1.5% in taxes alone. Santa Fe County charges only 5.75 percent in gross receipts tax and 4 percent in lodgers tax compared to the city, where you'll pay a 6.4375 percent gross receipts plus 5 percent lodgers tax.

BED AND BREAKFASTS

Vacation Rentals

LOOK FOR:
- Downtown
- County
- Agencies

Visitors looking to stay in Santa Fe for more than a few days, especially those who don't want to dine out every meal, might consider a vacation rental instead of a hotel, motel, or bed and breakfast. Vacation rentals come in several flavors: apartments, condominiums, *casitas* ("little houses"), or private homes. They're usually only available for short-term leases, though that can mean several months in some instances, especially in timeshares. Many require a minimum stay of two to three days. Some are pedestrian, others elegant. You can be sure that the style will be reflected in the price.

Vacation rentals are ideal for skiers who would rather spend money on the slopes than on their digs. Even cushy rentals can turn out to be downright reasonable for families or groups of friends. Ditto for opera buffs who don't mind digging into their pockets for season tickets but cringe at paying hundreds, if not thousands, of dollars on accommodations.

Some people prefer to do their own cooking, whether it's to save money or to accommodate special diets. Either way, you can easily recoup some of the cost of your chi-chi accommodations (if that's what you choose) by cooking at home. For those of you who fit into this category, *please* eat at least a few meals out. Visiting Santa Fe without tasting the local cuisine is like going to New York without catching a Broadway play. You could do it, of course. But why would you want to?

If smoking, pets, children or handicapped access are important issues for you, be sure to ask about them before you make your reservations. Unless we note otherwise, all the accommodations listed here accept major credit cards.

Price Code

Our legend is based on the lowest rate per night in peak season. Price ratings don't reflect lodging tax or other surcharges.

$	Less than $55
$$	$56 to $89
$$$	$90 to $139
$$$$	$140 to $199
$$$	More than $200

Downtown

Adelante Casitas
$$$ • 316 Staab St.
• (505) 988-2883,
(888) 340-2883

Just a few blocks from the Plaza and around the corner from the Georgia O'Keeffe Museum, Adelante Casitas consists of two two-bedroom units with large backyards suitable for children and pets—both of which are welcome. Done up in Southwestern style, the *casitas* have fireplaces, beamed ceilings, skylights, full kitchens, and washers and dryers. One has two queen-size beds, the other a king and a queen. Both are modern and clean.

Las Brisas de Santa Fe
$$$$ • 624 Galisteo St.
• (505) 982-5795,
(800) 449-6231

Las Brisas is a compound of 29 one-, two-, and three-bedroom condominiums—10 timeshares, the rest owner-occupied or rentals, and all of them pure Santa Fe: exposed adobe walls, *saltillo* tile floors, *viga* ceilings, *kiva* fireplaces, enclosed courtyards or patios, punched tin decorations, and other southwestern touches. For the truly decadent, there's even one with a whirlpool bath and an enclosed atrium with a skylight. All units are fully furnished and include dishwashers, microwaves, cooking and eating utensils, linens, stackable washers and dryers, and queen sleeper sofas in the living rooms. They do not include daily maid service. Las Brisas is around the corner from the state capitol and six blocks from the Plaza. Guests can rent by the night, the week, or the month, based on availability.

Otra Vez en Santa Fe
$$$$ • 202 Galisteo St. • (505) 988-2244, (800) 536-6488

At the corner of Galisteo and Water Streets, above two narrow intersecting roads in the heart of historic downtown Santa Fe, sits an elegant timeshare that few locals even know exist. Otra Vez—which means "again" in Spanish—occupies the second and third floors of an relatively "new" Santa Fe building, circa 1923, above Harry's, a chic men's store, and Foreign Traders, which sells high quality Mexican furniture, collectibles, and accessories.

Otra Vez doesn't have to advertise. It fills up its 18 one- and two-bedroom units by word-of-mouth. Among the attractions are a sun terrace with a year-round, outdoor hot tub and barbecues. The apartments are elegantly decorated in modern Southwestern style with handcrafted furniture. Each has a full kitchen with microwave, dishwasher, and cooking and eating utensils. The rates include daily maid service, access to free laundry facilities, and parking in a lot behind the building.

La Dulce Vida, Casitas on Grant
$$$ • 509 Grant Ave. • (505) 989-7964

La Dulce Vida ("the sweet life") is among the more recent additions to Santa Fe's choice rental list and one of Santa Fe's best-kept secrets. Just a five-minute walk from the Plaza, La Dulce

> ## INSIDERS' TIP
> Dogs are welcome in Santa Fe. In fact, they're about as ubiquitous as the kitschy bandana-clad howling coyote you'll see everywhere. Keep in mind, however, that a city ordinance requires all dogs to be leashed in public, even in parks and on trails. In the county, your pooch must be within voice command. For energetic canines, this could present a real hardship. Please consider this before taking Rufus with you to see—and, of course, smell—The City Different. He may be happier at home with a dog sitter or staying with a neighbor.

Vida consists of two attached, 600-square-foot one-bedroom *casitas* hidden behind an adobe-walled entrance. Each has its own private garden patio, one with a fireplace. Both have living/dining rooms with queen-size sleeper sofas and *kiva* fireplaces; full baths with Mexican tile and clawfoot tubs; well equipped kitchens that include microwaves and coffeemakers; cable televisions and VCRs; and fax facilities upon request. Also upon request, the owner will stock your refrigerator and handle other arrangements including dinner reservations, horseback riding or tours—all before you arrive. After check-in, you'll find fresh fruit, chilled wine, and two gallons of reverse osmosis water waiting for you.

Zona Rosa
$$$$$ • 209 W. San Francisco St. • (505) 988-4455, (800) 955-4455

Just one block from the luxurious Eldorado Hotel, the Zona Rosa Suites is an independently owned complex of nine luxury condominiums managed by the Eldorado. Each one-, two-, and three-bedroom suite features southwestern furnishings, an authentic *kiva* fireplace, *saltillo* tile floors, rustic *viga* ceilings, and Native American artwork. All contain a full kitchen, living room, a balcony or patio, separate entrance, and off-street parking. The two- and three-bedroom units each have two full bathrooms. Guests at Zona Rosa may use all the Eldorado Hotel facilities including the rooftop swimming pool, fitness center, and sauna.

> ## INSIDERS' TIP
> Check out ski vacation amenities. Ask the rental management about ski area shuttles, ski equipment lockers on site, and special ticket discounts.

County

Rancho Jacona
$$$ • Route 5, Box 250, Pojoaque • (505) 455-7948

The name of this vacation rental/farm comes from the Tewa Indian word *Saconai*—"the cliffs where the tobacco grows." Although tobacco no longer grows here, lots of critters do—rabbits, sheep, goats, burros, and birds. Kids love

VACATION RENTALS

Northern New Mexico offers an abundance of winter sports activites including skiing at Santa Fe, Taos, Angel Fire, and Red River. This makes winter a fine time to take a vacation in Santa Fe.

Photo: Ken Gallard

it. This is without a doubt a child-friendly place with lots to offer adults, too, including beauty, quiet, relaxation, and close proximity to the Santa Fe Opera (see Art and Culture), Bandelier National Monument, and a number of Indian pueblos, all within a half hour of town.

The farm's 10 self-catering *casitas*—Coyote, Frog, Lizard, Parrot, Piglet, Owl, Rabbit, Raccoon, Rooster, and Turtle—are cheerfully furnished, pueblo-style adobe houses with one or two bathrooms and from one to three bedrooms with a king or queen bed. All the *casitas* have fireplaces in addition to central heating; *portals* or patios for sitting, sunning, or barbecuing; fully equipped kitchens, including garbage disposals; washers and dryers; cable television; and private phones. The grounds feature a 60-foot heated outdoor pool set among lawns and trees, a pond, barn, and lots of pastureland. Rancho Jacona requires a three-day minimum stay. Prices drop between $10 and $20 per night for stays of one week or more. Seniors are eligible for discounts from November through March except during certain holidays.

Agencies

Kokopelli Residential Property Management
825 Topeka St.
• **(505) 988-7244, (888) 988-7244**

Kokopelli can match you up with a condo, *casita*, private home, or guest house with Santa Fe charm and modern conveniences. Homes, many built of adobe and featuring patios or decks, come with fully equipped kitchens, laundry facilities, linens, televisions, and VCR's. The agency will even provide wood for the fireplace.

The Management Group
320 Paseo de Peralta, Suite G
• **(505) 982-2823, (800) 283-2211**

The Management Group handles one-, two-, three-, and four-bedroom homes and condominiums throughout Santa Fe with prices ranging from $100 to $800 a night, depending on the season and length of stay.

VACATION RENTALS

Restaurants

Price Code

The dollar signs after each restaurant's name refer to the average price of a dinner entrée—no appetizers, desserts, side orders, wine—not even a Diet Coke. We also did not factor in tax or gratuity. If a restaurant is open only for breakfast and lunch, we made adjustments accordingly. And, of course, prices can change. If you're concerned, call to verify.

Our scale for dinner entrée:

$	Less than $6
$$	$7 to $12
$$$	$12 to $16
$$$$	$16 and over

People who live in Santa Fe are spoiled when it comes to good food. This community of some 65,000 residents has more than 250 restaurants. And among them are many that have received national acclaim— The Coyote Cafe, Santacafe, La Casa Sena, The Old House, Anasazi Restaurant, Geronimo, and others. Santa Fe consistently ranks in the top-25 culinary destinations in the United States as selected by both *Playboy* and *Money* magazines.

Variety marks Santa Fe's restaurant scene. You'll find many places that specialize in the tasty regional cuisine, ranging from elegant, like Café San Estevan, to charming and informal, like the Peppers and Maria's. If you decide you'd like to eat something that doesn't have chile in it, Santa Fe can accommodate you with first-rate American cuisine from deluxe dining at places like The Old House to laid-back spots such as the Zia Diner and the Cowgirl Hall of Fame.

"The key to successful restaurant is good consistent food and outstanding service," David Zlotnick, president of the Santa Fe Restaurant Association said. "Customers need to feel that they are receiving value for their money and that they are valued." His advice to visitors: "Try to sample our local New Mexican food and also some of the international cuisine that is available here. Experience the tremendous variety of food Santa Fe offers."

Tourism is important to Santa Fe restaurants, he said, but so is local business. "Competition is the commonality all restaurants face," he said. "Bad restaurants simply don't last here."

Santa Fe's luster as a food town is reflected in the city's many food-centered benefits and special events. The Wine and Chile Fiesta, a citywide celebration each September, brings nationally and internationally acclaimed chefs to town along with thousands of eager gourmands (see our Annual Events chapter). The city has a long-established, well-regarded cooking school, the Santa Fe School of Cooking, which frequently hosts guest chefs from around the country. The Taste of Santa Fe benefit honors local restaurants for the best selection in several categories— if you want to visit a place that's a justly proud winner, go to Paul's and ask to see their engraved award platter, which hangs on the dining room wall.

"Visitors are impressed with us," Zlotnick said of the city's restaurants. "Tourists are always telling me that they weren't aware that this high a level of food was here. Santa Fe is an eating haven."

This chapter offers some suggestions on where to eat. We mention only places unique to the area, figuring that you already know what to expect at the chains. We've organized the listings by style of food served. If you're unfamiliar with the New Mexican style of cuisine, see our close-up in this chapter, which explains and defines many of the foods and terms you'll encounter when dining out in Santa Fe. And we've separated "Mexican" and "New Mexican" on purpose because these cuisines are different.

Our advice on reservations is simple—make them whenever you can. Some places—like the perennially popular Tomasita's—don't take reservations. Others take them only for large parties. If you call these places ahead of time, they will gladly give you an idea of when to come to minimize your wait. After all, it's their business to make you happy.

Dress is casual here, although diners tend to dress better when they go to more expensive places. Nowhere in Santa Fe, however, requires a coat and/or tie for men. And if you want to eat outside in the summer—we recommend it—remember that you're at 7,000 feet and the air cools when the sun sets. Even if the day's high temperature has been in the 90s, you'll probably welcome a jacket or sweater in the evening.

Unless otherwise noted, restaurants listed in this chapter accept major credit cards and are open daily. However, many restaurants close for Christmas, Thanksgiving, New Year's Day, and other holidays—if you want to dine out on those days, please call ahead. Keep in mind that some places expand their hours during the summer or cut back during the winter.

American Food, Fine Dining

Anasazi Restaurant
**$$$$ • Inn of the Anasazi,
113 Washington Ave.
• (505) 988-3236
• www.INNoftheANASAZI.com**

This award-winning restaurant prides itself on food that is a feast for the eyes as well as the palate. The menu changes frequently but includes fresh fish, game, and a wonderful, eclectic assortment of appetizers and desserts. *Prix-fixe* meals and a la carte dining are available. Organic produce and free-range meats are used. Entrées include such dishes as "Cinnamon-Chile Rubbed Beef Tenderloin with White Cheddar-Chipotle Chile Mashed Potatoes and Mango Salsa." The staff knows wine and can competently suggest a selection to complement your food. The Anasazi serves breakfast, lunch, Sunday brunch, and dinner and also has a bar menu served after the dining room closes.

La Casa Sena
**$$$$ • Sena Plaza, 125 E. Palace Ave.
• (505) 988-9232**

Wonderful old Santa Fe ambiance combined with a creative approach to food makes La Casa Sena a longtime favorite place to celebrate special occasions. Try the trout cooked in adobe for a succulent and different dish. The patio is one of Santa Fe's nicest. For less formal and less expensive dining, visit the Cantina, where you'll hear waiters and waitresses present excerpts from Broadway shows. The restaurant has a full bar and a nice wine selection. It is open daily for lunch and dinner.

Coyote Café
**$$$–$$$$ • 132 W. Water St.
• (505) 983-1615**

The legendary Coyote Cafe helped put and keep Santa Fe on the gourmet map. Owner Mark Miller's food is an interesting and tasty mix of Tex-Mex, Pueblo Indian, Hispanic-New Mexican, and his own innovations—nouvelle southwestern cuisine. The menu changes often and the wait staff is always well informed. Even without the excellent food, the whimsical decor would capture your attention. Among the Coyote's trademark dishes are its griddled buttermilk corn cakes and the amazing 24-ounce New Mexico Cowboy Rib Chop—come hungry for this one, pardner! Both have been on the menu since the Coyote opened more than 10 years ago. Be sure to note the genuine cowhide chairs. This is a great place for celebrity watching. The Coyote is open for lunch Monday through Friday and dinner every night. In the dining room, service is exclusively *prix fixe*, three courses for $42.50—appetizer, entrée, and dessert.

From mid-April until mid-October, you can eat at the Coyote Cantina, a rooftop restaurant that offers more casual dining, including dishes with a decidedly Cuban influence, cocktails, and appetizers. You can order lunch and at the cantina a la carte. The Coyote has a full bar.

Fuego Restaurant
**$$$$ • 330 E. Palace Ave.
(La Posada de Santa Fe Resort and Spa)
• (505) 986-0000**

The well-trained, professional staff here add to your dining enjoyment. This recently remodeled restaurant offers pleasant patio dining as well as an elegant interior decorated in vivid colors with leather couches and, for winter, roaring wood fires. While you can choose some chile dishes for breakfast, the chef's focus for lunch and dinner is elsewhere. Signature dishes include the appetizer black tiger shrimp glazed with honey and garlic, which won honors at the Taste of Santa Fe, crab cakes, the oven roasted venison loin with lingonberry and cranberry compote, and the grilled halibut with shrimp and lobster sauce. You'll also find lamb, buffalo, beef, and chicken on the menu. Fuego serves three meals a day and brunch on Sundays.

Geronimo
$$$$ • 724 Canyon Rd.
• (505) 982-1500

Geronimo began to win our hearts from the start with a warm greeting by the host. "We're glad you decided to join us for dinner," he said. And, as it turned out, so were we.

It's for good reason that any list of Santa Fe's top ten restaurants includes this Canyon Road eatery, which recently received the Mobile Four Star rating. Housed in a landmark adobe with a long *portal* for outside dining, Geronimo carries on a fine tradition of good restaurants in this lovely site. Inside you'll find three fireplaces, gleaming, brass-plated tabletops, 24-inch-thick adobe walls, and huge beams high overhead. The food is creative and excellent and the service exceptional. The price is high, but the value outstanding, especially on the Chef's Selection dinners. The menus change frequently for lunch and dinner.

At lunch, look for unusual salads, burgers with toppings such as a chile-pineapple salsa and gruyere cheese, and good meat and chicken dishes. At dinner, try the lobster appetizer—a perfectly cooked lobster tail serve on al dente angel hair pasta with a drizzle of great spicy sauce. The elk, ranch raised in Texas, is one of the most popular dishes and the nightly special usually includes a fish choice. Desserts blend creative presentation with flavor—try the sweet mango napoleon with Swiss chocolate and casis coulis—yum. You can sit on the patio in the summer or request a table with a fireplace view in the winter. Geronimo is open for dinner daily and for lunch daily except Sunday and has a full bar.

Nellie's
$$$–$$$$ • Hotel Loretto,
211 Old Santa Fe Tr.
• (505) 984-7914

This isn't your usual hotel restaurant. For starters, the inside dining room is arranged for quiet and privacy. When the nights are cool, ask to sit near the fireplace. On the patio you're still pleasantly removed from the hustle of downtown Santa Fe. Depending on where you sit, you might get a view of the historic Loretto Chapel, which adjoins the hotel. Nellie's takes a fresh approach to food, which means the menus change often and offer a limited number of choices, each excellently prepared. The lunch menu may feature old favorites; evening offerings tend to be a little fancier. Try the lobster and Thai noodle spring rolls, the red chile raspberry pork tenderloin, or the molasses grilled rack of lamb. Nellie's has a full bar and a climate-controlled wine cellar with a collection of 150 varieties. It is open for breakfast, lunch, and dinner.

The Old House
$$$$• Eldorado Hotel,
309 W. San Francisco St.
• (505) 988-4455

The food here is both beautiful and original; the atmosphere upscale and peaceful. You'll find variations on New Mexican cooking such as a mustard and pepper crusted rack of lamb, framed by a pool of red chile. Or try the crispy seared Muscovy duck breast, served with while polenta and a Madeira-truffle sauce added at your table. Desserts not only taste great, but they're also beautiful. Chef Martin Rios was named chef of the year by the New Mexico Hospitality Industry. The Old House was also the only restaurant in New Mexico to receive the Four Diamond ranking from AAA. The Old House, which offers a full bar, is open for dinner only and is closed on Monday. The restaurant does not allow smoking. You can also eat at the Eldorado Court, which serves breakfast, lunch, and dinner and offers a less-gourmet, less-expensive menu. The Eldorado Court seating adjoins a sometimes-lively cocktail lounge.

Paul's
$$$ • 72 W. Marcy St.
• (505) 982-8738

This intimate bistro isn't afraid to try something new, and you'll find food with Southwestern influences as well as Provençal French inspirations. Paul's can get noisy, especially for lunch. But some would say that just adds to its charm. Lunches feature Caesar or Niçoise salads and sandwiches such as grilled eggplant with red peppers and melted cheese—stuff you probably wouldn't fix at home. In the evening, the food gets fancier with entrées such as the restaurant's trademark baked salmon in pecan-herb crust. Desserts get rave reviews. Paul's chocolate ganache, a rich and irresistible blend of white and bittersweet chocolate in a pecan crust, won the dessert category in the Taste of Santa Fe competition. The cheese cake crème brûlé gives new meaning to the word sophisticated. A lovely fresh strawberry napoleon with crispy pastry layers and just a touch of sweetness finishes your meal elegantly. Paul's is open daily except Sunday for lunch and dinner and accepts reservations for dinner. This is a non-smoking restaurant that serves beer and a simple but high-quality selection of wines.

The Pink Adobe
$$$ • 406 Old Santa Fe Tr.
• **(505) 983-7712**
• **www.thepinkadobe.com**

This restaurant has become a local tradition because of its beautiful Santa Fe–style dining room and the consistent quality of its food and service. Housed in a centuries-old building with 36-inch-thick walls and six fireplaces, the restaurant gets its name from its characteristic pink stucco exterior. The Creole Salad Bowl, with egg slices and velvety avocado, is a luncheon star. Or try Gypsy Stew, a wonderful concoction of chicken, green chile, tomatoes, and onions in a rich sherry flavored broth, served with fresh hot corn bread. At dinner, try the combination of juicy beef and the pep of green chile in Steak Dunnigan, one of the Pink's signature dishes. Save a little room to share a piece of apple pie with hot brandy sauce. The Pink Adobe is open for lunch Monday through Friday and dinner daily. The restaurant's bar, The Dragon Room, serves a limited menu and is frequently standing room only. Smoking is permitted in the bar, but the dining rooms are smoke free.

Santacafe
$$$$ • 231 Washington Ave.
• **(505) 984-1788**
• **www.santacafe.com**

This is one of Santa Fe's "don't miss" places, a casually elegant restaurant with a creative approach to food and fine service. The New York Times called it, "a restaurant to love, offering perhaps the best combination of inspired food and attractive surroundings in the city." The cuisine frequently blends Asian and Southwestern flavors with wonderful results. Lunch choices include a pasta special, succulent calamari (also available as an appetizer at dinner), and an omelet of the day. The red chile onion rings served with Judy's house-made ketchup and filet burger draw rave reviews. At night, listen for the fish specials or try the grilled filet mignon with tarragon butter, red chile mashed potatoes, and baby vegetables, a variation of the dish that made the cover of *Bon Appetit* magazine. The roasted poblano chile relleno with three mushroom quinoa and chipolte cream captures the flavor of Northern

New Mexico in a whole new way. The Santacafe occupies part of a restored hacienda, and its white walls, fresh flowers, and warming fireplaces add to the dining experience. It also has a lovely patio for quiet summer dining. Santacafe serves lunch Monday through Friday and dinner daily. The restaurant has a full bar.

American Food, Casual Dining

Atomic Grill
$–$$ • 103 E. Water St.
• **(505) 820-ATOM (820-2866)**

This casual place, secluded in an alley next to the popular Café Pasqual's, serves breakfast all day and offers some interesting choices such as raspberry-infused French toast. The menu is an eclectic mix of cuisines and flavors and includes wood-fired pizzas, fish tacos, burgers, quesadillas, and homemade desserts. Patrons include vegetarians who've just got to have an Earth Mama Garden Burger (they're delicious), a meatless Frito pie, or any number of other vegetarian delights. Carnivores might crave the Atomic Grill's half-pound All-Terrain Burger, a catfish sandwich, or any of the restaurant's other diverse specialties, including breakfasts served all day and fresh pastries and desserts. You'll find a fine selection of beers—including 80 or more from microbreweries—to accompany your meal. Try dining outside in the summer. The Atomic stays open until 3 AM daily except Sunday and is a popular late-night gathering spot. It sometimes offers live entertainment. No smoking is allowed.

Back Street Bistro
$, no credit cards
• **513 Camino de los Marques**
• **(505) 982-3500**

Just off the beaten track, this informal cafe serves first-rate soup, with 10 choices featured daily. The chef consistently wins Best Soup and Best Presentation at the Annual Souper Bowl Fundraiser. Try the sweet pepper bisque or the Hungarian mushroom. The hot or cold sandwiches, including New York corned beef, can be ordered by the half, so you'll have room for the top-notch pies and desserts. Daily soups are posted on white boards. The restaurant does not allow smoking or cell phones. An art exhibit that changes regularly adds to the ambiance. Expect to wait if you come at the height

A Beginner's Guide to Santa Fe Dining

Does a menu listing enchiladas, flautas, and chalupas tantalize your appetite? Or leave you in confusion?

Traditional New Mexican cuisine grows from simple, delicious ingredients.

First come the chiles, then pinto beans, both corn and flour tortillas, cheese, beef, chicken, pork, and often onions. From the mouth-watering aromas of steaming green chile to the sultry velvet texture of guacamole and the dollop of sour cream that blends and soothes the fiery red, traditional New Mexican food leaves few indifferent. Many crave it with such enthusiasm that they take recipes and ingredients home with them.

As you embark on this culinary adventure, take note that dairy products will quench the peppery fires of chile dishes: cheese, a glass of milk, and a dish of ice cream are your palate's best coolants. Restaurants that specialize in this spicy cuisine serve many chile dishes topped with chopped lettuce and tomato to help calm the heat. Bread, either flour tortillas or the puffy sopaipillas served with the meal, will also help. And if you're afraid the chile may be too hot, you can ask for a sample or have it served on the side.

Venture forth with good appetite; the rewards come in the eating!

What's What in New Mexican Food

Biscochito: An anise-flavored cookie.

Burrito: A flour tortilla rolled to enclose meats, beans, cheese, or a combination of these and often served smothered with chile sauce and melted cheese. Breakfast burritos may be filled with scrambled eggs, potatoes, and bacon.

Carne adovada: Cubes of marinated meat, usually pork, cooked in red chile, garlic, and oregano.

Chalupas: Corn tortillas fried into a bowl shape, filled with shredded chicken, beef, and/or beans, usually topped with guacamole and salsa.

Chile: The vegetable that puts the fire in traditional New Mexican cooking. Green chile is the fresh vegetable, which is roasted, chopped, and thickened to produce a sauce. Red chiles are mature green chiles, which are dried and used as seasoning or for a sauce. While red may look hotter, the spiciness depends not on the color, but on where the chile was grown and the weather conditions during the growing season.

Chile con queso: Green chile and melted cheese mixed together into a dip.

Chile relleno: A whole green chile roasted, peeled, and stuffed (usually with cheese), then dipped in a batter and fried.

Chorizo: A spicy pork sausage seasoned with garlic and red chile.

Christmas: The phrase that means you'd like to try both red and green chile on your dish.

Empanada: A turnover usually filled with a sweetened meat mixture or fruit.

Enchiladas: Corn tortillas filled with chicken, ground meat, or cheese and covered with chile sauce and cheese, often topped with shredded lettuce and tomato. The tortillas may be rolled with the filling inside or stacked with the filling in between. Either yellow-corn or blue-corn tortillas—made from a special variety of corn with blue kernels— are used. Enchiladas may be served topped with a fried egg and/or sour cream.

Fajitas: Strips of grilled steak, chicken, or sometimes shrimp with sautéed peppers, and onions, often served still sizzling in a metal fry pan. Warm tortillas and side dishes of salsa, cheese, sour cream, and guacamole are served alongside so you can make your own burritos.

Flan: Caramel custard dessert similar to créme caramel.

Flauta: Tightly rolled corn tortillas filled with meat and fried to a crunch, usually served with salsa and guacamole for dipping.
Frijoles: Beans, usually pinto beans; frijoles negros are black beans.
Guacamole: Mashed avocado, usually seasoned with chopped onion, garlic, lime juice, and chile powder. Served as a dip, a topping for some dishes, or even a filling for tacos.

Northern New Mexican cooking gets its integrity from ingredients that are grown locally—chile, corn, and beans. Dried chile, which turns red, also has wonderful decorative potential.

Photo: Don Strel/Southwest Assignments

Huevos rancheros: Eggs, usually fried, served atop corn tortillas and smothered with chile and cheese. A popular Santa Fe breakfast.
Menudo: A soup made with tripe and chiles. (It's known as the "breakfast of champions.")
Nachos: Corn chips topped with refried beans, melted cheese, and sliced jalapeños. If served "grande" they will probably include ground beef or shredded chicken, guacamole, and sour cream. Olives, fresh tomatoes, and onions may be added.
Natilla: Soft custard dessert.
Pico de gallo: Salsa with chopped fresh chiles, tomatoes, onions, and cilantro. It's usually spicier than traditional salsa.
Posole: Hominy stew, usually made with pork, onions, and oregano, usually served with chile sauce on top or on the side.
Quesadilla: A turnover made of a flour tortilla filled with cheese and sometimes beef, chicken, or other ingredients, then toasted, fried, or baked.

Refritos: Beans, usually pintos, mashed and fried.
Ristra: A bunch of chiles, usually red, hung to dry or for decoration.
Salsa: An uncooked mixture of chile, tomatoes, onions, cilantro, and other spices. Usually eaten as a dip.
Sopaipilla: Puffed, fried yeast bread served hot with honey or honey-butter and eaten with the meal.
Taco: A folded corn tortilla either fried crisp or soft and usually filled with meat or chicken and garnished with cheese, fresh chopped lettuce, onions, and tomatoes.
Tostadas: Corn tortilla chips. This term also means an open-faced fried corn tortilla covered with refried beans, salsa, cheese, and chopped lettuce and tomato.
Tortilla: A flat bread made of corn or wheat. Flour tortillas may be served with the meal in New Mexican cooking; corn tortillas tend to be incorporated in dishes and baked with sauce.

RESTAURANTS

of noon-hour business. There's ample parking along the street or in the lot behind the restaurant. Closed Sundays

Café Dominic
$ • 320 S. Guadalupe St.,
• (505) 982-4743
Looking for an affordable, tasty meal down-

town? Try Café Dominic. Open breakfast, lunch, and dinner, this restaurant invites you to come to the counter to place your order for blue corn pancakes, an enchilada plate, or baby back ribs. Take a number, have a seat, and wait for piping hot food to arrive at your table. You can get breakfast all day on Saturday and Sunday, in addition to the regular menu. You can get fancy coffee as well as beer and wine with your meal and desserts and pastries are displayed at the front counter. Although basically the same menu is available for lunch and dinner, dinner includes a few extras such as spicy Shrimp Diablo and Dominic's Ribs, served with slaw, fries, beans, and garlic bread. You can also have three varieties of half-pound burgers and the hard-to-find Monte Cristo sandwich. Dominic's has a children's menu and offers carry-out, a convenience for guests in nearby hotels and people who work in the area.

Carlos' Gosp'l Cafe
$, no credit cards • in the Plaza at the Interstate Bank Building, 125 Lincoln Ave.
• (505) 983-1841

The consistently good soup and fresh sandwiches made here make this one of the favorite lunch spots for folks who work downtown. The patio provides a pleasant place to enjoy lunch and conversation in the summer; inside the aromas that surround you are sure to make you hungry. Carlos' is famous for its Hangover Stew, a savory assembly of potatoes, corn, and green chile with Monterey Jack cheese. Meatloaf for the meatloaf sandwich is made on the premises. Don't get too full for dessert—the freshly baked lemon-meringue pie is worth loosening your belt a notch. The cafe lives up to its name by continuously playing gospel music and with the gospel singer mural inside. Seating includes shared community tables, and the place is usually crowded. The cafe is closed on Sunday.

Celebrations
$$–$$$ • 613 Canyon Rd.
• (505) 989-8904

As you're visiting Canyon Road, stop at Celebrations for lunch or dinner daily year-round or breakfast in the summer and on the weekends. Celebrations occupies an old house on this arty street, nicely redone as a restaurant, with peach-colored walls, colorful tile table tops, and soft music. Meals are served indoors and on the enclosed patio, which has a fireplace and heaters for use year-round. The menu changes frequently and might include butternut squash soup, lamb stew, sautéed sea scallops, crawfish etouffee, and New Mexican specialties. Try the marinated rack of lamb with Madeira sauce and the potato strudel. The restaurant has a full bar and a nice wine list. No smoking allowed. Celebrations is open daily

for breakfast and lunch and for dinner Wednesday through Saturday.

Cowgirl Hall of Fame Bar•B•Q and Western Grill
$$ • 319 S. Guadalupe St.
• (505) 982-2565
• www.cowgirl-santafe.com

The cowgirl theme of this restaurant comes through in a homey Old-West decor that includes some great old photos of real cowgirls. The signature dishes are the mesquite-smoked barbecue, although you can find fish and veggie offerings here, too, as well as traditional New Mexican chile-based food and a butternut

From bountiful breakfast buffets to elegant lunches and delectable dinners, Santa Fe is known for its first-class cuisine.

squash caserole. The menu also offers chicken fried steak, burgers, jerked chicken salad, gumbo, and other Louisiana specialties. Try the Salmon Tacos al Carbon, a juicy piece of grilled salmon folded into flour tortillas with jack cheese, chopped lettuce, and tomato, served with tomatillo salsa. And save room for the ice cream "baked potato"—a serving of vanilla ice cream coated with cocoa and served with pistachio "chives". Cowgirl's patio is busy in the summer, and the crowd often includes families with kids. Nightly entertainment features local singers and songwriters and sometime touring musicians. Cowgirl offers an extensive list of draft beers and a full bar. You can eat lunch or dinner daily and breakfast on weekends. No checks.

Harry's Roadhouse
$$ • Rt. 9, Box 52 D, Old Las Vegas Hwy.
• (505) 989-4629

The food is great here, but since the desserts are even better, we'll start with those. Everything is made fresh, from scratch. Fruit desserts such as strawberry rhubarb pie and apricot crisp, are made from fresh fruit and garnished if you wish with REAL whipped cream or premium or homemade ice cream. The banana cream pie with white chocolate, for example, comes in a crust so tender it's amazing it doesn't crumble before you can eat it. So, although the rest of the menu is full of temptations, save room! This comfortable, casual place is popular among locals and visitors. Unless you're a big party (and made a reservation) you may have to wait, but the service tends to be quick once you're seated. The extensive menu has something for everyone—barbecue, New Mexican food, blackened catfish, pizza, salads, juicy burgers with all the toppings, and even fish tacos. Harry's has a lovely landscaped patio and a full bar. The restaurant is smoke-free and open daily for all three meals.

Plaza Restaurant
$–$$ • 54 Lincoln Ave.
• (505) 982-1664

Location gives this diner a definite edge on the competition. You'll find big, Santa Fe-style breakfasts as well as lunch and dinner. The menu includes burgers and salads, enchiladas and tacos, and some Greek dishes. Try the Gyro Sandwich served with hot thick fries or the vegetable mousaka. Daily specials may include a Mediterranean plate or a chicken mole tamale. The atmosphere is reminiscent of the Fifties, complete with some interesting old photos on the walls. Expect to wait in the summer. The Plaza offers a kid's menu and beer and wine are available with meals for the parents. If you're lucky enough to get a window seat, you can watch life on the Plaza as you enjoy your food. This favorite spot of many longtime Santa Fe residents is open every day.

San Francisco Street Bar and Grill
$$ • 114 W. San Francisco St.
in Plaza Mercado
• (505) 982-2044

Established in 1985, this well-managed restaurant is a long-standing local favorite. People who work downtown and value good food at a good price eat here often, enjoying the famous green-chile cheeseburger. The menu features a huge Greek salad, fresh grilled seafood, daily pastas, steak, chicken, and sandwiches. The restaurant offers daily specials and a nice selection of wine by the glass. There's also a full bar. Although the restaurant is indoors, the tables in Mercado's open space have a patio feeling to them. Kids are welcome here seven days a week. The restaurant is smoke free.

Zia Diner
$–$$ • 326 S. Guadalupe St.
• (505) 988-7008

Locals eat here for the same reason that visitors are willing to stand in line to try it: The Zia offers generous portions of good food at fair prices. This is comfort food—potatoes and gravy, fish and chips, piñon meat loaf, an open-faced turkey sandwich with all the trimmings, cherry and other home-made pies, and ice cream drinks. But the menu is far from boring—or predictable. The chef offers humus with pita, Greek salads, spaghetti, enchiladas, and, on some days, Asian specials. Fish dishes tend to be creative and delicious. The Zia serves lunch and dinner daily and offers patio dining in the summer. You can also eat in the bar.

Asian

Chow's
$$$ • 720 St. Michael's Dr.
• (505) 471-7120
• www.mychows.com

Even though it looks like a shopping center

INSIDERS' TIP

Don't be shy about asking your waiter or waitress for recommendations. If you don't understand the menu, seek their advice, especially when it comes to New Mexican food. For example, they can tell you if the red or green chile is hotter.

---

storefront, Chow's offers gourmet Chinese food in a calm, upscale setting. The contemporary, eclectic Chinese cuisine is a long way from steam-tray chow mein. Appetizers include firecracker dumplings filled with vegetables, ground turkey, and chile, served with a pesto dipping sauce and wonderful barbecued ribs. The Santa Fe Won Ton Soup features turkey dumplings, sliced chicken breast, wild mushrooms, and fresh spinach in a light chicken vegetable broth. The Pearl River Splash, a steamed whole boneless trout in a delicate ginger and scallion sauce, makes a light healthy choice. The noodle dishes satisfy the appetite and the eye, and interesting vegetarian choices are available. Chow's makes everything without MSG. It's open Monday through Saturday for lunch and dinner. Beer and wine are available with meals in this smoke-free restaurant. Credit cards are accepted for meals that cost more than $20.

Dynasty
$$ • 500 Cerrillos Rd.
• (505) 983-2011

You can order from the menu, but what's fun at Dynasty is the Mongolian Barbecue Buffet. You'll find a spread of noodles, raw fresh veggies of all kinds, beef, pork, and chicken. Fill a bowl with what you'd like, then add sauces such as flavorful Mongolian barbecue, garlic, ginger, jalapeño, or about a dozen others. The chef will cook it for you. Soup, salad bar, and egg roll come with the buffet at lunch and dinner. You can even go back for more. The menu includes the expected Chinese offerings and some interesting specials, such as Strawberry Fish Filet or crispy shrimp with banana and coconut sauce. The restaurant is smoke free, open daily, and offers wine and beer with meals.

Hunan Chinese Restaurant
2440 Cerrillos Rd.
• (505) 471-6688

Red and gold are the color scheme here, and you're greeted by a dragon in the entryway. This is one of Santa Fe's largest Chinese restaurants and a popular place for locals. The daily luncheon buffet captures your attention with its multitude of choices, including seafood, chicken, beef, pork, and vegetarian offerings. No MSG is used. The menu includes family dinners and a combination plate. On the other end of the spectrum, Hunan will create Peking Duck for you with 24 hours advance notice. Service is usually prompt and efficient. You can order beer or wine with your food in this nonsmoking restaurant, located in a large shopping center on the south side of town.

The Kiva fireplace and beam-and-corbel ceiling add Santa Fe style to this dining room.

Saigon Vietnamese Kitchen
$ • 501 W. Cordova Rd.
• (505) 988-4951

Santa Fe's only Vietnamese restaurant, the Saigon offers an interesting variety of noodle dishes, some unusual cold salads with noodles, and a few other Vietnamese specials. The soups, including many varieties of rice noodle, egg noodle, vermicelli, and wonton, come to the table steaming hot and a feast for the eyes as well as the palate. The atmosphere is basic storefront Asian and the service informed and efficient. The servings are generous—if you invite a moderately hungry friend to join you for lunch and order two dishes to share, you'll both have something to take home. You can order beer and wine to go with your meals. The Saigon is closed on Sundays.

Shohko-Cafe
$$–$$$$ • 321 Johnson St.
• (505) 983-7288

Japanese food is the house specialty. Look on the board for the daily appetizer specials, which may include wonderful steamed dumplings. The sushi bar has a half-dozen tables in addition to counter seats, where you can watch chefs roll your sushi. There are two other dining rooms where you can order yakitori, superb sukiyaki, or even sushi made with green chile or green chile tempura. Try the Bento Box lunch. Beer and wine are available with meals in this nonsmoking restaurant. Shohko is open weekdays for lunch and daily except Sunday for dinner.

Ten Ten Chinese Buffet
$–$$
• 3005 Cerrillos Rd.
• (505) 438-2727

This is Santa Fe's largest Chinese buffet, and perhaps the best bargain. Decor is simple here—two big rooms with lots of tables and aquarium at the front door. The buffet is the centerpiece, with two long sections for hot food and a cold salad bar. The staff does a good job of keeping the buffet replenished, and there are dozens of offerings to choose from including chicken, shellfish, beef, vegetables, pot stickers, soups, and more. You'll find hearty lo mein noodles, fried rice, egg foo young, and more. If that doesn't suit you, they also have a menu.

Elegant presentation marks most of the city's upscale restaurants.

Service is attentive, and they have special rates for kids.

The Wok
$$ 2860 Cerrillos Rd.
• (505) 424-8126

We like the elegant feel of this place—the crisp linen on the tables and the walls tastefully decorated with owner Ming Zi Pais paintings. Ming may greet and serve you while her husband and partner Donald does the kitchen magic. Lunch is both delicious and a bargain. Dinner is a little more pricey, but still well worth the cost. Vegetarians have much to choose from including curry eggplant, orange tofu, and veggie mu shu. You'll also find your favorite beef and chicken dishes and nightly dinner specials. The chiletang of the spicier dishes pleases the Santa Fe tastebuds! Beer and wine is available. Luncheon meals are served on lovely lacquered trays and both lunch and dinner include a scoop of vanilla ice cream in a small goblet. The restaurant is closed Sundays.

INSIDERS' TIP

In 1835, La Dona Tules established a popular gambling saloon on the site where the Palace Restaurant now stands. In 1959, during excavation for the building of the Palace Restaurant, a doorknocker consisting of half a horseshoe and a woman's leg was discovered. Apparently, this relic was the original doorknocker of the old gaming house. It became the Palace's logo.

RESTAURANTS

Yin Yang Chinese Restaurant
$$ • 418 Cerrillos Rd.
(Santa Fe Design Center)
• (505) 986-9279

At Yin Yang you'll find a fresh and varied lunch buffet as well as an extensive menu. In addition to hot items, the buffet includes a salad bar with several kinds of fruit and, some days, cold shrimp. Our favorite dinner entrée is the Crispy Orange Scallops. The atmosphere is pleasant, especially during the day when sunlight from the large bank of windows facing Cerrillos Road adds to the restaurant's charm. You can order beer or wine with your meal, and parking is easy here at the Design Center. Yin Yang usually goes all out for Chinese New Year …watch for announcements.

Breakfast

Bagelmania
$ • 420 Catron Street
• (505) 982-8900

Just about any thing you can imagine eating for breakfast is here. And, as the name suggests, bagels are the specialty, from plain to "everything." The everyday brunch specials, great when you can't decide between breakfast and lunch, include a portabello frittata—an open faced omelet smothered with feta cheese, olives, peppers, tomatoes, and juicy mushrooms. You can get fancy coffee to go with your bagel, New Mexican breakfast burritos, or Papas Benedict—hash brown potatoes with eggs and a green-chile Hollandaise sauce. Bagelmania is open daily until 3 PM and also serves sandwiches and blue plate specials for lunch. Bakery and deli counter greet you at the door of this non-smoking establishment.

INSIDERS' TIP

For Santa Fe dining, make a reservation whenever possible. While during the off-season you may be able to slip into a popular place, don't count on it. If you want to eat somewhere that doesn't take reservations, you can call and ask when you're likely to have the shortest wait.

Cafe Pasqual's
$$$–$$$$
• 121 Don Gaspar Ave.
• (505) 983-9340 or (800) 722-7672
• www.pasquals.com

For a small café, Pasqual's gets the lion's share of attention. Eager diners line up outside for breakfast, lunch, and dinner throughout the day—the place seats only 50. Cafe Pasqual's has been serving original cuisine inspired by the culinary traditions of New Mexico, Old Mexico, and Asia, using fresh, seasonal, organic, and naturally raised foods for more than two decades. It has been honored with the James Beard America's Regional Cooking Classics Award. Pasqual's serves great lunches and dinners, but breakfast is its signature meal. Pasqual's is well-known for its freshly baked bread and freshly concocted chile sauces. Try the chorizo burritos or the breakfast quesadillas for a dining experience you won't get in Topeka. You can also order a breakfast trout, either grilled or served as smoked trout hash. Pasqual's has a community table where you're welcome to sit and join the conversation. You can order beer and wine, but just looking at this place, decorated with Mexican garlands and homages to San Pasqual, the patron of the kitchen, lifts your spirits.

Cloud Cliff Bakery-Cafe-Artspace
$–$$ • 1805 Second St.
• (505) 983-6254

If breakfast in a bakery strikes you as the right thing to do, Cloud Cliff can fill the bill. You can sit at the long bar and watch as your food is prepared or pick a table with a view of the art. Frequently changing exhibits of local paintings, collages, and other creations fill the walls. Portions are generous, although quality and service tend to be erratic. You can get fancy coffee here and enjoy your breakfast treats on the patio in the summer. The bakery sells a wide variety of scrumptious whole grain breads, rolls, muffins, cakes, pies, and cookies to take home with you, and also supplies baked goods to area groceries. Cloud Cliff also serves lunch. Beer and wine are available. The restaurant is smoke free.

Grant Corner Inn
$$ • 122 Grant Ave.
• (505) 983-6678 or (800) 964-9003

This charming bed and breakfast inn, known for its creative cuisine, welcomes the public (with reservations) for breakfast or lunch. In the summer, you can dine outside beneath the shaded porch of this old brick home—one of the few of its kind in Santa Fe. Breakfast includes granola, juice or fruit, pastries, and hot specials—eggs, potatoes, meats,

Yes, they're wearing ties, but most restaurants in Santa Fe don't require them.

or a breakfast burrito. You might find orange-granola pancakes or some version of eggs Benedict on Sunday, when breakfast stretches into brunch. The inn also serves holiday dinners and offers a special menu for children. Breakfast is served daily, and the restaurant is nonsmoking. Reservations are a good idea.

Guadalupe Cafe
$$ • 422 Old Santa Fe Tr.
• (505) 982-9762

The Guadalupe Cafe is justly famous for its great breakfasts, beginning with good coffee and friendly service. The restaurant bakes its own muffins and serves a variety of unusual offerings including migas, a combination of eggs, chile, cheese, and corn chips, and sausage and cheese enchiladas. The huevos rancheros are excellent. Lunch and dinner here are good, too—tasty soup and chile dishes, plus sandwiches heaped with meat. Servings are generous—you may have leftovers to take home. Desserts are made on the premises and are worth saving room for. The patio faces Old Santa Fe Trail; you can eat outside and watch a parade of tourists and locals go by. The Guadalupe serves breakfast, lunch, and dinner daily except Monday. Beer and wine are available with meals on request.

INSIDERS' TIP

Looking for appetizers? El Farol won the 2000 Taste of Santa Fe competition with its lobster and chorizo crepe.

Santa Fe Baking Company
$ • 504 W. Cordova Rd.
• (505) 988-4292

You won't mind standing in line to place your order here because you get to see all the fresh-baked goodies in the display counter. Muffins, Danish pastry, croissants, and fruit-filled turnovers may tempt you, but you can also get eggs, breakfast burritos, and other hot specials. Coffee drinks are a specialty and a juice bar adds to your options. The Baking Company also serves lunch and dinner. The restaurant is nonsmoking except for the patio and offers an interesting variety of newspapers and magazines you can peruse while you eat.

Tecolote Cafe
$ • 1203 Cerrillos Rd.
• (505) 988-1362

If breakfast is your meal—even after noon—this is definitely your place. Tecolote—it means "owl"—specializes in good food and quick service. They keep your coffee cup full while you wait for French toast made from a variety of breads or a simple order of fresh fruit you can enjoy by itself or add to your breakfast order. The chile is wonderful here, but not for the faint of heart. Pancakes—including the Tollhouse, with walnuts and chocolate chips—are another specialty. A basket of homemade sweet breads comes with your egg meal. You can also order any of the sandwiches, burgers, or other lunch items throughout the day—the enchiladas and black bean soup are worth a try.

Continental/ French

Bistro 315
$$$–$$$$ • 315 Old Santa Fe Tr.
• (505) 986-9190

This small French restaurant is big on imagination and service. The specials change daily and seasonally with usually eight to ten entrées offered at lunch and dinner. Bistro 315 serves a wonderful potato leek soup and a great warm spinach salad with house-smoked ham. Entrées might include grilled smoked chicken, Seafood Papillote, veal scallopini, or stuffed portabello mushrooms. Delicious desserts complement the food, so save room. Bistro 315 may have Santa Fe's best crème brûlée, finished at your table with a blowtorch! It's open for lunch and dinner. The dining room is smoke free, but you can dine and smoke on the patio in summer.

Ristra
$$$ • 548 Agua Fria St.
• (505) 982-8608
• www.ristrarestaurant.com

Expect first-rate food and service at this Guadalupe-area restaurant that offers a southwest variation on French cuisine. Ristra is known for its foie gras appetizer—farm-raised goose liver seasoned to perfection, grilled, and served with crispy toasted bread. Other house specialties are the black Mediterranean mussels in aromatic chipotle and mint broth, housemade country pate served with with tiny cornichon pickles and onion slices, and melt-in-your-mouth mesquite grilled filet mignon. Ristra does fish well and offers ranch-raised elk and/or venison with wonderful complimentary sauces. The menu changes frequently here, but the staff knows what's what and is pleased to help both with the food and with selections from an extensive wine list to compliment your meal. Housed in a former bungalow, Ristra's white-walled atmosphere is unassumingly plain. In the summer, try the patio. Reserva-

tions are recommended. Ristra is open daily for dinner only.

In a Class of Their Own

Corn Dance Cafe at the Hotel Santa Fe
$$$ • 1501 Paseo de Peralta
• (505) 982-1200

Come to the Corn Dance Cafe for cuisine with an American Indian focus served in a lovely dining room. The menu includes lighter dishes and hearty entrées. The chef's several nightly specials include unusual offerings such as rabbit stew or venison shanks simmered in a sauce with juniper berries. You'll find a roasted ear of fresh corn among the appetizers, and dinner starts with corn-bread sticks richly flavored with jalapeños. Don't miss the Kick Ass Chili—a Texas-style dish rich with meat. Try the Little Big Pies, a sort of pizza with toppings including caramelized onion and goat cheese or spicy shrimp. They make a nice light dinner if matched with a salad or a cup of the squash soup or the soup of the day, which might be red-pepper bisque. The names on the menu reflect some of the tribes that have influenced the menu—Potowatomi Prairie chicken or Tlingit salmon. Among the desserts you may find pumpkin cheesecake with piñon nut crust and a lovely strawberry-cranberry-rhubarb cobbler that's large enough for two. Corn Dance has a full bar and does not allow smoking. You may find music, including an American Indian flute player/guitarist, in the evenings.

India House
$$ • 2501 Cerrillos Rd.
• (505) 471-2651

A real find amid the fast-food country of Cerrillos Road, India House offers good food at a good value. The restaurant is nicely appointed with fresh flowers, tablecloths, and well-dressed and well-trained waiters. It's an oasis of calm from the noise the bustle outside. You can have a table or a private booth. India House's luncheon buffet, complete with tandoori chicken, vegetarian specials, salad, and dessert, is both elegant and satisfying. For dinner, take your

INSIDERS' TIP

Al Lucero, co-owner of Maria's New Mexican Kitchen with his wife Lori, is also an author. His *The Great Margarita Book*, published by Ten Speed Press, includes some 90 recipes and is available in local and national bookstores. Robert Redford wrote the introduction.

Santa Fe's fine restaurants have drawn national recognition.

choice of many entrées, including seafood and vegetarian choices. Try the appetizer platter for a nice sampling of the restaurant's fare. The mango lassi and rice pudding are recommended as good dishes for the little ones to enjoy. Beer and wine are available. The restaurant serves lunch and dinner daily except Sunday, when only dinner is served.

India Palace
$$ • 227 Don Gaspar Ave.
• (505) 986-5859
This may be the only East Indian restaurant in the country to be housed in an adobe building with Santa Fe charm inside and a mural of India on the outside. India Palace sits on the edge of a city parking lot across from the Hotel St. Francis. From certain tables, you can watch what's happening in the kitchen through a window. The food includes all the Indian specialties you'd expect, well flavored with garlic, ginger, cardamom, cloves, saffron and other spices. You can also order well-prepared tandoori meats and succulent lamb as well as vegetarian choices. The hearty luncheon buffet is a good value. Beer and wine are available with lunch and dinner, and you can dine on the patio in the summer.

Lola's Café Libertad
$$ • 311 Old Santa Fe Trail
(at the Desert Inn)
• (505) 983-8372
Lola's bright mix of Cuban flavors adds a welcome dimension to Santa Fe's dining scene. Open for breakfast, lunch, and dinner, Lola's has a nice selection of beers and wines by the glass to compliment your meal. Try the plantain cornbread as part of your breakfast, the fish tacos for lunch, and the Frutas del Mar, a seafood stew with rice and chile, for dinner. Be sure to ask about the specials—the monkfish steamed in a banana leaf with coconut/chipotle sauce and purple Peruvian potatoes is hard to beat! For dessert, the moist Kahlua chocolate torte should satisfy your chocolate craving. You can sit on the patio in the summer or eat indoors in an ambiance of Cuban music and Spanish posters of old U.S. movies. Brunch is available Saturday and Sunday; closed Mondays.

Whistling Moon Cafe
$$ • 402 N. Guadalupe St.
• (505) 983-3093
In this comfortable, casual restaurant, you'll find Mediterranean fare inspired by the cuisines of Morocco, Egypt, Turkey, Greece, and

elsewhere. If you're curious, a salad sampler plate offers a nice variety of flavors and textures. The soft pitas filled with grilled lamb,

Locals and tourists support the popular Burrito Company on Washington Ave, a half-block from the plaza.

Photo: Don Strel

falafel, or lemon-marinated chicken, and the pizzas, calzones, and pastas are all first-rate. Ask about the nightly specials, which often include fresh fish. And, whatever else you eat here, be sure to try the spicy French fries. Whistling Moon serves lunch and dinner daily, with beer or wine available, in smoke-free dining room.

Italian

Andiamo!
$$$ • 322 Garfield St.
• (505) 995-9595
Andiamo!, which means "let's go!," offers good, fresh food prepared with panache. The menu changes daily and may include an antipasto, such as freshly made mozzarella with appropriate accompaniments or crispy polenta set off with a topping of rosemary and gorgonzola. Each evening features a pasta special and desserts that are beautiful as well as flavor-packed. The

Caesar salad is one of the city's best, filled with flavor but not overpowering with either garlic or anchovies. Some say this is Santa Fe's best Italian food. The restaurant operates from an old bungalow redone in rich yellows and reds and crammed full of tables—eating outside will give you more space and privacy. No smoking is allowed inside. Andiamo! is open for dinner daily except Tuesday. Beer and wine are available and reservations recommended.

Julian's
$$$ • 221 Shelby St.
• (505) 988-2355

When Santa Fe folks are asked to name the city's most romantic restaurants, Julian's always makes the list. The beauty of the surroundings adds to the dining experience—soft jazz, stained glass, twinkling lights, enormous mirrors, large bouquets of fresh flowers, and, in the winter, warming fireplaces. The menu is filled with good choices. Try the Risotto della Mamma, rich with tender chicken cubes and wonderfully flavorful white beans. The duck here is also excellent. You can finish with tiramisu or a more unusual dolce and steaming espresso. Julian's is open for dinner daily. The restaurant has a full bar and is smoke-free except for the patio.

Osteria D'Assisi
$$ • 58 S. Federal Pl.
• (505) 986-5858
• www.osteriadassisi.com

The Osteria specializes in northern Italian cuisine, and you'll find good pasta here as well as nicely presented grilled dishes and pleasing desserts. The menu changes daily with fresh specials. Try the Canelloni di Magro, tender house-made pasta filled with cheeses mixed wild mushrooms and pine nuts and topped with a tomato basil béchamel sauce. The Farfalle al Salmone e Basilico—bowtie shaped pasta, fresh salmon, and creamy tomato basil sauce—looks as good as it tastes. The restaurant has a bright, open feeling to it and offers patio dining when the weather permits. You can order beer or wine to go with your lunch or dinner. Osteria also does take-out orders for sandwiches, entrées, pasta, sauces, and salads. Osteria is closed Sundays and is nonsmoking except for the patio.

The Palace
$$$ • 142 W. Palace Ave.
• (505) 982-9891
• http://palacerestaurant.com

This plush restaurant is another leading con-tender for a romantic rendezvous in the evening. During lunch, it serves as a hot spot for the Santa Fe equivalent of a power lunch. Red leather booths, white linens, and a well-trained staff complement the good food you'll find here. Luncheons include homemade pastas, fresh fish, sandwiches, prime rib, and a nice assortment of salads. For dinner, start with the Caesar salad prepared at your table. The New Mexico Roasted Rack of Lamb al Sasso, served with mint pesto and gorgonzola polenta makes a fine meal. And save room for dessert, which you can select from a cart of temptations rolled to your table. Our favorite is the tiramisu. The Palace is open Monday through Saturday for lunch and dinner and also serves dinner on Sunday. The Palace has a popular bar that offers live music on the weekends and a lovely patio for summer lunches and dinners.

Pastability
$$ • 418 Cerrillos Rd.
• (505) 988-2856

Casual is the tone for dining here. This friendly little restaurant inside the Design Center has the ambiance of a sidewalk cafe, but it's indoors. As you'd assume from the name, pasta is the specialty. You'll find penne, rigatoni, linguine, and more, all hot and fresh. Sauces include game hen and puttanesca—a combination of capers, olives, and anchovies. The menu also features antipasto selections and some desserts. The restaurant is smoke-free and serves dinner Tuesday through Saturday. There's plenty of parking in the Design Center lot.

Il Piatto
$$ • 95 W. Marcy St.
• (505) 984-1091

This downtown storefront makes the most of its available space to create a lively coziness. The tables, covered with white cloths topped with white paper and trimmed with fresh flowers, add a nice touch to the low-key decor. The menu is limited and excellent, and the values are especially good for dinner. You can choose from appetizers, soup, salads, pastas, and entrées or pick a special. The minestrone is packed with chunks of vegetables. Try one of the creative pasta dishes like risotto with duck, artichoke, and truffle oil or the beautiful homemade pumpkin ravioli. Another favorite is roast chicken with Italian sausage, potatoes, peppers, and onions. The zabaglione or the panettone bread pudding makes the meal complete.

Smoking is not allowed. Il Piatto is open for dinner nightly and lunch Monday through Friday.

RESTAURANTS

In addition to selections of wine from around the world, you may find offerings from some of New Mexico's own wineries on the wine list.

Photo: Chris Corrie

Pranzo Italian Grill
$$$ • Sanbusco Ctr., 540 Montezuma Ave.
• (505) 984-2645

Service at Pranzo is consistently professional, a skillful blend of friendliness and knowledge. The menu offers a nice selection of starters, pizza, delicious pasta, and original entrées to keep locals and visitors happy. In fact, Pranzo is consistently selected as the city's best Italian restaurant by readers of the *Santa Fe Reporter*. A good opener is the Antipasto Misto, a sampler plate that includes a head of roasted garlic, a grilled portobello mushroom, salmon, prosciutto, fontina cheese, and more. Salads are great here; we recommend the Gorgonzola dressing. The restaurant is nicely appointed, comfortable and classy— a very "in" place for lunch. The staff happily accommodates special food requests. Pranzo serves lunch Monday through Saturday and dinner nightly. You can get light food at the bar. Smoking is allowed in the bar and upstairs on the terrace.

Mexican

Bert's La Taqueria
$$ • 1620 St. Michael's Drive
(St. Michael's Village West)
• (505) 474-0791

Voted the best new restaurant in Santa Fe

for 1999, this is a great place to go for Mexican food that will remind you of Mexico City. Tacos pastor—succulent marinated pork served with a variety of house-made salsas and soft, fresh corn tortillas—put La Taqueria on the map, but other dishes are good here, too. The menu features a dozen varieties of tacos as well as other choices. Informal for lunch, the restaurant adds tablecloths and softer lighting for dinner. If you call ahead and ask politely, the chef will gladly consider requests for Mexican specialties not on the menu. The restaurant serves Mexican and American beers and wine and is closed on Sunday.

Old Mexico Grill
$$–$$$• College Plaza South
Shopping Ctr., 2434 Cerrillos Rd.
• (505) 473-0338

You'll find the true cuisine of Mexico here, not New Mexico's adaptations. Start with a classic ceviche—fish cooked in a lime-juice marinade. Arracheras—also known as fajitas—come to the table sizzling with fresh tortillas and all the accompaniments. You'll find Mexican moles, spicy and slightly sweet, along with an assortment of salsas. Watch the board for daily specials. You can sit at a booth, a table, or at the bar, which offers several flavors of Margaritas and an assortment of cold Mexican cervezas. Old Mexico Grill serves lunch Monday through Friday and dinner nightly. No smoking is permitted.

Mariscos "La Playa"
$$ • 537 Cordova Rd.
• (505) 982-2790
La Playa 2
2875 Cerrillos Rd.
• (505) 473-4594

After operating La Playa for three years, the Ortega family spread its wings to open a second restaurant, using the same successful recipes. These simple little eateries have an authentic, south-of-the-border feel. At the Cordova location, you can imagine you're on the beach as you look at the mural of white sand, waves, and para-sailers as you wait for your meal. Chances are the wait will be a quick one—the kitchen runs efficiently. You can choose cold selections, such as seafood cocktails or ceviche, or hot fish and shellfish entrées fixed many ways. The soups are filled with fish and vegetables, and the grilled platters are served hot and well seasoned. You can get fish tacos and shrimp burritos, along with soft, fresh corn tortillas. Try the Filete a la Plancha, baked snapper stuffed with shellfish, octopus, and cheese. The restaurants serve lunch and dinner daily except Tuesdays. You can order beer—Mexican or from the good ol' USA— with your meal. Reservations are accepted at the Cerrillos Road location, which sometimes has music.

Los Mayas
$$$ • 409 W. Water Street
• (505) 986-9930
• www.losmayas.com

Eating here is fun, especially in the summer when you and your family can be outside on the large patio. This is Mexican–style food and both tortilla dishes and seafood are well represented on the extensive menu. Try the enchiladas banana appetizer—two rolled tortillas stuffed with fried plantains topped with a nicely spiced mole sauce and cheese. Entrées include choose-your-own

INSIDERS' TIP
At last count, Santa Fe had about 200 sit-down restaurants, not counting fast food operations like the burger chains.

Santacafe is one of Santa Fe's more elegant dining spots.

Photo: Courtesy of Santacafe

RESTAURANTS

Traditional New Mexican, Asian, Noveaux cuisine . . . all provide a continuing unique dining experience for residents and visitors.

combination plates, fajitas, and grilled items. The Santo Domingo is a warm plate filled with skirt steak and jumbo shrimp split, grilled, and served in the shell. Beer and wine, including sangria, add to the fun. You'll find live music nightly. Los Mayas serves lunch and dinner seven days a week.

New Mexican

Blue Corn Cafe
$$ • 133 Water St.
• (505) 984-1800
Blue Corn Cafe and Brewery
$$ • 4065 Cerrillos Rd.
• (505) 438-1800

Start your meal with fresh chips and salsa, then, if you want New Mexican food, create your own combination plate or choose from those on the menu. The grilled corn and chipotle soup will spice up your day, and the blue corn posole is a nice touch. The fish and chips, served with a green chile tartar sauce, is another good choice. The Water Street location is downtown and offers window tables where you can watch the world walk by below you. The Cerrillos Road restaurant includes the brewery where they make their own beer, and is conveniently located near south side shop-

ping and movies. The brewery offers daily beer specials. Lunch and dinner are served daily.

The Burrito Company
$ • 111 Washington Ave.
• (505) 982-4453

This casual place, where you stand in line to place your order and bus your own table, is the bargain of downtown and a good spot to take kids. Not only is the food good, you can also get in and out quickly and have money left to buy your Santa Fe t-shirts. But don't let the casual atmosphere fool you—the chile is the real thing, with enough spark to get your attention. In addition to New Mexican favorites, you can order pastries, coffee drinks, and hot dogs. It's open for breakfast, lunch, and early dinner. Try the breakfast burrito—a warm flour tortilla stuffed with scrambled eggs and bacon and smothered with chile, and you'll be ready to explore the city for hours. The Burrito Company does not allow smoking and serves beer and wine with meals.

Café San Estevan
$$$ • 428 Agua Fria
• (505) 995-1996

You can enjoy lunch, dinner, or Saturday and Sunday brunch at this charming and beautifully appointed New Mexico restaurant. The white walls, coved ceiling, and polished flagstone floor invite you to relax. The walls and shelves feature local weaving and woodcarvings. The food is well presented—a pleasure for the eyes as well as the palate. The menu features New Mexican specialties and a few other choices such as roast breast of chicken, salmon, steak, and pork chops. Many patrons opt for the enchiladas here, and the guacamole also gets rave reviews. Try the Poblano Chile Rellano, a large green chile filled with cheese and onions with a crispy crust. The restaurant has an extensive wine list. And don't miss the raspberry chocolate cake, a wonderfully moist blend of flavors with a melt-in-your-mouth texture. For brunch, we enjoy the Blanquillos—a pair of poached eggs served over fresh spinach and sliced potatoes, surrounded by a moat of red chile. Beer and a good selection of wines are available and reservations are accepted. The restaurant is closed on Monday.

La Choza
$$ • 905 Alarid St.
• (505) 982-0909

Well-prepared, simple New Mexican food is the hallmark of La Choza. Operated by the same folks who run The Shed (choza means "shed"), this place has the same good food but a little more space for its diners. It's off the beaten path and, perhaps because of that, a favorite among locals. The carne adovada is one of the house dishes to die for. The enchiladas, served flat with chile to the edge of the plate, are another popular dish. Try them "Christmas" with a bit of red and green chile on top. La Choza is open for lunch and dinner daily except Sunday. Specials are posted on the blackboard. The restaurant is smoke free. When weather permits dining outside, the patio is lovely.

Diego's Cafe and Bar
$$ • DeVargas Center, 193 Paseo de Peralta
• (505) 983-5101

You'll find first-rate New Mexican food in this comfortable, unpretentious restaurant. The burritos are huge, the chile well seasoned, and the sopaipillas mouth-watering. The restaurant offers "light lunch" specials, which provide ample food for the average appetite. If you're hesitant about Santa Fe chile, try the chalupas—crisp tortilla cups loaded with beans and meat if you wish, and topped with guacamole and sour cream. You may have to wait to get in, but it's worth it. Diego's serves lunch and dinner daily and has a full bar.

Gabriel's
$$$ • U.S. Hwy. 285.,
15 miles north of Santa Fe
• (505) 455-7000

Getting to Gabriel's requires a quick drive, and the scenery along the way helps set the mood for a relaxing ambiance and well-prepared meal you'll be served here. Start with the ice-cold Margaritas and guacamole prepared at your table from a cart with avocados, fresh garlic, onions, cilantro, salt, lime juice, tomatoes, and jalapeños. In addition to New Mexican food, you can get a good steak and other non-ethnic dishes. The patio is gorgeous in the summer, with abundant fresh flowers, a bubbling fountain, and plenty of shade. Inside, Gabriel's has the spacious feel of an old home and easily accommodates parties or large groups. This is a great place to linger. It's open for lunch and dinner daily except Monday.

La Plazuela Restaurant
$$$ • La Fonda Hotel,
100 E. San Francisco St.
• (505) 982-5511

If a contest were held for Santa Fe's most charming dining room, La Plazuela would definitely be a finalist. Diners—among them hotel guests, visitors, and locals who work downtown—have a sense of timelessness as they relax in this bright space and enjoy the colorful painted windows, the mural of New Mexico pueblo life and the welcoming fireplace. The bright table settings and waitresses attractively dressed in flowing skirts and Santa Fe–style blouses add to the ambiance. Most diners favor the restaurant's New Mexican offerings, including a hearty combination plate and first-rate chile rellenos. You can order pork or vegetarian tamales topped with red or green chile. For vegetarians, the eggplant sandwich gets a gold star—grilled eggplant and a hint of pesto. La Plazuela is open for breakfast, lunch, and dinner and offers a full bar. Try the margaritas. The restaurant is non smoking. You can also have cocktails at the Bell Tower, a full bar upstairs on a patio that overlooks the city, or in La Fonda's lounge.

Maria's New Mexican Kitchen
$$ • 555 W. Cordova Rd.
• (505) 983-7929

Maria's is known for a lot of things—great luncheon specials, one of Santa Fe's best Margarita menus, and murals in the cantina by artist Alfred Morang, which the artist traded for food and drink. There's a lot of history in this place—it's been in business in the same location for 50 years and still has the original phone number! You can order dozens of types of Margaritas, made with different tequilas and complementary liquors, each served with panache. The food is tasty and affordable, and Maria's uses local chile and produce whenever possible. For a change, try the Green Chile Philly at lunch, a variation of a tradition Philly sandwich served on a flour tortilla with the spice of green chile as a special addition. You can watch the tortillas being made so you know they're fresh. Strolling musicians add to the ambiance in the evenings. Reservations are welcome— and a good idea. Lunch and dinner are served every day.

Peppers
$ • 2239 Old Pecos Tr.
• (505) 984-2272

Peppers' dining room, decorated in bright pink, peach, and yellow, with several (artsy) parrots on perches swinging overhead, sets the stage for fun. The menu is huge, presenting a vast assortment of well-prepared New Mexican dishes—combination plates, burritos, stuffed sopaipillas, and fajitas—as well as "American" offerings like salads, sandwiches, and items from the grill. Peppers serves Chimayó red and green chile from the green chile fields of Hatch, New Mexico. The carne adovada burrito, tender chunks of meat cooked in a wonderful red chile marinade, wrapped in a soft flour tortilla and smothered with more chile and cheese on top, is a great choice, served with a dollop of sour cream to cut the fire, a side of posole and a fresh sopaipilla. Vegetarian offerings, such as hard-to-find spinach enchiladas, are plentiful. Peppers has a bar with a view of the city lights at night and a large private dining room for parties. They serve breakfast, lunch and dinner daily and also do "to go" orders.

Rancho de Chimayó
$$ • 3 miles from the N.M. Hwy. 76
intersection with N.M. Hwy. 520,
32 miles north of Santa Fe, Chimayó
• (505) 984-2100 or (505) 351-4444

The drive from Santa Fe is part of the pleasure of dining in this long-established New Mexican restaurant. Allow yourself at least 45 minutes. Plan your reservations for just after

sunset and you'll have a chance to see the Jémez Mountains against a wonderful golden, crimson or peach-colored sky. Rancho de Chimayó gets an "A" for ambiance. Housed in a sprawling old hacienda, the restaurant sits near apple orchards and offers patio dining and a lovely bar with a fireplace. Try one of the house special drinks, a Chimayó cocktail. You'll find strolling musicians here most weekends. The fare is New Mexican with a few other choices for non-chile eaters, such as steak and trout. The sopaipillas here are light and crisp and they refill the basket as often as you ask. In 2000, *Hispanic* magazine honored this place as one of the top 50 Hispanic restaurants in the United States. From mid-May through mid-November the restaurant is open daily for lunch and dinner; otherwise it's closed Mondays. It's non-smoking except for the terraces.

The Shed
$$ • 113½ E. Palace Ave.
• (505) 982-9030

The Shed is housed in a part of Sena Plaza, a historic hacienda a block off the Plaza. The small rooms give you a feeling of Santa Fe ambiance, and the food will kindle your inner fire. Established in 1954, The Shed's signature dish is red chile enchiladas, served with a piece of garlic bread. Other specialties include green-chile stew with potatoes and pork and charbroiled "Shedburgers." The homemade desserts are fabulous—save room for the mocha cake. The Shed is open for lunch and dinner daily except Sunday. The restaurant is smoke-free and has a full bar.

Tia Sophia's
$ • 210 W. San Francisco St.
• (505) 983-9880

Come to Tia Sophia's for breakfast or lunch and experience good, well-priced food in nonpretentious atmosphere. You may have a short wait to get seated at one of the old wooden booths or a table. The green chile stew and daily Blue Plate Specials are ever popular, and the sopaipillas are some of Santa Fe's best. We love the breakfast burrito, a giant serving of shredded potatoes, eggs, bacon if you wish, and chile spicy enough to get your attention. To go orders are available. The servers are good natured and efficient, and when you're finished you can walk to the Plaza, enjoying the shops

INSIDERS' TIP
If a restaurant advertises that it serves beer and wine, that means it doesn't have a full liquor license.

and galleries on the way. No alcohol is available.

Tiny's Restaurant & Lounge
$$ • 1015 Pen Rd.
• (505) 983-9817

Serving Santa Fe residents and their visitors since the 1950s in several different locations, Tiny's is a community institution. You can order steaks and burgers here, as well as good Northern New Mexican food. The fajitas are a good choice and so are the baked chicken flautas with blue corn tortillas. Be sure to check the daily specials. Tiny's has a full bar and a cozy patio. You'll find a band for dancing Wednesday through Saturday and the music begins around 8:30 PM. The bar and dining area feature one of the Southwest's largest decanter collections. Name brands include Wild Turkey, Jim Beam, Ski Country, Lionstone, and Ezra Brooks, all done in fine china. You'll also find many works of art done by local artists, including Ramon Rice, Barry Coffin, Clark Hulings, Earl Biss, Frank Howell, Tommy Manscione, Ernesto Zepeda, R.C. Gorman, John Fincher, Peter de LaFuente, and others. This lively place is open for lunch weekdays and dinner daily except Sunday.

Tomasita's Restaurant
$$ • 500 S. Guadalupe St.
• (505) 983-5721

Although you'll seldom see an advertisement for this place—even in the telephone book—Tomasita's may be Santa Fe's most popular New Mexican restaurant. They don't take reservations so expect to wait if you decide to eat here—but you won't be disappointed. The red and green chile are both excellent, the sopaipillas light and tender, and the sangria and Margaritas will tempt you to linger. The daily specials make ordering easy— or ask your server for a recommendation. In addition to New Mexican food you'll find steaks, burgers and even stuffed grape leaves, but the chile here still steals the show. Located in a restored train station, Tomasita's serves lunch and dinner every day except Sunday. There's a full bar, which also serves as the smokers' dining room, and patio dining when the weather permits.

Tortilla Flats
$$ • 3139 Cerrillos Rd.
• (505) 471-8685

This is the place to go if you want to grab a bite without making a big production out of it.

Generous portions rule. You'll find great offerings for breakfast, including a hefty breakfast burrito and tender pancakes. The chorizo fold is perfect for smaller appetites, combining spicy sausage with scrambled eggs inside a warm flour tortilla, served with a side of light fresh salsa. For lunch or dinner the vegetable quesadilla with fresh carrots, broccoli, and two cheeses is a winner, as are the brisket burrito and the carne adovada. The atmosphere is casual, and the service, away from the bustle of downtown, is good. Children are made to feel welcome. Tortilla Flats is open for breakfast, lunch, and dinner and offers a full bar.

Pizza

Fabio's Pizza Oven
106 N. Guadalupe St.
• (505) 982-5533,
(505) 982-04464 to fax orders
• http://fabiospizzaoven.com

Conveniently located near all the major downtown hotels, Fabio's Pizza is a good meal at a good price. In addition to 12 kinds of pizza, Fabio's serves Pizza Pazza, a double-decker pizza with uncooked ingredients, such as fresh spinach, piled on the top. You can also get salads, soup, and sandwiches here. Try the homemade pasta or the grilled polenta stuffed with porcini mushrooms. The pizza oven is open daily for lunch and dinner and has free pizza delivery. Ask about nightly specials. Across the street is Fabio's other restaurant, Fabio's Seafood & Grill, 329 W. San Francisco, where you can get a complete Italian seafood dinner grilled fresh meats, gnocchi, ravioli, homemade pasta, and risotto.

Pizza Etc.
$ • DeVargas Ctr., 564 N. Guadalupe St.
• (505) 986-1500
or order by fax (505) 986-1035

You can enjoy several hearty salads and delicious calzones in this shopping mall cafe, but pizza is the house specialty. You might not expect to find gourmet fare here, but this is a first-rate eatery. Try the special pizzas, like the Greek with feta cheese, Kalamata olives, sundried tomatoes, fresh roasted garlic, and fresh cucumbers. Yummy. We like the Pontchartrain, complete with shrimp and Andouille sausage and the sweetness of caramelized onions. A large gourmet went for $24.50 in 2000, but you can have your friends bring salad and dessert! In addition to the standards, toppings you

Bert's Burge Bowl is a favorite of locals, serving green chile cheeseburgers, burritos, tamales, and shakes.

Photo: Don Strel

can add include soy cheese, ground buffalo meat, pine nuts, and shrimp. You'll also find pizza by the slice here. This little place does a good carry out business and has some tables for dining in. It's open for lunch and dinner daily and is smoke-free. They'll deliver for free within a two-mile radius, which includes most downtown hotels.

Upper Crust Pizza
$ • 329 Old Santa Fe Tr.
• (505) 982-0000

Open daily for lunch and dinner, Upper Crust is a Santa Fe tradition. The food is served hot and fresh, and you can order pizza with whole-wheat crust. The Grecian Gourmet, a succulent combination of feta cheese, Kalamata olives, mushrooms, garlic, and other pizza magic, is a good choice. Toppings available include green chile and chorizo, a spicy New Mexican sausage. In addition to pizza, Upper Crust serves meal-like salads, several sandwiches, and calzones. We love the whole-wheat crust. You can get a glass of wine with your meal or order from their interesting selection of micro-brews. In the summer, after you order at the counter, you can eat on the front porch and watch the crowds stroll by. The restaurant is smoke-free except for outdoors.

Il Vicino
$ • 321 W. San Francisco St.
• (505) 986-8700, (505) 820-0524 order fax

When you've had enough chile or too many fancy dinners, the casual, comfortable Il Vicino will fill the bill. Order at the counter, choosing among wood-fired pizzas, salads, soups, calzones, sandwiches, and maybe lasagna. The chicken pizza is a favorite here. You'll have to stand in line to order during busy times; phone or fax in your order to speed pick-up if you want pizza to go. You can select a beer—including their own microbrew—or wine from their extensive list. Smoking is allowed on the patio only.

Pubs

The Green Onion
$ • 1851 St. Michael's Dr.
• (505) 983-5198

This is one of Santa Fe's most popular watering holes, a blue-collar sort of place where you'll find college students and even some tourists. With TVs that offer all the games and nightly food and drink specials, the Onion is a popular hangout for local recreation league teams. You'll find traditional bar fare here, and the chile dishes are good. So is the pizza. You can order a deluxe burger with plenty of toppings and get fries, onion rings, or, if you must, a salad on the side. The nightly specials—often including a pasta selection—are posted by the door. St. Patrick's Day is a major event. The Green Onion is open for lunch and dinner daily.

Second Street Brewery
$$ • 1814 Second St.
- **(505) 982-3030**
- **www.secondstreetbrewery.com**

Off the beaten track, this neighborhood restaurant and brew pub recently won a gold medal in a state competition for microbrews and is frequently ranked as the city's number one brew pub. In addition to beer made on the premises, you can get sandwiches, desserts, and hot entrées at this neighborhood restaurant. Among the specialties are the London Broil, served with lots of mashed potatoes and gravy, an herb roasted half chicken, salmon cakes served with apple raisin chutney, and, of course, fish & chips. The atmosphere is as casual as you'd expect, and children are welcome. Lunch and dinner are served daily, and the restaurant is smoke free. You may find live music in the evenings.

Spanish

El Farol
$$$ • 808 Canyon Rd.
- **(505) 983-9912**

If you're looking for tapas, El Farol can fill the bill. You'll find cooking from many regions of Spain, with paellas as well as fresh seafood and El Farol's signature garlic soup. For lunch, you'll also find sandwiches and a few other entrées. The tapas, both hot and cold, offer plenty of options. Try the duck served surrounded by tasty carrot sauce or the portobello mushrooms in shallot-garlic-sherry sauce. Presentations are beautiful, and each dish can be shared— so you can sample more of the menu. For dessert, we like the dried figs and dates with marzipan and chopped pistachios, garnished with orange slices.

El Farol also has an extensive list of wines, sherries, ports, and brandies from the Iberian peninsula and elsewhere. The atmosphere here is that of an old Western bar inside a rustic, plank-floor adobe building. You can listen to live music and dance most nights. Patio dining is available in season and you can park in the city lot across the street. Open daily for lunch and dinner.

El Meson
$$$ • 213 Washington Ave.
- **(505) 983-6756**

Open for lunch, dinner, and Sunday buffet brunch, this Spanish restaurant serves tapas, paella, and a few other entrées. The house special tapas include shrimp in garlic sauce, fried calamari, spicy lamb brochettes, and manchego cheese in olive oil. Ask about the nightly specials, too, such as a wonderful stew of summer squash served with crisp toast for dipping. The saffron-infused Spanish paellas are available with seafood, chicken, and sausage or vegetarian. On a cold day, try the thick Spanish hot chocolate. And leave a little room for the creamy orange flan. You can get a beer or glass of wine with your meal, and patio seating is available. The restaurant is nicely appointed inside, with lace curtains and solid wooden furniture set off by the light walls.

Steaks

El Nido
$$$–$$$$ • C.R. 73 at Bishops Lodge Rd., Tesuque
- **(505) 988-4340**

A former dance hall and trading post, El Nido offers choice aged beef, fresh seafood, and a few local specialties. Only a five-minute drive from the Santa Fe Opera, El Nido is a summer favorite of opera fans. Consistency throughout the years has given El Nido a cadre of loyal customers. The small, lively bar adds to the restaurant's ambiance, as does the adobe building, complete with fireplaces. The menu is built on choice aged meat—prime rib, sirloin, lamb chops—plus fresh seafood and some other choices, such as duck breast

INSIDERS' TIP
Chile sparks New Mexico's regional cuisine. Some are harvested green—usually beginning in September—roasted until the skin blisters, then peeled. Chile enthusiasts claim that chopped green chile, sometimes thickened with a bit of flour to make a sauce, goes well with meat, fish, fowl, eggs, cheese, and vegetables. No one will think it unusual if you ask for a side of green chile with just about anything—even hash browns.

RESTAURANTS

While Santa Fe may be best known for its chile, diners can choose from a wide variety of cuisines.

and a New Mexican green chile stew. You'll also find several nightly specials—braised lamb shanks, perhaps—and some Asian touches. Start with the onion soup—they're famous for it. El Nido is open for dinner every day except Monday. Smoking is allowed in the bar and the restaurant. It's 2.5 miles from the U.S. 84/285 Tesuque exit and 7 miles from the Santa Fe Plaza.

Piñon Grill
$$$–$$$$ • Hilton, 100 Sandoval St.
• (505) 986-6400

If you're looking for meat, fish, or interesting salads, the Piñon Grill is the place to come. The menu offers plenty of choices for meat eaters, including a chile-wrapped and rubbed filet. Try the beef stuffed with wild mushrooms, blue cheese, and green chile. Caesar salad made at your table is a show as well as a good starter. If you book ahead, you can ask to sit in front

of the welcoming fireplace in the winter. The grill is open for dinner daily and has a full bar. The restaurant is non-smoking.

Steaksmith at El Gancho
$$$ • Old Las Vegas Hwy., 1 mile from I-25 Exit 387
• (505) 988-3333

This spacious restaurant, a Santa Fe standby since 1973, is well-known for its appetizers, including spinach-cheese balls and deep-fried avocado. The bar, with a fireplace and TVs is a lovely spot to relax. Steaks and seafood are the rule here, and dinners are served with a choice of salads and homemade soup. You can order green chile, piñon chile, or other sauces on the side. For dessert, try the sour cream apple walnut pie or ask if they have the fresh raspberry pie, which won the 2000 Taste of Santa Fe competition for best dessert. The Steaksmith is open

INSIDERS' TIP

Looking for a good cup of coffee and some local ambiance? Try Downtown Subscription, 376 Garcia St. You can have a pastry or even a sandwich with your espresso or cappuccino and relax surrounded by more than 1,600 different magazines and newspapers from around the world. Writers published and otherwise come here for inspiration. Don't miss the side patio!

for dinner every night. The view, which you'll notice from the parking lot, is one of Santa Fe's nicest vistas, puts the sparkling lights of the city on display each evening. The dining area is non-smoking.

Vanessie
$$$–$$$$ • **434 W. San Francisco St.**
• **(505) 982-9966**

There's not another place like this in town. With its soaringly high ceilings, huge fireplaces, and stylized antlers, Vanessie reminds some of an update on the medieval hunting lodge. The lounge features piano music and warming fireplaces, and winter or summer it's usually packed. The adjoining restaurant offers beef, lamb, fish, roasted chicken, salads, baked potatoes, rice, and vegetables, all served a la carte. The delectable onion appetizer resembles a huge basket of onion rings cooked into a loaf-like shape. Desserts are good here too—and most things are big enough to share.

Nightlife

If you're in search of a non-stop, highly varied nightlife, may we suggest you catch the next flight to Los Angeles, Miami, or New York? It's not that commercial nighttime entertainment doesn't exist in Santa Fe. In fact The City Different boasts a thriving nightlife. You just have to look a little harder for it than you would in other, larger cities. It's also somewhat limited in scope, especially as evening turns into night and night turns into morning. Except for bars, a few dancing locales, and a handful of cafés, Santa Fe rolls up the sidewalks after 10 PM. Many bars close at 11:30 or midnight during the week, some even on weekends.

Locals are resourceful, however. They create their own nightlife, much of which consists of meeting friends at favorite restaurants or bars which, like their denizens, have distinct personalities. For those who live to dance, there's one honest-to-goodness "disco" in town, several country and western venues, and a few Latino clubs. Many hotels also offer live entertainment, much of it homegrown—though that by no means rules out the occasional big-name act. Thanks to Santa Fe's magnetic attraction for artists, musicians, and celebrities off all ilk and notoriety, local talent is excellent and plentiful here.

For detailed information about how to fill your evenings in Santa Fe, check the "Comings and goings" section of *Pasatiempo*, the weekly arts and entertainment section of the local daily newspaper, *The Santa Fe New Mexican*. The free, weekly *Santa Fe Reporter* also contains day-by-day listings of nighttime entertainment in "Going Out," part of its "Culture" section while the *Albuquerque Journal* offers nightlife suggestions in "Revue," which comes out on Fridays, and daily in *Journal North*.

Coffeehouses, Restaurants and Late-Night Haunts

Atomic Grill
103 E. Water St.
• (505) 820-2866

Located one block south of the Plaza and open 'til 3 AM Monday through Saturday, the Atomic Grill attracts an interesting and varied cross section of Santa Fe, especially in the wee hours of the morning. You'll find vegetarian insomniacs who've just got to have an Earth Mama Garden Burger (and they're *good*), a meatless Frito pie, or any number of other vegetarian de-

lights—if they ever hope to get to sleep. Carnivore's might crave the Atomic Grill's half-pound All Terrain Burger, a catfish sandwich, wood-oven pizza, or any of the restaurant's other eclectic American specialties, including breakfasts served all day and fresh pastries and desserts from the Plaza Bakery next door. The restaurant is also a popular after-hours spot for people spilling out of the bars at the 2 AM witching hour; some folks need to sop up the booze before they drive, others are just plain hungry, while many simply aren't ready to stop partying. The Atomic Grill's beer and wine license means you can't drink there after 11 PM. Before then, however, you can choose from a selection of up to 80 beers and a half-dozen wines. Or try one of its hot drinks—a cappuccino, perhaps, or maybe an eggnog latte during the Christmas season—or a freshly made Italian soda. The arty, warehouse-styled restaurant offers live, mostly acoustic music on summer weekends. The Atomic Grill is open Monday through Friday from 9 AM to 3 AM, Saturday from 8 AM to 3 AM, and Sundays from 8 AM until midnight.

Aztec Street Coffee House
317 Aztec St.
• **(505) 983-9464**

The Aztec Street Coffee House is about as close as you can get in Santa Fe to an old-fashioned, European style café. It's one of those increasingly rare places where you can buy a single cup of coffee, get your one free refill, and spend the rest of the day reading, writing, composing, consulting, ciphering, or contemplating your navel without pressure to buy more, eat more, drink more, say more, do more, or leave. The minimalist, unpretentious—some call it downright funky—atmosphere attracts a clientele that runs the gamut from working and starving artists, musicians, filmmakers, and writers to students, slackers, local business people, New Agers, conspiracy theorists, tub-thumpers, gadflies, barflies, or anyone looking for what many patrons claim is the best cup of coffee in town. You can even buy the house blend by the pound. The Aztec serves vegetarian food including fresh breakfast burritos, bagels, pastries—many of them homemade, and scones starting at 7 AM Monday through Friday and 8 AM on weekends, and homemade soups, stews, *bruschette* (open faced grilled sandwiches), humus, and hot vegetarian entrées and daily specials until 7 PM Sunday through Thursday and 9 PM on Fridays and Saturdays.

The Aztec is a happy meeting ground for smokers and non-smokers, though not necessarily in the same rooms. The patio, however, is the equivalent of international air space and is open to both camps. Weekend evenings at the Aztec feature open-mike sessions for music, poetry, performance, or any other variation of the spoken word. The café runs a revolving art show on its adobe walls, showing the work of local artists and changing the exhibit monthly.

Cafe Oasis
526 Galisteo St.
• **(505) 983-9599**

Stepping into the ultra-eclectic Oasis is like stepping into a time warp. Is it the psychedelic '60s? Or is it *fin-de-siècle* Paris? Well, it all depends which room you're visiting. The "Mystic Room," an opium den without the opium, is for bare feet only with old Turkish rugs on the floor and not a chair in sight. You sit on pillows, eat at low tables, and ought probably to be listening to Ravi Shankar or perhaps some belly dancing music. If you prefer, you can climb in or sit under the loft and eat, drink, meditate, or write your memoirs. Down a hot-pink hallway decorated with painted flames you'll find the intimate "Victorian Room," aka the "Romantic Room," whose persimmon walls are decorated with turn-of-the-century John Waterhouse prints set off by antique furniture of that and other periods. You can sit at a clawfoot table, a 1950s booth, or on a comfortable couch with a low-lying table, perfect for a *tête-à-tête* over tea.

Tobacco users should head directly for the "Smoking Room," whose mosaic and wood-paneled walls are reminiscent of an old-fashioned pub. Or go no farther than the "Social Room," also called the "Tahiti Room" because of the Gauguin prints, a large, bright, fauna-filled salon at the entrance, where live music—blues, cowboy, flamenco, folk, jazz, Middle Eastern, and other genres—plays Wednesday though Sunday starting at 8 PM. You won't pay a cover charge for the entertainment though there is a $6 minimum that you won't mind spending on the café's natural food, including breakfast served all day. If you prefer, you can dine outdoors in the restaurant's spacious patio, which is encircled by plants of the Southwest and lighted with Tiki torches and candles. There's also a lovely garden up front with flagstone and mosaic benches and tables and a mosaic floor. Café Oasis is open 365 days a year. It stays open from 9:30 AM to midnight Sunday through Wednesday and until at least 2 AM Thursday through Saturday.

Downtown Subscription
376 Garcia St.
• **(505) 983-3085**

Though Downtown Subscription is primarily a daytime establishment, the coffeehouse/ international newsstand stays open an extra hour and a half or so every other Wednesday evening for poetry readings sponsored by a Santa Fe-based cultural education organization called Recursos de Santa Fe. Poets are chosen based on work they have submitted. Most are local, though some come from other cities and occasionally even other states. Readings start at 7 PM and last until approximately 8:30 PM. You might want to show up early because the readings get crowded—sometimes with up to 80 people, many of them sipping cappuccino, hot Mexican mocha made with ground Ibarra chocolate, tea, or any number of other hot or cold non-alcoholic drinks, perhaps accompanied by a lime bar, rugelah, Aunt Helen's sour cream coffeecake, or maybe even a sandwich. There is no cover charge for poetry readings. Downtown Subscription's regular hours are from 7:30 AM to 7 PM daily. The café, which is extremely popular among locals, sells magazines and newspapers from around the world with up to 2,500 titles in stock at any one time.

La Casa Sena Cantina
Sena Plaza, 125 E. Palace Ave.
• **(505) 988-9232**

You're just about to bite into your almond-crusted salmon while your partner is slicing into honey-glazed New Mexico pork loin. Suddenly, your waiter breaks into song. If it's Broadway, it must be La Casa Sena Cantina. No, that's not the number he's singing. It's a dinner club where the wait staff doubles as musical comedy performers usually after, though sometimes during, your meal. There are two seatings nightly—at 5:30 PM and again at 8 PM. The performance begins an hour or so after you arrive, probably about the time you're having dessert and coffee, and lasts approximately one hour. Prior to the show, live piano music plays in the background as you dine on any of a variety of innovative New Mexican

and Southwestern entrées, which range in price from $12 to $18 à la carte. There's no additional charge for the entertainment; it's included with your dinner. But do leave some extra cash in the tip bowl for the performers in addition to a gratuity for serving your dinner. They heartily deserve it. La Casa Sena Cantina is open seven nights a week, 364 days a year, closing only on Christmas day. Walk-ins are welcome, but we strongly recommend you make reservations, especially during the summer and on holidays. For Indian Market weekend (see our "Annual Events" chapter), people often book months in advance.

Country and Western

Fiesta Barn
Rancho Encantado, N.M. 592
• **(505) 982-3537**

The Fiesta Barn at luxurious Rancho Encantado (see our Accommodations chapter) is an honest-to-goodness barn that features live country and western music by popular local bands on Sunday nights from April through October. Erected about 20 years ago, the unheated Fiesta Barn is rustic and earthy, yet cozy and comfortable, with Mexican blankets adorn-

Relax and enjoy yourself—you're on vacation!

ing the beams and haystacks around the perimeter as well as picnic tables for chowing down on fresh barbecue. Beer seems to be the most popular item from the small, full-service bar—especially the ever-popular, all-American Budweiser—though some local microbrews give the Clydesdales a run for their money. But the dance is the draw. Literally hundreds of people show up to two-step, waltz, polka, and swing the night away to the sounds of South by Southwest (see "La Fiesta Lounge" in this section) and Hired Hands, both enormously talented bands. You'll see some darned good dancers here, but don't let that intimidate you. The wooden dance floor is big enough for everyone and the ambiance is friendly and fun, not to mention energetic and downright electric. In the end, it's pure country, right down to the fashions, which include lots of cowboy hats and boots and women in swinging skirts. Five bucks will get you into the Fiesta Barn, which is a separate building located in a wooded area near the main lodge with nearby outhouses. The faint of heart may use the bathrooms in the lobby, just a short stroll away along attractive, lighted paths. Once in the lobby, do take a minute to explore the lobby's curious but attractive blend of northern New Mexican and European charm, complete with huge log *vigas* on the ceiling, a couple of large fireplaces, overstuffed couches, and an eclectic mix of period furniture. And do show up some Friday at the Main Lodge between 5:30 and 7:30 PM to hear talented wranglers from the luxury resort's own stables read original poetry and sing songs.

On Sundays in the winter and Wednesdays in the spring and summer, Rancho Encantado features dinner dancing in its top-rated restaurant. The resort literally rolls up the carpet to expose the dance floor so diners can cut a rug to big band sounds. You'll see everything from swing and samba to the bossa nova and cha-cha. Casual elegance is the dress code for the night, which tends to attract a somewhat older audience, say 40 and above. The dinner dance goes from 5:30 to 9:30 PM and is open to the public, not just hotel guests. There is no cover charge. Check the newspapers for special events.

J.W. Eaves Movie Ranch
105 Rancho Alegre
• **(505) 474-3045**

If it's Sunday night and you suddenly realize your toes are tapping to the imaginary sounds of Gene Autry or Sons of the Pioneers, then it's time to put on your cowboy hat and boots and head on down to the J.W. Eaves Movie Ranch just off the Turquoise Trail. You'll find yourself amongst a mild-mannered crowd of people from 8- to 80-years-old two-stepping their way around one of the largest dance floors in Santa Fe. Located about 20 miles south of the Plaza, the movie ranch is an elaborate 27-acre Old West movie set built in 1969 for *The Cheyenne Social Club*, starring Henry Fonda, James Stewart, and Shirley Jones. Since that time, owner J.W. Eaves—an ornery but lovably old coot from Texas who earned millions in the trucking industry—has hosted more than 100 other productions, primarily oaters, including many that left behind structures and scenery they built for their films. Among them is the "Liberty Palace"—the larger of two saloons on the movie ranch and the one where dudes and dudettes dance every Sunday to the tunes of Syd Masters and the Swing Riders or various other local Western swing bands. For a $7 cover charge, you can cut a rug on the wooden floor from 7 to 11 PM, slaking your thirst between dances with beer from the Rio Grande brewery. Or you can opt for soft drinks and a hot dog at the snack bar.

When the Eaves Ranch held its first dance in April 2000, only 15 or 20 people attended. These days, the saloon attracts 75 to 80 people on Sunday nights with room for more. Many dress to suit the surroundings, as do some employees. You're just as likely to see someone decked out as a gunfighter as you are to find your bartender wearing garters on his sleeves. The saloon itself is fitted with swinging doors at the entrance, a long wooden bar inside and seating for about 70 people, including several tables outside for any overflow. Although the ranch hosts private parties in the Liberty Palace saloon, Sundays are reserved strictly for this event with one exception—the annual charity Buckaroo Ball (see our Events chapter).

Rodeo Nites
2911 Cerrillos Rd.
• **(505) 473-4138**

A friend of ours describes Rodeo Nites as "a party" for the "tight jeans crowd." We think that's as apt a description as any we've heard, at least as the night gets long. Actually, Rodeo Nites is almost two nightclubs in one. It starts out nearly every evening as a straight-ahead country and western club that attracts a loyal group of fairly genteel dancers who really know their way around the dance floor. They two-step, swing, line-dance, polka, and waltz until about 10:30 or 11 PM. Then the music gets louder and harder and younger—and so does the crowd. Between sets by almost invariably a country and western band, the later crowd also dances to ranchero, salsa, Tejano, and rock spun by two deejays on the brigs. Rodeo Nites has live music starting at 8 PM every night. It has brought in such national luminaries as Freddie Fender, Perfect Stranger, Neal McCoy and Sammy Kershaw as well as local and regional favorites like South By Southwest, Ricochet, Midnight Fire, and Wild West Band. The club charges $2.50 to get in the door on Thursdays and $3 on Friday and Saturday. The rest of the week there's no cover. Wednesday night is ladies' night but don't get your hackles up, fellas. The perks—mainly discounts on special drinks—apply to you, too. And every night is discount night at the shot bar, where you pay less for beers and shots by getting them yourself instead of waiting for table service. The ambiance at Rodeo Nites is strictly saloon with a brass rail separating the 90-foot oval dance floor from the raised platforms with tables and chairs. Rodeo Nites opens nightly at 5:30 PM and closes at 2 AM (midnight on Sundays).

Sports Bars

Green Onion Sports Bar
1851 St. Michael's Dr.
• (505) 983-5198

The Green Onion is exactly what you'd expect in a sports bar: lots of beer and other booze, lots of smoke, lots of rowdy sports fans, and, of major importance, lots of televisions—11 to be exact, including a 60-inch set used during parties for the Superbowl, the World Series, NBA playoffs, and other major televised sports events. Two of the sets are hooked up to the National Trivia Network, which runs half-hour trivia games of 15 questions in which players compete at no charge against other bars around the country. It's fun even for people who could care less about sports, though you'll certainly be in the minority. A staple in Santa Fe, the Green Onion is where sports fans of all sorts—including lots of blue collar workers, according to management—gather to watch games, and where local sports teams meet after their own games. Because it's not downtown, the Green Onion is truly a local bar, even a neighborhood bar, despite the fact that it's not in a bona fide neighborhood. Founded 25 years ago by an Irishman, the Green Onion is considered the only traditional "Irish" bar in Santa Fe, where St. Patrick's Day is treated like a national holiday with a huge party featuring bagpipes and other live music and the usual culinary suspects—corned beef and cabbage and Irish stew. The rest of the year, the Green Onion serves classic pub food, including hot and cold sandwiches, pizza, and excellent hamburgers as well as pretty darned good New Mexican dishes. The Green Onion is open Monday through Saturday from 11 AM to 2 AM and Sundays from 11 AM to midnight. The kitchen stays open until 9:30 PM on weeknights and 8:30 PM Saturday and Sunday.

Rocky's Bar & Grill
1201 Cerrillos Rd.
• (505) 986-1992

Rocky's is a family-owned lounge that is part sports bar, part dance bar. Its four television sets are tuned to sports channels at all times and are visible from most corners of the saloon, even by the pool tables, which rent out for $1 per person game. The owners host parties during big sporting events—Superbowl, World Series, NBA playoffs, etc.—with food and drink specials such as $1.99 super nachos and $2 bottles of domestic beer, $2.50 for imports and premiums, for parties of six or more. On Wednesday, Friday and Saturday nights, the bar turns into a cabaret with live local bands playing rock, blues, or R&B. Those nights command a cover charge of $2 or $3, depending on who's performing. The crowd changes with the music—younger people for alternative rock, baby boomers for blues. Sporting events cut across all age groups, though the owners say their sports clientele are primarily blue-collar workers. Rocky's tends to attract more locals than tourists because it's not a downtown bar. As a result, it has the feel of a neighborhood bar with a lot of regulars. As the name implies, Rocky's Bar & Grill also serves food, specializing in burgers and New Mexican dishes. Rocky's is open Monday through Thursday from 11 AM to midnight; Fridays and Saturdays from 11 AM to 2 AM. The bar is closed on Sundays.

Everything Else

Bar B
331 Sandoval St.
• (505) 982-8999

This tony bar adjacent to The Paramount is included with The Paramount bar, below.

Bull Ring
150 Washington Ave.
• (505) 983-3328

The Bull Ring steakhouse and lounge is *the* place to go if you like rubbing elbows with politicians. It's the "other" State Capitol, a second office of sorts for lawmakers when the state legislature is in session. Many New Mexico politicians and lobbyists head to the Bull Ring at the end of the legislative day to hang out, chill out and sometimes strike political deals. With its elegant, masculine dark green and wood décor, the upscale restaurant and lounge attracts a variety of primarily male professionals, many of whom mingle at the oaken and brass-railed bar until closing at 10:30 or 11 PM. Not only can you smoke cigars at the bar, you can buy them there, too. However, the dining room is strictly non-smoking. Voted the best steakhouse in Santa Fe by *Santa Fe Reporter* readers, the Bull Ring serves only USDA prime, corn-fed steaks from Chicago.

Catamount Bar & Grille
125 E. Water St.
• (505) 988-7222, (505) 988-7299
Catamount Bar Billiards Room

The Catamount Bar & Grille is a popular literal stomping ground for the 20- to 30-year-old set who come to dance, dine, and maybe meet the love of their lives—or at least some love for a night—in an Irish tavern-like atmosphere. The Catamount features live music on weekends—primarily rock, blues, and jazz, mostly by local talent (from Santa Fe, Albuquerque, or Taos) and occasionally a national band on tour. A cover charge, generally between $2 to $5, will get you in the door. Then it's up to you to find space on the packed tile dance floor. The grill offers standard pub fare including chicken breast, hamburgers, buffalo wings, and nachos while the bar bills its Margaritas as a specialty and carries locally made microbrews. Upstairs, the billiards room features six 9-foot Brunswick pool tables which rent for $8 to $10 an hour, depending on the time of day, plus $2 for each additional person. Smoking is allowed throughout the establishment, including cigars. The Catamount stays open until 2 AM Monday through Saturday and midnight on Sunday.

Club Alegría
2797 Agua Fría St.
• (505) 471-2324

Club Alegría is a live music and dance club. Beyond that, it's impossible to categorize. The club, on lower Agua Fría Street, is probably most famous, at least locally, for its Friday night salsa show starring Pretto y Paranda and featuring Father Frank Pretto—the Panamanian-born, piano-playing, singing, swinging priest of nearby San Isidro Catholic Church (See our Worship chapter). The minute the music starts,

the dance floor fills to the edges with men and women swaying their hips—some subtly, others wildly—to salsa, cumbia, merengue, and other Latin rhythms. This is tropical music, and when you're dancing to it, there's definitely a heat wave. Some couples actually know what they're doing. Many don't, but nobody cares. Everyone has fun. If you want to know how it's really done, show up an hour before the show for free dance lessons from 8 to 9 PM. Saturdays and Sundays at Club Alegría often feature *norteño* music, best described as Mexican cowboy music. During the week, the club occasionally books popular national acts—everything from rock, blues, and rhythm and blues to alternative, and country and western. Past performers have included Marcia Ball, Beausoleil, Bo Diddley (who lives in Albuquerque), Joe Ely, Beau Jocque and the Zydeco High-Rollers, Leon Redbone, Michelle Shocked, the Marshall Tucker Band, and many others. Show prices range from $5 to $25, depending on the act. Pretto y Parranda will cost you five bucks. It's a steal, and you'll probably even lose weight in the bargain by shaking it up on the dance floor. For those who'd rather shoot pool than dance, there are two $1 tables at the back of the club, conveniently located right next to the bar. There's plenty of free parking behind the club in a well-lighted lot with security. Club Alegría is open from 8 PM to 1:30 AM on Wednesday, Friday and Saturday and any night featuring a national act. Sunday hours are from 8 PM to midnight.

Cowgirl Hall of Fame Bar•B•Q and Western Grill
319 S. Guadalupe St.
• (505) 982-2565

The Cowgirl is a highly popular restaurant, bar, and mini-museum as well as an entertainment space for music, comedy, and improv theater. As you might expect from its name, the theme is Western with a capital W. The walls and mantels of the front room are filled about to capacity with all sorts of western knick-knacks and memorabilia, including rodeo crowns, covered wagon lamps, graphic old calendars, ads and magazine covers, early movie posters, new and used cowboy boots, spurs, and even a certified aerosol can of "Bullshit Repellent" behind the bar. The bar itself is a copper-topped half-rectangle made from barn board planking with some barstools constructed from tractor seats. Resting their boots on the iron footrest are real cowboys, urban cowboys, artists, bankers, cooks, doctors, EMTs, farriers, furriers, good ol' boys, and jus' plain folks. This room also serves as the smokers' dining room as well as the stage for free live music that might be blues, folk, country and western, or rock 'n' roll. You can hear the music in the large non-smoking dining room in the back whose glittered walls feature dozens of black and white archive photos of honorees inducted into the original Cowgirl Hall of Fame, now located in Fort Worth, Texas. In summertime, musicians often play on the spacious, attractive front patio from 9 PM to 1 AM. Food wise, the Cowgirl specializes in "deep Southwestern barbecue with a twist." In winter, the restaurant opens its Mustang Grill—reserved for private parties in the summer—to diners looking for a tonier atmosphere. See our Restaurants chapter for details. The Cowgirl stays open Monday through Friday until 2 AM and Sunday until midnight.

El Farol
808 Canyon Rd.
• (505) 983-9912

Located on chic Canyon Road, El Farol is as much a fixture in Santa Fe's nightlife as the Plaza is in the city's day-life, though the 400-year-old Plaza has a few years on El Farol. Established in 1968 in what was previously La Cantina del Cañon, the bar at El Farol is in a beautiful old adobe building that dates back to 1835. Look closely at the wooden floor and you'll see spots worn down by four decades of flamenco dancing. (Prior to 1959, the floor was dirt.) The front of the building is framed by an inviting old porch with pillars and *vigas* and, in summer, spills over with patrons. The inside is dominated by the murals of Alfred Morang, who traded artwork for drinks at La Cantina del Cañon as well as other Santa Fe bars. Many artists have frequented La Cantina, and later El Farol, largely because of its location in the midst of one of Santa Fe's most well-known artistic enclaves. As a result, it has always been a hip establishment, attracting an eclectic clientele, even today. You'll find well-known artists, actors, and other luminaries drinking with carpenters and farriers, secretaries and CEOs, and all variety of wannabes.

Famed for its inviting atmosphere, El Farol consistently runs neck-and-neck with the Pink Adobe Dragon Room Bar (see entry in this section) as the "friendliest bar" in the *Santa Fe Reporter's* "Best of Santa Fe." Some people come to drink and socialize, others to listen to music that's as eclectic as the patrons including blues, country, flamenco, folk, jazz, klezmer, and even the occasional belly dancing act. The bar is relatively small, but that has never stopped patrons from wearing out the floor yet few millimeters with whatever dancing suits the music. Live entertainment commands a cover charge of $2 to $5, depending on who's playing. The sounds tend to spill into El Farol's adjacent restaurant, famous for its *tapas* and Spanish cuisine (see our Restaurants chapter). The bar is open daily until 2 AM except Sunday, when it closes at midnight.

El Paseo Bar & Grill
208 Galisteo St.
• (505) 992-2848

Smack in the heart of downtown Santa Fe, El Paseo Bar & Grill beckons strollers to wander in and relax over a few brews and free live music—especially in summer when it's front window is open and the music and laughter and clinking of glasses sifts out into Galisteo Street. Although El Paseo is a relatively new saloon with only a few years under its belt, it already has that worn-in feel of a neighborhood bar. Its clientele is a mixture of ages and backgrounds including young service industry workers and older, well-heeled professionals who like to come in for a drink and some socializing after work, rugby players chilling out after a game, trustfunders and slackers alike looking for a haven from the world, and assorted other types drawn to El Paseo's friendly, boisterous atmosphere. During the week, El Paseo offers various drink specials to go with the variety of sounds: $1 Tecate beers on Tuesday, which is open mike night for singers and songwriters; $2 drafts on

INSIDERS' TIP

Until just a few years ago, Santa Fe still had "blue laws" on the books, which banned sales of packaged liquor on Sundays, certain holidays, and Election Day until after the polls closed. Although most of the arcane liquor laws have been struck off the books, the Election Day prohibition still stands. Nor can you buy packaged liquor on Christmas or Thanksgiving, so plan ahead if you're hosting a party or plan to bring wine to one you're attending. With those exceptions, you may buy packaged liquor every day, supermarkets included, between 7 AM and midnight Monday through Saturday and noon to midnight on Sunday.

Wednesdays when KBAC radio (see our "Media" chapter) tapes New Mexico rock 'n' roll, R&B or blues bands for playback on the air; just jazz on Thursday with $2 "oil cans" of Fosters; and rhythm and blues on Friday—dancing and all—despite the small space.

El Paseo serves a wide selection of microbrews on tap from throughout the Southwest, including some brewed locally and quite a few from Colorado. It also offers daily food specials from a full menu, which offers traditional pub fare as well as northern New Mexican dishes. For those of you who like to smoke your Havanas in the comfort of a warm room instead of being banished to the outdoors, this is a cigar-friendly saloon. In fact, there are plans afoot to sell cigars behind the bar. El Paseo stays open Monday through Saturday until 1:30 AM and until midnight on Sunday.

Espiritu
731 Canyon Rd.
• (505) 820-2226

Tucked among the galleries near the top of Canyon Road, Espiritu not only has darned good gourmet pizzas, but it's among the top venues in Santa Fe to hear live jazz—and in a smoke-free environment to boot. Espiritu's cabaret, which adjoins the fauna filled restaurant, has become home for cabaret vocalist Chris Calloway and her trio. The daughter of legendary jazz singer and dancer Cab Calloway—who made famous such songs as *Minnie the Moocher* and *Hi-De-Ho*—Chris croons, caresses, and belts out songs with a voice that alternates between honey and whiskey. Don't miss her on Friday and Saturday, when she performs two shows nightly. Guest performers have included jazz legend Mose Allen; flutist Herbie Mann, who lives in Santa Fe; and contemporary jazz musicians such as Eddie Daniels, Patricia Barber, and Alan Pasqua. Espiritu features a weekly singer's showcase for new vocalists and hosts frequent jam sessions. The cover charge generally ranges from $5 to $15—more for big names. The bar serves cocktails, wine, and beer, including imports and microbrews. Espiritu is open until 9 PM Monday through Wednesday and 10 PM Thursday through Saturday. Its sister restaurant on St. Michael's Drive is a dining establishment only.

Evangelo's Cocktail Lounge
200 W. San Francisco St.
• (505) 982-9014

Don't let the Harleys in front intimidate you. Evangelo's Cocktail Lounge is a friendly neighborhood bar with a mixed, youngish clientele that runs the gamut from bikers to bankers. Only one block west of the Plaza, Evangelo's practically owns the corner of West San Francisco and Galisteo Streets, attracting scores of tourists in summer who find themselves drawn to the lounge's walls of open windows and the crowd spilling out on to the street, day and night. Interestingly enough, the boisterous bar co-exists happily with several bookstores in the immediate vicinity and some rather pricey jewelry and clothing boutiques. During winter, Evangelo's belongs to the locals, who appreciate the nightly drink specials, including $2 domestic beers, $2.50 imports (of which there are over 30), the selection of Greek drinks including Metaxa and Ouzo, and the downstairs pool tables at 50 cents a game.

Regardless of season, weekends at Evangelo's are always a fun, happening time with live rock 'n' roll and rarely a cover. On New Year's, Fiestas, and other special events, you'll have to cough up $5 or so to get in the door, a small price indeed to behold the odd mixture of Polynesian, Greek, and Santa Fe decor. But it works, lending a unique personality to the bar, which has been featured in *The New York Times*, and other national dailies as well as in newspapers and magazines in Sweden, Norway and Japan.

Evangelo's first opened its doors in 1971 when Evangelo Klonis, a Greek immigrant and American World War II hero, decided to branch out from his restaurant business on the Plaza. Today his son, Nick Klonis, runs the bar. He attributes the popularity of Evangelo's to its being "the only bar left in Santa Fe where you can go have a drink, meet friends, have a good time, and not be pretentious." A number of Santa Fe bars would surely dispute the "only" in that sentence, though the rest is undoubtedly true. Evangelo's is open until 2 AM Monday through Saturday and until midnight on Sunday.

La Fiesta Lounge
La Fonda Hotel, 100 E. San Francisco St.
• (505) 982-5511

Located in the attractive Spanish/New Mexican-style lobby of Santa Fe's most historic hotel—legend has it that a *fonda*, or inn, has existed on that same corner since 1610—La Fiesta Lounge is a welcome haven for both the weary and the wired, a place to relax over a beer or a margarita or to dance 'til you drop. Whether you lean toward country and western, ranchero or Latin jazz, La Fiesta offers top quality live entertainment nightly, most at no charge. They include Bill and Bonnie Hearne, a local country and western duo transplanted from Austin who have achieved national prominence of late. They usually play La Fiesta Lounge on Wednesday and Thursday nights. The lounge also attracts a crowd of regulars on Monday and Tuesday nights when Yoboso—a four-piece band with congas, keyboard, drums, bass and vocals—plays salsa, marimbas, merengue, cumbias and other Latin sounds. Friday, Saturday and Sunday nights in the lounge feature Sierra, which plays country and western, Tex-Mex, ranchero and a variety of other regional music. For mellower sounds, visit the lounge during happy hour when Javier Padial plays Spanish classical guitar. La Fiesta Lounge is open Monday through Thursday until 11:30 PM, Friday and Saturday until 12:30 AM and Sunday from until 11:30 PM. From May to October, take time to sip a summer cocktail and view incredible sunsets in La Fonda's outdoor Bell Tower Bar on the hotel's fifth-floor roof.

LobbyBar
Hotel Loretto, 211 Old Santa Fe Tr.
• (505) 988-5531

The LobbyBar in the casual, upscale Hotel Loretto has two faces. Monday Night Football is a sacred event in the cozy lounge, a time when locals and guests sit back in overstuffed sofas and chairs, eyes glued to a 60-inch television tuned in to the game. Anyone who tampers with the dial does so at great personal risk. The rest of the time, the plush, comfortable LobbyBar offers free entertainment including a solo guitar player and vocalist for Friday and Saturday happy hour (5 to 8 PM) and contemporary Latin dance music on Friday and Saturday night from 9 PM to midnight. The LobbyBar attracts primarily locals on weekends and a mixture of residents and visitors the rest of the week. Among the attractions is a large fireplace, a ceiling decorated with hand-painted wood carvings and a track lighting system with which patrons are welcome to adjust. The bar serves sandwiches, salads and appetizers as well as seasonal drink specialties such as hot toddies and alcohol infused coffee drinks in winter, iced drinks in summer. The LobbyBar is open nightly until midnight.

Mañana Restaurant & Bar
Inn of the Governors, Alameda St. at
Don Gaspar Ave.
• (505) 982-4333

Located off the lobby of the Inn of the Governors a few blocks south of the Plaza, Mañana is popular among locals, tourists, and hotel guests because of its nightly "piano bar"—in quotes because you can't actually sit around the grand piano, though you can still hum along to your old favorites—and the giant picture windows that open up to the world outside. Its horseshoe bar, copper-topped tables and Southwestern-style decor create a warm ambiance enhanced in winter with a crackling fire in a large kiva fireplace, perfect after a day on the slopes, especially with a hot toddy or coffee drink. You could enjoy a full dinner from the adjacent restaurant without ever leaving the bar. Or you can choose from a large selection of appetizers before heading while you're waiting for your table. Mañana attracts primarily the over-30 set, including lots of professionals and a fair share of lawmakers during the legislative session. The atmosphere is friendly, though not for cigars. Sports fans can watch games on the bar's 32-inch television when there's no live entertainment. Mañana is open until 1 AM Monday through Saturday and until midnight on Sundays.

Mine Shaft Tavern
2846 N.M. 14, Madrid
• (505) 473-0743

For a taste of an honest-to-goodness mining-town bar, don't miss the Mine Shaft Tavern in Madrid, about 25 miles south of town. Once a booming coal mining village, Madrid (pronounced MAA-drid, oddly enough), turned into a ghost town after it fell on hard times in the 1950s. Two decades later, the village began enjoying a renaissance with the arrival of artists and craftspeople who converted many of the old buildings into galleries and shops, turning Madrid into a sightseeing mecca. The Mine Shaft, however, remains today pretty much as it was in 1946 when Oscar Huber, who owned the mining company that literally owned the town, built the tavern for the coal miners who worked for him. Perhaps the biggest change in the intervening half-century is the absence of the rail cars that used to travel directly from the mine to the bar.

The tavern is a cavernous rustic room with a 50-foot lodgepole-pine bar—the longest stand-up bar in New Mexico, the owners claim. On the wall above the fireplace hangs a buffalo head. Above the bar are paintings depicting Madrid's history. Gracing the wooden walls throughout the tavern is an eclectic collection of cowboy paraphernalia, Native American items, railroad memorabilia and mining accoutrements. The clientele is as eclectic as the decor. You'll find everyone from artists and old hippies to cowboys and Indians, Vietnam vets and yuppies, tourists and commuters, skiers and couch potatoes and even a few ghosts. Except for the ghosts, they come to drink, eat what the owners claim is the best burger west of the Mississippi and to dance to live music on the weekends. The Mine Shaft is open daily until about 10:30 PM on weeknights and until midnight or thereabouts on the weekend.

The Ore House on the Plaza
40 Lincoln Ave.
• **(505) 983-8687**

The Ore House bar and restaurant has both tourist and local appeal, not only because of its location, but also because of its large, heated balcony overlooking the Plaza. Inside, the decor is strictly Southwestern with *vigas* on the ceiling, *saltillo* tile on the floor, and a *kiva* fireplace in the restaurant. The Ore House offers free live music Thursday through Sunday. There's no official dance floor, however, customers occasionally annex the balcony for dancing. Bar patrons can order from an appetizer menu or from the restaurant's main menu, which features steak, seafood, and highly creative Southwestern specialties. If you have a favorite wine, it's a good bet you'll find it among the Ore House's award-winning selection. For those of you who like your liquor hot and sweet with a jolt of caffeine, try some of the Ore House's specialty hot coffee drinks such as the Choc' Full O' Nuts with Godiva chocolate liqueur and Amaretto; a Downtown Mexican Coffee with tequila and Kahlua; or an Ore House Mocha with Godiva liqueur, Bailey's Irish cream and either coffee or espresso—all topped with whipped cream. If those aren't enough to get your sweet tooth aching, there's the Balcony Snuggler, with peppermint Schnapps, dark Crème de Cacao, hot chocolate, and whipped cream. The Ore House also serves hot buttered rum, which appeals to the *après* ski crowd, and makes more than 40 different Margaritas with a variety of tequilas. For the connoisseur, the bar serves a $100 shot of tequila, though you'd probably want to drink that one straight. The Ore House closes at 11 PM Sunday through Thursday and midnight or 12:30 AM on Friday and Saturday.

Palace Restaurant and Saloon
142 W. Palace Ave.
• **(505) 982-9893**

The Palace is a Santa Fe institution. Around since 1835, the restaurant and bar got its start under the proprietorship of Doña Gertrudis Barcelo—a.k.a. Doña Tules ("Miss Trudy") or La Tules—who opened a gambling saloon that remained popular until her death in 1853. The details about what happened to the saloon after ter La Tules' died are sketchy, but popular myth has it that it was a bordello at some point in its post-Tules history. Fueling that belief was the discovery in 1959—the year the owners broke ground for the present establishment—of a horseshoe shaped door-knocker whose left side has been fashioned into a high-heeled, fishnet-stockinged leg in profile, complete with bare buttocks, and containing the inscription, "Burro Alley—1873." Burro Alley is a historic lane at the west entrance to the Palace that once housed a burro pen along with the old saloon. Today, the Palace is widely popular among locals—it certainly gets its fair share of tourists, too—who appreciate the fine bartending of Alfonso Alderette, a Cuban national who has been tending bar at the Palace for years and who often wins the title of "Best Bartender" in the *Santa Fe Reporter*'s annual "Best of Santa Fe" poll. When he gets to know you, he'll often surprise you with a drink he feels suits your taste or your personality. But it's not just Alfonso's drinks that are so good, it's his contagious laugh. Patrons also appreciate the atmosphere, which is unapologetically dark and, well, bordello-like, complete with red flocked wallpaper and pictures of reclining nudes. Many regulars, including state legislators when they're in session, hold court in the bar, which features a 140-year-old mahogany bar with a brass foot rail. There's often live background music—either someone playing the grand piano in the back of the room or perhaps a duet in front. Drinks are generous and there's always a dish of mixed nuts handy. If you need something more substantive, you can order upscale pub fare off the bar menu—a superb prime rib sandwich *au jus*, perhaps, or maybe some truffle duck mousse paté, escargot in garlic ragout or a truly delicious burger. You may also choose from the restaurant menu (see our Restaurant chapter for details). The Palace is open daily until midnight and, except for Sunday, sometimes until 1 AM.

Paolo Soleri Outdoor Theater
Santa Fe Indian School, 1501 Cerrillos Rd.
• **(505) 256-1777 or (505) 989-6300**

Designed by and named for the famed Italian architect who apprenticed under Frank Lloyd Wright, Paolo Soleri is an open-air amphitheater that's as popular among performers—Tracy Chapman, B.B King, k.d. lang, Lyle

Lovett, Ziggy Marley, the Neville Brothers, Steel Pulse, and James Taylor, to name just a few—as it is among audience members, who get to listen to world class music under the Santa Fe stars. It's also the only venue in town that gets such big name acts, which, for obvious reasons, are limited to summertime only. Tickets, available at various Ticketmasters around town, can be pricey, though, especially by Santa Fe standards—usually in the $ 30 to $50 range. But we've rarely heard anyone grumble that their money was ill-spent after a concert here. For more information, call the number listed above for Big River Productions which, along with Evening Star Productions, has been producing these concerts since 1978. You can also check Evening Star's website at www.eveningstar.com. or *Pasatiempo* (see *The Santa Fe New Mexican* in our "Media" section) for performers, times, and prices.

The Paramount
331 Sandoval St.
• (505) 982-8999

This is Santa Fe's only true "disco" where men and women put on their spandex and dance, dance, dance. The Paramount—which readers of the *Santa Fe Reporter* consistently vote the best nightclub in town—caters largely to gays and lesbians, but everyone is welcome provided they have a healthy attitude. You'll see everything here from dreadlocks to drag queens and lawyers to lipstick lesbians. Some come to strut their stuff—perhaps in a G-string or something equally scanty, and even on stage if they so desire—others play the voyeur. Whichever end of the spectrum you find comfortable, Paramount is definitely not for the peevish.

Every night of the week brings a different brand of entertainment at The Paramount, and often a different crowd. Mondays feature a dance party called "Soulscape" in the club's chic Bar B lounge while Tuesday is swing night for all ages with Lucky's Belvedere Lounge. Wednesday is one of the hottest nights of the week with "Trash Disco," a retro chic dance party featuring music from the 70s and 80s and fashions to match. Thursdays sizzle with salsa, cumbia, and merengue. Weekends are also big nights at The Paramount, as you might expect: Fridays are a revolving showcase for big name acts, both local and national, while Saturday is OXYGEN night with resident deejay Oona, who often hosts Grammy Award-winning guest deejays from across the country and across the globe. For the country and western set, Sundays are sacred. They South By

Southwest, a hugely popular local band with a large and loyal following that follows them from dance hall to dance hall. They arrive dressed to dance and dressed to kill—the men in jeans, western style jackets, cowboy boots and hats, and even the occasional neckerchief, women in boots and "country chic" dresses or skirts, sometimes adorned at the waist with *concho* belts. What you wear is less important than your enthusiasm for the dance, whether it's the two-step or the western waltz. It's truly a sight to behold such a dandied up crowd genteelly gliding around the dance floor. In addition to voting the Paramount the best nightclub in Santa Fe two years in a row, locals named the club the best place to dance, hear live music and meet singles.

For a toned-down—and downright tony—experience, stroll into The Paramount's adjoining Bar B. From the moment you walk in the door, it's as if the clock has turned back some 60 or 70 years. You half expect to see Nick and Nora Charles sipping martinis and swapping repartees or chatting wittily with one of the bartenders at the small, curved bar whose lighting from below gives it an other-worldly quality. Indeed, everything about the Bar B screams the 1930s and '40s—from the stylish, art deco chandeliers and faux leopard skin chairs and bar stools right down to the understatedly elegant mica shades on the table lamps. The entertainment often fits the bill, too, with live jazz, rhythm & blues or a down-tempo version of whatever's playing in The Paramount's main room. Bar B also features an occasional evening of drag bingo as well as experimental theater and comedy. Regardless of the genre of entertainment, you can keep to the retro mood with Bar B's award-winning Vesper—Stolichnaya vodka and Bombay gin à la James Bond, i.e., shaken not stirred—or one of its famous Cosmopolitans made with Absolut Citron, Triple Sec, a splash of cranberry juice and a preserved sweet bing cherry. Whatever you're drinking, don't be afraid to ask for your favorite brand. The lounge takes pride in its extensive premium bar, which has won second for "best bar" two years running in the *Santa Fe Reporter*'s "Best of Santa Fe."

The cover charge at The Paramount or Bar B normally falls in the $3 to $15 range, though some acts might command more. A Paramount Pass allows bearers to get in free most nights and entitles them to drink specials and access to the club's $1 pool tables. The Paramount and Bar B are open daily from 5 PM to 2 AM, midnight on Sundays.

The Bell Tower Bar provides an opportunity to catch stirring sunsets from the top floor of the La Fonda Hotel.

Pink Adobe Dragon Room Bar
406 Old Santa Fe Tr.
• (505) 983-7712

Attached by a driveway to the Pink Adobe, a fine New Mexican restaurant that's been a staple in Santa Fe since 1944, the Dragon Room is an extremely popular bar among locals, especially the 30-and-older crowd, who enjoy its informal atmosphere and warm camaraderie—not to mention the help-yourself popcorn from the movie theater-style popper near the door. Just a few doors down from the State Capitol building, the Dragon Room also packs in state lawmakers during the legislative session. It's no wonder *Newsweek*'s 1988 international edition named the Dragon Room one of the top 10 bars in the world. Readers of the *Santa Fe Reporter* consistently the lounge as among the friendliest bars in town and the best place to meet singles.

Regardless of why you're here, you'll find service with a smile from a professional wait staff that keeps regulars coming back and welcomes newcomers. But the warmth is not merely metaphorical. During winter, the bar keeps two fireplaces burning, one each in the front and back rooms, making it a truly cozy place for a beer or a bourbon. There are often so many bodies here, however, that the fireplaces can be superfluous heat-wise, though they're always a welcome addition to the ambiance. There's still more fire on Christmas Eve when a traditional *luminaria* (bonfire) burns on the sidewalk in front of the bar for *farolito* viewers and passersby to warm themselves. The Dragon Room even burns its own effigy of Zozobra (see our Annual Events chapter) during Fiestas. The rest of the year, the lounge features live music until 9 or 10 PM. While you're listening to the music, glance around the room at the paintings by the recently deceased owner, Rosalea Murphy, who also hand-painted the tables. And do try some of the food from the bar menu which, while admittedly limited, is creative with such offerings as gypsy stew—a hearty one-dish meal made with chicken, tomatoes, onions, and pepper. If you're in a decadent mood, try the escargot or the artichoke with dipping sauce. And by all means, do try the Pink Adobe restaurant, which serves superb New Mexican style food. (See our Restaurant section for details). The Dragon Room is open Monday through Saturday until anywhere between midnight and 2 AM and Sundays until midnight. Parking is at a premium in the lot behind the bar. We recommend you park in the state office building lot across the street.

Second Street Brewery
1814 Second St.
• (505) 982-3030

A relatively new addition to Santa Fe's food, drink, and night scene, Second Street Brewery is a locally owned brew pub with some of the best beer in Santa Fe. But don't take our word for it. The brewmaster, originally from Oregon, has won numerous awards at the Great American Beer Festival in Denver—the Superbowl of beer festivals in the United States. The food is darned good, too, with such traditional English pub fare as fish and chips (the real thing, served with malt vinegar), shepherd's pie, chicken pot pie, and London broil, as well as classic American dishes including burgers, Philadelphia cheese steaks, Reuben sandwiches, and a number of creative vegetarian offerings. Second Street offers live entertainment—anything from folk and Celtic music to good old rock 'n' roll—throughout the week in an attractive yet unpretentious setting. The crowd ranges in age from college students to septuagenarians. While it's located a bit off the beaten path—in other words, neither downtown nor on one of Santa Fe's main drags—Second Street Brewery is well worth the extra time to get there. The pub is open daily until midnight. The kitchen serves food until 10 PM.

The Staab House Lounge
La Posada de Santa Fe, 330 E. Palace Ave.
• (505) 986-0000

The Staab House Lounge is an oh-so-genteel and ver-ry Victorian drinking establishment that's extremely popular among locals, in part because it's remarkably unpretentious despite its rarefied decor. That's because the lounge doesn't pretend to be anything more than it is—a lovely grouping of old-fashioned, recently refurbished parlors with brocade loveseats and settees, leather chairs, square fireplaces—all merely steps from the bar room. Some of the parlors feel like smoking rooms, others like a maiden aunt's sitting room. In any you'd feel just as comfortable drinking tea as tequila. The latter is in good supply in the barroom, whose centerpiece is a graceful Victorian cherrywood bar with a brass foot rail.

Under new ownership, La Posada still receives visits from Julia Staab, whose ghost manifests itself fairly frequently in and around the bar with flying glasses, swinging chandeliers, banging in the lounge bathroom, and even a curl of smoke by a particular chair, as if someone were sitting there holding a lighted cigarette. She can't object much to an expanded liquor selection that now includes up to 30

INSIDERS' TIP

Santa Fe restaurants and bars that participate in the county's Designated Driver program will provide soft drinks on the house to a table's designated driver. Some establishments even offer the entire table free snacks.

tequilas, a larger collection of single malt scotches, and extensive collection of cordials, ports, brandies, and cognacs. Nor is it likely she'd be upset with the upscale bar menu featuring such items as smoked trout- and shrimp-stuffed rellenos or chips with avocado salsa. But one can only wonder how many more glasses flew off the shelves when the old Staab library turned into a piano lounge, the Rose Room; the original Staab family dining room turnedinto a private dining room and wine cellar; and the Mason Room transformed into a cigar lounge complete with humidor. The Staab House Lounge is open daily from 11 AM until at least 11 PM or midnight and, except for Sundays, even later if business warrants remaining open.

Summerscene
Santa Fe Plaza
• (505) 438-8834,
(505) 983-2261

During the summer, some of Santa Fe's most popular and accessible nightlife is on the Plaza—and it's free. It's called Santa Fe Summerscene, a community program partially funded by the City of Santa Fe Arts Commission and staged by a nonprofit group of the same name. Summerscene is an outdoor nightclub without walls or alcohol. People of all ages are welcome to dance under the stars to everything from bluegrass to opera. Very occasionally, Summerscene brings in a dance troupe to perform. Performances take place on Tuesdays and Thursday from noon to 1:30 PM and again from 6 to 8 PM beginning the last week in June and continuing through the last week in August. We recommend you dine al fresco with a picnic lunch or supper.

INSIDERS' TIP

You're considered legally drunk in New Mexico if your blood-alcohol level is 0.08 percent or greater for adults. New Mexico is coming down hard on people who drink and drive. Weekend and holiday drivers have a good chance of encountering unannounced police checkpoints, where officers may test a driver's alcohol level if they suspect drunkenness.

Tiny's Restaurant & Lounge
1015 Pen Rd.
• (505) 983-9817/1100

As Insiders, we would be remiss if we didn't include Tiny's Restaurant and Lounge in our Nightlife chapter. Located in an unassuming little strip mall that also houses a pizzeria, a bakery, and a locksmith, Tiny's isn't merely a dining and drinking establishment, it's an ex-perience—especially in the lounge. Let's get one thing out of the way first. The New Mexican food at Tiny's is authentic and it's darned good. But we've dealt with that in our Restaurant chapter. Here we're concerned with only two things: drinking and dancing—and we don't mean Coca Cola and rock 'n' roll.

As the restaurant nears closing, the lounge takes on a life of its own with an older crowd that really knows how to cut a rug, whether they're listening to country and western or old standards. They put their younger brethren to shame, dancing non-stop, arm-in-arm, with honest-to-goodness certified dance steps from swing to salsa to two-step. The atmosphere is, well, kind of bare bones with bright lighting, Formica tables. a television set over the bar and another above the dance floor. But when the musicians play, nothing else matters. The performers and the audience have a ball! And it's contagious, even if neither the music nor the dancing is your usual style. While you're sitting one out, take a gander at the hundreds of decanters around the bar and the restaurant. The barkeep, a professional who has been tending bar for nearly three decades, will tell you they belonged to the original owner, Tiny Moore, who opened the restaurant and nightclub in 1950 and began collecting the bottles in the late '50s. Tiny's son-in-law, Jimmie Palermo, has been running the restaurant since 1959, which is why you'll hear many old-timers call the place Jimmy and Tiny's. But he's kept the restaurant in Tiny's name—and kept the decanters, too—as a tribute to his father-in-law, who died in 1984. Tiny's stays open until 2 AM Monday through Saturday. Sunday hours are from 11 AM to 6 PM. You can hear live music Friday and Saturday nights.

Vanessie of Santa Fe Restaurant and Piano Bar
434 W. San Francisco St.
• (505) 982-9966

Vanessie is a very sophisticated, very upscale, and surprisingly very comfortable place to have a cocktail, whether you're sitting at the bar watching the bartender mix magic or sitting around the grand piano singing to timeless standards. *Esquire* magazine named Vanessie one of the best piano bars in America. Indeed, it's a perennial favorite in Santa Fe, especially among largely well-heeled professionals of all ages, though older locals who have been sitting around the piano for the past couple of decades have claimed Sunday as "their" night. While every night is special at Vanessie—this is a place where you truly feel you're stepping out in style—New Year's Eve is an elegant gala affair for which people fly in from around the world to listen to music, drink champagne and dine on Texas-size servings of prime rib. All of Vanessie's classic American cuisine—steak and seafood, salads, baked potatoes, its famous onion loaf, cheesecake, etc.—come in obscenely large portions, beautifully presented (see our "Restaurant" chapter for details).

Behind the bar, Vanessie keeps a computer file with hundreds of drink recipes, many with creative—and occasionally risqué—names such as a "slippery nipple (a.k.a. "Butterbaby"), made from Baileys Irish Cream and butterscotch liqueur. While you're sipping your drink or digging into your 16-ounce steak, you're likely to spot Jack Palance or perhaps Harry Connick, Jr., Gene Hackman, Barbara Hershey, Neil Sedaka, Tom Selleck, or any number of stars who either live in Santa Fe or frequent the restaurant when they're in town. Vanessie is open nightly until 2 AM, except Sundays and winter weekdays when it closes at midnight.

INSIDERS' TIP

Too tipsy to drive home from a restaurant or bar? Ask the manager or bartender about SafeRide Home. He or she will summon a taxi, which will deliver you safely anywhere in Santa Fe County at no charge.

Teen Scene

Sadly, Santa Fe doesn't have much to offer in the way of nightlife for teenagers. The under-21 set is pretty much left to its own de-vices to create evening entertainment. For many, that usually means hanging out in the Plaza or skateboarding until curfew when the weather permits. The rest of the time, teens like to frequent the malls or the movies. There are the occasional "raves"—all-night warehouse teen parties with non-stop dancing, usually advertised by word-of-mouth. For teens who aren't into—or allowed to attend—raves, here are a few other suggestions:

Silva Lanes Bowling Center
1352 Rufina Circle
• (505) 471-7250

Silva Lanes is great evening entertainment for all ages, including teens, who like to go here on weekends or even on week nights when school is out. And the price is right, too, starting at $2.75 a game plus $1 to $1.75 to rent shoes. See our Recreation chapter for more. information.

Warehouse 21
1614 Paseo de Peralta
• (505) 989-4423

Founded in 1990 as CCA (Center for Contemporary Arts) Teen Warehouse, Warehouse 21 helps the void of youth-oriented activities in Santa Fe for 10- to 21-year-olds. During the day, the organization sponsors free after-school workshops and seminars in the arts—from knitting and puppetry to acting, deejaying, guitar, photography, silk-screening, and tai chi. It also forges apprenticeships, internships, and mentorships. At night, Warehouse 21 produces shows and dances most weekends, including comedy shows, theater, and performance art. Music ranges from alternative rock to blues, jazz and punk. Days and times vary, so call ahead of time or check *The Santa Fe New Mexican*'s weekly entertainment section, "Pasatiempo."

Shopping

The most difficult decision about shopping in Santa Fe is where to start. The clusters of stores and the shopping plazas in the downtown area can lure even the most shopping-resistant travelers. The city's unique shops delight visitors and draw return local business. Often located in former homes, many of the specialty shops downtown and on Canyon Road are built around pleasant courtyards with fountains and well-tended gardens. Of course, like Any Town, U.S.A., Santa Fe also has malls, chain stores, a flea market, and outlets to fill all kinds of shopping needs.

In this chapter we describe Santa Fe's main shopping areas, followed by a listing of specialty stores. We couldn't possibly list all of the fine places to shop, but we've done our best to include a representative sample. Santa Fe has such an eclectic and plentiful arts and crafts market that we've included those types of stores in their own chapter, Regional Arts, and in the "Galleries" section of our Arts chapter. Retail businesses can change quickly, so don't be shy about checking out a shop or boutique that may have opened since we finished this guide.

Cash, credit cards, and traveler's checks are welcome in most of the area's specialty shops, malls, plazas, boutiques, and shopping centers. Most shops are open from 9 or 10 AM until 5 or 6 PM Monday through Saturday, and some are open Sunday afternoons.

Santa Fe is a great place to find items you might not be able to buy at home—locally made crafts, chile-based products, or cookbooks that specialize in the cuisine of the region. The city is an active artistic community, and many shops carry handmade work at affordable prices. And, of course, there's no reason to go home without a Santa Fe T-shirt!

LOOK FOR:
- Shopping Areas
- Malls
- Specialty Shops
- Bargain Shoppping
- Yardsales
- Bookstores
- Books
- Specialty Foods and Health Products

Shopping Areas

Downtown/The Plaza

The Plaza sits between San Francisco Street, Old Santa Fe Trail, Palace Avenue, and Lincoln Avenue, and the Downtown area stretches two or three blocks from the Plaza in all directions. You'll find city-owned parking lots on Water, San Francisco, and Marcy Streets. There's limited on-street parking, and some private lots are available for shoppers.

As the last stop along both el Camino Real and the better-known Santa Fe Trail, the Plaza has been a shopping paradise since the days when wagons unloaded their imported treasures here. If you time your visit right, you can still shop here on days when the city hosts outdoor arts and crafts shows or during Spanish or Indian Market (see our Annual Events chapter). The Plaza pulses with activity, especially in the summer, hosting community events of all shapes and sizes, some with parades and music. And the Plaza's shady benches offer an ideal place to take a break while shopping.

We think the best guide for shopping in the Plaza area is to follow your nose. Stroll along the streets just off the Plaza: Marcy Street, Galisteo Street, Don Gaspar Avenue, Water Street, Shelby Street, and others. It's easy to stumble into the most delightful places and find just what you weren't looking for sweetly beckoning. The nooks and crannies in this easily walked area can provide days of just-poking-around entertainment.

In this central location you won't find many "deep discounts." Downtown shops pay steep rent for the privilege of high accessibility to visitors.

The overall tenor of Santa Fe's downtown area is galleries, American Indian goods, and tourist souvenirs such as T-shirts and coffee mugs, but you'll discover an interesting variety of upscale merchandise here. The best place to start your downtown shopping expedition is the Plaza area itself

If you want American Indian wares, the most intriguing spot for buying is under the *portal* of the **Palace of the Governors on Palace Avenue** (see our Attractions chapter). Here you can purchase directly from the Indian artists. Another first-rate place for Indian merchandise is **Packard's Indian Trading Co.**, on the corner of Old Santa Fe Trail and San Francisco. The sales staff at this long-established business can give you a great education in Indian-made items.

Next to American Indian treasures and souvenirs, clothing stores dominate downtown. You'll find many chic and original clothing stores as well as Santa Fe representatives of national chains. For an idea of the variety, look for casual **Chico's**, 135 W. Palace (and at two other downtown locations) and elegant, playful **Susan K's**, 229 Johnson St. near the O'Keeffe Museum. **Mimosa**, at 52 Lincoln Ave., has sold elegant Santa Fe-style clothing for more nearly 20 years.

Santa Fe Dry Goods, 53 Old Santa Fe Trail, has been a steady fixture in downtown merchandizing, and features tasteful shoes, scarves, and clothing for men and women.

A few nationally known stores usually found in malls add to the downtown. You'll find places like **Banana Republic**, 123 W. San Francisco Street, for the casual look; **Gap**, 78 E. San Francisco Street, for the young look. In Lincoln Place, a shopping complex at 130 Lincoln Avenue you'll find most of the familiar with **Talbots** for the stylish look; **J.Crew** for the sporty look; **Eddie Bauer** for the outdoor look; and **Ann Taylor** for the professional look. But keep looking—Santa Fe's downtown/Plaza area has much more shopping ahead.

If you're in the market for souvenirs, visit **Dressman's Gifts**, 58 Lincoln Avenue, just across the Plaza from Packard's. This longtime business is geared for the tourist who wants to

take back some inexpensive reminders of Santa Fe. You'll find Indian jewelry, a large selection of T-shirts, and some suprising items you probably weren't expecting. Trust us.

Just down the street, **Ortega's on the Plaza** has sold fine Indian jewelry for 25 years. You may find a pot by the famous San Ildefonso Pueblo potter Mariá Martinez here. Other downtown shops with Indian goods are the **Eagle Dancer**, **Virginia Trading Post**, **Desert Blossom**, **Pueblo Traders Inc.**, and the **Santa Fe Indian Trading Company**.

As an example in what shopping downtown is all about, let's take an imaginary walk west from the Plaza on West San Francisco Street. You'll pass coffee shops, galleries, small boutiques, and major retail business.

You'll find the **Plaza Mercado Shopping Plaza** at 112 W. San Francisco Street. This complex spans a solid half-block and includes an interesting variety of shops and restaurants arranged over three stories. **Nambé Foundry** has a shop here selling the beautiful, silver-colored metalware they've been designing and manufacturing since 1951. You'll find everything from heavy baking dishes to Christmas ornaments, and you can also buy seconds. The Mercado complex includes the **Santa Fe School of Cooking**, with its shop that has all you need to make your own New Mexican recipes. **The White House**, 112 W. San Francisco Street, is an intimate woman's shop with sleek dresses, blazers, and slacks all in white or light beige.

But don't stop now (unless you want to). Also on West San Francisco you'll also the upscale women's clothing store **C.P. Shades** and **The Collected Works Bookstore**. Need a chocolate break? Head for the **Rocky Mountain Chocolate Factory** at 217 W. San Francisco. The wafting aroma of freshly made candy flows all the way out to the sidewalk. What an enticement!

Origins, 135 W. San Francisco, has been around for 25 years and feels a little like a folk art/textile museum, showing dolls, puppets, jewelry, and wearable art from around the world. You'll find clothing from Africa, Pakistan, India, and Thailand as well as creations by local designers. Just walking in makes you feel elegant.

Around the corner on Don Gaspar Avenue you'll find more shops including **Spirit of the Earth**, 108 Don Gaspar, which features jewelry by Tony Malmed, clothing, and collectibles. And don't miss the eclectic **Doodlet's Shop**, 120 Don Gaspar. This long-time local business has wonderful gifts collected from around the world.

More surprises await you the next street over, Galisteo, which runs parallel to Don Gaspar to the West. At 223 Galisteo you'll find **Lucille's**, a store packed full of those long flowing skirts you see Santa Fe women wearing, with blouses, vests, jackets, and more to mix and match. **The Sheepskin Overland Company**, 217 Galisteo Street, a mainstay in the area, carries the most luscious coats and bags and rugs out of sheepskin and many different leathers. **Artesanos Import Co.**, 222 Galisteo Street, displays an intriguing pottery selection and other items for home decorating and remodeling in Mexican and Southwestern style. Next door, **Harry's**, 202 Galisteo, carries fine men's clothing and shoes as well as some great items for the ladies.

Shady Marcy Street, a block north of the Plaza has numerous attractions. At 101 W. Marcy, the **Design Warehouse** has been around nearly two decades, offering comfortable and affordable home furnishings and kitchenware. At the **Marcy Street Card Shop**, 75 W. Marcy Street, you can choose from more than 500 postcards and then move on to cards for birthdays, anniversaries, getting well, first communions, retirements, and more. **Gloriana's Fine Crafts**, 55 W. Marcy Street, delights bead lovers with jars and bags and strands of every shape, size, and color.

For a look at wonderful hand-carved folk-art animals, take a step into **Davis Mather's Folk Art Gallery** on at 141 Lincoln Avenue. Be cautious: The fanciful wooden snakes beg to go home with you!

Another place not to miss downtown is a Christmas shop, called **The Shop**, 116 E. Palace, selling the most ornaments this side of the North Pole, many in the Pueblo Indian style and many handmade.

Sena Plaza
121-135 Palace Ave.
• **no central phone**

Although it's downtown, Sena Plaza deserves mention all its own because of its special shopping ambiance. This former family home, one block east of the Plaza on Palace Avenue, offers a variety of shops as well as a first-class restaurant. There is limited complimentary parking available behind the building. It's easy to find Sena Plaza: a photogenic wooden portal covers the sidewalk running in front. Originally part of a 1697 land grant, the place still has that old Spanish ambiance. The

two-story building was once the gracious home of the Senas, a prominent family. Myriad rooms run under long portals, all facing an enclosed, beautifully landscaped patio.

The original adobe rooms now house galleries and specialty shops with a diversity that can keep you browsing for hours. **Goler Fine Imported Shoes** tempts the most sophisticated feet with snazzy shoe styles, and **Taos Mountain Candles De Santa Fe** offers an array of shaped, colored, and scented candles. The cleverly named **Soap Opera** carries a wide range of fragrances, lotions, massage oils, and items for the bath. **Gusterman Silversmiths** shows a fine collection of original affordable jewelry. The long established women's clothing store Zephyr, specializes in unique, contemporary fashions.

Susan's Christmas Shop gets the prize for best use of a tiny space. You'll find ornaments from around the world with a nice selection of handmade Southwestern items. The shop changes its name to suit the season, becoming "Susan's Valentine Shop" or "Susan's Easter Shop" with merchandise appropriate to the coming holiday.

Canyon Road

Best known for its galleries, this scenic, narrow street is worth a visit. Canyon Road begins just east of Paseo de Peralta and runs roughly parallel to Alameda Street. You can walk from downtown hotels. Historically important and currently quaint, the road began as a trail down from the mountains. People would lead their burros this way into town to sell or trade their wares.

The area teems with Santa Fe charm: thick adobe walls draped with vines, sidewalks shaded from large cottonwood trees, lovely gardens, and a mix of residential and commercial uses—shops, restaurants, and galleries. You can easily spend a day moseying along the road, taking your time, learning how to slow down Southwestern style.

Canyon Road is famous for its galleries that line the street for blocks and blocks (see our Arts chapter). Interspersed, you'll discover clothing, jewelry, leather and other specialty stores. Most of the retail shops cluster near the intersection of Camino del Monte Sol. A walk of just a few blocks on either side of this corner will take you to most of the stores.

Gypsy Alley, 708 Canyon Road, can lure even the most leg-weary tourist. This once dusty place, now lined with flower beds brimming with color in summer, has been renovated into a row of shops (and of course more galleries).

In an area where many shops and galleries may only survive for a seasons, **Judy's Unique Apparel**, 714 Canyon Road, deserves its name for longevity as well as the quality of the merchandise. Judy's has offerings for both men and women; colors and textures of the clothes will make you want to linger, touch, and try things on.

Artisan/Santa Fe, 717 Canyon Road, an art-supply store packed to the gills, has what you need to satisfy your own creative urge. The owners boast that Georgia O'Keeffe used to come here for all her paints and brushes. They've been in the same location for more than 20 years. A small parking lot for patrons is on the west side of the building.

Desert Son, 725 Canyon Road, another old-timer on this street, has been selling belts, buckles, hats, and silver buttons for 20 years. Its custom boots are snazzy to say the least. Wind down a path and find **Canyon Road Pottery**, 821 Canyon Road, a store filled with handsome glazed and originally designed contemporary pots.

Visitors know the **Canyon Trading Post**, 670 Canyon Road, as "the belt place." In business at this location for more than two decades, the store welcomes shoppers with the distinctive scent of rich leather. In addition to a selection of 18,000 belts, you can buy tin ornaments, cactus lamps, and antler chandeliers.

If you can't walk from your hotel to shop Canyon Road, first try parking along the main road and side streets. A few stores have small lots for patrons, and a public lot is available at the intersection of Canyon Road and Camino del Monte Sol.

Guadalupe Street
Between Agua Fria and Garfield Streets.

This shopping area, also an easy walk from downtown, attracts locals and visitors.

In the '70s, Guadalupe Street was the place where several counter culture types tried their hand at retail—often selling their own arts and crafts—fitting their shops in among the garages and upholstery shops. Renovation has been extensive, and Guadalupe is now a street of the modern commercial age. You'll find restaurants, a movie theater, a historic church, and a train station. During the summer, the Farmers' Market is nearby (see our Attractions chapter) and the **Farmer's Market Store** operates year-round. You'll also find a variety of original shops selling everything from furniture to fancy underwear.

Vendors sell their crafts on the north side of the Plaza across from the Palace of the Governors.

Photo: Don Strel

One of the area's trademark businesses is **Cookworks**, 316, 318, and 322 Guadalupe Street. Here, you'll find all those new gadgets every cook worth her salt longs for, as well as pots, skillets, and kettles for your serious cooking. The buyers keep up with the latest trends—if it's "in" they've got it. The store has been so successful, it's expanded to two other outlets on the same street. **Cookworks Gourmet**, 318 Guadalupe Street, sells coffees, baking mixes of all sorts, jellies, special cooking oils, and pastas. **Cookworks Tableware and Gifts**, 322 Guadalupe, offers a great selection of high-end dinnerware and flatware. Exquisite salad bowls, soup tureens, and pitchers in deep colors and rich styles imported from Italy, France, Morocco, Mexico, and Peru will take your breath away.

Another landmark business is **The Flower Market**, at Guadalupe and Manhattan Streets. Wonderful fresh-cut flowers by the stem are the specialty here. The market shares its building, an old house, with **Cardrageous**, a place to find unusual greeting cards of all kinds as well as wrapping paper, journals and gifts.

On the corner of Guadalupe and Read Streets at 435 S. Guadalupe is **Placita Guadalupe**, where the **High Desert Angler** sells everything an angler needs. Kicks, right next door, sells everything a dancer needs. **Street Feet** carries everything a woman needs—shoes, clothing, and accessories. (Well, not quite everything . . . .)

For a decade, the **Rio Bravo Trading Co.**, 411 S. Guadalupe, has specialized in "American Indian and Western relics—collectible cowboy stuff," to use the words of the owner. Saddles, spurs, hats, chaps, Indian jewelry, and Old West posters abound.

When strolling along Guadalupe Street, be sure to take a slight detour up Garfield Street to **Fairy Queen/Wild Things**, 316 Garfield Street. This is the place where dresses hang from the porch. Inside is stuffed with goodies. The owner, Tobi, says her place is "totally hip—with antique, vintage, ethnic, trippy clothing." She's been in business in Santa Fe for many years, and customers come here for the best of period pieces.

Santa Fe Pottery, 323 S. Guadalupe Street, had a Guadalupe address before the street was

---

INSIDERS' TIP

It's Christmas all year around at The Shop, 116 E. Palace Ave. and at Susan's Christmas Shop, 115 E. Palace. The Shop is the larger of the two, Susan's the cozier. You'll find ornaments galore here along with nativity scenes, lights, garlands, gingerbread people, angels, and more.

---

a shopper's paradise. The owners started the business back in the 1960s as a studio and watched it grow into a showcase of strictly contemporary American crafts. The shop specializes in dinnerware and one-of-a-kind ceramics by local potters. You'll find colorful, whimsical pieces here, things that are useful as well as pretty, ranging in price from less than $10 to several hundred. They will gladly take special orders.

The shopping compound at corner of Guadalupe and Montezuma Avenue, 328 S. Guadalupe Street, has several stores of interest including **Southwest Spanish Craftsman**. This stylish furniture store has served Santa Fe residents and their visitors since 1927. Shoppers with a longing to live in Santa Fe will find everything here they need in Southwestern carved furniture. Next thing you know, you'll have to buy a house to put it in!

Next door, **Paper Unlimited** offers a rich supply of cards, ribbons, gift boxes, and bags. **Horizons, The Discovery Store**, a nature-focused shop that's been around since the early 1980s, has telescopes, compasses, nature kits, bird feeders, and toys, all with a scientific bent. Locals shop here for unusual, practical gifts for the nature lovers. Children love this place, too. And be sure to be lured into **Allure**, a high-end lingerie shop with an interesting variety of the feminine and sensuous. On the north side of Southwest Spanish Craftsman, **Form and Function** has sold lights and an impressive variety of lampshades for more than a decade. **Chico's** clothing has another outlet here, and the well-appointed windows tempt you inside. **Le Bon Voyage**, whose owners advertise themselves as "the Bag Ladies," has a great assortment of travel accessories—portable alarm clocks and coffee warmers and the like in addition to luggage. A bookstore specializing in travel guides, **The Travel Bug**, conveniently adjoins them. Travel Bug hosts free presentations by Santa Fe travelers or guest speakers about unusual travel destinations. Watch the newspapers for information.

Limited metered parking is available along Guadalupe Street. Some of the stores have free parking in very small lots. If you can walk from your hotel—and you can if you're staying downtown—that's your best bet.

Villa Linda Mall on the southside of Santa Fe offers several anchor storesand a variety of smaller stores. It also houses two complexes of movie theatres.

Photo: Don Strel

Sanbusco Market Center
500 Montezuma Ave.
- **(505) 989-9390**
- **www.sanbusco.com**

From Guadalupe Street, the Sanbusco Market Center is just a block to the west. The building that now houses these shops originated in 1882 as part of Santa Fe's warehouse district. Renovation in the 1980s made it a bright addition to Santa Fe's shopping options. Complete with restaurants and a spacious across-the-street parking lot, Sanbusco is home to professional offices, small, upscale shops, and, expected in the fall of 2000, Santa Fe's first Cost Plus World Market. You can also get a bite to eat at restaurants here or nearby that share the parking lot.

Boutiques come and go here, but **Bodhi Bazaar** is a longstanding tenant. This women's store offers natural fiber clothing, and the linen and cotton attracts a strong local clientele.

Another local favorite is **Teca Tu**, a store for pets. The owner is fond of both cats and dogs, and her array of bowls and brushes, beds, collars, fancy dog blankets, and leashes gives you plenty of choice for your pet. There's also a small collection of books and cards and soft, cuddly stuffed animals and cute dog vests.

On Your Feet is a fun places to shop for shoes. They carry Wolky and Sebago and other name-brand footwear. The tasteful displays feature shoes on slatted willow crates or set on old Spanish tables. The **New Territory**

Leather shop carries an amazing selection of fine leather bags, Western jackets, and vests. Its tapestry coats definitely say "original." The merchandise changes with the seasons. **Victoria Cacti & Orchids** offers a nice selection of succulents, orchids of all colors and varieties, cacti to suit all tastes and other plants and accessories. The **Reel Life/Orvis Outfitter** sells flyfishing supplies, and also offers classes. **Borders Books** has one of its trademark stores here, complete with books of all sorts, magazines, music, videos, and a cafe.

Malls

While some longtime locals may complain that malls lack Santa Fe style, they have to acknowledge the convenience malls offer. Where else can you use your J C Penney, Sears, and Dillard's cards? Parking is no problem here, and you'll find specialty shops with Santa Fe style as well as national chains. At all three of Santa Fe's major malls, you can buy New Mexican foods, spices, and other treats as well as American Indian arts to remind you of your Santa Fe vacation. In addition to these, the city has other shopping centers, usually anchored by a grocery store, with auxiliary shops mostly geared toward local business, offering those who live nearby convenience and a chance to chat with their neighbors over the produce.

DeVargas Center Mall
564 N. Guadalupe St.
• **(505) 982-2655**
• **www.devargascenter.com**

At the corner of Guadalupe Street and Paseo de Peralta, DeVargas Center is Santa Fe's oldest mall. Relatively small at 246,000 square feet and easy to negotiate, DeVargas is anchored by Albertson's Food Center on the northeast side and Office Depot on the southeast side. You'll find a post office, movie theaters, a candy shop, restaurants, antique stores, pharmacies, shoe stores, jewelry stores, and several women's clothing boutiques.

Stag Tobacconist, one of the mall's longest-established merchants, sells pipes, canes, postcards, and, of course, special kinds of tobacco. **Las Cosas Kitchen Shop** offers a great variety of pots and pans and many nifty gadgets for the cook. You'll find top-of-the-line, restaurant-quality merchandise. Be sure to ask about the cooking classes. **Radio Shack**, **Ross Dress for Less**, and **Christine's** bridal and tuxedo shop are here, along with **Roberto's**, a small shop that sells delightful imported dresses with exotic flavors. You can shop for jewelry at **Zale's** or **Chavez Fine Jewelers. Gameco** offers a place for people, mostly teens, to play "Magic" and other games and to buy game cards and supplies. A large **Hastings** has a wide selection of music, magazines, books and videos, and a coffee bar. On the north end of the mall, the **Mail and Parcel Center** will ship your packages home. You can stop at **Rachel's Bakery** counter for a sweet treat or head to **Starbucks** or **Baskin Robbins 31 Flavors** ice cream and yogurt store. DeVargas Center is surrounded by a large parking lot regularly patrolled by security officers.

Villa Linda Mall
4250 Cerrillos Rd.
• **(505) 473-4253**

With more than 80 shops, this is Santa Fe's largest mall, the place where teens hang with their friends and folks buy their back-to-school clothes. South of town at the corner of Rodeo and Cerrillos Roads, Villa Linda is a great central place to get all those normal, necessary things. Of course some fun, unnecessary things can be found here too. Villa Linda has a food court, two six-screen movie theaters, and a video arcade.

Anchors include **Sears** on the southwest end, **J C Penney** on the east, **Dillard's** on the north, and **Mervyn's** on the west. Between the big department stores, scores of shops offer accessories, jewelry, shoes, sports equipment, software, home furnishings, gifts, and books.

Clothing stores are scattered throughout the mall **Lerner New York** carries women's styles at reasonable prices. You can walk into **Victoria's Secret** and fulfill that slinky fantasy. **Lane Bryant** offers women's casual apparel. **Para Niños** is exclusively for young children and carries some hard-to-resist dressy outfits. **Miller's Outpost** and **County Seat** carry clothing with a cowboy touch for men and women, as does the **Western Warehouse**, a store to help you dude up with pearl-button vests, jeans, shirts with fringe, fancy skirts, and boots. Sports Mania has sports caps galore, jackets, T-shirts, and jerseys—all with your favorite team's name. Walk into **Gadzooks** and feel like you've stepped out of Santa Fe and into a shop on some big-city block. The clothing here is designed for the fast lane. The front end of a VW bug in the center of the store sets the tone. Teens will love this place!

Villa Linda has shoe stores galore include **Payless ShoeSource, Lady Foot Locker, Athletic Express, Foot Locker,** and **Footaction USA**.

Two interesting accessories shops in the mall are **Afterthoughts** and **Claire's Boutique**. Both carry a delightful array of inexpensive things for the hair and ears. For more jewelry, try **Zales** and **Jewel Time**.

In the center of the promenade running the length of the mall are booths, carts, and islands, those pagodas that offer everything from seasonal specialties like Christmas ornaments or Halloween costumes to fancy reading glasses, lighters, knives, and specialty foods. At

> ## INSIDERS' TIP
> Santa Fe is a good place to find Nambé ware—beautiful, practical and decorative items which have won awards for their design. Made from a metal alloy containing no silver, lead, or pewter, Nambé possesses the beauty of sterling combined with striking durability of iron. The lustrous alloy does not crack, chip, peel, or tarnish and can retain heat and cold for hours. Nambé has outlets at 924 Paseo de Peralta and 104 W. San Francisco St. and a Web site, www.nambe.com.

Southwest Expressions, you can pick up Indian kachinas, Christian angels, and Spanish concha belts.

For gifts, *Trevors* has country throw pillows and silk flowers. **Chili Pepper Emporium** sells Southwestern ristras, wreaths, and jars of cactus jellies and jams. The **Coach House** offers candles, beads, T-shirts, and gift bags. At **Joni's Hallmark** store you'll find cards, photo albums, pens, and more. Need to get your glasses adjusted? **Lenscrafters** has a large store here.

The post office has a substation in the mall that makes mailing all your packages easy. A **Walgreen Drug Store** is on the northwest side. The **General Nutrition Center**, for all your health needs, sells supplements and supplies. You'll also find a branch of the **Santa Fe Public Library** here. Because the storefront space is small, the library calls it a Bookstop or even a "twig."

Like malls everywhere, Villa Linda also has a food court with a variety of offerings. If you want something a little quieter, the Mall also offers **Luby's Cafeteria** and **Ceci's Pizza**.

Constructed in 1985, Villa Linda encompasses 573,000 square feet and is the fifth largest mall in the state. A large parking lot surrounds the entire mall, and security officers are always on duty, sometimes patrolling on horseback.

Santa Fe Premium Outlets
8380 Cerrillos Rd. (at I-25)
• **(505) 474-4000**

This out-of-the-way outlet center offers about 40 factory stores selling a wide variety of name-brand merchandise at a discount. You'll find clothing, shoes, luggage, gifts, and housewares. There also are also some purely local shops. The stores all open onto a central outdoor patio, and are all on one level. You can get a bite to eat at the café here too.

Some of the name-brand stores are **Levi's, OshKosh b'Gosh, Brooks Brothers, Jockey, Jones New York, Bugle Boy,** and **Liz Claiborne.** The clothing available ranges from casual to professional to conservative for both men and women. Tastefully displayed items make it hard to resist the deals. You'll also find clothing for children.

Sissel's—Fine Indian Jewelry, Pottery and Kachinas—carries just what the sign says and lots of it. With a sharp eye you can get some good buys. Try **Zale's** jewelers for diamonds. The **Peruvian Connection** sells textiles from that South American country.

For home furnishings, among the stores you'll find are **Dansk, Springmaid,**

Wamsutta, and **Harry and David.** Looking for shoes? Try on styles from **Bass, Nine West,** or **Famous Footwear.** Top-quality luggage and leather goods are available at **Coach** and **Samsonite/American Tourister.** There's plenty of parking here, and the views of the mountains are marvelous.

Specialty Shops

Here's a brief introduction to some of Santa Fe's more interesting shops.

Antiques and Home-Decorator Items

Antique Warehouse
530 S. Guadalupe St., #B at the Railyard
• **(505) 984-1159**

This store's name isn't trendy; it really is a warehouse in Santa Fe's original warehouse district. You'll find more than 600 sets of doors and shutters, along with gates and windows from Mexico. Telephone inquiries are welcome, but it's fun to come and look. It's closed on Sunday.

Artesanos Imports Co.
222 Galisteo St.
• **(505) 983-1743**

Mexican imports are the specialty in this store, which has been in the same location for more than 30 years. The quantity and variety are dazzling. Artesanos has lights, tile, glass, and pottery items, some stored in a large outdoor lot. You'll find genuine pigskin furniture as well as hundreds of types of tile for the floor, bath, or countertop. Artesanos says it is the largest distributor of Mexican tile in the United States. It's closed on Sunday.

Foreign Traders
202 Galisteo St.
• **(505) 983-6441**

Heavy carved tables and other furniture, glassware of all sorts, and other items imported from Mexico are in abundance at Foreign Traders. This shop was originally established in 1927, just across the street from its present location, by Tony Taylor, Lady Bird Johnson's brother.

Jackalope Pottery
2820 Cerrillos Rd.
• **(505) 471-8539**

You can spend hours here poking around

and looking at all the imported pots, figurines, weavings, clothing, and decorations. Jackalope's international collection of goodies occupies several large buildings, including one that looks like an old church. "Folkart by the truckload" is their motto! You may find music on the patio in the summe and you can get a bite to eat at the Jackalope café. This company, which began in Santa Fe in 1975, now has several other outlets and a catalog business.

El Paso Import Company
Design Center, 418 Cerrillos Rd.
• (505) 982-5698
This business has been around many years, carrying an extensive selection of old and new furniture shipped in from Mexico. Tables, wardrobes, bed frames, and other large items are a specialty.

Christopher Selser, American Indian and New Mexican Antiques
830 Canyon Rd.
• (505) 984-1481
You can pick up some good deals here among the top-quality wares. The collection is well displayed to show the antiques and art to optimum advantage. Selser, a national expert on Indian antiques, has been a featured appraiser on a PBS special.

Southwest Spanish Craftsman
328 S. Guadalupe St.
• (505) 982-1767
In business since 1927, this store specializes in heavy Southwestern carved chairs, tables, beds, and sofas. The look that characterizes the selection is one of carefully constructed solidity. You'll also find Southwestern tinwork here. It's closed on Sunday.

Stephen's, A Consignment Gallery
2701 Cerrillos Rd.
• (505) 471-0802
Voted "Best Place to Buy Used Furniture" by the readers of the *Santa Fe Reporter*, Stephen's includes antiques and art among its treasures. The large store is packed with all sort of items, from mirrors and dressers to knickknacks of every type imaginable. They also will appraise and buy either single items or estates.

The Santa Fe Look— Women's Apparel

The following list of shops, by no means complete, provides a few places where you can find the items you might need to complete your Santa Fe look—flowing skirts, concha belts, boots, velvet or satin blouses, and turquoise jewelry. Also included are some places that sell wearable art. If your favorite isn't here, just let us know, and we'll try to include it the next time.

Back At The Ranch
235 Don Gaspar
• (505) 989-8110
Satisfy your passion for unique cowboy boots at this downtown store. In business 10 years, this shop carries beautiful hand-made boots by Rocketbusters, Stallion, and Lucheesi. If you don't see a design that grabs you, you can order custom-made boots to express your own style. You can also find "Santa Kleese" Christmas boots (they're really stockings) by Rocketbusters, in a variety of designs; our favorites are Day of the Dead and the Virgin of Guadalupe.

Judy's Unique Apparel
714 Canyon Rd.
• (505) 988-5746
A fire in the fireplace welcomes visitors to Judy's on winter days. The lovely clothing—from casual to evening wear, from practical to romantic, from pampering silks to linens to cozy jackets—occupies several rooms. You'll find hats, belts, and unique jewelry patterned after antiques.

The prices are such that locals remain among Judy's longtime clientele and recommend this place to friends and visitors. There's also a menswear section and plenty of places for non-shoppers to wait comfortably. The staff is helpful and will let you wander through the store at your own speed. Judy Broughten started the business in 1978 as a painted-T-shirt shop in one of the rooms Judy's now so nicely occupies.

Hopalong Boot Company
3908 Rodeo Rd., just West of Richards Ave.
• (505) 471-5570
This place, off the beaten

INSIDERS' TIP
If you travel from Santa Fe to Taos in the summer or fall, you'll notice roadside produce vendors selling farm-grown fruits and vegetables from the backs of their trucks or fruit stands. Stop and see what's for sale. You might find ristras (bunches of chiles strung together), honey, and other treats too.

track and out of the high-rent district, bills itself as "A First-Class Second-Hand" Western Shop—where you'll find "broken-in" cowboy boots, vintage clothing, and collectibles. Hopalong has something for cowgirls and cowboys of all ages. Look for the big purple double gates with the rabbit mural, you can't miss it! Open 10 AM to 4 PM, Monday through Saturday.

Lucille's
223 Galisteo St.
• (505) 983-6331

A front-porch sale rack welcomes shoppers here. Lucille's specializes in Santa Fe style and its creative variations, with plenty of flowing skirts, dresses, silk T-shirts, blouses, and tops. Natural fibers are the rule, with merchandise imported from India and elsewhere. Shoppers like the ranges of styles, colors, and sizes—including clothing that looks great on full-figured women. Lucille's also has a tempting collection of earrings and fanciful necklaces from Africa and India. The shop carries sweaters all year long.

Maya
108 Galisteo St.
• (505) 989-7590

If you're shopping for something different, the fashions hanging outside this downtown store are sure to catch your eye. Indoors, you'll discover two stories packed with folk art and fashion. In addition to easy-to-wear blouses, pants, skirts, dresses, and vests imported from around the world, you'll find all sorts of jewelry, belts, and hats. This eclectic shop also offers international folk art including carvings from India, milagros—charms from Latin America that are said to aid in healing—and a wonderful assortment of Day of the Dead figures from Mexico.

Origins
135 W. San Francisco St.
• (505) 988-2323

This is one of those stores that compels you to go inside—even if there's absolutely nothing you think you need. For starters, the windows skillfully combine art and marketing, displaying the clothing and accessories in combination with folk art for eye-catching results. Among the plentiful merchandise are creations especially designed for this shop, wearable art by local and world-renowned artists from elsewhere in the United States and Europe. Evening wear and the more casual fashions include styles and sizes that look great on every woman, not just the size 2s. The jewelry, including 18- and 24-karat gold, and objects from around the world will demand your attention. Watch for sales!

Just off the Plaza, this ice cream shop is probably the most patronized store in town.

Photo: Don Strel

Pat Peterson's Blue Rose
101 W. Mary
• (505) 989-9594

Don't miss this shopping treasure chest, now in a new location with a street-front show window. If you're looking for handmade, one-of-a-kind fashions, seek it out. Blue Rose represents 25 New Mexico fabric artists on consignment, with creations ranging from handwoven vests and shape-flattering jackets to lacy, flowing skirts that make you want to dance flamenco. Peterson has been in business since 1990 and has added a catalog to her marketing tools.

Purple Sage
110 Don Gaspar Ave.
• (505) 984-0600

Handwoven clothing is a specialty here, and you'll find styles from Santa Fe chic to elegant silks. Ask about the sueded rayons, designed and handmade by a local fabric artist. Be sure to take a look at the nice assortment of handbags. Contemporary hand-woven jackets and shawls in rayon chenille are one of Purple Sage's trademarks. Another is the colorful handblown glass that makes this store not just another fashion shop. More than 35 glassblowers show their wares, including many perfume bottles, platters, and vases. You'll also find gift items along with an impressive assortment of kaleidoscopes. For non-shoppers, Purple Sage has couches, magazines, TV, and candy. Can't decide? Take home a catalog for phone orders.

Sign of the Pampered Maiden
123 W. Water St.
• (505) 982-5948

In business since 1968, this tasteful women's clothing and accessory store specializes in what the owner aptly describes as comfortable, beautiful clothing you can wear every day. You'll find her inventory on the romantic side, with plenty of velvet, lace, and silk. Granddaughters, moms, and grandmothers can shop together here—and each take home something they'll like. In addition to clothing, this downtown shop also offers a variety of accessories to complement the fashions.

INSIDERS' TIP

For unique candy, visit Senior Murphy Candymaker in two locations. The piñon concoctions, including piñon brittle, piñon fudge and a piñon log, are hard to find outside of Santa Fe. The candy is made at the Santa Fe factory, but the candymaker will gladly ship it for you as long as the weather isn't too hot. For a special, non-melting treat, try the red chile peanut brittle or the chile jelly.

Spirit of the Earth
108 Don Gaspar Ave.
• (505) 988-9558

In business in Santa Fe for more than a decade, Spirit of the Earth sells clothing that could be described as wearable art and jewelry by designer Tony Malmed in gold with precious stones and festive opals. Malmed's bracelets, rings, necklaces, earrings, and the like are one-of-a-kind pieces, which means if you like it and it fits your budget, take it home because you'll never find it again. The fashions are soft and sensual in cut velvets, lace, and sueded rayons with a feminine flowing look. You'll find an abundance of color and luscious tactile fabrics. The sales staff knows how to be helpful without being pushy and are happy to help you make the right choice to complement your figure and coloring.

Bargain Shopping

Act 2
839 Paseo de Peralta, Suite A
• (505) 983-8585

At Act 2 you'll discover vintage and modern clothing, jewelry, and accessories. You might have to hunt for this shop—it's slightly off the beaten path—but it's worth the search. A consignment shop, Act 2 has great clearance sales.

Double Take
320 Aztec St.
• (505) 989-8886

This shop, on Aztec Street just off Guadalupe Street, labels itself "eclectic," with styles for men, women, and children. The items are carefully chosen and well displayed—you don't have to wade through junk. The management mixes a few new items with the old, and the layout makes going through the racks exciting. You'll also find shoes and other accessories. Double Take has two other consignment stores nearby. Double Take at the Ranch, 319 S. Guadalupe, features classic cowboy clothes and other Western items. At Double Take Hacienda, 317 S. Guadalupe, you'll find furniture and home accessories.

Santa Fe Premium Outlets, south of Villa Linda Mall features name brand outlets at discounted prices.

Photo: Don Strel

Encore 505
505 Old Santa Fe Tr.
• (505) 983-5055

This upscale consignment shop is in the Kaune's Market Center. You'll find nice women's clothing and colorful and unusual accessories to make you feel like a million dollars. Encore has been in business since 1981, and is only open afternoons.

Goodwill Industries Store
927 Baca St.
• (505) 983-7156

Careful shoppers can discover old favorites or something they've always wanted to read in the book racks at Goodwill. The sales are hard to beat. This store, unlike many thrift stores in Santa Fe, tends to have furniture. Proceeds benefit Goodwill and its rehabilitation work.

Hospice Center Thrift Store
1303 Cerrillos Rd.
• (505) 995-9901

Recently reinstalled at a new location, Cerrillos Rd. at Baca, the Hospice originally established its thrift store as a fund raising/community service program in 1993. The store's bright, big space features clothing, furniture, artwork, housewares, appliances, and more. You find all sorts of secondhand treasures— some of the nicest things you'll see in the recycled world. Items for sale have been appraised, so you know you're getting your money's worth. The funds raised help the nonprofit Hospice Center continue its highly respected work with the dying and their families.

Open Hands Thrift Store
851 W. San Mateo Rd.
• (505) 986-1077

Open Hands' well-stocked store has lots of choices in clothing and household goods at good prices. The donations and sales receipts go for a worthy cause—operation of the adult day care and other programs for the elderly.

St. Vincent De Paul Thrift Store
1088 Early St.
• (505) 988-4308

At this granddaddy of an operation, affectionately known as La Tiendita, you'll find racks and racks of goodies, all at low prices. Operated by a Catholic auxiliary, money raised through this business benefits Santa Fe's poor.

Salvation Army Thrift Store
1202 Camino Carlos Rey
• (505) 473-7735

This is Santa Fe's largest thrift store. You'll find everything from furniture to wedding dresses and racks of clothing for the whole family. The Salvation Army's programs provide crucial help to Santa Fe's children and poor families. In addition to holiday meals, one popular project provides back-to-school clothing for children.

Pueblo of Tesuque Flea Market
U.S. Hwy. 84/285,
7 miles north of Santa Fe
• **(505) 660-8948 or (505) 983-2667**

This huge flea market sits on Tesuque Pueblo land northwest of Santa Fe, right next to the Santa Fe Opera in one of those wonderful Santa Fe juxtapositions. The market is open Friday, Saturday and Sunday from 8 amto 5 pm May to December. Connoisseurs say this is one of the best markets of its kind around. You'll find whole sections of antiques, imports from Africa, Bali, South and Central America, vintage and handmade clothing, and more. Depending on the season, you might be able to take home watermelons, apples from northern New Mexico orchards, or fresh flowers. You'll see tables by commercial dealers who specialize in Indian jewelry, rainsticks, or collectible fishing tackle as well as neighbors who've pooled their junk and brought it here rather than having a yard sale. Nonprofit agencies rent space to sell donated treasures and raise a few bucks. It's easy to spend hours and money as you amble among the stalls. If you get hungry or thirsty, you can buy what you need from the concession stand. Parking and admission are free.

Yard Sales

Santa Fe residents love their yard sales. If you read *The New Mexican* any weekend during the summer, you're likely to find scores of yard sales, estate sales, multifamily sales, garage sales—junk and treasure recycling opportunities by any name you can think of. Clothing, toys, furniture, books, treats, and necessities for baby, exercise bikes, antiques, plants, knick-knacks, and all those things you don't know how you managed to live without await you. Saturday is the big sale day, but some folks extend buyers the opportunity to visit Sunday as well.

The best selection goes to those who arrive early, but please respect the "no early birds" advisory. Real bargains can come to those who shop late, waiting until the seller would rather make a sweet deal than repack his or her items to save them for another sale or donate them to Salvation Army or Open Hands. While May

INSIDERS' TIP

Santa Fe Village, a collection of shops at 227 Don Gaspar Avenue, includes some unusual offerings such as Keshi, a store that specializes in fetishes, or small carved animals, from Zuni Pueblo.

A "must visit" is the Tesuque Flea Market, voted one of the top 10 in the US. A visitor can find drums, garage sale booths, traders from Africa, and Indian jewelry.

Photo: Don Strel

The downtown area offers some of the finest clothing shops in Santa Fe featuring the latest in women's fashions.

Photo: Don Strel

through September is Santa Fe's prime yard sale season, you'll find a sprinkling of sales sooner and later in the year, depending on the weather. Take small bills and change; the seller will smile at you. Be sure to poke through boxes and bags—while families tend to display their best stuff, taste varies. And if you see something you like that you think is overpriced, make an offer. If the seller refuses, you can leave your phone number for him or her to call later if the item hasn't sold.

Bookstores— New Books

Ark Books
133 Romero St.
• **(505) 988-3709**
• **www.arkbooks.com**

Ark Books is a mainstay for New Age books and tapes, but the store has a good selection of material on self-improvement, anthropology, cultural studies, women's issues, and more. You'll find nice jewelry and stones as well as drums and tarot cards. Authors sometimes come here to speak and sign. The Ark, operating out of a converted home in a largely residential area, opened in 1980, survived a fire and came back bigger than ever.

Book Warehouse, Inc.
Santa Fe Premium Outlets,
8380 Cerrillos Rd.
(I-25 at Cerrillos Rd.)
• **(505) 473-5508**

You'll find discounts on already discounted books at the Book Warehouse. Good deals await in children's books, former bestsellers, big photo books, cookbooks, and more!

Borders Books & More
500 Montezuma in the Sanbusco Center
• **(505) 954-4707**

Like its sister stores, this Borders offers a lot of everything. You'll find a selection of fiction and non-fiction of the Southwest. You'll also find bilingual selections (English and Spanish predominate) and an assortment of periodicals. The store hosts a variety of special events, author talks and signings, weekend programs for children, and evenings with local musicians. You can get coffee and a light meal in the café.

The Collected Works Bookstore
208-B San Francisco St.
• (505) 988-4226

This store gets the prize for Santa Fe bookstore longevity; it's been in the same downtown location since 1978. You'll find healthy Southwestern and Indian sections as well as a good selection of nature, travel, and children's books in this easy-to-browse store. Local and regional authors sometimes sign here. The staff is great with special orders, and they will ship your orders.

Garcia Street Books
376 Garcia St.
• (505) 986-0151

This locally owned and operated bookstore has a wide variety of books and a great computer system that helps you find what you need. Book people work here, and they can answer your questions and recommend titles. The store is an easy stroll from Canyon Road. Garcia sometimes hosts autograph parties.

INSIDERS' TIP

Looking for well-made, comfortable, shoes that (surprise!) also look good? Walking on Water, 207 West Water St., a locally owned, one-of-a-kind store specializes in fine shoes for women and men. At this family-operated store you can find clogs, slippers, and shoes from Canada, England, Switzerland, France, and the good ol' U.S.A. The business also sells over the Web.

Hastings Books and Music & Video
2414 Cerrillos Rd. in College Plaza
• (505) 473-5775
542 N. Guadalupe St. in DeVargas Ctr.
• (505) 988-3973

In addition to the bestsellers and selections for kids, these stores carry good representations of books about the Southwest. Don't miss the clearance tables—you could find a treasure! You can rent videos, buy cards and magazines, and shop for CDs and tapes here too. The College Plaza store is the larger of the two.

Horizons —The Discovery Store
328 S. Guadalupe St.
• (505) 983-1554

Peruse an outstanding collection of nature books for children and adults in this science store. You'll find guidebooks galore, along with a nice assortment of globes, atlases, binoculars, and gifts for children and adults with an interest in the natural world around them.

Sanbusco Center, next to the railroad yards, houses a variety of shops, including Borders Book Store and a specialty pen shop.

Streetside vendors offer their wares to passing tourists. This merchant sells chile ristras.

Photo: Don Strel

La Fonda Newsstand
La Fonda Hotel, 100 E. San Francisco St.
• **(505) 988-1404**

How do they pack so much interesting stuff into such a small space? Especially designed for tourists, La Fonda has a collection of Southwestern books covering the most often requested titles. You'll also discover some unusual magazines as well as old favorites.

St. John's College Bookstore
1160 Camino de la Cruz Blanca
• **(505) 984-6056**
• **www.sjcsf.edu**

This store is a wonderful place to browse. As one would expect from a college that focuses on the "great books," you'll discover an excellent selection of the classics here as well as mainstream titles and more experimental literary offerings. While you're here, take a look at St. John's College's attractive campus.

Travel Bug
328 Montezuma Ave.
• **(505) 992-0418**
• **mapsofnewmexico.com**

This outlet specializes in travel books, maps, guides, travel journals, and has the complete USGS map series for New Mexico and Colorado. The store also has all the topographic maps of

New Mexico on CD ROM! You'll also find what they call "airplane books"—easy-to-read fiction you don't mind leaving at the airport.

Waldenbooks
Villa Linda Mall, 4250 Cerrillos Rd.
• **(505) 473-4050**

While your buying your vacation wardrobe, you can pick up a book or two to take along on your trip. At Waldenbooks you'll find all the best sellers, a nice section of regional books, an extensive travel section, and more. The convenient mall location makes this a popular weekend spot.

Books—Used, Rare, and Hard to Find

Blue Moon Books and Video
329 Garfield St.
• **(505) 982-3035**

In an old house turned bookstore, Blue Moon's books and rooms seem to go on and on—it's easy to lose yourself in the stacks. Not only will you find your way out again, but you'll also discover a great selection of videos to rent or buy, and a staff that knows the inventory. Spiritual traditions of the east and west, books on the occult, and books about film are among their specialties.

Books and More Books
1341 Cerrillos Rd.
• (505) 983-5438
A well-stocked, well-organized bookstore, Books and More Books offers pre-owned treasures in categories ranging from art to science. You can browse to your heart's content or ask the owner, a poet, for his recommendations on a specific topic.

Book Mountain
Used Paperback Exchange
2101 Cerrillos Rd.
• (505) 471-2625
This one-room space is crammed with paperbacks of all kinds, including some books you probably never heard of. You'll find a good selection of mysteries and romances as well as bestsellers, Westerns, and even comic books. You can pick up some inexpensive vacation reading and trade them in for something else when you're done.

INSIDERS' TIP

January is a great month for sales in Santa Fe. In addition to major savings on clothing, many shops selling Indian arts and crafts also reduce their prices with sales following the holiday buying madness.

Nicholas Potter
Bookseller
211 E. Palace Ave.
• (505) 983-5434
Proprietor and own Potter has made use of all the available space—and then some—to the delight of his established customers and newcomers who might chance on the store. A selective and savvy book dealer, Potter has been in the book business for some 30 years. Located in an old house on historic Palace Avenue, the store is inviting—a great place to spend a quiet afternoon.

Specialty Foods and Health Products

Santa Fe is home to two major national natural foods stores. The newest, Whole Foods (Cerrillos Road at Garfield), has liquor, including some hard-to-find micro-brewed beer, as well as all the produce, chemical free meats, non-animal-tested cosmetics, and bulk foods you'd expect at a store like this. Founded in

Irresistible marketplace items will tempt even the most frugal shopper.

Photo: Don Strel

The Farmers Market is a summer event where buyers can sample fruits and jams and treat themselves to coffee and sweet rolls.

Photo: Chris Corrie

Austin, Texas, in 1980, Whole Food is the largest national retailers of organic and organic foods. The other major player is Wild Oats, with Wild Oats Community Market, 1090 S. St. Francis Drive, and an Alfalfa's Market, 333 W. Cordova Road. Wild Oats is a quickly growing national enterprise that began in Colorado. All of these supermarket-size stores have extensive restaurant/deli sections, great salad bars, and places where you can settle in for lunch. Besides wonderful freshly baked bread, you can get vitamins, hair products, dairy products and dairy alternatives, fresh flowers, gift items, and goodness knows what else.

INSIDERS' TIP

Santa Fe shopping trips can be difficult to end...if you are planning a day out shopping with small children plan to bring strollers, backpacks and plenty of items to entertain.

Alfalfa's Market
333 W. Cordova Rd.
• (505) 986-8667

This supermarket-sized food store also has an extensive restaurant/deli and one of Santa Fe's best salad bars. You can buy treats to go or settle in for lunch. Besides chemical-free meat and veggies and wonderful freshly baked bread,

you can get vitamins, hair products, dairy products, and dairy alternatives.

Wild Oats
Community Market
1090 St. Francis Dr.
• (505) 983-5333

This big, clean, well-lit store is a cross between a mainstream supermarket and a health-food store. Everything exotic you need, like those little Chinese roots called for in some esoteric recipe, can be found here. The store has been a great carry-out food section and a place to eat in the store. The store frequently hosts workshops on various aspects of health and nutrition. Wild Oats is a quickly growing national enterprise that began in Colorado.

Here are some smaller, home-grown places we find of interest:

Herbs Etc.
1345 Cerrillos Rd.
• (505) 982-1265

Jars of dried leaves, stems, and flowers cover the shelves at Herbs Etc. You can find tinctures, oils, and infusions as well as herbs packed in capsules just like Tylenol. The people who work here can answer health questions from an alternative perspective.

Kaune Food Town
511 Old Santa Fe Tr.
• (505) 982-2629

This is a great place for the gourmet shopper. You'll find out-of-the-ordinary sauces and mustards and imported crackers and caviar to spread on them. Kaune's carries jars and cans of everything you need to fix that unique Asian, Italian, or otherwise one-of-a-kind meal. This locally owned grocery is packed with the unusual and exotic, but you can also buy milk, eggs, and, if you must, sliced white bread. It carries a fine selection of fresh meat and welcomes holiday orders.

Kaune's Grocery Co.
208 Washington Ave.
• (505) 983-7378

This store always offers some excellent buys on wines and spirits. It also has all the basics, fresh meat, and a nice assortment of fancy food. It's within walking distance to several downtown accommodations—a blessing for visitors staying downtown. Despite the names, the two Kaune's are not under the same management or ownership.

Kokoman Circus
301 Garfield St.
• (505) 983-7770

Many would argue that Kokoman is the closest thing Santa Fe has to a real stand-alone delicatessen. In addition to meat, cheeses of all sorts, olives, and the rest, Kokoman has a nice selection of uncommon beers, wines, and spirits as well as fresh bread and fine chocolates. You can relax and enjoy a drink, sandwich, a cup of soup, or a latte in the sunny dining room here or get your order to go. If you eat here, save room for dessert—they usually have at least half-dozen tasty things to choose from.

The Market Place Natural Grocery
627 W. Alameda St.
• (505) 984-2852

Santa Fe's oldest health-food store, The Market Place and its local ownership and management help it fill an important niche. This small alternative grocery (compared to Whole Foods or Wild Oats) stocks an amazing array of food, including an interesting section of prepared carry-home items. The friendly staff happily answers your questions.

INSIDERS' TIP

Parts of The Original Trading Post, downtown at 201 W. San Francisco Street, date back to 1836. At various times, the building was used as a saloon, grocery store, and meat market. Today, you'll find all varieties of Santa Fe souvenirs and American Indian arts here.

Regional Arts

LOOK FOR:
- American Indian Art
- Traditional Spanish Art

In addition to its deserved reputation as one of the best cities in the nation to buy fine art, Santa Fe also offers a host of wonderful places to purchase work by American Indian and Hispanic artists. There are many ways to approach this kind of shopping, and they're all fun.

Some visitors spend time learning as much as they can about such things as traditional Indian jewelry, pottery, kachinas, baskets, and weaving. Others, fascinated by the city's Spanish heritage, gravitate toward the Hispanic santos, tinwork, and straw inlay. These savvy shoppers try to find out who are the best among the modern practitioners of these indigenous crafts and then search Santa Fe's shops for their work.

Other shoppers just follow their eyes to bracelets, earrings, bolo ties, pots of all sizes, shapes, and design, and masterful hand-woven rugs. They discover a wealth of other American Indian arts and Hispanic treasures.

Whatever method you pick, you'll find that Santa Fe offers dozens of attractive options. There's no problem finding beautiful shops that sell first-quality Indian-made items; places to buy traditional Hispanic arts are harder to come by but worth the search.

Among the good places to shop for American Indian items are the Native American Vendors Program beneath the portal of the Palace of the Governors, 107 W. Palace Avenue, and the shop operated by the Museum of New Mexico Foundation at the Palace—where you may also find some Hispanic art. You can see and buy interesting Indian jewelry, pottery, and weavings as well as a fine selection of books at the shop at the Museum of Indian Arts and Culture, 710 Camino Lejo. The shops at the Institute of American Indian Arts Museum, 108 Cathedral Place, and the Wheelwright Museum, 704 Camino Lejo, also offer authentic handmade Indian items. You'll find Hispanic arts and crafts and other interesting items at the shops at the Museum of International Folk Arts (MOIFA) and at El Rancho de las Golondrinas a few miles out of town in La Cienega. The MOIFA has expanded its book selections with the recent lobby and shop renovation. A percentage of the sales at all these interesting little stores benefits the respective museums. The volunteers on staff know about the artists and their works. (See our Attractions and Arts chapters for more about these museums.)

If your timing is right, you'll enjoy shopping at Indian Market in August or at the Spanish Market and the Eight Northern Pueblos Arts and Crafts Show both in July (see our Annual Events chapter). At any of these shows, you can get an education while you make a purchase. Ask the artists about their work; the more you understand, the more you'll appreciate these longstanding traditional art forms.

You can see excellent examples of early New Mexican Spanish arts at the Museum of International Folk Art. Indian arts and artifacts are exhibited and explained at the Museum of Indian Arts and Culture and elsewhere. (See our Attractions chapter.) Scholars have written shelves full of books about Indian arts and crafts—their origins, the interconnectedness of themes and materials, the evolution of certain designs, family heritage in various arts, use of native or commercial materials, innovation in design, and much more. If you're seriously interested, bookstores around Santa Fe offer wonderful resources. Although less has been written on the traditional Spanish Colonial art forms, there are several fine published sources of information available. Our purpose in this chapter is to provide a basic overview of the local artistic styles and forms to help visitors encountering them for the first time.

American Indian Art

Jewelry

When you think of Indian jewelry, do you expect turquoise and silver, feather designs and strands of beads? Well, you'll find that—but that's only the beginning. How about a butterfly pendant with a pearl head and diamond-edged wings? Or a sophisticated bracelet with a finely crafted miniature ear of corn with coral kernels in a golden husk?

Even a quick look at Santa Fe's shops and galleries or a walk along the Vendors Market at the portal of the Palace of the Governors will help orient you to the vast and varied world of American Indian jewelry. This is a kingdom in which traditional designs and materials share their popularity with innovative approaches building on long-established traditions of craftsmanship.

Much of the jewelry you'll see for sale in Santa Fe comes from the surrounding pueblos, including Santo Domingo, San Felipe, Cochití, and San Juan. You'll also find work by Navajo and Hopi artists. The Navajo learned to work silver from Mexican silversmiths in the second half of the 19th century. The concha belt, named after the Spanish word for shell, is among their best-known designs. The belts are a collection of silver discs, sometimes with inset stones, connected on a leather belt.

While American Indian jewelry can be made from many different materials and in a huge spectrum of styles, authentic pieces are crafted by hand and are usually one of a kind. The jeweler normally begins with metal. While silver is the most common metal used, you'll also see American Indians working in gold.

Jewelers create through cutting, shaping, hammering, soldering, texturing, stamping, roller printing, and embossing metal. Stamping involves using a steel tool to press a decoration into the surfaces of metal. Casting is a metalsmithing method that gives the jewelry both surface texture and shape. Molten metal is poured into a mold and hardened to make a jewelry form. Jewelers use both tufa casting, which employs porous rock made of volcanic ash, and the lost-wax method to make their creations.

Turquoise and coral are traditional Indian jewelry stones. Turquoise, reminding us of our clear blue sky, has been New Mexico's official gem for 30 years. According to some, turquoise is the creator's way of telling us that earth and sky are one, inseparably linked. Indian jewelers have used this wonderful stone for centuries. During an early exploration of Chaco Canyon's Pueblo Bonito—one of the world's most extensive American Indian ruins—workers found 56,000 pieces of turquoise, mostly beads and pendants. The turquoise found at Chaco may have come from the mines in Cerrillos just outside of Santa Fe. The Pueblo Indians mined turquoise long before the Spanish arrived. They used the stone as currency, as a valuable trade item, and in all sorts of jewelry. Because New Mexico's native supplies of turquoise were largely depleted in the 1980s, most jewelers now get their stones from traders who buy it in Arizona, Colorado, Nevada, or even China. Turquoise comes in a variety of colors, from intense blue to pale green.

But you'll find more than turquoise in Indian jewelry. During your exploration of Santa Fe you're likely to see Indian jewelry made with lapis, diamonds, rubies, ironwood, opal, jet, and about any other stone you can think of.

In addition to setting them in metal, jewelers may use turquoise, coral and shell as the basis for lapidary work, shaping the raw materials into beads, some so delicate they seem fragile. Beads may be formed and smoothed using a hand drill; other jewelers tool them on machines. Indian jewelers also incorporate stones, coral, and shell for inlay work, setting a decorative pattern of various colors into a base of silver or other material.

Indian Market, held in August, draws more than 100,000 visitors to Santa Fe. Jewelry, pottery, sculpture, and beadwork are among the finds.

Photo: Don Strel

Silver overlay, a technique developed in the 1940s, is a distinctive Southwestern procedure used by the Hopi people of Arizona and other American Indians. The jeweler cuts a design into a sheet of silver, then places the design over a solid layer of silver. The jeweler then solders the pieces together and allows oxidation to darken the bottom layer that shows through to make the design more pronounced.

Here are a few tips for jewelry shopping:

• Look at the craftsmanship. Check to see that the edges are smooth and the stones securely fastened, that the stamp work is deep, sharp, and even, and that the finish is consistent.

• Try on the bracelet, necklace, or bolo before you buy it. Make sure it's comfortable to wear and of the appropriate size and weight for you. Look at it in a mirror; get a friend to give you an opinion.

• Ask about the materials and techniques the jeweler used.

• Fine jewelry will have the stamp or signature of its creator.

Pottery

New Mexico's Pueblo Indians were skilled potters for generations before the Spanish arrived. Today, collectors the world over prize pueblo pottery for its craftsmanship, design, and intrinsic beauty and because of the continuity with its traditional roots each piece represents.

A generation ago, it was easy to tell where a potter came from because the pottery from one pueblo differed sometimes markedly from another in color and design. Today, the definitions are less rigid, but pueblo potters still follow their ancestors' traditions in the type of clay they use, the symbols incorporated in the design, and in many other ways. But each potter also is an individual, and the final work reflects this artist's creativity, inspiration, and even sense of humor.

Picurís, Isleta, and Taos Pueblos specialize in micaceous ware. They make it using clay that has bits of mica in it, which gives the finished pots a lovely sparkle. Potters may add relief bands, handles, and lids. They commonly make large jars and pots, along with animal figures. These tribes also make storytellers—ceramics that feature a central character such as a grandmother covered with smaller characters, like grandchildren, listening to a story. These pueblos also make undecorated ceramics.

Acoma, Cochití, Laguna, Santo Domingo, Santa Ana, and Zia pueblos traditionally make white or buff slipped vessels with black and brick colored motifs, usually with a reddish-brown base. Larger, earth-tone vessels are also popular. Their design elements may include stylized rain, lightning and clouds, humans and animals as well as crosshatching and geometric patterns. Acoma is famous for its black and white fine-line pots. You'll find storytellers and animal figurines there as well as at Cochití.

Nambé, Pojoaque, San Ildefonso, San Juan, Santa Clara and Tesuque traditionally make black or red polished jars, wedding vases—tall pots with two spouts—water and storage jars, nativity scenes and bowls. They carve, etch or paint the finished pot, which tends to be black, red or a combination of both colors. These pueblos also make some micaceous ware.

Jemez, a pueblo in the Jemez Mountains between Santa Fe and Albuquerque, is known for buff or red-slipped wares with buff, white, or red designs. Storytellers, clowns, and animal figures are among the pueblo's specialties.

Hopi pottery, made by the Pueblo people of the Arizona mesa land, tends to be warm amber colored with designs that include stylized birds, kiva steps, and rain symbols.

Zuni Pueblo traditionally makes large bowls and jars with brownish, black, and red designs painted on a white or buff slip. The rain bird, plants, and animals form the basic designs. Owl effigies and designs created by adding clay relief figures to the surface of the vessel are also common.

Although best known for their weaving and jewelry, the Navajo also make some pottery. It tends to be dark with a shiny finish and is usually unpainted.

Just like jewelers, potters approach their craft with tremendous variation and innovation within their tribal tradition. You'll find vessels inlaid with turquoise, exquisite miniatures, and carved and etched pots. Indian artists make all sorts of animals and figures and decorate their work, large and small, with everything from geometric designs to kachina figures to acrobats.

The innovative artist who made a pot on display at the Museum of Indian Arts and Culture in Santa Fe, for example, decorated it with dinosaurs.

Traditional artists fire their pots in shallow pits. After they place the pots inside and cover them with wood bark and animal dung, they ignite the fuels, and the vessels smolder. Some set the pottery on a metal crate atop stones or old cans rather than in a fire pit. Fire clouds, or dark spots on the surface, are a result of these firing methods. In traditional firings as much as 25 percent of the pottery can break. Other potters use kiln firing, a sometimes controversial innovation, which reduces the breakage but also changes the finish of the pot.

Basketry

Basket-making is the oldest and most widespread of all the American Indian crafts. Archaeologists have found evidence that Indians were making baskets as early as 9,000 B.C. Baskets traditionally had many functions, and the variety of the modern craft reflects this heritage.

Indians coiled or twined large cylindrical baskets for carrying food and fuel. They used broad, shallow trays to help winnow seeds. Basket bowls of many depths and shapes were used for food preparation and eating. Large, lidded baskets stored food; open baskets were used for washing corn. Tribes also made basket cradles to carry their babies. Other baskets had special ceremonial uses.

Baskets can be woven from many different materials, but American Indian baskets are usually crafted from plant stems, either whole or split. The materials produce an interesting range of natural color, and some basket-makers also use dyes, both commercial and vegetable, to enhance their work. Basket-makers use three basic techniques to make their art: twining, plaiting, and coiling. Because of the hundreds of hours involved in creating the basket—a good one can take five months—a beautiful, well-made piece will demand a high price.

Among the Pueblo people, the Hopi are the best-known basket-makers, with different colors and designs reflecting the artistry of each village. Flat plaques and shallow bowls as well as deep containers characterize this work. The coiling is done from right to left. The Hopi also make

REGIONAL ARTS

Native American artists and craftspeople sell their wares under the portal of the Palace of the Governors.

Photo: Chris Corrie

In addition to traditional art forms, American Indian artists also work with contemporary media and topics.

Photo: Don Strel

some plaited wicker baskets. The design may include kachina or spirit figures, traditional abstractions, or birds.

Navajo basket-making underwent a renaissance in the 1970s, with more practitioners taking up the craft and more commercial-quality baskets created. Navajo baskets come in many sizes and shapes in both new, original designs and in the historic tradition.

The Jicarilla Apaches, whose reservation is in northern New Mexico near Chama, have been known for their superbly crafted baskets for centuries. The term jicarilla means finely made baskets. Their cylindrical and hamper-shaped baskets, which they tend to decorate with geometric forms, catch collectors' eyes and get top dollar.

Weaving

While most people think "Navajo" when they think of American Indian weaving, the Pueblo people, including the Hopi of Arizona, also create fine textiles. Early evidence of pueblo weaving dates to turkey feather and fur blankets and to items of clothing made from the native cotton that grew in the Rio Grande Valley and in irrigated fields in Arizona. An early account of the Spanish encounters with the Hopi mentions their cotton dresses.

The arrival of the Spanish meant the arrival of sheep's wool, looms, and a new approach to an old craft. By the 18th century, wool weaving was an established pueblo tradition. When commercial cloth became available with the opening of the Santa Fe Trail, the pueblos near Santa Fe de-emphasized weaving, but in the more isolated Hopi country the tradition continued. The Hopi helped supply the woven articles other pueblo people needed.

Pueblo men traditionally are the weavers, although women also weave. Hand-woven clothing is used in pueblo dances and is also sold commercially.

When the Navajo people migrated into the Southwest, they learned weaving from the agricultural Pueblo Indians. The Navajo soon became sheepherders, a livelihood ideally adapted to their traditional nomadic way of life. They transformed the skills they had acquired with cotton to the working and weaving of wool. By 1800 they were masters of the craft and had moved away from the pueblo tradition to create their own patterns and designs. They made blankets, rugs, sashes, and even bridles for their horses. Weavers created items for their family's own use and for trade. The weavers, who were usually women, dyed the wool with natural dyes as well as chemicals. Their work utilized traditional designs and colors, creating textile styles that were influential in the development of weaving in the American Southwest.

By the early 20th century, Navajo weaving had become so famous and important that museums were collecting samples. Designs range from geometric patterns of all styles to depiction of Navajo figures or Yeis, to pictorial weaving, which might have trains, trucks, or whatever else catches the weaver's fancy. There are no machine-made Navajo or pueblo weavings—all the work is done by hand.

Kachinas

Kachinas, or ceremonially costumed dolls, were originally an element used in the Pueblo peoples' complex and private religion. They are most common among the Hopi people and are also known as katsinas. For the Hopi, kachinas are sacred religious objects modeled after tribal deities. They were traditionally carved by Hopi men to give to women or children to remind them of what the deities looked like during the time of year when no ceremonies are performed. Traditionally children were encouraged to believe that the kachina spirits themselves made the dolls.

The kachinas offer a way to represent forces outside of human control, to maintain the balance between the natural world and human world. They help the people learn about a hierarchy of power and responsibility but are not similar to Christian icons.

Visitors have a chance to buy award-winning art at Santa Fe's major Indian art shows.

Photo: Don Strel

Kachinas come with a wide range of forms, colors, costumes, and attitudes. Some represent creation and life; death and war; lightning and storms; stars and planets; water and air; mountain peaks; the important foods of corn, squash, and beans; other tribes; and animals, birds, and insects. There may be various depictions of the same kachina. Carvers generally craft kachinas from cottonwood roots and dress them with feathers, animal hides, and hand-woven fabric.

The oldest dolls were simple with painted faces and uncomplicated bodies. Hopi and Zuni kachinas were known for the most figurative detail. Earliest kachinas hung on walls, but after World War II, collectors sought figures that showed more action, and the carvers responded with kachinas that could stand on flat surfaces. Kachina art has become a source of income for tribal artists as the market for the carvings has grown among collectors over the past 30 years. Hopi work can be recognized by its meticulous attention to detail. The figures have passed from religious icons to fine art.

Each kachina is unique; buyers should make sure they know who the artist is and that the work is guaranteed as Indian-made and made by hand. The name of the artist and the kachina should be on the piece. In buying kachinas, look for graceful positioning of the body, attention to details in the carving, and skilled use of paint and costuming. The price, as with all American Indian art, depends on the age and quality of the piece and the renown of the artist.

Although they were not part of the Navajo tradition, the Navajos make some "kachinas" today. The Navajo carvings, which some collectors and dealers prefer to call dolls, are inspired by traditional and contemporary Pueblo kachinas but, because they are do not have religions significance to the Navajo artist, may include colors, costumes, or poses that are particular to the individual artist. The Navajo work tends to be less expensive than the Hopi.

Pricing

As you shop for jewelry, pottery, textiles, baskets, kachinas, and other American Indian arts and crafts, you'll probably notice a tremendous variety of prices. Some of the differences may be due to the quality of materials used, the artist's skill in design or his or her reputation and popularity. If a piece seems too inexpensive to be authentic, ask where it came from and how it was made. Likewise, if the price seems excessive, ask why. A reputable dealer or legitimate artist will be delighted to tell you.

Traditional Spanish Arts

Although not as well-known as American Indian art forms, the northern New Mexico Hispanic tradition of handmade items, many of them religious, is honored in Santa Fe.

In the centuries before New Mexico became part of the United States, the settlers here had to use their own resourcefulness and creativity to produce what they needed for daily life. In addition to useful items, this included images of Jesus and the saints to help bring them closer to their god. The traditions of wood carving, straw inlay, embroidery, and weaving that were brought from Spain and Mexico grew into a unique indigenous art form. The Museum of International Folk Art, 706 Camino Lejo, has one of the most important collections of Spanish Colonial art, with pieces dating from the late 1700s to the present.

Among the Spanish Colonial arts you may find in Santa Fe or elsewhere in northern New Mexico are religious figures carved from wood or painted on wooden panels; loom weavings from hand-spun, vegetable-dyed yarn; and decorative and utilitarian furniture usually made from pine. Wheat-straw and corn-husk applique, applied to wood in intricate designs is usually found at several booths. Other artists work in metal: tin that they have cut, punched, and worked into useful and/or decorative objects; forged iron used for tools and household objects; and gold and silver filigree jewelry.

As you shop for traditional northern New Mexican Spanish items, you may come across these terms:

Bulto - A statue or three-dimensional image of a saint

Colcha - A distinctive embroidery style

Reredos - An altar screen. (This is actually a French term—in Spanish they were called retablo mayor for the main screen and retablo colateral for the side screens.)

Retablo - A painting of a saint on a wooden panel

Santo - A saint

A final word of advice: Follow your heart. If you love it and can afford it, buy it. If you don't, someone else probably will and chances are you may never see its likes again.

Santa Fe has dozens of wonderful commercial shops in addition to the nonprofit museum shops mentioned in the introduction to this chapter. The following selection, which also includes places to buy Hispanic arts

INSIDERS' TIP

Interested in American Indian jewelry? The Indian Arts and Crafts Association offers buying tips:

• Look for the artists' hallmark stamped on jewelry.

• If you're considering silver, look for a stamp that says "sterling."

• Ask the seller to certify that the item was Indian made. By law, a member of a state or federally recognized tribe or an artist who is tribally certified must create any item sold as such.

• Genuine handmade Indian jewelry is often expensive. If the price seems too good to be true, it probably is.

and crafts, is provided for your convenience. Unless otherwise noted, these places accept credit cards. Most shops are open from 9 or 10 AM until 5 or 6 PM Monday through Saturday. Some may be open on Sunday, especially during the summer.

Shopping Guide

Andrea Fisher Fine Pottery
211 W. San Francisco St.
• **(505) 986-1234**
• **www.andreafisherpottery.com**

This classy shop specializes in just one thing: Southwestern Indian pottery. You'll see fine examples from New Mexico's pueblos, including historic work by Maria Martinez. You'll also find exquisite work by New Mexico's contemporary potters. Fisher, the owner, arranges her contemporary and historic pieces by area, to give the viewer a sense of place. They're also grouped according to age and then by families, sometimes showing seven generations of pots by one family. The owner says a visit is an educational experience—we wish education was always this much fun!

The Clay Angel
125 Lincoln Ave.
• **(505) 988-4800**

This downtown shop presents work by New Mexico Hispanic artists along with imports from around the world. You'll find aspen, pine, and cottonwood bultos, painted retablos, and altar screens by Anita Romero-Jones. Just a short walk from the Plaza, the store specializes in ceramics, glassware, and flatware, but you'll find a variety of other fine crafts here too. Ask to see work done by New Mexicans.

Cristof's
420 Old Santa Fe Trail
• **505-988-9881**

This shop is known for its first-rate Navajo weavings, collected from throughout the reservation. The staff can help you understand what you're looking at—and lookers are welcome. You'll also find a nice selection of jewelry, pottery, sculpture, kachinas, storytellers, and sandpaintings.

Dewey Galleries Ltd.
53 Old Santa Fe Tr.
• **(505) 982-8632**

Dewey Galleries is one of Santa Fe's best-known places to buy historic Native American weavings, pottery, jewelry, and artifacts. It will do appraisals and handle estates and collections. They are also the Santa Fe representative for the estate of renowned sculptor, Allan Houser. Dewey Galleries is on the second floor of the building.

La Fonda Indian Shop and Gallery
La Fonda Hotel, 100 E. San Francisco St.
• **(505) 988-2488**

This gallery features fine art by American Indians from throughout the Southwest. La Fonda acquires private estates and collections on a consignment basis. You may find beautiful etched miniature pots or Indian jewelry made from gold and opals as well as silver and turquoise.

Good Hands Gallery Ramón José Lopez y Familia
700 Paseo de Peralta
• **(505) 982-3352**

In business for 30 years and recently moved to a former Santa Fe home several blocks from the Plaza, this shop features a wide variety of contemporary and traditional North American artists such as Andy Burns, Ricardo Chavez-Mendez, and Roger Montoya. You'll also find paintings, sculpture, bultos and retablos, along with "treasure necklaces" by Nancy Lopez. Watch for the festive openings.

Helen Hardin Estate/Silver Sun
656 Canyon Rd.
• **(505) 983-8743**

Santa Clara Pueblo artist Helen Hardin, who died in 1984, left a wonderful legacy of artwork, which is featured in this gallery along with the sculpture of Gerard Tsonakwa and delicate Acoma and Mata Ortiz pottery. You'll also find Indian jewelry at a wide range of prices. The shop's jewelry specialty is high-quality, natural American turquoise stones in custom-designed silver and gold settings, created by their own Navajo silversmiths. It also sells pottery by Jacquie Stevens, rugs, fetishes, and carvings.

Indian Trader West
204 W. San Francisco St.
• **(505) 988-5776**

This place feels like an old-time trading post, with items available in many price ranges. You'll find everything that will say Indian and Southwest when you get back home—top-quality clothing, art, and souvenirs.

prices are good and the staff can answer your questions. They're open 7 days a week.

Kiva Fine Art
El Centro Mall,
102 East Water Street
- **(505) 820-7413**
- **www.kivaindianart.com**

This shop may be off the beaten path, but it's well worth the visit. In business for 10 years, it specializes in contemporary Native American art, including sculpture, paintings, textiles, pottery, and kachinas. Some of their many artists include C. S. Tarpley, Yellowman, Benjamin Nelson, and David K. John. You'll also find a display of old studio art from 1930 to about 1960, along with vintage rugs and jewelry.

Davis Mather Folk Art Gallery
141 Lincoln Ave.
- **(505) 983-1660**

This tiny gallery is packed full of wonderful animal woodcarvings by New Mexican Hispanic artists and American Indians from instate and elsewhere. Among the craftspeople featured are Josefina Aguilar, Ron Rodriguez, Paul Lutonsky, David Alvarez, Doreen Herbert, and Joe Ortega. The gallery has been in business since 1975 and is open daily.

Montez
125 E. Palace Ave.,
Stes. 33 and 34
- **(505) 982-1828**

Traditional-style arts and crafts by New Mexico's leading Hispanic artists are on display in this gallery, including both contemporary and antique items. The owner, from a family of santeros himself, knows his business. You'll find wood carvings of the saints, tin work, santos, and other lovely and unusual items. The shop is in Sena Plaza near the northwest corner.

Morning Star Gallery
513 Canyon Rd.
- **(505) 982-8187**

Morning Star promotes itself as the largest

Beautiful, original art awaits you in the city's many galleries that specialize in American Indian and Hispanic art.

Photo: Don Strel

Keshi—The Zuni connection
Santa Fe Village Mall, 227 Don Gaspar
- **(505) 989-8728**

This shop, originally started by Zuni Indians, has been in business for 19 years, and is a direct outlet for the Zuni Pueblo. You'll find Zuni jewelry exclusively and the largest collection of authentic Zuni fetishes in the Santa Fe area. The gallery in the country devoted exclusively to antique Native American art. In business 15 years, the gallery occupies an old Canyon Road hacienda. The inventory includes a variety of material from the major cultural areas of North America. The emphasis is on Plains beadwork, quill work, ledger drawings and parfleche, Southwestern pottery, baskets, textiles, and jewelry.

Robert F. Nichols Gallery
Contemporary Clay
419 Canyon Road
• (505) 982-2145
• www.robertnicholsgallery.com

Celebrating its 20th year on Canyon Road in 2000, this gallery's primary emphasis is contemporary work in clay by Native American artists of the American Southwest. Artists represented are Diego Romero, Les Namingha, Bill Glass, Nathan Begay, and the Ortiz family. This is a destination for established collectors, with a broad enough price range to include those just starting out.

Ortega's On The Plaza
101 W. San Francisco St.
• (505) 988-1866.

In business for 25 years, Ortega's sells fine Indian jewelry from all the pueblos. You'll also find Pendleton blankets, old Navajo rugs, baskets, and even a pot by the famous San Ildefonso Pueblo potter Marià Martìnez. The merchandise is beautifully presented, and the staff is knowledgeable. The gallery is open seven days a week.

Packard's Indian
Trading Co.
61 Old Santa Fe Tr.
• (505) 983-9241

On the plaza since 1920, Packard's offers the finest Native American art and crafts, including exquisite jewelry, katsinas (also known as kachinas), weavings, pottery, evening bags, and gift items. To learn more about katsinas, attend one of their popular 1-hour educational seminars at noon each Tuesday during the summer. Packard's is open daily.

The Rainbow Man
107 E. Palace Ave.
• (505) 982-8706

At the Rainbow Man you'll find works by regional Hispanic folk artists, including some of the people who show at Santa Fe's annual Spanish Markets. Don't miss the wood carvings with nice touches of fantasy. The shop also has an interesting selection of early Chimayó and Rio Grande Weavings as well as an extensive collection of Native American arts and crafts—including miniature kachinas. All the way to the back of the shop you'll find an enormous selection of Edward Curtis photographs of Native American Indians. The store is open daily.

Relics of the Old West
402 Old Santa Fe Tr.
• (505) 989-7663

In business since 1959, this shop carries top-quality antique American Indian art and sells baskets, rugs, and other items to collectors and museums. Included are exceptional Two Grey Hills weavings from Toadlena Trading Post. It also carries Spanish Colonial items as well as Egyptian, Greek, and Roman treasures.

Sun Country Traders
123 E. Water Street
• (505) 982-0467

Open since 1979, this lovely shop offers a beautiful selection of Native American jewelry and is well known for its large display of Taos drums as well as drums from the Cochití and Santo Domingo Pueblos, and even some from the Sioux tribe. Look for the bright yellow awning at the east end of Water Street.

INSIDERS' TIP

The non-profit Spanish Colonial Arts Society, the group which presents the Traditional Spanish Market, maintains one of the largest and most comprehensive collections of Spanish colonial art in the world. The society's long-held goal of having a facility in which to display its 2,500-item collection will become a reality. Construction of a new 4,600-square-foot Spanish Colonial Arts Society Museum will provide a place for exhibition and preservation of the collection.

Attractions

We're the first to admit it. Santa Fe thrives on its contradictions, and one of the most basic is this: Why is it that a town that prides itself on its mañana attitude offers more things to do than a place three or four times its size? Don't worry if Santa Fe's many options to spend your time seem overwhelming—they are!

The diversity of attractions here, coupled with the community's natural beauty, bring visitors back year after year. The most recent figures place Santa Fe's visitors at 3 million annually—or 50 tourists for every resident!

As you explore Santa Fe, you'll find many superlatives: the biggest adobe office building, the oldest bell, the largest sculpture garden in New Mexico, the largest collection of contemporary American Indian art, the only museum dedicated to a woman artist of international stature . . . and that's just for starters.

Santa Fe offers so much that if you're making your first trip, we recommend that you take a city tour. You can take walking tours of all sorts, ride an open-air tram or climb aboard a big bus. A few hours with a well-trained guide will not only give you a better appreciation for the tremendous historic and cultural riches you'll find here, but it can also help you avoid spending any of your precious vacation time getting lost or searching for a parking place.

In this chapter you'll find the attractions divided into logical categories for Santa Fe: churches, museums, historic buildings and districts, other attractions, tours, and visitor information. In addition to information here, please take a look at our Arts, Recreation, and Kidstuff chapters for more ideas.

We've done our best to include up-to-the-minute information about hours and admission fees of the attractions we list, but if you're on a tight budget or a tight schedule, please call to see if anything has changed since our book was published.

LOOK FOR:
- **Historic Buildings**
- **Historic Churches**
- **Historic Districts**
- **Museums**
- **Other Attractions**
- **Tours**
- **Near Santa Fe**
- **Worth The Trip**

Historic Buildings

**Lamy Building
(State of New Mexico
Santa Fe Welcome Center)
491 Old Santa Fe Tr.**
- **(505) 827-7336**
- **vcenter@state.nm.us**

Visitors who stop here for information are literally stepping into history. Named after Archbishop Jean Lamy, the building was erected in 1878 as part of St. Michael's College, the oldest private school in New Mexico. (See our Education and Child Care chapter.) The three-story structure had classrooms and community rooms on the first two floors and a dormitory for the boys who came from throughout northern New Mexico on the third floor. With its tower, portico, galleries, veranda, and mansard roof, the building is typical of many 19th-century New Mexico buildings, most of which have now disappeared. In 1926, fire almost completely destroyed it, but the students saved the day by forming a fire brigade. The Lamy Building's graceful two-story portal is one of the few remaining in Santa Fe. The visitors center is open from 8 AM to

5 PM daily with very few exceptions, but your best view of the building is from outside.

National Park Service— Southwest Office
1100 Old Santa Fe Tr.
• (505) 988-6100

Curious about what lies behind Santa Fe's pervasive adobe walls? This attractive building, a National Historic Landmark, can help satisfy your curiosity. Not only is it beautiful, but also it's the largest known adobe, or mud brick, office building and one of the largest secular adobe buildings in the United States.

The Park Service building derives its significance from its architecture, art collections, and association with the federal relief programs of the New Deal era. The sculptural, massive quality of the adobe walls, the lovely patios, and the hand-worked wooden beams and corbels reflect some of the characteristic elements of "Santa Fe Style," a type of architecture that began here around 1910 and continues to be popular today. To do the construction, the Public Works Administration provided the materials and skilled labor, and the Civilian Conservation Corps provided unskilled workers, a crew of unmarried men ages 17 to 23. They earned about $1 a day for their work and had to send home at least $22 a month. The men made the structure's 280,000 adobe bricks by hand. From the artisans they worked with they learned woodwork, stone and foundation masonry and traditional tinwork to decorate and enhance the building. The government completed the job by acquiring paintings by local artists, Navajo rugs, and Pueblo pottery. That collection remains on display.

Although the offices are closed to visitors-after all, people are working there—the patio, lobby and conference room give you a fine feeling for the building's wonderful architecture and skillful finishing touches. You can visit between 8 AM and 4:30 PM Monday through Friday. There's no charge, and you'll find a brochure for a self-guided tour in the lobby.

New Mexico State Capitol
Paseo Peralta at Old Santa Fe Tr.
• (505) 986-4589
• http://legis.state.nm.us (legislature)

Visit the New Mexico State Capitol and in the process learn a lot about New Mexico's history, politics, and its rich artistic community. The Capitol, nicknamed the Roundhouse for its circular shape, was built in 1966 and remodeled at a cost of $34 million in 1992. The architectural design comes from the Zia Pueblo

sun sign or circle of life, the same symbol you'll notice on New Mexico's red and yellow state flag. The current Capitol is New Mexico's fourth, following the Palace of the Governors and a downtown building constructed in 1887 and reconstructed in 1890 after it burned in a fire.

The Capitol has four levels, three above ground. In the basement (which is not open to the public) are the House and Senate chambers. The second floor, at ground level, contains a visitor information office and the rotunda, where visitors find changing art exhibits. The floor of the rotunda displays the state seal. All of the semiprecious stones decorating the seal and the marble of the surrounding walls and floor were mined in New Mexico. Old photographs of past legislators line the walls of the third floor House and Senate galleries, the area where visitors may watch laws being made. During the legislative sessions—the 30-day financial session and 60-day general session in alternating years—the Roundhouse is filled with students on field trips, lobbyists, and interested residents who come from around the state to observe their elected representatives in action. Recent hot topics have included Indian gaming, prison construction, and highway funding. The legislature convenes beginning at noon on the second Tuesday in January.

On the fourth floor, the Governor's Gallery features art by New Mexicans in exhibits that rotate often. Walls elsewhere in the building display paintings, photographs, weaving, and mixed media work by some of New Mexico's best known artists. On the Capitol grounds, you'll find monumental sculptures by Allan Houser, Glenna Goodacre, and others. Docents offer free guided tours at 10 AM and 2 PM Monday through Friday. The Capitol building is open from 8 AM to 5 PM Monday through Friday.

Randall Davey Audubon Center
1800 Upper Canyon Rd.
• (505) 983-4609

You might see a bobcat track in the snow at this quiet sanctuary, only a 10-minute drive from the Plaza. In 1847, at the beginning of the U.S. occupation, the first sawmill in the territory was built here, providing planks for the construction of Santa Fe's Fort Marcy, where U.S. troops were garrisoned. At the turn of the century, Candelario Martinez farmed this land until he sold the property to artist Randall Davey in 1920. Davey converted the mill into a two-story home and used the Martinez hacienda for his studio. The house still contains a representative sample of Davey's work and his furnishings. You can tour the Davey home on Mondays between 1 and 4 PM in the summer and otherwise by appointment.

The Audubon Society acquired this property in the mid-1980s and operates it as a nature center and the group's New Mexico headquarters. Included is land along the Santa Fe River. The center's trails begin in the piñon and juniper woodlands and meadows and climb up to cool ponderosa pine forest. More than 100 species of birds have been observed here, along with coyote, black bear, mountain lion, and mule deer. In addition to the do-it-yourself nature trails, the center offers guided hikes, wildlife interpretive programs, and summer activities for children. The center's gift shop sells birdseed, books, and other items of interest to naturalists.

To reach the center, follow Canyon Road past the intersection of Camino Cabra at Cristo Rey Church to Upper Canyon Road. The center is the very last structure on Canyon Road. The center is open from 9 AM to 5 PM daily. The trail fee is $1 for adult nonmembers and 50 cents for children 12 and under. The grounds are also available for rent for outdoor weddings.

Sena Plaza
100 Block of E. Palace Ave.
•**No central phone**

One of the city's most popular courtyards, this beautiful place gives you a feel for the old Territorial days when Santa Fe was still a village. With its beautifully landscaped patio and fountain, this spot entices you to sit and relax, smell the flowers, or watch the snow fall and enjoy the day. From the Palace Avenue portal, you won't know this oasis is here unless you come through the narrow entranceway and take a few steps inside.

The property was originally part of a land grant from Don Diego de Vargas, the man who brought the Spanish back to New Mexico after the 1680 Indian revolt, to one of his captains, Arias de Quiros. In 1844, the property, which included a small house and patio, was bequeathed to the mother of José D. Sena, a major in the U.S. Civil War who was later to inherit it. Sena expanded the living quarters into a 33-room house, which he eventually occupied with his family. The second story was added to the east and north portions of the estate in 1927 when the building was sold and remodeled into shops and offices. (See our Shopping chapter.) Visitors are welcome, free of charge, from 10 AM to 10 PM.

El Zaguan
545 Canyon Rd.
• **(505) 983-2567 (Historic Santa Fe Foundation)**
• **www.historicsantafe.org**

This long, rambling Territorial-style house

You can get a feel for Adobe architecture with a self-guided tour at the National Park Service—Southwest Office.

Photo: Don Strel

ATTRACTIONS

has long been regarded as one of New Mexico's showplaces. The old hacienda with its lovely garden was named El Zaguan, "the passageway," because of the long hall running from the patio to the garden. James Johnson, one of the first Yankee merchants to settle permanently in Santa Fe, purchased the property, which included a small house, in 1849. In the Santa Fe pattern, the building was enlarged and remodeled several times. Early floor plans show two patios, a central patio that served as the entry from the street with larger, more formal rooms opening onto it, and an east patio, which was the center of household activities. The house, today with 14 rooms, once had 24 rooms, including a chapel, a "chocolate room," and a library that once housed the largest collection of books in the territory. Servants' quarters were across the street. The garden was reportedly laid out by Adolph Bandelier—the writer and archaeologist for whom Bandelier National Monument is named—with peony bushes from China and two large horse chestnut trees brought from the Midwest.

In 1962 the property was purchased for preservation by El Zaguan Inc., and today one of its apartments is an office shared by the Historic Santa Fe Foundation and the Old Santa Fe Association. The Foundation, incorporated in 1961 to receive tax-exempt donations for historic preservation, conducts research to identify worthy buildings and preserves and maintain landmarks in Santa Fe and the nearby communities. The foundation office is open to visitors 9 AM to noon and 1 to 5 PM Monday through Friday; the garden area is open Monday through Saturday, 9 AM to 5 PM. For information on renting the boardroom or the garden area for special events, call (505) 983-2567.

Historic Churches

Archbishop Lamy's Chapel Bishop's Lodge Resort
1292 Bishop's Lodge Rd. N.
• (505) 983-6377

Santa Fe's remarkable Archbishop Jean Baptiste Lamy prayed in this lovely little chapel that he built as a retreat beginning in the late 1860s. The building, about 3 miles from the Santa Fe Plaza, reflects both European and traditional Hispanic New Mexico architectural styles. The walls are adobe, or mud brick, but the spire looks like something from New England. Changes over the years included replacing the rafters with white-washed vigas and

covering the floor with cement. But the wooden entry doors and their hardware are original.

In addition to his role as religious leader and promoter of education (see our Education and Child Care chapter), Lamy attempted to transform Santa Fe from an adobe village to a more European-looking city. He contracted stone masons and artisans from France and Italy who in 1869 began to build the St. Francis Cathedral. He also guided the construction of Loretto Chapel.

Today, the Bishop's chapel is virtually surrounded by Bishop's Lodge Resort. The chapel is open to visitors during daylight hours free of charge. Visitors can arrange for weddings, baptisms, and other religious ceremonies in the chapel.

Cristo Rey Church
1120 Canyon Rd.
• (505) 983-8528

The parish of Cristo Rey uses this church, America's largest adobe building, for regular worship, but visitors are welcome. A classic example of New Mexico mission architecture, Cristo Rey was built of 200,000 adobe bricks made from soil at the church's site. The 1940 construction commemorated the 400th anniversary of Coronado's exploration of the Southwest, which led, of course, to the founding of Santa Fe. In addition to the architecture, notice the restored painted stone reredos, a sculpted Spanish Colonial-style altar screen with images of the saints. Crafted in 1760, the 18- by 40-foot screen originally was commissioned for an old military chapel situated near the Plaza. Admission is free. The church is open to visitors from 7 AM to 7 PM daily.

Loretto Chapel
207 Old Santa Fe Tr.
• (505) 984-7971
• www.lorettochapel.com

This chapel, dedicated to Our Lady of Light, was the first Gothic structure west of the Mississippi. Today, the chapel is one of Santa Fe's top visitor attractions and a popular place for weddings and concerts.

Built for the Sisters of Loretto, the style of this jewel-like chapel testifies to the influence of Santa Fe's first bishop, Frenchman Jean Baptiste Lamy. The Sisters came to Santa Fe at the request of Lamy to establish a school for young women downtown. Their Loretto Academy occupied the site upon which the Loretto Hotel now stands.

The French influence includes the white altar, beautifully adorned sanctuary, rose windows, and architectural beauty modeled after Paris' Sainte Chapelle. The chapel's claim to fame, however, is a graceful spiral staircase that winds to the choir loft with no center support and not a single nail. Legend has it that work on the chapel was nearly done when the sisters realized no room remained for a traditional staircase. They prayed to St. Joseph for guidance and believed he answered their novena when a carpenter arrived. He agreed to build the staircase. Using only a saw, a carpenter's square and tubs of hot water to soften and shape the wood, he crafted a beautiful circular staircase. He then disappeared before he could be paid. The story recently captured the attention of the producers of *Unsolved Mysteries* and got national television exposure.

The chapel is administered by the Sisters of Loretto but maintained by the Historic Santa Fe Foundation. Admission is $2.50 for adults, $2 for kids 7-13, and $2 for seniors over 65; children under 6 get in free. The chapel is open from 9 AM to 6 PM Monday through Saturday, and from 10:30 AM to 5 PM Sunday.

San Miguel Mission
401 Old Santa Fe Tr.
• (505) 983-3974

Many people believe this mission is the oldest church in the United States. Construction began in 1610 by the Tlaxcalan Indians who came from Mexico as servants of the Spanish soldiers and missionaries. The job was completed in 1625. When the Pueblo Indians drove the Spanish from New Mexico in 1680, they nearly destroyed the mission and burned all records of its early history. The sturdy adobe walls remained unharmed, however. When the Spanish returned, they ordered the church rebuilt and construction was finished in 1710. For many years it served the surrounding Barrio Analco, one of Santa Fe's most historic neighborhoods.

Inside you can see traditional religious images crafted by Hispanic artists. The wooden reredos, or altar screen, dates to 1798 and holds paintings from the early 18th century. You'll see rare and ancient images of Jesus on buffalo and deer hides, testimony to the faith and ingenuity of frontier artists. Among the chapel's drawing cards is the San Jose bell, cast of silver, copper, iron, and gold. Touted as the oldest bell in America, some historians date its fabrication to 1356. Spanish churches used it before it was shipped to Mexico and then hauled to Santa Fe by oxcart in the 19th century.

A helpful staff of Christian brothers and a six-minute audio presentation that runs continuously as a recorded tour will help orient you to the mission. It's open Monday through Saturday from 9 AM to 4:30 PM and Sunday

ATTRACTIONS

The mill at Los Golindrinas is a popular attraction.

Photo: Don Strel

from 1:30 to 4:30 PM. Admission is free. Mass is celebrated here Sunday at 5 PM.

Change may come to the chapel in the future; at press time a search was underway for a new director who might take the historic little church in a new direction in terms of programs and policies.

Santuario de Guadalupe
100 Guadalupe St.
• (505) 988-2027

At one time this Santa Fe-style building resembled something straight out of Colonial New England. In another incarnation, it was

San Miquel Mission, Santa Fe's oldest church, sits next to another historic building, the original home of St. Michael's High School, now a state office building.

Photo: Don Strel

California mission-style. Today, the unassuming adobe church looks much like it did when it was first built, between 1776–96. It is the oldest shrine to Our Lady of Guadalupe in the United States. Our Lady of Guadalupe is a name given by the Catholic Church to the apparition of the Virgin to an Indian outside of Mexico City in the 16th century. This Madonna speaks of the Virgin's love for native people of the Americas. You'll find her representations throughout New Mexico, on everything from T-shirts to the hoods of lowrider cars.

Franciscan missionaries oversaw the construction of the original church, which had a dirt floor, no pews, and a simple ladder leading to the choir loft. In the 1880s, Archbishop Jean Lamy assigned a French priest to the little church and made it a regular parish. Father James DeFouri (for whom nearby DeFouri Street is named) supervised extensive remodeling, the first of many for the structure. It took on a pitched roof, steeple, and a white picket fence. The church was modified again in the 1920s following a fire, this time redone in California mission style. In the 1960s, the growing Guadalupe parish built a new church next to the mission. The old church retained its California look until 1976, when a restoration brought the building back to its simple mission origins—but this time with a floor and seats. The restoration covered the original adobe walls, which ranged from 3- to 5-feet thick, with two layers of hand-plastered adobe finish. The lintels above the windows and the front door are original. The ceiling includes some original beams, but the building's roof, brick parapets, and bell are new. You can see pictures of the Santuario in its incarnations in the history room.

Among the Santuario's art is a 1783 oil-on-canvas altar painting of Our Lady of Guadalupe by Mexican baroque artist Jose' de Alzibar, a renowned Mexican painter. It is one of the finest and largest oil paintings of the Spanish Southwest. It came to Santa Fe in pieces and was reassembled on site. The nonprofit, nonsectarian Guadalupe Historic Foundation operates the Santuario as museum, performing arts center and occasional art gallery. The Santa Fe Desert Chorale has performed most of its summer and Christmas concerts here since 1982. You can visit the Santuario Monday through Saturday from 9 AM to 4 PM. It's closed weekends from November through

April. Admission is free. Mass is celebrated here once a month.

St. Francis Cathedral
213 Cathedral Pl.
• (505) 982-5619

In this city of flat-roofed adobe buildings, the towering cathedral stands out from the crowd. Constructed from New Mexico's golden brown sandstone, St. Francis Cathedral was the first church between Durango, Mexico, and

The Plaza welcomes the community and visitors during the year.

Photo: Don Strel

St. Louis, Missouri, to be designated a cathedral. Archbishop Jean Lamy supervised its construction, recruiting artisans from Europe and working on the plans himself. Lamy died before the workers finished. (He is buried beneath the cathedral's altar.)

Built beginning in 1869, the cathedral arose around an earlier mission church on the same site. The cathedral's Romanesque-style stained glass imported from Clermont, France, and dual bell towers stand in sharp contrast to New Mexico's simple adobe churches.

The exterior was completed in 1884, but work went on inside for many years after that.

The builders erected Corinthian columns leading to a ribbed vaulted ceiling. Frosted glass chandeliers illuminate the sanctuary. The windows depict the 12 apostles; today, painted stations of the cross in the New Mexican folk art santero style hang on the wall beneath them, a fitting reminder that this is Santa Fe, after all.

In a small chapel—all that remains of the original church on this site—the cathedral shelters a religious icon greatly revered by New Mexico's Hispanic Catholics and others who treasure the state's religious history. This small wooden statue of the Virgin Mary was for years known as La Conquistadora and now is also called Nuestra Señora de la Paz, or Our Lady of Peace. It is the oldest representation of the Madonna in the United States. Spanish friars brought the image from Mexico City to Santa Fe and carefully took it out of New Mexico again when they fled during the Pueblo Revolt. La Conquistadora returned to Santa Fe with Don Diego de Vargas during the reconquest and is carried in procession as part of the religious commemorations of the Santa Fe Fiesta.

When you visit the cathedral, it's hard to overlook the massive bronze double doors out front. They chronicle more than four centuries of the Roman Catholic religion in New Mexico. Each panel weighs 25 pounds. Notice La Conquistadora in the "1680" panel. The cathedral is open to visitors from 6 AM to 5:45 PM. Admission is free. Mass is celebrated daily.

Historic Districts

Barrio Analco
E. De Vargas St. between Don Gaspar Ave. and Old Santa Fe Tr.

Believed to have been one of the first parts of Santa Fe to be settled by the Spanish, this area was named "analco" or "other side of the river" because it sits across the Santa Fe River from the Palace of the Governors. The early residents were the Mexican Indians who came to Santa Fe in the early 1600s with the Spanish settlers, missionaries and soldiers. The Spanish lived closer to the thick-walled haven of the Palace. Because of its vulnerability, angry Pueblo Indians were able to totally destroy this area during the

INSIDERS' TIP
A call from Santa Fe to most other New Mexico communities - Albuquerque, Pecos, Las Vegas or Espanola for example—is long distance. A call to Los Alamos is not.

ATTRACTIONS

revolt of 1680. The neighborhood was rebuilt when the Spanish returned and as years went by became a more class-inclusive kind of place. Today state buildings dominate this area, but some of the old charm remains. The homes are privately owned and not open to visitors, but a stroll along E. DeVargas Street gives you a sense of Santa Fe in its early days.

Canyon Road
From Paseo De Peralta to Camino Cabra, roughly parallel to E. Alameda and Acequia Madre

If you only have a weekend in Santa Fe, you ought to spend at least part of it walking along Canyon Road, exploring some of the many shops and galleries, observing the historic homes that still dot the area, and getting a feel for old Santa Fe. The best way to explore Canyon Road is on foot; wear your walking shoes. Don't worry if you get hungry, there are restaurants here, too. If art interests you, you'll discover a variety of styles, media, and prices here. Many of the road's galleries and shops occupy former homes.

Several nearby streets—Camino del Monte Sol, Garcia Street, and Acequia Madre—are also worth a look. Primarily residential, they offer another glimpse of Santa Fe's classic beauty. In the spring and early summer, the lilacs and fruit trees here are spectacular. Acequia Madre means "mother ditch," a name that comes from the irrigation ditch that runs along the street. In pre-Spanish times, Indians used this footpath to travel between the Santa Fe River valley and Pecos Pueblo. Later it was the conduit for haulers bringing their loads of firewood from the mountains to sell in town. Farmers grew chiles, beans, and peaches, drawing the water for irrigation from acequias, or communal ditches. Sheep and goats grazed on the nearby hillsides.

Canyon Road owes part of its fame to a group of artists who came to Santa Fe in the 1920s. They called themselves "Los Cinco Pintores" (The Five Painters) and built homes along Camino del Monte Sol, just off Canyon Road. Their paintings often reflected a romantic Santa Fe. (See our Arts chapter.) The artists became neighbors of Canyon Road's long-established Hispanic families. The cultures intermixed, and the area saw little visible change until recent years, when some longtime residents began selling their land, in part because of rising taxes. Today, this area, known as the East Side, is one of Santa Fe's most desirable and pricey neighborhoods. (See our Real Estate and Neighborhoods chapter.)

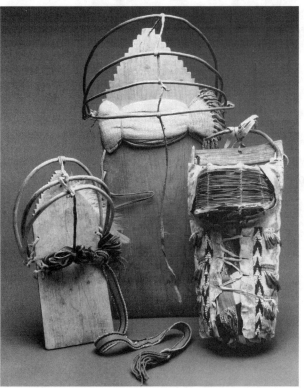

Canyon Road offers a variety of interesting galleries, including some that specialize in American Indian art.

Photo: Blair Clark/courtesy of Museum of New Mexico

Artist Olive Rush, said to be the first female Anglo artist to move to Santa Fe, lived and worked in a studio at 630 Canyon Road for 40 years. A Quaker, Rush left her home to the Santa Fe Society of Friends at her death, and it is still used for Quaker Meetings. El Zaguan, 545 Canyon Road, is among the street's historic buildings. (See separate write-up in this chapter.)

Parking in the Canyon Road area can be a challenge, especially in the summer. You can look for parking places along the street or in the city lot, 225 Canyon Road, near the corner of Canyon Road and Camino del Monte Sol.

The Plaza/Downtown

Directly across from the Palace of the Governors, the Plaza is bordered by Lincoln Avenue to the west, Washington Avenue to the east, San Francisco Street to the south, and Palace Avenue to the north. The downtown area extends several blocks from the Plaza in all directions.

The Plaza, a shady expanse of trees, grass, benches, and monuments, is the core of old Santa Fe, the city's "Central Park." It's one of four sites in Santa Fe listed on the National Register of Historic Places. (The others are the Palace of the Governors, the National Park Service Southwest Headquarters, and the Barrio Analco near the San Miguel mission.) To many residents, despite all the changes over the past decades, the Plaza is still the community's sentimental place of the heart. A few years ago, the city sponsored a program of free entertainment on the Plaza appropriately called "El Corazon de Santa Fe" (The Heart of Santa Fe).

For many visitors, time spent exploring the Plaza and downtown Santa Fe with its museums, shops, restaurants, and historic attractions, forms one of their most vivid memories of this unusual city. The Plaza is Santa Fe's favorite place for festivals and fairs. You'll find Spanish Market, Indian Market, Fiesta de Santa Fe, the Christmas drama Las Posadas, and many other events here. They fill the Plaza and spread into the surrounding streets, bringing Santa Fe residents and visitors downtown. In the summer the city traditionally blocks traffic on San Francisco Street and Lincoln Avenue to make the area more pedestrian friendly.

The Plaza has several monuments that present pieces of its long, rich history: The small stone marker on the north side, just across the street from the Palace of the Governors, notes the arrival of Gen. Stephen Watts Kearny with the Army of the West in 1846 during the war between Mexico and the United States. Kearny claimed Santa Fe for the U.S. government without firing a shot; Santa Fe's Mexican governor may have believed the resistance was useless.

The monument on the south side of the Plaza marks the end of the Old Santa Fe Trail and provides an idea of the historic route from Missouri to Santa Fe. The Santa Fe Trail brought wagons filled with tons of goods to New Mexico between 1822 and 1870. The wagons' bounty was sold or traded for furs and pelts, gold, and silver. Interstate 25 follows the same route from Santa Fe to Denver. The old trail brought contact with the United States that ultimately led to New Mexico becoming a state. The Plaza also marks the end of an older commercially important trail, El Camino Real, the trade route to Santa Fe from Mexico.

At the center of the Plaza, the obelisk commemorates Civil War battles in the area. Although most visitors may not realize it, the Civil War reached New Mexico in 1861. The Confederacy, in an effort to take the West, sent soldiers from Texas up the Rio Grande to capture New Mexico's Fort Union, the garrison established by the U.S. Army to protect wagons along the Santa Fe Trail from Indian marauders. The Confederacy controlled both Albuquerque and Santa Fe by 1862, setting up headquarters in the Palace of the Governors. The rebel plan would have succeeded except for the pivotal Battle of Glorieta on March 28. Major John Chivington took some Union soldiers and destroyed the Confederates' central supply base, leaving them with no support and no choice except to abandon the area.

Surrounding the Plaza are narrow streets and distinctive buildings that represent three and a half centuries of continuous civilization, beginning with the 1610 establishment of the city as the seat of the government of Spain's northern frontier. Architectural styles range from Spanish Pueblo to Territorial and European. Strict building codes govern what you

INSIDERS' TIP

For researchers, scholars and artists, the collections of the Museum of International Folk Art (MOIFA) provide an invaluable resource for cultural understanding and artistic inspiration. The collections of the museum have grown to about 125,000 pieces, in four categories: the Spanish Colonial collection (17th to 19th centuries), the contemporary Southwestern Hispanic art collection (20th century), the international textiles and costumes collection, and the international collection of folk objects (late 19th and 20th centuries). With examples from more than 100 different countries, these holdings constitute the most important collection of cross-cultural folk art in the world.

can design, erect, or demolish. Rents are high, and as a result, in addition to museums, you'll find shops that handle exclusive and expensive merchandise and shops that make their money on heavy sales of less expensive items. The Hägen-Dazs ice cream store on San Francisco Street, for example, is reputed to be the busiest such outlet in the United States.

Parking in the Plaza area can be difficult. The city operates several downtown lots (see our Getting Around chapter), and some private businesses offer limited parking. There also are a few spaces along the street. Your best bet, if you're staying downtown, is to walk from your hotel. If you're outside the downtown area, you can take a city bus, hotel shuttle, or a taxi.

Museums

Archdiocese of Santa Fe Museum
223 Cathedral Pl.
• **(505) 983-3811**

Because the Spanish government wanted converts as well as gold from New Mexico, the Catholic faith played a vital role in the area's history (see our Worship and Spirituality chapter). This unimposing little museum features historic documents, photographs, and artifacts that trace the development and role of the Catholic Church in New Mexico.

You can see the beautiful chalice used by Archbishop Jean Lamy when he said mass more than a century ago and the proclamation formally re-establishing the Spanish presence and Catholicism in Santa Fe, dated June 20, 1692, and signed by Don Diego de Vargas. The museum is open from 8:30 AM to 4 PM Monday through Saturday. Admission is by donation.

Bataan Memorial Military Museum and Library
1050 Old Pecos Tr.
• **(505) 474-1670**
• **bataanmm@cs.com**

Organized through the efforts of the New Mexico National Guard, the Bataan Veterans Organization, and many other interested parties, this museum displays artifacts collected by the state's military veterans and honors all New Mexicans who have done military service. The museum occupies an old armory and displays items dating from World War I through Desert Storm. The highlight is a tribute to the Bataan veterans, the 200th Coast Artillery Regiment that was sent to the Philippine Islands to furnish anti-aircraft support. The regiment was later divided to form the 515th Coast Artillery Regiment. The men saw enemy action on Bataan when the Japanese overran the Philippines in 1942. The 200th is officially credited with firing the first shot and being the last to surrender to the Armies of Japan. The 200th consisted of 1,800 men when deployed. After three and a half years of brutal captivity, less than 900 men returned to their families in New Mexico. The state has a government office building named in honor of these brave fighters, and a perpetual flame burns for them just outside it.

The museum has 30,000 artifacts, an extensive research library, and an archive of military documents relating to New Mexico's history. It's usually open Tuesday through Friday from 9:00 AM to 4:00 PM, and Saturday from 8:00 AM to 1:00 PM, but hours can change with seasonal visitors and tour groups. There is no admission charge.

Institute of American Indian Arts Museum
108 Cathedral Pl.
• **(505) 983-8900**
• **www.iaiancad.org/ museum/museum.html**

If you're interested in contemporary American Indian art, be sure to visit this downtown attraction. The museum is affiliated with the Institute of American Indian Arts, which has long been one of America's leading schools for Indian arts. Among the teachers and students whose work has put the IAIA on the national map are Allan Houser, Dan Namingha, Estella Loretto, Linda Lomahaftewa, and T. C. Cannon. With more than 6,500 pieces in the collection representing 3,000 artists, the museum is the largest repository of contemporary Indian art in the world. Painting and sculpture and traditional crafts such as beadwork, pottery, weaving, and basketry are displayed in the museum's five galleries. The museum offers educational programming and the outdoor Allan Houser Art Park for large sculpture. The IAIA Museum is open June through September 9 AM to 5 PM; October through May, 10 AM to 5 PM, Monday through Saturday; Sunday, 12-5. Admission is $4 for adults, $2 for seniors and students with an ID, and free for IAIA members and children younger than 16.

El Rancho de las Golondrinas
334 Los Pinos Rd., La Cienega
• (505) 471-2261

It's easy to imagine the relief of the tired travelers along the famous Camino Real, the main trade route connecting New Mexico to Mexico, when they reached this shady oasis. The ranch was the last stop before Santa Fe on the grueling journey from Mexico City to the northern province of New Spain. Centuries later, the natural beauty remains.

Approximately 15 miles southwest of Santa Fe, El Rancho de las Golondrinas, "the ranch of the swallows," offers a vivid re-creation of the area's 18th- and 19th-century history. The restored buildings—built on original foundations—have been furnished as appropriate to the period. You can visit an 18th-century placita house, a home built around a patio with thick walls and defensive towers. You can see a wa-ter-powered mill, feel the heat in a blacksmith shop, visit a school house, hike through the mountain village, and notice the solemnity in the morada, a chapel/meeting house used by an influential religious society.

Santa Fe residents like to bring their out-of-town visitors to the museum for its popular festivals and Civil War weekend. During these lively events, volunteers dress in traditional costumes, chat with visitors, and demonstrate many of the skills early settlers needed to survive on the frontier. The museum comes alive with dancing, music, sales of food and crafts, and activities of all sorts. You can see, taste, smell, hear, and touch the life of Spanish Colonial and Territorial New Mexico. El Rancho de las Golondrinas also presents theme weekends throughout the summer, focusing on topics such as arts, oral history and storytelling, Colonial traditions, the Catholic faith as it shaped the area's arts, and the animals the Spanish brought with them.

From June through September, you can tour the ranch on your own. Admission is $5 for adults; $4 for seniors (62 and older), teens, and military personnel; and $2 for ages 5 through 12. Children younger than 5 get in free. The

INSIDERS' TIP
If you don't want to sound like a tourist, please call the Plaza, "The Plaza," not "The Town Square."

ATTRACTIONS

The Wheelwright Museum is privately owned and operated.

Photo: Don Strel

museum's self-guided tour involves about a 1.5-mile walk over roads and trails that are sometimes steep and rocky. You should allow at least an hour and a half for the tour. During the festivals or Civil War Weekend, admission is $7 for adults; $5 for seniors (62 and older), teens and military; $3 for children ages 5 to 12 and free for children younger than 5. To reach the ranch from Santa Fe, take I-25 S. to Exit 276 and bear right on N.M. Highway 599. Turn left at the traffic light onto the frontage road and right just before the racetrack on Los Piños Road. The museum is 3 miles from this intersection.

School of American Research Indian Arts Research Center
660 Garcia St.
• **(505) 982-3584**

Although not, strictly speaking, a public museum, the public can view this extensive collection of American Indian art of the Southwest, including textiles, pottery, basketry, and jewelry once a week on a special tour. Docents will explain the SAR's fascinating history and role in American archaeology in addition to offering insights into the beautiful objects you'll see. Tours, by reservation only, are $15 and are normally held Fridays at 2 PM.

Wheelwright Museum of the American Indian
704 Camino Lejo
• **(505) 982-4636, (800) 607-4636**
• **www.wheelwright.org**

The story of the Wheelwright Museum is a tale of amazing transition, one which testifies to this institution's ability to adapt to the times. Mary Cabot Wheelwright, who founded the museum as the Museum of Navajo Ceremonial Arts in 1937, came to the Southwest from New England, bringing with her an outsider's appreciation for what she found and the economic and social connections to create a new institution. Her collaborator in the establishment of the museum was Hastiin Klah, an esteemed and influential Navajo singer or "medicine man." Klah was born in 1867 when most of the Navajo people were held as prisoners of war by the United States government. Klah had witnessed the decades of relentless efforts by the government and missionaries to assimilate the Navajo people into mainstream society. To Klah, the future of traditional Navajo religious practices appeared bleak.

Traders Frances "Franc" and Arthur Newcomb introduced Wheelwright and Klah, and the two became close friends. They were determined to create a permanent record of Klah's and other singers' ritual knowledge. Klah dictated and Wheelwright recorded the Navajo Creation Story and other great narratives that form the basis of Navajo religion. While Wheelwright concentrated on the spoken word in Navajo ritual, Franc Newcomb focused on the sandpaintings the singers create and destroy during the healing ceremonies. She re-created versions of them in tempera on paper. Klah, who was also a skilled weaver, recorded the sandpaintings in tapestry.

By the early 1930s it was clear to Wheelwright and Klah that a museum would be needed, not just as a repository for the manuscripts, recordings, paintings, and sandpainting tapestries but also to offer the public an opportunity to sense the beauty, dignity, and profound logic of the Navajo religion. The architect they chose, William Penhallow Henderson, based his design for the building on the hogan—the traditional eight-sided Navajo home and the setting for Navajo ceremonies. The museum's earliest names were the Navajo House of Prayer and House of Navajo Religion, but soon after it opened its official name became the Museum of Navajo Ceremonial Art.

Times changed, and, far from becoming assimilated, the Navajo people became one of the most powerful Indian groups in the United States. The resilient Navajo culture proved that the apprehension Wheelwright and Klah shared about the death of the Navajo religion was unfounded. In the 1960s and 1970s, the Navajo Nation exerted its independence in a number of ways, including the establishment of its own community college system. Also at that time, Navajo singers founded the Navajo Medicine Men's Association. The teaching of traditional Navajo religion enjoyed a revival, and its practitioners began to express their concerns about the sacred items and information in museums throughout the country.

In 1977, the Navajo Museum's board of trustees acknowledged the wisdom and authority of the Navajo Medicine Men's Association by voting to repatriate several Navajo medicine bundles and other items sacred to the Navajo people. The Navajo Nation now maintains them at the Ned A. Hatathli Cultural Center Museum at Navajo Community College in Tsaile, Arizona. With the repatriation in 1977, the museum changed its name to the Wheelwright Museum of the American Indian and now showcases art by contemporary American Indian artists.

Although it is no longer actively involved in the study of Navajo religion, the Wheelwright Museum maintains world-renowned collections and archives that document Navajo art and culture from 1850 to the present. (Scholars may view the collections through special arrangements with the museum director.) Exhibitions in the main gallery include contemporary and traditional American Indian art with an emphasis on the Southwest. The exhibits rotate every four months. A second gallery presents one-person exhibitions. The entrance displays outdoor sculptures by Allan Houser and others. Special activities include storyteller Joe Hayes on Saturday and Sunday evenings in July and August. Hayes entertains in a tipi; visitors sit on blankets and listen to tales that reflect Santa Fe's Indian, Hispanic, and Wild West heritage. The museum also hosts a children's pow-wow in the fall. The Case Trading Post has a wonderful selection of art work, jewelry, pottery, books, and unusual items. The museum is open from 10 AM to 5 PM Monday through Saturday and 1 to 5 PM on Sunday. Admission is free.

Museum of New Mexico Hours and Prices

The four museums operated by the Museum of New Mexico—Palace of the Governors, Museum of Fine Arts, Museum of International Folk Art, Museum of Indian Arts & Culture/Laboratory of Anthropology—follow the same pricing schedule and hours. Instead of repeating this information in each entry, we've put it here for your convenience.

Daily admission for one museum is $5; $10 for a four-day pass for unlimited admissions to all four Santa Fe museums; $1 on Sunday for New Mexico residents with I.D.; Wednesday is free to New Mexico seniors with I.D. Free admission is offered daily to youth 16 and younger. Annual passes are available for $25.

All branches of the Museum of New Mexico are open from 10 AM to 5 PM Tuesday through Sunday. The Palace of the Governors and the Museum of Fine Arts are also open from 5 to 8 PM for Free Friday Evenings. The museums are closed Mondays, New Year's Day, Easter, Thanksgiving and Christmas. For information about the Museum of New Mexico's events and attractions call the 24-hour information line, (505) 827-6463

The Museum of New Mexico
Administrative offices, 113 Lincoln Ave.
- **(505) 827-6451**
- **www.museumofnewmexico.org**

Headquartered in Santa Fe, the state's museum system includes research libraries, artifact conservation, archaeological research, education programs, and traveling exhibits, the American Indian portal vendors "living exhibit," the Museum Press, and El Palacio magazine. Operated with state funding, private grants, and money earned though admission fees, the museum system is managed as part of the New Mexico Office of Cultural Affairs. The four Santa Fe-based museums are the Palace of the Governors, Museum of Fine Arts, Museum of International Folk Art, Museum of Indian Arts and Culture/Laboratory of Anthropology. The Palace and the Fine Arts Museum are downtown. Museum of Indian Arts and Culture and the Museum of International Folk Art are about 2 miles from the Plaza on Camino Lejo, just off the Old Santa Fe Trail.

Museum of Fine Arts
107 W. Palace Ave.
- **(505) 827-4468**
- **www.museumofnewmexico.org**

The Museum of Fine Arts is easy to find once you're on the Plaza. It's right across the street from the Palace of the Governors at the corner of Lincoln and Palace Avenues. Its classic Santa Fe style makes the museum one of the city's most-photographed buildings. The collections focus mainly on art from the Southwest and New Mexico and include both traditional and contemporary work in a variety of media. The museum owns and displays creations by many well-known artists, including the Santa Fe and Taos master painters who first brought the art world's attention to New Mexico as well as Georgia O'Keeffe and Peter Hurd. (See our Arts chapter.) The museum's galleries change exhibits fairly frequently and usually include cutting-edge work by living artists as well as shows that draw on the collections. A recent exhibit invited the viewer to ask "What is art?" with an eclectic display ranging from a gilded bomb to an experimental motorcycle and a house covered with ceramic tile.

Like its sister, the Palace of the Governors, this museum attracts attention for its architecture as well as its archives. Completed in 1917, the museum is a beautiful example of the Pueblo Revival style of construction, complete with split cedar *latillas* (roof supporters), hand-hewn *vigas* (log roof beams) and corbels. The gracious style reflected in the thick walls, pleasantly landscaped central courtyard, smooth interior plaster, and other finishing touches became synonymous with "Santa Fe Style."

The Museum of Fine Arts offers art classes for kids, an extensive program of lectures, and gallery talks. The Santa Fe Chamber Music Festival makes its home in the museum's St. Francis Auditorium during the summer.

Museum of Indian Arts and Culture
710 Camino Lejo
• **(505) 827-6344**
• **www.miaclab.org/**

This museum's pride and joy is its permanent exhibit, "Here, Now and Always," which opened with tremendous fanfare and blessings from Indian leaders in August 1997. The exhibit goes on the must-see list for anyone interested in American Indians and their arts, culture, and history. Housed in a large new wing, "Here, Now and Always" tells the story of the Native American presence in the Southwest with more than 1,300 objects and a multimedia production created during the eight-year period the museum spent in collaboration with Native American elders, artists, scholars, teachers, builders, and writers. These consultants worked with a team of Indian and non-Indian museum curators and designers to develop an exhibit that combines the actual voices of contemporary American Indians with ancient artifacts. The architectural design helps bring centuries of culture and tradition to life.

The exhibit uses stone and silver, clay and wool, feast days, fairs, and family stories to tell of the enduring communities of the Southwest. To orient visitors, it incorporates the landscape itself, mesas and settlements, plazas, and sacred peaks. Visitors proceed by theme through the galleries. You can visit a pueblo kitchen, an Apache wickiup, a Navajo hogan, a 1930s trading post, and a contemporary vendor's booth at a tribal feast day celebration. The stories in "Here, Now and Always" are told on videotape by 24 American Indians.

The Museum of Indian Arts and Culture was established in 1987 next to its adjoining research facility, the Laboratory of Anthropology. In addition to exhibits, the museum has a resource center with looms, magazines, books, maps, and other useful tools. The museum is noted for its prehistoric and historic pottery, basketry, woven fabrics, and jewelry. The museum offers a "Breakfast With the Curators" program, daytrips, and other special events.

Museum of International Folk Art
706 Camino Lejo
• **(505) 827-6350**
• **www.state.nm.us/moifa**

Just as the Museum of Indian Arts and Culture provides a fascinating and informative orientation to the American Indian cultures of the Southwest, the Folk Art Museum does the same for New Mexico's Hispanic culture. And that's just one of its exhibits! The Hispanic Heritage Wing features Spanish Colonial folk art and an interactive computer program in its "Familia y Fe/Family and Faith" exhibit. The finely crafted displays delineate the central position of extended family relationships and the Catholic faith in northern New Mexico's Hispanic culture. The exhibit also underlines the resourcefulness of the pioneer families who lived for more than a century in tremendous isolation from manufactured goods, European medicine, and formal education.

In addition to insight into New Mexico's Hispanic past, museum visitors can come away with a better sense of the world as a whole. This museum is the repository for the world's largest collection of international folk art. In the "Multiple Visions: A Common Bond" exhibit, for example, you'll find objects from more than 100 countries displayed in fascinating dioramas. Toys from 19th-century Europe, Chinese prints, embroidered Indian mandalas, Mexican Day of the Dead mementos, and examples of early 20th-century Americana are among the treasures. This exhibit alone includes more than 10,000 pieces of folk art, all donated by the Girard Foundation Collection.

Opened in 1998, the Neutrogena Wing

INSIDERS' TIP
The Museum of International Folk Art maintains a research library (open to the public) of more than 11,000 books and subscribes to nearly 100 journals. Its holdings relate directly to collections and provide extensive information on textiles, costumes, Spanish Colonial art and life, and folk art and cultures around the globe. Other branches of the Museum of New Mexico also have libraries, which are open to the public, and librarians who can help with your research.

houses an impressive array of textiles, costumes, and masks donated by Lloyd Cotsen and the Neutrogena Corporation. Get an up-close look at riches from the collection with a visit to "Lloyd's Treasure Chest" where you will have an opportunity to examine cherished objects and watch the collection's staff as they work behind the scenes.

The museum hosts changing exhibits and a variety of special events, some ready-made for children and families. Check with the museum about docent-guided tours, which are free with admission.

Palace of the Governors
105 E. Palace Ave.
- **(505) 827-6483**
- **www.palaceofthegovernors.org**

With its chronicle of more than 450 years of European presence in the Southwest, the Palace presents a first-class historic introduction to Santa Fe and northern New Mexico. Built in 1610, this massive adobe building sits as simple testimony to New Mexico's long, rich. and fascinating history. It's the oldest public building in the United States and has been in continual use since shortly after the day its builders, probably Indian slaves, laid the last adobe or mud brick.

Despite the name, don't be surprised that this building doesn't look much like a storybook palace or the grand structures of Europe. Santa Fe's Palace, a single-storied, earth-colored building with a long front portal and a shady interior courtyard, suited the place and the time of its construction. It speaks more of early New Mexico's entrepreneurial, frontier style than the glory of mother Spain. The Spanish used the Palace until the Pueblo Revolt of 1680, when consolidated forces of Pueblo Indians seized the building and drove the Europeans out of New Mexico. (See our History chapter.) The Indians remained in control for 12 years, then the Spanish returned and the Palace again became their Territorial headquarters. When Mexico won its independence, taking New Mexico with it, the Mexican flag flew here. The U.S. government seized control during the Mexican-American War. Confederate forces occupied the Palace during their attempt to win the West. Territorial Governor Lew Wallace wrote part of Ben Hur here.

The building was replaced as a governmental seat in 1909 after it had housed 60 New Mexico governors. It then became Santa Fe's first museum. Apart from any of the displays, the building itself is rich with history because of the many events and decisions crucial to the history of New Mexico that were born inside these thick mud walls. Whenever changes to

In most years, Northern New Mexico boasts a bountiful fall harvest.

Photo: Don Strel

the building that are more than superficial are made, archaeologists discover more treasures and historic tidbits beneath its floors. The rooms display thousands of treasures, including Indian pottery made before the Spanish "discovered" this place, written accounts of the Coronado Expedition, a reconstruction of a 17th-century Spanish cart, and maps of 18th-century Spanish America. You'll have a chance to see, horse-drawn hearses, a full-scale reproduction of a mountain village chapel, a chuck wagon dating to the mid-19th century, and a book bindery and presses from an old print shop.

Period rooms, including the 1846 New Mexico Governor's Office and a much more ornate parlor used in 1893 by Gov. L. Bradford Prince, re-create the Palace of the past. The American Indians who sit in front of the museum along the portal are an attraction that draws international attention. (See our Close-up in this chapter.) The museum also has a fine shop that offers unusual merchandise and a good selection of books. The Palace hosts lectures and book signings with pleasant frequency and offers a variety of special programs including Christmas at the Palace and the Mountain Man Rendezvous (see our Annual Events chapter).

Georgia O'Keeffe Museum
217 Johnson St.
• **(505) 995-0785**
• **www.okeeffemuseum.org**

Georgia O'Keeffe is New Mexico's best-known artist—even people who don't know a pastel from a poster have heard of O'Keeffe and seen reproductions of her famous paintings of the city's most popular destinations for visitors.

The Georgia O'Keeffe Museum is America's first museum dedicated to the work of a woman artist of international stature. O'Keeffe visited New Mexico in 1917 and came here permanently in 1949, settling in an old adobe home in the small village of Abiquiú (see our close-up in the Arts chapter). She lived there, inspired by the landscape and the light, for nearly 40 years before moving to Santa Fe a few years before her death in 1986 at age 98.

The Georgia O'Keeffe Museum houses the world's largest permanent collection of her work, including many pieces the artist kept for herself that have never exhibited previously. At the museum, you'll see work O'Keeffe produced between 1916 and 1980. Flowers and bleached desert bones, abstractions, nudes, landscapes, city-scapes, and still lifes are all here. The museum's galleries trace O'Keeffe's artistic evolution follow the depth and breadth of her long, productive career.

As a secondary goal, the museum collects and hosts guest exhibits of works by contemporaries of O'Keeffe who were part of her artistic community. Anne and John Marion, philanthropists who also funded the new visual arts center at the College of Santa Fe, endowed the 13,000-square foot museum. The building itself allows plenty of room for the paintings. The display throughout the museum's 10 galleries is simple and unpretentious, just as O'Keeffe would have liked. The museum offers guided tours, educational programming, and special events. You can watch a short video about O'Keeffe's life and learn about her contribution to American art.

The Georgia O'Keeffe Museum is open 10 AM to 5 PM Tuesdays- Sundays and 10 AM to 8 PM Fridays. It is closed Mondays, New Year's Day, Easter, Thanksgiving and Christmas. Admission is$5 for a one-day pass, $10 for a four-day, five-museum pass that allows unlimited admission to all museums in the Museum of New Mexico system. Admission is $1 on Sundays for New Mexico residents with ID. Free admission is offered daily to ages 16 and under. Wednesday are free days for New Mexico seniors (60 and older with ID). And Fridays from 5 PM to 8 PM everyone gets in free.

Other Attractions

The Cross of the Martyrs and Commemorative Walkway
Paseo de Peralta at Otero St.
•**No phone**

You feel like you're walking through history as you climb the winding brick path that takes you to the Cross of the Martyrs. Informative plaques line the walkway, summarizing the city's early history and the events that led to the deaths of the Franciscan missionaries who are commemorated by a 20-foot white metal cross at the path's end. From the top of the hill, you get a lovely view of the city and a panorama of the Sangre de Cristo, Jemez, and Sandia Mountains—a reward for your energetic effort. Santa Fe's annual Fiesta ends with a candlelight procession from the cathedral to the cross. And on Christmas Eve, bright bonfires, or luminarias, surround it. There are no official visiting hours, and no fees are charged.

The Planetarium
**Santa Fe Community College,
6401 Richards Ave.**
• **(505) 428-1707**

The Planetarium, one of the city's newer, out-of-the-way attractions, offers a changing schedule of productions intended to give the audience a better feeling for the night sky. The Celestial Highlights program the first Thursday of each month provides an introduction to the stars and constellations that will be visible for the next 30 days. Show time is 7 PM. The planetarium is on the upper level in the west wing of the Community College. From June through August, the planetarium's Wednesday programs are designed to entertain general audiences. Thursdays are "kids night out" with a different program each week. On both evenings, the entertainment begins at 7 PM. From September through May, the planetarium offers its live "The Current Research Series" on Wednesdays, "Celestial Highlights" on the first Thursday and "Celestial Sounds," an in-house concert series on the second Thursday. Tickets are $5 for adults, $3 for children 12 and younger and for seniors 65 and older and for SFCC students with a current ID. Concerts are $8 and $5 respectively. Tickets go on sale a half-hour before showtime. Call (505) 428-1777 for the current show listing.

Santa Fe Botanical Garden
6401 Richards Ave.
• **(505) 428-1684**

Santa Fe Botanical Garden doesn't have a full-fledged public garden site quite yet, however a permanent home at the entrance to Aldea, a residential development in west Santa Fe, is currently in the works. Once established, the 25-acre facility will be a place for ongoing education and research as well as a celebration of the region's rich botanical heritage and biodiversity. Meanwhile, Santa Fe Botanical Garden still has plenty of year-round offerings for resident and visiting garden aficionados alike.

From May to October docent-led tours of Leonora Curtin Natural History Area, a 35-acre wetland area south of Santa Fe, are regularly scheduled. A working preserve and outdoor laboratory overseen by the Garden, Leonoroa Curtin is a sanctuary for native plant and animal species which affords birders and nature lovers a unique experience. Another recent addition to Santa Fe Botanical Garden's stewardship is a pristine 1,350-acre wilderness preserve in the Ortiz Mountains. Escorted visits to this extraordinary area may also be arranged through the office. Santa Fe Botanical Garden offers regular programs and classes on various aspects of gardening and horticulture, tours of private gardens in and around Santa Fe and numerous other events throughout the year. A quarterly newsletter and reduced event fees are among member benefits.

Santa Fe Farmers' Market
Santa Fe Railyard near Sanbusco Center
• **(505) 983-4098**

Farmers' Market brings fresh area produce along with homemade salsa, baked goods, herbal remedies, cheeses, organic meat, fragrant cut flowers, plants for landscaping, and more. What you discover in the farmers' booths depends on the season and how early you show up. But you can be assured that you'll find a crowd of Santa Fe residents and curious visitors. The vendors come from throughout northern New Mexico and as far east as Ft. Sumner, nearly 200 miles away. When you buy here, you not only get delicious food, you're supporting small business. Music, free samples, coffee, and baked goods for sale mark most morning markets. The market is open from 7 AM to noon on Saturday; a Tuesday morning market is held at the same times starting mid-May. Those who come early find the best selection. The market usually runs from the end of April until the end of October. Potential buyers and their children are admitted free. A new "satellite" market has been added on Rodeo Road at the County Extension building and will be open on Thursdays, 3:30 PM to dusk, from mid-June through the end of September.

INSIDERS' TIP

In the Plaza area you'll find artists who'll do your portrait as a souvenir of your visit to Santa Fe. These entrepreneurs and others who sell on the Plaza are licensed by the city.

Santa Fe Horse Park
Go west on Airport Rd. to C.R. 56;
the entrance of the Santa Fe Horse Park
is 2 miles from the intersection on the
right-hand side
• **(505) 424-7400, Clubhouse,**
(505) 424-7656 Polo
• **www.horsepark.com/clinics.html**

Year-round polo and other horse events are the attraction here, along with a breath-taking location. Most events are free to spectators and offer visitors a fine chance to see great horsemanship and beautiful horses in a variety of contexts. The outdoor polo season runs from May to end of September; indoor polo runs from January to March. Other activities include hunter-jumper and dressage competitions, team roping, barrels, and team penning. Call for information about the Old West cowboy mounted shooting, an event that involves shooting targets from the back of a running horse! Clinics for dressage riders by well-known instructors and clinics for polo umpires leading to certification have been hosted here. The horse park also offers boarding facilities and riding lessons.

With its stuffing views of Sangre de Cristo Mountains, the Santa Fe Horse Park provides a picturesque backdrop to all kinds of outdoor entertaining, and the facility can be leased for special events.

Shidoni Foundry and Gallery
P.O. Box 250, Bishops Lodge Rd., Tesuque
• (505) 988-8001
• www.shidoni.com

Established in 1971, Shidoni is one of the world's leading fine-art casting facilities and showplaces. Sculpture produced here represents leading artists from throughout the world. On Saturday (times vary, please call), you can watch 2,000-degree molten bronze as it's poured into ceramic shell molds for casting. The foundry is open for visitors who'd like to walk through from noon to 1 PM Monday through Friday and from 9 AM to 5 PM on Saturday. The self-guided tours are free. Shidoni also offers an 8-acre sculpture garden with 500 works, the largest outdoor sculpture display in New Mexico. You can stroll among monumental sculptures in a variety of styles and media year round from 8 AM to sunset. Shidoni makes its grounds available for private parties and fund-raising events. Two contemporary art galleries are located on the property. One features painting and crafts and the other highlights sculpture. The galleries are open from 9 AM to 5 PM Monday through Saturday. Shidoni is in Tesuque, about 5 miles north of the Plaza in Santa Fe

Ski Santa Fe Chairlift Rides
Santa Fe Ski Area, 16 miles northeast of Santa Fe on N.M. Hwy. 475
• (505) 983-9155, (505) 982-4429
• www.skisantafe.com/

The Super Chief Quad, a four-person chairlift, takes sightseers to the top of Aspen Peak at an elevation of 11,000 feet. The stunning view from this part of the Santa Fe National Forest includes the Jemez and Sandia Mountains, Mount Taylor, San Antonio Peak, and the Rio Grande valley. A descriptive sign with tubes you can look through helps identify major landmarks. Even in the summer, it's a good idea to bring a sweater or jacket—the air can be cool up here in God's country. If you're feeling energetic, you can continue hiking through the spruce, fir and ponderosa pine. You may see marmots, dozens of different wildflowers, and colorful mushrooms. Afterwards you can buy lunch, a snack, or a cold drink at the ski area's La Casa Cafe Grill near the base of the chairlift.

The chairlift operates weekends and holidays from 10 AM to 3 PM July 4 through Labor Day and again in the fall. Round-trip rates are

$7 per person. Children shorter than 46 inches may ride for free accompanied by a paying adult; seniors 72 or over may ride for free. One-way trips for hikers are $5.

Pueblo Casinos

Camel Rock Casino
Tesuque Pueblo, U.S. Hwy. 84-285, 10 miles north of Santa Fe
• (800) GO-CAMEL (505) 984-8414
• www.camelrockcasino.com

Named for the distinctive rock formation just across the highway, this casino has one of the nicest locations in northern New Mexico. The attractive, 60,000-square-foot building includes a large bingo hall, dining area, gift shop, plenty of slot machines and gaming tables, and you can enjoy live entertainment, from local bands to headliners. Minors can eat at the buffet but otherwise are not allowed in the casino. The casino is open Sunday through Thursday, 8 AM to 4 AM, and 24 hours on Friday, Saturday and federal holidays. In addition to a huge lot for parking, free valet parking is available.

Cities of Gold Casino
Pojoaque Pueblo, U.S. Hwy. 84-285, 15 miles north of Santa Fe
Hotel reservations (877) 455-0515
• www.citiesofgold.com

The early Spanish explorers sought the legendary cities of gold when they came to the Southwest. Gamblers here hope to have luck. In addition to the usual attractions, this casino includes a sports bar, more than 600 slot machines, video poker and keno, live blackjack, craps, roulette, a spacious poker room, and a 400-seat bingo hall. A free shuttle makes several daily pickups at downtown and Cerrillos Road motels. The casino, which is open 24 hours a day, seven days a week, does not allow minors. If you get hungry you can visit the buffet and snack bar.

Ohkay Casino Resort
2 miles north of Espanola on NM 68, about 40 minutes from Santa Fe
• (800) PLAY-AT-OK, hotel reservations 1-877-829-2865
• www.ohkay.com/

This 127,000 square foot casino—New Mexico's Largest casino-resort—has slot machines and table games including live action blackjack, roulette, craps, poker, and bingo. You can try your luck at any of 750 slot machines.

The casino features comedy acts on Tuesday nights at the Silver Eagle Lounge, and bands play a variety of music from 8 PM to 1 AM. The lounge has a full bar with appetizers on some nights; smoking is allowed. If gambling has stirred up your appetite, the Harvest Café has a buffet menu every night and a margarita brunch from 10 AM to 4 PM on Sundays. You can catch professional boxing matches, concerts, and other events in the casino dome, just north of the main casino. Casino hours are 8 AM to 4 AM Sunday through Wednesday; open 24 hours Thursday through Saturday. Special event tickets are available at the casino gift shop and at Ticketmaster outlets. The resort offers an attached 101-room Best Western hotel.

San Felipe's Casino Hollywood
I-25, Exit 252, 30 miles south of Santa Fe
• (505) 867-6700 1-87-PLAY2WIN
• www.sanfelipecasino.com/

Located between Albuquerque and Santa Fe, Casino Hollywood offers 530 slot machines, blackjack, Pai Gow poker, roulette and Wheel of Madness 21. The machines include Filthy Rich, Jackpot Party, Boom, Reel'em In and Chicken. Video poker, video keno, video blackjack and many more games here welcome your nickels, quarters, dollars, and five-dollar tokens.

The casino, which will let you try your luck 24 hours a day, seven days a week, is usually busy. There's plenty of convenient parking for cars, recreational vehicles, and busses. The place is handicapped accessible and, its web site claims, virtually smoke free.

San Felipe Pueblo opened Casino Hollywood in November 1995, providing some 350 jobs for tribal members and New Mexico residents as well. Casino employees consist of 42.5 percent San Felipe members, 17.5 percent other American Indians and the rest non-Indians.

Tours

Afoot in Santa Fe Walking Tours and The Loretto Line Tram Tours
211 Old Santa Fe Tr. at the Loretto Hotel
• (505) 983-3701

In business since 1990, this tour company prides itself on hiring guides who know their history and have a good sense of humor. Owner Charles Porter has conducted tours for groups from the National Parks Foundation and the Smithsonian. The walking tours involve more history; the driving tours on the Loretto Line trolley cover more sightseeing territory. The

walking tour, which encompasses about 2 miles of the city's nooks and crannies and takes about 2 hours, leaves daily year-round at 9:30 AM. Fee is $10 per adult and free for children younger than 16 with a parent.

The open-air trams leave at 10 AM, 11 AM, noon, 1, 2, and 3 PM, with additional tours added during the busiest summer weeks. The one hour and 15-minute tour costs $12 for adults and $6 for children 12 and younger and lasts about 75 minutes. The trolleys normally run from April through October depending on the weather. No reservations are needed for either tour. All tours depart from the Loretto Hotel. Pay parking for tour guests is usually available at the hotel.

Art Walking Tours
Museum of Fine Arts, 107 W. Palace Ave.
• (505) 476-5072
• www.museumofnewmexico.org/calendar

Every Monday in the summer when the museum is closed, you can join trained docents on an interactive walking tour of downtown Santa Fe. Learn about Santa Fe's outdoor sculptures, Frederico Vigil's mural in the County Courthouse, WPA murals in the Federal Building and the art collection at La Fonda Hotel. The walk begins at 10 AM and is $10 for adults. Accompanied children 16 years and younger are free. Proceeds support the Museum of Fine Arts Library and Education Department. Tour participants meet at the Museum of Fine Arts Shop steps.

Historic Walks of Santa Fe
Leave from La Fonda Hotel,
100 Ea. San Francisco, and the Plaza Galleria,
next to Simply Santa Fe
• (505) 986-0122, (505) 986-8388
• www.historicwalksofsantafe.com/

These walking tours give visitors a chance to learn local history, shop, or discover Santa Fe's art scene. The history tours depart morning and afternoon daily for $10–which includes admission to the Miraculous Staircase. No reservations are required. The company's other tours do require reservations and may require minimum numbers. The shopping tour includes lunch and the gallery tour includes refreshments.

The "Ghostwalker" tour presents ghost lore with good-humored guides who take these hair-raising legends just seriously enough to make the tours fun. The deluxe ghost walk takes you down to the Santa Fe River, where, if you're lucky (and every group seems to be) you might see La Llorona, northern New Mexico's infamous weeping woman who haunts river-beds looking for her lost children. Bring your cameras. Ghostwalker tours are held on Friday evenings.

Fees for the special tours range from $10 for the regular ghost tour to $35 for shopping and lunch.

Outback Tours
P.O. Box 961, Santa Fe 87504
- **(505) 820-6101, (800) 800-JEEP**
- **www.outbacktours.com**

These jeep tours focus on the natural history, ecology, and archaeology of the Santa Fe area. All guides have advanced degrees in fields such as botany, geology, and archaeology. The tours are fully insured and the company has been in business for seven years. Regularly scheduled trips, such as into the Jémez Mountains, to Taos or into the national forest above Santa Fe, are offered from March through October, with custom tours available other months. Prices begin at $48, and reservations are necessary. You may be able to arrange for pick-up at your hotel.

Palace Walks History Tours
Palace of the Governors
105 E. Palace Ave., Santa Fe
- **(505) 827-6483**
- **www.nmcn.org/features/walkingtours/index.html**

During the summer and fall, the Palace of the Governors hosts tours of historic down-town Santa Fe. Each walk is personalized by the specially-trained guide and reflects his/her particular area of interest. The walk covers history beginning in the 17th century and ending with current assessment of contemporary life in Santa Fe.

The tour takes about 1½ hours and departs from the Blue Gate of the Palace of Lincoln Avenue at 10:15 AM, Monday-Saturday, May-October. Fee for adults is $10. (Accompanied children younger than 17 are free.) All proceeds benefit the museum.

Rojo Tours
P.O. Box 15744, Santa Fe 87506
- **(505) 474-8333**
- **tours@rojotours.com**

Rojo offers a variety of customized tours and arranges packages for convention and meeting planners. In addition to Santa Fe driving and walking tours, they will take visitors to cave dwellings and Indian pueblos. Rojo offers an O'Keeffe country tour and a visit to fine-art studios and sculpture gardens. They'll also drive you to Taos, to Hispanic and Indian villages along the Rio Grande, and even to Chaco Canyon in a 12-hour extravaganza. Balloon rides, whitewater rafting, backpacking excursions, and more are available. Prices range from $50 to $350, depending on the trip. Please call to find out where to join a specific tour.

Santa Fe Detours
54 E. San Francisco St.
- **(505) 983-6565, (800) DETOURS**
- **www.sfdetours.com**

In town or out of town, by foot, raft, or railroad, Santa Fe Detours has served visitors and residents for more than 15 years. This locally owned and operated company handles the bookings for the Roadrunner, the open-air yellow trolley that cruises Santa Fe's historic neighborhoods. This company will also arrange horseback riding, private guides for hiking and biking, Grayline bus tours, and even help find tickets to popular performances. Prices depend on the services selected; they offer a comprehensive package that includes a ride on the Roadrunner and a walking tour for $17. Their central reservation service can also help with accommodations from luxury suites to cozy vacation rentals.

Santa Fe Southern Railway
410 S. Guadalupe St.
- **(505) 989-8600**

Take a trip from the city to the neighboring community of Lamy, about 20 miles away, on the comfortable vintage coaches of a working freight train. The train leaves from the Santa Fe Depot in the Guadalupe Street area—a great place for shopping—and travels south over the old Atchison, Topeka, & Santa Fe line. You'll see the northern New Mexico high desert ringed by the blue Jemez, Sandia, and Sangre de Cristo Mountains. The train stops in the village of Lamy, home of the Lamy Depot, which is used by the Amtrak line. Passengers spend 90 minutes in Lamy enjoying lunch, either a picnic they've brought with them or catered items for sale on the train—please call to determine which days the caterer is available! After lunch, the train takes you back to the Santa Fe depot. November through March, the trains leave at 11:00 AM Tuesday, Thursday, and Saturday, and 1:00 PM on Sundays. April through October, trains depart at 10:30 AM Tuesday, Wednesday, Thursday, and Saturday and 1 PM Sunday and Monday. From April through October you can enjoy New Mexico's spectacular sunsets and clear, starlit skies on the Friday evening "High Desert Highball" trip. Departure is 6:15 PM April through Labor Day; after Labor Day it's 5:45 PM. You'll be back in Santa Fe by 8:30 PM. On Saturday nights, you can join fellow passengers for a campfire barbecue, April through October; the train leaves at 6:15 PM and returns at 10:45 PM.

Rates depend on the trip you select. Scenic-day tickets are $25-$40 for adults; seniors are $20-$35; children ages 3-13 are $13-$28; tots under 3 ride free.

Aboot About/Santa Fe
624 Galisteo, No. 32
• **(505) 988-2774**
• **www.abootabout.com**

This company offers walking tours with guides who are archaeologists, artists, and anthropologists. In addition to the popular Santa Fe orientation tour, the company offers ghost and mystery walks, literary walking tours, artist and gallery tours, and a full range of half- and full-day adventures throughout New Mexico. The basic historic walking tour is a two-and-a-half-hour stroll to Santa Fe's significant sites. Tours leave daily at 9:45 AM and 1:45 PM from the Hotel St. Francis, 210 Don Gaspar Avenue. Fee is $10 per person, and people younger than 16 go along free if accompanied by an adult. You can park in city lots across the street from the hotels.

Southwest Safaris
P.O. Box 945, Santa Fe 87501
• **(505) 988-4246, (800) 842-4246**

These unique air/land tours take visitors by aircraft and land vehicle to some of the Southwest's most magnificent landmarks and ruins, providing a detailed look at the area's geology, archaeology, and natural history. One-day expeditions are offered from Santa Fe to the Grand Canyon, Monument Valley, Canyon de Chelly, Mesa Verde, and Arches. On the one-day trip to Cannyon de Chelly, for example, safari travelers fly over the Rio Grande and the Jémez Mountains. They see the San Juan Basin, the rugged Chuska Mountains, and picturesque Canyon de Chelly before landing in the heart of the Navajo Reservation. Passengers rendezvous with a ground tour and Navajo driver for exploration of the canyon, famous for its cliff dwellings and sheer sandstone walls. Fee for the tour is $359 per person. The trip departs Santa Fe at 7 AM and returns by 3:30 PM.

Want a shorter tour? Try a half-day safari

to Aztec Ruins National Monument. After a one-hour flight over the enchanted vistas of northern New Mexico, travelers land and are met by an archaeologist/anthropologist who serves as personal guide through the pueblo ruins of the Monument. The cost is $279 per person, and the trip leaves Santa Fe at 7 AM, returning by 12:30 PM. Pilot/guide Bruce Adams will also arrange custom trips. All trips are by reservation.

WingsWest Birding Tours
2599 Camino Chueco
• **(505) 473-2780, (800) 583-6928**
• **www.collectorsguide.com/wingswest**

WingsWest Birding Tours offers customized trips throughout the northern half of New Mexico. Bird watchers select from among 4-hour, 7-hour, or all-day expeditions. Company founder Bill West, an avid birder for 35 years, has spent the last two decades in New Mexico. Because of the diversity of habitat and the change of seasons found in the Land of Enchantment, visitors can enjoy northern New Mexico's birds year round. West and company welcome beginners as well as experienced birders on the excursions and provide loaner binoculars. Fees are $185 for full day, $125 for half day, and $80 for quarter day. Rates are the same for one or two visitors. There is a small per person charge for groups bigger than two.

Visitor Information

La Bajada Visitor Center
I-25 at the La Bajada exit #268,
17 miles south of Santa Fe
• **(505) 690-6610**

La Bajada, Spanish for "the descent," was clearly named by travelers heading south to Rio Abajo or the lower Rio Grande country— rather than those making the arduous climb up hill from Albuquerque. The newly-renovated La Bajada Visitor Center, serving more than 140,000 travelers a year, offers the largest assortment of free publications about Santa Fe and northern New Mexico and the state of New Mexico's comprehensive free vacation guide. It's a logical first stop for travelers arriving from Albuquerque. For added comfort, the center has public restrooms and telephones maintained by the state highway department and serves free coffee until 4 PM daily. Take an extra minute here and enjoy the view of glittering Santa Fe below you with the blue Sangre de Cristo Mountains towering in the background. The center is open from 8 AM to 6 PM daily from Memorial Day to the end of October and from 8 AM to 5 PM the rest of the year. It's closed on Thanksgiving, Christmas, and New Year's Day.

Plaza Information Booth
62 Lincoln Ave. in the portal window of the First National Bank on the Plaza
• No phone

Volunteers from the Santa Fe Chamber of Commerce staff the Plaza Information Booth as a service to Santa Fe's multitude of visitors during the peak of the tourist season. You'll find brochures of all kinds and free copies of locally published visitor guides. They can give you a list of restaurants and lodging possibilities. Even better, you'll find people who live here and can answer your questions. Mid-May through mid-September, the booth is open from 9 AM to 4 PM Monday through Friday.

New Mexico Public Lands Information Center
1474 Rodeo Rd.
• (505) 438-7542
• www.publiclands.org

This interagency program offers books, maps, permits, and licenses for people interested in outdoor activities and audiovisual information about recreational opportunities on all of the state's public lands. A partnership between the Bureau of Land Management and the Public Lands Interpretive Association established and maintains the center. In addition to first-rate materials you can buy, you'll find many free publications. The staff knows the area well. The center is open 8 AM to 5 PM Monday through Friday; there's plenty of parking.

Santa Fe Chamber of Commerce Information Center
510 N. Guadalupe St. at DeVargas Center North
• (505) 983-7317
• www.santafechamber.com

If you're considering a move to Santa Fe, stop here for information about real estate, taxes, the business climate, and more. The Chamber of Commerce has a separate room devoted to all kinds of free material provided by members. You can order a comprehensive relocation packet online or by phone for $25 including shipping. A Santa Fe Membership and Business Directory is available for $10 plus shipping.

Santa Fe Convention and Visitors Bureau
Sweeney Center, 201 W. Marcy St.
• (505) 984-6760, (800) 777-2489
• www.santafe.org

You'll find a variety of information about Santa Fe here along with a schedule of events for Sweeney Center, one of Santa Fe's most popular spots for conferences, conventions, trade shows, and public events. If luck is with you, you'll be able to get a parking place in the city-owned lot right next door. The bureau is an easy walk from the Plaza and downtown hotels. You can pick up information between 8 AM and 5 PM Monday through Friday.

State of New Mexico Santa Fe Welcome Center
491 Old Santa Fe Tr.
• (505) 827-7336

Conveniently located near the corner of Old Santa Fe Trail and Paseo de Peralta, right across the street from the State Capitol, this is one of Santa Fe and New Mexico's most comprehensive sources for visitor information. The free maps, brochures, and visitor guides are arranged by county. The friendly and knowledgeable staff can answer your questions, or at the very least, refer you to someone else who can. And if you time it right, you might be able to find a shady parking place for your RV while you gather the information you need. Best of all, this center is open from 8 AM to 5 PM (until 7 PM after Memorial Day) seven days a week! The center occupies the historic Lamy Building (see the listing in this chapter).

Near Santa Fe

Hyde Memorial State Park
7.5 miles northeast of Santa Fe on N.M.Hwy. 475
• (505) 983-7175

With its hiking opportunities and cross-country ski trails, a cold stream to splash in, and plenty of picnic tables, Hyde Park draws a nice crowd of Santa Fe residents and visitors into the Sangre de Cristo Mountains year-round. Backpackers and Nordic skiers use Hyde Park to begin their explorations of the adjoining Santa Fe National Forest. Campsites, including areas for large groups, and the park's playgrounds are popular in the summer. In the winter, there's a sledding slope and tubing run. The road from Santa Fe to Hyde Park and beyond is designated as a National Scenic Byway, and the trip takes you through beautiful mountain country over a paved, two-lane highway that is steep and twisty in some places. Day use is $4; the fee for camping is $10 per day for a tent site or $14 per day for a site with electricity.

J.W. Eaves Movie Ranch
About 25 miles south of Santa Fe, CR 45, off NM 14
• **(505) 474-3045**

The Eaves Ranch has served as a movie set for decades. Stars such as Jimmy Stewart, Henry Fonda, Shirley Jones, John Wayne, Clint Eastwood, Kevin Costner, Johnny Cash, and others came here to work on westerns. The town is open from 10 AM to 5 PM, Friday through Sunday. Western swing dancing runs from 7 to 10:30 PM on sundays. Tours are available. Admission is $10 for adults; $5 for children and $7 for the Sunday dances.

Santa Fe National Forest
Headquarters, 1474 Rodeo Road
• **(505) 438-7542**
• **www.publiclands.org**

This sprawling forest has five ranger districts throughout northern New Mexico, but the area closest to Santa Fe is among the most scenic and popular. This section of the Santa Fe National Forest begins at the northern border of Hyde Park, 7.5 miles northeast of Santa Fe and stretches for miles into the Pecos Wilderness. You might see a deer or even a black bear. You'll find campgrounds and cross-country ski trails here as well as the Santa Fe Ski Area, which operates on a forest service lease. Campgrounds include Aspen Basin, Aspen Vista, and Big Tesuque. Camping fee is generally $10 per night in most campgrounds. The Santa Fe National Forest Headquarters offers a wonderful source of information on public lands in New Mexico, along with BLM maps, Forest Service maps, hiking books, and a variety of fun things for kids. (See earlier listing in this chapter.)

Worth the Trip

Abiquiú

The Georgia O'Keeffe House
P.O. Box 40, Abiquiu
• **(505) 685-4539**

If homes reflect the personalities of their owners, you won't find a better example than the Abiquiu house of the late Georgia O'Keeffe. Like the artist herself, the 7,000-square-foot adobe is strikingly beautiful yet austere and even aloof. Despite its cool, almost disengaging personality, the residence reveals magnitudes about O'Keeffe and her work. Once off-limits to the public, the mesa-top home and its magnificent views are now available by appointment only.

No doubt O'Keeffe, who treasured her privacy nearly as much as the stones and skulls she collected on her countless high-desert hikes, would be appalled at gawking strangers traipsing by the dozen through her home to glean some small nugget of information about the enigmatic artist.

The public, however, apparently does not share that opinion. Literally thousands of O'Keeffe admirers have visited the artist's house and studio since the Santa Fe-based Georgia O'Keeffe Foundation began giving tours in 1994. Few are disappointed with the four-bedroom, three-bath residence, which remains essentially as O'Keeffe left it in 1984 when she moved to Santa Fe—and nearer to medical care—for the last two years of her life. One certainly comes away from the house understanding O'Keeffe's keen sense of simplicity, balance, and focus. Her home inspires a soothing, inviting calm with clean, simple lines and muted colors that draw in and celebrate the glorious Southwestern panorama that so captivated O'Keeffe.

Tours of O'Keeffe's home and studio are by reservation only, and you should make reservations well in advance. To schedule a tour contact the Georgia O'Keeffe Foundation, P.O. Box 40, Abiquiu, NM 87510, (505) 685-4539. The foundation limits tours to 12 people at a time, but may accommodate larger groups with advance notice. Tours take place Tuesdays, Thursdays, and Fridays from April through November. The minimum requested donation is $22 per person. Proceeds benefit the Georgia O'Keeffe Foundation and are tax deductible. Abiquiu is approximately one hour northwest of Santa Fe—out of our normal coverage area but well-worth the trip.

Albuquerque

Albuquerque Aquarium and Botanic Garden
2601 W. Central Ave. N.W.
• **(505) 764-6200**
• **www.cabq.gov/biopark/aquarium/, www.cabq.gov/biopark/garden/**

The Albuquerque Aquarium, one of Albuquerque's most popular attractions, stands

ATTRACTIONS

out as one of the few aquariums in the country that isn't located near the ocean. Visitors flocked to the place when it opened in 1996, and they're still coming! Children can have an encounter of the skin-to-skin kind with whelks, sea urchins, sea stars, and other invertebrates at the education station—the marine equivalent of a petting zoo. You'll get a kick out of the eel cave with its large population of scary-looking moray eels. The "Inside the Wreck" exhibit features a replica of a 16th-century Spanish ship. But the aquarium's most popular attraction is the 285,000-gallon shark tank, where about 20 sand, tiger, brown, and nurse sharks circle and watch the people who've come to watch them. The aquarium's newest exhibit features seahorses and seadragons.

The Rio Grande Botanic Garden is just across the plaza from the aquarium and in the summer, the two facillities often share live performances in the evening, free with the price of admission. The aquarium is open from 9 AM to 5 PM Tuesdays-Sundays. Closed Mondays. Admission is $4.50 for adults ages 16 to 64, $2.50 for seniors and children ages 3 to 15. Kids younger than 3 are admitted for free.

Indian Pueblo Cultural Center
2401 12th Street NW
- **(505) 843-7270**
- **www.indianpueblo.org**

Among the attractions here is a museum that traces the beginning of the Pueblo Indians through modern times, focusing on each of the state's 19 pueblos. The Indians tell their own version of the Spanish conquest. You'll also find a children's center with hands-on activities. The cultural center's biggest draw is its dances, held every Saturday and Sunday at 11 AM and 2 PM along with a crafts demonstration. At the gift shop, you can shop for jewelry from the various pueblos as well a pottery, rugs and books. The museum's restaurant offers authentic Southwestern cuisine such as huevos rancheros, or eggs served on a tortilla covered with a chile sauce.

The cultural center is open from 9AM to 5:3 PM

daily. Admission is $4 for adults, $1 for students and free for those 4 and younger.

National Atomic Museum
Kirkland Airforce Base, entrance at
Louisiana and Gibson
- **(505) 284-3243**
- **www.atomicmuseum.com**

The National Atomic Museum is Congressionally chartered as the "official" Atomic Mueum of the United States, with an extensive collection of unclassified nuclear technology. The museum not only serves as a readily accessible repository of educational materials and information relecting the Atomic Age, it does a fine job of interpreting and exhibiting its collections in an educational and entertaining way.

As America's museum resource for nuclear history and science, the museum's exhibits tell the story of the people behind the science that led not only to the development of the atomic bomb but also to nuclear medicine. The diversity of individuals and events that shape the historical and technical context of the nuclear age come to life here in both permanent and a variety of temporary exhibits on science, technology, history, and the atomic age. Be sure to take a look at the timeline for the Road to the Atomic Age, the Russian display and the replicas of atomic bombs. The museum is open daily, 9 AM to 5 PM except for New Year's Day, Easter, Thanksgiving and Christmas. Admission fees are: Adults 19–54 are $3; 55+ and youth 7–18 are $2; children under 6 are free.

Rio Grande Zoological Park
903 10th Street S.W.
- **(505) 764-6200**
- **www.cabq.gov/ biopark/zoo/**

The Rio Grande Zoo's beautifully landscaped grounds include an aviary, elephants, petting opportunities, and a reptile house with 6-foot cobras, 20-foot pythons, and Komodo dragons. The zoo has a new $2.2 million exhibit where polar bears cavort in an 11-foot-deep pool, lounge by a stream, play under four waterfalls, slip down a water slide, and enjoy an

INSIDERS' TIP

In 1998, the skull of a dinosaur that once roamed northern New Mexico, a Coelophysis, was carried into space aboard the Space Shuttle Endeavour. The Coelophysis, which looks something like a miniature version of Tyrannosaurus rex, lived 215 million years ago, weighed 50 to 100 pounds, ate meat and walked on its hind legs. The skull came from Ghost Ranch in Abiquiu and is the oldest dinosaur of North America. You can see models of the Coelophysis at the Museum of Natural History and Science in Albuquerque.

El Museo Cultural de Santa Fe

Santa Fe's newest museum lies a little off the beaten trail—and that's not the only thing unusual about it.

El Museo Cultural de Santa Fe occupies a former warehouse at 1615-B Paseo de Peralta. The museum began operating in April 1998 and has been gaining momentum ever since.

The independent, nonprofit organization has big plans for the development of a Hispanic Cultural Center and Museum. The museum focuses both on nurturing local talent and on bringing in appropriate performances and exhibits from elsewhere.

"We consider ourselves to be a center of Hispanic culture and an experiential museum. Our audience is both native Hispanic people and residents and visitors with a desire to learn more about the Hispanic culture," Museum director Valdez Abeyta y Valdez said.

The museum, located at the Santa Fe rail yard property just off Paseo Peralta, opened with a community festival that included mariachi musicians, children's performances and an exhibit of art by native Hispanic artists from throughout Northern New Mexico.

El Museo offers art and dance programs for children and youth, but its broad outreach also includes workshops and classes for adults. The schedule for 2000 and 2001, for example, featured a spring theater show of vignettes by Hispanic playwrights, "Ojos Hispanos" which featured photography by Hispanic artists, La Voz Festival—nine days of contemporary Latin American artists and performers—and an exhibit of quilts. In the fall of 2000, the museum hosted the Matriz Conferencia, a conference for women to examine a variety of personal and cultural issues. A lecture series emphasizing Hispano literature, classes in language, and presentations in music, dance, and folklore that highlight the value of the area's cultural past and the need for its preservation are part of the museum's focus.

In addition to providing avenues for Hispanic artists to exhibit, the organization offers scholarship funds to students at the Santa Fe Community College and works with the public schools to help Hispanic students learn

Both the traditional and contemporary Hispanic art have their place at El Museo Cultural.

Photo: Miquel Gandert /purchase of Maxwell Museum, courtesy of The Clay Angel

(Continued on next page)

ATTRACTIONS

about their roots. Education programs have included the Adobe Project in which school children were taught the history and practice of traditional mud-brick homebuilding and made their own small casitas using miniature adobe bricks.

The multiple uses the museum now makes of its current large-but-nothing-fancy space through exhibitions and performances give visitors an idea of what the board hopes will come to be when the building is remodeled to better serve the community's needs. The renovation will reflect the museum's two branches of emphasis: the focus on exhibitions, performance, and presentations of contemporary artistic creations and its support for the preservation of Hispanic culture, history, language, and traditions through education. The finished museum will include a professional-looking gallery area, large conference space ,and a kitchen for teaching students how to cook traditional dishes and preparing native foods. An entry court and jardin, based on the Spanish building concept of gardens and plazas, will add to the elegance. There will be room for a library and a mercado/theater where artists can demonstrate their work and sell to visitors.

The museum has received financial help from the City of Santa Fe, and is also raising funds on its own to makes its dreams come true.

In addition to the renovation project, the museum has other plans for the future. Events include participation in national non-political caucuses on Hispanic issues and offer local community forums to promote cultural awareness. The Museo will host the 2001 conference of the National Association of Chicana and Chicano Studies, which is expected to bring 1200 participants to Santa Fe. The museum also hopes to continue to be the main home for many of the exhibits, lectures and performances held in conjunction with La Voz, Festival of the Americas, each June. (Please see our Events chapter.)

"We're not exclusive, we're inclusive," director Valdez said. "It's about the sharing of culture. It doesn't matter what other culture one belongs to, you're welcome here."

The museum is open daily except Monday from 1 to 5 PM. Although there was no admission charge at the time of this writing, the museum may begin to charge in the fall of 2000. For more information call 505-992-0591.

air-conditioned ice cave. Australian animals, Mexican wolves, a primate area, and a new Tropical America add to the zoo's attraction. Free animal encounter shows, story hours, animal discovery demonstrations, concerts, and other summer programs are part of the zoo's regular events. Call for a schedule.

The zoo has won praise from wildlife specialists for its innovative design techniques that help ensure the animals' physical and psychological well being. The zoo invites visitors to become foster "zoo parents" by sponsoring or "adopting" certain animals. The zoo also raises money with special events, including "Saturday Night Wild," in mid-June, which welcomes visitors in the cool of the evening to see the animals when some of them are most active. Contests, face-painting, international food, musicians, puppets, clowns, and music add to the fun. Admission to the event is $8.

If seeing all the animals makes you hungry, you can buy food at the mid-park Cottonwood Café or pack a picnic. The zoo is open from 9 AM to 5 PM Tuesday through Sundays. Zoo admission is free to children younger than 3, $2.50 for seniors and ages 3 to 15 and $4.50 for ages 16 to 64. Children 12 and younger must be accompanied by an adult.

Explora Science Center and Children's Museum of Albuquerque
#98 Winrock Center (near the food court), Indian School at Louisiana and Wyoming
• (505) 842-1537

Once separate museums, these two programs moved to a shared space in late 1997 and more recently moved to this popular Albuquerque shopping mall. Children enjoy the hands-on exhibits, which are especially designed for ages 2 to 12. Weekends bring storytellers, musical performances, science and art workshops, dance concerts, and more. The museum is open 10 AM to 9 PM Monday through Saturday and from noon to 6 PM on Sunday. Admission is $2 for ages 2 to 12 and for visitors older than 62; it's $4 for ages 13 to 62 and free for children younger than 2.

New Mexico Museum of Natural History and Science
1801 Mountain Rd. N.W.
• (505) 841-2800
• www.nmmnh-abq.mus.nm.us/

This attraction, fondly known as "the dinosaur museum," recently got even better with two new additions. The LodeStar Astronomy Center, operated by the University of New Mexico, features permanent astronomy exhibits, a planetarium, a Virtual Voyages simulation theater, and an observatory with a 16-inch telescope. LodeStar is the first planetarium in the world to showcase high-definition digital video imaging over an entire domed projection screen. The dome is 55 feet in diameter—it makes for quite a show! And the museum expanded its Dynamax Theater with a larger screen, better projection and sound, and more seats.

But the dinosaurs here still steal the show. From the life-size sculptures of Spike the Pentaceratops and Alberta the Albertosaurus to the FossilWorks Laboratory where kids can watch scientists extract real dinosaur bones from rock, this is New Mexico's version of dinosaur heaven. You can stand next to the skeletons of real dinosaurs that actually lived in what is now New Mexico and see casts of their footprints. The museum's other attractions include a habitat of New Mexico's ancient seashore, a walk through a simulated volcano, and ride in an "Evolator" that takes you back to the days when arid Albuquerque was a rain forest.

The museum's hands-on learning center gives kids (and adults) a chance to look through microscopes, test their sensory perception, and ask science questions. Dynamax theater presents movies every hour on the hour from 10 AM until 5 PM. Recent topics included wolves and Mt. Everest. The museum is open from 9 AM to 5 PM daily except Christmas and non-holiday Mondays in January and September. Admission is $5 for adults, $4 for seniors and students, and $2 for ages 3 to 12. Tickets to the Dynamax Theater, the LodeStar Virtual Voyages, and the LodeStar Planetarium are extra. You can save money if you buy a combination tickets package.

Los Alamos

Bradbury Science Museum
15th St. at Central Ave., Los Alamos
• (505) 667-4444
• www.lanl.gov/worldview/museum/

The development of the atomic bomb and the role Los Alamos played in the process is a key focus here. The museum offers visitors the opportunity to play with a laser, see Fat Man and Little Boy atomic bombs, learn about DNA fingerprinting, work with computers and interactive video, and watch a 20-minute movie about the development of the atomic bomb. Operated by Los Alamos National Laboratories, the museum shows the role Los Alamos played in the atomic bomb's creation and offers interactive exhibits explaining the scope of its nuclear research today. Even if you're not especially interested in the nuclear weapons world, anyone curious about science will enjoy the hands-on displays and lively demonstrations and shows. The museum is open daily except Thanksgiving, Christmas and New Year's Day. Hours are 1 to 5 PM Saturday, Sunday and Monday and 9 AM to 5 PM Tuesday through Friday. Admission is free.

Bandelier National Monument
5 miles south of Los Alamos on N.M. Hwy. 4 (45 miles northwest of Santa Fe)
• (505) 672-3861
• www.nps.gov/band/

You'll find ladders to climb and caves you can crawl into at this popular National Park,

---

INSIDERS' TIP

Santa Fe' many historic districts and neighborhoods contain more than 100 individual sites which are recognized on the National Register of Historic Places and the State Register of Cultural Properties. As you explore these areas, you may notice plaques installed by the Historic Santa Fe Foundation. The Foundation has selected more than 50 Santa Fe buildings the group judges to be worthy of preservation. Most of these structures are included in the New Mexico State Register of Cultural Properties.

ATTRACTIONS

all the while getting a first-hand look at the way an ancient people lived. The monument encompasses more than 1,000 Indian dwellings, homes to people who may have been the ancestors of some of the modern Pueblo Indians. A good place to start is with a walk through the visitors' center, where displays introduce this prehistoric Pueblo Indian ancestral culture. Then head out along the self-guided ruins trail that begins in back of the museum. You'll walk on the narrow paths formed by Indian feet hundreds of years ago. If you wish, you can climb ladders to reach the upper cliff dwellings and step inside caves where Indian families slept or stored their food and belongings many hundreds of years ago. Be sure to notice how smoke from the ancient fires blackened the cave ceilings and watch for petroglyphs carved along the cliffs.

One of New Mexico's most famous and popular attractions, the area now known as Bandelier was occupied as early as A.D. 1100. The people who lived here were farmers and hunters. Since they had no written language, much of their culture remains a mystery. The monument preserves a wealth of archaeological ruins covering about 450 years of human history. Large pueblos, medium-sized house clusters, single-room shelters, and cave dwellings are all here; Bandelier National Monument was established to protect and preserve this priceless heritage.

The monument is named for Adolph Bandelier, an explorer, historian, and author who visited here on five different occasions. Bandelier's novel The Delight Makers used one of these ancient pueblos as its setting.

When you've seen enough ruins, you can picnic along the stream or hike to a waterfall —most of the park is wilderness. Overnight camping is allowed, and summer campfire programs explain the wildlife, plants, and people of the area. (Please call for a schedule.) The park is about an hour's drive from Santa Fe through some of northern New Mexico's most interesting geologic country. The monument is open from dawn to dusk. Entry fee is $10 per vehicle.

Pecos

Pecos National Historical Park
25 miles southeast of Santa Fe on I-25,
Exit 299 then
2 miles east on
N.M. Hwy.63
• **(505) 757-6032**
• **www.nps.gov/peco**

In this park, you'll get a fascinating introduction to the life of the Pueblo people prior to and after the Spanish arrived. Before touring the ruins, stop at the museum for displays that explain the 15th-century pueblo and its mission church, built under the guidance of Spanish friars. In the museum, you and your kids can touch ancient Indian artifacts and watch a short, exciting film about the Spanish exploration of New Mexico. Then walk the trail through the ruins, which begins just outside the museum. Don't miss the kiva, the Pueblo's ceremonial center, where you can push a button to fill the room with American Indian music. The mission, now reduced to only low mud walls, was once described as "the most magnificent church north of Mexico City." During the summer, the park often has demonstrations of Indian or Hispanic arts and crafts. (Call for a schedule.) The park is open daily from 8 AM to 6 PM Memorial Day through Labor Day and until 5 PM the rest of the year. Admission is $2 for adults (children get in free) or $4 per carload, whichever is less.

INSIDERS' TIP

Looking for a good deal? At all Santa Fe branches of the Museum of New Mexico and the Georgia O'Keeffe Museum, admission is $1 on Sundays for New Mexico residents with ID. Free admission is offered daily to ages16 and under. Wednesday are free days for New Mexico seniors (60 and older with an ID to prove it). And Fridays from 5 PM to 8 PM everyone gets in free!

ATTRACTIONS

Kidstuff

Keep them busy! Every parent knows that activity is a key to sibling peace and parental sanity. If children are playing, reading, exploring, and discovering new things, they don't have the time or energy to fight with each other or argue with you. That's true in Santa Fe, too.

In this chapter, you'll find a variety of events, attractions, camps, excursions, and programs for children in the Santa Fe area. Despite its reputation as a cultural mecca and sophisticated town, Santa Fe also welcomes kids with all sorts of fun things to do. Not only will they be busy, but they'll also learn something here, too!

Like adult visitors, children have two basic sets of options: things to see and to do in town and attractions and adventures in the big outdoors surrounding Santa Fe. Among the highlights...the city has a museum designed and constructed just for kids, complete with a special child-size door. Santa Fe has a river to walk along, parks to explore, an Audubon Center, swimming pools, and a new ice skating rank that's open year-round, places to Rollerblade and skateboard, and a bowling alley. The new Genoveva Chavez Center on Rodeo Road offers lots of family fun—swimming, diving, a big-screen TV, the above-mentioned ice rink, and classes galore. The mountains and foothills surrounding Santa Fe are rich with opportunities for family picnics, hiking, skiing, and mountain biking. If you didn't bring bikes, you can rent them in town. And don't forget the sunscreen!

In the spring and summer, parents and kids can take a raft trip, spending a day on the Rio Grande or Rio Chama having fun and getting wet. Many commercial rafting companies are based in Santa Fe and offer a variety of options from gentle floats to white-water excitement. Please call first and ask if there are age requirements; some trips don't accept the youngest children. (See our Recreation chapter for more on rafting.) Horseback riding is another popular option. Trail rides through a variety of terrains, breakfast trips, and campfire rides are available from several businesses and resorts in the area. Many stables also offer riding lessons for children.

Fishing, surprisingly to some people, is as much a part of summer here as it is anywhere in the USA. Children younger than age 12 can fish for free in New Mexico. In the Santa Fe area, opportunities for lake fishing—which is often easier for young children—include the Cochití, Abiquiú, Santa Cruz, and Monastery Lakes. Nambé, Santa Clara, and San Juan Pueblos have public fishing lakes (see our regional map in the front of this book). If you want your kids to try stream or river fishing, the Rio Grande between Santa Fe and Taos off N.M. Highway 68 — especially near Pilar—is worth a visit. Or cast your lines into the Pecos River and streams that flow into it in the Santa Fe National Forest outside the community of Pecos, off Interstate 25 on N.M. Highway 63 about 30 miles east of Santa Fe.

In the winter, you and your kids can have fun together at the Santa Fe Ski Area, which offers an extensive program of classes for children, or along cross-country trails in the Santa Fe National Forest and elsewhere. You can go sledding or tubing in Hyde Park, north of Santa Fe on N.M. Highway 475. Take a look at our Recreation chapter for other activities and destinations that are ideal for children.

LOOK FOR:
- Be a Happy Camper
- Be Dramatic/ Get Arty!
- Catch Some Culture
- Get Moving!
- Join the Club
- Just for Fun
- Kid-Friendly Museums
- Kid-Style Events
- On the Road

Because Santa Fe boasts one of the country's most vibrant arts communities, our children benefit. Kids can study everything from painting and pottery to drama and dance. We've mentioned a few of these schools in this chapter, but be sure to check the phone book or specialized publications for children for more suggestions. Santa Fe children can put on their own shows or go to professional theater, opera, and music productions. Some groups offer special free concerts just for children. Many of the city's events include children in wonderful ways. The Fiesta de Santa Fe, a community celebration each September, invites kids to walk in their own parade. Both the Spanish and Indian Markets, major summer arts and crafts shows, have exhibitor spaces dedicated to children who are also artists.

And, if Santa Fe seems a little too different at times, please realize that our community has the comfortable old standbys—franchised and independent video rental outlets, movie theaters, video arcades, and a mall where teens can meet their friends. For more information, *The Santa Fe New Mexican*, (505) 995-3839, offers a "Family Attractions" category in its "Pasatiempo" calendar each Friday and "Best Bets for Kids," on Thursdays. Two specialized free publications, *New Mexico Kids!*, and *Tumbleweeds*, present pages of ideas, suggestions and insights into services and activities for children in the Santa Fe areas. (See our Media chapter.)

We've done our best to make sure all information in this chapter is current, but the phone numbers are listed for your convenience if you wish to double check on any information. In addition to the information here and in our Recreation chapter, you'll find more suggestions in our Attractions and Arts chapters. Have a good time and remember: Before you know it, your little ones will be all grown up.

Be A Happy Camper

In addition to the programs listed here, many of the agencies offered under our "Get Arty" section offer summer programs.

Audubon Summer Camp
Randall Davey Audubon Center
1800 Upper Canyon Rd.
• **(505) 983-4609**

These popular summer nature programs fill up quickly and rightly so. Kids ages 5-11 get to spend time outside learning about such things as animal camouflage and disguises, nocturnal creatures, tracking, and native birds. Themes include nature detectives, flight, water, maps, and treasure hunts as well as stories, art, and games with an Audubon focus. Sessions are held mornings and afternoons, with lunch provided for full-time campers. Session usually run from mid-June to mid August.

Brush Ranch Camp
Brush Ranch, P.O. Box 5759,
Santa Fe 87502
• **(505) 757-8821, (800) 722-2843**
• **www.brushranchcamps.com**

This long-established camp along the Pecos River in the Sangre de Cristo Mountains east and north of Santa Fe offers an assortment of programs: all sorts of kids' camps for ages 6 to 15 and camps kids and parents can attend to-gether. You'll find traditional camp and adventure camp for older children, Mountaineers sessions for 9- to 12-year-olds, Trailblazers for 6- to 8-year-old first-time campers and family camp for all ages from grandparents on down. The setting amid the ponderosa pines is beautiful and convenient to Santa Fe. Sessions run one to eight weeks from mid-June through mid-August. Call for prices.

Children's Adventure Company
P.O. Box 146, Tesuque 87574
(mailing address only)
• **(505) 989-8424**

This popular program offers an extensive summer camp, overnight camping, and after-school programs for children ages 5 up through the 9th grade. Summer day camps include nature trips, cooking, swimming, and art with field trips to Albuquerque. The fee for 2000 was $170 a week. There's also a 6-day water-skiing trip to Lake Powell, including a houseboat, for $450. Prices began at $180 for a three-day trip. The company also offers enriched after-school programs for kindergartners through 6th graders at $230 per month, with price adjustments for children who don't attend every day.

College of Santa Fe Day Camp
College of Santa Fe, Driscoll Fitness Center, 1600 St. Michael's Dr.
• **(505) 473-6370**
• **www.csf.edu/dfc/daycamp**

Kids ages 5 to 12 can spend as much as 10

A young visitor scales the museum's 16-foot-high technical climbing wall that simulates rock climbing in natural settings.

Photo: Don Strel/Courtesy of Santa Fe Children's Museum

weeks here enjoying aerobics, arts & crafts, basketball, creative dance, racquetball, rock climbing, soccer, volleyball, swimming, tennis, theater, games, and field trips. Each two-week session runs from 8 AM to 5 PM Monday through Friday. Fee for the program is $325 per session and includes snacks, hot lunches, and a T-shirt. Campers are grouped by age in two-year spreads, and each group contains no more than 20 children. The camp director recommends reservations; programs fill up fast.

Camp Elliott Barker
Girl Scouts – Sangre de Cristo Council
450 St. Michael's Drive, Santa Fe
• (505) 983-6339 or
1-877-983-6339 toll free

The Sangre de Cristo Girls Scout council, which serves 13 counties in Northern New Mexico and one in Colorado, does a lot more than sell cookies. One of the most popular scouting activities is also open to non-scout girls—camping at Camp Elliott Barker in

Angel Fire. The camp offers one- and two-week sessions for girls from age 6 up to seniors in high school. The camp also hosts family weekends and sessions for mothers and daughters and dads and daughters. Here, in the cool and beautiful Sangre de Cristo Mountains, girls can ride horses, try their skill in a ropes challenge course, backpack, learn New Mexico crafts and culture, build rockets, and, most importantly, have fun. Camping experience is available in three, six, or 10-day sessions. Please call for prices.

New Mexico Dance & Theater Ranch
22 Camino Cerro Chato, Cerrillos, N.M.
• (505) 982-1662

This residential program for boys and girls, ages 10 to 16, draws young dancers from throughout the country. To attend, a student must have at least three years of prior training. In addition to classical ballet, pointe, modern dance, flamenco, Irish dance, and more, the young students also have an opportunity to ride horses, visit museums, hike, swim, ice skate, and attend campfire cookouts. The camp is held in mid-June and ends with a student performance open to the public. Fee for the 2000 session was $700. Pearl Potts, a well known Santa Fe dance teacher, is the camp director.

Be Dramatic/ Get Arty!
Classes and Workshops

Art Academy de los Niños
2504 Calle de los Niños
• (505) 473-3003

The August through May after-school programs here focus on many different art media. Private sessions can also be arranged. The teacher is a longtime art educator who works with students to help develop and release their innate creativity. Media range from drawing and painting to sculpture and pottery. Classes are $45 a month for weekly 90-minute sessions, including all materials.

Art and Clay Studio
851 W. San Mateo Rd., Ste. 4
• (505) 989-4278

This comprehensive art school offers programs for ages 6 through adults and has separate classes for teens. Professional artists teach all arts and crafts activities. Students may work with a potter's wheel or try sculpture, painting, printmaking, tie dying, silk-screening, puppet making, paper making, bookbinding, comic

A special day for preschoolers at the Santa Fe Children's Museum provides magnet fun.

Photo: Courtesy of Santa Fe Children's Museum

book illustration, and more. The studio offers after-school, holiday, and summer programs. The fee for seven weeks of class is about $130.

Art is Fine
Museum of Fine Arts, 107 W. Palace Ave.
• (505) 476-5072

Fourth through 8th graders can take classes in various forms of the fine arts at this venerable and beautiful museum. A recent session offered 10 Saturday mornings of painting with acrylics, beginning with stretching and priming canvases and culminating with an exhibit at the museum. Fee is $100 for the 10-week session.

The Children's Dance Program
**Railyard Performance Center,
430 W. Manhattan Ave.**
• (505) 982-1662

Ballet, modern dance, tap, jazz, hip-hop, flamenco, Irish dance, programs for mothers and daughters, and more are offered here for boys and girls ages 3 to 15. Kids can go to class after school or on weekends, with special summer workshops available. Classes begin with movement exploration and move on to advanced combinations that help the young dancers build their skills and their imaginations. Fee per class is $15 with discounts available depending on the number of classes taken.

The Georgia O'Keeffe Museum Art and Leadership Program for Girls Summer Intensive
123 Grant Avenue
• (505) 954-4393

The O'Keeffe Art and Leadership Program for Girls Summer Intensive, an interactive program for pre-teen and adolescent girls, incorporates skill building and problem solving in the areas of identity, creativity, and self-esteem. In 1999 more than 60 girls participated in the summer intensive sessions. Opening circles provided the time to share ideas, feelings, and dreams as explored in independently completed home assignments. Artist and New Mexico resident Georgia O'Keeffe and several contemporary women artists function as strong role models. The three- to six-day education programs

included a hike in O'Keeffe's Ghost Ranch country followed by an overnight stay in Ojo Caliente, New Mexico. The participants' artwork was displayed in a public exhibition at the end of the program in 1999.

This event is sponsored by the Museum in collaboration with CRIZMAC. Founded in 1985, CRIZMAC Art & Cultural Education Materials, Inc. is a publishing company dedicated to art education and appreciation. They sponsor art-related programs for children and adults throughout the U.S. For information you can contact CRIZMAC at (800) 913-8555 or by e-mail at crizmacinc@aol.com.

Children ages five to 12 and their parents explore pertinent themes in art by looking at works on exhibit in the galleries and participating in multi-disciplinary, hands-on art activities on Saturdays. Guest artists joint the Museum's director of education, Jackie M., to present programs, concentrating on a different theme each session. The participants use O'Keeffe's paintings on display in the museum's galleries, as examples for study and discussion and then create their own works of art. In addition to traditional visual forms such as drawing and painting, children and their parents explore art making using movement, writing and storytelling. The hands-on activities reinforce the ideas formed in the galleries. During the summer the program runs twice per month. The sessions are free and open to the public. Call for times.

School group tours of the museum are offered by appointment on Mondays, when the Museum is closed to the public and at 9 AM on Tuesdays, Thursdays, and Fridays. Schools should contact Faith Strongheart at (505) 954-4393 ext.1007 to set up a tour. Tours can include hands-on lessons from the interdisciplinary curriculum.

Santa Fe Dance Foundation
550B St. Michael's Drive
• (505) 983-5591

Children ages 3 through their teens can study ballet, modern dance, creative movement, and jazz here. Adult classes are also available. The students dance in at least one annual

> **INSIDERS' TIP**
> Originally started as part of a museum exhibit, the All Children's Powwow has taken on a life of its own, and now draws participants between the ages of 2 and 15 to Santa Fe from Arizona, Colorado, Oklahoma, and Wyoming. In addition to dancing, children make their own costumes. The event, held in October, is sponsored by the Wheelwright Museum.

KIDSTUFF

public performance. A single class costs $10; the rate goes down depending on the number of classes taken. An annual performance of the Nutcracker and a spring recital give the students on-stage experience. The school also offers a summer intensive in June.

National Dance Institute of New Mexico
P.O. Box 22988, Santa Fe 87502
• **(505) 983-7646**

This exceptional program works with several Santa Fe Public elementary schools each year to offer the students an introduction to movement and dance. Lessons culminate with a public performance at Greer Garson Theater for parents, friends, and the community in general. The 2000 Santa Fe show will include more than 600 children from throughout New Mexico. The National Dance Institute of New Mexico was founded to help children develop discipline, a standard of excellence, and a belief in themselves that will carry over to other aspects of their lives. Participation is free thanks to grants and volunteers.

Catch Some Culture

Santa Fe Opera Youth Night and Backstage Tours
Santa Fe Opera Theater, 7 miles north of Santa Fe on U.S. Hwy. 84/285
• **(505) 986-5900, (800) 280-4654**
• **http://www.santafeopera.org**

Youth Night at the Opera provides children and young adults an opportunity to attend dress rehearsals of the opera productions at low cost. A special adjunct, the Pueblo Opera Program, brings pueblo children and their parents to the opera. (For more information on the Opera, see our Arts chapter.) The kids see a real opera—not a watered-down production. Tickets are $25 for one adult chaperone and three children or $40 for two adults and four children. Each additional child's ticket is $5. Tickets for young adults who may come without chaperones (ages 15 to 22) are $5. Most youth night performances sell out early.

Children ages 7 to 15 can accompany a parent free of charge on the Opera's Monday through Saturday back stage tours. Docents show visitors costumes, sets, scenery, and props and explain how the Opera makes them. Tours run from late June through the end of the Op-

era season, usually the third week in August, at 1 PM. People older than 15 pay $6.

Santa Fe Stages
100 N. Guadalupe St.
• **(505) 982-6683**
• **www.santafestages.org**

Santa Fe Stages brings world-class performances in theater, dance, and music to town each summer and hosts special events periodically other times of the year. While all their shows aren't appropriate for children, many of them are. Past productions have included singer Amanda McBroom, the Parsons Dance Company, and Guadalupe!, a musical presented by young actors, dancers, and musicians based on stories collected from Santa Fe grandmothers. If you wait until the day of the show, you can buy one or two tickets for only $8 each. Sometimes shows sell out, however, so if there's something you really want your kids to see, plan ahead. Regular-price tickets range from $20 to $37.

You can learn more about Santa Fe Stages in our Arts chapter or from the company's website. The website includes a parents' guide, which differentiates among shows designed as family entertainment, those acceptable for all ages, and those with mature themes.

Santa Fe Chamber Music Festival Youth Concerts
St. Francis Auditorium, Museum of Fine Arts
• **(505) 983-2075**
• **http://www.santafechambermusic.org/ SFCMF.html**

The festival's youth concerts, founded in 1993, bring music to children in free performances during July and August. Past programs have included jazzy string music, a presentation about violin making, a flamenco-inspired piece for chamber ensemble and dancers, and a program that highlighted young musicians. The concerts are free thanks to private foundations and support from the City of Santa Fe and the state. The Festival's Passport program gives kids a free ice cream cone and a T-shirt if they attend 4 or more concerts.

Santa Fe Performing Arts School & Theatre
Armory for the Arts, 1050 Old Pecos Tr.
• **(505) 982-7992**

These after-school and summer programs provide training in music, dance, and drama for Santa Fe kids ages 3 to 18. Company members use the skills and techniques they learn in the workshops to present four annual productions, two designed for and acted by younger children and two for older company members. Past shows have included *Annie Get Your Gun*, *Peter Pan*, and *Little Shop of Horrors*. Tickets for performances are $5 to $12; watch the newspapers for a schedule.

Southwest Children's Theatre Productions
Resident Children's Company of the Santa Fe Playhouse
Santa Fe Playhouse, 142 E. DeVargas St.
• **(505) 984-3055**

Quality children's plays and theater education are offered by this nonprofit group, founded in January 1988. Children learn improvisation, creative dramatics, voice and body training, and characterization. Adult professionals join the students for two main-stage productions each year, one in the spring and one in the fall. Each summer, the company presents an all-student production—written, produced and starring the summer theatre students. After-school programs welcome kindergartners through 8th graders, and outreach to area schools offers even greater access to the theater arts for all of Santa Fe's youth. Tickets

to the big cast shows are $5 for adults and children.

Get Moving!

Rockin' Rollers Event Arena
2915 Agua Fria St.
• **(505) 473-7755**

Kids and their parents can rent skates here and roll on to the rhythms that roll out over the sound system. Rink staff teaches skating classes, and if you get tired of skating you can play in the video arcade. On the weekends, the rink sometimes hosts free all-ages evening concerts presenting local bands or a live DJ with music and accompanying videos on what's advertised as Santa Fe's largest screen. You can also reserve the space for parties.

The arena is open for skating on Wednesday from 3 to 5 PM, Friday, Saturday, and Sunday afternoons from 1 to 3 PM with an additional Friday session from 3 to 5 PM. Friday from 7 to 10 PM is available for public skating except when the club is hosting teen dances. Hours may change—call to confirm.

Admission is $3.50. Skaters can bring their own skates—in-line or four-wheelers. Or they can rent a pair of quads for $.50. The conces-

Pueblo youngsters after a morning of traditional dancing.

Photo: Don Strel

KIDSTUFF

sion stand offers a large variety of reasonably priced snacks, and the club is smoke free.

Santa Fe Climbing Gym
825 Early St.
• (505) 986-8944

This indoor, air-conditioned gym welcomes children as young as 5 as well as more experienced customers. The weekly Kids Climb program provides fully supervised instruction by climbers who are also trained teachers. The gym also presents outdoor climbing excursions in northwestern New Mexico. Summer programs include wilderness experiences, low-impact camping, ecological expeditions, and more. Helmets, shoes, ropes, and all other equipment are provided. Rates range from $15 for a Kids Climb session to $225 for a five-day camp. Normal operating hours are from 5 to 10 PM Monday through Friday; Saturday & Sunday gym, 1 to 6 PM; Saturday Kid's Climb, 9 to 11 AM.

DeVargas Skateboard Park
W. De Vargas St. at Sandoval

A 6-foot-deep bowl, ramps, a half-pipe, and a smaller bowl for beginners are part of Santa Fe's downtown skate park, which opened in 1996. Due to its popularity, the city expanded the park in 1997, and it now includes 5,000 square feet of places to skate. This is a great place for middle-school kids, and you'll find older teens and adults here too. Skateboarders have to bring their own wheels. The park charges no fees and is open during daylight hours.

News flash! The city may build a second skate park on the south side of town at the Franklin Miles Park on Camino Carlos Rey, a few blocks east of Cerrillos Road. The park would include a street plaza, combination bowls, advanced double bowls, rail slides, and spine runs. The project could be finished as soon as the fall of the year 2000, if all goes as scheduled.

Silva Lanes Bowling Center
1352 Rufina Cir.
• (505) 471-2110

The 32-lane Silva Lanes offers junior bowling programs including scholarship leagues and scholarship tournaments for competitors as young as 3. Small shoes and light balls make the sport easier for children. The youngest bowlers can try bumper bowling—and be assured of no frustrating gutter balls! This is also a popular spot for Santa Fe's younger set to hold birthday parties. You'll find a full service pro shop, snack bar and video games. The bowl-

ing alley is open from 10 AM to 2 AM daily. Fees are $2.25 per game per person for adults and $2 per child. Shoe rental is $1.75 for adults and $1 for kids. In the spring, Silva Lanes traditionally hosts the Big Brothers/Big Sisters bowl-a-thon, a fund raising program for a great nonprofit agency.

City of Santa Fe
Public Swimming Pools
Fort Marcy Complex, 490 Washington Ave.
• (505) 984-6725
Genoveva Chavez Community Center, Rodeo Road,
• (505) 438-4000
Salvador Perez Pool, 601 Alta Vista St.
• (505) 984-6758
Tino Griego Pool, 1730 Llano St.
• (505) 473-7270
Bicentennial Pool, 1121 Alto St.
• (505) 984-6773 (open summers only)

The city's pools score big with Santa Fe kids. The pool at the Chavez Center is a youngsters' favorite. They can use the waterslide to splash down through the mouth of a frog into warm water. Older children and adults have a larger slide and their own section of the pool to enjoy. Another area is reserved for diving or lap swim. The center also has childcare for tots whose parents want to work out.

Fort Marcy has a tot pool with warmer water and a shallow bottom for minnows 5 and younger and the Bicentennial Pool has a toddler section. Other pools start at 3 feet. The pools all set aside special times for recreational swimming and family fun. Each pool has different hours for open swimming, and schedules vary seasonally; please call for information and to find out about classes. Swimming costs $1.85 for adults 18 and older, $1.50 for students with IDs, $.75 for children 8 to 13 and for seniors older than 60 and free for children younger than 7.

Santa Fe City Parks and Recreation Programs
Locations vary
• (505) 438-1485 for park and park program information;
(505) 984-6573 for summer and after school recreation programs
• http://www.ci.santa-fe.nm.us/sfweb/index.htm

The City of Santa Fe offers an extensive summer recreation program and an assortment of other events during the year. Children can learn to swim and play tennis or spend the day in a park with a program of sports, games, and arts and crafts. All offerings are free or inexpensive—$20 for a month of daily half-hour swimming classes, for example. Kids also can compete in basketball and football contests, races, and fun walks. The city sponsors summer gymnastics, cheerleading camps, a diaper bash, pumpkin-carving contests, and an Easter egg hunt. Listing all the specifics would take the rest of this chapter. But if you visit any of the city recreation centers, the public library or call the city recreation office at the number above, you can get a free printed schedule—a booklet, actually—with all times, dates, prices, and addresses.

When it comes to parks, Santa Fe had 49 at last count, and all of them welcomed kids. Many have swings, slides, tot equipment, tennis courts, basketball hoops, and fields for sports. Salvador Perez, 610 Alta Vista Street, (505) 984-6755, provides a fine, fenced tot lot where toddlers can swing, slide, play in the sand, and explore to their hearts content. The park, next to the Salvador Perez Pool, has a train locomotive engine (fenced for safety) as its centerpiece. The Villa Linda Park, 4250 Cerrillos Road, offers swings, slides, and climbing bars as well as a picnic area and a multipurpose field that's perfect for Frisbees. The Monica Roybal Center, 737 Agua Fría Street, (505) 984-6750, has lit outdoor basketball courts and offers programs for kids after school and during the summer. The Roybal Center stresses family involvement through many of its programs. At the Fort Marcy Complex, 490 Washington Avenue, (505) 984-6725, you'll find a gym for basketball, fitness classes for kids, a weight room, and outdoor fields for soccer, baseball, and other sports in addition to a pool. The city's newest recreation center, the Genoveva Chavez Community Center, Rodeo Road, (505) 438-4000 includes Santa Fe's first public indoor ice rink along with swimming pools, a fully equipped gymnasium, classrooms, racquetball courts, and more. (Please see our Recreation chapter for all the details.)

For a different kind of park, visit the Arroyo Chamisa Trail. The paved path stretches from Yucca Road to Villa Linda Mall and past the Monica Lucero Park with its ballfields, playground and tot lot at 2356 Avenida de la Campanas. The trail meanders along the Arroyo Chamisa, a major wash that is dry 99 percent of the year, and past a colorful mural painted by Santa Fe youth. The trail draws families from all over town. The route can be used by strollers and tricycles and is especially inviting at sunset. And don't forget the Frenchy's Field Park, Agua Fría Street and Osage Avenue, a passive park with walking trails, picnic areas, and its own pond.

DeVargas Skateboard Park located downtown offers youngsters a chance to hone their skills skateboarding, BMX biking, or on inline skates.

Photo: Don Strel

Join the Club

Santa Fe Boys and Girls Club
730 Alto St.
• **(505) 983-6632**

This longtime Santa Fe youth center finished an extensive remodeling job in 1997 and launched some new programs to help serve Santa Fe kids for decades to come. Established in 1942, the club now serves about 4,500 Santa Fe county children and teens with special events and activities. Programs include basketball, music, dancing, photography, boxing, computer labs, tutoring of all sorts, and job training. The club staff also works with members on substance-abuse prevention and personal and social skills, including conflict management. Children and teens can study for scholarships and college placement tests or prepare for their high school diplomas.

In addition to the main building on Alto Street, the Boys and Girls Club offers programs in other locations in Santa Fe county. The members are ages 6 to 17. The club is open after school until 6 PM and from 7:30 AM to 6 PM during spring and winter break and during the summer. Membership, on a sliding scale, ranges from $30 a week during the summer to $30 a year.

Girls Inc.
301 Hillside Ave.
• **(505) 982-2042**

Girls Inc. and its predecessor, the Santa Fe Girls Club, have served Santa Fe girls since 1957. Part of a national organization to help girls, Girls Inc. offers after-school programs, a summer camp, and special camps during the schools' winter holidays and spring break. Programs are designed for girls ages 6 to 12 and include arts and crafts, sports, cooking, field trips, guest speakers, community service projects, and more. Among recent program highlights is Girls Dig It!, a project offered in conjunction with the Office of Archaeological studies. Participating girls went on field trips to dig for artifacts for seven weeks and learn about the artifacts they found. The summer and holiday camps work with girls from 7:30 AM until 6 PM Monday through Friday and are popular among parents who

INSIDERS' TIP

Altitude can have an effect on children too. Make sure that your kids get plenty of sleep—or at least rest—during your visit to Santa Fe. They'll need their energy to handle the 7,000-foot elevation, not to mention all the things you'll want to do.

Dinosaur fans of all ages travel to the New Mexico Museum of Natural History in Albuquerque.

Photo: Dick Kent

KIDSTUFF

work at the State Capitol or City Hall because of the club's downtown location near Hillside Park. Membership fee is $10 annually. The camps are offered on a sliding fee scale.

Warehouse 21 Santa Fe Teen Art Center
1614 Paseo de Peralta
• (505) 989-4423

The closest thing Santa Fe has to a teen hangout, Warehouse 21 offers teens a place to learn about photography, flamenco, music recording, radio announcing, various forms of theater, and more. Programs are open to young people ages 12 to 21. Friday evenings bring comedy or music from local acts or touring bands. Classes, some of which are free and others low cost, vary with the season and availability of teacher, and have included papermaking, swing dance, beading, guitar, and computer graphics.

The Warehouse, with typical teen bravado, gives itself the subtitle "The Future of Art in Santa Fe." Artists- in-Residence workshops give interested teens a chance to work with a professional artist. Recent programs included sculpture with latex polymers using molds, a youth monothon printmaking festival at the College of Santa Fe's Printmaking Center, and "environmental art." The Warehouse gets lots of support for its good work, including funding from the City of Santa Fe, the Santa Fe Arts Commission, the Rotary Foundation, and several private nonprofit foundations with a special interest in kids.

Just for Fun

Engine House Theatre
Melodrama Engine House Theatre,
2846 N.M. Hwy. 14, Madrid
• (505) 438-3780

Kids and adults can have fun together at the Engine House Theatre. The company presents classic Victorian melodrama, inviting the audience to cheer the hero and hiss the villain. They pattern the plots after old-time shows: A sweet young thing in distress is threatened with loss of home and virtue by a sinister, blackhearted scoundrel, but in the nick of time, the handsome hero . . . you get the picture. The show runs weekends and holidays from Memorial Day through mid-October. Curtain time is 3 and 8 PM on Saturday and 3 PM on Sunday and Monday holidays, with matinees only during October. Tickets are $9 for adults, $7 for seniors and $4 for children younger than 12.

Allow at least a half-hour to get to the theater from Santa Fe. The drive, along what's known as the Turquoise Trail, will take you past the historic village of Cerrillos and into Madrid, an old mining town.

Jets Arcade
Villa Linda Mall, 4250 Cerrillos Rd.
• (505) 471-2909

Santa Fe's largest video arcade, Jets offers a variety of games, including Laser Storm. Junior-high and high-school kids like to hang here, testing their skill against each other and the video geniuses who invent these games. Kids drop in quarters to play and win tickets, which they exchange for prizes. The arcade has a party room for birthday celebrations and nonviolent games suitable for younger children. The arcade is open from 9:30 AM to 10 PM on weekdays, from 9:30 AM to 11 PM on Friday and Saturday and from 11 AM to 10 PM on Sunday.

Quiggy's Playland
Cerrillos at Rodeo Road
• (505) 424-6200

An arcade for the younger set, this boisterous indoor playground keeps the elementary school crowd and their younger brothers and sisters entertained with active fun in its huge playhouse. The games run on tokens you buy at the front desk, and you can also buy drinks and food here. The establishment is state licensed and open 10 AM to 9 PM daily, except Sunday, when the hours are 11 AM to 7 PM.

Santa Fe Southern Railway
410 S. Guadalupe St.
• (505) 989-8600, or (888) 989-8600

If your children are interested in trains, you can satisfy their curiosity here. The vintage coaches of this working freight train leave from the Guadalupe Street area, travel to the neighboring community of Lamy, stop 60 to 90 minutes for lunch and then come back; total trip time is approximately 4.5 hours. The railway also offers special rides, including some with Santa and clowns—call to find out if they have any scheduled. November through March, the trains leave at 11 AM Tuesday, Thursday, and Saturday, and 1 PM on Sundays. April through October, trains depart at 10:30 AM Tuesday, Wednesday, Thursday, and Saturday, and 1 PM Sunday and Monday. From April through October enjoy New Mexico's spectacular sunsets and clear, starlit skies on the Friday evening "High Desert Highball." Departure is 6:15 PM April through Labor Day; after Labor Day it's

KIDSTUFF

5:45 PM. You'll be back in Santa Fe by 8:30 PM. The railroad offers a campfire barbecue on Saturday nights, April through October; the train leaves at 6:15 PM and returns at 10:45 PM. Tickets are $25 to $40 for adults; seniors are $20 to $35; children ages 3 to 13 are $13-$28; children under 3 are free. Group rates, charters, private car facilities, and school rates are available.

Stories at the Tipi
Wheelwright Museum, 704 Camino Lejo
• (505) 982-4636

Affable Joe Hayes entertains children and grownups with stories drawn from Hispanic and American Indian traditions and the Wild West. Join this professional writer and yarn-spinner on summer evenings for first-class entertainment. You can carry along a picnic, and be sure to bring a blanket or cushion to sit on. The program usually lasts about an hour, and even the youngest children stay attentive because of Hayes' skill at presenting the different accents and voices of the characters he's talking about. The audiences especially love stories about La Llorona, Santa Fe's legendary weeping woman, and funny tales of Coyote the Trickster. Hayes entertains on at 7 PM on Saturday and Sunday from July through August. Admission is free.

Toy Lending Center
Santa Fe Community College,
Division of Early Childhood,
6401 Richards Ave.
• (505) 428-1612

Parents can borrow toys and equipment free of charge here, selecting from among more than 2,000 items. The center offers a good assortment of toys for infants, toddlers, and preschoolers, with some choices for kindergartners and school-age children. Among the possibilities are blocks, riding toys, easels, chalkboards, and musical instruments. Best of all, the center will loan you the toys and equipment you want for free once you've completed the registration forms. The center is open ev-

A variety of "hands on" activities entertain and educate youngsters.

Photo: Courtesy of Santa Fe Children's Museum

KIDSTUFF

ery Wednesday, 1 to 5 PM. It has expanded hours the second Wednesday of each month, when it's open until 8 PM. The center is open the second Saturday of the month, 9 AM to 1 PM.

Kid-Friendly Museums

El Rancho de las Golondrinas
334 Los Pinos Rd., La Cienega
• (505) 471-2261

The geese, goats, sheep, and burros are waiting for your kids here. Frogs croak and swim in the ponds, and lizards sun themselves on rocks nearby. Animals are a big attraction of this living ranch and museum, where hands-on activities are encouraged. Kids may have a chance to sample bread freshly baked in an horno, an outdoor beehive-shape oven, and to grind corn with mano and metate, the stone tools used by the early settlers. They can also meet costumed villagers who will explain what it was like to live in New Mexico 200 years ago. "The ranch of the swallows" offers a vivid re-creation of the area's 18th- and 19th-century Hispanic history. The ranch wasn't built for tourists; this was the last stop on El Camino Real before Santa Fe on the grueling journey from Mexico City to the northern provinces of New Spain.

Children can walk inside the restored buildings—built on original foundations and furnished as appropriate to the period. They can sit in a Colonial schoolhouse and marvel at the lack of playground equipment and computers. The museum's self-guided tour involves about a 1.5-mile hike over roads and trails that are sometimes steep and rocky. There's plenty of shade, but it can still be a major expedition for a preschooler. You should allow at least an hour and a half. If you're in luck, you'll be able to bring your kids to Golondrinas on a festival day, when the museum buzzes with excitement. Volunteers chat with visitors and demonstrate many of the skills early settlers needed to survive on the frontier. Lively dancing, foot-stomping music, and scrumptious food add to the fun.

El Rancho de las Golondrinas also presents theme weekends throughout the summer, including one that focuses on storytelling and another about the animals the Spanish brought with them to New Mexico—both fine events for children. (Check with the local papers or call the museum for the dates.) Admission fees vary depending on what's happening at the museum. From June through September, you can tour the ranch on your own and bring a picnic. Admission then is $5 adults, $4 seniors (62 and older), teens, and military, and $2 for ages 5 through 12. During the festivals or Civil War Weekend, admission is $7 adults, $5 seniors, teens, and military, and $3 for children 5 through 12. Children younger than 5 always get in free.

To reach the ranch from Santa Fe, take I-25 S. to Exit 276 and bear right on N.M. Highway 599. Turn left at the traffic light onto the frontage road and right just before the racetrack on Los Pinos Road. The museum is 3 miles from this intersection.

Santa Fe Children's Museum
1050 Old Pecos Tr.
• (505) 989-8359

Children—especially those 12 and younger—get a chance to learn by doing here. The "exhibits" are hands-on activities that involve water, magnets, live snakes and giant cockroaches, bubbles you can stand inside, a climbing wall, microscopes, magnets, pulleys, beading and weaving looms, and a place outside to make bread in "hornos." Environmental educators offer garden-based biology and environmental education projects such as making miniature gardens, including a "pizza garden", nature prints, and seasonal wreaths made from natural materials. There's even a special garden planted with flowers that attract hummingbirds! Founded in 1989, Santa Fe Children's Museum was the first museum just for kids in the state. It receives more than 60,000 visitors a year. Children from all 50 states and 49 foreign countries have played inside these walls. Because it treasures toddlers, too, the museum has a special climbing structure for them and sets aside time each week when toddlers and their parents have the place all to themselves.

The Children's Museum complements its

> **INSIDERS' TIP**
> The Santa Fe Children's Museum hosts an annual birthday party each February, with free admission and a big birthday cake to thank everyone who makes it the city's most popular museum among the younger set. The night before the family party, the museum hosts a benefit dinner and auction to raise some of the money needed to keep its doors open.

exhibits with special monthly evening performances for families. The museum invites guest artists to lead children in a variety of hands-on activities. Sundays, visiting scientists introduce astronomy, physics, electricity, and biology in ways that can make kids giggle. For parents, child development specialists are on hand on Fridays and Saturdays to answer common parenting questions.

The museum is open from 10 AM to 5 PM Thursdays through Saturdays and noon to 5 PM Sundays from September through May. June through August, it's also open on Wednesdays. The museum is closed from Labor Day through the second Wednesday in September. Please call for special holiday hours and programs. Admission is $3 for adults and $2 for children younger than 12.

Museum of International Folk Art
706 Camino Lejo
• (505) 827-6350
• http://www.nmmnh-abq.mus.nm.us/
mnm/mnm.html

Even kids who think they don't like museums will enjoy the treasures of "Multiple Visions: A Common Bond" in the Girard Wing. It's the largest collection of dolls, toys, and miniatures ever assembled by a private citizen. Collector Alexander Girard's folk art gems shine even more brightly because the museum displays them in "environments" resembling miniature cities, village markets, even Heaven and Hell. Windows cleverly placed at a child's eye level enable the smaller visitors to see on their own. The museum also has the Neutrogena Wing, which houses an impressive array of textiles, costumes, and masks donated by Lloyd Cotsen and the Neutrogena Corporation. You and your kids can get an up-close look at riches from the collection with a visit to "Lloyd's Treasure Chest" where you will have an opportunity to examine cherished objects and watch the collections staff as they work behind the scenes.

Also of interest to kids is "La Casa Colonial," a Spanish Colonial home from the early 1800s, which is staffed with docents who can explain what life was like back then. La Casa Colonial is an interactive, hands-on exhibit that allows the visitor to experience 19th century living, handling tools and materials that were both homemade and brought as trade items from other areas of the world.

Daily admission is $5 or $1 on Sunday for New Mexico residents with I.D.; Wednesday is free to New Mexico seniors with I.D. Admission is always free for children 17 and younger. The museum is open from 10 AM to 5 PM Tuesday through Sunday. The museum is closed Mondays, New Year's Day, Easter, Thanksgiving, and Christmas. For information about the Museum of New Mexico's events and attractions call the 24-hour information line, (505) 827-6463.

Museum of Indian Arts and Culture
710 Camino Lejo
• (505) 827-6344
• http://www.nmmnh-abq.mus.nm.us/
mnm/mnm.html

You and your children can get a wonderful introduction to the richness of American Indian culture in the "Here Now and Always," exhibit. This multimedia presentation lets children hear Indians speaking their own languages and look at a pueblo kitchen, an Apache wickiup, a Navajo hogan, a 1930s trading post, and a contemporary feast day vendor's booth. The museum is next to the Museum of International Folk Art; if you're judicious in your looking, you can easily take your children to both on the same day.

Daily admission is $5 or $1 on Sunday for New Mexico residents with I.D.; Wednesday is free to New Mexico seniors with I.D. Admission is always free for children 17 and younger. The museum is open from 10 AM to 5 PM Tuesday through Sunday. The museum is closed Mondays, New Year's Day, Easter, Thanksgiving, and Christmas. For information about the Museum of New Mexico's events and attractions call the 24-hour information line, (505) 827-6463.

The Palace of the Governors
105 E. Palace Ave.
• (505) 476-5100
• http://www.nmmnh-abq.mus.nm.us/
mnm/mnm.html

Kids can see authentic armor like that worn by the conquistadors and Old West stage-

INSIDERS' TIP
You'll notice murals throughout the city created by the Santa Fe Youth Mural project. The program teaches teenagers the basics of art, teams them with professional artists, and decorates walls and utility boxes with a variety of paintings. Buses and even garbage trucks have been painted as part of the project

The Santa Fe Pet Parade brings out the young and old to show their pets and strut on Palace Avenue.

Photo: Don Strel

coaches that traveled the Santa Fe Trail. Among the museum's displays, you'll spot tools used by the Spanish settlers, traps used by the early fur traders, and fancy party dresses worn by Santa Fe senoritas centuries ago. The artifacts help bring the state's story to life. The collections here will be of interest to older children, especially those who know something about New Mexico's days as a Spanish territory or who are curious about the past. The Palace hosts a wonderful holiday party for children and their families each December, bringing the old building to life with music, theater, and refreshments.

Daily admission is $5 or $1 on Sunday for New Mexico residents with I.D.; Wednesday is free to New Mexico seniors with I.D. Admission is always free for children 17 and younger. The museum is open from 10 AM to 5 PM Tuesday through Sunday. The museum is closed Mondays, New Year's Day, Easter, Thanksgiving and Christmas. For information about the Museum of New Mexico's events and at-

tractions call the 24-hour information line, (505) 827-6463.

Kid-Style Events
April

All Species Day
On the Plaza and at Fort Marcy Park, 490 Washington Ave.
• (505) 988-2637

You can watch—or join—a parade of costumed characters through Santa Fe's downtown, attend an ecology-oriented family festival, watch puppet theater, listen to music, dance, and even get some education about other cultures at All Species Day.

After a long hiatus, the community celebration returned for Earth Day 2000, and promised to reinstate itself as a popular annual event. Among the usual

INSIDERS' TIP

The New Mexico Children's Foundation is a nonprofit, charitable organization that makes grants to other nonprofit agencies that serve children and families in Santa Fe and throughout the state. For more information, call (505) 986-2043.

participants will be students from Santa Fe's schools, performance troupes, community youth groups, and families interested in making costumes or creating projects. All Species Day also offers would-be participants access to a free public art studio (locations may vary) where people of all ages can make masks, giant puppets or banners, or work on floats, using advice and materials from the All Species Day staff.

The event begins with the late morning opening ceremony at the Santa Fe Plaza followed by the All-Species-Can-Dance parade to Fort Marcy Park, near the corner of Washington Avenue and Artists Road. Fort Marcy Park is the focus of afternoon activity, with plays, puppet shows, and a "creature congress" where participants are invited to speak on behalf of the creatures they represent.

May

CommUNITY DAY in Santa Fe
On the Plaza
• **(505) 984-6568**
• **http://sfweb.ci.santa-fe.nm.us/**

Face-painting, chalk-drawing, balloons, music, food, and more add sparkle to this annual event, designed to bring local families back to the Plaza. The activities pack the Plaza with friendly folks, including children, grandparents, and even some teenagers. The Santa Fe Public Schools may use the occasion to highlight special projects in the works in their buildings all over towns. Nonprofit agencies that help families and children use the festival to get the word out about their services. Children's performing groups from local schools often add to the day's mix of live entertainment. The program varies from year to year, but the goal is the same: a day of relaxed, free fun. Watch for Community Day on a Saturday in mid-May.

June

Santa Fe Air Show
Santa Fe Airport, Airport Rd. S.
• **(505) 473-7243**

Children love this event because they can see the planes up close and even climb right inside some of them. Among the air show's drawing cards are flybys, stunt pilots doing aerobatics, and a sizeable display of military aircraft. The event has simple objectives: family fun, promoting and educating people about aviation, and raising money for local charities, including those that work with kids and fami-

lies. The show is held the first weekend in June. The show is ideal for strollers and wheelchairs— once you reach the airstrip, everything is paved and flat. Visitors can buy T-shirts and a variety of aviation memorabilia and nosh on hot dogs and other festival-type food. Bring a hat and wear your sunscreen: It can get hot on the tarmac! Tickets are $5; children younger than age 5 get in free. Parking fee is $1.

Rodeo de Santa Fe
Santa Fe Rodeo Grounds, Rodeo Road
• **(505) 471-4300**

The rodeo offers four evening performances and a Saturday matinee. After years of fighting the July rains, the rodeo recently moved to June— the 2000 dates were the 21st through 24th. In general, look for it the third week of the month. The event features local and area talent, Turquoise Circuit cowboys, and some nationally ranked performers, including Mark Gomes, Steve Dollarhide, and Ty Murray in past years. In addition to all of the regular cowboy and cowgirl acts and intermission trick riding, the rodeo spotlights special events just for the little wranglers. A calf scramble on Saturday, invites kids to grab for a ribbon tied to the tail of a calf. In nightly "mutton busting" selected youngsters try their skill at riding uncooperative sheep. Registration is free, but only a limited number of kids can join the fun: It's first-come, first-served.

Kids love the Rodeo parade that kicks off the event each year at 10 AM on the Wednesday morning before the first evening's performance. The Plaza is a good place to watch; be sure to bring water, sunscreen and a hat!

Tickets for rodeo performances, 7:30 PM. with an addition al 2:30 PM show Saturday, range from $7 to $30, and parking is free. Kids get a discount for the Saturday matinee on box seats and chair seats; under 12 are always free in the grandstand and bleachers. The Rodeo takes place at the Santa Fe Rodeo Grounds, Rodeo Road at Richards Avenue. You can buy snacks and beverages from vendors who stroll the stands or from booths on the rodeo grounds. For an extra touch of Western, enjoy the Chuckwagon BBQ nightly beginning at 5:30 and Saturday at noon.

July

Fourth of July Pancakes on the Plaza
On the Plaza
• **(505) 983-7317**

Santa Fe families often plan to meet their friends on the Plaza for this festival event. Food

Traditional dress is required of those performing in Native American Dances.

Photo: John Running

and festivities are the centerpieces of this day of community fun, a fund-raiser for United Way of Santa Fe County. Hundreds of community volunteers cook pancakes and ham, serve coffee, orange juice, and milk, and chat with the crowd. On the bandstand, continuous entertainment ranges from mariachi music to dancing grandmothers. Red, white, and blue balloons make the Plaza look festive, and you can buy a commemorative T-shirt for yourself and your brood to mark the day. Breakfast tickets are $4 in advance at United Way, and $5 at the event. Watch the papers for other sales locations.

Eight Northern Indian Pueblos Arts and Crafts Show
At a Northern Pueblo
• (800) 793-4955

The largest Indian-run art show in the country, the annual Eight Northern Pueblos Arts and Crafts Fair doesn't leave kids out. Young American Indian artists have their own booth at this huge outdoor event and get to meet potential buyers and talk about their work. Children also share space in family booths throughout this huge outdoor show and sale. Usually held the third weekend in July, this show attracts top American Indian artists from throughout New Mexico, the Southwest, and the nation. A variety of live performances of American Indian music and traditional dancing adds to the festival, and many of the dance groups include children. You can buy food and drinks here as well as jewelry, pottery, baskets, weavings, paintings, designer clothing, and other arts and crafts. Various northern pueblos take turns hosting the show, but none is far from Santa Fe. Wear sunscreen, a hat, and sturdy shoes—you may have to hike several blocks from the parking area to get to the show grounds. In conjunction with the show, Eight Northern Indian Pueblos also sponsors the Popay Foot Race/Walk, in honor of the Indian leader who organized the Pueblo Revolt. Children have their own division in the event.

Traditional Spanish Market/ Contemporary Hispanic Market
On the Plaza
• (505) 983-4038

Work by children and teens is included in the traditional market, both in conjunction with their families and at a table devoted exclusively to youth. Santos (painted images of the saints), bultos (carved religious images), tinwork, silver filigree jewelry, secular wood carving, weaving, straw inlay, and embroidery are all here. The youths' creations are especially popular among market shoppers who may be looking to discover the next major santero. The traditional market celebrates Santa Fe's Spanish heritage; the contemporary market allows the artists more leeway to experiment with new materials and techniques. Both are juried. Children also enjoy the demonstrations of ancient craft techniques including rope making and blacksmithing. Traditional Hispanic dancing, music and food add to the fun. Admission is free.

August

Ice Cream Sunday
Santa Fe Children's Museum, 1050 Old Pecos Tr.
• (505) 989-8359

If there's any better way to sweeten a summer afternoon than with a bowl of ice cream, it involves adding the goodies you need to turn your vanilla into a sundae or even a banana split. The museum goes all out for this annual family-style fundraiser. The sticky fun begins at noon, traditionally on the first Sunday in August, and continues until 5 pm—or until the ice cream runs out. Santa Fe celebrities, including the mayor, the superintendent of schools, and chief of police, have helped with the scooping. Some years, a big red fire truck is on hand, and the firefighters offer the little ones an up-close look. You'll also find music and performances by children here throughout the day. Kids can also get their faces painted, ride donkeys, or jump themselves silly in the bounce-a-matic—one of those rubber rooms filled with balls. All the money goes directly for new exhibits at the museum, the only one in Santa Fe dedicated to kids. There's no admission fee, and ice cream is $3 a serving.

Mountain Man Trade Fair
Palace of the Governors, 105 E. Palace Ave.
• (505) 476-5100

The mountain men, traders and trappers who lived by their wits and spent long months of time in the backcountry, are a colorful part of northern New Mexico's history. The Palace

INSIDERS' TIP
If your child is interested in organized sports, Santa Fe is filled with opportunities. Here are some resources for you: Little League Baseball, ages 6-12, Cliff Garley, (505) 983-4186; ages 13-18, Toni Chavez, (505) 983-4643. Santa Fe Children's Football League, ages 6-13, Eddie Webb, (505) 989-4593. Northern New Mexico Soccer Club, (505) 982-0878. Basketball offered through the Boys and Girls Club, (505) 983-6632. Hockey, Santa Fe Trailrunners Youth Hockey Program, (505) 986-1552.

KIDSTUFF

of the Governors, once the center of New Mexico's political life and now a popular history museum, hosts this annual fair as tribute to Santa Fe's role as a trade center. Modern mountain men—and mountain women—come in costume to sell handmade items that are often reproductions of the tools, weapons, and domestic items these traders would have sold a hundred years ago. Demonstrations of mountain-man skills, such as tomahawk tossing and musket firing, and a program on animals such as beaver, fox, and mink are guaranteed kid pleasers. Please call for specific events and a schedule. The fair is usually held mid-month in the museum's central courtyard. Admission is free.

Santa Fe County Fair
Santa Fe County Fair Grounds,
Rodeo Rd. at Richards Ave.
• **(505) 471-4711**
Santa Fe County 4-H plays a major role in this event, and youth exhibits are one of its major attractions. Children can see goats, rabbits, ducks, and lambs. You might find llamas walking an obstacle course, pygmy goats, or a watermelon-eating contest. Kiddie rides, entertainment, and concessions sold by bright-eyed 4-Hers add to the fun. The frog-jumping contest invites teams of four people to encourage their frog to win the contest; afterwards, they get to keep the frogs. Spanish dance performances, Mariachi music and chili cook-off and salsa contest are also part of the fair's attractions. Watch for it in early August. Admission fees and parking change from year to year but are never more than a few dollars.

Indian Market
On and around the Plaza
• **(505) 983-5220**
• **http://www.swaia.org/index.htm**
Although this event is primarily aimed at adults with an interest in American Indian art, several features may appeal to kids. The tented area in Cathedral Park next to St. Francis Cathedral, 131 Cathedral Place, displays work produced by youth who participate in a special outreach and mentorship program though the Southwestern Association for Indian Arts, the group that presents Indian Market. SWAIA opens this area free of charge to talented young people who do not have family members exhibiting at Indian Market. (Those with family may share their booth.) Children also may be interested in the fashion show, usually held on Sunday afternoon of Market weekend, and the

musical events on Friday and Saturday nights. The entertainment and its locations change annually—please call or check the local newspapers for detailed information.

Another kid-friendly facet of the market is the demonstrations that are offered continually both Saturday and Sunday of the show. Children can watch American Indian artists make pottery, do silverwork, weave a basket, create intricate beadwork, or shape a sculpture from a chunk of stone. And kids love the food, which ranges from green-chile cheeseburgers to Indian tacos—dinner-plate-size pieces of quickly fried yeast bread topped with ground beef, onions, chile, tomatoes, lettuce, and cheese. You can also buy hot dogs and sodas. To make the market less overwhelming, SWAIA publishes a guide that lists every artist by name and category and includes a map of booth locations. You can get a free copy at the SWAIA office or at their booth on the Plaza during the event. Indian Market is always the weekend following the third Thursday of the month. Admission is free. (Please see our Annual Events and Festivals chapter for more information on Indian Market.)

September

New Mexico State Fair
State Fair Grounds,
300 San Pedro Blvd. N.E.,
between Central Ave. and Lomas Blvd.,
Albuquerque
• **(505) 265-1791, (800) 867-FAIR**
• **http://www.nmstatefair.com/**
If you've never been to the New Mexico State Fair, the size will impress you right off the bat. The fair is huge, 236 acres of displays and attractions, and it's a long, varied show, opening the first Friday after Labor Day for 17 days. Every day offers different shows and events, in addition to a continual program of commercial attractions. If you're bringing a toddler, don't forget the stroller! A favorite attraction is the midway with its rides and games. A special section, the Kid's Kingdom midway, is dedicated to younger kids with less-intense rides just the right size for half-pints.

In addition to the rides, you can spend time at the petting zoo and in the Villa Hispana and Indian Villages where you'll find entertainment, exhibits, and food. At the Youth Hall, young exhibitors have their own competitions in categories from model building to sewing. In the evenings, the rodeo performances, complete with top-of-the-line country singers and national recording artists, are also great family fun.

And everyone likes the food, served by more than 100 vendors in virtually every corner of the fairgrounds. You'll find corn on the cob, all sorts of New Mexican treats, freshly baked pies, cool snow cones, cotton candy, hot dogs and burgers, Greek specialties, barbecue, and more. The State Fair usually runs from early to mid-September. You can pick up a free schedule of each day's events and a map of the grounds at the information booth. Admission in 1999 was $1 for early birds Monday through Thursday; $4 after 2 PM and on Fridays and weekends. Children ages 3 to12 are $2 and those two and younger are free. Parking fees are $4 to $8.

Fiesta De Santa Fe
On the Plaza and other locations
• (505) 988-7575

Not only do kids have their own event at the Fiesta, the entire festival is kid-friendly. The Fiesta, held the weekend following Labor Day, commemorates the Spanish resettlement in Santa Fe after the Pueblo Revolt chased the conquistadors back to Mexico. (See our History chapter.) It's the oldest continuous community celebration in the United States.

Children love Fiesta, especially the burning of Zozobra and a fireworks show. In 1999, the city and the Kiwanis moved the event from Friday evening to Thursday, and kept the Thursday date for 2000—and probably beyond. You'll pay $5 (kids get in free) to watch from the field, which is usually VERY crowded. Santa Fe artist Will Shuster created Zozobra, a 44-foot tall puppet with glowing eyes and a gravelly voice, to personify the disappointments and mistakes of the year. (His nickname is Old Man Gloom.) Crews of volunteers build Zozobra the week before Fiesta and erect the giant puppet on a huge pole at Fort Marcy Park, 490 Washington Avenue. As the sky grows dark, the puppet comes to life, moaning, growling, and waving his hands. (Very young children may be scared.) Finally, after a performance by the Fire Dancers and children dressed as Little Glooms, Zozobra disappears in flames to a rowdy chorus of cheers.

One of the Fiesta's most charming events, the Pet Parade, or *Desfile de los Niños*, "Parade of the Children," happens Saturday morning. Children, parents, and pets ranging from cats and dogs to llamas, circle the Plaza and walk along downtown streets. Many of the humans wear costumes to be real or imaginary animals; many

of the animals are also dressed up. Watch from the shade of the Plaza or in front of the Palace of the Governors, just across from the Plaza bandstand. Come early for a good seat. Watching and participating are both free.

Throughout Fiesta weekend, the Plaza is alive with free entertainment provided by a variety of local and area music and dance groups, including some composed only of children. A commercial carnival at the Rodeo Grounds adds to the weekend's merriment.

October

Albuquerque International Balloon Fiesta
Balloon Fiesta State Park, between Alameda and Tramway N.E., west of I-25, Albuquerque
• (505) 821-1000, (888) 422-7277
• www.aibf.org/

Children love this festival, which fills the Albuquerque sky with hundreds of balloons of all colors, shapes, and sizes, including some whimsical flying creatures. You can attend four mass ascensions, several evening balloon glows (in which the balloons are inflated but stay on the ground like giant light bulbs), contests that test pilots' skill, and a special shape "rodeo." More than 100 of the special shape balloons can be found at the Fiesta; in the past participating pilots have brought giant macaws, flying tennis shoes, dragons, and pink pigs. The Balloon Explorium, a tent at the launch site, gives kids a chance to learn about balloon operations from inflation through flight and landing. The history of the sport and safety aspects of ballooning also get attention here. The exhibit is open during ballooning events and there is no charge. About 1.5 million people attend this event over its nine-day run. In addition to the balloons, the Fiesta presents live music including jazz, country-western, and mariachi. Food and shopping concessions await visitors. Admission is $4 for adults; kids younger than 12 get in free. Parking is $5. (See our Annual Events and Festivals chapter.)

Annual All Children's Powwow
Location to be determined
• (505) 982-4636 (Wheelwright Museum)
• http://www.wheelwright.org/

The oldest children's powwow in the country, this event attracts more than a hundred young American Indians who perform intertribal, blanket and social dances on either the first or second Saturday of the month. Prizes go to the winners in different age groups, and spectators are welcome to take pictures. Public events usually begin at 11 AM and run until dusk. If you can't stay the whole time, the Grand Entry that opens the powwow is especially colorful and photogenic. An all-volunteer staff does the organizing. The event was held at the Wheelwright Museum, which sponsors it, until it grew too large and was moved to the football field at the Santa Fe Indian School in 1999. Please call for site information. The event is free. You'll also find American Indian crafts and food sales.

December

Christmas at the Palace of the Governors
Palace of the Governors, 105 E. Palace Ave.
• **(505) 476-5100**

Musicians, carolers, storytellers, and dancers carry the spirit of the holiday season to this big, free party. Christmas at the Palace draws hundreds of Santa Fe families and lucky visitors with good timing. It's an ideal event for children. The celebration includes a visit from Santa and activities that fill nearly every room of this sprawling old museum. Although the party is free, in keeping with the spirit of the season donations of nonperishable food for the poor are welcome. The event, funded in part by the city's arts commission, is usually held on a Thursday and Friday evening in mid-December.

Down the street at the Museum of Fine Arts, children may be interested in the annual Baumann Marionette performances, which are usually held on a weekend in mid December. Please call the Museum of Fine Arts for details, (505) 476-5072.

Nature, Anyone?

Chairlift Rides Santa Fe Ski Area
16 miles northeast of Santa Fe on N.M. Hwy. 475
• **(505) 983-9155, (505) 982-4429**

Kids feel all grown up when they ride to the top of the mountain on this comfy, four-person chairlift. The lift, which is also great for anyone else who might enjoy the chance to see a magnificent view without a big hike, takes passengers to the top of Aspen Peak at an elevation of 11,000 feet. If you're energetic, you

can continue hiking through the spruce, fir, and ponderosa pine. You may see marmots, bushy-tailed woodchuck-like creatures also known as "whistle pigs" for their high-pitched barks. You'll find dozens of different wildflowers and colorful mushrooms. When you're ready, you can ride the lift back down.

The chairlift operates from 10 AM to 3 PM on weekends and holidays from July 4 through Labor Day and again in the fall for aspen viewing, with the dates determined annually based on the weather. Round-trip rates are $7 per person. Children shorter than 46 inches may ride for free accompanied by a paying adult; seniors 72 or over may ride for free. One-way trips for hikers are $5.

The Planetarium
Santa Fe Community College, 6401 Richards Ave.
• **(505) 428-1677**
• **http://www.santa-fe.cc.nm.us/community.html**

One of Santa Fe's favorite attractions for children and families, the Planetarium offers a changing schedule of productions intended to give the audience a better knowledge of the night sky. Each month's programs explore a new theme that includes some history, some astronomy news and maybe even some physics. The planetarium presents children's programs on selected Saturdays at 10:30 AM. Big Bird and Oscar have been among the celebrities who help introduce the young audience to the wonders of astronomy. The planetarium schedules shows of interest to adults as well as children on the first Thursday of most months and on Fridays, usually at 6:30 PM and 8 PM. About 10,000 children visit the planetarium for free each year through a special arrangement with the Santa Fe Public Schools. Tickets are $5 for adults, $3 for preteens and for seniors 65 and older and for community college students with a current ID; free for members. Tickets go on sale a half-hour before show time. For up-to-date recorded information, call the SFCC InfoLine, (505) 428-1777. Press option 6, then 1, to get show information.

Randall Davey Audubon Center
1800 Upper Canyon Rd.
• **(505) 983-4609**

The popular summer nature programs here fill up quickly and rightly so. Kids get to spend time outside learning about such things as animal camouflage and disguises, nocturnal creatures, tracking, and native birds. But you don't

KIDSTUFF

have to sign up for a workshop to enjoy this beautiful spot. Families take pleasure in walking along the nature trail—it's a nice stroll even for the youngest ones. You might see a coyote, and you'll probably spot several different varieties of birds. The center's trails begin in the piñon and juniper woodlands and meadows and climb up to the cool ponderosa pine forest. The gift shop sells birdseed, books, and other items of interest to naturalists. One of the center's attractions is its convenience; it's only a 10-minute drive from the Plaza. Follow Canyon Road past the intersection of Camino Cabra at Cristo Rey Church to Upper Canyon Road. The center is the very last structure on Canyon Road. It is open from 9 AM to 5 PM daily. Trail fee is $1 per person.

Santa Fe Farmers' Market
Sanbusco Market Center Parking Lot, 500 Montezuma St.
- **(505) 983-4098**

If your kids think peas come from a can and carrots from a bag, a trip to Farmers' Market will open their eyes and please their taste buds. You can see and buy fresh area produce, colorful cut flowers and freshly baked treats here two days a week, usually from mid-May until sometime in October. You'll find live music at the market most mornings, sometimes with children as part of the performance. The market sometimes hosts special demonstrations and events and sponsors an annual tour to working farms. It's open from 7:00 AM to 11:30 AM on Tuesday and Saturday, but those who come early find the best selection. Potential buyers and their children are admitted free.

On the Road
Albuquerque

Albuquerque Aquarium and Botanic Garden
2601 W. Central Ave. N.W.
- **(505) 764-6200**
- **www.cabq.gov/biopark**

The Albuquerque Aquarium, one of Albuquerque's most popular attractions, stands out as one of the few aquariums in the country that isn't located near the ocean. Kids flocked to the place when it opened in 1996, and they're still coming! Children and their parents can have an encounter of the most direct kind with whelks, sea urchins, sea stars, and other inver-

tebrates at a hands-on education station—the marine equivalent of a petting zoo. Kids get a kick out of the eel cave with its large population of scary-looking moray eels. The "Inside the Wreck" exhibit features a replica of a 16th-century Spanish ship. But the aquarium's most popular attraction among visitors of all ages is the 285,000-gallon shark tank, where about 20 sandtiger, brown, and nurse sharks circle and watch the people who've come to watch them. The aquarium's newest exhibit features seahorses and seadragons from around the world. Children also enjoy the cool pond outside the building where cartoonlike iron fish, frogs, and pelicans splash. The Rio Grande Botanic Garden is just across the plaza from the aquarium. The aquarium is open from 9 AM to 5 PM Tuesdays through Sundays. Closed Mondays. Admission is $4.50 for adults ages 16 to 64, $2.50 for seniors and children ages 3 to 15. Kids younger than 3 are admitted for free.

Rio Grande Zoological Park
903 10th Street S.W.
- **(505) 764-6200**
- **www.cabq.cov/biopark**

The Rio Grande Zoo makes a nice day trip for northern New Mexico families and for Santa Fe visitors. The zoo offers everything you'd expect and more. The beautifully landscaped grounds include an aviary, elephants, petting opportunities and a reptile house with 6-foot cobras, 20-foot pythons and Komodo dragons. The zoo has a new $2.2 million exhibit where polar bears cavort in an 11-foot-deep pool, lounge by a stream, play under four waterfalls, slip down a water slide, and enjoy an air-conditioned ice cave. Australian animals, Mexican wolves, a primate area, and a new Tropical America add to the zoo's attraction. Free animal-encounter shows, story hours, animal discovery demonstrations, concerts, and other summer programs are part of the zoo's regular events. Call for a schedule.

The zoo has won praise from wildlife specialists for its innovative design techniques that help ensure the animals' physical and psychological well being. The zoo invites children and their parents to become foster "zoo parents" by sponsoring or "adopting" certain animals. The zoo also raises money with special events, including "Saturday Night Wild," in mid-June, which welcomes visitors in the cool of the evening to see the animals when some of them are most active. Contests, face-painting, international food, musicians, puppets, clowns, and

The Rodeo Parade is a kid-friendly part of Rodeo de Santa Fe, which has been held since 1949.

Photo: Don Strel

music add to the fun. Admission to the event is $8. If seeing all the animals makes you hungry, you can buy food at the mid-park Cottonwood Café or pack a picnic. The zoo is open from 9 AM to 5 PM Tuesday through Sundays. Zoo admission is free to children younger than 3, $2.50 for seniors and ages 3 to 15 and $4.50 for ages 16 to 64. Children 12 and younger must be accompanied by an adult.

Explora Science Center and Children's Museum of Albuquerque
**#98 Winrock Center
(near the food court),
Indian School at Louisiana
and Wyoming**
• **(505) 842-1537**

Once separate museums, these two programs moved to a shared space in late 1997 and more recently moved to this popular Albuquerque shopping mall. Children enjoy the hands-on exhibits, which are especially designed for ages 2 to 12. Weekends bring storytellers, musical performances, science and art workshops, dance concerts, and more. Kids are welcome to have birthday parties here. The museum is open 10 AM to 9 PM Monday through Saturday and from noon to 6 PM on Sunday. Admission is $2 for ages 2 to 12 and for visitors older than 62; it's $4 for ages 13 to 62 and free for children younger than 2.

New Mexico Museum of Natural History and Science
1801 Mountain Rd. N.W.
• **(505) 841-2800**
• **www.nmmnh-abq.mus.nm.us**

This attraction, fondly known as "the dinosaur museum" by New Mexico kids, recently got even better with two new additions. The LodeStar Astronomy Center now features permanent astronomy exhibits, a planetarium, a Virtual Voyages simulation theater, and an observatory with a 16-inch telescope. LodeStar is the first planetarium in the world to showcase high-definition digital video imaging over an entire domed projection screen. The dome is 55 feet in diameter—it makes for quite a show! And the museum expanded its Dynamax Theater with a larger screen and more seats.

But from the life-size sculptures of Spike the

Children have their own events at Rodeo de Santa Fe.

Photo: Bob Stoval Photography

Pentaceratops and Alberta the Albertosaurus to the FossilWorks Laboratory where kids can watch scientists extract real dinosaur bones from rock, the dinosaurs here still steal the show. Children can stand next to the skeletons of real dinosaurs that actually lived in what is now New Mexico and see casts of their footprints. The museum's other attractions include a habitat of New Mexico's ancient seashore, a walk through a simulated volcano and ride in an "Evolator" that takes you back to the days when arid Albuquerque was a rain forest.

The museum's hands-on learning center gives kids a chance to look through microscopes, test their sensory perception and ask science questions. Dynamax theater presents movies every hour on the hour from 10 AM until 5 PM. Recent topics included whales and their migrations and the rain forest. The museum is open from 9 AM to 5 PM daily except Christmas and non-holiday Mondays in January and September. Admission is $5 for adults, $4 for seniors and students, and $2 for ages 3 to 12. Tickets to the Dynamax theater, the LodeStar Virtual Voyages and the LodeStar Planetarium are extra. You can save money if you buy a combination tickets package.

Los Alamos

Bradbury Science Museum
15th St. at Central Ave., Los Alamos
- **(505) 667-4444**
- **www.lanl.gov/external/museum**

Children with curiosity about science enjoy this museum for its hands-on displays and lively demonstrations and shows. The museum offers visitors the opportunity to play with a laser, see Fat Man and Little Boy atomic bombs, learn about DNA fingerprinting, work with computers and interactive video, and watch a 20-minute movie about the development of the atomic bomb. Operated by Los Alamos National Laboratories, the museum shows the role Los Alamos played in the atomic bomb's creation and offers interactive exhibits explaining the scope of its nuclear research today. The museum is open daily except Thanksgiving, Christmas, and New Year's Day. Hours are 1 to 5 PM Saturday, Sunday and Monday and 9 AM to 5 PM Tuesday through Friday. Admission is free.

Bandelier National Monument
5 miles south of Los Alamos on N.M. Hwy. 4 (45 miles northwest of Santa Fe)
- **(505) 672-3861**

Kids will find ladders to climb and caves to crawl inside at this popular national monument, all the while getting a firsthand look at the way an ancient people lived. The monument encompasses more than 1,000 Indian dwellings, homes to people who may have been the ancestors of some of the modern Pueblo Indians. A good place to start is with a walk through the visitors center, where displays introduce this prehistoric Pueblo Indian ancestral culture. Then head out along the self-guided ruins trail that begins in back of the museum. Children enjoy walking on the narrow paths formed by Indian feet hundreds of years ago. They can climb ladders to reach the upper cliff dwellings and step inside caves where Indian families slept or stored their food and belongings many hundreds of years ago. They'll see how smoke from the ancient fires blackened the cave ceilings and notice petroglyphs carved along the cliffs.

One of New Mexico's most famous and popular attractions, the area now known as Bandelier was occupied as early as A.D. 1100. The people who lived here were farmers and hunters. Since they had no written language, much of their culture remains a mystery. The monument preserves a wealth of archaeological ruins covering about 450 years of human history. Large pueblos, medium-sized house clusters, single-room shelters, and cave dwellings are all here; Bandelier National Monument was established to protect and preserve this priceless heritage.

The monument is named for Adolph Bandelier, an explorer, historian, and author who visited here on five different occasions. Bandelier's novel The Delight Makers used one of these ancient pueblos as its setting.

When you've seen enough ruins, you can picnic along the stream or hike to a waterfall —most of the park is wilderness. Overnight camping is allowed, and summer campfire programs explain the wildlife, plants, and people of the area. (Please call for a schedule.) The park is about an hour's drive from Santa Fe through some of northern New Mexico's most interesting geologic country. The monument is open from dawn to dusk. Entry fee is $10 per vehicle.

Pecos

Pecos National Historical Park
25 miles southeast of Santa Fe on I-25, Exit 299 then 2 miles east on N.M. Hwy. 63
- **(505) 757-6032**

In this park, children and their parents will get a fascinating introduction to the life of the Pueblo people prior to and after the Spanish arrived. Before touring the ruins, stop at the museum for displays that explain the 15th-century pueblo and its mission church, built under the guidance of Spanish friars. In the museum, kids can touch ancient Indian artifacts and watch a short, exciting film about the Spanish exploration of New Mexico. Then walk the trail through the ruins, which begins just outside the museum. Don't miss the kiva, the Pueblo's ceremonial center, where you can push a button to fill the room with American Indian music. The mission, now reduced to only low mud walls, was once described as "the most magnificent church north of Mexico City." During the summer, the park often has demonstrations of Indian or Hispanic arts and

Traditional dances are held every half-hour at the Eight Northern Indian Pueblos Arts and Crafts Show.

Photo: Don Strel

crafts. (Call for a schedule.) The park is open daily from 8 AM to 6 PM Memorial Day through Labor Day and until 5 PM the rest of the year. Admission is $2 for adults (children get in free) or $4 per carload, whichever is less.

Near Santa Fe

Hyde Memorial State Park
7.5 miles northeast of Santa Fe on N.M. Hwy. 475
• **(505) 983-7175**

With its hiking opportunities and cross-country ski trails, a cold stream to splash in, and plenty of picnic tables, Hyde Park draws a nice crowd of Santa Fe residents and visitors into the Sangre de Cristo Mountains year-round. Backpackers and Nordic skiers use Hyde Park to begin their explorations of the adjoining Santa Fe National Forest. Campsites, including areas for large groups, and the park's playgrounds are popular in the summer. In the winter, there's a sledding slope and tubing run. The road from Santa Fe to Hyde Park and beyond is designated as a National Scenic Byway, and the trip takes you through beautiful mountain country over a paved, two-lane highway that is steep and twisty in some places. Day use is $4; the fee for camping is $10 per day for a tent site or $14 per day for a site with electricity.

Santa Fe National Forest
Headquarters, 1474 Rodeo Road
• **(505) 438-7542**
• **www.publiclands.org**

This sprawling forest has five ranger districts throughout northern New Mexico, but the area closest to Santa Fe is among the most scenic and popular. This section of the Santa Fe National Forest begins at the northern border of Hyde Park, 7.5 miles northeast of Santa Fe and stretches for miles into the Pecos Wilderness. You might see a deer or even a black bear. You'll find campgrounds and cross-country ski trails here, as well as the Santa Fe Ski Area, which operates on a forest service lease. Campgrounds include Aspen Basin, Aspen Vista, and Big Tesuque. Camping fee is generally $10 per night in most campgrounds. The Santa Fe National Forest Headquarters offers a wonderful source of information on public lands in New Mexico, along with BLM maps, Forest Service maps, hiking books, and a variety of fun things for kids.

INSIDERS' TIP
Don't let the price of admission stop you from taking your children to any branches of the Museum of New Mexico. Young people 16 and under are always free. For information about exhibits call the 24-hour information line at (505) 827-6443.

Annual Events and Festivals

Arts festivals, celebrations deeply rooted in the area's history and traditions, family events, and even a dog show just for mutts: Santa Fe's schedule of special events is unmatched in communities twice its size.

As is true in most places, summer means more activities. But there's something to do year-round. Many events here are benefits for one good cause or another, a testament to Santa Fe's generosity.

August brings Santa Fe's most popular event, Indian Market. The market, a two-day show and sale, highlights the best in American Indian arts from throughout the country, packs Santa Fe's hotels and restaurants, and sends some locals packing, too! Galleries around town honor their best and best-selling artists on market weekend with exhibits and gala openings. Indian Market includes a growing performing arts component, offering a chance for Native American musicians, storytellers, and dancers to perform before an appreciative audience.

While Indian Market draws the most visitors, Fiesta wins hands-down as Santa Fe's oldest celebration and takes the honors as a favorite with residents. Held the weekend following Labor Day, Fiesta commemorates Santa Fe's Spanish heritage with parades and pageants, music, dancing, and food galore. Fiesta also has a strong religious element, celebrating the contribution of the Franciscan missionaries and the city's deeply rooted Catholic heritage.

Christmas in Santa Fe also showcases the community's rich traditions. Farolitos—little bags filled with sand and lit with a small candle—and luminarias, or bonfires, line the streets and light the way for the Christ child and for neighbors and churchgoers on Christmas Eve. A troupe of Spanish-speaking actors present an ancient Christmas pageant, *Las Posadas,* each December on the Santa Fe Plaza.

Spring brings the annual Easter pilgrimage to the historic church at Chimayó, about 40 miles north of Santa Fe. Pilgrims from throughout New Mexico walk to the shrine on Good Friday as a testimony to their faith or to ask for divine blessings.

Summer offers a full schedule of performing and visual arts events—too many to list separately in this chapter. From June through August, the city buzzes with choices ranging from Shakespeare to modern theater, from storytelling in a tipi to lectures on culture and history, and from ballet to flamenco performances. The visual arts scene sparkles with gallery openings and outdoor art shows and fairs. Please see our Arts chapter for more specific information about the Santa Fe Opera and other concerts. And whenever you're planning to visit, check the local papers to see if a big-name jazz artist, a reggae concert or who-knows-what-else has arrived for the weekend.

We've organized this list of the year's highlights based on when the event usually occurs. Unless otherwise noted, prices are per adult ticket, and parking is free. (During Indian Market and Fiesta, some entrepreneurs and nonprofit groups may set up lots and charge for parking. If you don't want to pay, you can park elsewhere for free, but you'll have a longer walk.)

You'll notice that many events happen on the Plaza. You'll find the Plaza, Santa Fe's town square, downtown at the northern end of Old Santa Fe Trail, at the corner of Lincoln and Palace avenues.

In addition to this calendar, don't forget the public events at the Indian pueblos near Santa Fe, which are listed in the Pueblo Culture section of our Local Cultures chapter.

January

Souper Bowl
**Sweeney Convention Center,
210 W. Marcy St**
• (505) 471-1633

This event combines fun and fundraising. Those who attend have an opportunity to sample soups from more than 25 of Santa Fe's finest restaurants and vote for their favorites. Proceeds from the admission fee ($15/$5 for children under 12) benefit the Food Depot, Santa Fe's local food bank, which provides food to more than 60 nonprofit agencies in northern New Mexico. Watch for it around the football Super Bowl weekend.

The Edible Art Tour
Santa Fe art galleries and studios
• (505) 982-1648

The Santa Fe Gallery Association and ARTsmart combine efforts for this event, a fund raisers for ARTsmart's work in the Santa Fe schools. You can celebrate the art of food and food as art. Some of Santa Fe's top chefs are paired with galleries to create beautiful, edible art. Begun in 1998, the tour grows more popular every year. The offerings in prior years have included venison gumbo, miniature sweet potato pies and homemade sausage. The price? $20. For 2001 and beyond, the event may be expanded. Stay tuned.

Jessie Helms Cabaret, Dinner, and Ball
Hotel Loretto 211 Old Santa Fe Trail
• (505) 986-1838

Sponsored by the Human Rights Alliance, this event parodies the honorable Republican senator form North Carolina, a gentleman known for his stand against federal arts funding and money for AIDS. Among the sponsors, you'll usually find liberal politicians and gay rights advocates. The Ball includes a comedy show, dancing, and silent auction and raffle

for about $25 advance or $30 at the door. A buffet dinner and cabaret performances precede the ball for an additional $45.

February

Jimmie Heuga Ski Express
**Santa Fe Ski Area, 16 miles northeast
of Santa Fe on N.M. Hwy. 475**
• (505) 982-4429
• www.skisantafe.com

This event raises money for scholarships to send New Mexicans with multiple sclerosis to the Jimmie Heuga Center in Colorado. At the center, people with MS learn about diet, exercise, and attitude adjustments that can make their lives more pleasant. Jimmie Heuga, an Olympic medallist who has MS, founded and directs the program. Santa Fe hosts New Mexico's oldest and only Express.

Skiers compete on three-person teams for prizes that include a trip to Vail to represent the Santa Fe Ski Area in the finals. Santa Fe's Express usually includes a race through the gates and an endurance event or treasure-hunt type rally. Santa Fe skiers have placed among the top 10 teams at the finals. The date of the event varies according to snow conditions; call the number above to find out the year's date. To enter, each three-member team must contribute a minimum of $1,000. Spectators and volunteers are welcome but must be able to ski and purchase ski lift tickets.

INSIDERS' TIP
Santa Fe has a lively schedule of concerts, plays, and art show openings all year long. For information please see our Arts chapter, or check the local newspapers when you're in town.

The Great Cookie Caper
Quail Run, 3101 Old Pecos Trail
• (505) 983-6339

Desserts steal the show at this event, which benefits the Sangre de Cristo Girl Scout Council. Chefs from some of Santa Fe's finest restaurants use Girl Scout cookies as the basis for elaborate and delicious sweet treats. Those in attendance sample the entries and pick the winner. The evening also includes a cookie jar auction and dinner. Proceeds help the scouts run their summer camp and operate other programs. Admission in 1999 was $40.

Monothon
College of Santa Fe Print Making Center
CSF campus, 1600 St. Michael's Drive
• **(505) 473-6564**

A marathon of monotype printmaking sessions, this long-standing event also includes sales of prints to raise funds for art student scholarships and to support the College of Santa Fe's Printmaking Center. Adult sessions are usually held the second and third weekends of the month. Special attractions for children may also be included. Call for information on times, fees, and public receptions and a big art exhibit of the work held in March.

Winefest
La Fonda 100 E. San Francisco
• **(505) 988-4640**

This long-standing event combines good food with wine and beer tastings and an auction, all to benefit Santa Fe Pro Musica. In past years more than a dozen breweries and about that many wineries have participated. Food comes from Santa Fe's top restaurants. After the tasting, you can buy your favorites by the case at a silent auction. Stick around for the live auction and bid on artwork, vacations, and

all sorts of services. Tickets are $25 in advance and $30 at the door if any remain.

March

Gladfelter Bump Contest/Southwest Snowboard Championships
Santa Fe Ski Area, 16 miles northeast of Santa Fe on N.M. Hwy. 475
• **(505) 982-4429**
• **skisantafe.com**

The area's best mogul skiers and snowboarders compete for glory and prizes in the annual Gladfelter competition. The Snowboard Championships include jumps, half-pipes, and a slalom course and draw snowboarders from throughout the region. Both events are held in late March or early April, depending on snow conditions. Spectators are welcome, but you have to be able to ski or snowboard to get to the course, and you'll need a lift ticket. Registration for the competition is usually around $10 plus the cost of a lift ticket.

Oscar Night Gala
College of Santa Fe
• **(505)473-6244**

Sip champagne, enjoy a generous buffet, and watch the Academy Awards presentation in style on multiple screens. This black-tie party

The Santa Fe Fiesta includes a parade among its activities.

Photo: Chris Corrie

The Plaza is a great place to people watch or have an ice cream cone and chat.

Photo: Don Strel

raises money for scholarships and is sponsored by the College of Santa Fe's Moving Image Arts Department. (For more information on CSF, see our Education chapter.) Santa Fe residents love this party; tickets go fast, and it's usually sold out. This is always held on the night of the Academy Awards, usually late in the month or in early April, so mark your calendar. Tickets cost $75 per person in 1999. For another small donation, you can vote on who you think will take home the big prizes.

April

Chimayó Pilgrimage
Santuario de Chimayó, Chimayó, N.M.
• **no phone**

Every Holy Week beginning on Thursday, thousands of pilgrims walk to the Santuario de Chimayó, about 40 miles from Santa Fe. Christians, a few of them carrying wooden crosses, walk to this beautiful adobe church to repay a solemn vow or to ask for Christ's blessings. Pilgrims travel along U.S. Highway 84/285 through Santa Fe to the Nambé junction at N.M. Highway 503 and then on to Chimayó on N.M. Highway 76. The majority of the devout walk late on Holy Thursday and on Good Friday. Area law enforcement pays close attention to traffic to keep the pilgrims safe. If you're driving this route, please slow down and be careful. If you'd like to join the pilgrims for your own spiritual reasons, by all means do so.

People walking at night should bring a flashlight and wear light-colored clothes. Day or night, carry plenty of water, wear sturdy shoes, and watch for cars.

All Species Day
On the Plaza and Fort Marcy Park, 490 Washington Avenue.
• **(505) 988-2637, (505) 820-0493**

A parade of costumed characters and funky bands marching along through Santa Fe's downtown, an ecology-oriented family festival, puppet theater, dance and even some education about other cultures—that's All Species Day. Usually held around Earth Day, the event attracts students from Santa Fe's schools, performance troupes, community youth groups, and families. Participants make their own floats and costumes, assemble at the Santa Fe Plaza and parade through the streets to Fort Marcy Park on Washington Avenue for food and more festivities. The opening ceremony usually begins around 11 AM, and the fun lasts until dusk.

May

Partners in Education Ball
Sweeney Center, 201 W. Marcy St.
• **(505) 474-0240**

You can get dressed up, schmooze with the city's other movers and shakers, enjoy a good meal, and dance the night away—all for a fine cause. The Ball, inaugurated in 1997, raises money for the Santa Fe Public Schools and promotes community awareness of and involvement in the work the schools do. High school volunteers serve as greeters, ushers, and servers and provide the music. Partners in Education sponsor the event, usually held the first Saturday in May. Partners is a nonprofit group dedicated to helping teachers and students succeed in the classroom. The cost was $85 per person in 2000.

All Species Day is an ecologically centered celebration with costumes, homegrown marching band, food, and booths.

Photo: Don Strel

Micaceous Pottery Market
Museum of Indian Arts and Culture, 710 Camino Lejo
• **(505) 827-6344**
• **www.miaclab.org**

Northern New Mexico's Pueblo Indians have made pottery for centuries. Micaceous pottery sparkles because it's made from clay with mica and the market features potters who specialize in this ancient form. At last count, roughly 60 potters receive invitations to the market; participation varies each year. You talk to the potters about their creations and can buy directly from the artists.

Bach Festival
Various venues.
• **(505) 988-4640**
• **www.santafepromusica.com/**

Santa Fe Pro Musica treats Santa Fe residents and visitors to several evenings of the music of J.S. Bach and his talented sons. A recent program featured performers on instruments from Bach's time presenting *St. Matthew's Passion*. Santa Fe Pro Musica musicians were joined for the performance by the Smithsonian Chamber Players. Chamber music and cantatas are among the festival's highlights along with sonatas and concertos of all sorts. Concert locations include the historic Loretto Chapel and Santa Maria de la Paz Catholic Community Church. Festival tickets are usually $25 to $30.

AIDS Walk Santa Fe
Begins on the Plaza
• **(505) 989-WALK**

If you live in Santa Fe long enough, chances are you'll be asked either to join this AIDS walk or to sponsor someone who's walking. Santa Fe has a high percentage of people with AIDS and HIV, and the community offers a variety of services for them (see our Healthcare chapter). The AIDS Walk, usually held in early October, assembles hundreds of walkers, including children, babies in strollers, teens from area churches, people with AIDS, and those who care about them. After warm-up exercises and a blessing, the walkers start off on a 5-mile loop that brings them back to the Plaza for lunch and music. Participants not only have fun, but they also raise money to help Santa Fe Cares continue its support of AIDS services throughout northern New Mexico.

Taste of Santa Fe
Sweeney Center 201 W. Marcy St.
• **(505) 983-4823**

On the first Tuesday in May each year, more than two dozen Santa Fe restaurants strut their stuff, competing for attractive plaques and the bragging rights that go to the winners. But the real winners are the hungry people who attend and the Museum of New Mexico's Palace of the Governors, which receives the proceeds. Ticket holders get to sample and vote on everything from appetizers to desserts. Chefs go all out for this event, and the food ranges from relatively simple New Mexican dishes—Santa Fe's comfort food—to the fancy, exotic, and sublime. A no-host bar where you can buy your favorite libation and a coffee booth are part of the evening's festivities. A "nonessential auction," which usually includes trips and meals in private homes, is part of the evening's fun. Tickets cost around $25 per person.

CommUnity Day in Santa Fe
The Plaza
• **(505) 986-6942**

Designed to bring local families back to the Plaza and celebrate Santa Fe's multicultural heritage, CommUnity Days began in 1994. The event, sponsored by the city and produced with the help of volunteers, features plentiful entertainment, activities for kids, food booths, and information about dozens of nonprofit agencies that make Santa Fe a better place to live. City and state officials use the opportunity to mingle with residents, especially during an election year. Newcomers get an excellent orientation to the community and longtime residents get a kick out of seeing old friends and reminiscing about the days when the Plaza truly was the city's center. The event is free.

The Santa Fe Century Ride
Ride begins at Capshaw Middle School, 351 E. Zia Rd.
• **(505) 982-1282**

Bicyclists, more than 2,000 of them, come from throughout New Mexico and elsewhere to ride 100 miles of history on this trip. Cyclists who are in for the "century" pedal down the Turquoise Trail, through the old mining towns of Madrid and Golden, across the Estancia Valley to the villages of Cedar Grove, Stanley, and Galisteo and back into Santa Fe. You also can sign on for 25-, 50-, or 75-mile loops. The idea here is to have fun, and toward that end organizers offer detailed maps, sag wagons (vans to pick tired riders), and a van

with a bike mechanic. You can stop for snacks and water along the route and purchase a hearty pancake breakfast or an organic pasta lunch at the beginning and end of the trail. The ride traditionally happens on a Sunday mid-month. The cost to enter is around $15 and the money benefits the Leukemia Society of America. A strong rider completes the trip in four or five hours, to the cheers of friends and family who may be waiting at the finish line.

A Day at the Opera Ranch
The Santa Fe Opera, U.S. Hwy. 84/285, 7 miles north of Santa Fe
• **(505) 986-5909**
• **santafeopera.org**

Continuous entertainment showcasing talented children and teens from Santa Fe and elsewhere in New Mexico is one of the attractions for this event. The entertainment, which lasts from 10 AM until 2 PM , includes student musical performances, dancing, and excerpts from plays. Visitors can tour a gallery of Santa Fe Opera costumes, art from set and costume designs, and get a guided backstage tour to see where some of the magic is made. But the biggest drawing card is the beautiful opera grounds, a grassy oasis in the arid foothills of Santa Fe. The opera's administrative offices and training studios are known as the "ranch," and visitors can picnic on the grounds as part of the fun. The Guilds of The Santa Fe Opera Inc. have hosted this event for years, usually on the Saturday of Memorial Day weekend. You can buy drinks and picnic food such as hot dogs and Frito pies. Be sure to bring a hat and sunscreen. The event is free.

Civil War Weekend
El Rancho de las Golondrinas, 334 Los Pinos Rd., La Cienega
• **(505) 471-2261**
• **www.golondrinas.org**

Families can step back in time to the days of the Civil War and New Mexico's Battle of Glorieta at the annual Civil War Weekend festival at this living history museum just south of Santa Fe. (See our Attractions chapter for more information on the museum.) Between 10 AM and 4 PM both days you'll have an opportunity to watch artillery and marching demonstrations, experience camp life, and see reenactments of the historic 1862 battles around Glorieta, New Mexico, between Union and Confederate troops. This event is co-sponsored by the New Mexico Civil War Commemorative Congress. In addition to the demonstrations and information, visitors can stroll the lovely grounds and visit the historic buildings on this old ranch, a stop on El Camino Real, the main trail from Santa Fe to Mexico City. Food is available. Admission is $7 for adults; $5 for seniors (62 and older), teens and military; and $3 for children 5 to 12. Children younger than 5 always get in free. To reach the ranch from Santa Fe, take Exit 276; follow signs for "Racetrack/Museum" and then "Las Golondrinas."

June

Santa Fe Botanical Garden's Garden Tours
Various locations
• (505) 438-1684

From Memorial Day through Labor Day, Santa Fe's non-profit Botanical Garden offers glimpses of some of the most interesting and beautiful private gardens in Santa Fe and other nearby communities. Scheduled tours might include artists' gardens or xeric sites, which use drought-tolerant plants to great advantage. The tours are self-guided and, due to their popularity, have been known to sell out, so book early. The cost per tour is around $10 for members and $15 for nonmembers. Advance tickets are discounted to members. A tour of fall garden gems is often offered as well.

Spring Festival
El Rancho de las Golondrinas,
15 miles south of
Santa Fe in La Cienega at 334 Los Pinos Rd.
Take exit 276 off I-25
• (505) 471-2261
• www.golondrinas.org

During this two-day celebration on a weekend in early June, the old ranch comes to life with dancing, music, and demonstrations of the skills necessary for successful living in early New Mexico. Among the things you'll see are hand shearing of the curly-horned churro sheep; a procession honoring San Isidro, the patron of New Mexico farmers; a working blacksmith shop; and bread baking in traditional outdoor ovens. Music, dance, art, and entertainment add to the fun. Ad-

mission is $7 for adults; $5 for seniors (62 and older), teens and military; and $3 for children 5 to 12. Children younger than 5 always get in free.

La Voz, Festival of the Americas
Various locations, including El Museo Cultural de Santa Fe
1615-B Paseo de Peralta
• (505) 995-0738
• www.lavozfestival.com

This festival presents a variety of artists from Latin America in programs that include visual arts, lectures, music, theater, film, and more. Joining them to entertain and educate during the festival's ten-day run are local groups that perform in Spanish, English, and bilingually. The 2000 event opened with a parade, complete with puppetry and clowns, and live music on the Plaza. Other highlights included the music of Corazón de Mono, who mixed Caribbean, Brazilian, and Argentinean sounds with a contemporary twist, and a visit from Chusma, a three person team of Chicano/a activists and performers from Los Angeles in the tradition of circus tent slapstick comedy. Other entertainers came from Caracas, Venezuela, and Spain. Some programs are free; in 2000 paid admission ranged from $5 to $12.

Rodeo de Santa Fe
Santa Fe Rodeo Grounds, Rodeo Rd.
at Richards Ave.
• (505) 471-4300

Santa Fe loves its rodeo and has supported this event since 1949. Sanctioned by the Professional Rodeo Cowboys Association, the rodeo runs for four days in late June.

You'll find all the required competitions here—bareback and saddle bronc riding, steer wrestling, barrel racing, and the ever-popular bull riding. Cowboys come from throughout the Southwest to test their skill, and the rodeo also attracts a fair share of local talent. Unlike most professional sports, the cowboys aren't paid. Not only do they have to come up with their own entry fees, but they also cover the cost of transporting and feeding their horses, overnight rooms, medical and rehab bills, and all other expenses. For

INSIDERS' TIP

Festival Santa Fe is a clearinghouse for information about the city's major performing groups who entertain during the summer. Santa Fe Chamber Music Festival, Santa Fe Stagers, Santa Fe Desert Chorale, Maria Benitez Teatro Flamenco, The Santa Fe Opera, and Shakespeare in Santa Fe form the coalition. For information call toll free 877-222-3022 or check www.festivalsantafe.org.

some, a good year is breaking even. Those who don't place in the money go home with only their memories—and the appreciation of the Santa Fe audience.

The rodeo features evening shows and a matinee. A rodeo queen and princess are crowned one evening, and the royalty from Fiesta de Santa Fe are featured guests at another performance (see the Fiesta listing under September in this chapter).

Rodeo de Santa Fe has always welcomed families. Some little buckaroos watch from right behind the fence. Kids can compete in mutton busting, which gives them a chance to ride a bucking sheep. Or they can join a calf scramble, the goal of which is to capture a red ribbon from the tail of an uncooperative calf.

Before the rodeo starts, there's live entertainment on the grounds, and you can buy the food that goes with the fun—a complete chuckwagon dinner, burgers, hot dogs, popcorn, cotton candy, cold drinks, and hot coffee. Ticket prices range from $8 to $16, with a limited number of box seats available. Kids get a discount and can attend Saturday's matinee free with a paid adult. Parking is free.

Buckaroo Ball
Eaves Movie Ranch, Cerrillos, N.M.
• **(505) 992-3700**
Founded in 1993, the Buckaroo Ball takes the honors as Santa Fe's single most profitable fund-raising event. Loosely modeled after the Cattle Baron's Ball in Dallas, the Buckaroo Ball is an upscale gala evening with first-rate food, exotic auction items, and stunning entertainment. Recent events, for example, have featured singer Patty Loveless and Asleep at the Wheel. A casually glitzy/Western-looking crowd of about 1,200 enjoys spectacular hors d'oeuvres from Santa Fe's finest restaurants, dinner, and a fabulous silent and live auction including such things as trips to Bali, France, Tuscany, and Africa and television guest spots. A committee disperses the money as grants to nonprofit groups working with children in Santa Fe and Northern New Mexico. As of 2000, almost $4 million has been awarded in grants. Despite the price ($650 a person in 2000), tickets sell quickly and usually disappear long before party night.

Santa Fe Stages
100 N. Guadalupe St.
• **(505) 982-6680, Box office**
(505) 982-6683
• **www.santafestages.org/**
Santa Fe Stages features a potpourri of live

professional entertainment from early June to late August. The international festival of theater and dance productions has included performers Tomas Kubinek, Compay Segundo, Amanda McBroom, The Parsons Dance Project, Paul Taylor Dance Company, the Buena Vista Social Club, and others. Ticket prices begin at $8.

Maria Benitez Teatro Flamenco
Radisson Hotel, 750 N. Francis Dr.
• **Box office: (505) 982-1237,**
(505) 982-5591, (800) 905-33151
• **www.mariabenitez.com**
This world renowned, internationally acclaimed dance group is choreographed by Maria Benitez whom *Dance Magazine* has called "The generation's greatest flamenco dancer!" An ensemble of leading Spanish dancers, singers, and guitarists from the United States and Spain reflects the passionate and dramatic world of Spanish dance. Performances in 2000 included special guest dancers from Tango USA. The season runs from late June through Labor Day weekend and includes six performances per week at 8:30 PM nightly except Tuesday. Tickets cost $16 to $36.

Shakespeare in Santa Fe
St. John's College, outside Peterson Hall in the Courtyard,
1160 Camino Cruz Blanca
• **(505) 982-2910**
• **www.shakespearesantafe.org**
These outdoor performances are a long-time Santa Fe summer favorite. After a tradition of one show per season, the company offered two separate productions in 2000: *Measure for Measure* and *Midsummer Night's Dream*. The season runs from mid June until the third week in August, with shows on Friday and Saturday evenings and Sunday matinees. Productions are professionally acted and directed and well staged. Tickets range from $10 to $28 (for reserved seats up front.) If you can't afford a ticket, you can bring a blanket and recline on the grass for free. Productions begin with free entertainment in the spirit of Shakespeare by The Festival Faire starting at 6 PM. You can enjoy pre-play dinners, either catered or brought from home, on the college lawn before the productions begin.

Santa Fe Desert Chorale
Various venues
• **(505) 988-7505, 800-905-3315**
• **www.desertchorale.org/**
The Desert Chorale, New Mexico's only professional vocal ensemble, sings under the

direction of Dennis Schrock, also director of the Canterbury Choral Society. The summer season offers more than 25 performances of four separate concert repertoires throughout July and early August. Since its inception in 1983, the Desert Chorale has been noted for its effective programming and virtuoso performances. Critics and audience members have consistently praised the chorale for presenting some of the world's most significant and engaging repertoire—from the ancient to the modern. Summer concerts begin at 8 PM nightly except Sunday, when the ensemble performs at 6 PM. The company also offers a winter season and a Christmas holiday series. The Desert Chorale performs many of its concerts at the Santuario de Guadalupe and the Loretto Chapel, two settings as beautiful as the music. Tickets for most performances are about $30.

Annual West Muttster Dog Show
College of Santa Fe,
1600 St. Michael's Dr.
• **(505) 983-4309**

Dogs don't need a pedigree for this show, but they might need a costume. The Santa Fe Animal Shelter and Humane Society sponsors a day of fun, usually a Saturday in mid-June, as a reunion for the dogs that have gone to good homes thanks to the shelter's work. Contests may include dog and owner lookalikes, "old dog, new trick/new dog, old trick," "most extraordinary tail," "most spots," and "stands out in a crowd." Dog obedience demonstrations, music, food, and face painting add to the mix. Admission is free.

Arts and Crafts Show
The Plaza
• **(505) 988-7621**

Challenge New Mexico, a group that works with people with disabilities and sponsors a popular and a successful horseback therapy program, benefits from this show. You'll find arts and crafts from all disciplines. Everything is handmade by professional artists. You can chat with the artisans, and food and live music add to the weekend's festivities. The mid-month event attracts artists from throughout the region. Admission is free.

INSIDERS' TIP

If you go to Albuquerque for the International Balloon Fiesta—and you should—take a jacket or sweater. October mornings are warmer in Albuquerque than in Santa Fe, but you can still expect temperatures in the 40s. Don't complain: Balloons can stay afloat longer in the cool air.

Fiber Arts Festival of Traditional Cultures of the Southwest
Museum of Indian Arts and Culture
708 Camino Lejo
• **(505) 476-1250**

Usually held the last weekend in June, the the Museum of Indian Arts and Culture originated the Fiber Arts Festival to highlight the tradition of weaving among both Indian and Hispanic cultures in Northern New Mexico. The festival, an invitational event for participants, includes weaving demonstrations, sheep shearing, and yarn dyeing. At the open marketplace you can buy finely crafted woven products as well as traditional New Mexico foods and Native music. Each year, artisans who have contributed to the weaving profession are honored at a special ceremony.

Opening Night, Santa Fe Opera
Santa Fe Opera Theater,
U.S. Hwy. 84-285, 7 miles north of Santa Fe
• **(505) 986-5900, (800) 280-4654**
• **www.santafeopera.org**

Opening night at The Santa Fe Opera means tails and tailgate parties, black ties and caviar. For the most part, Santa Fe isn't a dress-up town, but you'd never know it tonight. Denim with diamond studs, velvet capes, lace and satin, cowboy boots shined to a high polish, the latest New York fashions, and thousands of pounds of turquoise come out for the occasion. The glitter of the audience rivals that on stage. A variety of public and private parties precede the night's operatic performance—watch the papers or call the opera to find out what's on the schedule. After the opening night soiree, (which is either the last Friday in June or the first Friday in July), the opera season continues through late August with five productions in repertory and some special concerts by apprentice artists. (See our Arts chapter.)

July

The Event at Goose Downs
Goose Downs Farm, Galisteo, N.M.
• **(505) 466-8771**

Top riders from through the country come

Nationally ranked riders compete in the Rodeo de Santa Fe, held in June, which offers barrelback steer wrestling, bull riding, and more.

Photo: Don Strel

to Galisteo for this two-day horseback competition, which benefits Challenge New Mexico, a program for mentally and physically disabled children. The contests, which include dressage, jumping, and a cross-country course, bring together past champions and future contenders. Events start around 8 AM, usually the last weekend in June or first weekend in July. Admission is free to spectators, and a published program helps you figure out who's who.

New Mexico Wine Festival
El Rancho de las Golondrinas
334 Los Pinos Road, La Cienega,
15 miles south of Santa Fe on I-25
Take Exit 276 to La Cienega and
follow the signs
• **(505) 471-2261 or 1-888-888-0882**
• **nmwine.net**

Believe it or not, New Mexico has 21 wineries producing almost 350,000 gallons of wine a year. Between noon and 6 PM on a Saturday and Sunday in early July you can sample some of these New Mexico wines while enjoying a variety of food and entertainment. The event, sponsored by the New Mexico Wine Growers' Association, also includes continuous live entertainment, agricultural product tastings and sales. Admission is $10 for adults, which includes a commemorative wine glass, and $4 for those 13 to 20. Children 12 and younger are free.

Fourth of July Pancake Breakfast
The Plaza
• **(505) 982-2002**

Food is the centerpiece of this day of community fun, a fund-raiser for United Way of Santa Fe County. Hundreds of community volunteers cook pancakes and ham, serve coffee, orange juice, and milk and chat with the crowd. On the bandstand, entertainment ranges from mariachi music to flamenco dancing. A vintage car show presented by Santa Fe Vintage Car Club lines the streets. You can even sleep late if you want; the grills stay hot, and the pancakes keep coming until noon, or as long as the batter lasts. The price is $5 per person.

Behind Adobe Walls House Tours
Various dates and locations
• **(505) 983-6565, (800) DETOURS**
1-800-732-6881

The Santa Fe Garden Club presents this annual event, which offers visitors and residents an up-close look at some of the city's finest homes and gardens. A recent tour, for example, visited a historic Canyon Road property with mature landscaping beautifully designed to complement the home's architecture and location. Participants enjoyed the soothing sound of the acequia, which watered the flowers, trees, shrubs, and colorful groundcover plants, and marveled at the showpiece apple tree, the largest of its kind in Santa Fe county. Two tours are offered each summer, usually in late July. Buses load at a downtown hotel. Money from ticket sales goes to community beautification projects. The cost is $45 per tour and early reservations are required—the tour sells out quickly.

Contemporary Hispanic Market
The Plaza
• **(505) 983-4780**

Running simultaneously with the Traditional Spanish Market (see next listing) this contemporary art show features a wide range of styles and media by artists from Santa Fe and elsewhere. First organized in 1986, this continues as the largest annual exhibit of contemporary Hispanic work in the Southwest. Expect to see the works of some 80 artists. It's a diverse show in terms of sophistication and content with works in water color, photography, silkscreen, jewelry, sculpture, drawing, lithography, and more. Admission is free and El Museo Cultural sponsors the show.

Traditional Spanish Market
The Plaza
• **(505) 983-4038**
• **www.spanishcolonial.org**

Unique work in the Spanish Colonial tradition fills the Plaza for a weekend in late July. Much is religious—carved and painted images of the saints that reflect New Mexico's long isolation from the religious art of Mexico and Spain. Some 300 artists also display handsome tinwork, silver filigree jewelry, woodcarvings, weaving, straw inlay, and embroidery. A special youth division showcases the creative efforts of more than 100 children and teens. Many of the artists featured here don't show in galleries; the Spanish Market and the Winter Market in December offer two of the few opportunities to see and purchase their work. Prizes go to the best entries in each medium. Music, dance, food, and pageantry add to the fun. Artists' demonstrations continue throughout both days. Admission is free.

The Santa Fe Opera
Community Concerts
St. Francis Cathedral, 131 Cathedral Pl.
• **(505) 986-5924**
• **www.santafeopera.org**

Each summer, The Santa Fe Opera and cooperating sponsors present free public concerts in Santa Fe and Albuquerque featuring apprentice artists from The Santa Fe Opera. The concerts, about an hour of arias, duets, and ensemble music, offer a no-risk introduction to operatic music—and you don't even have to drive to the theater. The project started as a way to reach the elderly, disadvantaged, and children. Everyone is welcome. Admission is free. Usually two performances, one in late morning and the other in early afternoon of the same day, are held on a weekday late in the month.

Storytelling in the Tipi
Wheelwright Museum, 704 Camino Lejo
• **(505) 982-4636**
• **www.wheelwright.org/**

Beginning in mid-July and continuing for much of August, master storyteller Joe Hayes spins his web of fantasy and excitement each week at the museum. Hayes tells Native American legends, Hispanic cuentos, and tall tales that leave the audience spell bound and coming back for more. Hayes has been telling stories at the Wheelwright each summer for many years. He has compiled many of the stories into books and also recorded them on tape. You can bring a picnic dinner and a blanket and watch the sunset—stories usually begin around 6 PM. Best of all, the event is free, although donations are welcome.

Eight Northern Pueblo:
Arts & Crafts Show
Held at one of the Northern Pueblos, call for location
• **(800)793-4955 or (505) 852-4265.**
• **Artnewmexico.com/eightnorthern**

If you're in the market for a unique American Indian event, this is it.(See our Close-up in this chapter.)The annual show is held in mid-July at one of the northern pueblos. (The 1999 and 2000 events were at San Juan Pueblo.) It offers the opportunity to see work by some 1,500 top American Indian artists from throughout New Mexico. Admission is $5 for adults or $8 for a two-day pass. Children ages 6 to 12 are $2 on Saturday and $1 on Sunday. Ages 5 and younger are admitted free.

Santa Fe Chamber Music Festival
**St. Francis Auditorium in the
Museum of Fine Arts, 107 E. Palace Ave.**
• **(505) 983-2075**
• **www.santafechambermusic.org/
SFCMF.html**

The Santa Fe Chamber Music Festival was founded in 1972 and has grown in size and stature to become one of the leading performance organizations of its kind in the United States. During the first season, fourteen artists performed six Sunday concerts in Santa Fe and toured to several New Mexico and eastern Arizona communities. That season, Pablo Casals served as the Festival's honorary president, and a 20-year series of Georgia O'Keeffe posters and program covers began.

Today, the Festival presents more than 80 events during its annual summer season—including concerts, adult and youth education/outreach presentations, free open rehearsals, concert previews, and roundtable discussions with composers and musicians. The season runs from mid-July through the third week in August. In addition to what most people think of as "chamber music" the season features jazz and world music performed by musicians from the world's stages. Guest musicians have included Pinchas Zukerman, Jaime Laredo, Herbie Mann, Eddie Daniels, R. Carlos Nakai, and many more. Tickets start at $15; many concerts sell out.

August

Arts and Crafts Fair
The Plaza
• **(505) 982-2042**

From early morning to dusk, usually on the first weekend in August, the Plaza is filled with all sorts of arts and crafts from more than 240 exhibitors who come to Santa Fe from throughout the country. Girls Incorporated of Santa Fe, a nonprofit organization that offers programs for girls during the school year and over the summer, benefits from the booth fees. Santa Fe residents and visitors can see and buy paintings, handmade clothing, original toys, jewelry of all sorts, stained glass, and more. Admission is free.

Summer Festival and Frontier Market
**El Rancho de las Golondrinas,
334 Los Pinos Rd., La Cienega**
• **(505) 471-2261**
• **www.golondrinas.org**

The museum comes to life the first weekend in August with an old-fashioned Mountain Man market and a festival celebrating the bounty of summer. Events include costumed characters as mountain men, soldiers, traders, and gunfighters. Music, dance, art, entertainment, and fun for the whole family mark the event. You can buy snacks and drinks. Events run from 10 AM to 4 PM both days. During the festival, admission is $7 for adults; $5 for seniors (62 and older), teens, and military; $3 for children 5 to 12. Children younger than 5 always get in free. To reach the ranch from Santa Fe, take Exit 276; follow signs for "Racetrack/Museum" and then "Las Golondrinas."

Santa Fe County Fair
Santa Fe County Fair Grounds,
Rodeo Rd. at Richards Ave.
• **(505) 471-4711**

Santa Fe County 4-H plays a major role in this three-day event, which draws produce, livestock, and other entries from throughout rural Santa Fe County. Among the highlights are the frog-jumping contest, a llama show, a herding-dog exhibition, and, of course, the livestock auction. Kiddie rides, entertainment, and concessions sold by bright-eyed 4-Hers add to the fun. Don't miss the music and Western dancing or the chile and salsa cook-off. Watch for it in early August. Admission is free, but parking costs $1.

Ice Cream Sunday
Santa Fe Children's Museum,
1050 Old Pecos Tr.
• **(505) 989-8359**

If there's any better way to sweeten a summer afternoon than with a bowl of ice cream, it involves adding the goodies you need to turn your vanilla into a sundae or even a banana split. The museum goes all out for this annual family-style fundraiser. The sticky fun begins at noon, traditionally on the first Sunday in August, and continues until 5 PM—or until the ice cream runs out. Santa Fe celebrities, including the mayor, the superintendent of schools, and chief of police, have helped with the scooping. Some years, a big red fire truck is on hand, and the firefighters offer the little ones an up-close look. You'll also find music and performances by children throughout the day. Kids can also get their faces painted, ride donkeys, or jump themselves silly in the bounce-a-matic—one of those rubber rooms filled with balls. All the money goes directly for new exhibits at the museum, the only one in Santa Fe dedicated to kids. There's no admission fee, and ice cream is $3 a serving.

Mountain Man Rendezvous and Trade Fair
Palace of the Governors, 105 E. Palace Ave.
• **(505) 476-5100.**

The Palace of the Governors, once the center of New Mexico's political life and now a popular history museum, hosts this colorful fair as a tribute to Santa Fe's history as a trade center. Demonstrations of mountain man skills and other events that may change from year to year are part of the event. The Mountain Men—contemporary versions of the original mountain men who lived off their wits and the bounty of the Western mountains as trappers, guides, hunters, and traders—display a variety of handmade items. You'll find examples of the goods their counterparts traded a century ago. And, yes, Mountain Women are also represented. Free.

Haciendas—A Parade of Homes
Various locations
• **(505) 982-1774**

The Santa Fe Area Home Builders Association offers this tour of more than a dozen new homes to showcase their members' most professional and creative work. A map guides visitors to the homes, built in various Santa Fe neighborhoods, from working class to millionaire territory. The tour features homes represent many varieties of building products as well as new styles. You can pick the winners of juried competitions for Best Floor Plan, Best Kitchen, Best Craftsmanship, and other categories in each price range. The association also awards a "Best of Show" prize in each price category and an overall winner, the "Grand Hacienda." After you've seen the homes, you can vote for your favorite. You might even want to buy it! Tours are free.

Wheelwright Museum Auction
Wheelwright Museum, 704 Camino Lejo
• **(505) 982-4636**
• **www.wheelwright.org/**

Jewelry, paintings, and pottery by contemporary Native American artists will be on the auction block here, along with dinners donated by some of Santa Fe's finest restaurants. Art appraisals, spa treatments, or tax advice also are offered. But the real reason this event attracts a crowd is the high-quality Indian art sold to benefit the museum, one of Santa Fe's favorite institutions. The Wheelwright, a small, private museum devoted to contemporary Indian art, uses the auction as its main moneymaking event. The sale opens with a preview party on Thursday evening and a silent auction. The live auction usually begins on Friday about 1 PM. Some 80 lots of antique and contemporary pottery, jewelry, Navajo textiles, kachina dolls, beaded goods, paintings, baskets, and more are featured. The auction audi-

A mountain man shows off his wares and outfit at the annual "Mountain Man Rendezvous" on the Palace of the Governors.

Photo: Don Strel

ence gathers in a big tent on the museum grounds, usually the Thursday before Indian Market. You can meet the artists and authors and watch demonstrations. Admission is about $10.

Indian Market
On and around the Plaza
• **(505) 983-5220**
• **www.swaia.org**

Serious collectors and the curious flock to Santa Fe for this show and sale, always held the weekend following the third Thursday of the month. One of Santa Fe's most famous and popular events, the market features a wide selection of the finest American Indian art from 1,200 exhibitors. Dancing, food sales (including favorites such as mutton stew), and demonstrations of various craft techniques add to the market's attraction. Indian Market includes a Fashion Showcase, a juried clothing show open to artists working in wearable art, sewing, weaving, and beadwork. A youth market

occupies nearby Cathedral Park. Admission to the market is free.

The Southwestern Association for Indian Arts Inc. has presented Indian Market since 1922. It is the largest contemporary American Indian art event in the world, generating some $130 million in revenue for artists, galleries, and the tourism industry. (The average amount spent on Indian arts and crafts during the market is about $735 per visitor, organizers say.) The market has become a driving force in setting prices and standards for first-class American Indian art. Indian Market's awards program distributes more than $60,000 in prizes in 350 categories. Artists cherish the awards for the prestige they carry. There's a long waiting list of artists to join the market; these folks may have a chance if the artists first chosen sell out early during the market.

To make the market less overwhelming, SWAIA publishes a guide that lists every artist by name and category and includes a map of booth locations. You can pick them up at the SWAIA office, 125 E. Palace Ave, Suite 65. Since the market draws about 80,000 visitors, expect crowds.

Serious collectors become members of SWAIA for a chance to preview the prizewinning works before they go on sale the next morning. Memberships can be purchased at Sweeney Center, 210 W. Marcy Street, on Friday night before the preview. Having seen what they want, collectors line up long before the booths open for a chance to purchase the winning pieces.

During Indian Market, parking downtown is at a premium, and the city runs shuttles from outlying lots to reduce downtown congestion and frustration. Special shows and gala openings in most of Santa Fe's galleries and exhibits in Sweeney Center and many area hotels also are part of Indian Market weekend. Speaking of hotels, make reservations early—some 70 percent of those in attendance come from outside New Mexico; the majority of these visitors say that Indian Market was the primary reason for their visit.

Fiesta Melodrama
Santa Fe Playhouse, 142 E. DeVargas St.
• **(505) 988-4262**

This funny, spunky show has a different plot each year but always features the same general tone—poking fun at Santa Fe's foibles.

An anonymous committee puts together an original script about contemporary Santa Fe, structuring the show to resemble an old-time melodrama. The villain is always terrible, the heroine always in big trouble, and the good guys always win. The story itself draws on the city's freshest controversies and might include contentiousness among city, county, and state officials, Santa Fe's ongoing saga of street repair and crazy traffic, the water situation, the latest uproar in the arts, school politics, or New Age hype as subjects of its comic ridicule. The show usually opens in late August and runs through the Santa Fe Fiesta weekend in mid-September. Although some of the jokes might be rated PG-13, children are welcome. Tickets cost about $12 for adults and $10 for children, students, and seniors.

Santa Fe Bluegrass and Old Time Music Festival
Santa Fe Rodeo Grounds, Rodeo Rd. at Richards Ave.
• (505) 471-2413, (505) 298-8727
• www.inetserv.com/swp/Festival_2000.html

For more than 20 years, folks who enjoy banjo and fiddle music and other traditional fare have gathered at the Rodeo Grounds for three days of great music in late August or early September. A series of Friday evening concerts opens the festival, followed by two days of workshops, band scrambles, jam sessions, and contests on Saturday and Sunday. The festival is a labor of love for the Southwest Traditional and Bluegrass Music Association, also known as Southwest Pickers. Among the highlights are original song-writing performances and concerts by the prior year's winners in the Bluegrass Band and Old Time Band contests. Don't miss the children's fiddle contest, which is usually held on Saturday morning. As part of the multi-stage event, the grounds are open to "rough" camping (no hookups). Tickets are $35 for a three-day pass, $10 for the Friday concert or $20 for all-day Saturday or Sunday. Children younger than 12 are free and those older than 65 receive a $2 discount. You can buy food and beverages.

University of New Mexico Lobos Football
University Stadium University and Cesar Chavez Blvds., Albuquerque
• (505) 925-LOBO, (505) 925-5626, (800) 905-3395
• www.GoLobos.com

The Lobos may be the University of New Mexico's team, but Albuquerque loves them. So do UNM alumni around the state. Terance Mathis and David Sloan played football here. Brian Urlacher, whom *The Sporting News* called the nation's top strong safety in 1999, and arguably the best all-around player to ever put on a New Mexico uniform, joined the Chicago Bulls after graduation in the 2000 draft.

Football, with a season that runs from late August to November, is the second-most popular campus sport after basketball. On warm fall days fans come early to enjoy tailgate picnics in the massive parking lot. The Lobos play both afternoon and evening games. It can get chilly at night or late in the season, so come prepared. Early season afternoon games can be hot, so bring your hat and sunscreen. Welcome to New Mexico!

Tickets for football are to $12 to $19 for reserved adult seats. Parking is free, but unless you come early, expect to walk a block or so to the stadium. Game-day traffic can be intense. If you're driving from Santa Fe, leave two hours before game time.

INSIDERS' TIP

For winter 2000, The Santa Fe Opera planned to offer *The Beggar's Opera* at El Museo Cultural in the Santa Fe Rail Yards as part of the opera's community outreach program. Depending on the success of *The Beggar's Opera*, other outreach programs—programs held in Santa Fe rather than at The Santa Fe Opera Theater—will be scheduled for subsequent years.

September

Labor Day Arts and Crafts Show
The Plaza
• (505) 988-7575 (number also includes Santa Fe Fiesta information)

Jewelry of all styles and materials—from delicate silver earrings to bolo ties like the ones cowboys wear—is one of the highlights at this end-of-summer show. You'll also find oil and watercolor paintings, sculptures, ceramics both useful and decorative, one-of-a-kind clothing, and more. Proceeds from the Plaza booth rentals benefit the Santa Fe Fiesta Council, the volunteer group who present the community's biggest party, La Fiesta de Santa Fe. As with all Plaza art shows, artists have to submit their work to a jury and may sit on the waiting list before they get one of the coveted spaces to show and sell their creations. Since Labor Day brings a fresh wave of visitors to town, this show is especially popular.

New Mexico State Fair
State Fair Grounds, 300 San Pedro Blvd. N.E. between Central and Lomas Aves., Albuquerque
• **(505) 265-1791, (800) 867-FAIR**
• **www.nmstatefair.com/**

The New Mexico State Fair is one of the state's most popular events, and the fair's attendance records usually top all but two other shows in the West. (It's exceeded by the Texas State Fair and the Houston Livestock Show and Rodeo.)

The State Fair runs from early to mid-September. You'll find free schedules of each day's events and a map of the grounds at the information booth. Kids flock to the midway; the cowboy crowd loves the rodeo and accompanying country music concerts in Tingley Coliseum; and the cultured set is drawn to several galleries. Everyone likes the food, dished out more than 100 vendors in virtually every corner of the fair grounds. Don't miss Indian Village, Villa Hispaña, and Pioneer Village, all of which serve up tasty ethnic dishes and pleasing entertainment. The fair also offers a day of bull riding and daily horse shows.

Animal exhibits include a large petting farm for the little ones. At the Creative and Home Arts exhibits, you'll find everything from dolls to homemade donuts. The Kid's Park midway for ages 12 and younger features its own gentler rides and two stages for performances, including a magic show and puppet theater. Admission in 1999 was $1 for early birds Monday through Thursday; $4 after 2 PM and on Fridays and weekends. Children ages 3 to12 are $2 and those two and younger are free. Parking fees are $4 to $8.

Fiesta De Santa Fe
The Plaza and other locations
• **(505) 988-7575**
• **www.zozobra.com/zozobra.html**
(Zozobra information)

Fiesta is one of Santa Fe's favorite parties. Held the weekend following Labor Day, Fiesta commemorates the Spanish resettlement in Santa Fe after the Pueblo Revolt chased the conquistadors back to Mexico (see our History chapter). It's the oldest continuous community celebration in the United States.

Each year at the Santa Fe Fiesta, the city remembers the contribution of Don Diego de Vargas and the Catholic Church to the community's survival. The Fiesta began as a religious commemoration, but parties, parades, a fashion show, and Zozobra, a giant puppet that is burned with great fanfare, were added as the community changed and grew.

Even before Fiesta officially begins, Santa Fe starts celebrating. The Fiesta Melodrama (see August events), appearances by the Fiesta Queen and the Caballeros de Vargas, pre-Fiesta shows, and mariachi concerts are part of the fun. Throughout Fiesta weekend, the Plaza is alive with free entertainment provided by a variety of local and area music and dance groups. The Gran Baile de la Fiesta, or Fiesta Ball, a show of historic fashions and a commercially operated carnival at the Rodeo Grounds add to the merriment. Admission to the ball is usually around $10; the fashion show costs $5. Plaza events are free.

For most revelers, Fiesta begins with the burning of Zozobra. In 1999, the city and the Kiwanis moved the event from Friday evening to Thursday. You'll pay about $5 to watch from the field, which is usually VERY crowded. Santa Fe artist Will Shuster created Zozobra, a 44-foot-tall puppet with glowing eyes and a gravely voice, to personify the disappointments and mistakes of the year. (His nickname is Old Man Gloom.) Crews of volunteers build Zozobra the week before Fiesta and erect the big white puppet on a huge pole at Fort Marcy Park, 490 Washington Avenue. As the sky grows dark, the puppet comes to life, moaning, growling, and waving his hands. (Very young children may be scared.) Finally, after a performance by the Fire Dancers and children dressed as Little Glooms, Zozobra disappears in flames to a rowdy chorus of cheers.

One of Fiesta's most charming events, the Pet Parade, or Desfile de los Ninos, begins around 10 AM on Saturday. Children, parents, and pets ranging from cats and dogs to llamas and snakes circle the Plaza and walk along

INSIDERS' TIP
Change happens, even in a town as filled with tradition as Santa Fe. If you'd like to plan your vacation around a specific event, please call the sponsor or the Santa Fe Convention and Visitors Bureau, (800) 777-2489, to double check dates and other specifics.

ANNUAL EVENTS AND FESTIVALS

Eight Northern Indian Pueblos
Arts and Crafts Show

If you're in the market for a unique American Indian event, this is it.

Held the third weekend in July at a pueblo near Santa Fe, the Eight Northern Indian Pueblos Arts and Crafts Show offers the opportunity to see work by some 1,500 top American Indian artists from throughout New Mexico, the Southwest, and the nation.

Initially organized in 1972 with a group of 100 artists, the show has grown in popularity among exhibitors and the public. As many as 40,000 visitors now come to shop, chat, and buy during the two-day event.

Several things make the ENIP show unique. For starters, it's the largest Indian-run art show in the world. It's held outdoors at a pueblo where some of the participating artists live and work—not at a gallery, conventional center, hotel meeting room, or even the Santa Fe Plaza. Various northern Indian pueblos take turns hosting the show, but none are far from Santa Fe. Buyers and exhibitors don't have to worry about imitation/machine-made Indian art here. To be accepted, the artist must demonstrate, either in person or on video, that he or she can create the work represented. Every piece in the show is handmade by the artist and reviewed for quality; awards go to the best work in a variety of categories.

You'll find all manner of beautiful things here, from traditional heishi, or shell jewelry, to very contemporary creations. Pottery ranges from miniatures to huge sculptural pieces, some crafted closely following tribal tradition and some with a more contemporary edge. Beadwork, painting, drums, clothing, leatherwork, kachinas, and more are here. The show attracts many of the same artists who participate in Santa Fe's Indian Market. Lonnie Vigil of Nambé Pueblo, Pablita Velarde and Toni Roller of Santa Clara Pueblo, Glenn Gomez of Taos and Pojoaque Pueblos, and Connie Tsosie of Picurís Pueblo are among the artists. Exhibitors represent more than 36 tribes. In addition to Pueblo people, Hopi, Sioux, Pawnee, Comanche, Chippewa, Cherokee, Navajo, and Apache artists usually participate.

As another special feature, the weekend's events include a footrace commemorating the Pueblo hero Popé, the leader who instigated the 1680 Pueblo Revolt, the only successful uprising by Native people against European occupation. The race is open to all comers, with separate categories for children and walkers.

During the show, visitors and artists can pause from their shopping to watch a variety of American Indian dances. Although the dancers vary from year to year, you'll usually see children's troupes from many New Mexico Pueblos as well as adult dancers in wonderfully colorful costumes. Drummers and singers accompany them with ancient rhythms. Dances often performed include the Buffalo Dance, Deer Dance, Rainbow Dance, and Corn Dance.

And, unlike at many events at New Mexico Pueblos, you are welcome to take photographs here provided you purchase a permit. (The fee was $10 in 1999). You can freely take photos of the dances, but please ask permission before taking a picture of an artist or his or her work. Video cameras and sounding recording equipment are not allowed.

Finally, the show offers nourishment for the body as well as the spirit. You can buy food, from homemade tamales to fresh Indian bread—loaves baked brown in *hornos,* or beehive-shaped, wood-fired ovens. Indian tacos, fry bread with honey or powdered sugar, roasted corn, and Pueblo fruit pies are among the treats that await.

For 2000, admission to the show was $5 for adults or $8 for a two-day pass. Children ages 6-12 are $2 on Saturday and $1 on Sunday. (Ages 5 and younger are admitted free.) Wear sunscreen, a hat and sturdy shoes—you may have to hike several blocks from the parking area to get to the show grounds.

The evening before the Arts and Crafts Show, event organizers host a benefit auction to raise money for awards and for the Eight Northern Indian Pueblos youth programs. The auction is open to all comers for the price of a ticket (usually around $15) and you can bid on all sorts of beautiful Indian arts as well as services and meals donated by area businesses. Place and time may vary; the Eldorado Hotel hosted the 2000 event.

For information about the Eight Northern Indian Pueblos Arts and Crafts Show and the auction, please call (800) 793-4955 or (505) 852-4265.

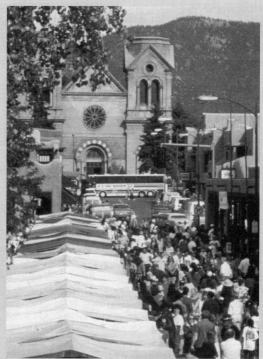

Many famous artists who show at the Santa Fe Indian Market can stay home to take part in the Eight Northern Indian Pueblos Show.

Photo: Chris Corrie

downtown streets. Many of the humans wear real or imaginary animal costumes , and many of the animals are dressed up too. Watch from the shade of the Plaza or from in front of the Palace of the Governors, 105 E. Palace Avenue, just across from the Plaza bandstand. Arrive early for a good curbside seat.

Among Sunday's highlights is the Historical/Hysterical parade. The parade, which features floats, marching bands, horses and politicians, begins at 2 PM. It starts in the parking lots at DeVargas Mall, North Guadalupe at Paseo de Peralta, continues to the Plaza, and returns using a different downtown route.

A final review of Fiesta celebrities—Don Diego de Vargas, his court, and the Fiesta Queen—follows the parade. At 7 PM comes the Fiesta Mass of Thanksgiving at St. Francis Cathedral, 213 Cathedral Place, followed by a candlelight procession from the church to Cross of the Martyrs, north of Palace Avenue off of Paseo de Peralta. The soft light of hundreds of candles as the procession makes its way up the hill is a beautiful sight and an appropriate ending to the weekend's events.

Viva la Fiesta!

Aspen Viewing
Santa Fe Ski Area, 16 miles northeast of Santa Fe on N.M. Hwy. 475
- **(505) 982-4429, (505)983-9155**
- **www.skisantafe.com**

Ride the chairlift to enjoy shimmering golden aspen, fall wildflowers, and a stunning view. The aspen schedule depends on the weather; some years the viewing lasts from the mid-September through mid-October. You can, of course, also see the aspen from your car and from other spots along N.M. 475, including the well-named Aspen Vista hiking and picnic area. From the chairlift, however, you get an eagle's-eye look at the trees and panoramic views of mountains as far away as the Colorado border. You can purchase a one-way ticket and hike down through the spruce, aspen and wildflowers or ride both ways. Lunch and snacks are served at the outdoor grill on the Ski Area deck near the chairlift. Bring a jacket—it's cool up here at 12,000 feet! Call for rates—expect to pay between $5 and $10. Children shorter than 46 inches will ride for free if accompanied by a paying adult.

Wine and Chile Fiesta
Various venues
- **(505) 438-8060**
- **www.santafewineandchile.org/**

Food and wine tastings featuring Santa Fe's finest restaurants and dozens of the world's best vineyards, cooking demonstrations, food tours, a wine auction, seminars, and even golf and horseback riding—what more could you want in a gastronomic extravaganza? The annual Santa Fe Wine and Chile Fiesta has grown in size and stature since its founding in 1990. The Big Event, subtitled The Grand Food and Wine Tasting, includes more than 200 varietals to compliment the chile-inspired cuisine prepared by some 70 of Santa Fe's best restaurants. Organizers anticipated 2,500 at The Big Event in 2000. Usually held over a five-day period in late September, the festival's smaller events (those limited to 25 guests) sell out quickly and even the Big Event closes some two weeks before showtime. Reservations are usually due three weeks in advance. Events are priced separately, with fees ranging from $35 for a Santa Fe Chefs demonstration to $125 for a Georgia O'Keeffe country tour and wine luncheon. No one under 21 is admitted.

October

Harvest Festival
El Rancho de las Golondrinas,
334 Los Pinos Rd., La Cienega
- **(505) 471-2261**
- **www.golondrinas.org**

The Harvest Festival gives modern visitors a chance to see what the harvest season of the Spanish Colonial era was like. Harvest meant hard work in early New Mexico, but the visitors at the re-enactment get to have fun. Special events for this weekend in late September or early October depict life on an old ranch using volunteers in the costumes of the time. Music and dancing, artists, and craftspeople selling their work, and the baking and sampling of bread and bizcochitos, New Mexico's famous anise and sugar cookies, add to the fun.

Visitors can see a wheelwright at work, attend an outdoor mass, and join a procession in honor of San Ysidro. Adding to the harvest ambiance, volunteers demonstrate techniques for stringing chiles into ristras, preparing fruits and vegetables for drying, making sorghum molasses, shelling corn and making chicos (dried corn to last the winter), crushing grapes for wine and threshing wheat. The farm's animals—burros, horses, goats, sheep, turkeys, geese, ducks, and chickens—are always popular with children. Events run from 10 AM to 4 PM and food is available!

During the festival, admission is $7 for adults; $5 for seniors (62 and older), teens, and military; $3 for children 5 to 12. Children younger than 5 always get in free. To reach the ranch from Santa Fe, take Exit 276; follow signs for "Racetrack/Museum" and then "Las Golondrinas."

Albuquerque International Balloon Fiesta
Balloon Fiesta Park,
between Alameda and Tramway N.E.,
west of I-25, Albuquerque
- **(505) 821-1000 or (888) 422-7277**
- **www.aibf.org**

If you're anywhere near New Mexico during the first two weeks of October, make it a point to visit this spectacular event. Not only is the Albuquerque International Balloon Fiesta worth the 60-mile drive from Santa Fe, it's also worth getting up before dawn to get there! The world's largest ballooning event, the Balloon Fiesta drew more than 900 balloons from around the world in 1999—and plenty of eager spectators. Pilots compete for prizes in precision events and fly for fun.

The nine-day festival includes mass ascensions held on the four weekend mornings and gala events that fill the sky with balloons of every shape, size, and color. The ascension begins at dawn—other attractions are even earlier. The mass ascensions are the festival's most popular draws among spectators and you can usually see balloons as late as 10 AM. Festival vendors peddle coffee, hot chocolate, breakfast burritos, and other morning treats to help you enjoy the show wide-eyed. About 1.5 million people attend this event over its nine-day run. In addition to the balloons, the Fiesta presents live music, including jazz, country-western, and mariachi.

If dawn is too early for you, don't despair. You can get a taste of the Fiesta at the evening balloon glows. The enormous colorful balloons

Annual All Children's Powwow
Location to be determined
• **(505) 982-4636**
(Wheelwright Museum)
• **www.wheelwright.org/**

The oldest children's powwow in the country, this event attracts more than a hundred young American Indians who perform intertribal, blanket, and social dances on either the first or second Saturday of the month. Prizes go to the winners in different age groups, and spectators are welcome to take pictures. Public events usually begin at 11 AM and run from late morning until dusk. If you can't stay the whole time, the Grand Entry that opens the powwow is especially colorful and photogenic. An all-volunteer staff does the organizing. The event was held at the Wheelwright Museum, which sponsors it, until it grew to large and was moved to the football field at the Santa Fe Indian School in 1999. Please call for site information. The event is free. You'll also find American Indian crafts and food sales.

Barkin' Ball
Sweeney Center, 210 W. Marcy St.
• **(505) 983-4309**
• **www.sfhumanesociety.org**

Barkin' Ball is THE annual fundraising event for the Santa Fe Animal Shelter and Humane Society. Any well-behaved dog is welcome to attend. The event includes cocktails, dinner, dancing (with or without your dog), canine costume contests, the shelter store, door prizes, and more.

Human attire ranges from black tie to blue jeans, and costumes are encouraged (for both 2- and 4-legged attendees). Tickets, $35 in 1999, are available at the shelter, 1920 Cerrillos Road. They always sell out quickly.

Spanish Colonial Arts Market and Meem Library Book Sale
St. John's College Great Hall,
1160 Camino Cruz Blanca
• **(505) 984-6104**
• **www.sjcsf.edu/**

This market, not to be confused with the Spanish Market held in downtown Santa Fe in July, features some 20 of the area's best known

The Albuquerque International Balloon Fiesta draws more than one million visitors each October.

Photo: Terry Moore, courtesy of Albuquerque Convention and Visitor's Bureau

lit by the flame of their propane burners against the dark sky resemble oversized light bulbs lined up on the launch field.

Everyone loves the special-shape balloons so much that the balloons have been given events all their own—a special-shape mass ascension and a balloon glow "rodeo." Dinosaurs and dragons, flying shoes and bottles, fantasy castles, and a cow jumping over the moon delight the audience during each Fiesta.

Albuquerque hosts the Balloon Fiesta from the first Saturday through the second Sunday of October at the Balloon Fiesta Park near Osuna Road and west of I-25. Don't worry about getting lost if you're coming from Santa Fe—signs, the steady flow of vehicles, and traffic cops will help you find the field. Admission is $4 for adults; kids younger than 12 get in free. Parking is $5.

The Fourth of July Pancake Breakfast on the Plaza also offers a vintage car exhibit with over 100 cars displayed for viewing; exotics, hot rods, and classics are available to "look don't touch."

Photo: Don Strel

Hispanic artists working in the traditional style. The art sale, often accompanied by Spanish guitar music, is held on a Saturday midmonth. The book sale, hosted by the college's Meem Library, is also that Saturday and Sunday. Admission is free, but bring your checkbook!

Santa Fe Festival of the Book
Sweeney Convention Center,
210 W. Marcy St., and other locations
• **(505) 995-4866**
• **www.ci.santa-fe.nm.us/sfpl/festival.html**

Presented by the Santa Fe Public Library and a troop of volunteers, the book festival offers something for readers of every age and inclination. The three-day event includes author presentations, writing workshops, poetry readings, a book trade show, student presentations, and author interaction, as well as book-related performances. Admission to all programs and exhibits is free. For the year 2000, the scheduled keynote speaker was author Ana Castillo, winner of numerous awards for her work. The trade show gives readers an excellent opportunity to get signed copies of work by their favorite southwestern authors.

Santa Fe Jazz Festival
James A. Little Theater,
1060 Cerrillos Road
(New Mexico School for the Deaf campus)
• **(505) 989-8442**

Listen for a Who's Who of contemporary jazz musicians in 34 ensemble concerts at this two-week event. The 2000 festival featured Marc Copland, Eddie Daniels, Eliane Elias, Fred Hersch, Dave Holland, Wayne Krantz, Herbie Mann, and many more. The Open Arts Foundation sponsors the festival, which also includes events for children. Call for ticket prices.

New Mexico Scorpions Hockey
Tingley Coliseum, New Mexico State Fair Grounds, 300 San Pedro N.E., Albuquerque
• **(505) 881-PUCK (800) 4-SCORPS**
• **www.scorpionshockey.com**

The Scorpions, New Mexico's first-ever hockey team, played their inaugural season in 1996–97 as one of the six original teams in the new Western Professional Hockey League. They made their debut with 10 consecutive victories. The Scorpions competition includes the Austin Ice Bats, Amarillo Rattlers, and the

El Paso Buzzards. They were Western Division Champions in 2000. Go Scorps!

The team plays more than 60 games a season, half at home and half on the road. The season runs from mid October to early May. The Scorpions transform Tingley Coliseum, which hosts the New Mexico State Fair Rodeo and rock concerts, into a hockey stadium for their games. What a surprise to find ice where sawdust used to be!

Tickets ranged from $9 to $20 for the 1999-2000 season. Parking is free.

Artists' Studio Tours
Many northern New Mexico communities see area newspapers for details

Fall is a wonderful time to visit Santa Fe and the surrounding communities, not only for the scenery but also for the visual arts celebrations throughout the area. The dates and itineraries change from year to year, but you can usually expect El Rito/Ojo Caliente, Taos, Los Alamos, Madrid/Cerrillos, Abiquiu, Galisteo, and other communities to participate. Artists open their studios to visitors, sometimes offering refreshments as well as an opportunity to buy work directly from the maker. You might discover the next star; and at the very least you'll have a chance to see some beautiful things and enjoy some of the wonderful landscape beyond the city limits.

November

Open Hands Benefit Auction
St. John's College Great Hall,
1160 Camino Cruz Blanca
• (505) 982-4258

Open Hands is one of Santa Fe's best-loved organizations, and as a result the auction usually gathers great donations and a friendly crowd of bidders. Items available include meals at some of the city's nicest restaurants, weekend get-aways, private concerts, and other pleasures for the mind and body. In addition to a live and silent auction, the afternoon includes refreshments, wine, and entertainment. Tickets in 1999 were $35.

Lobos Basketball
University Arena University Blvd at Cesar Chavez Blvd., Albuquerque
• (505) 925-LOBO (505) 925-5626
• www.golobos.com/

The Lobos seldom disappoint anyone who's looking for good college basketball. As members of the Mountain West conference, the Lo-

Mariachis entertain outside a local business during Fiesta.

Photo: Don Strel

bos face tough competitors, and the crowd appreciates their fighting spirit. Men's basketball begins in mid-November and ends in mid-March. The Lady Lobos' schedule roughly coincides.

The Lobos play all home games in University Arena, fondly known as The Pit. A game in the Pit is a worthy experience even if, God forbid, the Lobos lose. There's not a bad seat in the house, although some are a long view to the floor. Lobos fans are famous for their rousing support, which is recorded on a noise meter that's part of the scoreboard. The volume can go to the top of the scale during games with the Lobos men's major rivals, Utah, University of Texas at El Paso, and Arizona. Because of the men's basketball success in recent years, games may sell out. If you think you'll be around to watch, call to check on ticket availability and make a reservation.

Lobo men's coach Fran Fraschilla completed his first season at New Mexico in 1999–2000. Fraschilla led the Lobos to an 18–14 record and a second-round showing in the NIT. Fraschilla became just the third coach to take UNM to the postseason in his first year and his 18 wins were the third-highest total of any Lobo boss in his inaugural season.

The Lady Lobos posted their fourth winning season in a row in 1999–2000 under head coach Don Flanagan. The Lobos also advanced to the postseason Women's NIT for the second year in a row and participated in a post-season tournament for the third consecutive year.

Tickets are $11 for reserved adult seats. Parking is free, but unless you come early, expect to walk a block or so to the stadium. Game-day traffic can be intense. If you're driving from Santa Fe, leave two hours before game time.

New Mexico Slam basketball
Tingley Coliseum,
New Mexico State Fair Grounds,
300 San Pedro N.E., Albuquerque
• **(505) 830-2255**
• **www.nmslam.com/**

The Slam is part of the International Basketball League and is New Mexico's only professional basketball team. The team, which initially included several former University of New Mexico Lobos, played its first season in 1999. Albuquerque is the smallest of the 10 IBL cities, but enthusiasm for the Slam has grown as the team has begun to mature. The season consists of 64 games, and coincides with Lobo men's and women's basketball, high school hoops, and the New Mexico Scorpions hockey team, with whom the Slam shares Tingley Coliseum. The season runs from late November until May. The team is owned by Gil Burciaga, one of the founding members of the International Basketball League, who envisioned the team's games as "a source of affordable family entertainment." Tickets range from $8 to $25. Children ages 4 to 12 are half price with a paying adult.

Ski Swap
Sweeney Center, 210 W. Marcy St.
• **(505) 982-9958**

The Santa Fe Ski Team, kids who like to ski race, sponsors this event to raise the money they need to travel from Santa Fe for races during the year. You'll find great buys on used, and some new, equipment here. You can recycle your outgrown, unneeded skis, boots and whatever else in the sports equipment category and help a good cause. Volunteers include people who work in the ski business. They can give you advice on how to buy boots and skis that suit your style. This is also a good place to find children's equipment. Admission is about $2 during regular hours Saturday and Sunday or $25 and $5 for each additional family member for the preview on Friday evening before the sale officially begins.

> **INSIDERS' TIP**
> The Wheelwright Museum offers its "Looking at Indian Art" series every Saturday morning. The program, which varies weekly, talks about techniques used in making Indian jewelry, how to identify different styles of pottery, the meanings behind traditional designs and symbols, and more. Coffee and donuts are offered and the program is free at the museum, 704 Camino Lejo.

Opening Day at the Santa Fe Ski Area
Santa Fe Ski Area, 16 miles northeast of Santa Fe on N.M. Hwy. 475
• **(505) 982-4429**
• **www.skisantafe.com**

If the snow gods smile on us, the ski area opens on Thanksgiving Day. In good years, the lifts might start a little sooner; in snow-free seasons the opening is delayed. Sometimes just the beginner slopes are in good shape; some years the whole mountain is gloriously covered in sweet powder. Santa Fe's snow pattern differs from that of Colorado or Taos Ski Valley. The skiers usually frolic through mid-April. (See our Winter Sports chapter.) Adult all-day all-lift tickets are $40; the new teen (13 to 20 years old) all-lift ticket is $34. Half-day tickets, morning or afternoon, are $28. The beginner chair is $20. Children age 12 and younger and skiers between the ages of 62 and 71 pay $28 for an all-day, all-lift ticket. Children shorter than 46 inches tall in their ski boots and super seniors 72 and older ski for free.

AID and Comfort Gala
ElDorado Hotel, 309 W. San Francisco St.
• (505) 989-3399

Santa Fe gets into the holiday spirit with this festive, big-hearted event, always held the Saturday after Thanksgiving. In addition to fabulous buffets of tasty finger foods, AID and Comfort features a glittering assortment of entertainment, music for dancing, an auction of Christmas wreaths and other wonderful things, and a sale of Christmas trees decorated for the occasion. This is one of the few occasions when Santa Fe folks dress up grandly, and it's one of the favorite social events of the season. The proceeds benefit those with AIDS. Tickets cost $45 per person.

December

Winter Spanish Market
Sweeney Center, 201 W. Marcy St.
• (505) 983-4038
• www.spnaishcolonial.org

Like its sister event, the Traditional Spanish Market in July, Winter Market showcases work in the Spanish Colonial tradition by artisans from throughout New Mexico and southern Colorado. You'll find holiday gifts you can't buy anywhere else and a special booth of work by children. When they're not making sales, most of the artists are happy to explain the history behind their art. The Spanish Colonial Arts Society sponsors this event, which is usually held the first weekend of the month. Admission is free and the show runs from 9 AM to 5 PM each day

Christmas at the Palace of the Governors
Palace of the Governors, 105 E. Palace Ave.
• (505) 827-6483
• www.palaceofthegovernors.org/

Usually held on a Thursday and Friday evening in mid-December, Christmas at the Palace draws hundreds of Santa Fe families and lucky visitors. This annual community celebration brings the museum to life with music, stories, dance, puppet shows, a visit from Santa, and more. Volunteers serve hot cider and *biscochitos*, New Mexico's traditional anise sugar cookies. The museum sparkles with *farolitos* and other decorations. Although the party is free, donations of nonperishable food for the poor are welcome.

Las Posadas
The Plaza
• (505) 827-6483

Wear your hat and gloves when you come to see this traditional New Mexican folk drama, which presents the story of Joseph and Mary and their search for shelter. (*La posada* means "the inn" in Spanish.) A troupe of actors performs this ancient play in original archaic Spanish beneath the stars, or amid falling snowflakes, usually on the second Sunday of December. The pageant concludes in the courtyard of the Palace of the Governors with hot chocolate for everyone. Spectators are asked to bring a candle or a flashlight. No flash photography is allowed. The event is free.

Holiday concerts
Various venues.
See the local papers for details.

December is a wonderful month for music in Santa Fe, with nearly every performance group offering something to make your holiday season brighter. The Santa Fe Symphony and Chorus, Desert Chorale, Santa Fe Pro Musica Chamber Orchestra, and the Santa Fe Women's Ensemble offer performances to warm your December evenings. New Mexico Pro Coro, Sangre de Cristo Chorale, and Music One (Santa Fe Concert Association) also usually schedule special performances for the holidays. For more information, please check the newspapers or see our Arts section.

Annual Baumann Marionette Performances
Museum of Fine Arts
107 West Palace Ave.
• (505) 476-5072
• www.museumofnewmexico.org/

Created by well-known Santa Fe artist Gus Baumann, these puppets gave their inaugural performance in 1932. The ancient marionettes come out on stage only once a year to entertain children and their parents in St. Francis

The Orion String Quartet performs in the courtyard of the Museum of Fine Arts during the Santa Fe Chamber Music Festival.

Photo: Don Strel

auditorium at the Museum of Fine Arts. The free shows, usually one on Friday night and a second on Saturday afternoon the week before Christmas, are part of the museum's holiday presentation, which is also held at the Palace of the Governors.

12 Days of Christmas
Inn of the Anasazi, 113 Washington Ave.
• (505) 988-3030

This series, which concludes on Christmas Eve, features daily activities at one of Santa Fe's most luxurious downtown hotels. You'll find music, storytelling, crafts demonstrations, slide presentations, and other events that reflect holiday traditions of the region. The programs culminate with a lighting ceremony and caroling on Christmas Eve. From here it's an easy stroll to the Plaza to see the city's Christmas decorations. The events are free; please call to verify schedules.

Farolito Walk
Hillside Ave., Acequia Madre,
Cross of the Martyrs and elsewhere
in the downtown/Canyon Rd. area
• no phone

On Christmas Eve, old Santa Fe twinkles with the light of thousands of tiny candles. The city's ancient neighborhoods are decorated with *farolitos*, little paper bags weighted with sand and lit with a candle. They line sidewalks and the tops of adobe walls. Neighbors and neighborhoods join to create this subtle, beautiful reminder of the days when Santa Fe was primarily a Catholic town where residents lit the way for Baby Jesus. *Luminarias*, or bonfires, stand on corners to warm the walkers. Because of the number of pedestrians along Garcia Street and Acequia Madre, the city closes roads in this area to all but resident traffic. The closure means that you don't have to walk through gasoline fumes and suffer bright car lights to enjoy the sights—but be sure to dress warmly. Some households or merchants along the way serve hot cider to passersby. Strangers often congregate to sing Christmas carols.

The Cross of the Martyrs, at the top of the hill just off Paseo Peralta near Marcy Street, is another fine place to see *luminarias* and *farolitos*. In addition, many churches decorate with farolitos for the Christmas Eve services, and private homes throughout the city keep the tradition alive.

While you're cruising, don't forget to take a look at the Plaza, which sometimes has holiday ice sculptures in addition to its decorations. And the Loretto Hotel, a downtown hotel designed to resemble an Indian Pueblo, does Christmas up right with electric *farolitos* to highlight its many levels. All of the sights are free.

The Arts

Long before "cultural tourism" became a catch phrase, the arts and culture drew tourists to Santa Fe. Although the city is best known for its visual arts, as reflected in its nationally recognized museums and some 200 galleries, you'll also find opera, chamber music of all sorts, and vocal music. You'll discover theater, both homegrown and imported, and a smattering of dance, including world-famous flamenco by María Benítez. Santa Fe has everything from free performances to $100-a-ticket extravaganzas.

The arts here encompass the traditional and the modern. The petroglyphs in the Galisteo area and along the rock canyons of the Santa Fe River south of the city reflect the antiquity of Santa Fe's attraction as an arts center. The descendants of the city's founding families set the stage for Santa Fe's development as an art mecca with their indigenous arts—the colcha embroidery, delicate straw inlay, painting, and carving. The Spanish brought the arts of silversmithing, ironsmithing, and weaving to New Mexico. These early Europeans, who used their skills to create religious images and beautiful, practical items for the home and ranch, must have been inspired, as visitors are today, by the pottery and jewelry created at the nearby Indian pueblos.

Santa Fe's blue skies, incredible light, and diverse landscape began to draw painters and photographers from the east at the start of the 20th century. The artists found plenty to inspire them—buildings that seemed to grow from the earth itself, narrow twisting streets, the blue bulk of the mountains and foothills framing the city to the east, and the fiery sunsets against the Jémez Mountains to the west.

Many of the earliest artists came seeking better health. The same sunshine and dry air that made them feel better also captured their eyes and imaginations. Carlos Vierra, for example, came for his health and made Santa Fe his permanent home. Vierra, a painter and photographer, worked with the School of American Archaeology (now the School of American Research) and helped develop a unique style of architecture drawn from Santa Fe's antiquity and practical use of available materials. Vierra and other artists also pushed for the restoration of historical buildings. He painted some of the murals that you can still see on the walls of St. Francis Auditorium at the Museum of Fine Arts. Before World War I, Sheldon Parsons, Victor Higgins, Gerald Cassidy, William Penhallow Henderson and his poet wife, Alice Corbin Henderson, B.J. O'Nordfeldt, and many more artists came to Santa Fe, enriching the city with their art and energy.

The establishment of the Museum of Fine Arts in 1907 gave Santa Fe artists a boost, helping them financially by making studios available and professionally by displaying their work. The new museum opened with an exhibit of art by Santa Fe and Taos painters. The artists donated paintings to the museum, forming the basis of its now expansive permanent collection. Many of those featured are regarded as the most important U.S. artists of their time.

In the 1920s, Will Shuster—now best known for creating Zozobra, a giant puppet that is burned as part of the Santa Fe Fiesta—and four other Santa Fe painters became known as Los Cinco Pintores (The Five Painters) and spread the glory of Santa Fe's scenery and people with their art. Even earlier, John Sloan, George Bellows, and Leon Kroll—important names in 20th-century American art—had visited and painted in Santa Fe. Edward Hopper and Marsden Hartley lived here in the 1920s and 1930s, as did Robert Henri and Andrew Dausburg. Writers "discovered" Santa Fe too. Mary Austin, Willa Cather, Jack London, H.L. Mencken, Ezra Pound, Witter Brynner, and many others either lived here or were frequent visitors.

The Santa Fe Concert Band, which traces its founding to 1869, is the community's oldest performing organization still in existence. The all-volunteer band includes amateurs and some retired professional performers who still get a kick out of playing before an audience. The group performs several times a year, usually in public parks or on the Plaza, and all concerts are free. (Call 505-471-4865 for information.) Santa Fe Playhouse, formerly Santa Fe Community Theater, is another long-established amateur company, founded in 1922, just 10 years after statehood. Music One/Santa Fe Concert Association has brought classical music to Santa Fe audiences for more than 60 years.

Santa Fe's arts community took a step into the national spotlight in 1957, when the Santa Fe Opera staged its first performances. The Santa Fe Opera, with its commitment to nurturing American talent and offering a venue for new works, is a major player in the operatic world and draws opera fans and the curious from throughout the world for its summer season. Composer Igor Stravinsky spent more than 10 summers here, in part because of his affection for the outdoor Santa Fe Opera. (Please see our Close-up in this chapter). The Opera's success inspired other performance companies, with the Santa Fe Chamber Music Festival, the Santa Fe Desert Chorale, and Santa Fe Stages adding to Santa Fe's artistic reputation. María Benítez, one of the nation's best-known flamenco dancers and choreographers, has spent summers here dancing with her company for some 30 years.

St. Francis Auditorium, an attractive, shoe-box-shaped hall, is a popular venue for musical groups. Acoustics are good here, but some audience members may have trouble seeing. The same is true for the beautiful but small Loretto Chapel and the Santuario de Guadalupe, an old church that has been graciously rented out for music and theater, as well as some visual art shows. Sweeney Center, the city's all-purpose public space, can seat large crowds and offers convenient parking. The James A. Little Theater at the New Mexico School for the Deaf and Greer Garson Theater are among Santa Fe's most frequently used venues, in part because they were actually built to be theaters! Coming in 2001, Santa Fe should have a new performing arts space downtown in the Lensic Theater. Another new space, El Museo Cultural (see our attractions section), is raising funds for a remodeling to become an all-purpose center for Hispanic art and cultural events.

New Mexico's best-known painter, Georgia O'Keeffe, lived in Santa Fe in the years immediately preceding her death in 1986 and is honored with her own museum. O'Keeffe followed a long tradition of artists from the east migrating to Santa Fe, Taos, and nearby communities. Now, by some estimates, more than a thousand artists—some famous, some unknown but hopeful—live in Santa Fe and the surrounding area.

The Museum of Fine Arts, The Georgia O'Keeffe Museum, and the exhibits at SITE Santa Fe add to the city's standing as a visual-arts center. The city estimates there are between 200 and 300 art galleries here, making Santa Fe one of the nation's leading places to buy and sell art. Among the galleries are those that show work by well-known national and international artists, those that look for emerging artists and cutting-edge work and some that strive to display paintings and drawings that average buyers can afford. From traditional cowboy paintings and sculpture to work by Santa Fe and Taos painters of the 1920s and 1930s to contemporary art and even some avant garde creations—if it calls itself art, you probably can buy it here.

But galleries don't have a monopoly on art. The long-established Indian Market brings leading American Indian artists and craftspeople from throughout the coun-

INSIDERS' TIP

Jazz flute maestro Herbie Mann has a home in Santa Fe. You can catch his performances from time to time—check the local papers.

try to Santa Fe each summer. Spanish Market, held in July and December, offers a rare occasion to see work patterned after traditional Spanish Colonial arts created with fresh inspiration by living Hispanic artists. Santa Fe's Plaza hosts a parade of summer arts and crafts shows, which make shopping for art—or just looking—accessible to the whole family. (See our Annual Events chapter for more information on seasonal art fairs.)

The city of Santa Fe's mural program has resulted in murals at City Hall, on street corner signal boxes, municipal buses, and even on garbage trucks. The Aspen Santa Fe Ballet launched its first season in 2000, as did the Santa Fe Jazz Festival. Arts of all sorts intermingle as part of the fabric of contemporary Santa Fe. From subtle chamber music to lively bilingual theater, it's hard to find a weekend without a concert, lecture, film or recital to entice you. Enjoy!

The following listings offer a look at some Santa Fe arts organizations. For logical use, it is arranged alphabetically. Where possible we've given addresses for performance locations.

Community Arts Centers

Plan B Evolving Arts
Armory for the Arts, 1050 Old Pecos Tr.
• **(505) 982-1338**

Plan B is an all-purpose arts center, providing the Santa Fe community with a movie theater featuring foreign and art films, a performance stage dedicated to new and exciting dance and theater projects, and two visual arts galleries that feature emerging as well as internationally recognized artists. Plan B is passionate about presenting cutting-edge, experimental, and simply beautiful art.

You'll find detailed descriptions of all Plan B's events in BLATT!, its bi-monthly newsletter. Its film program in the Cinematheque has long been a favorite for movie-hungry Santa Feans and was voted Best of Santa Fe in the Santa Fe Reporter's Reader's Poll for 1999. Plan B is open weekdays from noon until 9 PM and weekends according to the movie schedule. There's plenty of free parking.

El Museo Cultural de Santa Fe
1615-B Paseo de Peralta
• **(505) 992-0591**

The museum and arts center, located at the Santa Fe rail yard property just off Paseo Peralta, offers art and dance programs for children and youth, but its broad outreach also includes workshops and classes for adults, visual art shows, performances, and special events. (See our Close-up in Attractions.)

The multiple uses the museum makes of its current large-but-nothing-fancy space through exhibitions and performances give visitors an idea of what the board hopes will come to be when the building is remodeled to better serve the community's needs. The renovation will reflect the museum's two branches of emphasis: the focus on exhibitions, performance, and presentations of contemporary artistic creations and its support for the preservation of Hispanic culture, history, language, and traditions through education. The finished museum will include a profes-

sional-looking gallery area, large conference space, and a kitchen for teaching students how to cook traditional dishes and prepare native foods. An entry court and jardín, based on the Spanish building concept of gardens and plazas, will add to the elegance. There will be room for a library and a mercado/theater where artists can demonstrate their work and sell to visitors.

The museum is open daily except Monday from 1 to 5 PM. Although there was no admission charge at the time of this writing, the museum may begin to charge in the fall of 2000.

SITE Santa Fe
1606 Paseo de Peralta
• **(505) 989-1199**
• **www.sitesantafe.org**

SITE Santa Fe is a private, not-for-profit contemporary arts organization committed to providing an ongoing venue for regional, national, and international exhibitions and interdisciplinary programs. Although best known as a visual arts space, SITE Santa Fe also hosts lectures and literary programs. The website offers a useful calendar of events to keep you up to date on pending activities. The art space is open Wednesday through Sunday, 10 AM to 5 PM and Friday, 10 AM to 7 PM. Admission is $5/adults, $2.50/students and seniors. Individual events are separately priced.

Dance

Aspen Santa Fe Ballet Company
Various venues
• **(505) 983-3262,**
or for tickets (505) 851-6060
or (800)905-3315 or tickets.com
• **www.aspensantafeballet.com**

The only professional dance company in New Mexico, the Aspen Santa Fe Ballet started in 1996 and has slowly grown. The company, with administrative headquarters in Aspen, Colo., presents three concerts a season, from August through March. The 2000–2001 programs included "Mixed Repertory" performed with guest stars from the San Francisco Ballet; *The Nutcracker* with students and professionals and Prokofiev's *Romeo and Juliet*. Tickets range from $18 to $36.

María Benítez Teatro Flamenco/ Institute for Spanish Arts
Radisson Hotel, 750 N. St. Francis Dr.
• **(505) 983-8477, (800) 905-3315; Protix, (local box office, opens mid-June): (505) 982-1237; Tickets.com; and Culturefinder.com**

Talented and passionate about her art, María Benítez has brought flamenco dance to Santa Fe each summer for many years. Benítez performs with her company of dancers, singers, and musicians from late June through early September at the Benítez Theatre, Radisson Hotel. In addition to engagements with the company, Benítez frequently appears as a guest artist and choreographer with the Santa Fe Opera and the Metropolitan Opera in New York, among others. María Benítez Teatro Flamenco tours nationally and internationally and has been broadcast in all 50 states and on PBS-TV. The Institute for Spanish Arts, the non-profit organization that Benítez co-directs with her husband, Cecilio, presents workshops and classes in Spanish dance and music and operates a regional Spanish dance company, Estampa Española, as well as María Benítez Teatro Flamenco.

New Mexico Dance Coalition
Performance locations vary
• **(505) 820-2636**

Organized in 1986 by some of the state's leading dancers and dance companies and based in Santa Fe, The New Mexico Dance Coalition's mission is to develop and promote dance arts within the state. The group also works as advocates for dance, dancers, and dance companies and provides networking, information sharing, and administrative services to the dance community. Although primarily a service organization for dancers, the coalition produces two events: MonoMundo, a free ethnic dance festival in August on

INSIDERS' TIP

Santa Fe is becoming increasingly known as a literary mecca. The city has 25 or so publishers and more than a dozen general interest bookstores. The College of Santa Fe is one of only a few private U.S. schools offering an undergraduate creative-writing degree. The Lannan Foundation, which moved to Santa Fe from Los Angeles in 1997, offers grants and fellowships to writers.

Santa Fe's more than 200 art galleries range from contemporary to traditional, from experimental to realistic. You'll see work by newcomers along with that of established professionals.

Photo: Chris Corrie

the Santa Fe Plaza, and an annual Choreographers' Showcase in November, featuring professional and novice dancers performing innovative works. NMDC publishes a quarterly newsletter, *High Altitude Dance*, and promotes educational programs throughout the state for youth, adults, and professional dancers.

Santa Fe Dance Foundation (The Official School of Aspen Santa Fe Ballet)
550 B St. Michael's Drive,
Performance locations vary
• (505) 983-5591

Gisela Genschow, a dancer born and trained in Germany, has danced professionally in Germany and France and founded this dance school in 1992. Ballet classes are offered for children and adults, including intensive training programs each summer. The students also participate with professional dancers in an annual holiday performance of *The Nutcracker*, presented by the Aspen Ballet.

Film

Cinematheque Program
Plan B Evolving Arts, 1050 Old Pecos Tr.
• (505) 982-1338

Plan B's Cinematheque was voted Santa Fe's Favorite Art Film Theater in the *Reporter's* Reader's Poll 1999 and screens some of the world's best movies, including classic black and white films, beautiful foreign films and mind-blowing documentaries. Recent offerings include films from China, Israel, Iran, India, France, and Britain. Popular series include the annual Film Noir festival in July and the Santa Fe Film Festival in November. A new film opens every Friday and runs at least one week. Tickets are $7 with discounts for students, seniors, and members. Please call for a schedule and show times. Plan B has plenty of parking.

Grand Illusion
St. Michael's Village West Shopping Ctr.,
1614 St. Michael's Dr. at Llano St.
• (505) 471-8935
• www.transluxmovies.com

During the summer, Grand Illusion becomes Santa Fe's family theater with a continuous long run of a Disney feature or otherwise appropriate movie for kids and their parents. Evenings and during the rest of the year, Grand Illusion offers foreign-language films and some mainstream movies. You'll find a synopsis of the current feature on the website and parking in the shopping center lot.

Jean Cocteau Cinema and Coffee House
418 Montezuma St.
• (505) 988-2711 (Recording),
(505) 988-9781 (Manager)
• www.transluxmovies.com

A first-rate coffeehouse sets this downtown art theater apart from the crowd. This cozy, classy little theater isn't your usual movie palace. You'll find foreign films, alternative American productions, and mainstream classics here. Jean Cocteau Cinema uses a customer wish list to help with its programming. The coffeehouse is open from 3 PM until midnight and offers live music before the midnight movies. You can park along the street or in nearby lots. They'll send you're their schedule via e-mail. The Cocteau offers discounts for children and seniors and has a VIP screening room you can reserve for parties.

St. John's College Film Society
St. John's College Great Hall,
Peterson Student Center,
1160 Camino Cruz Blanca
• (505) 984-6158

Varied programming of classic films marks this series, which draws students as well as film buffs from the community. Shows are on Wednesdays and Saturdays; a recent Wednesday featured a slate of modern French films including *The City of Lost Children,* a film about a sleepless monster that kidnaps children to steal their dreams. The weekend series runs on Saturday nights starting at 7 PM with an old-fashioned cartoon, followed by the main feature. Sometimes there's a second feature at 9:15 PM. For you sentimental folks, *It's A Wonderful Life* is always shown the first Saturday in December. Admission is only $3, $4 if a double feature is on the program—one of the biggest movie bargains in town.

United Artists Theaters
United Artists DeVargas Center 6
 DeVargas Ctr., 562 N. Guadalupe St.
(Guadalupe St. at Paseo de Peralta)
• (505) 988-2775
United Artists North, 4250 Cerrillos Rd.
(Villa Linda Mall)
• (505) 471-3377
United Artists South, 4250 Cerrillos Rd.
(Villa Linda Mall)
• (505) 471-6066

United Artists is the central force in Santa

Fe commercial cinema, with as many as 20 Hollywood products on display—the movies that get the expensive TV commercials and whose stars are interviewed on talk shows and profiled in *People*. United Artists North and South are on the appropriate sides of Villa Linda Mall. You'll find lines of teens here most weekends. Parking at Villa Linda is easy in the mall's sprawling lots and there's horseback security. The DeVargas theater means that people who live on the north side of town and visitors staying in the downtown hotels don't have to drive south to Cerrillos and Rodeo Road to catch a commercial hit. Abundant parking also awaits at DeVargas Center—especially in the evenings.

Literature

Book Signings

Santa Fe is a literary center and has played host to such writers as Willa Cather, Carl Sandburg, Tony Hillerman, Vachel Lindsay, Robinson Jeffers, Thornton Wilder, Evan Connell, Robert Frost, and many more. Some only visited, some stayed for years, others live here still. Most weekends at least one author, either local or imported, is celebrating the long-awaited arrival of a new book with an autograph party at any one of the local bookstores. Author talks and signings are also a favorite fund-raising tool and a vital part of Santa Fe's annual Festival of the Book. (See our Annual Events chapter.) All three Santa Fe newspapers publish author interviews and information about signings. Sometimes in addition to signings, authors will also read from their new works. Please see our Shopping chapter for the addresses and phone numbers of the bookstores.

Readings & conversations
Site Santa Fe, 1606 Paseo de Peralta, and other venues
• Lannan Foundation: (505) 954-5149
• www.lannan.org

An outstanding group of poets and novelists read and discuss their work in this enormously popular and well-attended series. Past participants have in-

cluded Pulitzer Prize-winning poet Mark Strand, novelists Peter Matthiessen and Jamaica Kincaid, and others. Guest writers read from their work and then are interviewed by a knowledgeable host such as the editor of a national literary magazine or public radio or television book program. Best of all, tickets are inexpensive, just $5 adults or $2 for students. Advance purchase is a good idea; call the foundation for more information. Videos of the series also are available.

Recursos de Santa Fe Southwest Literary Center
826 Camino de Monte Rey
• (505) 982-9301

Founded in 1984, Recursos is a nonprofit educational organization that includes among its missions the encouragement of good writing. To this end, Recursos Southwest Literary Center presents seminars, conferences, expositions, study tours, and academic and artistic projects. The Writers Reading Series gives Santa Fe a regular opportunity to hear poets, novelists, and nonfiction writers read from their works. Sponsored by grants, including support from the Witter Brynner Foundation for Poetry, a national organization based here, the free programs bring writers and readers together twice a month. The series has included Paula Gunn Allen. A Discovery Reading presents less-familiar voices, winners of the national Discovery Writing Competition that Recursos sponsors annually.

In addition, each year the nonprofit organization conducts about six writers' workshops, which draw attendees from throughout the country. Recent topics have included Writing Women's Lives with Western States Book Award novelist Demetria Martinez and Pam Houston, who won the same award for her short-story collection. George Johnson, former editor of the *New York Times News of the Week in Review* joined other top writers for Writing Science Today, a seminar for professional science writers. Recursos also brings many major writers to Santa Fe each summer for its annual Santa Fe Writers Conference. Student participants are selected based on written submissions; attendance is limited to allow for more individual attention at this popular and successful series. Faculty members have included E. Annie Proulx, Tony Hillerman, John Nichols, and many other published writers of national and international reputation. Fee for conferences is approximately $450 for a five-day program.

New Mexico Book Association
310 Read Street
• (505) 983-1412

This Santa Fe-based organization works to nurture the growing literary and publishing scene throughout New Mexico. In recent years many small presses publishing fine works by local writers have emerged, tested their dreams against reality, and survived in pleasingly strong numbers. NMBA publishes a lively newsletter, *Libro Monthly,* with plenty of news from writers and publishers in Santa Fe, New Mexico, and even out of state. The group hosts monthly luncheons for publishers, writers, and readers. They also publish New Mexico's *Book World: A Resource Guide,* a directory of book people and services in the state.

PEN New Mexico
2860 Plaza Verde
• (505) 473-4813
• www.pennm.org

Chartered under the U.S.A. PEN Los Angeles Chapter, this group started in 1991. A nonprofit professional organization, PEN sponsors local readings, seminars, regional conferences, and other events relevant to writers and the literary world. Among recent activities, PEN NM sponsored the conference "Censorship in Cyberspace," and hosted a dinner meeting for interested members with literary agents from California. PEN NM plans a series of videos by famous contemporary writers and poets as evenings of socializing and discussion. The group and its members participate in the Santa Fe Festival of the Book. PEN

also supports *The Reading Sampler,* an author interview and reading radio program on KSFR Santa Fe Public Radio (KSFR 90.7 FM).

Music

(In addition to the musical organizations listed here, please see our Nightlife section of more information on popular performance venues. And the area casinos frequently host musical acts as part of their entertainment. Check the newspapers to find out who may be in town or our Attractions chapter for additional information.)

Collaborations
College of Santa Fe,
Greer Garson Theatre Center,
1600 St. Michael's Dr.
• (505) 473-6511

This music series features an eclectic mix of contemporary performances in the intimate space of the Weckesser Studio Theater inside the Greer Garson Theater Center. Performers may be New Mexicans or visitors from out of state. Ticket prices range from $8 to $12. Performances are scheduled during the school year; call for a schedule of events.

St. John's College Concert Series
St. John's College
Peterson Student Center,
1160 Camino Cruz Blanca
• (505) 984-6104

Concerts here tend to stress piano music. Musician-in-residence Peter Pesic offers informal noon performances in the spring and fall in the Junior Commons Room with commentary about the music. The programs are free. The college also hosts visiting musicians in evening programs, to which admission may be charged. Included in the range of performances have been the Borromeo String Quartet, a medieval music ensemble by Paul Hillier, founder and director of Theatre of Voices, and the College's Chamber Choir Performances.

INSIDERS' TIP

The Santa Fe Opera has joined with the Salzburg Festival and the Theatre du Chatelet in Paris to co-commission and co-produce *L'amour de Loin* (Love from Afar) by the Finnish composer Kaija Saariaho. The internationally known director Peter Sellars, in his Santa Fe Opera debut, will stage this new work. American singers, Dawn Upshaw and Lorraine Hunt Lieberson will sing the major roles. Each has extensive international credits, as well as prior appearances with The Santa Fe Opera. The co-production will open in the Salzburg Festival's 2000 season, be performed in Paris in 2001 and then travel to Santa Fe for the American premiere in the company's 2002 season. The opera has also commissioned two other full-length works.

The Santa Fe Opera's New Frontier

There's a big change in store for the Santa Fe Opera for the 2001 season and beyond.

After more than 40 years, the Santa Fe Opera's founder and general director, John Crosby, has stepped down. Crosby, the company's first and only general director, built the Santa Fe Opera into a world-renowned company.

The new general director, Richard Gaddes, has announced a series of major initiatives including world premieres, a co-production with the Salzburg Festival and Pours Theatre du Chatelet, and more programs with a community/regional focus. But the underlying vision of the Santa Fe Opera as a company that welcomes talented young American singers and new or seldom-heard operatic works remains in place.

Crosby founded The Santa Fe Opera in 1957, building a small open-air theater seven miles north of Santa Fe. The first summer the company presented seven operas: three from the standard repertory, three seldom-heard works, and one contemporary premiere. This something-old, something-new combination has become the company's hallmark. Each summer, Crosby has conducted at least one opera. The theater, rebuilt after a fire in 1964 and completely remodeled for the 1998 season, sits on 55 acres with full view of the Sangre de Cristo and Jémez Mountains. In a typical season it attracts more than 70,000 visitors from throughout the United States and around the world.

The company has established a reputation for adventurous programming, high performance standards, and nurturing outstanding young artists and technicians. Singers, directors, technicians, orchestral musicians, and staff work together during an intense three-month period to produce five operas. By the end of the 2000 season, The Santa Fe Opera had presented 118 operas. The repertoire includes nine world premieres—eight of which were Santa Fe Opera commissions—and 39 American premieres including Alban Berg's *Lulu*. The company has performed all the major operas of Richard Strauss and has featured artists including Ben Heppner, Bryn Terfel, Kiri TeKanawa, Tatiana Troyanos, James Morris, Samuel Ramey, Catherine Malfitano, and Sylvia McNair.

(Continued on next page)

A model of the new Santa Fe Opera theater.

Photo: Courtesy of The Santa Fe Opera

"Thanks to the leadership of John Crosby, the Santa Fe Opera has a well-earned reputation for quality and creativity," Gaddes said. "I look forward to building on that tradition as we raise our performance standards and artistic aspirations even higher."

Gaddes, who has been the company's associate general director since 1995, took the helm on Sept. 30, 2000. He first came to the company in 1969 as artistic administrator. He left Santa Fe in 1976 to establish the Opera Theatre of St. Louis, where he earned commendations for discovering young singers and giving them opportunities to perform important roles. He returned to the Santa Fe Opera in 1994.

Born in England, Gaddes studied at Trinity College of Music in London. After leaving Trinity he formed his own artists management company and later joined Artists International Management and represented musicians worldwide. It was there that he met John Crosby, who invited him to come to Santa Fe as the company's artistic administrator. Gaddes was instrumental in Dame Kiri Te Kanawa's American debut at the Santa Fe Opera. He is a former vice president of Opera America, has served on opera and music panels of the National Endowment for the Arts and frequently judges national and international voice competitions including the Metropolitan Opera National Council auditions.

Asked if he planned changes for the Santa Fe Opera, Gaddes said: "We are going to be more aggressive in seeking out and bringing to Santa Fe the most dynamic young talent from this country and abroad. An important part of my vision for the company is to present major artists in significant new stage roles for the first time in their careers. Each season we'd like to feature American debuts by exceptional singers from around the world."

To serve local and regional audiences in new ways, in the fall of 2000 the company began its Showcase Production Series with *The Beggar's Opera*. The series, to be staged annually during the fall and winter, expands Santa Fe Opera performances outside the Santa Fe Opera theater. With popular-priced tickets, Gaddes hopes to attract new audiences to opera in general and to the Santa Fe Opera in particular.

Other initiatives include an expanded website, special ticket offers, shuttle service to and from the Opera, and pre-performance activities such as free preview discussions.

But Santa Fe Opera audiences haven't seen the last of John Crosby. An internationally recognized champion of the Richard Strauss canon, he planned to conduct the 2001 production of *The Egyptian Helen*.

MusicOne: The Santa Fe Concert Association
Performance locations vary,
usually St. Francis Auditorium,
Museum of Fine Arts, 107 W. Palace Ave.
• (505) 984-8759, (800) 905-3315
(Tickets.com)

Since 1937 Santa Fe Concert Association has made Santa Fe a more cultured place to live by bringing in nationally known artists. Before the Opera and the Chamber Music Festival, the top-quality musicians who came to town under this nonprofit group's sponsorship offered city residents their only chance to hear national artists without a road trip. This group's impressive performance list draws the best musicians and singers from around the world. The association arranges a dozen or more events from September to May with performances ranging from soloists to string quartets, trios to chamber orchestras. Past guests have included pianist Andre Watts, the Prague Chamber Orchestra, Czech violinist Josef Suk, and pianist Radu Lupu. The Concert Association's Christmas Eve and New Year's Eve concerts presented by local and visiting musicians have been a regular and very popular addition to Santa Fe's musical life since 1981. Ticket prices range from $16 to $60.

Paolo Soleri Amphitheater
Santa Fe Indian School campus, 1501 Cerrillos Rd.
• (505) 989-6318, tickets from Ticketmaster (505) 993-7800
• www.eveningstar.com

This open-air theater, designed by the renowned architect Paolo Soleri, hosts popular concerts during the warmer months, usually beginning about May and extending to early October. Among the singers who've performed here are k.d. lang, B.B. King, Dan Fogelberg, Ziggy Marley, James Taylor, and Lyle Lovett. The theater is frequently the venue for native Roots & Rhythms Festival, a performance component that accompanies Santa Fe's annual Indian Market. Most concerts start with warm-up groups around dusk. Food, drinks, tapes, CDs, T-shirts, and other concessions may be sold. Ticket prices vary with the groups. (See our Nightlife chapter.)

The Paramount
331 Sandoval St.
• (505)982-8999

This is the place for live nightclub entertainment. You'll find all sorts of music here, from Irish folk groups to punkabilly, R&B, bluegrass, swing, zydeco—you get the idea. Depending on the name, seating may be tableside with room for dancing or theater style to maximize the size of the audience. Tickets tend to be in the $10 to $20 range depending on who's playing. The music usually starts between 8 and 10 PM. You can get a schedule and buy tickets at Bar B, a smaller, intimate performance space that adjoins the Paramount, after 5 PM, or through Ticketmaster. (See our Nightlife chapter.)

Sangre de Cristo Chorale
Various venues
• (505) 662-9717
• www.sdc-chorale.org

The Sangre de Cristo Chorale is a volunteer choral ensemble established in 1978 to provide high-quality vocal ensemble music for the Northern New Mexico community. The musicians, who come from Santa Fe and Los Alamos,

picked the name of the local mountain range to identify strongly with the area. The group selected Sheldon Kalberg, then Choral Director at Los Alamos High School, as musical director, and he continues in that capacity.

Through the 1999–2000 season, the Chorale had presented 55 major concerts in 158 performances primarily in Santa Fe, Los Alamos, and Albuquerque. The chorale usually performs in December, March, and May. The December concert in Santa Fe includes a holiday dinner. In 1999, the dinner concert cost $40 regular admission or $35 for senior citizens and students. (It sells out in November.) For other concerts, expect $12 regular admission or $10 for seniors and students. Recordings of the chorale are available; call for information or see their website.

Santa Fe Chamber Music Festival
St. Francis Auditorium, Museum of Fine Arts, 107 W. Palace Ave. and SITE Santa Fe, 1606 Paseo de Peralta
• (505) 983-2075, (505) 982-1890(summer)
• www.santafechambermusic.org

One of Santa Fe's most esteemed musical groups, the Chamber Music Festival began in the summer of 1973 and has grown into an event with an international following. The Festival draws consistent critical acclaim for the depth of its programming and its vision in commissioning new pieces and presenting seldom-heard works. Each summer, performers at the Festival include established musicians and up-and-comers. A typical season features more than 30 concerts, composers-in-residence, emphasis on American music and attention to masterworks. Jazz continues to play a major role. But the classics, performed by such musicians as Ani Kavafian, The Orion String Quartet, Leon Fleisher, and Pinchas Zukerman, form the festival's lifeblood. Repertoire ranges from the works of J.S. Bach to the world premiere of Bright Sheng's Festival commission, The Silver River. New programming includes the addition of two contemporary music concerts at Site Santa Fe, and two world music concerts featuring the music of Indonesia and India. The Festival offers master classes each season with musicians such as Leon Fleisher, Ralph Kirshbaum, Michael Tree, and Pinchas Zukerman.

The Festival arranges its programming in separate series to make it easier for patrons to hear the music they like best. The music is taped and frequently broadcast over public radio and on classical stations.

To help inform the audience, the Festival presents free concert previews about the music and artists. Immediately before the concerts, these discussions feature guest composers, artists and musicologists reviewing the day's repertoire. The public can sit in on selected daytime rehearsals free of charge. As another part of its outreach, the Festival's musicians often give free concerts to senior citizens, residents of rehabilitation centers, and hospitals. The Chamber Music Festival offers a special series for children, also for free.

Concerts are rehearsed and performed in St. Francis Auditorium, and the Festival looks forward to performing in the Lensic Theatre upon completion of its renovation, perhaps as early as the summer of 2001. The season runs from the second weekend in July through mid-August. Seating is reserved, and individual tickets cost from $15 to $36. Student tickets are $10 and half-price tickets are offered a half-hour before the concert, subject to availability. You may also order tickets through the website.

Santa Fe Desert Chorale
Various venues
• **(505) 988-7505 (box office),**
(800) 905-3315 (Tickets.com)
• **www.desertchorale.org/**

The Santa Fe Desert Chorale, a fully professional chamber chorus, presents two seasons each year. The summer season offers more than 25 performances of four separate concert repertoires throughout July and early August. The Winter Season offers performances of "A Merry New Mexico Christmas" during the week before Christmas and "A Baroque Treasury" during the week following Christmas.

The chorale performs in some of the most beautiful and historic sites of Santa Fe and Albuquerque, including the Loretto Chapel, Santuario de Guadelupe, and San Felipe de Neri in Albuquerque. In addition, newer sites—Santa Maria de la Paz, St. John's Episcopal Cathedral, and the Albuquerque Academy—are no less appealing in architectural design or acoustical sonority. Since its inception in 1983,

the Desert Chorale has been noted for its effectiveness of programming and virtuosity of performance. Critics and audience members alike have consistently praised the Chorale for presenting some of the world's most significant and engaging repertoire—from the ancient to the modern.

The Chorale, New Mexico's only professional vocal ensemble, sings under the direction of Dennis Schrock, also director of the Canterbury Choral Society. The summer season offers more than 25 performances of four separate concert repertoires throughout July and early August. The chorus has many recordings, including numerous American and world premieres.

Summer concerts begin at 8 PM nightly, except Sunday, when the ensemble performs at 6 PM. Call for information about the winter season and Christmas holiday series. Tickets for most performances are about $30, except for Santa Maria concerts, which range from $12 to $27. A 50 percent student discount is available for all single-ticket and subscription orders.

The Santa Fe Opera
Santa Fe Opera Theater,
7 miles N.W. of Santa Fe on
U.S. Hwy. 84-285
• **(505) 986-5955, (800) 280-4654**
• **www.santafeopera.org**

The Santa Fe Opera, a summer opera festival, achieved international stature soon after its inception. The fame is due to the high-quality performances and the company's sense of adventure in tackling new and rare works. The Opera presents a combination of classics, rarely heard works, and an American or world premieres in beautiful productions that attract opera lovers from around the world. The Opera opened on July 3, 1957, in a 480-seat theater. Its founder, John Crosby, stepped down as general director at the conclusion of the 2000 season—the longest-tenured operative in that role in America. The original theater burned in 1967 and was replaced with a 1,889-seat open-air theater by the start of the next season. That theater served the company through the 1997 season. The Santa Fe Opera completely rebuilt the theater beginning in the fall of 1997 to preserve the open-air ambiance while offering the audience more protection from the elements. The new theater, designed by Polshek Partnership of New York, has won a number of important awards for its design and has drawn mixed reviews among the locals. The redesign completely roofed the audience seating area and extended the roofline farther on the sides. The

*Outdoor sculpture is occasionally featured
outside galleries, in parks, and around the
state capitol building.*

Photo: Don Strel

debut season, The Santa Fe Opera has presented 118 operas. Nine were world premieres, and of that number, eight were Santa Fe Opera commissions. Thrity-nine operas received their American premieres in Santa Fe, including Alban Berg's *Lulu*. Friday and Saturday performances frequently sell out in advance. Normal repertoire includes a familiar opera such as Verdi's *La Traviata;* a work by Mozart; a Richard Strauss opera; an older, seldom-heard work, such as Handel's *Semele;* and an American or world premiere.

In addition to its willingness to take a chance on a new work, the Santa Fe Opera also takes a chance on new talent with its extensive apprentice singer and technician programs. Apprentices, chosen by audition, appear in the productions as chorus members and understudies for major roles. They learn the many facets of opera from some of the world's best conductors, directors and coaches. Well-known singers including Samuel Ramey, Ashley Putnam, and James Morris are among the program's graduates. Kiri te Kanawa made her American debut here, as did Bryn Terfel. Each August the Opera gives the apprentices the stage on their own, in two performances that showcase their talents with a variety of opera vignettes. Technical apprentices learn lighting, costumes, sets, wigs, makeup, and more.

Backstage tours through the costume shop and production area continue June through August, Monday through Saturday at 1 PM, and reservations are not required. Since the company makes most of its own sets, props, and costumes, there's plenty to see. The company offers elegant pre-performance buffets with guest speakers. The theater has two bars that serve light fare and libations. At the gift shop you can buy tote bags, sweatshirts, and other merchandise with the distinctive SFO logo, and a portion of the sales benefit the company.

Tickets for the Santa Fe Opera performances range from $20 to $118 Monday through Thursday and from $28 to $128 on Friday and Saturday. Standing room is $8. The season runs from late June or early July through the last week in August.

new theater seats 2,128 patrons with additional standing-room designation. The remodeling added 37 lavatory fixtures, five drinking fountains, and three public telephones. The reconstruction, a $19.5 million project, also included better handicapped accessibility and an electronic literary system which provides an English translation of the dialogue on stage on a small screen located directly in the front of each seat. Patrons can turn the screen on or off as they wish. Behind the scenes, the Santa Fe Opera has a wetlands sewage treatment and water reclamation system to harvest rainwater from summer thunderstorms.

The theater sits atop a hillside in the Sangre de Cristo Mountains with a stunning view of the Jémez Mountain range. Performances begin just after sunset so you can enjoy the natural light show first.

The Opera operated on a budget of $110,000 its first season; for the 2000 season, the budget was approximately $13 million. The Santa Fe Opera makes its musical magic with the assistance of more than 600 company members at the height of its summer season. Since the 1957

Santa Fe Pro Musica Chamber Orchestra and Ensemble
Performance locations vary
• **(505) 988-4640, (800) 960-6680**
• **www.santafepromusica.com**

This group consists of a 35-member chamber orchestra and a more intimate chamber ensemble series. The orchestra performs without a conductor in a long-standing tradition of chamber orchestras of the 18th century. Pro Musica presents concerts from October through May and offers an annual Mozart & Haydn Festival, Santa Fe Bach Festival and popular Baroque Christmas Concerts in the historic Loretto Chapel. The ensemble presents Santa Fe Bach Festival performances on period instruments—wooden rather than metal flutes, string instruments using gut strings rather than steel. Pro Musica engages some of the world's leading soloists including Ani Kavafian, David Jolley, John Elwes, Allan Vogel, Kurt Ollmann, and Van Cliburn piano competition winner Jose' Feghali. The group covers an impressive repertoire, with works from Beethoven and Vivaldi as well as contemporary masters who celebrate the concerto and symphonic forms. Santa Fe Pro Musica performs in Loretto Chapel, 207 Old Santa Fe Trail; the St. Francis Auditorium, 107 W. Palace Avenue and Santa Maria De La Paz Catholic Community, 11 College Way. Concerts will return to the Lensic Theater in its incarnation as the newly renovated Lensic Performing Arts Center in downtown Santa Fe in the spring of 2001. Tickets range from $16 to $40. Full-time students are always half-price.

Santa Fe Symphony and Chorus
Performance locations vary
• **(505) 983-1414 (box office),**
(800) 480-1319

Since it's founding in 1984, the symphony has become known for its outstanding performances by New Mexican musicians and has featured such guest artists as Andre Watts, Elmer Bernstein, Marilyn Horne, and Dave Grusin. The symphony has been heard nationwide on National Public Radio's *Performance Today* series. The group won Santa Fe's appreciation for presenting the inaugural local performances of such masterpieces as Berlioz's *L'Enfance du Christ,* the complete Brandenburg Concerti by J.S. Bach, and Handel's *Messiah.* Premieres, including Mark O'Connor's Fiddle Concerto are also part of the repertory. The season runs from October through June with nine concerts, including such annual favorites

INSIDERS' TIP

Nearly 300 feature films have been shot in New Mexico, starting with silent pictures in 1898. The diverse landscape, incredible light, and rich blue skies top the list of why the state was chosen. Santa Fe and northern New Mexico have long been popular with moviemakers—more than half of the state's movies have been shot within the city's mountain and mesa vistas.

as Holiday Traditions and the Beethoven Festival, as well as new presentations such as The Music of Spain and Mexico and an expanded Beethoven Festival spotlighting talented local soloists. Tickets range from $10 to $45.

Santa Fe Women's Ensemble
Loretto Chapel, 211 Old Santa Fe Tr. and Santuario de Guadalupe, 100 Agua Fría St.
• **(505) 954-4922**

This 12-voice group has delighted Santa Fe audiences since 1980 and attracts an enthusiastic audience. The women sing two concerts a year, their Spring Offering and a Christmas Offering. Past concerts have included Gerald Near's *The Storke* and Dean Roush's *Stabat Mater.* Performances are held at Christmas in the jewel-like Loretto Chapel (downtown next to Hotel Loretto), which sets off the voices in splendor; the Spring Offering is performed at the historic Santuario de Guadalupe.

Serenata of Santa Fe
Santuario de Guadalupe, 100 Agua Fría
• **(505) 989-7988**

Another of Santa Fe's long-established musical groups, the Serenata has two goals: to present chamber music to audiences of all economic resources in an informal, friendly way and to provide an opportunity for musicians to get together to perform pieces they love. All programs are presented in the Santuario de Guadalupe and range from solo music to octets. Ensemble members may chat with the audience about the music and composer prior to concerts. The ensemble's players change, and guest performers may be added depending on the pieces in rehearsal for any of their four or more annual concerts. But the group prides itself on not compromising on rehearsal time and not shying away from challenging works. Tickets are $15 by phone or $12 at the door (an incentive to be spontaneous!).

20th Century Unlimited
Performance locations vary, Tickets:
Nicholas Potter Books, 211 E. Palace Ave.
• **(505) 820-6401**
• **www.20thcenturyunlimited.org**

20th Century Unlimited presents leading

musical artists performing some of the great music of our times as well as new works of special interest and merit. The series features local and international musicians in ensemble settings and frequently presents pre-concert lectures by leading musicologists. In addition to its diverse repertoire of chiefly 20th century classical music, 20th Century Unlimited has commissioned and premiered eight compositions since its inaugural season in 1997. In collaboration with Theaterwork, they offered a staged performance of Stravinsky's *A Soldier's Tale* in 1998, and regularly take interactive musical programs to the Santa Fe Public Schools.

20th Century Unlimited's season features seven concerts. All tickets are only $5.

Theater

(Companies that offer performances and classes for children are featured in our Kidstuff chapter.)

Engine House Theater
Melodrama Company
2846 N.M. Hwy. 14, Madrid
• (505) 438-3780

For unadulterated fun, it's hard to top the Madrid melodrama. Since 1982, the company based in the old theater next to the MineShaft Tavern has drawn enthusiastic crowds to cheer for the heroes and hiss at the bad guys. Bags of marshmallows to toss at the villain are included

with admission. The plays are 1800s-style melodramas that fit in well with this old one-time mining town. The season runs weekends from Memorial Day through mid-October. Curtain time is 3 and 8 PM on Saturday and 3 PM on Sunday and Monday holidays, with matinees only during October. Tickets are $9 for adults, $7 for seniors, and $4 for children younger than 12. Allow at least a half-hour to get to the theater from Santa Fe. The drive from Santa Fe, along what's known as the Turquoise Trail because of the historic turquoise mines here, will take you past the village of Cerrillos. Madrid, an old mining town, is now rich with unique shops and galleries. Leave early and poke around a little.

Greer Garson Theatre Center
College of Santa Fe, 1600 St. Michael's Dr.
• (505) 473-6511
• www.csf.edu
(go to "Performing Arts" section)

The 500-seat Greer Garson Theatre is the venue for four yearly stage productions by the College of Santa Fe's nationally recognized Performing Arts Department. The shows, including a musical, feature student casts and usually have faculty members as directors. (The college offers majors in contemporary music, theater, acting, design/theatre technology, and musical theater.) Recent seasons have included *Lend Me a Tenor, Dracula, A Midsummer Night's Dream, Dames at Sea, The Diary of Anne Frank, You Can't Take it With You,* and a musical ver-

This peaceful sculpture is found outside Plaza Resolana, 401 Old Taos Highway.

Photo: Don Strel

sion of *The Importance of Being Earnest.* Tickets range from $8 to $17. Greer Garson—the actress whose generosity is recognized with buildings in her and her husband Buddy Fogelson's names throughout the campus—joined the student company for a production or two. The college is generous about allowing other performance companies access to the theater and to the smaller Weckesser Studio.

Santa Fe Performing Arts
Armory for the Arts Theater,
1050 Old Pecos Tr.
• **(505) 982-7992,**
(505) 984-1370 (box office)
• **www.sfperformingarts.org**
Santa Fe Performing Arts' year-round programming includes performing arts classes for ages 6 to 18 and an adult resident company that performs four productions per year. The children's company presents six productions per year. Recent performances include *The Fantasticks,* and *As Bees In Honey Drown.* Tickets range from $5 to $15.

Santa Fe Stages
100 N. Guadalupe Street
• **(505) 982-6683 (box office),**
(505) 982-6680
• **www.santafestages.org**
Founded in 1995, Santa Fe Stages holds a unique position in New Mexico's performing arts community. Critically acclaimed as "cool" by *Time* magazine and "stunning" by the *Los Angeles Times*, Stages is the primary presenter of modern dance in Santa Fe. Stages also produces and presents a wide variety of cutting-edge and classic theater, solo performance artists, cabaret performers, and Latin music in what has become Stages' signature eclectic programming mix. Since its first season, Stages has mounted more than 70 different productions, including six world premieres, nine North American premieres, and two United States premieres. They recently unveiled their intimate new 200-seat theater, Santa Fe Stages at the Firestone Plaza, located only blocks from the Plaza. Other performance venues are the Greer Garson Theater at the College of Santa Fe, Santuario de Guadalupe and the Paolo Solari amphitheater.

Recent performances include *Guadalupe!,* a musical celebration of the community featuring young performers and a chorus of grandmothers, an evening of cabaret with Amanda McBroom, and an original production of Ariel Dorfman's psychological thriller *Death and the Maiden.* Performances are scheduled year-round and ticket prices range from $20 to $50; for children under 16, tickets are half price, and student discounts are available. A limited number of tickets are available for $8 on the day of a performance.

Actors perform a scene from **Measure for Measure.**

Santa Fe Playhouse
142 E. DeVargas St.
• (505) 984-3055,
(505) 988-4262 (box office)
• www.santafeplayhouse.org

The oldest continuously running theatre company west of the Mississippi, the Santa Fe Playhouse was founded in 1922. The company dedicates itself to presenting works that give voice to New Mexico's varied cultures and communities as envisioned by the founder, Mary Austin, in 1918. The Playhouse offers year-round theatre with musicals, comedies, dramas, murder-mysteries, and classics in the mix. Located three blocks from the Plaza in Santa Fe's ancient Barrio de Analco—one of the oldest neighborhoods in America—the Playhouse theater is an intimate 100-seat historic adobe building.

The Santa Fe Fiesta Melodrama, which pokes fun at the city's events, politicians, celebrities, and quirks in the guise of an old-time melodrama, is the group's best-known production. Other theater groups frequently use this space as well. Tickets for most shows range from $12 to $15, or $10 for senior and students. Admission is $8 on Thursdays, and Sundays are "pay what you wish" performances.

Shakespeare in Santa Fe
Outdoors near the John Gaw
Meem Library, St. John's College,
1160 Camino de la Cruz Blanca
• (505) 982-2910
• www.shakespearesantafe.org

Shakespeare in Santa Fe adds to the city's cultural scene with summertime outdoor performances from the English language's most famous playwright. The company presents two different shows each summer from mid-June to mid-August. Since the company's beginning in 1987 as Shakespeare in the Park, the professional actors and directors have staged a wide selection of the Bard's comedies, tragedies, and romances. Original music and Southwestern settings add to the fun, all under the colorful sunsets and starry skies of the Meem Courtyard at St. John's College, a picturesque setting nestled in the foothills of the Sangre de Cristo Mountains. The company also hosts an intern program that welcomes select high school and college students to work with the performance

and technical aspects of the productions and produce and perform in their own production of an original musical in August. Shakespeare in the Schools, another venture of this company, tours New Mexico schools each year with programs specifically designed to introduce local students to Shakespeare in an entertaining, non-intimidating way.

Tickets range in price from $10 to $28, with two-show discount packages available, and grass seating is always available at no cost for those who might otherwise be unable to attend. The grounds open early for a pre-show Festival Faire, and you can buy dinner from food vendors or bring your own picnic supper. Performances are Friday, Saturday, and Sunday evenings, with additional performances in August. Call for details.

> **INSIDERS' TIP**
>
> The McCune Charitable Foundation, the second-largest grant-making institution in New Mexico, is based in Santa Fe and supports many local arts groups, including the International Folk Art Foundation.

Theater Grottesco
Various venues
• (505) 474-8400

Founded in Paris in 1983, Theater Grottesco began as a touring company and moved to Santa Fe in 1996. They've been busy ever since. In addition to continuing their national tours, the company has become an active player in the city's theatrical world. During their May-June season, Grottesco has produced original full-length plays and short pieces, presenting its work in various performance spaces around town. The company focuses on homegrown talent in terms of writers, actors, and designers and has plans for an expanded season. Ticket prices are in the $15 to $17 range.

Theaterwork
1336 Rufina Cir.
• (505) 471-1799

Theaterwork is a non-profit theater company that offers a season from September through June. Since moving to the Rufina address in 1996, the company has presented 38 full-length productions ranging from the classics and operas to original new works by local playwrights. The theater also hosts play and poetry readings of area writers. The company members offer classes in acting, design, play writing, and story collecting for children and adults. Theaterwork also has a conservatory program for teens who are interested in learning about all aspects of theater. Tickets for most performances are $12 or less.

Visual Arts

Noncommercial Galleries and Museums

(For more information about Santa Fe's museums please see our Attractions chapter.)

College of Santa Fe Fine Arts Gallery
1600 St. Michael's Dr.
• (505) 473-6555

You'll find exhibits by students as well as local, regional, and nationally known artists in this space in the college's Southwest Annex, just across from the Fogelson Library. Among the annual highlights are thesis exhibitions and faculty shows. In October, the gallery features indoor sculptures that are part of the art department's annual Sculpture Project Outside, the campus displays monumental contemporary sculpture throughout the year. Most exhibits open with an artist's reception and usually run for a month. The gallery is normally open Tuesday through Friday from 1 to 5 PM, but extended hours are offered for some exhibits. Admission is free.

In addition to the Fine Arts Gallery, CSF's new $11 million Visual Arts Center houses the Atrium Gallery in the Anne and John Marion Center for Photographic Arts. Designed by renowned Mexican architect Ricardo Legorreta, the Visual Arts complex also includes many courtyard exhibition spaces.

Georgia O'Keeffe Museum
217 Johnson St.
• (505) 995-0785
• www.okeeffemuseum.org/

The Georgia O'Keeffe Museum is America's first museum dedicated to the work of a woman artist of international stature. Georgia O'Keeffe is New Mexico's best-known artist—even people who don't know a pastel from a poster have heard of O'Keeffe and seen reproductions of her famous paintings. O'Keeffe visited New Mexico in 1917 and came here permanently in 1949, settling in an old adobe home in the small village of Abiquiu. She lived there, inspired by the landscape and the light, for nearly 40 years before moving to Santa Fe a few years before her death in 1986 at age 98.

The Georgia O'Keeffe Museum houses the world's largest permanent collection of her work, including many pieces the artist kept for herself and have never been exhibited previously. At the museum, you'll see work O'Keeffe produced between 1916 and 1980. Flowers and bleached desert bones, abstractions, nudes, landscapes, city-scapes, and still lifes are all here. The museum's galleries trace O'Keeffe's artistic evolution follow the depth and breadth of her long, productive career.

As a secondary goal, the museum collects and hosts guest exhibits of works by contemporaries of O'Keeffe who were part of her artistic community. Anne and John Marion, philanthropists who also funded the visual arts center at the College of Santa Fe, endowed the 13,000-square foot museum. The museum offers guided tours, educational programming, and special events. You can watch a short video about O'Keeffe's life and learn about her contribution to American art.

The Georgia O'Keeffe Museum is open 10 AM to 5 PM Tuesdays through Sundays and 10 AM to 8 PM Fridays. It is closed Mondays, New Year's Day, Easter, Thanksgiving, and Christmas. Admission is $5 for a one-day pass and $10 for a four-day, five-museum pass that allows unlimited admission to all museums in the Museum of New Mexico system. Admission is $1 on Sundays for New Mexico residents with ID. Free admission is offered daily to ages 16 and under. Wednesday are free days for New Mexico seniors (60 and older with ID). And Fridays from 5 AM to 8 PM everyone gets in free.

The Governor's Gallery
New Mexico State Capitol, Fourth Floor,
Old Santa Fe Tr. at Paseo de Peralta
• (505) 827-3028

Exhibits here feature New Mexico artists and change with some frequency. Receptions for the artists are always open to the public. These exhibits bring people to the State Capitol and introduce the many Roundhouse visitors and state workers to a wide assortment of visual art. The gallery also hosts an annual ex-

INSIDERS' TIP

For on-line information about Santa Fe's arts groups and an calendar of events go to www.santafe.org/. The Santa Fe Visitors and Convention Bureau maintains the site.

A state supported museum, The Museum of Fine Arts houses works by New Mexico's early artists. Exhibits include early and comtemporary painting, sculpture, and photography.

Photo: Don Strel

hibit of work by the winners of the Governor's Awards for Excellence in the Arts, a program to recognize New Mexican painters, writers, musicians, dancers and others whose creative work makes the state a better place to live. An outreach of the Museum of Fine Arts, the gallery is open 8 AM to 5 PM Monday through Friday. Admission is free.

Institute of American Indian Arts Museum
108 Cathedral Pl.
• (505) 988-6281

American Indian art as an expression of contemporary life—that's one of the underlying themes you'll find in the art displayed here. Or, as the curator of exhibits once said, the museum shows Indian art through Indian eyes. The museum designs its exhibits to give viewers a sense of the appreciation the artists and their communities feel for the works created. With more than 6,500 pieces in the collection representing 3,000 artists, the museum is the largest repository of contemporary Indian art in the world. Paintings, sculpture, and traditional crafts such as beadwork, pottery, weaving, and basketry are displayed in the museum's five galleries. The museum also offers educational programming and the outdoor Allan Houser Art Park for large sculpture.

The museum is in an attractive adobe building that formerly housed Santa Fe's main post office. It is part of the Institute of American Indian Arts which has worked with American Indians and Alaskan Natives here since 1971. (See our Education and Child Care chapter.) Among the teachers and students whose creative talent has put the IAIA on the national map are Houser, Dan Namingha, Estalla Loretto, Linda Lomahaftewa, and T.C. Cannon.

The IAIA Museum is open June through Sept. 9 AM to 5 PM; October through May, 10 AM to 5 PM, Monday through Saturday; Sunday, 12 to 5 PM. Admission is $4 for adults, $2 for seniors and students with an ID, and free for IAIA members and children younger than 16.

The Museum of Fine Arts
107 W. Palace Ave.
• (505) 827-4468
• http://www.museumofnewmexico.org

The Museum of Fine Arts opened in 1917, the second site for the Museum of New Mexico. It played a pivotal role in helping establish Santa Fe as an arts center. Stately and beautiful in classic Pueblo-Revival style, the Museum of Fine Arts isn't just another pretty adobe. The

museum's open-door exhibition policy in the 1920s gave Santa Fe and Taos artists, many of whom had moved here from the Eastern United States, a convenient place to show their work and begin establishing their reputations in the West.

The museum's collections focus mainly on art from the Southwest and New Mexico and include both traditional and contemporary work in a variety of media. You may find on display creations by many well-known artists including the Santa Fe and Taos master painters who first brought the art world's attention to New Mexico. You'll also discover work by Georgia O'Keeffe and Peter Hurd. The museum's galleries change exhibits fairly frequently and usually include provocative work by living artists as well as shows that draw on the collections.

The Museum of Fine Arts' St. Francis Auditorium, with its lovely murals and church-like atmosphere, provides one of the city's most popular venues for musical performances and other productions.

Adult admission is $5 for one day or $10 for a four-day pass that provides unlimited admissions to all branches of The Museum of New Mexico. On Sundays adult admission for New Mexico residents with an ID is $1. From 5 to 8 PM on Fridays, admission is free. The museum is open from 10 AM to 5 PM Tuesday through Sunday and on Friday evenings. It is closed Mondays, New Year's Day, Easter, Thanksgiving, and Christmas.

Museum of Indian Arts and Culture
710 Camino Lejo
•(505) 827-6344
• http://www.miaclab.org/

If you're not used to thinking of historic American Indian pottery, weavings, and the like as "art," the collections on display here will leave you with something to consider.

The museum's pride and joy is its permanent exhibit, "Here, Now and Always," which tells the story of the Native American presence in the Southwest with more than 1,300 objects and a multimedia production. The museum is noted for its prehistoric and historic pottery, basketry, woven fabrics, and jewelry.

In addition to exhibits, the museum has a resource center with looms, magazines, books, maps, and other useful tools.

Adult admission is $5 for one day or $10 for a four-day pass that provides unlimited admissions to all branches of The Museum of New Mexico. On Sundays adult admission for New

Mexico residents with an ID is $1. The museum is open from 10 AM to 5 PM Tuesday through Sunday and on Friday evenings. It is closed Mondays, New Year's Day, Easter, Thanksgiving, and Christmas.

Museum of International Folk Art
706 Camino Lejo
• (505) 827-6350
• http://www.state.nm.us/moifa

Familiarly known as the Folk Art Museum, this is one of the locals' favorite spots to take visitors, including those with children in tow. The museum is the repository for the world's largest collection of international folk art. In the "Multiple Visions: A Common Bond" exhibit, for example, you'll find objects from more than 100 countries displayed in fascinating dioramas. Toys from 19th-century Europe, Chinese prints, embroidered Indian mandalas, Mexican Day of the Dead mementos and examples of early 20th-century Americana are among the treasures. This exhibit alone displays more than 10,000 pieces of folk art, all donated by the Girard Foundation Collection. And you still have the rest of the place to explore!

The Neutrogena Wing houses an impressive array of textiles, costumes, and masks donated by Lloyd Cotsen and the Neutrogena Corporation. Get an up-close look at riches from the collection with a visit to "Lloyd's Treasure Chest," where you will have an opportunity to examine objects and watch the collections staff as they work behind the scenes. Also of special interest here is the Hispanic Heritage Wing which features Spanish Colonial folk art and an interactive computer program in its "Familia y Fe/Family and Faith" exhibit.

The museum hosts changing exhibits and a variety of special events, some ready-made for children and families. Adult admission is $5 for one day or $10 for a four-day pass that provides unlimited admissions to all branches of The Museum of New Mexico. On Sundays adult admission for New Mexico residents with an ID is $1. The museum is open from 10 AM to 5 PM Tuesday through Sunday and on Friday evenings. It's closed Mondays, New Year's Day, Easter, Thanksgiving, and Christmas.

St. John's College Gallery
Second Floor, Peterson Student Center, 1160 Camino de la Cruz Blanca
• (505) 984-6199

This small exhibit space hosts shows from faculty members and artists of national reputation and also promotes local artists. There's an annual student show, judged by members of the college's Fine Arts Guild, as well as an annual juried faculty-and-staff show. The hours

The Passing Storm Navajo Country—*a painting by Gerald Cassidy in the Museum of Fine Arts.*

Photo: Don Strel

fluctuate, but the gallery is normally open from 5 to 8 PM Friday and Saturday and from 1 to 5 PM on Sunday and by appointment. Admission is free.

SITE Santa Fe
1606 Paseo de Peralta
* **(505) 989-1199**
* **www.sitesantafe.org**

Established in 1995, SITE Santa Fe occupies a former warehouse on the edge of the Guadalupe Street neighborhood—a walkable distance from the downtown museums. Created around the concept of the European kunsthalle, this nonprofit visual arts organization, with no permanent collection, has the flexibility to bring important exhibitions and innovative programs to the community in a manner that's both accessible and affordable. Public opening receptions for artists are usually held on Fridays from 5 to 7 PM.

Major exhibits are accompanied by lectures, films, performances, and symposia on similar topics. You may find interactive art, including work that uses cameras and projections, interdisciplinary presentations, focused-theme exhibits, and one-person shows. SITE Santa Fe also produced *Now Eleanor's Idea*, a four part opera that featured lowriders (see our Local Cultures chapter for an explanation of lowriders).

SITE Santa Fe has an international mission and national affiliations as well as strong connections with private galleries and public museums. Go with an open mind! In 1999, SITE Santa Fe presented the third International Biennial: Looking for a Place, which featured 28 artists from 24 countries who created work depicting a sense of place especially for the SITE Santa Fe space. SITE Santa Fe's Fourth International Biennial, a major exhibition of contemporary art, is set to open in the summer of 2001.

The artspace is open Wednesday through Sunday from 10 AM to 5 PM, and Friday from 10 AM to 7 PM. Admission is free on Friday, and on other days it's $5 for adults and $2.50 for seniors, teachers, and students; admission is free to SITE Santa Fe members. Free docent tours are available on Saturdays and Sundays at 2 PMand Fridays at 6 PM. The artspace will gladly offer tours in Spanish by appointment.

Wheelwright Museum of the American Indian
04 Camino Lejo
* **(505) 982-4636, (800) 607-4636**
* **www.wheelwright.org/**

You'll find work by living American Indian artists showcased at this private, not-for-profit institution which is just a short walk away from the Museum of New Mexico's Camino Lejo museum complex. The Wheelwright build-

The Georgia O'Keeffe Museum houses the largest permanent collection of this artist's work. It is the first museum in the United States to honor a woman artist.

Photo: Don Strel

ing itself is part of the joy of being here. The museum was designed by William Penhallow Henderson, a noted Santa Fe painter and architect, to resemble a Navajo hogan, or log home. The entrance faces east, toward the rising sun.

Exhibitions in the main gallery include contemporary and traditional art with an emphasis on the Southwest. A second gallery presents one-person shows, usually with opening receptions where the public can meet the exhibitor. Recent main gallery exhibitions have included contemporary basketry, a recreation of the studio of sculptor Allan Houser, paintings by Harry Fonseca, the art of Pablita Velarde, and contemporary Navajo pictorial weaving. Main gallery exhibitions change twice a year. Smaller galleries feature one-person shows by Native American artists and photographers, or items relating to the main gallery exhibition. The museum and the Case Trading Post museum shop sponsor talks, seminars, meet-the-artist receptions, and other events.

The museum makes good use of the natural beauty of its site and the entrance displays outdoor sculptures by Allan Houser and others. The Wheelwright is open Monday through Saturday from 10 AM to 5 PM and Sunday from 1 to 5 PM. Admission is free. (See our Attractions chapter for more information.)

Private Galleries

Santa Fe has many private galleries where you'll discover an exciting variety of visual arts. What we offer here is just a small sampling of them. Many of the galleries listed here are members of the Santa Fe Gallery Association. Galleries that feature predominately American Indian and/or Hispanic arts are featured in the Regional Arts chapter.

Michael Atkinson Gallery
120 W. San Francisco St.
• **(505) 820-0411**

This gallery, one block west of the Plaza, showcases nationally known watercolorist and sculptor Michael Atkinson. Also displayed are life-size bronzes, landscapes, colorful abstracts

on canvas, carved-wood sculptures, turned-wood vessels, and a large variety of graphics and posters. The gallery is open by appointment only.

Cline Fine Art Gallery
526 Canyon Rd.
• **(505) 982-5328**
• **www.clinefineart.com**

Cline Fine Art specializes in 20th century American art with a focus on early American modernism and regionalism. The gallery exhibits works by Arthur Dove, John Marin, and Joseph Stella, as well as regionalist works by Emil Bisttram, Fremont Ellis, Raymond Jonson, and Alfred Morang. Cline Fine Art also represents a small and distinguished group of contemporary artists including Tony Abeyta, Francisco Benitez, Evelyne Boren, and Jim Vogel. The gallery represents the estates of Alexandre Hogue and of William Lumpkins. You can visit Monday through Saturday from 10 AM to 5 PM and from noon to 4 PM on Sunday.

Dreamtime Gallery
223½ Canyon Rd.
• **(505) 986-0344**
• **www.dreamtimegallery.com**

In business since 1995, this is the only gallery in the United States to exclusively represent Australian Aboriginal art. The exhibits change monthly, selected from the work of more than 100 Australian artists. You can park in front of the gallery. Dreamtime is open Monday through Saturday from 10 AM to 5 PM.

Linda Durham Contemporary Art
Across from the Galisteo Inn, Galisteo
• **(505) 466-6600**
• **www.artnet.com**

Located in the picturesque village of Galisteo, about a half-hour drive from Santa Fe, this gallery shows serious, abstract contemporary New Mexico-based artists. The owner has been in business since 1977, knows her stuff, and is considered a forerunner of contemporary art in New

THE ARTS

Mexico. The gallery is open Tuesday through Saturday from 10 AM to 5 PM.

The Allan Houser Compound
P.O. Box 5217, Santa Fe, NM 87502
- **(505) 471-1528**
- **www.allanhouser.com**

The Allan Houser Compound located 20 minutes south of Santa Fe, features gardens devoted to the presentation of the sculpture of Apache artist Allan Houser, one of the best known American Indian artists in the world. Before his death in 1994, Houser constructed a sculpture studio, visitors center, and sculpture garden. The project has grown and the studio expanded into a complete bronze foundry. The sculpture garden now displays both the family collection of Houser's work and available bronze editions. The 104-acre compound is open by appointment Monday through Saturday year-round except holidays. Tours of the sculpture walk, private family collection and showroom are available to individuals and groups.

Charlotte Jackson Fine Art
200 W. Marcy St., Ste. 101
- **(505) 989-8688**
- **www.charlottejackson.com**

Carving her own niche in Santa Fe's diverse art market, Charlotte Jackson represents "concrete" and radical painters from the United States and Europe. These large monochromatic works are seldom seen in the United States. Sculpture and paintings that focus on the exploration of light and surface are also in the collection. Exhibits rotate throughout the year. The gallery also hosts lectures and sponsors publications. It is open Monday through Friday from 10 AM to 5 PM and Saturday from 11 AM to 4 PM.

LewAllen Contemporary
129 W. Palace Ave.
- **(505) 988-8997**
- **www.lewallenart.com**

One of the largest contemporary galleries in the Southwest, with more than 10,000 square feet of exhibit space, LewAllen hosts monthly rotating exhibitions of contemporary artworks in all media by regionally, nationally and internationally celebrated artists. You'll see are works by Forest Moses, John Fincher, Emmi Whitehorse, and Judy Chicago. The gallery has been in Santa Fe since 1977. It's open Monday through Saturday from 9:30 AM to 5:30 PM. In July and August the gallery is open on Sunday.

The Marcus Gallery
213 Galisteo St.
- **(505) 982-936**
- **www.marcusgallery.com**

Since 1983 this gallery has offered a carefully chosen selection of contemporary and tra-

Film productions is one of the core industries in Santa Fe.

Photo: J.B. Smith

ditional art, exhibiting 20 recognized and emerging artists working in media ranging from watercolor and oil to bronze and clay. You'll find high quality fine art, equitable prices and exemplary customer service here. The gallery represents Nelson Boren, James Roybal, Mikki Senkarik, and Walker Moore, among others. It's open Monday through Saturday from 10 AM to 5:30 PM and on Sunday from 11 AM to 4 PM during the summer.

Nedra Matteucci Galleries
1075 Paseo de Peralta
• **(505) 982-4631**
• **www.matteucci.com**

You'll discover contemporary and historic art in this sprawling gallery, along with a variety of Native American antiquities and Spanish Colonial furniture. The gallery features paintings from California regionalists and work by the Hudson River, Ashcan, and Brandywine schools. And New Mexico isn't ignored; you'll find first-rate, museum-quality bronzes and paintings by the Santa Fe and Taos artists who put New Mexico on the cultural map more than 50 years ago. The gallery displays work by Joseph H. Sharp, E. Martin Hennings, Walter Ufer, Victor Higgins, Nicolai Fechin, Leon Gaspard, and Fremont Ellis. Outside, monumental sculpture by Dan Ostermiller, Glenna Goodacre, and many others is featured in the gallery's beautifully landscaped garden, complete with a large pond. The gallery is open Monday through Saturday from 8:30 AM to 5 PM. Nedra Matteucci Galleries, formerly Fenn Gallery, has been in business for more than 25 years. You can park in front of the gallery.

Meredith-Kelly Latin American Art
135 W. Palace Ave.
• **(505) 986-8699**

This gallery specializes in Latin American masters and contemporary Latin sculptors, including Diego Rivera, Francisco Zuniga, and Rodolfo Morales. There's no other like it in Santa Fe. Call for hours.

Leslie Muth Gallery
221 E. DeVargas St.
• **(505) 989-4620**

In business since 1980, this gallery represents outsider, visionary, and self-

taught contemporary American artists with an emphasis on Southwest artists such as Nicholas Herrera. Navajo folk art is also included among the exhibits. The gallery is open by appointment only.

Gerald Peters Gallery
1011 Paseo de Peralta
• **(505) 954-5700**
• **http://www.gpgallery.com**

For some 25 years the Gerald Peters Gallery has been a must-see destination for serious art lovers, first in its historic Canyon Road home and now in larger, grander headquarters. Dedicated to the research, exhibition, and sale of important American paintings of the 19th and 20th centuries, Peters' well-designed 32,000-square-foot gallery space puts many museums to shame.

When it opened in August 1998, Gerald Peters gallery was heralded by the *Dallas Morning News* as a symbol of new vitality in the Santa Fe art world. More than 9,000 people passed through opening weekend. Located downtown near Canyon Road, the gallery was designed in traditional Pueblo style, with a lush sculpture garden, attractive landscaping, and 8,500 square feet of museum-quality exhibition space.

Beginning with his interest in art of the American West, Peters built a collection centered around the Taos Founders and the Santa Fe art colony and included the artists of classic Western painting and sculpture. In addition to these works, the gallery also displays American Impressionists, American Modernists (including Georgia O'Keeffe), abstract expressionists, contemporary realists, contemporary sculpture, and vintage and contemporary photography.

The gallery is open Monday through Saturday, 10 AM to 5 PM. The adjoining lot offers ample parking.

Peyton Wright Gallery
237 East Palace Ave.
• **(505) 989-9888 or (800) 879-8898**

Peyton Wright Gallery, located in the historic Spiegelberg house at the corner of Palace Avenue at Paseo de Peralta, features both contemporary and historic works of art. You find extensive offerings of

Spanish Colonial, African, Russian, Native American and Pre-Colombian art and antiquities in an ambience of museum quality. Exhibitions change monthly and include contemporary painting, sculpture, and works on paper by emerging, mid- and late career artists of both national and international repute. Established in 1989, the gallery is open Monday through Saturday from 9 AM to 5 PM and Sunday by appointment.

Reflection Gallery
201 Canyon Rd.
• **(505) 995-9795**
This gallery is at the base of Canyon Road in a 75-year-old adobe home. It features traditional, realist, and impressionist works by artists such as Dalhart Windberg, Vladimir Naso-nov, Robert Cook, Jan Saia, Yuri Novikov, and Jei Wei Zhou. Patrons can park in the rear. The galley is open daily from 10 AM to 5:30 PM.

Running Ridge Gallery
640 Canyon Rd.
• **(505) 988-2515**
A contemporary fine crafts and fine-art gallery, Running Ridge exhibits art works in ceramics, fiber, glass, metal, and wood, as well as paintings, prints, sculpture, jewelry, and lovely handcrafted vessels. Of the 100 artists represented in the gallery, James Lovera, jeweler Carolyn Morris Bach, and glass artist Hiroshi Yamano are included. Fabric-collage artist Amanda Richardson is shown, along with the original characters of Laidman Dogs by Roberta Laidman. In an adobe building more than a century old, the gallery has had the same owners since 1979. Special arrangements can be made for parking on pre-mises; call in advance. There's a handicapped parking space in front of the gallery. Running Ridge is open Monday through Saturday from 10 AM to 5 PM. The gallery is also open Friday nights until 7 PM in the summer and fall and for special holidays. Sunday hours are noon to 5 PM.

Laurel Seth Gallery
1121 Paseo de Peralta
• **(505) 988-7349**
• **www.sethgallery.com**
Laurel Seth Gallery continues a 20-year tradition of presenting outstanding

Southwestern art. Featured artists include Vallerie Graves, Geoffrey Landis, Angie Coleman, Teresa Archuleta-Sagel, and many more. The intimate gallery also specializes in the work of early Taos and Santa Fe artists. Openings here are festive, cozy affairs. Parking is available behind the gallery. It's open from 1 to 5 PM Tuesday through Saturday.

Andrew Smith Gallery Inc.
203 W. San Francisco St.
• **(505) 984-1234**
Andrew Smith Gallery has an exclusive focus on fine American photography and has been in business for 25 years. You'll discover a broad and deep selection of work by the major photographers of the 19th and 20th centuries. The gallery carries original classic photography of the American West by E.S. Curtis, Charles Lummis, and others—along with work by Ansel Adams, Eliot Porter, Edward Weston, and more. The gallery is open Monday through Saturday from 10 AM to 5:30 PM and Sunday from noon to 4 PM.

Support Organizations

New Mexico Arts
La Villa Rivera Building, 228 E. Palace Ave.
• **(505) 827-6490**
• **www.nmarts.org**
New Mexico Arts, an arm of state government, offers many resources for artists and arts organizations, from grants to tips on networking and other types of technical assistance. The division supports programs throughout New Mexico and has been zealous in its determination to spread the state's artistic wealth among smaller communities. Major programs include Arts in Public Places, which allocates one percent of building funds for public art in public buildings, and programs that use artists, musicians, writers, and actors to teach art, music, writing, and drama in New Mexico schools. The agency also administers The Governor's Awards for Excellence in the Arts, a tradition since

INSIDERS' TIP
Santa Fe will have a new performing arts space in the spring/summer of 2001. The Lensic Performing Arts Center, 211 W. San Francisco St., will be the reincarnation of an old downtown movie house that originally opened in 1931 as a vaudeville theater. A nonprofit corporation expects to spend some $7.5 million on the project. The new center will house eight local arts groups as well as touring performers, meetings and other activities.

1974. Awards have gone to New Mexico artists working in all media and honorees include Georgia O'Keeffe, potter María Martínez, playwright Mark Medoff, author Tony Hillerman, and visual artists Fritz Scholder, Luis Jimenez, and Allan Houser. New Mexico Arts is part of the state's Office of Cultural Affairs.

Santa Fe Arts Commission
120 S. Federal Pl.
- **(505) 955-6707**
- **www.ci.santa-fe.nm.us/arts**

This arm of city government administers grants to local nonprofit arts and cultural groups, commissions artworks for city-owned facilities, and advocates for arts education in the public schools. In collaboration with local arts organizations, it also offers professional development for teachers. The Commission provides general information on Santa Fe–area arts activities and publishes a good list of arts and crafts shows.

Santa Fe Council for the Arts
P.O. Box 8921, Santa Fe, NM 87504
- **(505) 424-1878**

A grassroots organization composed mainly of visual artists, the Santa Fe Council for the Arts produces fine arts exhibitions, including the summer New Mexico Arts Market in Cathedral Park, and an annual Our Lady of Guadalupe exhibit. The group also produces workshops, and an annual lecture series titled, "A Dialogue Among Peers," where artists discuss the creative process. The nonprofit organization began in 1978 and has about 400 members.

Santa Fe Gallery Association
P.O. Box 9248, Santa Fe, NM 87504
- **(505) 982-1648**

The Santa Fe Gallery Association is dedicated to supporting the artistic and cultural heritage of the greater Santa Fe area by striving to improve the business conditions for Santa Fe galleries and art dealers. The association provides a forum for communication between galleries and art dealers and supports charitable organizations and causes directly related to the arts. The Association's primary charity, ARTsmart, raises funds for art supplies for Santa Fe's elementary school children.

The Natural Environment

Santa Fe's charm begins with the sky.

On a July afternoon, for instance, you can watch the thunderheads build, a symphony of towering clouds sometimes accompanied by a wispy chorus of higher, drier formations.

These billowing clouds that create Santa Fe's summer thunderstorms also bring incredibly rich sunsets. It's not unusual to see cars pulled to the side of U.S. Highway 84-285 near the Old Taos Highway or along Artist Road. People park, climb out, and look westward, watching the sky change minute by minute. Sunsets confound the eyes with a palette of color—pinks and oranges, magentas and golds, lilacs, and vivid reds.

Winter skies can be equally startling. After a February snowstorm, for instance, the brilliant blue of the heavens is as intense as the turquoise the Indians sell under the portal along the Plaza. The snow glistens like spun glass in the intensity of the sun's light. To the east, the frosted Sangre de Cristos shine a brilliant white against a cloudless blue backdrop.

The night sky weaves its own magic. Go outside on a moonless evening and look up. When your eyes adjust, you'll see layer on layer of sparkling stars, planets, and constellations. If you watch a little longer, you may see meteors, passing satellites, and the blinking red lights of planes on their way to Los Angeles or Denver. Some nights the sky looks black; other times it's a deep indigo.

The natural environment makes Santa Fe special. The skies, the mountains, the beauty of the place, take people by surprise.

Climate and Weather

At an elevation of 7,000 feet, Santa Fe is the highest state capital in the United States. The air is clear here, thanks to the economic base of tourism and government, and the sun shines at least part of the day 300 days a year.

Average temperatures range from a low of 4 in January to a high of 91 in July and August. It's not uncommon for evening temperatures to drop below zero in the winter and for the heat to soar into the mid-90s in the summer, but such extremes tend to last only a day or two. Few traditional Santa Fe homes have air conditioning. If you keep the windows closed during the heat of the day and let the cool evening air come in, you'll be comfortable most of the time. Even in summer, nighttime temperatures may dip into the 40s. And the dryness makes summer's warm days easier to take. Humidity usually registers at 50 percent or less.

Most summers, the thunderstorms begin around the Fourth of July and continue through August. This isn't constant rain. The clouds start to build in late morning, clumps of thunderheads piling like cotton candy atop the Sangre de Cristos and Jemez Mountains. By late afternoon, lightning may bounce from one cloud to the next, making them glow as if under strobe lights. Great spear-shaped flashes or slender slivers of energy crack toward the ground. The show can go on for hours. New Mexico and Florida lead the nation as lightning centers, but this is a dangerous beauty. Lightning strikes start several forest fires near Santa Fe each summer and occasionally kill hikers.

Spring is the worst time for fires here, especially after a dry winter. In May 2000, the Santa Fe National Forest and the community of Los Alamos, a 45-minute drive from the Santa Fe Plaza, were devastated by the worst fire in New Mexico's history. The blaze destroyed 260 homes, forced the evacuation of 18,000 people, and left tens of thousands of acres of forest charred and blackened.

INSIDERS' TIP

Want to see the stars? The city and county of Santa Fe have ordinances to help by restricting light pollution in order to keep the night sky bright. If you want an even sharper view, head up Hyde Park Road to further diminish the city's glare.

In an average summer, Santa Fe gets about 14 inches of rain—as much as might fall in Houston in a single stormy weekend. The rest of Santa Fe's precipitation comes in six or eight major winter snowstorms. Average total snowfall in town is 2 to 3 feet. The snow usually melts after a few days, (10 inches of snow equals about 1 inch of water) but accumulates to greater depths in the mountains. The Santa Fe Ski Area reports an average snowfall of 210 inches a year. Much to the delight of skiers, snow here tends to be light powder (see our chapter on Winter Sports).

New Mexico is one of the nation's driest states because of its inland location. In the summer, storms born over the Pacific Ocean or in the Gulf of Mexico have a long trajectory across dry land areas before they reach Santa Fe. In the winter, most Pacific storms that head eastward across the United States pass too far north to have much impact here.

Despite its southerly latitude—about the same as that of Casablanca and Baghdad—Santa Fe is colder in the winter and the summer than one might expect because of the influence of elevation on temperature. Hotel concierges tell stories of January visitors who come with shorts

THE NATURAL ENVIRONMENT

From the 6,000-foot valley floor to the 12,000-foot peaks, the climate and seasons are very much a part of the Santa Fe scene.

Photo: Don Strel

and tennis rackets instead of the appropriate skis and parkas. Sometimes by late February, however, you can enjoy both sports in the same day.

As the snow melts in the mountains the Santa Fe River, usually a tiny trickle, becomes a rushing creek. Some years, it's even stocked with fish for a weekend or two, to the delight of local children. The acequias, a system of irrigation ditches that date to Spanish times, flow with springtime water that residents who have access divert to their gardens.

The Landscape

Technically, Santa Fe sits on the edge of the Transition or Mountain life zone and the Upper Sonoran life zone. "Life zones" describe variations in living conditions caused by elevation and temperature. Each zone has distinctive plants and animals. New Mexico has six of the seven recognized life zones, missing only the lowest tropical zone. This means the variety of plants and animals that can live in the state is virtually unsurpassed.

The Sangre de Cristo Mountain Range, which rises from Santa Fe's backyard, is the southernmost portion of the Rocky Mountains. The mountains lie to the northeast of town, providing a good point of orientation. The name Sangre de Cristo means "Blood of Christ."

First-time visitors, especially those who expected Santa Fe to resemble the prairie, find the mountains something to write home about. Artists often delight in the contrast between the blue slopes of the Sangres and the dusty tan look of the town. The collection at the Museum of Fine Arts includes many paintings that depict the Sangre de Cristos and their gentle foothills.

If you drive up into the Sangres and ride the chairlift to the top of Aspen Peak, you'll look out on a panoramic view with the town of Santa Fe far below. The Sandia Mountains near Albuquerque, the Ortiz Range with their gold-mining scars, and the gentle Cerrillos Hills rise to the southwest. To the north, you can see San Antonio Peak, a rounded blue mass on the Colorado border.

To the west on a clear day you can see the ancient volcanic Mount Taylor rising to 11,300 feet. This place plays a major role in the origin stories of the Navajo Indians. Closer lies another volcanic range, the Jemez Mountains, which were home to the ancestors of some of New Mexico's Pueblo Indians. Volcanic Black Mesa, a striking, square-shaped formation beloved by many of the Rio Grande Pueblo people, stands in dark contrast to the reddish hues of the Rio Grande Valley.

INSIDERS' TIP

The Lamy Garden, next to the Archdiocese of Santa Fe Museum, 223 Cathedral Place, is part of the museum's program and reminiscent of the garden originally established by Archbishop Jean Lamy. Lamy's spring-watered, four-acre plot produced vegetables, fruit trees, and flowers. The pond, which is now gone, covered half an acre. Lamy's flowers included French lilacs started from cuttings the bishop himself brought from France. In 1995, the last of the trees Lamy planted were removed. Pine, apple, almond, and apricot trees—some dead, some diseased—were replaced by bing cherry, pine trees, and others. The wood was given to local wood carvers.

Vegetation

At the ski area, besides the stunning views, you'll notice ponderosa pine, spruce, aspen, columbine, wild strawberries, and other plants suited to the cooler, damper climate at 12,000 feet. As you head down toward Santa Fe through the Santa Fe National Forest and Hyde State Park, the vegetation changes. In less than 20 minutes, you're in the warmer, drier piñon/juniper zone. Natural vegetation throughout most of the county includes ricegrass, sagebrush, and western wheatgrass. You don't have to be a botanist to notice that all the plants here are not cactus!

Piñon, a small pine tree, produces edible nuts popular among both animals and humans. Junipers have purple berries that attract birds. Both common in the Santa Fe area, they are tough, slow-growing evergreens. They tolerate heat and below-freezing temperatures and, once established, survive in a climate where rain is always a blessing. They grow slowly. A 12-foot piñon tree may be 100 years old; piñon can live up to 400 years. Piñon trees alive today were growing when the Spanish occupied the city of Santa Fe. Some people use juniper in their fireplaces; it's a slow-burning wood with a wonderful, crisp aroma.

Because of the elevation, wildflowers of the Santa Fe area have more in common with those of southern Colorado than with their Albuquerque cousins just 60 miles south. You'll find the vivid blue of delicate-looking flax, the deep purple, scarlet and pale pink penstemon, the white blooms and feathery seeds of Apache plume and cheery orange and red blanket flowers. In the fall, watch for the brilliant yellow of the chamiso framed by pale purple wild asters. And the aspen trees in the Sangres and the Jemez Mountains put on a wonderful golden show beginning in mid-to-late September.

Santa Fe is a four-season city. You can feel the stirring of spring as early as February, even though the last snowstorm often comes in May, burying the daffodils and covering the apricot blossoms. If the snow has been deep or the city gets spring rain, tulips and hyacinth, fruit trees, and iris bloom in abundance. New Mexico's state flower, the yucca, grows in and around Santa Fe. Yuccas generally begin to bloom in May. The large, bell-shaped flowers rise in magnificent showy overstatement. You may notice the cream-colored display as you drive along Interstate 25 between Santa Fe and Albuquerque.

Just before summer hits in full force comes the sweet smell of Russian olive blossoms, tiny yellow flowers among greenish-gray leaves. Wisteria and lilacs flourish, and migrating hummingbirds return. Native grasses turn green. The cholla cactus explodes with magenta blossoms.

Santa Fe does have big trees like cities elsewhere. Walk along the Santa Fe River, for instance, and you'll see towering cottonwoods, trees so big it takes two adults holding hands to encircle their trunks. Fruit trees, especially those bred to bloom late, thrive in backyards and in orchards where they get the water they need. Water always makes the difference.

Landscaping designed to conserve water is called xeriscaping, and you'll see many lovely examples of it in Santa Fe. While gardeners may not be able to grow the same things they did in Topeka

The high county provides a close and quiet refuge from city life.

Photo: Don Strel

Don't Let Altitude and Allergies Get You Down

When some people talk about how Santa Fe takes their breath away, they mean it literally.

Because Santa Fe is perched at 7,000 feet the air is thinner here. Your lungs and heart have to work harder to do their jobs, and the result can be headaches, lack of energy, nausea, nosebleeds, and other uncomfortable symptoms. People with chronic illnesses such as heart disease or high blood pressure need to pay close attention to how they feel here; if you have any questions about the effect altitude may have on your health, ask your doctor.

Another thing that may leave you breathless is allergies. While Santa Fe ranks low in visible air pollution, the pollen from native plants such as juniper, elms, sage, and cottonwood can make your throat scratch, your eyes itch, and your nose run.

Since more visitors are likely to notice the altitude, we'll talk about that first.

Altitude

Altitude sickness is odd in its unpredictability. A healthy 20-something person may be slowed down here for a few days; another who might be older and not in the best of shape could notice nothing. Travelers who live at an elevation of 3,000 feet or lower may be listless and headachy, dizzy or light-headed, and have trouble falling asleep or staying that way. More serious symptoms of altitude sickness include appetite loss, nausea, vomiting, heart palpitations or a pounding pulse, congested lungs, and trouble breathing. All this signifies that your body hasn't adjusted to life in the high country.

There are some things you can do.

Before you come, try to get enough rest, drink plenty of fluids, and eat a diet higher in protein.

Give your body extra time to adjust. If you're flying to New Mexico from Los Angeles or Houston, you might consider spending a night in Albuquerque. At roughly 5,000 feet, Albuquerque treats you a little more gently. It's a good place to let your system begin to adapt.

Take it easy. Don't exercise vigorously until you've adjusted to the altitude. If you feel like a nap in the afternoon, indulge yourself.

Drink plenty of water. Beside being thin, the air here is dry. Dehydration will only add to your discomfort.

Stay at this elevation until you feel better instead of going higher. If you leave Santa Fe for a drive to see the aspens or go skiing, expect the symptoms to worsen.

In addition to altitude sickness, higher altitudes also mean more solar radiation and a decreased tolerance for alcohol. People who study these things say one drink at 7,000 feet is the equivalent of three at sea level. So remember your hat and sunscreen when you sit on the patio, and slowly sip your afternoon Margarita.

Most people adjust to the altitude in a few days. If you stay in Santa Fe long enough you'll notice a pleasant side-effect when you return to sea level. You may have more energy for a day or two.

Santa Fe is always in color, from springtime blossoms of cherry and lilac to the changing of the aspen in the fall.

Photo: Don Strel

Allergies

The body's reaction to pollen is just as unpredictable as its response to altitude. About 1 in 20 people is allergic to pollen of some sort. If you move to a different climate, doctors say it usually takes about two years to develop new sensitivity to native plants. Many people who are not initially allergic find they develop allergies after living here a while—sometimes after 20 or 25 years.

A person who's allergic responds to pollen by acting as if the pollen were a virus. Juniper, one of the area's most annoying pollens, usually begins to bother people in February and continues for several weeks. Other pollens that aggravate come from elm and cottonwood trees, ragweed, and native grass. The good news? Most people are not allergic to the flowers here. And Santa Fe usually ranks low in mold spores because of our dry climate.

If pollen here catches you off guard, there are things you can do besides reach for the antihistamines:

Most pollen is released in the morning. If you can plan your activities so you aren't outside early you'll lessen your exposure. What a great excuse to sleep late!

Wind is the enemy. Stay out of it.

Besides giving you shade from Santa Fe's intense sun, sunglasses help keep pollen out of your eyes.

A change in elevation may help. The plants that grow near the ski area differ from those you'll find at the rodeo grounds.

Santa Fe has a wealth of natural food stores that sell herbal remedies. Ask the staff what they recommend to take the discomfort away.

or San Diego, hundreds of plants thrive in cultivation despite low rainfall and the city's restrictions on watering.

If you're interested in native plants and how to grow them, visit a Santa Fe nursery. Most sell attractive and hardy flowers, shrubs, trees, and grasses that survive just fine without much water. You can also take a look at the xeriscape demonstration gardens at Santa Fe Greenhouses, 2904 Rufina Street, (505) 473-2700. Santa Fe Botanical Gardens, with offices at the Community College, (505) 438-1684, offers tours of established gardens and workshops for gardeners from beginners to experts. The Santa Fe Botanical Garden's Leonora Curtin Natural History Area, south of Santa Fe in La Cienega, is a 35-acre preserve and one of the few relatively intact example of riparian vegetation left in New Mexico. The area's bird list includes 128 species; you might see red-tailed hawks, wintering duck, crows, jays and magpies, northern flickers and ladder-backed woodpeckers, black-capped chickadees, bushtits, towhees, juncos, and various sparrows. Some 34 species of butterfly have been spotted there along with 200 different plants. Please call (505) 428-1684 for information.

Birds and Animals

One of your best resources for learning about the birds and animals that live here is the Randall Davey Audubon Center, less than 4 miles from the Plaza (see our Attractions chapter). While hiking along the center's trails, bird-watchers have identified more than 140 species of birds, ranging from hawks to hummingbirds.

The big birds with iridescent blue wings that you'll see commonly in Santa Fe are piñon jays. In the fall, they scout the foothills in noisy flocks, looking for their favorite meal, the rich nuts of the piñon trees. Colorful northern flickers, several types of swallows, ravens, mountain chickadees, and robins all are common here. You'll find cottontail rabbits, jack rabbits, coyotes, squirrels, skunks, and several kinds of lizards here too. You probably won't see a rattlesnake, unless you're hiking outside of town in rocky areas. (Despite their reputation, rattlers tend to be shy creatures. If you leave them alone, they'll return the favor and continue to do their part to keep the rodent population in check.)

The Public Service Company of New Mexico gave the Randall Davey Audubon Center and the people of the southwest a wonderful gift in 1999—a 190acre nature preserve adjacent to the center's existing property. The land, which had been part of the Santa Fe Canyon Watershed, will be available for hiking, bird watching and other activities.

INSIDERS' TIP
In August, Santa Fe Greenhouses sponsor the annual Hummingbird and Butterfly Festival. As part of the festival, the nursery spotlights those plants that attract these visitors. Common hummingbirds in northern New Mexico include the rufous and the blackchin.

You won't have to look far in Santa Fe to find one animal you may not be used to seeing—the prairie dog. Related to ground squirrels and marmots, prairie dogs eat roots and seeds and live in burrows underground in vacant lots around Santa Fe. The sentry dogs stand on their hind feet at the edge of the burrows, watching for danger or, maybe, enjoying the view. Prairie dogs communicate with different barks and warn each other of an advancing owl or a coyote. When a person approaches, the little tan creatures disappear with a flick of their short black tails.

A large colony of prairie dogs lives on the city-owned railyard property, and you may spot them near the railroad tracks just west of Cerrillos Road between Guadalupe Street and St. Francis Drive. The Jackalope store, 2820 Cerillos Road, (505) 471-8539, has a Prairie Dog Village on its grounds (see our Shopping chapter). A few years ago, the animals claimed squatters' rights to the DeVargas Junior High School athletic field. Volunteers from Prairie Dog Rescue relocated as many of the critters as they could catch and the holes were filled, saving students from the possibility of broken legs. A prairie dog is depicted as part of the statue honoring St. Francis, the patron saint of Santa Fe, downtown in front of City Hall.

Parks and Recreation

From birding to whitewater rafting, baseball to volleyball, disc golf to Ultimate Frisbee, Santa Fe either has it or can get you to it with little fuss. Santa Fe city and county are veritable playgrounds for the young and old, the rich and the poor, the active and the sedentary. You'll find an abundance of city parks here, many with athletic fields, some just for sitting back and taking in the sunshine. We have a national forest in our backyard with literally dozens of hiking trails ranging from easy to strenuous. And there's biking galore, each hairpin turn yielding magnificent vistas. Santa Fe is a gateway to world class hunting and trout-filled streams that draw anglers like iron to magnets. If hot-air ballooning is your passion, you're just an hour away from one of the best places in the world to do it—Albuquerque, home of the International Balloon Fiesta.

From A to Z—well, okay, B to W—we've included in this chapter a good-sized sampling of what Santa Fe and environs have to offer in the way of public lands as well as indoor and outdoor recreation. A mere glance through this chapter ought to convince even the most-die-hard couch potatoes to put down the television remote and explore Santa Fe's recreational bounty.

LOOK FOR:
• City Parks
• State Parks
• National Parks
• Recreation

City Parks

The City of Santa Fe maintains 50 parks on more than 400 acres, including 235 acres of manicured grounds. Some city parks offer extensive facilities and organized activities such as sports, community events, and holiday festivities. Others offer little more than a bench or two, some grass, perhaps a sculpture, and a quiet, restful place to eat lunch, paint a picture, or contemplate your navel. Whatever you fancy, there's a park in town to meet your needs and desires. For a list of all city parks, call the City of Santa Fe Parks and Recreation Department, Parks Division, at (505) 955-2106.

The Plaza
63 Lincoln Ave.

Not simply located in the heart of downtown Santa Fe, the Plaza is the heart of downtown Santa Fe. Without a doubt, it's the most popular of all city parks. Adult readers of the Santa Fe Reporter have consistently voted the Plaza the best place to bring visitors, walk dogs, people-watch, spot celebrities, or simply "hang out." It's also the choice spot to begin and/or end parades, make speeches, hold community festivals and dances, play Hacky Sack, or take a noon-time snooze, if you can wrangle one of the white-painted wrought iron benches for yourself.

Salvador Perez Park
601 Alta Vista St.
• (505) 955-2604

Kids have voted Salvador Perez their favorite city park in the Santa Fe Reporter's annual "Best of Santa Fe" survey. Maybe it's the imposing, authentic locomotive car on the centrally located property. Perhaps it's the recently renovated indoor heated pool. Or it could be the park's cool new playground with lots of equipment made from recyclables. There's also a Little League field with tons of room to run and jump—enough even for grown-ups, who borrow the field in summer for mush ball. With several tennis courts, volleyball courts, barbecue grills, and lots of picnic tables, Salvador Perez is an ideal spot for a family outing.

Alto Park and Bicentennial Pool
1043 Alto St.
• (505) 955-2650

Located next door to the City of Santa Fe Division of Senior Services and the Mary Esther Gonzales Senior Center, Alto Bicentennial Park and Pool has something for everyone: Little League; Young American Football for kids 13 and under; noon-time mushball for city, county, and state employees; tennis courts for whoever gets there first; and, of course, the pool. Open Monday through Friday from 6 AM to 3 PM and 3:30 PM to 8:30 PM and weekends from 9 AM to 7 pm, the Bicentennial Pool reserves weekday mornings and evenings for lap swims with group and recreational swimming in between. On weekends, recreational swimming is the order of the day, except for the first swim of the morning. The tot pool stays open all day for recreational swimming. Parents who like to swim with their kids will be happy to know that children in diapers must wear water-proof diapers and rubber pants.

Fort Marcy Complex
490 Washington Ave.
• (505) 955-2500

Among the most heavily frequented parks in Santa Fe—after the Plaza, of course—is Fort Marcy Complex. Located in downtown Santa Fe just a few blocks north of the Plaza, Fort Marcy features a large indoor/outdoor recreation center with a ballpark and other outdoor fields, an indoor heated pool, a gym and weight room, racquetball courts, and a jogging/walking path. It also offers a wide variety of classes from swimming and aerobics to dancing and martial arts. The complex is open weekdays from 6 AM to 8:30 PM and 8 AM to 6:30 PM on weekends. Fort Marcy is also the site of the burning of Zozobra—"Old Man Gloom"–at the end of fiestas in September. (See our Annual Events chapter for details.)

Franklin E. Miles Park
1027 Camino Carlos Rey at Siringo Rd.

The city's largest park, Franklin E. Miles offers a wide variety of facilities including softball

fields, soccer fields, basketball and volleyball courts, an enormous playground, barbecue grills, plenty of picnic tables, and good lighting at night.

Herb Martinez Park
2240 Camino Carlos Rey

Herb Martinez is another well-used park with good sports facilities. Its soccer fields serve school and youth leagues from March through November. The park also features softball fields, tennis courts, basketball courts, a small playground, barbecue grills, and tables.

Ragle Park
Zia Rd. and Yucca St.

Ragle Park, in a residential area near Santa Fe High School, has the largest adult softball complex in Santa Fe. See our Softball section for details. The park also contains a decent playground, perfect for softball players with little ones in tow.

Passive Parks

Cornell Park/Rose Garden
1203 Galisteo Parkway

While you can find an appropriate spot in any park to celebrate a quiet moment, some are more conducive than others to meditation and aloneness. Among them is Cornell Park, a lovely refuge from the world located a couple of miles south of downtown Santa Fe. A small park—it's about as wide and as long as a city block—in a residential neighborhood, the Rose Garden is aptly named for the rose bushes that come to life in spring and summer, scenting the air with their fragrant blossoms. The promenade is lined with old trees, making it a favorite among dogs and their owners.

Amelia E. White Park
981 Old Santa Fe Trail

Sitting prettily at the crossroads of Camino Corrales and Old Santa Trail—mere blocks from the Wheelwright Museum of the American Indian, the Museum of Indian Arts and Culture, and the Museum of International Folk Art—Amelia E. White Park is an ideal spot for a picnic lunch or simply to relax and enjoy the day. You might even catch a painter in action as you sit under a grape arbor admiring the sky.

Tom Macaione (Hillside) Park
301 E. Marcy St.

Despite its location along heavily trafficked

Paseo de Peralta, Tom Macaione Park is a little oasis of greenery among a long line of low-slung adobe or faux-adobe buildings. If you're willing to walk the three short blocks northeast of the Plaza, you're likely to have this tiny park, also called Hillside Park, all to yourself—or nearly almost any time of year except summer. Then it's put to good use by Girls Inc. (see our Kidstuff chapter) next door. Otherwise, you'll probably share it only with a bronze sculpture of the much-loved, eccentric, impressionist painter for whom the park is named. Macaione died a few years ago and the town is still mourning his passing.

East Santa Fe River Park
726 E. Alameda St.

Located only a few blocks south of the Plaza, East Santa Fe River Park is a lovely, narrow stretch of land that begins in front of the Supreme Court Building at Don Gaspar Avenue and continues for about a mile to East Palace Avenue. The park offers shaded, tree-lined walkways and picnic tables along the banks of the Santa Fe River, attracting local and visiting brown-bag diners when the weather permits.

State Parks

Hyde Memorial State Park
740 Hyde Park Road
• (505) 983-7175

Located 12 miles northeast of Santa Fe and a mere three miles below the Santa Fe Ski Basin, Hyde Memorial State Park contains 350 beautiful acres filled with Ponderosa pine, aspen, and meadows at an elevation of 8,500 feet. It's a favorite among locals for hiking and picnicking and a popular base for backpackers heading into the Pecos Wilderness. The park's campground accommodates both RVs and tents and provides drinking water and toilet facilities, but not showers. However, for $1.85, you can shower at Fort Marcy (see entry later in this chapter) and even get in a swim, if you're so inclined.

National Parks

New Mexico is a veritable outdoor paradise with stunningly beautiful public lands, many of them wild and woolly, some of them tame and comfortable. Santa Fe, which is surrounded by more than 3 million acres of public forest, is a doorway to many of these. In fact, nearly half the state's national wilderness areas are in north central New Mexico. These include the popular Pecos Wilderness—233,333 scenic acres featuring some of the state's highest peaks, glacial lakes, and 150 miles of rivers and streams; the 5,200-acre Dome Wilderness adjacent to the Bandelier Wilderness in Bandelier National Monument (see entry below) and providing access to the canyonlands as well as 8,200-feet-high St. Peter's Dome; and the lesser known—and lesser used—San Pedro Parks Wilderness northeast of Cuba, New Mexico, with 41,132 spectacular acres of aspen, evergreen forest, and meadows and altitudes reaching into the 10,000-foot range. Sadly, all are recovering from recent devastating wildfires that burned close to 90,000 acres. Call or visit the Public Lands Information Center, 1474 Rodeo Road, (505) 438-7542, for information about conditions, closures, and fire regulations.

These and a fourth wilderness area—the Chama River Canyon Wilderness—are located within the Santa Fe National Forest whose more than 1.5 million acres comprise some of the finest mountain scenery in the Southwest. They offer 1,000 miles of mapped trails, 620 miles of trout streams, abundant hunting, camping, picnicking, skiing, and scenic drives where you'll experience mile-after-mile of breathtaking beauty. The Rio Grande divides the Santa Fe National Forest into two distinct sections. To the west lie the Jémez Mountains, a canyon- and mesa-filled range with elevations from 5,300 feet in White Rock Canyon to 12,000 feet at the summit of Chicoma Peak. It's in this section that you'll find the Dome and San Pedro Parks wilderness areas as well as Valle Grande—an immense grassy depression that represents only a portion of the 14-mile-wide Valles Caldera formed a million year ago by a volcanic eruption. Also within these mountains are the ancient Indian ruins and cliff dwellings at Bandelier National Monument and its high-tech, think-tank neighbor, Los Alamos National Laboratory.

East of the Rio Grande and much closer to home, the rugged Sangre de Cristo Mountains loom watchfully over Santa Fe—especially Truchas Peak, which reaches a magnificent 13,101 feet at the summit. The Sangres nur-

INSIDERS' TIP

Get to your campsite early, especially during peak season, or you may find yourself sleeping in your car instead of a tent.

PARKS AND
RECREATION

ture large, aspen-ringed meadows, splendid canyons, trout-filled streams and rivers, crystal-clear glacial lakes, a huge variety of wildlife, and recreational opportunities galore.

Bandelier National Monument
HCR1, Box 1, Ste. 15, Los Alamos 87544
• (505) 672-3861, ext. 517 (visitors center),
(505) 672-0343 (24-hour information)

Located along N.M. 4 on the Pajarito Plateau of the Jémez Mountains near the towns of Los Alamos and White Rock, Bandelier National Monument encompasses 32,737 acres of scenic wilderness and striking land formations that contain prehistoric cliff houses and the ruins of multi-storied, pueblo-style dwellings inhabited between the 12th and 16th centuries by the ancestors of today's Pueblo Indians. Although the 47,000-acre Cerro Grande fire began here in May 2000, only a couple hundred acres of Bandelier burned.

You might pass a few hours on the main trail exploring ruins, kivas (round, underground ceremonial rooms), and Ceremonial Cave, which is accessible only by ladder. Or you could spend days, even weeks, hiking Bandelier's 70-plus miles of pet-free backcountry trails. If you do hike the backcountry, be sure to get a wilderness pass at the visitors center, where all trails begin. Located at the bottom of Frijoles Canyon where a creek by the same name provided water to the ancient Indians who lived and farmed there. The visitors center is open year-round except for Christmas and New Year's days. It features exhibits on prehistoric and historic Pueblo culture as well as information on the monument and nearby attractions. Hours are 8 AM to 6 PM in summer; 9 AM to 5:30 PM in fall and spring; and 8 AM to 4:30 PM in winter. Juniper Campground stays open from March through November and accommodates RVs and tents. Entrance fees run $10 per car for a seven-day permit. Campers pay $10 a night per campsite. Call for group rates. During the summer, the park offers regularly scheduled guided walks, evening programs and lectures, and "interpretive" talks. To get to Bandelier from Santa Fe, take I-25 north to 84/285,

head west in Pojoaque to N.M. 502 and cross the Rio Grande to N.M. 4. From there, follow the signs to Bandelier.

Pecos National Historical Park
P. O. Box 418, Pecos
• (505) 757-6032 (visitors center);
(505) 757-6414 (administrative offices)

Just 25 miles southeast of Santa Fe, the 6,000-acres Pecos National Historical Park embraces 10,000 years of history including the ancient Pecos Pueblo, two Spanish Colonial missions, parts of the original Santa Fe Trail and the site of the Civil War battle of Glorieta Pass. Visitors may take a 1¼-mile self-guided tour through the old Pecos Pueblo and the mission ruins. Groups can arrange guided tours in advance. The visitors center contains exhibits in both English and Spanish, including a 10-minute introductory film. The park offers special summer programs including weekend cultural demonstrations and night tours. It also holds an annual Feast Day Mass the first Sunday in August. You can picnic in the park but you can't spend the night. However, the USDA Forest Service operates six campgrounds within a 20-mile radius of the park. Pecos National Historical Park is open all year except Christmas Day. Hours are 8 AM to 5 PM Memorial Day to Labor Day and 8 AM to 6 PM from Labor Day to Memorial Day. Entrance to the park is $4 per car, $2 per person. To get there from Santa Fe, take I-25 to exit 299 (Pecos Village) and continue south for two miles.

INSIDERS' TIP

Each year, a few people die of exposure in the mountains here. Don't be one of them. Take plenty of warm, waterproof clothing on the trail with you, even if you're just going out for a couple of hours. The mountains here are unpredictable and unforgiving. A few hundred feet could mean a sudden and unexpected snow storm—even in late spring or early fall—so be prepared. You should also take some sort of shelter (a space blanket), plenty of water, matches, some food, and a topo map. This is not being alarmist—it's being safe.

Recreation

What Santa Fe lacks in spectator sports, it more than makes up for in recreation and participatory sports. You could come to Santa Fe and do nothing but play—outdoors, indoors, solo, or on teams. For league sports such as baseball, basketball, football, mushball, soccer, softball, volleyball, etc., the City of Santa Fe Parks and Recreation Department, 1142 Siler Rd., (505) 955-2100, is your best single source of information, though it may take some patience and persistence to reach the right person. The

This National Park Service building was built to blend in with surrounding rocks and trees.

Photo: Don Strel

baseball teams, its recreation division can probably point you in the right direction for youth and little league, semi-pro, and seniors' baseball. Be prepared, however, to do some legwork on your own to find a team. For little league, (505) 983-4186, that will depend upon where the child lives. Eastside kids play on American Little League, west-siders on the Metropolitan league, and south-central children on the National Little League team. Teens play in the Santa Fe Amateur Baseball Congress, (505) 988-2584, comprising four divisions—Connie Mack for ages 17 and 18, Mickey Mantle for teens age 15 and 16, Sandy Koufax for age 13 and 14, and PeeWee Reese for 10, 11, and 12—with a Willie Mays division in the works for kids under 10. Teams play at Ragle, Fort Marcy, and Franklin E. Miles ballparks and occasionally use the high schools (Capital, Santa Fe, or St. Michael's) as backup fields.

Santa Fe's only semi-professional baseball team, the Expos, may have bitten the dust in 2000, but that's not to say it won't be resurrected for the 2001 season. Call the city for updates and a contact name and telephone number, if available. Also defunct, at least temporarily are the Los Alamos Bombers, (505) 672-0262, an appropriate name for a team from the birthplace of the atomic bomb. Both the Expos and the Bombers have been members of the Greater Albuquerque Baseball League.

Santa Fe baseballers age 28 and older play for the Santa Fe Cubs, (505) 989-8261, part of the Men's Senior Baseball League. The Cubs play 30 games a season on Sundays. Like most Santa Fe teams, they play home games at Fort Marcy Ballpark (Fort Marcy/Mager's Field Sports Complex), adjacent to but not part of the Fort Marcy, 490 Washington Ave., (505) 955-2500. Away games are almost always at one of the Albuquerque public high schools, though the University of New Mexico occasionally hosts a game at Lobo Field, a NCAA-quality ball-park. (505) 955-2500.

department can usually provide details about adult and youth sports and recreational activities in Santa Fe—even those it doesn't sponsor because chances are good that non-city leagues play in city parks or other municipal facilities. The department's annual Activity Guide is another good place to learn about city-sponsored sports and events. In addition to participatory sports, this section will also deal with a host of other recreational activities, from hiking, biking, and horseback riding to flying, rock climbing, and scuba.

Baseball

Santa Fe Parks and Recreation Department, Recreation Division
1142 Siler Rd.
• (505) 955-2100

Although Santa Fe has no city-sponsored

Basketball

Twelve of the city's 50 parks have outdoor basketball courts. You can get a list from the from the Parks and Recreation Department on Siler Road or by calling (505) 955-2100.

City of Santa Fe Parks and Recreation Department
1142 Siler Rd.
• (505) 955-2508

The City of Santa Fe sponsors a number of basketball-related activities throughout the year, including men's and women's summer and winter basketball leagues; girls' and boys' basketball leagues and clinics; basketball camp; and such special events as the Hot-Shot competition, in which participants ages 7 to 12 try to make as many baskets as possible from various hot spots on the court, and Free-Throw in which 7- to 12-year-olds attempt 25 shots in each of two rounds. The city also sponsors several adult basketball tournaments, including 3-on-3 and 5-on-5 competitions.

Biking

Talk about cycling in the Southwest and zealots will tell you it can only mean one thing: mountain biking. Indeed, northern New Mexico is undoubtedly among the best places in the world to pedal in the mountains and along backcountry trails. Ranked as one of the most popular sports nationwide, mountain biking is especially suited to this area because of our beautiful and varied terrain, from high-desert plateaus and mesas to alpine forests and flower-filled meadows. The region is flush with public lands—literally thousands of acres criss-crossed with thousands of miles of trails, many of them open to mountain bikers. Although more and more states are banning mountain bikes from all but a few designated trails, New Mexico is bucking that trend and will likely continue to do so provided cyclists respect trail etiquette, i.e., yield to hikers, horseback riders, and uphill traffic; practice low-impact cycling by treading lightly and remembering that "skids are for squids;" and avoid getting so terribly lost that a search and rescue team is required. Do note, however, that all designated wilderness areas—the Pecos near Santa Fe, Taos County's Wheeler Peak, or Sandia Peak east of Albuquerque, for example—and the trails leading to them are always off limits to mountain bikes. If you violate the rules, you risk losing your wheels. For more information on New Mexico's bicycle laws, contact the state Highway and Transportation Department, 1120

Northern New Mexico offers many opportunities for mountain biking.

Photo: Ben Blankenburg

You can rent a bike just one-half block from the Plaza and tour the downtown and Canyon Road.

Photo: Don Strel

Cerrillos Road, (505) 827-5100 or (800) 432-4269.

A locally popular and scenic route for both mountain and touring bikes goes straight up N.M. 475—variously called Artist Road, Hyde Park Road, or Ski Basin Road, depending on the particular section—to the Santa Fe Ski Area. Starting at the Fort Marcy/Mager's Field Sports Complex, 490 Washington Ave., it's a 15-mile uphill ride to the ski basin—or 8 miles to Black Canyon, a nice midway stopping point. The road gets quite narrow and practically shoulder-less as you near the ski slopes and you'll encounter numerous hairpin turns and sometimes-heavy traffic. But the stunning views are worth every whiff of carbon monoxide, not to mention the trail of impatient cars at your back. Take warm clothing, as it can get quite chilly in the higher elevations. Also, bring rain gear, in case of a sudden thunderstorm, and plenty of water, especially if you're unaccustomed to an arid climate.

A comfortable ride for beginners that's popular even among experienced mountain bikers—and one that only recently received official sanctioning after years of illicit use by bik-

ers, hikers, and equestrians—is the Lamy Trail, known locally as the Santa Fe Rail Trail, which runs between Santa Fe and the Lamy depot. The 11.5-mile dirt trail runs alongside the train tracks originally laid by the Atchison, Topeka, & Santa Fe Railway in 1880, used today by the Santa Fe Southern Railway that runs between the downtown Santa Fe and Lamy depots. Make your way to S. St. Francis Drive and head south until it turns into Frontage Road. Continue southbound to the train tracks and follow them to Lamy. Along the way, you'll pass over a trestle bridge that one devote happily describes as "pretty scary." If you're lucky, or you plan it right, you might even meet up with a train. From Lamy, you can either bike back to town or catch the Santa Fe Southern Railway and ride back in style in a restored 1920s passenger coach.

If you're looking to explore the hinterlands, the Jémez Mountains provide spectacular scenery for cyclists, both on- and off-road. One of the more popular loops begins at N.M. Highway 501—about 35 miles northwest of Santa Fe—in the parking lot of Los Alamos National Laboratory. Continue south along N.M. 4 to the Los Alamos "Truck Route,"—an otherwise unnamed road belonging to LANL's overseer, the U.S. Department of Energy—and finally back to the lab. The 26-mile trek will take you past the ancient pueblo ruins at Bandelier National Monument and Tsankawi and open up to remarkable vistas.

If you choose to go south, the Turquoise Trail to Albuquerque via the Sandia Crest Scenic Byway offers a route as rich in history as it is in scenery. The 52-mile journey begins on N.M. 14, called the Turquoise Trail because of the turquoise mined in the mountains there. You'll pass through a number of old mining villages, some of them long-deserted ghost towns while others, like Madrid and Cerrillos, are thriving artistic communities. Once in Albuquerque, do go the extra 12 miles to Sandia Crest, a 3,700-foot climb along the Sandia Crest Scenic Byway (N.M. 536), to an elevation of 10,678 feet at the summit. On the way up, be sure to observe how the desert vegetation changes to ponderosa pine forests because you'll be too busy catching your breath on the way down to notice.

If you're here the third Sunday in May, you might want to try your hand—er, feet—at the 100-mile Santa Fe Century, or the 75-mile route to Stanley and back, 50 miles to Galisteo, and 25 miles to Eldorado. The Century is a challenging, scenic ride that starts at Capshaw School on Zia Road just east of St. Francis Drive, heads south down N.M. Highway 14 along the lovely Turquoise Trail to Golden. If you survive "Heartbreak Hill"—a half-mile killer climb between Golden and Edgewood that's steep enough to force many cyclists to walk their bikes—you'll head west toward Stanley, then north through Galisteo and Lamy to Eldorado, returning to Santa Fe via I-25. The Century will take you anywhere from five to eight hours, depending on your stamina, strength, and skill. Or you could take one of the shorter routes for 25, 50, or 75 miles. The Century, which the National Leukemia Society has adopted as a nationwide fundraiser, drew well over 2,000 riders in 2000, including 400 cyclists from around the country and our own tri-athlete governor, Gary Johnson, Many of the outings we've suggested here are geared toward off-road vehicles. For information about on-road biking, call Sangre de Cristo Cycling Club at (505) 982-0664. Otherwise, you can get information on trails and tours as well as rent bikes and other equipment from most bike rental shops in town. Some specialize in guided tours, including the following:

Known World Guide Service
NM Highway 582, No. 702, Lyden
• (505) 983-7756, (800) 983-7756

Known World offers a variety of mountain bike adventures from single-day trips to multi-day excursions throughout northern New Mexico. The company will arrange bike tours for all ages and skill levels—from gradual climbs on logging or ranch roads for beginners to steep, gnarly trails for experts. Trips run from $48 for a half-day trip up to about $100 per full day, depending on the itinerary, Known World provides the bicycle, helmet, water, and healthy gourmet food—snacks for half-day trips, lunch for all-day rides, and all meals for camping tours. Multiple-day trips range from overnights to 10-day truck-supported adventures. Known World will also arrange custom tours and/or custom catering.

New Mexico Mountain Bike Adventures
49 Main St., Cerrillos
• (505) 474-0074

Located in scenic, artistic Cerrillos in the Ortiz Mountains south of Santa Fe, New Mexico

INSIDERS' TIP
The unwritten code of the West is to leave things as you found them. If you open a gate, close it behind you. If the previous "tenant" left a pile of dead wood at your campsite, leave some for the next camper. Of course, if you find garbage or other unwanted remnants at your camp or on a trail, by all means tote it out along with your own.

Mountain Bike Adventures offers a variety of scenic and historic rides throughout New Mexico. It specializes in custom bike tours exploring Indian pre-history, ancient turquoise mines, El Camino Real, and 19th century railroads in and around Santa Fe County. It will also arrange tours in the Jémez Mountains as well as the Apache and Gila National Forests. Customers can choose from half-, full- and multiple-day bike trips for all riding abilities. Half-day trips, including bike rentals, start at $50; full-day trips start at $100, including bike rental and lunch. Multiple-day trips run between $115 and $135 per day, including meals, but not bike rentals. Ask about group discounts.

New Mexico Bike N' Sport
1829 Cerrillos Rd.
• (505) 820-0809

New Mexico Bike N' Sport rents front-suspension mountain and road bikes starting at $14 for a half-day, $22 for a full-day trip, and $34 for two days. The staff is closed-mouthed about their favorite trails, no doubt in hopes of keeping them from becoming over-populated. Perhaps that's why lots of hard-core mountain bikers frequent the store, which boasts its own 10-person racing team sponsored by local businesses and national bike manufacturers. In past years, Bike N' Sport has co-sponsored with the City of Santa Fe the annual La Tierra Torture Race in September. The 10-, 20- and 30-mile course features a women's open and men's beginning, intermediate, and pro category. Although the city opted out of its sponsorship in 2000, Bike N' Sport may sponsor the race on its own, though that was still undetermined by the time this book went to press.

rob & charlie's
St. Michael's Village West,
1632 St. Michael's Dr.
• (505) 471-9119

A trusted locals' favorite, rob & charlie's is Santa Fe's longest reigning bike and skateboard shop (see our skateboarding section in this chapter). In business since 1979, rob & charlie's has earned a reputation for being friendly, helpful and, most importantly, knowledgeable about all aspects of bicycles—from buying one to riding one and, inevitably, repairing one. The store car-

Locals as well as tourists use the bicycle as a means of exercise and transportation.

Photo: Don Strel

ries a large selection of mountain bikes, road bikes, BMX bikes, and kid's bikes from Giant, Raleigh, Schwinn, Redline, S E Racing, and Trek, to name just a few brands. It also sells roof racks, parts, and all manner of accessories and accouterments from clothing, shoes, and water bottles to books, magazines, and maps. Priceless to those who don't have it, yet free for the asking at rob & charlie's, is the skinny on bitchin' biking trails from the most popular to the lesser known. rob & charlie's is open Monday through Saturday from 9:30 AM to 6 PM.

Birding

New Mexico is home to a number of bird sanctuaries, including one right here in Santa Fe and several within a few hours drive. But you need only venture to any open space outside the city limits to observe hawks soaring in search of prey or, if you're especially lucky, a bald eagle either in flight or repose. In spring and autumn, Santa Fe hosts an astounding number of migrating birds because of its location along a major migratory pathway.

Bosque del Apache National Wildlife Refuge
San Antonio, N.M.
• (505) 835-1828
One of the top birding sites in the U. S., Bosque del Apache, ("woods of the Apache") is

well worth the 2½-hour drive from Santa Fe, even if you're not a card-carrying birder. Within the 57,191-acre Bosque, as New Mexicans familiarly call this gorgeous wildlife refuge, are 13,000 acres of moist bottomland at a wide spot of the Rio Grande. There, tens of thousands of birds gather each autumn and stay through the winter. At dusk, you can witness flocks of snow and Arctic geese, eagles, sandhill cranes, and even whooping cranes—one of a number of endangered species that winter at Bosque del Apache—returning to roost in the marshes. During the spring and fall, you'll see migrant warblers, flycatchers, and shorebirds. In summer—the season for nesting songbirds, waders, shorebirds, and ducks—the Bosque returns to its quiet existence as an oasis of ponds, marsh, riparian cottonwood, willow, and tamarisk on the northern edge of the Chihuahuan desert. Year-round residents include mule deer, coyote, porcupine, muskrat, Canada Goose, coot, pheasant, turkey, quail, and New Mexico's state bird, the roadrunner.

To get to Bosque del Apache from Santa Fe, take I-25 south to Exit 139 at San Antonio. Head east on U.S. Highway 380 for a half-mile, then take N.M Highway 1 south another eight miles to the refuge.

Las Vegas National Wildlife Refuge
Route 1, Box 399, Las Vegas
• (505) 425-3581
Located about 70 miles east of Santa Fe, Las

Vegas National Wildlife Refuge consists of 8,672 acres of marsh and water, native grasslands, cropland, timbered canyons, and streams providing habitat for a wide variety of plant and animal life—up to 271 species observed since 1966, when the refuge had only been in official existence for a year. Among its feathered visitors are Neotropical migrants, a species that nests in the U.S. or Canada, spending the winter primarily south in Mexico, Central or South America, or the Caribbean. They include colorful hawks, hummingbirds, warblers, and orioles, as well as shorebirds, flycatchers, and thrushes. The existence of the refuge helps preserve their habitat, which is essential to the survival of many of these birds.

Maxwell National Wildlife Refuge
P.O. Box 276, Maxwell
• (505) 375-2331

With 200 species of birds observed over the years around its largest compound, the Maxwell National Wildlife Refuge is the winter home to large concentrations of ducks and geese and to the burrowing owl in summer. Migrating birds are attracted to the many irrigation impoundments that serve this primarily agricultural area in the northeastern corner of the state. To get to the refuge, take U.S. 25 due north for about 150 miles and get off at the Maxwell exit, between the towns of Springer and Raton.

Boating/Canoeing

New Mexico may be desert, but there's still plenty of recreational water on which to play. Getting there from Santa Fe, however, will take a bit of traveling. Nearest to Santa Fe are Cochití Lake, (505) 465-0307, 26 miles southwest of the city; and Abiquiú Lake, (505) 685-4371, a beautiful, winding 45 miles northwest of Santa Fe—both managed by the U.S. Army Corps of Engineers. Cochití is a no-charge, no-wake lake with paved boat ramps and a no-frills slip-rental marina managed by Cochití Pueblo, (505) 465-2219. There are no boat rentals at the lake itself, but you can rent a craft in Santa Fe and take it with you. Among the most popular water sports at Cochití are sailing, fishing, windsurfing and, in summer, swimming. To get there, take I-25 south to the turnoff for N.M. 16, which is near the bottom of a long and notoriously steep hill called La Bajada ("the descent"). From N.M. 16, turn right on N.M. 22, which will take you directly to the lake.

Abiquiú Lake, located about seven miles northwest of the village of Abiquiú, provides a stunning sight from U.S. 84, its shimmering aqua color a lovely contrast to the red hills that surround it. The lake, which has two paved boat ramps on its north side, is a popular site for water-skiing, fishing, Jet Skiing, and sim-

Tent Rocks offers a great hike close to Santa Fe.

Photo: Don Strel

ply cruising. Swimmers also take advantage of the lake in summer, despite its lack of developed swimming areas. From Santa Fe, take U.S 84/285 north to Española. Turn left at Dandy Burger, where the highway splits. Follow U.S. 84 for 18 miles to Abiquiú and another seven miles to the turnoff for Abiquiú Dam, which is on your left. To rent a kayaks, call Active endeavors, 328 S. Guadalupe Ave., (505) 984-8221, open M-F 10 AM to 7 pm, Sat. 10 AM to 6 PM, Sun. Noon to 5 PM.

Bowling

Silva Lanes
1352 Rufina Circle
• **(505) 471-2110**

With 32 lanes, Silva's is larger than your average bowling alley. That's because it's the only one in town and, as such, is always buzzing with activity. A non-smoking establishment, Silva Lanes is home to literally dozens of sanctioned children's leagues. Kids from age 3 and up can earn money for college with every game they play. Of course, adults can play, too, in men's, women's, and co-ed leagues. For those who like a little dazzle in their game, Silva's features "Cosmic Bowling," complete with black lights, fluorescent pins, and disco music. Or they can play blacklight pool or air hockey in the new game room, as well as video games on any of a dozen different machines. Silva's has both a snack bar and a glassed-in lounge that welcomes smokers and offers hosted karaoke nightly. Silva Lanes is open 10 AM to midnight five nights a week and to 1 AM on Friday and Saturday. Prices range from $ $2.75 to $2.95 a game plus $1 to $1.75 to rent shoes. Hourly rates for groups up to six people start at $15.50 without shoe rentals.

Camping

Most of New Mexico's parks, national monuments, and forests have campsites ranging from primitive to developed sites with running water and restrooms. Some also have RV hookups, occasionally even with cable television! Public campsites are usually open from May through October on a first-come, first-serve basis and cost a few dollars. You don't need a permit to camp in national forest wilderness areas, but you do in national parks and monuments. They're available free from the visitor's center so make sure you stop in to register. Check with the National Park Service, P.O. Box 728, (505) 988-6012, for additional information about permits.

In Town

Los Campos RV Resort
3574 Cerrillos Rd.
• **(505) 473-1949, (800) 852-8160**

Five miles southwest of the Plaza on Cerrillos Road, Los Campos offers the gamut from tent camping all the way up to 50-amp service for extra-large RVs. The 11-acre, year-round trailer park has 95 sites, a coin laundry, groceries, a heated pool, and a playground. Costs start at $25 per night. Weekly and monthly rates are available.

Trailer Ranch
3471 Cerrillos Rd.
• **(505) 471-9970**

This is a combination RV and senior mobile home park, with the first third of the park reserved for up to 45 RVs with full hookups, including cable television, public showers, coin laundry, a heated, seasonal swimming pool, and a community house with a pool table, library, and card tables. The back two-thirds of Trailer Ranch is a seniors-only mobile home park with a minimum age of 55. Daily rates range from $25 to $28 with discounts for senior citizens.

Out of Town

Rancheros de Santa Fe
736 Old Las Vegas Highway
• **(505) 466-3482, (800) 426-9259**

With 131 campsites on 22 acres, including 30 sites for tents only, Rancheros de Santa Fe is the largest camping facility in the area. Amenities include a swimming pool, a recreation room with nightly movies, a game room, a hiking trail, coin laundry, and a playground. Guests can buy groceries, gifts, and propane on site. Rates start at $17.95 for up to two people plus $2 for each additional person. Be sure to ask about available discounts. Located 10.5 miles east of the Plaza on Frontage Road, the campgrounds are open March through November.

Santa Fe KOA
934 Old Las Vegas Highway
• **(505) 466-1419, (800) 562-1514**

This KOA offers 23 tent sites, 51 RV hookups and 10 "Kamping Kabins" on 8.5 acres in lovely Apache Canyon, located 11 miles southeast of Santa Fe. Rates for two people start at $19.95 for tents, $23.95 for RVs, and $33.95 for cabins, which sleep four. There's a $2 surcharge for each additional person. Campers have access to a coin laundry, recreation room with nightly movies during the summer, convenience store, upscale gift shop, and a playground. Propane is also available on-site. The camp is open March through November.

Santa Fe National Forest
N.M. 475
• **(505) 753-7331**

The Santa Fe National Forest has three campsites close to Santa Fe, all located off N.M. 475 on the way to the Santa Fe Ski Basin. From the lowest elevation to the highest—which, of course, is the order in which you'll first encounter them—they are:

Black Canyon, 8,400 feet. Open May-October, Black Canyon has 42 campsites, restrooms, drinking water, and trailer parking. Fees are $7 per night for a maximum of 14 days.

Big Tesuque, 9,700 feet. The absence of trailer parking makes the Big Tesuque a particularly pleasant place to park one's tent, despite a lack of drinking water. The seven campsites here are available free of charge for 14-day maximum stays between May and October.

Aspen Basin, 10,300 feet. For the truly hardy, Aspen Basin has six no-fee campsites open year-round with restrooms, drinking water, and picnic tables. Maximum stay is 14 days.

Hyde Memorial State Park
Hyde Park Rd.
• **(505) 983-7175**

Located 7.5 miles northeast of Santa Fe on N.M. 475, Hyde Memorial State Park has 50 year-round campsites, including seven with electric hookups. You'll find drinking water, restrooms, a dump station, a playground, and even a skating rink. Fees run $10 a night for tents, $14 for electric hookups.

Disc Golf

Dead Plastic Society
Ashbaugh Park,
Cerrillos Rd. and Fourth St.
• **(505) 982-8079**

The Dead Plastic Society is a loose organization of people of all ages, genders, and skill levels who play golf with a Frisbee-like disc tossed from tee boxes into stationary metal baskets provided by the City of Santa Fe and configured by a course pro. Santa Fe's disc golf course is one of about 1,100 around the world. The sport, which originated in California (of course), has gained tremendous popularity over the last few decades and is still growing. You can catch the Dead Plastic Society in action in the city's Ashbaugh Park (Cerrillos Road and Fourth Street), usually on Sundays starting between 9:30 and 11 AM. Members (and we use the term loosely) also play doubles on Wednesday night starting at about 5 PM. The times fluctuate with the season—and that includes winter, when players swap their sneakers for Sorels. Even in winter, you'll find anywhere from 10 to 40 people tossing around those little gray discs. (They cost about $8 each.) Some people cart around bags of them, just like traditional golfers do with their clubs. In fact, many golfers also play disc golf, though being good at traditional golf doesn't necessarily mean you'll be good at disc golf, which requires an athletic throwing arm. But don't be intimidated. The Dead Plastic Society welcomes all players, including first-timers, who will get a handicap commensurate with their experience. Who knows, after some practice you might find yourself competing in tournaments against teams from Albuquerque.

Fishing

New Mexico is an angler's paradise. Our rivers and lakes are home to a variety of coveted freshwater game fish, including Rio Grande cutthroat trout—the state fish, and one for which New Mexico is rightly famous—as well as brown trout, rainbow trout, brook trout, and lake trout. You can also fish for Kokanee salmon, black bass, white bass, and striped bass; largemouth, smallmouth, and spotted bass; panfish, catfish, walleye, bluegill, black crappie, and carp.

While there's little fishing to speak of in Santa Fe—though it's not unheard of to catch a stocker or two in the pretty-but-piddling Santa Fe River—the county is a gateway to superb fishing. Only 35 minutes southeast of Santa Fe, the Pecos River offers fine trout fishing, especially upstream from the Village of Pecos or in Villanueva State Park south of I-25. If you're willing to hike, you might venture into the Pecos Wilderness, where the Pecos River originates. You'll find that native cutthroat and rainbow trout thrive in streams such as the Rio Del Medio near Pecos Baldy. If you

Lakes, rivers, and streams offer the angler an opportunity to catch brown, brook, rainbow, and lake trout.

Photo: Ben Blankenburg

Taos, offers some fine fishing. So does the Taos Box of the Rio Grande, about two hours north of Santa Fe along N.M. 68, though you're likely to find yourself competing with whitewater rafters there. You might also try the Rio Santa Barbara, a medium-sized river that starts in the Pecos Wilderness near Truchas Peak and flows into Peñasco, a 52- or 67-mile drive northeast of Santa Fe, depending on which route you take.

If you're willing to travel a couple of hours or more, the northern part of the state has some of the best trout fishing in New Mexico. In the northwest region, the San Juan River below Navajo Dam offers excellent trout fishing year-round, often yielding trout longer than 20 inches. The most fished part of the San Juan is designated as a "special trout" or "quality" (protected) water with restrictions that limit anglers to artificial flies and lures; single, barbless hooks; and bag and possession limits. In northeastern New Mexico near the Colorado border, the Valle Vidal unit of the Carson National Forest— open for fishing from July 1 through Dec. 31 only—

plan to fish in this area after September, be prepared for severe winter weather, which can hit with little warning at any time.

The Rio Grande, which starts in Colorado and heads south to the Gulf of Mexico, is your other choice if you want to stick close to Santa Fe. Take note, however, that it's a temperamental river where fishing is a delight one day and impossible the next. We don't recommend you even attempt fishing the Rio Grande during spring runoff, when the water is far too swift and muddy.

On a good day, the Orilla Verde Recreation area north of Pilar, off N.M. 68, which heads to

offers outstanding trout fishing, as does the Red River south of Questa, part of which is designated as quality water with special restrictions. La Junta, the confluence of the Red River and the Rio Grande in the Upper Taos Box, has some of the best fishing on the Rio Grande, though its swift and wild waters are recommended for experienced anglers only. Be warned that it will take some serious hiking to get down to the river and even more serious hiking to get back to your car. For anglers with an eye for luxury, Ted Turner's Vermejo Park Ranch, (505) 445-3097, located Immediately adjacent to Valle Vidal, charges $350 a day for a minimum two-night stay to fish in any of its 23 lakes and 20-plus miles of streams between April and September. The price includes lodging, meals, horseback riding, and skeet shooting.

Perhaps the single most important piece of advice before dropping your line in the water is to get a copy of the state fishing proclamation wherever you pick up your license. You can buy a license at the New Mexico Department of Game and Fish or at any of more than 200 vendors statewide, including outfitters, some hardware and grocery stores, and Wal-Mart. An annual fishing license costs $17.50 for residents, $39 for non-residents. A one-day license is $8 for everyone, while a five-day permit costs $16. Seniors and juniors are eligible for discounts. We strongly recommend you pay the extra $5 for a wildlife habitat improvement stamp that allows you to fish on federal lands. Be prepared to pay a $1 vendor fee. If you have any questions about the rules and regulations, call or visit the New Mexico Department of Game and Fish, 408 Galisteo St., (505) 827-7911. The department can also provide you with a copy of New Mexico Public Fishing Waters, which includes a map as well as a comprehensive description of streams and lakes throughout New Mexico. You can also call the department's toll-free, 24-hour telephone number—(800) ASK-FISH (275-3474)—for up-to-date fishing and stocking reports and information on regulations, special waters, boat access, etc. For additional information on stocking, call (505) 827-7905 or visit the website, www.gmfsh.state.nm.us, updated each Friday afternoon for the past week.

If you're interested in looking at fish but not catching them, the Department of Game and Fish operates six fish hatcheries that are open for touring. They include Lisboa Springs at Pecos; Red River near Questa; Seven Springs near Jémez Springs; and Parkview near Chama in the northern part of the state. South of Santa Fe, you can tour the Glenwood hatchery near the Gila Wilderness and Rock Lake in Santa Rosa, which is the nearer of the two. Call the Fisheries Division at (505) 827-7905 for additional information.

A number of local operators offer guided fishing trips.

High Desert Angler
435 S. Guadalupe St.
• (505) 98-TROUT (988-7688)

In business since 1987, High Desert Angler was Santa Fe's first full-service fly-fishing shop. It sells high quality fly-fishing equipment and supplies, including popular site-specific fly patterns. It also offers guided fly-fishing trips throughout northern New Mexico and rents

Santa Fe's five golf courses offer varied terrain and spectacular scenery.

Photo: Chris Corrie

all manner of fly-fishing gear, including Sage rods and a variety of reels, waders, and pontoon boats. High Desert Angler can supply you with maps, guidebooks, licenses, and the latest fishing reports, including some that are first-hand.

Known World Guide Service
NM Highway 582, No. 702, Lyden
• **(505) 983-7756, (800) 983-7756**

Known World offers a variety of fly-fishing trips on many of northern New Mexico's best trout waters, including the Pecos, Rio Grande, and Red Rivers as well as high alpine lakes and smaller creeks. Guides try to avoid crowds and provide personalized service. Most trips last all day and sometimes into the night. Full-day trips include a light breakfast and hearty lunch. Known World also rents out equipment including rods, reels, waders, and boots.

The Reel Life
Sanbusco Center, 510 Montezuma St.
• **(505) 995-8114, (888) 268-FISH (3474)**

The Reel Life, which has stores in Santa Fe and Albuquerque, is an outfitter endorsed by the Orvis Company to guide fishing trips and sell Orvis' high quality fishing and outdoor gear. It also carries other brands and stocks hundreds of patterns and sizes of flies for freshwater and saltwater fishing as well as material and instructions to tie your own. The store offers guided fishing trips to many of the fine waters of New Mexico including the San Juan River, the Rio Peñasco, Taos area streams, and private lakes in Chama.

Fitness Centers, Gyms, Health Clubs, and Recreation Centers

Carl & Sandra's Physical Conditioning Center
DeVargas Center, 153-A Paseo de Peralta
• **(505) 982-6760**

Under the direction of former U.S. and Olympic weightlifting coach Carl Miller, Carl & Sandra's Physical Conditioning Center is the only gym in town that offers Olympic-style weightlifting as well as aerobic and anaerobic weight training programs for all ages, from children to seniors. Carl & Sandra's specializes in cardiovascular circuit training to build both strength and endurance with creative, individu-

alized programs updated every six to seven weeks. Training and nutritional counseling focus on weight loss or gain, stress reduction, specific sports, flexibility, bone density, pregnancy, rehabilitation, and Olympic-style weightlifting, for which owner Carl Miller holds U.S. and international records. The gym occasionally hosts sanctioned Olympic-style weightlifting competitions and schedules regular "fun meets," all of which the public may attend.

Carl & Sandra's recently expanded gym is light on frills—it has a small co-ed sauna and separate dressing rooms with showers and lockers—but heavy on well-maintained equipment. You'll find free weights, weight stack pulley systems similar to Universal, hydraulic resistance machines, Concept II rowers, Schwinn Aerodyne stationary bikes, gymnastic rings, a two-lane, indoor track for sprinting, equipment for plymetrics, and a host of other gadgets and machines designed to exercise every conceivable muscle and joint in the body along with the cardiovascular system. Staff members are dedicated and well-trained and work out regularly. Miller, a guru of sorts for many members, holds a master's degree in health, physical education, and recreation with specialties in exercise physiology, biomechanics, and nutrition. His wife, Sandra Thomas is an accredited teacher, has been a mountaineer for more than 30 years, and is a former search and rescue team and EMT team member.

Memberships at Carl & Sandra's Physical Conditioning Center run about $1,200 a year. Ask about family, group and senior citizen discounts. Guests of members may work out for $12 a day, $33 a week. Walk-ins pay $15 a day and $40 per week. The gym is open from 6 AM to 1:30 PM and 3:30 to 8 PM on Monday, Wednesday and Friday; 8 AM to 1:30 PM and 3:30 to 8 PM Tuesday and Thursday; 9 AM to 4 PM on Saturday; and 11 AM to 4 PM on Sunday.

Club International Family Fitness Center
1931 Warner Ave.
• **(505) 473-9807**

Located off St. Michael's Drive, one of Santa Fe's major commercial strips, Club International is a 25,000-square-foot fitness center with four racquetball courts; a basketball court; free weights; and a variety of resistance and electronic cardiovascular and weight machines including Nautilus, Concept II rowers, Stairmasters, Nordic Trak, Lifecycles, and StarTrac. The club has an indoor heated swimming pool, hot tub, steam room, and dry sauna. It offers classes in aerobics, yoga, stretching, and, for an additional cost professional racquetball instruction, tanning beds, and supervised childcare. Call for information about membership rates, including corporate and group rates. Daily guests pay $10. Club International is open 5:30 AM to 9 PM Monday through Friday, 9 AM to 5 PM on Saturday and 10 AM to 5 PM on Sunday.

El Gancho Fitness, Swim and Racquet Club
Old Las Vegas Hwy.
• (505) 988-5000

Located south of Santa Fe, adjacent to the Steaksmith restaurant on the scenic Old Las Vegas Highway, this beautiful 18,000-square-foot health club describes itself as a "complete health, tennis, and sports activity center." The facilities include indoor and outdoor tennis courts with resident pros available for instruction and adult and junior tennis programs; squash, racquetball, basketball, and volleyball courts; an outdoor running/walking track; a strength and conditioning center with free weights, Universal, and a variety of cardiovascular machines including Stairmaster, Cybex, and Schwinn; aerobics classes, body toning, and sports conditioning classes; indoor and outdoor heated swimming pools with certified swimming instruction available; kiddy and wading pools; hot tubs, steam rooms, and saunas. Among the services the club offers are personal fitness trainers, nutrition counseling, massage therapy, childcare, and a kids' summer day camp. Special programs include fitness evaluations, yoga, swim play, martial arts, and CPR. El Gancho memberships start at $70 a month for individuals with a one-time initiation fee of $300, with special rates and initiation fees for couples, families, single families, children, and corporations. The club is open 6 AM to 9:30 PM except on Tuesday, when it opens at 2 PM.

Fitness Plus
1119 Calle Del Cielo
• (505) 473-7315

The only all-women's gym in town, Fitness Plus describes its mission as providing women in Santa Fe with a "special place in which they can comfortably acquire better health and enhanced self esteem." The club has free weights, Nautilus, Universal, stretch-and-tone tables, and something it calls a "cardio theater" in which you can hook up to any of

Santa Fe hosts a number of fitness facilities. This one is the Women-only Fitness Plus.

Photo: Don Strel

six televisions and a variety of audio equipment while sweating on Versaclimbers, rowers, steppers, treadmills, and other cardiovascular equipment. Amenities include a new sauna and daily lockers with locks. Members get discounts on aerobics and yoga classes, massage, European body wraps, salt glows, and tanning beds. Fitness Plus offers two standard annual memberships. Both require a $65 initiation fee and come with a 30-day money back guarantee. A basic membership costs $44 a month and includes three sessions with a personal trainer. A complete membership costs an additional $199 and includes all of the above plus the Apex System—an individualized plan for altering one's body composition with guaranteed results. Ask about discounts for students, seniors and families. Daily guest passes run $12 per visit. The club is open Monday through Friday from 5:30 AM to 8:30 pm, Saturday from 8 AM to 5 pm, and Sunday from 10 AM to 5 PM. Owners Joe Oliaro an Barb Petkus are doctors of naprapathy, a gentle form of chiropractic. Oliaro is also a Doctor of Oriental Medicine, certified in acupuncture and herbology.

Fort Marcy Ballpark/ Mager's Field Sports Complex
490 Washington Ave.
• **(505) 955-2500**

The city-run Fort Marcy/Mager's Field Sports Complex has an indoor pool; separate gym and weight rooms; a racquetball court; outdoor fields and tracks; dance and fitness classes; body sculpting and stretching classes; swimming classes for all ages from infants to seniors; and martial arts. The complex also hosts various one-time competitions throughout the year in a variety of sports, including basketball and football. Fort Marcy offers a variety of memberships to suit nearly every user, including a $44 -a-year user fee card that allows partial use of the facility with additional per diem rates for the pool or other facilities. An unlimited individual membership costs $52 a month or $126 for three months; families pay $75 per month or $180 per quarter. Weight room, gym, or racquetball membership each run $23 a month, $51 per quarter, or $33 a month for any two activities, including the pool. Pool memberships by themselves range from $150 a year for adults to $23 for seniors and children ages 8 through 12 with per diem fees costing anywhere from $4 to 90 cents, depending on your age. Fort Marcy is open Monday through Friday from 6 AM to 8:30 PM, Saturday from 8 AM to 6:30 PM and Sunday from noon to 5:30 PM.

Genoveva Chavez Community Center
3321 Rodeo Rd.
• **(505) 955-4001**

A pull-out-all-the-stops grand opening welcomed this $27 million recreation center that opened in March 2000. Its centerpiece is a regulation-sized ice rink—complete with spectator seats and concession stands—for which figure skaters and hockey players throughout the area have been clamoring for years. The 170,000-square-foot municipal facility boasts three swimming pools: a 50-meter lap pool, a leisure pool with a triple-loop slide and "lazy river," and a therapy pool. A full gym houses three basketball/volleyball courts; two racquetball courts; an indoor, three-lane running track; an aerobics/dance room; weight training area; and locker-filled locker rooms for women, men, and families. Be sure to use a good lock to deter the opportunistic petty thieves who have been helping themselves to wallets, cell phones, shoes, etc. The city has promised to ratchet up security both inside and outside the center. We expect the city will have ironed out most of the wrinkles in short order. Annual passes range in price from $175 for a child under 10 to $640 for a family, with daily admission fees between $2 and $4, depending on age.

INSIDERS' TIP

An abundance of crosswinds, not to mention city ordinances, make hot air ballooning in Santa Fe an iffy proposition at best, though some balloonists will venture into the Santa Fe sky in July and August when the air is at its calmest. Your best bet for getting airborne is in Albuquerque, and Santa Fe Detours will be happy to arrange the adventure. In summer, you'll probably be aloft by early morning when the air is still cool enough to ensure the balloon will rise. In cooler seasons, you're likely to be in the air by noon, so pack a lunch if one hasn't been provided for you. Santa Fe Detours traditionally celebrates landings with a champagne toast and presents guests with a souvenir pen and, when appropriate a first-flight certificate. The company charges $135 per person; ask about group and other discounts. You can contact Santa Fe Detours at 54½ E. San Francisco St., (505) 983-6565, (800) DETOURS (338-6877)

PARKS AND RECREATION

Mandrill's Gym
708 W. San Mateo (at Pacheco)
• (505) 988-2986

Formerly Gold's Gym, Mandrill's came under new ownership—and a new name—in 1991 when body-builder Martin Sanchez decided he wanted to put his own stamp on the gym. Still big on bodybuilding—many members compete in the sport—Mandrill's is also a family gym for general fitness. It's equipped with free weights, Universal, resistance machines, and cardiovascular equipment including steppers, climbers, treadmills, and rowers. Among the amenities at Mandrill's are a dry sauna, dressing rooms with showers, $1 towel rental,s and a variety of drinks and supplements for sale. Membership, which costs anywhere from $42 a month to $365 a year, includes personal training from the staff. Or you can pay a private trainer, choosing from among those who work out at the gym. Mandrill's charges $5 for a daily pass. It's open Monday through Friday, 5:30 AM to 9 PM, Saturday from 8 AM to 5 PM and Sunday from 9 AM to 5 PM.

Municipal Recreation Complex
205 Caja del Rio Rd.
• (505) 955-4470

Open only since 1998 and still under construction, this long-awaited outdoor sports complex thus far contains five regulation adult soccer fields, two of which also serve as flag football fields; six softball fields, including four equipped for night games; three sand volleyball courts; a baseball field; and a special events field for disk golf, disk football, ultimate Frisbee, and rugby—the latter only until the summer of 2001, when the two rugby fields currently under construction are expected to be finished. Also scheduled to open by summer 2001 are seven youth soccer fields and an equestrian center. The 1,260-acre complex also features a BMX (bicycle/motocross) trail and a two-mile running/jogging path. The MRC's star attraction is the Marty Sanchez Links de Santa Fe golf course and driving range. (See the "Golf" section below for details.) There are even concession stands where you can slake your thirst or fuel up for the next round of activity. To get there from downtown Santa Fe, drive south on Cerrillos Road, turn right on Airport Road, right again on U.S. 599 and left at Caja del Rio Road. The sports complex is located about 1.5 miles from the turn on the east side of the road.

Quail Run Fitness Center
3101 Old Pecos Trail
• (505) 986-2222, (800) 548-6990

Quail Run Fitness Center is part of a pri-

Summer brings out the convertibles, bikes, Harleys, and trikes.

Photo: Don Strel

vate luxury development in southeast Santa Fe, but the public is welcome to join. The center features a 65-foot heated indoor lap pool, a hydrotherapy pool and two hot tubs. It also has two outdoor tennis courts, a weight room, cardiovascular equipment, and a 1.75-mile jogging trail around the Quail Run Golf Course (see our Golf section below). The club offers on-going classes in low-impact, step, and water aerobics; stretching; tai chi; and yoga. Personal training runs $30 per hour, with special group rates available. Swimming lessons and tennis lessons cost $25 per half-hour, $40 per hour with discounts for groups. The club also offers massage, spa services, facials and manicures by special appointment.

Individual membership in Quail Run's fitness center require a five-year initiation fee ranging from $2,500 for a silver membership to $3,500 for a gold membership, which includes use of the golf course. Monthly dues are $105 for silver memberships and $140 for gold. Families pay a $4,000 initiation fee for a silver membership and $5,000 for the gold plus $145 or $190 a month respectively. Call for information about corporate memberships. To get on the membership waiting list, you will need to put down a $500 deposit. Once accepted, members have access to the billiards room, card room, banquet facilities and the restaurant, which charges a minimum of $35 a month, whether you use it or not. So, go ahead and have that Margarita! Quail Run is open Tuesday through Sunday from 6 AM to 9 PM.

William C. Witter Fitness Education Center
Santa Fe Community College, 6401 Richards Ave.
• **(505) 428-1615**

Named after the college's founding president, who died in 1993, the William C. Witter Fitness Education Center is among the larger indoor physical fitness centers in Santa Fe and one of the best deals in town. For the price of a single physical education course—a requirement to use the facilities—anyone can take advantage of the 25-meter lap pool, indoor and outdoor tracks, basketball and volleyball courts, four tennis courts, large resistance training cen-

ter with hydraulic and free weights and cardiovascular equipment, and outdoor playing fields. PE classes for residents cost $21 a credit—few are more than one-credit classes—plus a $55 lab fee. Non-residents pay $50.40 per credit hour, plus the lab fee. The college also sells five-day guest passes for $25, $15 for seniors. The fitness center offers instruction in a wide variety of activities including aerobics, badminton, basketball, martial arts, tennis, volleyball, walking, weight training, and yoga. There are also many different swimming classes from which to choose, including water safety instructor certification. The center is open Monday through Friday from 6:30 AM to 9 PM and Saturday from 9 AM to 3 PM during the semester and, during interim sessions, Monday through Friday only from 6:30 AM to 8 PM.

Flying

Zia Aviation
405 Airport Rd.
• **(505) 471-2700, (800) 757-9030**

Zia Aviation provides flight training that will take a beginner and turn her into a private pilot after an average of 60 hours in the air. The school's FAA-certified instructors charge $30 per hour to teach students in a Cessna 172, which rents for $69 an hour including fuel. Each flight lesson includes approximately one hour on the ground and an hour in the air. Zia recommends students fly at least twice a week for optimum learning and retention. The company offers an introductory flight over Santa Fe for $49.95 in which students may take the controls. Zia is open seven days a week from 6 AM to 10 PM. Call ahead for an appointment.

Football

Santa Fe Parks and Recreation Department
Municipal Recreation Complex, 205 Caja del Rio Rd.
• **(505) 955-4470**

After a long void, the City of Santa Fe is once again sponsoring adult football. It orga-

PARKS AND RECREATION

nized a men's flag football league in 1999 to coincide with the completion of five regulation soccer fields at the new Municipal Recreation Complex (see entry in this chapter). The league has 14 teams, each of which pays $315 to join. The teams play against each other on Wednesdays, Saturdays, and Sundays during a season that runs from September through November.

The city also sponsors an annual Punt, Pass, & Kick competition for youths at the Fort Marcy/Mager's Field Sports Complex, 490 Washington Ave., (505) 955-2500. Participants from age 8 to 15 get three tries at punting, passing, and kicking a football, with each attempt measured for distance. The highest scores in each category are added together. Contestants with the three highest total scores win trophies. The competition costs $10.

Young America Football League de Santa Fe
1750 Cerrillos Rd.
• (505) 820-0775

This 30-year-old private co-ed league is part of a statewide organization for young footballers from age 6 to 13. Four hundred youths, the vast majority of them boys, participate in the Santa Fe league, which sponsors 14 teams that play in the city's Franklin E. Miles Park (Siringo Road and Camino Carlos Rey) and Ashbaugh Park (Cerrillos Road and Fourth Street) from August through October. The season starts with four weeks of rigorous conditioning and practice before players are allowed to have physical contact with each other. After that, teams rotate practice Monday through Friday between 5:30 and 7 PM. They play two games per night on Tuesdays, Wednesdays, and Thursdays from about 6 to 9 PM and three games on Saturdays between 9 AM and 1 PM. The league discourages stardom and a "winning is everything" mentality. Instead, it concentrates on teaching kids the rules of the game and sportsmanship.

INSIDERS' TIP
It's unlawful and disrespectful to remove pottery shards, arrowheads, or other artifacts from public lands. You can look at them, but don't pocket them.

Golf

Not only do Santa Fe golf courses offer lots of hills, varied terrain, and spectacular scenery, but they have a unique feature that any golfer has to love: the high elevation drives the ball farther than the same effort would get you at sea level. Combine that with the high quality bluegrass and bent grass that local courses use on their greens and fairways—not to mention relatively mild weather that allows you to play golf somewhere nearby all year long—and you can see why Santa Fe attracts golfers of all stripes.

Sun Country Amateur Golf Association
100-35 Country Club Land NW, Ste. 5, Albuquerque
• (505) 897-0864

This is the governing body of amateur golf in New Mexico and can provide you suggestions about where to play and how.

Pueblo de Cochití Golf Course
5200 Cochití Hwy., Cochití Lake
• (505) 465-2239

Located in the foothills of the Jémez Mountains, this 18-hole, par 72 course ranks in the top 50 nationwide among public golf courses. Golfers play roughly 50,000 rounds a year here on scenic bluegrass fairways and bent grass greens and tees. Championship tees play at 6541 yards, men's tees at 5996 yards, and ladies' tees at 5292 yards. Those numbers will have increased by July 2000 following major renovations on and off the green, including a new, three-level clubhouse with a restaurant and full-service pro shop. Guests pay a $25 greens fee during the week and $32 on weekends or they can pay an annual greens fee of $900. Carts cost $11 per player. Pueblo de Cochití Golf Course is open sunup to sundown year-round, weather permitting.

Quail Run Golf Course
3101 Old Pecos Trail
• (505) 986-2255, (800) 548-6990

Quail Run is a luxury, gated community with a private 9-hole/par 32 golf course that's open year-round, weather permitting, to guests from reciprocating country clubs with prior approval of the golf pro. The Arthur Jack Snyder–designed course, opened in 1986, features native grasses, bluegrass fairways, and tees measuring between 2,600 yards and 1,800 yards. Visitors pay $50 a day, including cart fees, to golf at Quail Run, where some 9,000 holes are played each year. The club has a pro shop that offers lessons as well as food and beverages. Hours are Tuesday through Sunday from 6 AM until dusk.

Santa Fe Country Club
Airport Road
• **(505) 471-0601**

Founded in 1946, this is a wide-open, 18-hole/par 72 public golf course. Golfers play about 45,000 rounds here each season, which runs from February through December. The course measures between 7,098 yards from the championship tees to 5,862 yards at the forward tees and offers a putting green, pitching green, and practice range. State residents pay between $90 a year for a social membership to $195 for a full membership. Non-residents can join for a flat $145 a year. Guests from New Mexico pay $25 a day to golf during the week, $35 a day on weekends, plus an $11 cart fee. Out-of-state guests pay $55 a day plus the cart fee. The club is open Tuesday through Sunday from 6 AM to about 8:30 PM between May and October and 8 AM to 5 PM the rest of the year.

Marty Sanchez Links de Santa Fe
Recreation Complex, 205 Caja del Rio Rd.
• **(505) 955-4470**

Named for a young Santa Fe golf champion who died of cancer at age 25, Marty Sanchez Links de Santa Fe is only 20 minutes from the Santa Fe Plaza and offers some of the best golfing in northern New Mexico with stunning backdrops on every tee. It features an 18-hole/par-72 championship links course with five tee-box locations measuring between 7415 yards from the championship tees to 5045 yards from the front tee boxes. It also has a 9-hole/par 3 course called a "Great 28." New Mexico residents pay $19 a day for 18 holes, $10 for nine holes, and an $11 cart fee. Seniors pay $25 and $10, respectively, including the cart fee. Junior residents can play 18 holes for $10, nine holes for $5. For non-residents, 18 holes cost $49 plus the $11 cart fee while nine holes are $17 plus cart fee. All golfers must purchase a $10 "resident card," which earns discounts at the pro shop.

Hiking

Santa Fe's backyard is a beautiful maze of trails, some forging deep into the mountains, others meandering easily in and around grassy, flower-filled meadows. Hyde Memorial State Park is just minutes away from downtown Santa Fe and offers a variety of trails, some easy, others strenuous. Among the most popular is the Winsor Trail, which leads into the

The foothills outside Santa Fe give riders a fine choice of trails.

Pecos Wilderness, though you needn't take it that far. It shares its bottom trailhead with the Borrego Trail, a very easy 4-mile hike that takes you through rolling meadows and forested hills. Simply follow N.M. 475 about 8.5 miles north to a parking lot where you'll find the trailhead.

If you're looking for a strenuous hike, the trail to Lake Katherine will give you spectacular views of Santa Fe Baldy, Penitente Peak, the upper Pecos Basin, the Rio Grande Valley, and the Jémez Mountains. This is a 14.5-mile hike requires 7 to 8 hours of hiking plus additional time to rest and eat. In that time, you will climb 3,200 feet. In about half the time, you can climb Atalaya Mountain, which literally is in Santa Fe's backyard. Starting at St. John's College (see out Education chapter), park in the visitor's parking lot, where you'll find the trailhead. (Take note: This is a favorite haunt for thieves who have no compunction about smashing car windows, so either carry all valuables with you or leave them at your digs.) Follow the signs, which will take you along and across an arroyo and eventually across and up a moderately steep hillside leading to a private road. There you'll begin your ascent up Atalaya, which starts off gently only to become quite steep in the middle and at the end of the trail. You'll be rewarded with magnificent, sweeping views of the entire city. Watch out for scree on the downhill portion of your hike. We recommend wearing hiking shoes with good tread. For more information on trails and conditions, call or visit the New Mexico Public Lands Information Center, 1474 Rodeo Rd., (505) 438-7542. Or call the Santa Fe chapter of the Sierra Club, Plaza Desira, 621 Old Santa Fe Trail #10, (505) 983-2703, and leave a message on the answering machine. Someone really will get back to you. You might also check the "Outdoors" section of Thursday's Santa Fe New Mexican, which lists Sierra Club outings for the upcoming weekend and phone numbers of the group leaders. If you're a serious hiker, by all means buy a copy of the local Sierra Club group's self-published Day Hikes in the Santa Fe Area. Now in its fifth printing, this 228-page paperback describes in delightful detail 45 hikes ranging from easy to strenuous, some in Santa Fe, others up to 85 miles away. If you're not the do-it-yourself type, there are numerous guides in

Santa Fe that will be happy to guide you on half-day to multiple-day hikes.

For more information about hikes in this area, see our Parks section in this chapter.

Horseback Riding

The Bishop's Lodge
North Bishops Lodge Rd.
• **(505) 983-6377, ext. 500;**
(800) 732-2240, ext. 500

Just three miles from Santa Fe Plaza, the Bishop's Lodge was once the private retreat of Santa Fe's famed 19th century Archbishop Jean Baptiste Lamy—the father, as it were, of St. Francis Cathedral in the downtown area. Today, the lodge is a resort on 500 acres of private land in a lush valley nestled into the foothills of the Sangre de Cristo Mountains. Its backyard is a natural piñon-juniper forest with a maze of scenic trails through which wranglers lead small groups, from beginners to experienced riders, on horseback for up to an hour and a half. You'll be riding along narrow mountain trails, so you'll rarely go faster than a trot, though you may be able to canter on the roads leading to the trails.

The stables offer regularly scheduled rides at 9:30 AM and 2 PM. They're open for business seven days a week, except for Sunday afternoons, from April through Thanksgiving, weather permitting. Lodge guests pay $28 an hour or $35 for 1.5 hours. Rides for non-guests cost $35 and $45, respectively. If you're not staying at the lodge, be sure to call ahead—a day or two is best—to guarantee a spot because lodge guests otherwise get first dibs. Don't plan on taking children younger than 9. Nor will the stable allow anyone who weighs more than 220 pounds to ride their horses, most of which are quarter-horse mixes.

Broken Saddle Riding Company
Vicksville Rd., Cerrillos
• **(505) 470-0074**

South of Santa Fe, about 26 miles from the Plaza, Broken Saddle is the only stable in the state that offers smooth-riding, gaited horses like Tennessee Walkers and Missouri Fox Trotters that use all four legs for power. With horses

> **INSIDERS' TIP**
> The City of Santa Fe changed its phone system in late spring 2000 and was still trying to work out the kinks at this writing. All city phone numbers now begin with 955. State numbers still begin with the prefix "827."

like these, it goes without saying that, unlike many stables, Broken Saddle allows riders to trot, canter, and even gallop. That's a big draw, especially for experienced riders who want to feel the wind in their face. With 5,500 acres in the Cerrillos Hills south of Santa Fe, Broken Saddle is instantly familiar with dozens of beautiful trails in juniper and piñon country you'll recognize from classic Western movies. Perhaps you'll ride to Devil's Canyon with its beautiful rock formations or to one of the 221 old mines in the Cerrillos Hills—maybe even Old Grand Central Silver Mine, one of the bigger ones, Or you might wend your way up to the Madrid (emphasis on the first syllable) Overlook with 360-degree views of five mountain ranges. Guided rides average two hours and cost $50 per person for up to five people. Beginners are welcome; riders shorter than 4'10" are not. The stable is open for business year-round. Summertime is especially busy, so call two to three days in advance.

Rancho Las Palomas
27A Calle Peligroso, Cañoncito
• **(505) 989-1474**

At the top of Glorieta Mesa southeast of Santa Fe (20 minutes from the Plaza), Rancho Las Palomas is the old homestead of owner/wrangler Bob Romero's grandfather. Romero will take up to 10 people for scenic rides on any of a dozen trails in the Santa Fe National Forest—through wide open valleys with up to 300 head of cattle grazing in the summer right on into the mountains. Rides run $40 an hour, $45 for 1½ hours and $60 for two hours. You can also make special arrangements for half- and full-day rides. Depending on their size, children age 6 and up are welcome as long as they're accompanied by an adult. Experienced riders may canter and gallop at the wrangler's discretion. The stables are open year-round from Tuesday through Sunday with rides by appointment from sunrise to sunset. While you can show up and take your chances, it's best to call ahead of time—up to a day or two in summer.

Makarios Ranch
198 Camino Querencia, Cerrillos
• **(505) 473-1038**

In the old mining town of Cerrillos, Makarios caters primarily to experienced riders of all ages who are looking for adventure on the back of a horse. Be warned, this is not easy riding. You'll be traveling on rough, mountain terrain at high speeds, either on your own horse

or on one belonging to the ranch. Your journey may take you into the lovely Galisteo Basin area or deep into the Cerrillos Hills or the Ortiz Mountains. This is wild country with Indian ruins and old mines, some of which you might want to stop and explore. Rides are by appointment only and cost $50 for two hours, more for half-day and daylong rides.

Hunting

NM Dept. of Game and Fish
408 Galisteo
• **(505) 827-7911, (800) 862-9310**

Northern New Mexico offers excellent trophy hunting for elk, deer, antelope, and limited bighorn sheep on state, federal, Indian, and private land. Any would-be hunter's first step should be to get a copy of the New Mexico Game and Fish Department's annual Big Game Proclamation, which comes out in mid-winter. The proclamation outlines rules and regulations as well as license fees. Be sure to read the pamphlet carefully because it's extremely—some would say ridiculously—dense and complicated. Hunters should be aware that the application deadline for special hunts, which include most big game, is in early spring. Ask the Game and Fish Department for its list of certified outfitters as well as its list of guides about whom complaints have been received or whose licenses have been revoked. Guides and outfitters must have permits from the appropriate agency if they will be guiding on federal (national forest, Bureau of Land Management) or State Trust lands. Prospective clients should insist that any outfitter provide names of prior customers and should follow-up by checking all references. They may also get additional information from the New Mexico Council of Outfitters and Guides (160 Washington St., SE #75, Albuquerque, N.M., 87108).

For elk, which is becoming the top game in New Mexico, the Valle Vidal Unit of the Carson National Forest in northeastern New Mexico is about as good as it gets on public land anywhere in the United States. The Sargent and Humphries wildlife areas near Chama, in northwestern New Mexico, also offer record book heads. Competition is fierce in both areas for limited slots. If you don't mind paying to hunt on private land, Vermejo Park Ranch, (505) 445-3097—contiguous with the Valle Vidal and recently purchased by media magnate Ted Turner—has one of the finest elk herds in the country, second, perhaps, only to the national

PARKS AND RECREATION

Rafting is a popular summer sport and the "Taos Box" is a special treat.

Photo: Chris Corrie

elk refuge in Jackson, Wyoming. Vermejo Park's is a natural herd managed for even age distribution, which allows elks to reach maturity. The ranch also offers world class accommodations and is priced accordingly. Weeklong guided rifle hunts for mature bulls can cost up to $13,000, including lodging and food. That compares to $750 for non-resident hunters going after trophy elk on public land, such as the already mentioned Valle Vidal unit or, further south (and much closer to Santa Fe), the Pecos Wilderness, which offers good hunting for those willing to hire a guide with the necessary horseback transportation. Please see the paragraph above regarding outfitters.

On the other side of the Rio Grande, hunters are finding increasing success in the Jémez Mountains, northwest of Santa Fe, as the state elk herd continues to expand. The Baca Ranch (Baca Land and Cattle Company, 505-662-2270 or Baca Outfitters, 800-456-6620), in Valle Grande near Los Alamos, ensures an even better success rate, though you'll pay top dollar— up to $11,000 for a guided bull elk hunt. On the same side of the Rio Grande, north of Dulce near the Colorado border, the Jicarilla Apache Tribe (505-759-3255) offers trophy animals and high success rates. The Jicarilla recently purchased a first class lodge in Chama featuring some 30,000 acres of prime habitat for elk and deer. The tribe offers guided hunting trips as

well as fishing trips on well-stocked private lakes.

Compared to elk, hunting mule deer on New Mexico's public lands is an iffy proposition. Many experts say increasing numbers of elk have pushed out their smaller brethren. Hunters seeking trophies can expect to work hard for them, climbing high, rough country far from paved roads. You may not come home with a trophy—or even a non-trophy animal, for that matter—but you'll see some stunning country. Farmington, in the northeast corner of the state, is among the better deer hunting areas in New Mexico. The terrain may not be the only challenge deer hunters face in New Mexico. While they may still purchase licenses over-the-counter, New Mexico is increasingly going to a system requiring hunters to apply through a lottery system for a limited number of permits. Again, applications for drawings are due in early spring. Check the proclamation for the exact dates.

If it's bighorn sheep you're after, the odds of drawing a license are precipitously against you. If you manage to land a permit, do yourself a favor and hire a good outfitter to make the most of a rare opportunity. A handful of hunters each year is lucky enough to get licenses for bighorn sheep in the Pecos Wilderness. These animals, frequently so tame as to eat snacks from the hand of passing backpackers, may offer their biggest challenge in the drawing of the permit. Similarly, would-be antelope hunters have the option of facing long odds in public drawings or paying ranchers, who often advertise in local newspapers. Eastern New Mexico on both sides of Interstate 40 offers trophy heads of the keen-sighted animals.

Spring and fall are hunting seasons for wild turkey, designated as big game in New Mexico. Locals addicted to this challenging—many say impossible—pastime find some success in the lower hills of the Pecos Wilderness and in the northern mountains.

Small game season varies according to the species. September, when hunting season opens for a number of small game species, is a perfect time for those who want to combine a lovely hike in the autumn woods with bringing home supper—perhaps a squirrel or grouse.

Martial Arts

Santa Fe is a beacon for alternative lifestyles, so it's not surprising that the city has an enormous selection of martial arts studios to appeal to those with eastern sensibilities. You'll find Aikido in styles ranging from soft to stringent; judo, karate, kenpo, kung fu, tae kwon do, tai chi, chi kung, tang soo, and a variety of others in the telephone book listed under "martial arts" or the specific activity.

Mushball

Santa Fe Parks and Recreation Department, Recreation Division
1142 Siler Rd.
• (505) 955-2500

Don't let the name put you off. This is a very popular co-ed sport among Santa Fe adults, particularly women. Except for the ball, which is the size of a grapefruit, the game is similar to softball. The Recreation Division can give you information about city-sponsored and private leagues, all of which play in various city parks. The city's mushball league runs from May through August and charges $315 per team.

Racquetball

A number of gyms in town have racquetball courts and offer lessons. These include the Genoveva Chavez Community Center, 3321 Rodeo Rd., (505) 955-4001; William C. Witter Fitness Education Center at Santa Fe Community College, 6401 Richards Ave., (505) 428-1615; Club International Family Fitness Center, 1931 Warner Ave., (505) 473-9807; and El Gancho Fitness, Swim and Racquet Club, Old Las Vegas Hwy., (505) 988-5000. See our Fitness Centers/ Gyms/Health Clubs section in this chapter for additional information on these facilities.

Fort Marcy/Mager's Field Sports Complex
490 Washington Ave.
• (505) 955-2500

The City of Santa Fe sponsors summer and winter racquetball leagues based out of the Fort Marcy/Mager's Field Sports Complex, which features two racquetball courts. The leagues play a 12-game schedule and hold post-season tournaments in which first- second- and third-place winners receive awards and all participants get T-shirts—not bad for $35. The summer league begins in June or July, the winter league in December or January. Call Fort Marcy or pick up a city Activity Guide for specific dates.

Rock Climbing

Santa Fe Climbing Gym
825 Early St.
• (505) 986-8944

While northern New Mexico is not exactly a mecca for rock climbers—there's precious little granite in the state; the rocks here tend to be sandstone and crumble easily—there are still enough challenges in the region to keep local climbers active and happy between trips to Yosemite or the Tetons. Closer to home, you can find excellent, frequently climbed local crags, especially in the Los Alamos/White Rock area in the Jémez Mountains northwest of Santa Fe. Before you go, you might want to spend some time in the Santa Fe Climbing Gym, the only place of its kind in town. The Climbing Gym emphasizes sport climbing, which is less about discovery and the technical aspects of climbing than the athletic or gymnastics. The gym is located in a large, new warehouse with 3,500-square-feet of artificial climbing walls. The main room has a 40-foot-wide wall that reaches 28 feet at its highest point and contains dozens of different holds as well as inclines and overhangs. Students practice climbing with their hands and with ropes, alone, and in groups. The floor is padded with carpeting over rubber to cushion falls, which are inevitable.

The Santa Fe Climbing Gym holds weekly, three-hour introductory classes for $40 each, including gear, intermediate classes for $20 and advanced classes for $50. It also offers classes and clinics for advanced climbers that in the past have featured such renowned climbers as Timy Fairfield, ranked No. 1 in the US; Bobi Bensman, who is one of the top women climbers in the country; and Lise Noel, a French climber who competes in World Cup competitions and is among the best climbers in the world. Seminars change every season so be sure to call the gym for descriptions, schedules and prices.

Adult climbers have a variety of membership options, including unlimited use of the facilities for $50 a month, three-month passes for $100, a 10-visit "punch pass" for $95 and day passes for $12 day, $6 for bouldering only (no ropes). Private instruction costs $20 an hour. The gym has open climbing Monday through Friday from 5 PM to 10 pm, Saturday and Sunday from 1 to 6 PM. Children under 14 can climb Saturdays from 9 AM to 11 AM. Weekdays at the Climbing Gym are reserved for public and private school classes and after-school programs. The gym also holds a weekly "kid climb"—a two-hour class for children age 7 and up at $15 per session, $75 for six visits or $120 for 10 visits. Parents and guardians need not be present. The Climbing Gym also offers summer programs. Ask for details.

Rollerskating

Rockin' Rollers Event Arena
2915 Agua Fría St.
• (505) 473-7755

Santa Fe youth have long complained—and rightfully so—that there's little or nothing for them to do in Santa Fe, especially at night. Rockin' Rollers Event Arena has come to the rescue. Located on Agua Fría Street, 50 feet south of Siler Road, Rockin' Rollers is a fantasy in purple that features a 3,500-square-foot tiled skating rink—yes, the floor is purple, too—with purple walls, including one with a mural of extraterrestrials skating on sea-green waves. Friday and Saturday nights at Rockin' Rollers feature dances with an in-house deejay or live local bands. All ages are welcome, but this place is a favorite of the younger set, so we've included a more extensive write-up in our Kidstuff chapter.

Rugby

Rio Grande Rugby Union, Santa Fe Club
1216 Parkway Dr.
• (505) 988-2205

Santa Fe has a very active all-male rugby club, the Santos, which will celebrate its 30th anniversary in 2002. A member of the Rio Grande Rugby Union—which encompasses the area from El Paso, Texas, to Durango, Colorado, and takes in all of New Mexico—the Santos have hosted a number of international clubs and many of its members have ventured abroad themselves to England, Ireland, New Zealand, and Vancouver The 23-man club boasts a number of high-profile members, including long-time state senator Shannon Robinson. Most teammates are 35 and younger; older members are called the Anasazi after the ancestors tribe of Pueblo Indians. While it doesn't have the depth of many clubs—some of its members have only been playing rugby five years though they have backgrounds in football, soccer, wrestling, and other aggressive sports—the Santos' overall athleticism is on par with any rugby club in the country. Their temporary home has been a turned field at the new Municipal Recreation Complex, 205 Caja del Rio Rd., (505) 955-4470, where construction of two rugby fields is in progress. The club plays home games on Saturday starting at 1 PM. Members practice Tuesdays and Thursdays starting at 5:30 or 6 PM. The Santos play primarily in fall and spring, though the club won't say no to summer games in the Colorado Rockies, where the weather is still comfortably cool. The spring season starts in early March, weather permitting, and continues through mid-May. The fall season begins in September and goes through November. The club sponsors an annual Labor Day weekend rugby tournament, which begins at 9 AM on Sunday with finals at about 5PM. It won the 1997 tournament, the first featuring a women's bracket. The Santos coach youth teams from Santa Fe and Los Alamos—the Rio Grande Union's next generation of rugby players who have cut their teeth in games against Denver, both at home and away.

Running/Walking

The beauty of Santa Fe is that practically anywhere you live, you can step outside your door and within a few minutes find yourself away from cars and people and, depending on the part of town, even pavement. If you're lucky enough to be in a relatively undeveloped part of town, or if you don't mind driving to your run or your walk, Santa Fe offers umpteen unpaved roads and trails, some in town, others in the county; some with respectable inclines, others downright intimidating. And practically anywhere you go, you'll find beautiful scenery and attractive architecture—unless, of course, you hate either real or faux adobe. In that case, move to Minneapolis.

Santa Fe offers nearly ideal weather for running and walking—even in the winter for zealots who won't let a little snow or slush stop them. There's nothing quite as beautiful as getting out first thing in the morning after a night's snowfall when the trees and adobe walls are outlined in soft shelves of white snow that muffle all sounds, including those of your shoes hitting the ground. Do be careful about slipping, however. The snow may cushion the thud, but it probably won't provide adequate cushioning for your back or hips.

The downside of running or walking in Santa Fe is that it's not a particularly pedestrian friendly town, except perhaps for the area in and around the Plaza. The city has a dearth of sidewalks, so you'll find yourself sharing the road with cars and bicycles or treading on terribly uneven shoulders that threaten twisted ankles or worse. The best defense is a pair of off-road running or walking shoes that provide lots of ankle support. For runners and walkers both, it's always a good idea to run facing traffic, especially on Santa Fe's many curving roads. Ideally, you want to find a place that has very little car traffic. That way you avoid carbon monoxide as well as possible accidents. If you run or walk at night, wear something reflective and be sure to ask around to make sure the area you choose is safe. Running or walking in groups certainly lessens the odds of being a crime victim, though for some it defeats the purpose entirely. If you prefer to run or walk in company, we've included a few suggestions here.

Villa Linda Mallwalkers
Villa Linda Mall, 4250 Cerrillos Rd.
• (505) 471-3895

Formed in 1984 by St. Vincent Hospital and a small group of seniors in search of exercise and companionship, the Villa Linda Mallwalkers today boasts up to 100 people, most of them elderly, who walk laps around the interior of the Villa Linda Mall. There's almost always a small crowd already at the doors when the mall, located at the intersection of Cerrillos and Rodeo Roads, opens at 7AM Monday through Saturday. After their morning constitutional, the walkers meet at Luby's Cafeteria, (505) 473-7084, on the north side of the mall, for 25-cent cups of coffee with free refills until 9:30 AM. On Fridays, Luby's serves the walkers cinnamon rolls for only 50 cents. One Friday a month, a speaker from either St. Vincent Hospital or Lovelace Health Systems (see the Wellness chapter) leads a 45-minute discussion on a variety of health topics of particular interest to seniors.

In addition to being an exercise group, the Mallwalkers has also turned into an ad hoc support group, helping members get through illness and deaths of loved ones. Many long-lasting friendships have been forged along the 0.6-mile course. Members socialize at parties and have even taken cruises together.

A smaller group meets at the opposite end of town in DeVargas Center, at North Guadalupe St. and Paseo de Peralta. Call the mall at (505) 982-2655 for more information.

Santa Fe Parks and Recreation Department
1142 Siler Rd.
• (505) 955-2509

The city sponsors a number of races throughout the year including the Santa Fe Run-Around in June, a 5k run and 1-mile walk co-sponsored by the Santa Fe Striders (see entry below), and the annual Sylvia Pulliam Memorial "Hot Chile Run" in August, a 5k and 10k run starting at Salvador Perez Park, 601 Alto St., and, in September, the 5k/10k Old Santa Fe Trail Run–begun in 1978, which makes it the oldest race in town.

Santa Fe Striders
P.O. 1818, Santa Fe, 87504
• (505) 983-2144

Affiliated with Road Runners Club of America, Santa Fe Striders is a local running club for everyone from the casual runner to 100-mile ultra-marathoners. The club has approximately 70 members of varying ages, from their 20s to their 70s, who promote running, sponsor races, and gather for informal runs open to anybody who's interested. Every Wednesday at 6 pm, members gather on the Plaza for a 5- to 7-mile run followed by beer and a bite to eat. Anywhere from three to a score of runners usually show up, regardless of weather. Most are members, but all are welcome. The Wednesday night runs always start and finish in or around the Plaza.

Competitive runners meet Tuesday nights at the Santa Fe High School track for speed workouts. Another group meets for occasional long-distance runs on weekends to prepare for marathons or just for the heck of it. Members also like to meet at least once a year at La Bajada—a steep incline along U.S. 25, about 20 miles south of Santa Fe—to run along the old Camino Real (see History or Overview). Sometimes they hold informal races from Santa Fe to Lamy in which the first team of two runners and a cyclist to arrive, wins. The club organizes other informal runs, often followed by a picnic, a pot-luck, or dinner at a restaurant.

The Santa Fe Striders sponsor several 5k and/or 10k races a year, including the club's flagship event, the Santa Fe Run-Around in June (see the previous entry); a charitable 5k run on the Saturday before Thanksgiving to benefit the Salvation Army; and the Corrida de Los Locos ("Run of the Crazies") in late January, an unsanctioned 4.2k race for which contestants pray for the worst weather possible. For the truly loco, there's even a snowshoe race in mid-January. Those who prefer less inclement weather might consider joining the club's Big Tesuque run in early October, an 11.6-mile mountain run from Aspen Vista to the radio towers at the top of Tesuque Peak and back down again—great training for endurance runners. All races cost between $10 and $15 and are advertised in the club's newsletter as well as in an annual calendar available from New Mexico USA Track and Field, 31 Sandhill Rd., Los Lunas, NM 87031, (505) 865-8612. You can also call the Santa Fe Striders directly for its schedule or suggestions on where to run.

For visitors, the club often recommends running around St. John's College, which sits directly in the foothills of the Sangre de Cristo Mountains. It also sends runners up Hyde Park Road (a.k.a. Artist Road), the beginning of a long uphill stretch that ends up at the ski slopes; along winding, scenic Bishop's Lodge Road; or up Atalaya Mountain—a 3.5-mile run with an elevation increase of 1,780—for some "light" spring, summer, and autumn running.

Skateboarding

It took some political finessing, but in 1995, Santa Fe opened its first "official" skateboard park on public land—an unusual gesture for any city to make and yet one more reason that Santa Fe deserves its nickname, "The City Different." Located downtown in West De Vargas Park at De Vargas and Guadalupe Streets, the park has concrete ramps and culverts galore, making it a popular destination for skaters as well as cyclists and rollerskaters. Skaters once practiced in and around the Plaza—to the consternation of many and the fascination of a few. Now, however, they'll have two parks from which to choose. At the time of this writing, the city was putting the finishing touches on a new skateboard park scheduled to open by August 2000 in Franklin E. Miles Park (see our write-up in the Parks section of this chapter). With 13,000 square feet, the new skateboard park is two-and-a-half times the size of its older sibling. It has plenty of bowls and even a street plaza, giving park habitués a birds-eye view of the talent. As in all city parks, skaters must observe the 10 PM curfew. This seems to pose few hardships—except, of course, in summer when avid skaters can never get enough of their favorite pastime. To find other good skateboard locations, ask any skater or just follow the rail marks.

Beyond Waves Mountain Surf Shop
333 Montezuma St.
• (505) 988-2240

When they're not in Skateboard Park, you're likely to find skaters in Beyond Waves Mountain Surf Shop, one of only two specialty stores in Santa Fe—and the only one located downtown—that sells skateboards and accessories, including apparel. On rainy days, you're likely to see groups of kids just hanging out at Beyond Waves, conveniently located down the street from Skateboard Park. You'll find some watching any of the store's more than 150 skating or snowboarding videos, others listening to music, and some exploring the wares. The store sponsors an annual summer skateboard contest in which participants in various age groups are judged for ability. Winners receive trophies, skateboards, T-shirts, and other goodies. Everyone gets a free bumper sticker. The event usually gets some radio and television coverage. Beyond Waves is open seven days a week, 10 AM to 7 PM in summer with an 8 AM opening time in winter to rent out snowboards. During the winter, the store closes Sundays at 6 PM.

Soccer

America has long played catch-up with Eu-

The Popay Foot Race is held every year in July.

Photo: Don Strel

due to open in summer 2001. Adults belong to the Santa Fe Soccer Club, (505) 471-3004, a member of the New Mexico State Soccer Association headquartered in Albuquerque. The club has nearly 600 members and 36 men's, women's, co-ed, and seniors teams for players 30 and older. Before the MRC fields opened in 1999, the soccer club used the football fields at Fort Marcy Park in downtown Santa Fe and Villa Linda Park south of town, forcing them to play in summer—Tuesday, Wednesday, and Thursday nights starting at 6:15—and putting them at odds with the state soccer association. Now that they have their own dedicated fields, the club will eventually ease into the normal soccer season. The Santa Fe Soccer Club also runs an indoor, no-walls adult soccer league called 5-a-Side that in 1999 had 51 teams. They play from December to March at Santa Fe Preparatory School, 1101 Camino Cruz Blanca, (505) 982-1829. Call for details.

Capital Soccer Club, (505) 982-6186), is the select club for youths from 1st through 8th grades. Beginning players belong to the Northern New Mexico Soccer Association (505-982-0878, 505-471-3743, and 505-982-8294—summer camps). The clubs register kids in May and play from August through October in a variety of locations—Fort Marcy (490 Washington Avenue), Villa Linda Park (Rodeo Road and Mall Circle), Salvador Perez Park (601 Alta Vista), and Ashbaugh Park (Cerrillos Road and Fourth Street), depending on the team, and MRC in future when youth fields are done.

rope in its appreciation for the game of soccer. In Santa Fe as elsewhere in the country the sport is rapidly gaining popularity with some 1,700 local kids and upward of 500 adults playing the game. Along with this popularity have come increasingly more vocal demands for equal time—and equal playing fields—with other sports. Accused for years of treating soccer players like second class citizens, the City of Santa Fe has finally risen to the challenge with five adult soccer fields, the only ones in the city dedicated to the sport, at the new Municipal Recreation Complex with seven youth fields

PARKS AND RECREATION

Softball

Greater Santa Fe Softball Association
3238 Nizhoni Dr.
• **(505) 473-3933**

The Greater Santa Fe Softball Association is a private organization that last year had 2,700 registered players from age 15 (with parental consent) to 67 in women's, men's, and co-ed leagues. Teams start practice in March with games beginning in April and continuing through September five nights a week. Tournaments take place on the weekend at the Tom Aragon baseball field at the Municipal Recreation Complex. The league plays three games per night starting at 6:15 PM with a new game on the hour and a quarter. Lights go out after 10 pm, precluding any extra innings.

Swimming

The City of Santa Fe has four indoor heated swimming pools with schedules, classes, and prices unique to each facility. Call the individual pool or pick up a copy of the City of Santa Fe Parks and Recreation Department's annual Activity Guide, which has a complete schedule for each pool. Check with the Recreation Division (505-438-1485) for special programs and teams. (For private pools, look under the "Fitness Centers/Gyms/Health Clubs" section in this chapter.)

Bicentennial Pool, 1121 Alto St.,
    (505) 955-2650

Fort Marcy Swimming Pool,
    490 Washington Ave., (505) 955-2500

Genoveva Chavez Community Center,
    3321 Rodeo Road, (505) 955-4001

Salvador Perez Park and Pool,
    601 Alta Vista St., (505) 955-2604

Tino Griego Pool, 1730 Llano St.,
    (505) 955-2660

Tennis

Santa Fe has public tennis courts throughout the city, all of them outdoors. Call the individual facility, if possible, or the City of Santa Fe Parks Division (505-955-2106) for hours,

lighting, rules, etc., as well as for information about instruction for children and adults. There is no charge to use the courts, which are available on a first-come, first-served basis only.

Alto Park & Bicentennial Pool,
    1043 Alto St., (505) 984-6773

Atalaya Park, 717 Camino Cabra

Chamisa Tennis Courts,
    Dr. Richard Angle Park, Calle Medico

Fort Marcy/Mager's Field Sports Complex,
    490 Washington Ave., (505) 955-2500

Galisteo Tennis Courts, 2721 Galisteo Street

Herb Martinez/La Resolana,
    2240 Camino Carlos Rey

Larragoite Park, Agua Fría Street and
    Avenida Cristobal Colon

Salvador Perez Park & Pool,
    601 Alta Vista St., (505) 955-2604

Private Courts

El Gancho Fitness, Swim and Racquet Club
Old Las Vegas Hwy.
• **(505) 988-5000**

El Gancho is a members-only club with the largest tennis facilities in Santa Fe. They include seven outdoor courts, of which two are clay and three are lighted, and two permanent indoor courts for an extra fee of $6 per half-hour in summer and $12 per half-hour in winter. El Gancho has four on-site tennis pros, leagues, and tournaments. For details on membership, see our write-up under the Fitness Centers and Gym section in this chapter.

Sangre de Cristo Racquet Club
1755 Camino Corrales
• **(505) 983-7978**

Sangre de Cristo Racquet Club is a private tennis club with five outdoor courts—including one clay court and another with lights and heat—and an indoor court in a fabric "bubble." The club also has an outdoor heated swimming pool for seasonal use only. Individual memberships require a $600 initiation fee and monthly dues of $83 . Family memberships cost $800 for initiation and $115 a month. Junior memberships run $54.25 per month plus a $300 initiation fee. The per-diem fee for non-members is $20. Sangre de Cristo has two tennis pros, a full-service pro shop, and two sanctioned tournaments.

Santa Fe Country Club
Airport Road
• **(505) 471-3378, ext. 22**
The Santa Fe Country Club offers three outdoor courts in a beautiful setting surrounded by trees. Although primarily for members, the tennis courts are open to non-members for $10 an hour for singles, $15 for doubles. The club has a full-service pro shop on the premises and one U.S. Professional Tennis Association-certified pro. She charges $45 an hour for private lessons, $12.50 per person for group lessons. Every summer the country club hosts an adult tournament and a junior tournament, both open to the public. The country club is closed on Mondays. See the entry under Golf for membership fees,

Shellaberger Tennis Center
College of Santa Fe, 1600 St. Michael's Dr.
• **(505) 473-6144**
Located on the campus of the College of Santa Fe, Shellaberger Tennis Center is the only club in Santa Fe exclusively for tennis. The center has seven outdoor courts including four with tournament-quality lighting. Members can join leagues, compete in tournaments, and take lessons from pros. The club has anywhere between one and four pros on site, depending on the season. The club will even arrange matches for you with a day's notice. Membership begins with a $325 initiation fee and costs $39 monthly. Non-members pay $5 per day for a maximum of six days per year.

Ultimate Frisbee

Santa Fe Ultimate
PO Box 23103, Santa Fe, 87505
• **(505) 988-4005**
There are only a two requirements to play for Santa Fe Ultimate, the only ultimate Frisbee team in Santa Fe: lots of enthusiasm and an ability to run. Of course a strong, controlled throwing arm won't hurt, either. But mostly, the idea is to have fun at the game, which is like a blend of football and soccer using a Frisbee instead of a ball. There's no tackle in this game, nor can you run with the disc. The goal is to get the Frisbee from one end of the field to another by tossing it from player to player. Santa Fe Ultimate is sanctioned by the Ultimate Players Association, based out of Colorado. The team has a roster of about 15 steady players, most of them outdoor sports enthusiasts (rock climbers, mountain bikers, etc) who show up regularly at Ashbaugh Park (Cerrillos Rd. and Fourth St.), where the team plays Monday, Wednesday, and sometimes Friday (if enough people come) from about 6 PM to dark, three seasons out of the year. Another 10 show up "when they feel like it," according to one player, who added, "This is Santa Fe. People have their own agenda." Weekends are reserved for tournaments, usually four or five a year, including one the team hosts annually that attracts more than 20 teams from throughout the Southwest.

Volleyball

Santa Fe Parks and Recreation Department
1142 Siler Rd.
• **(505) 955-2508**
The City of Santa Fe sponsors both a co-ed and an all-women's volleyball team in a season that begins in early October and ends in early March with tournaments. Register early because the Parks and Recreation Division has only 200 slots and they fill up early.

Santa Fe Volleyball Club
• **(505) 471-0409**
The Santa Fe Volleyball Club is a private outdoor league whose teams pay $250 to $300 for fall league play at St. Michael's High School, 100 Siringo Road, (505) 983-7353. In summer, club members meet at Gregory Lopez Park, 1230 San Felipe Avenue, to play doubles and fours for $20 per person. Non-members are welcome.

Whitewater Rafting, Kayaking, Canoeing, and Floating

Right here in the high desert of northern New Mexico, you'll experience some of the finest whitewater rafting in the West. Come spring, with the melting of winter's snowpack, the Rio Grande, Red River and Rio Chama swell their banks with churning, fast-moving water that makes for some mighty hairy rapids. Even

PARKS AND RECREATION

Fall colors along the Rio Grande support the notion that New Mexico is a special place.

Photo: Don Strel

the most jaded rafter will get a thrill—and some astoundingly beautiful scenery along the way. Try it for yourself and see why Congress officially designated these magnificent rivers as "wild and scenic." Among the more popular rafting spots is the Taos Box of the Rio Grande, so-called because you'll pass through class IV rapids boxed in by the sheer cliffs—some of them 1,000 feet high—of the Rio Grande Gorge. For a somewhat more sedate ride—and we do mean "somewhat" because you'll still run into several rapids—head northeast for El Vado and float down the Rio Chama through canyons of pink, red and mauve sandstone or Ponderosa pine.

Because of the unpredictability of the rivers, you're advised to do some careful research and advanced scouting should you decide to venture out on your own—and even then, you should do so only if you're highly experienced. The Rio Grande has some dangerous and, in certain sections, impassable stretches of water. You'd be wise to invest $3 in the state Parks and Recreation Division's New Mexico Whitewater: A Guide to River Trips, and by all means call the Bureau of Land Management in Taos, (505) 758-8148, for up-to-date information on the rivers. Or hire a professional outfitter, whose business it is to know the rivers and equip you with good gear and knowledgeable guides. You can choose trips lasting from a half day to five days, from flat-out easy to downright dangerous. Call the BLM at (505) 758-8851 for a list of New Mexico whitewater touring companies or try any of the local outfits listed below:

Known World Guides
NM Hwy. 582, No. 702, Lyden
• **(505) 983-7756, (800) 983-7756**

Known World offers a variety of rafting excursions in northern New Mexico including custom trips and moonlight floats. Your rafting trip can last anywhere from a half day in the Taos Box, for example, to a week in the upper Rio Grande from the Colorado border to the Lower Gorge. Or perhaps you'd prefer to float with your kids through White Rock Canyon, New Mexico's deepest canyon, which borders Bandelier National Monument (see Parks in this chapter) and offers up-close sightings of Anasazi petroglyphs. Known World river trips range from $50 for a half-day trip on the Rio Grande to $140 per day on the Canadian River in the northwest quadrant of the state. Prices

include all food and equipment except clothing and sleeping gear. Ask about group rates and multiple day discounts.

Kokopelli Rafting Adventures
541 Cordova Rd.
• **(505) 983-3734, (800) 879-9035**

Kokopelli Rafting Adventures' menu of river trips has something for everyone—from folks looking to kick back and relax to adrenaline junkies who can't get enough of those class IV rapids. You could spend anywhere from a half-day to eight days navigating the Rio Chama, Rio Grande, or other New Mexico rivers. Among Kokopelli's offerings is a two-day float down a rarely traveled portion of the upper Rio Grande. Starting at Ute Mountain located about 150 miles north of Santa Fe at the New Mexico-Colorado border, you'll experience 25 miles of a designated Wild and Scenic section of the river before winding up at Lee Trail after a night under the stars at Costilla Creek. River trips cost anywhere from $40 for a half-day to $195 for the two-day Ute Mountain trip. Call Kokopelli for information about longer trips. And let them worry about things like camping equipment, meals, soft drinks, and water. The company will provide them on day trips and snacks for half-day trips.

Santa Fe Rafting Company
1000 Cerrillos Rd.
• **(505) 988-4914, (800) 467-7238**

Santa Fe Rafting Company provides a variety of trips to make everyone from families to whitewater enthusiasts happy. Certified guides not only lead you through rapids, but can also identify the flora, fauna and geological attractions along the way. You can paddle yourself or sit back and let your guides do the rowing

Southwest Wilderness Adventures
2124 Camino Polvoso
• **(505) 983-7262, (800) 869-7238**

Enjoy the thrill of whitewater or the serenity of a float on a half-day, full-day, or overnight trip with Southwest Wilderness Adventures. Southwest offers trips in the Rio Grande Gorge, including the exciting Taos Box; in White Rock Canyon, which is suitable for the whole family; and down the "wild and scenic" Rio Chama. Quality meals are included with your trip. Discounts are available for groups of 10 or more.

Winter Sports

For some, the idea of "winter" in Santa Fe may stir images of short-sleeved golfing and tennis. After all, this is the Southwest isn't it? Well, yes—but we're not Phoenix. Santa Fe gets a real winter, complete with snow and frigid temperatures. Winter usually begins in late October, settles in to stay in January—the coldest month of the year here—and disappears sometime in March or April. In good snow years, you can still see patches of snow on the Sangre de Cristo Mountains above Santa Fe on the Fourth of July. Thanks to our elevation and the surrounding mountains, snow on Memorial Day is not unheard of. And, due to our relatively southerly location, neither is sweatshirt weather in March. Even in winter, some 70 percent of the days here are sunny. A normal winter brings only a few below-zero spells, but freezing nights and scrape-the-frost-off-the windshield morning are also the norm. To put it simply, "sunny" doesn't necessarily mean "warm".

Since it has snow and mountains, northern New Mexico boasts the lion's share of the state's ski areas. Old-timers say that running a ski area is like running a farm. In the end, your success depends on the weather. And for the winters of 1998–99 and '99–2000, the weather brought New Mexico a snow drought. As a result, all areas had few skiers and snowboarders than in good years and lower revenues—which means less money for improvements. But you have to be an optimist to be a farmer or run a ski area. Here's to good snow for the coming seasons!

Within a three-hour drive from Santa Fe, you have access to the Santa Fe Ski Area, Taos Ski Valley, Angel Fire Ski Resort, Red River Ski Area, Ski Rio, Sipapu Ski Area, and Sandia Peak Ski Area. You'll also find The Enchanted Forest cross-country ski area and many places to head off on your own for Nordic skiing, snowshoeing, or winter hiking.

You can bring your sled or inner tubes up to Hyde State Park, just outside of Santa Fe on N.M. Highway 475. If you don't want the drive on a snowy road, try city parks such as Patrick Smith Park at 1001 Canyon Road, or Herb Martinez Park, 2240 Camino Carlos Rey, which have hills that make good tubing runs.

Safety Tips and Planning

Before you go off skiing, snowshoeing, or winter hiking, please keep these tips in mind.

You're at a high altitude here, which affects your heart, lungs, and overall energy. Give yourself time to adjust before you do anything excessively strenuous. Santa Fe sits at 7,000 feet—the top of the Santa Fe Ski Area is 12,000 feet above sea level.

The weather can be volatile. Never assume that the clear, sunny early morning conditions will remain. Be prepared for weather changes, especially if you're headed for the backcountry. Tell people where you're going and when you plan to be back. Take a backpack with extra clothing, matches, a space blanket, food, water, and whatever else you'll need if you have to spend the night in subfreezing temperatures.

The sun shines brightly here, even in winter. Wear sunscreen and take an extra supply with you for a midday application. If there's snow on the ground, protect your eyes from the intense glare with sunglasses.

Northern New Mexico's air is dry, and winter exertion can require a lot from your body. Drink fluids whenever possible. And remember, alcohol has stronger effects at higher altitudes and can contribute to dehydration.

If you want to ski during the Christmas holidays or spring break, plan ahead. New Mexico's ski areas are popular and, like ski resorts everywhere, tend to attract more visitors these times of year.

Need to rent equipment? Renting at the ski areas is the most convenient, but on busy days you may have to wait and occasionally—say during the Christmas holidays or over spring break—all the rentals in your size may be gone before you get there. Our advice: Arrive early during peak ski times (it makes parking easier too) or rent ahead of time at an in-town ski shop. Most will let you rent your equipment the night before at no additional charge. Some will even loan you a ski rack to take it up to the mountain. What a deal!

Driving can be treacherous after a winter storm. Although all the ski areas and the state highway department do their best to keep roads clear, some days you'll be happier with chains on your tires or four-wheel drive vehicles.

If you plan on snowshoeing or Nordic skiing, dress in layers. Begin with long underwear that will wick perspiration away from your body, then continue with light, comfortable, insulated clothing that will move with you. Top it all off with a breathable waterproof shell or sleeveless vest. And don't forget a hat.

Downhill Skiing

Skiing is big business here and an important boost to the state's economy during the off-season, visitor-wise, for all concerned. (Except the town of Taos Ski Valley, which is busiest when the skiers come.) On average, more than a million skiers a year explore the pleasures of the state's generally uncrowded slopes, sunny winters, and abundant snow. The sport had an economic impact of $250 million on New Mexico in the 1996–97 season, counting everything from lift tickets and lunches to gasoline and hotel rooms. (For the next two seasons, the Snow Gods did not smile on New Mexico, and as a result fewer skiers hit the slopes.) According to a study by the University of New Mexico, the average skier who comes from out-of-state stays 4.5 days.

Santa Fe makes an excellent base for a ski vacation. The Rocky Mountain extension known as the Sangre de Cristos, the Jemez Mountains, and the Sandia Mountains are our playground. You can spend a day at any of the state's seven northern ski areas or head to Sandia Peak Ski Area outside of Albuquerque and easily accessible to the south. After a day of fun on the slopes, come back to Santa Fe for lodging and dining.

In most years, the downhill ski areas open around Thanksgiving and close in mid-April. Most operate from 9 AM to 4 PM daily during the ski season and offer food and snacks, lockers, emergency first aid, and a shop where you can buy sunscreen, goggles, and whatever else you need for a day of skiing or snowboarding. (But no snowboarding at the Taos Ski Valley.) All the areas have rental shops with a variety of equipment for children and adults, and offer instruction. To rent equipment, you usually need to leave a deposit on a credit card and perhaps a driver's license.

Most areas offer morning and afternoon lessons, and private and semiprivate sessions can be arranged on request. Some ski areas promote bargain weeks, early or late-season discounts, special deals for first-time skiers, multi-day discounts, and other enticements to persuade you to come. Children and older skiers usually get a break on ticket prices. Don't be shy— ask about discounts when you call to make your reservations.

If you've never skied or tried a snowboard before, be sure to inquire about beginner packages. The ski areas encourage people to take up the sport by offering the lessons, rentals, and lift tickets at a good price. And if you don't have clothes for skiing and don't want to make a big investment, check around. Some ski shops will also rent you a ski bib, insulated ski pants, and a jacket. You can also outfit yourself and your kids inexpensively by shopping at resale stores, of which Santa Fe has several.

In this section, we offer you a glimpse of the ski areas near Santa Fe. Unless otherwise noted, all prices are for the 2000–2001 season.

Santa Fe Ski Area
16 miles northeast of Santa Fe on Hyde Park Rd. (N.M. Hwy. 475)
• (505) 982-4429 (office), (505) 983-9155 (snow information line), (505) 857-8977 (recorded information), (800) 776-SNOW
• www.skisantafe.com

The Santa Fe Ski Area, with a 12,000-foot elevation at the mountaintop, offers visitors the chance to ski one of the 10 highest ski peaks in the United States. From the wide slopes of Broadway to the challenging, tree-studded Tequila Sunrise, Santa Fe has terrain to please skiers and snowboarders of all abilities. The area's variety keeps strong intermediate and advanced skiers interested and gentle trails are perfect for beginners.

Part of the Santa Fe Ski Area's appeal lies in its convenience. The slopes are an easy (most of the time) 45-minute drive from the Santa Fe Plaza. Skiers from Santa Fe, Albuquerque, and elsewhere in New Mexico as well as visitors from Texas, Oklahoma, California, other states and even other countries enjoy themselves here. It's not unusual for conventioneers who come to town between Thanksgiving and Easter to stay an extra day just for the skiing.

The ski area covers 550 acres of the Santa Fe National Forest and is leased from the USDA Forest Service. There are 43 named trails: 20 percent "easiest," 40 percent "more difficult," and 40 percent "most difficult." Lift capacity is 7,800 skiers, but normal business is a comfortable 3,500 skiers a day.

One of Santa Fe Ski Area's strengths is its family focus. The youngest children head for Chipmunk Corner Children's Center, a safe and convenient place to learn the sport or to be cared for while their parents ski. The full-service facility offers convenient separate ticketing and equipment rental for kids, a tow all their own, a cozy lunchroom, a playroom, and more. The outdoor learning area is fenced for snow play as well as beginning skiing. Instructors receive special training for helping the little ones. Chipmunk Corner instruction is reserved for ages 4 to 9. For children too young to ski, the area offers a nursery with day care and snow play. Day-care slots are limited, so be sure to make reservations.

When they graduate from Chipmunk Corner, children can try Adventure Land, a ski playground complete with roller-coaster bumps, an obstacle course and the opportunity to "ski the trees." A child must accompany adults who want to ski here. The area is just off the Lower Broadway run beneath the Super Chief Chairlift.

For older children who live in Santa Fe and the surrounding area, the ski area features popular weekend lesson programs—Pre-White Tornado, White Tornados, Thunderbirds, Roadrunners, and Saturday Shredders—all designed to accommodate a variety of needs and abilities. The seven-session classes run from January through March on Saturdays and Sundays. The Tesuque Peak Flyers provide recreational racing coaching and contests for advanced intermediate skiers ages 7 to 13. The Santa Fe Adventure Team offers skiing challenges for children of the same ages and ability who are not interested in racing. In conjunction with area schools, the Santa Fe Ski Area also offers classes during the week for groups of elementary school children at a special rate. It's a great way for children to learn the sport.

Finally, serious young skiers of intermediate ability or better can join the Santa Fe Ski Team. The team begins its dryland training in October and starts to work on the snow when the ski area opens. A board of parents and community volunteers handles the team's business, and their financial support comes from training fees, race revenue, and fund-raising events such as the Santa Fe Ski Swap. Held each November, the Swap is a great place to pick up used equipment. (See our Annual Events chapter.)

Now that the kids are taken care of, let's go skiing!

To get skiers to the mountain top, the area offers a quad chairlift, a triple chairlift, two double chairs, a poma, and two "mighty mite" surface lifts for beginners. Many skiers are surprised to learn that the top of the triple chair unloads at the state's highest elevation for skiing—12,000 feet. If you ski a short way from the apex, you'll find one of several stunning views. Look down toward Santa Fe, west to Mount Taylor and north toward the Colorado border. The vista of mountains and valleys, mesas, and riverbeds weaves together, sometimes with a band of low-lying fog or misty clouds, in blues and tans, reds, pinks, and warm beige.

Average annual snowfall here is 225 inches and snowmaking covers 30 percent of the mountain. On a winter night, if you look toward the Sangre de Cristo Mountains from Santa Fe, you'll see the lights of the snowcats bobbing back and forth as the big machines groom the slopes for the next day's skiing. The Santa Fe Ski Area frequently receives overnight storms that drop light powder snow. If you want to make first tracks in the powder, leave extra early. The new snow delights skiers—but not drivers. At the other end of snow scale, the area is known for its grooming, a way that Santa Fe makes the most of the snow it gets in limited snow years.

If you break a ski or need advice while you're on the mountain, members of Santa Fe's professional ski patrol can help. For more serious situations, they can use their extensive knowledge of first aid, CPR, mountain rescue, and other emergency skills. Patrol members also enforce safety rules and have been known to pull lift tickets from out-of-control skiers.

If you get hungry while you're on the mountain, you can grab a bowl of soup, a burger, the daily special, or a plate of pasta at La Casa Cafeteria and Outdoor Grill at the base area. The restaurant is open from 9 AM to 4 PM and serves a variety of hot and cold snacks as well as full meals. Totemoff's at mid-mountain offers an outdoor grill with burgers and other ski fare

Northern New Mexico offers a number of ski areas. The region is noted for its champagne powder snow.

Photo: Don Strel

WINTER SPORTS

from 11 AM to 2 PM. Totemoff's also is the only place to buy beer or wine at the ski area.

Need a trail map or have questions? Skier Service personnel are usually available near the lockers in the main building and at the stone hut near the base of the quad lift. They'll help with lost and found items, distribute maps and even offer sunscreen to those who came unprepared. You can buy sunscreen, extra socks, or a stylish new ski outfit at the Wintermill in the main La Casa building.

For rental equipment, the Santa Fe Ski Area's rental shop offers an inventory of 1,400 skis and 75 snowboards from beginner to high-performance and demo models. Skis, poles, boots, and bindings are available.

How about a lesson? The Santa Fe Ski Area has more than 70 ski and snowboard instructors, all professionally certified. Group lessons begin at 10 AM, noon, and 2 PM. Or you can work with a private instructor; private lessons can be arranged hourly, and reservations are required.

Just as it does for kids, the Santa Fe Ski Area offers special ski programs for grownups, including classes for women with women instructors, classes designed to help people who want to race, classes just for older skiers, and more. Inquire at the ski school.

Depending on the weather and the amount of snow, the Santa Fe Ski Area builds a snowboard park with jumps, bowls, half-pipes, and all the other attractions boarders love. More often than not, Santa Fe's black diamond runs develop respectable moguls for those who want to try their skill in the bumps. The Santa Fe Ski Area has recreational racing on a coin-op course, which is normally open Thursday through Sunday. Recreational racers may be pre-empted for special events.

Special annual events at the Santa Fe Ski Area include the Gladfelter Memorial Bump Run for mogul hounds, the Southwest Snowboard Championships and the Jimmie Heuga Ski Express to benefit people with multiple sclerosis. (See our Annual Events chapter.)

But no matter how much fun you're having, you can't spend the night. The Santa Fe Ski Area is strictly a day resort with no slope-side lodging. If you're staying at a hotel, ask if it has a ski shuttle. After all, you're on vacation!

Here is a summary of Santa Fe Ski Area rates:

Adult all-day all-lift tickets cost $40; half-day tickets, morning or afternoon are $28. Beginner chairlift tickets are $20.

For children (age 12 and younger) all-day, all-lift tickets cost $28. Children shorter than 46 inches tall in their ski boots can ski for free. Super seniors, ages 72 and older, ski free; for other seniors, ages 62 to 71, all-day, all-lift tickets are $28.

Equipment rental per day for skis, boots, and poles is $15 for adults and $12 for children. Snowboard rental is $22 or $30 with boots. Children's ski school for ages 4 through 9 costs $69 a day with instruction, lifts, and lunch.

Unlike many ski areas, Santa Fe doesn't offer off-site ticket purchase. The only place to buy your ski tickets is at the ski area itself. For more information write or drop by the Santa Fe Ski Area's in-town office at 2209 Brothers Rd., Ste. 220, Santa Fe, NM 87505.

Here's a look at other New Mexico ski areas easily accessible from Santa Fe:

Angel Fire Resort
95 miles north of Santa Fe,
22 miles east of Taos, N.M. Hwy. 434,
Angel Fire
• (800) 633-7463 (information and snow report)
• www.angelfireresort.com

New Mexico residents and visitors delight in the broad runs and relaxed atmosphere of this popular resort. Legend (perhaps invented by a shrewd PR person) has it that the name comes from the way the mountain looks in a certain light—as if the angels had set them ablaze.

The resort prides itself on keeping visitors happy. It's the only ski area in the state, and one of just a select few in the country, to offer a money-back guarantee to skiers for both lift tickets and lessons. If you don't like the condition of the runs on any given day, report back to the ticket office within an hour of buying your ticket, and you'll get a free ticket to return another time. If you're disappointed in your ski lesson, the area promises to give you another, free-of-charge, no questions asked.

Angel Fire also attracts visitors with major investments in improvements over the years, and the effort shows. Since the 1998 season, the resort has added 10 new runs and expanded snowmaking to cover 52 percent of the mountain. The area installed the state's only two high-speed detachable quad chairlifts, the fastest in all of New Mexico. A new summit restaurant is set for completion for the 2000–2001 season, and a 6,000 foot children's ski and snow board school complex opened last year. The area has a new summit terrain park for skiers and snowboarders.

Snowboarding is very popular at Angel Fire Resort.

Photo: Ben Blankenburg

Angel Fire has the state's only snowbike program. Snowbikes, an Austrian invention, arrived for the 1999–2000 season. Instead of wheels, these pedal machines run on skis. The instructors will reassure you that the sport is easy to master with just a few hours of practice. All bike rentals include a lesson on how to ride safely without looking foolish or taking too many spills. Accomplished snow bikers can tackle the moguls or plunge into powder.

Beginners, be they skiers, snowboarders, or snowbikers, especially love Angel Fire because they have their own easy slope and their own chairlift. For those just finding their snow legs or adjusting to the altitude, the poetically named Dreamcatcher lift offers a slow-moving ride that reduces anxiety and makes learning easier. Beginners can get a feeling for the snow and the equipment at their own pace, without pressure from more advanced skiers.

Children feel comfortable here in this family-friendly atmosphere. The programs are so popular, in fact, that reservations for children's classes are often required a minimum of two days in advance. The Angel Fire Resort Day Camp Program offers structured, supervised, creative activities for non-skiing kids and accepts infants as young as 6 weeks and children as old as 11. At the day camp, kids have fun indoors and outside with activities including art, music, movies, games, and more. But for kids eager to learn a new sport, the Children's Ski and Snowboard Center offers classes for ages 3 to 12. The package includes lessons, lift tickets, equipment rental, snacks, and lunch with full-day programs. The area groups youngsters by age and ability. Older children can join the Mountain Adventures Program or, if they want to snowboard, the Angel Fire Riders.

Angel Fire is a fine place for adults to learn to ski, too. The ski school has between 70 and 85 instructors. You can take a group lesson with people of your same ability level or request a private class. Angel Fire also offers equipment and instruction to accommodate skiers with physical and mental disabilities, and the staff includes instructors who can teach in languages other than English

For skiers and snowboarders of all ages, Angel Fire's biggest claim to fame is New Mexico's first and only high-speed detachable quad lifts, the four-person Chile Express and the Southwest Flyer. The Express, installed for the 1996–97 season, whisks you up the mountain in nine minutes. The Flyer, installed during the summer of 1999, unloads at the highest point on the mountain, offering access to all the area's runs. Less time on the lift, of course, means more time on the snow.

Angel Fire Mountain offers a nice mix of

WINTER SPORTS

skiing challenges. You can cruise more than 10 miles of skiable terrain, including smooth broad slopes, bumps and steeps. Of the area's 68 named runs, 31 percent are suitable for beginners, 48 percent for intermediate skiers, and 21 percent for more advanced skiers or boarders. The resort has three double chairs and a rope tow in addition to the high-speed quads. Angel Fire has a vertical drop of 2,077 feet, with a base elevation of 8,600 feet. Annual snowfall is 210 inches on average.

Angel Fire's trademark event is the annual Shovel Race, which draws competitors and spectators from around the country and television coverage from ESPN. Angel Fire's World Shovel Race Championships was recently voted "The Most Unique Event of the Year" by Event Business News. The race has three major categories. Competitors in the Production Class, the simplest event, slide down the hill on plain, waxed snow shovels. In the Modified Speed Class contenders build aerodynamic contraptions around the shovel, aiming for speed. It's often hard to find the shovel in these sleek machines, but it has to be in contact with the snow during the race for the machine to qualify. Finally, the Modified Unique Class uses the shovel as the base for a sort of snow-country artwork—a ski-slope float like those you might see in a parade. Designs have included a chicken sandwich, the Taj Mahal, and an entire living room. The race, usually held in early February, always draws crowds of enthusiastic spectators.

When the lifts close, you can still have fun on the slope-side tubing run. Between 5 and 7 PM you can rent a tube for $7 and slip and slide beneath the lights to your heart's content. (You have to be age 6 or older to join the fun.) The tubing hill is open from mid-December through mid-March.

The resort also offers snowmobiling, ice fishing, sleigh rides, helicopter rides, hot-air balloon rides, and more. At the base of the ski mountain, facilities include the ticket sales office, a rental and repair shop, the ski school and ski patrol offices, retail shops, and the Angel Fire Resort Hotel. The hotel has convenient slope-side lodging, an après-ski lounge, an indoor pool and hot tub, and two restaurants. You can ride the town shuttle to other businesses and lodgings.

For the 2000–2001 season, adult all-day all-lift tickets cost $42. Adult half-day tickets, morning or afternoon, are $34. Seniors age 65 and older and children under 6 ski free. The area also offers special rates for teens 13–17 and youth, ages 7–12. To encourage repeat visitors, Angel Fire offers a club card which, for $20, gives the user a $5 discount on a full-day lift ticket, a chance to go directly to the lifts without waiting in a ticket line, and the fifth ski day is free.

Established in 1966, Angel Fire is a year-round resort offering golf, fishing, mountain biking, and a range of special events in the summer.

Pajarito Mountain Ski Area
45 miles from Santa Fe,
7 miles from Los Alamos off
N.M. Highway 501 on Camp May Rd.
• (505) 662-5725 (office),
(888) 662-SNOW (snow conditions and general information)
• www.skipajarito.com

Pajarito stands out from New Mexico's other ski areas in several respects. For starters, the nonprofit tax-exempt Los Alamos Ski Club, a venerable and enthusiastic group of men and women, runs it. The club began more than 50 years ago to enliven the winter for the scientists and GI's working on the atomic bomb in Los Alamos, a beautiful, isolated spot in the Jemez Mountains. The club moved from an earlier site in search of better snow and came to Pajarito Mountain in the early 1960s. Volunteers cleared trees for the runs, built a cozy lodge, and installed the first lift. Today, volunteers still play a key role here.

The club now has some 3,500 members who elect a board of directors that hires the general manager and other paid staff. To be a member you must live or work in Los Alamos, but to ski here you just need the price of a ticket. (If the slopes get so crowded that the members have to wait in line any significant amount of time, the area will reduce its solicitations to nonmember skiers.)

Other things of less historic and, perhaps, more

INSIDERS' TIP

For information on ski conditions at all New Mexico resorts, call the Ski New Mexico Snow Phone, (505) 984-0606. For winter road conditions throughout New Mexico call (800) 432-4269. Also check out Ski New Mexico's website at www.skinewmexico.com. For Santa Fe Ski Area snow conditions, call (505) 983-9155; to reach the ski area: (505) 982-4429 or visit http://www.skisantafe.com/snowreport.html

practical interest differentiate Pajarito from northern New Mexico's other ski havens. The area is not a resort, but a ski hill. You won't find overnight accommodations, valet parking, ski shuttles, hot tubs, massages, day care, or après-ski activities here— or even a beer to go with your lunch. You will discover a challenging mountain with enough cruiser runs to keep intermediates and beginners happy too.

"We're a skiers' mountain with a good variety of slopes and groomed and ungroomed areas, nice runs through the trees and good bumps," said Sara Kauppila, the area's spokeswoman. Pajarito began marketing itself for the 1996–97 season, but it is still largely undiscovered and never plans to become a "ski resort."

Perched on a ridge above Los Alamos National Laboratory, the area receives an average snowfall of 143 inches. There's no snowmaking equipment here. Since the area depends totally on the natural stuff, Pajarito is usually among the last of New Mexico's ski areas to open, normally getting sufficient snow by mid-December. Pajarito usually closes some time in April. (Lack of snow kept the area closed for the 1999–2000 season.) The lifts operate only on Wednesday, Saturday, Sunday and federal holidays except Christmas Day. On Wednesday, the mountain is about 50 percent open.

The mountain has a peak elevation of 10,441 feet, a vertical drop of 1,410 feet, and 37 trails, of which 80 percent are rated either intermediate or "most difficult." Pajarito's skiers ride their choice of five lifts—three doubles, a triple, and a quad—to the mountain top. The views are wonderful. From the top of the Aspen chairlift, skiers can see part of the Valle Grande, a huge volcanic crater that now forms an expansive valley. The lifts can accommodate 6,500 skiers per hour, but don't except to see that kind of crowd except, perhaps, over Christmas vacation.

The area's cafeteria and ski school occupy a 13,000-square-foot lodge, and the ski patrol office is nearby in a separate building. Pajarito is one of the few mountains that still used an all-volunteer ski patrol.

You can get lessons in telemark skiing, cross

INSIDERS' TIP

Never tried downhill skiing before? Not to worry. Your best bet is to take a lesson (preferably more than one) from a certified instructor. All New Mexico areas offer ski schools that welcome beginners of all ages. Unlike your friends or spouse, these instructors have worked with countless newbies, helping them master the sport safely and have fun while learning. They won't lose their temper or laugh at you. Go for it!

country skiing, and snowboarding as well as alpine skiing here. The area has private lessons and group classes for children and adults. On Wednesday, you'll find lots of children here taking advantage of the area's classes for school groups from Española, Pojoaque, and the Jemez Valley. The Los Alamos Ski Racing Club operates a youth racing program. Challenge New Mexico uses Pajarito to introduce disabled children and adults to the world of skiing.

The major event of the year at Pajarito is Skiesta, held the end of March. The welcome-to-spring party comes complete with ski-boot dances, fun races, and costumes.

Athough the area did not open in 1999–2000 because of poor snow conditions, these were the set rates: Adult all-day all-lift tickets cost $33 on weekends and $26 on Wednesday. Beginner lift tickets are $22 or $17 for a half-day. Adult half-day tickets (afternoon only) are $24 on weekends or $20 on Wednesday. Seniors age 65 to 75 and children 12 and younger ski for $22 on weekends and $18 on Wednesday. Seniors age 75 and older ski free with ID.

The area does not offers an inclusive children's ski school package, but lessons for children are available.

Equipment rental per day for boots, skis, and poles is $13 for adults, $9 per child. Snowboard rentals cost $19 or $26 with boots. You can rent a helmet for yourself or your children at $5 a head. Please check with the area for updated prices.

Red River Ski Area
**106 miles from Santa Fe,
N.M. Hwy. 38, Red River**
• **(505) 754-2223, (505) 754-2220 (snow phone), 1-800-331-snow (reservations)**
• **RedRiverSkiArea.com**

There aren't many ski towns where you'll find old mines on the slopes—and that's only one of the things that makes Red River Ski Area special. Established in 1959, this family-oriented area has been compared to a dude ranch for skiers. The ski mountain towers above a town settled more than 100 years ago by hardy souls in search of gold. The setting gives Red River its Old West flavor. Some visitors have compared a visit to Red River to a trip back in history, to the simpler days when everything you needed was on Main Street.

Red River has been attracting happy skiers, many of them from Texas, Oklahoma, and Louisiana, for decades. A key to the resort's success is that the area offers plenty of easily accessible diversions for non-skiers. If Grandpa doesn't ski, he can watch the grandkids take a few runs on the slopes, then walk or ride the free trolley back to Main Street. He can explore the shops, arrange a snowmobile ride or a Nordic ski lesson, enjoy a pleasant lunch, curl up with a book, schedule a massage, or even take a nap. Red River boasts the most consistent skier attendance in the Rockies, in part because of the range of activities the village and the ski area offer. It's busy here even during years when the snow gods don't send New Mexico their blessings. The area reports that 43 percent of lift tickets during the 1999–2000 season went to people younger than 19.

Red River has 57 trails, evenly divided among expert, intermediate, and beginner, and three mountain restaurants. The trails are served by seven lifts—four doubles, two triples, and a surface tow. Lift capacity is 7,920 per hour, second only to Taos, so skiers hardly ever have to wait.

To supplement the average snowfall of 252 inches, snowmaking covers about 85 percent of the Red River mountain. The area has a vertical drop of 1,600 feet and a peak elevation of 10,350 feet. Before you ski down, you can stop at the Ski Tip Restaurant on top of the mountain for hot chocolate, lunch, or a snack. The restaurant is a favorite rendezvous place for families. From there, beginners can ski easy runs all the way to the base area. They get to see the views from the top of the mountain AND come down safely. Advanced hot doggers can take the more challenging runs.

Another place that adds to Red River's charm is the Moon-Star Mining Camp, an attraction that's especially popular with children. You can ski right up to an old miner's cabin and through a teepee. The reconstruction of the Old Buffalo Mine includes a plaque that discusses its operation and some of the old equipment. The camp also has tree houses for kids to explore and an old Western-style fort complete with wooden cows. The camp stands in an aspen grove, and the terrain is flat enough that even the most novice skiers usually have little trouble. The camp adds to Red River's extensive beginner area—some might call it beginner paradise. The Red River Willows welcomes snowboarders and offers a terrain park. New for the 2000–2001 will be expanded snowmaking.

You can take lessons at Red River, choosing from a range of classes for children and

Annual events and races on the slopes are fun for both spectators and skiers.

Photo: Don Strel

WINTER SPORTS

adults. The snowboard school at the Bobcat Terrain Park provides beginning and advanced lessons. The youth center hosts ski programs for ages 4 and older, and Buckaroo Child Care Center cares for infants and children ages 6 months to 4 years. Red River's adult programs include all the basics as well as specialty workshops for bumps, powder snow and racing. The area offers recreational racing on the NASTAR course.

Special events include torchlight parades every Saturday night and Mardi Gras, held each February coinciding with Mardi Gras in New Orleans. The area's single biggest event, Mardi Gras includes family costume balls featuring a band brought in from Houma, Louisiana. A slope-side parade complete with floats on skis, Cajun cooking and other activities add to the fun. Mardi Gras brings a capacity crowd to Red River, but it's normally easy to find a room here. Special rates and discounts are available throughout the season, including half-price weekends, bargain days, and the popular Kids Ski Free/Stay Free program. To make it less expensive for families to enjoy the sport, many hotels and lodges participate in the Kids Ski Free/Stay Free program. For each paying parent who stays a minimum of three nights and purchases at least a three-day lift ticket, one child stays for free and receives free lift tickets for the same number of days. You can find details on these programs, as well as discounts on rentals, on the website or by calling Red River Ski Area.

While there are more challenge places for experts to ski, visitors appreciate Red River for its convenience. To start with, you won't have to hunt for a parking place because 90 percent of the lodges sit within walking distance of the slopes. Two of the six chairlifts rise directly from town. If you need rental equipment, the ski area itself operates two rental shops, one on Main Street and one in the Ski Chalet at the area's base. You can book packages of lessons and lift tickets there and rent what you need for skiing, including high performance packages that include the latest ski designs.

For the 2000-2001 season, adult all-day all-lift tickets cost $42, and adult half-day tickets are $32. Seniors age 60 to 69 ski for $28 or $21 for a half day; seniors age 70 and older ski free. For teens, all-day, all-lift tickets are $37 or $27 for a half-day. Children's (age 4-12) all-day, all-lift ticket cost $28; children's half-day tickets are $21. A children's ski school package is $73 per day all-inclusive (lessons, rentals and lunch) for ages 4 to 10. Equipment rental per day for boots, skis and poles is $15 for adults and $10 per child. Snowboards rent for $25 including boots.

The area hosts some 500,000 people during the summer and about 200,000 in the winter. As a popular summer destination, Red River offers scenic chairlift rides, jeep tours, horseback riding, camping, hiking, biking, fishing, and more.

Sandia Peak Ski Area
35 miles from Santa Fe on N.M. Hwy. 536
• **(505) 242-9133, (505) 857-8977 (snow report)**
• **www.sandiapeak.com**

Albuquerque skiers appreciate the convenience of this area, and most of the folks who ski here are from "just down the hill." You can make the ride to Sandia Peak unique if you forego the twisting, scenic road to the ski slopes and instead take the Sandia Peak Tramway, a spectacular trip up the face of the Sandia Mountains to Sandia Crest.

Located in the Cibola National Forest about 30 minutes from Albuquerque, Sandia Peak has 30 runs, 35 percent of them for beginners, 55 percent for intermediates and a few expert trails. Skiers chose from six lifts—four doubles and two tows. Capacity is 4,500 skiers per hour. Vertical drop is 1,700 feet. The area encompasses 200 acres and has snowmaking equipment for 30 acres of the runs. The base elevation here is 8,678 feet, and the peak is 10,378 feet. Though Sandia Peak is high, it is farther south and it tends to have a shorter season, generally opening in mid-December and closing in March, depending on the snow.

Sandia Peak's base lodge offers rental service and a cafeteria. Kids have their own warming hut and a separate area in which to learn to ski safely. Sandia also offers a package of lessons for senior skiers. The staff teaches all types of lessons through the ski school, but there's no on-site day care. Your best bet is to make arrangements for baby-sitting in Santa Fe or Albuquerque.

Among the area's special activities is Ski and Tee Day, an event that combines a morning ski race with nine holes of golf at a course in Albuquerque the same afternoon.

Adult all-day, all-lift tickets cost $34 or $25 for a half-day. Children's tickets are $25 all day or $18 for a half-day, and kids shorter than 46 inches in ski boots ski free. Seniors age 62 to 71 ski for $22 all day or $14 for a half-day. Seniors age 72 and older ski free. For children (age 12 and younger), all-day, all-lift tickets are $25;

half-day tickets are $14. The Children's Ski School costs $60 a day for rentals, lessons, and lunch for ages 4 through 10. Equipment rental per day for boots, skis and poles is $15 adults and $12 per child. Snowboard rental packages are $30.

In addition to the ski area itself, you can buy your tickets, sign up for classes and rent equipment at the Ski Service Center, 2225A Wyoming Boulevard in Albuquerque's Hoffmantown Center, (505) 292-4401.

Sipapu Ski Area
65 miles from Santa Fe, 22 miles southeast of Taos on N.M. Hwy. 518
• (505) 587-2240 (snow conditions and information), (800) 587-2240 (reservations)
• www.swcp.com/paradise

This little skiing village hidden in a canyon in the Sangre de Cristo Mountains exudes a woodsy, family-friendly atmosphere. Telemarkers have discovered Sipapu with a passion and love its trails cut through the trees and uncrowded conditions. They share the slopes with skiers and snowboarders.

Owned and operated by the Bolander family, who founded it in 1952, Sipapu caters to folks looking for value and a noncommercial skiing experience. Tired of overmarketed glitsy area? Sipapu may be just your ticket.

The area's 20 runs offer something for everyone: 25 percent are classified beginner; 50 percent are intermediate; and 25 percent are advanced. Skiers can ride a triple chair or two tows, with a capacity of 2,900 skiers an hour.

Sipapu's base elevation is 8,200 feet, and its peak is at 9,065 feet. There are 40 skiable acres here. The season usually opens the week before Christmas and runs through March. Average snowfall is 110 inches, supplemented with snowmaking on 70 percent of the trails.

If you're a novice and want to improve more quickly, classes here tend to be very small and offer an opportunity for personalized learning—even in a group setting. Sipapu guarantees that you'll be able to accomplish your skiing goals at the end of the lesson or you get another lesson for free. In addition to traditional downhill classes, the area offers telemark and cross-country skiing and snowboard classes. Besides teaching visiting families, Sipapu offers ski lessons to students at more than 35 nearby northern New Mexico schools. More than 2,000 students participate each year. Because of the area's small staff, day care is available only through prior arrangement.

Among the special ski events, Sipapu goes all out for Presidents' Day in February with races, games, music, a costume contest, and Clowns Day. A huge castle built completely of snow provides a centerpiece for the event.

At the base area you'll find a folksy lodge with a big fireplace, a restaurant that serves New Mexican food as well as standard American offerings, a lounge, a shop for equipment rental, a gift shop, and a place to buy groceries and gasoline. The area has accommodations for 240 people at a motel, in family-style cabins and a dormitory. In the summer—beginning about mid-May when the snow has disappeared—you can play disc golf on Sipapu's 18-basket course. The game, something like regular golf only played with Frisbees and baskets, is appropriate for players of all ages. Best of all, there is no charge to play on the Sipapu course.

Adult all-day tickets are $31 or $25 for a half-day. Children's tickets are $25 all day or $21 a half-day. Children age 5 and younger ski free. Seniors between 65 and 69 pay $20; those 70 and older ski free. Children's ski school, including equipment rental and lessons, is $42 per day. Rental of skis, boots, and poles is $12 a day for adults and $10 for children. Snowboards with boots rent for $25; snowshoes or cross-country skis, boots, and poles rent for $10 per package for adults or children.

INSIDERS' TIP
Have you seen those "Free Taos" bumper stickers? The issue is snowboarding. Taos is one of the few areas in the country, and the only one in New Mexico, that says "no" to snowboarders. So far, the snowboaders complaints haven't swayed Taos Ski Valley management to reconsider.

Ski Rio
110 miles from Santa Fe on N.M. Hwy. 196, 8 miles east of the junction with N.M. Hwy. 522
• 1-800-2ASK-RIO (reservations), 1-877-505-SNOW (snow conditions)
• www.skirio.com

Nestled in the Sangre de Cristo Mountains practically at the Colorado border, Ski Rio is the northernmost ski area in New Mexico.

With 2,150 feet of vertical drop and a peak elevation of 11,650 feet, the resort includes 910 skiable acres. In an average year, Ski Rio expects to get 260 inches of snow and supplements that with snowmaking. The area has 83 named trails, of which 30 percent are beginner, 50 percent intermediate, and 20 percent expert. Otherwise, skiers reach the slopes on six lifts—two triples, a double, and three tows. The area can accommodate 5,500 skiers per hour and you'll seldom find a lift line here. The longest run is 3.5 miles. If you're having too much fun to come back to the base for lunch, you can eat at Zapatas Mid-mountain Restaurant at the top of B lift.

Ski Rio welcomes snowboarders and snowbladers, and built two terrain parks, Full Tilt and Powderhound Pete, to keep them happy. Ski Rio has hosted the majority of New Mexico's competitions in the United States Amateur Snowboard Association, on the state's only groomed halfpipe. Competitors in the New Mexico series have advanced to the national competition in halfpipe, boardercross, and slopestyle categories.

Before heading for the slopes, at the base area you can enjoy a cup of hot chocolate at the day lodge or Piñatas Cantina. Right outside the cantina is the area's new heated outdoor swimming pool. When you've had enough skiing you can take a dip while your friends make their final runs. You'll find the Pizza and Play Parlor, popular with the younger set, on the upper floor of the day lodge cafeteria. You'll also find lift tickets, ski rentals and a sports shop. The Blue Moon grill located in the Paradise Hotel offers continental and southwestern cuisine Santa Fe-style ambiance.

As you'd expect, Ski Rio has a full-service ski school with classes for children and adults, group and private lessons, in skiing, snowboarding, and snowskating. The area's Guaranteed Learn-to-Ski program for the never-ever skiers will help you get the hang of the sport your first day on the slopes. The children's programs are divided by age, and taught by instruction who receive special training to make things fun for the little guys.

On-mountain accommodations include two hotels, condominiums and casitas, many of which feature either kitchenettes or full kitchens and can serve up to eight adults. Group rates are available. If you don't want to drive back to Santa Fe after a day of skiing here, Ski Rio accommodations are a good choice.

A perfect day at Taos Ski Valley.

Photo: Ken Gallard

Governor Gary Johnson (left) and Hilary Lindh, world champion gold and Olympic silver winner, race down the slope at the Santa Fe Ski Area.

Photo: Don Strel

Ski Rio is open daily from mid-December to the end of March depending on snow conditions—as is true with all areas. For the 1999-2000 season, adult tickets were $35 for all day; juniors (7-12) are $25 for a full day. Children 6 and younger ski free, and discounts are offered to seniors and active military personnel. Multi-day tickets are sold at the discount. For the most current information on prices, snow conditions, and specials either call the area or visit the website.

Taos Ski Valley

80 miles from Santa Fe on N.M. Hwy. 150, 18 miles northeast of Taos
• **(505) 776-2291(information),**
(505) 776-2916 (snow conditions),
(800) 776-1111 (reservations)
• **www.skitaos.org**

When visitors think of skiing in New Mexico, they usually think of Taos, the state's most famous ski resort. Skiing Magazine consistently ranks Taos Ski Valley in the top 10 resorts in the United States and Canada, with references to fun in the steeps and thrills on the bump runs.

Taos Ski Valley's longstanding popularity among skiing fanatics confirms the media's praise. Visitors return year after year, in part because of the resort's well-regarded Ernie Blake Ski School and its popular learn-to-ski week. Taos also attracts many first-time visitors who learn about it through the area's extensive national marketing program, ads in major ski publications, an active group sales program, and through the area's clever website.

Founded in 1956 by Swiss skier and entrepreneur Ernie Blake and now run by his family, Taos Ski Valley established its fame on the challenge of its terrain and the European quality of the resort itself. With a base elevation of 9,207 feet and a peak elevation of 11,819 feet, Taos has a vertical drop of 2,612 feet. The longest run is more than 5 miles.

Taos boasts 312 inches of snow in an average year and is famous for its light, dry powder. The area can supplement nature's efforts with snowmaking on 95 percent of the beginner and intermediate terrain.

To reach the slopes, the area offers skiers four quad lifts, a triple, five doubles, and two surface lifts. The 12 lifts can handle 15,300 skiers per hour—the largest skier capacity of any New Mexico ski area. Al's Run, directly under the No. 1 lift, is a marathon of bumps where you'll find hard-core, hard-muscled mogul hounds. Taos offers chutes, bowls, and cruising runs. Experts who enjoy a challenge love to ski the ridge, an area above the named runs that involves a strenuous climb before you start to ski.

Although the mountain is a skilled skier's paradise, there's more than enough terrain here for beginners and intermediates. Of the 72 named runs, 49 percent are ranked as "blues" or "greens."

While some who ski here go home with stories of the steep High Traverse or the powder challenge on Lower Stauffenberg, others can speak of their skiing breakthroughs during the Learn to Ski and Learn to Ski Better weeks. Ski Magazine has ranked Taos' Ernie Blake Ski School as one of the best in the United States. The Ski Week programs, offered throughout the season, match students of similar ability with a teacher who can help them move on to the next level of skiing. Taos also offers special programs for women, older skiers, telemarkers, and teens. Super Ski Weeks welcome intermediate or advanced skiers who want intensive drills and exercises and specific instructions in racing, moguls, and adventure skiing. You can also take a single class or a workshop in racing or mogul skiing. For the most novice, Taos's traditional Yellowbird Programs cater to first- and second-day skiers with morning and afternoon lessons, a lift ticket, and rentals for $55 a day or $100 for two days. Private and group lessons are available.

Taos KinderKare provides a safe atmosphere for children six weeks to 2 years of age at $57 per day. The Junior Elite ski program teaches youngsters ages 3 to 12 how to ski. The children's programs have an 18,000-square-foot center with its own ticket counter, ski rental and accessory shop, and cafeteria.

Recent improvements at the area include reshaping and re-contouring some runs to improve skiing and reduce congestion. But what hasn't changed here is the prohibition of snowboarders. Taos is one of the few areas in the country where skiers don't have to share the slopes. The resort has an independent, noncorporate spirit. In addition to the Blake family, other skiing families own the lodges in the valley, and there's not a franchise outfit among them. Most of the innkeepers, not surprisingly, are skiers themselves who found the valley's conditions irresistible.

As if the skiing itself wasn't enough, special events add to the Taos Ski Valley's attraction. In early December, Taos Ski Valley offers a Brewmaster's Festival at the Resort Center featuring about 25 microbreweries from throughout New Mexico and the Southwest. Participants can sample food from Taos and TSV restaurants, enjoy live entertainment, and take home a souvenir glass, all for the price of admission ($15 in 1999). The area's most popular tradition, the Winter Wine Festival during the third week in January, is one of the oldest ski/wine festivals in the country. Started in 1985, the weeklong festival involves some 36 winemakers and includes on-mountain tastings, seminars, winemaker dinners, and Le Grande Tasting and the Taste of Taos, which includes food from local restaurants.

At the Resort Center, you'll find places to purchase equipment and sportswear and to rent skis, boots, and poles, including high-performance and demo models. You can eat at Tenderfoot Katie's Cafeteria or Rhonda's Restaurant. At the Martini Tree Bar you can have a cocktail and listen to live music. You can also eat at two on-mountain restaurants, The Phoenix and Whistlestop Cafe.

Want to spend the night instead of driving back to Santa Fe? You can stay in slope-side accommodations within walking distance of the lifts or elsewhere in the valley. You'll find about 20 lodges, but no high rises. Most lodges have their own restaurants and offer aprés-ski and evening entertainment. Be advised, however, they tend to fill up fast, especially over the holidays. Another popular option is to stay in the town of Taos and ride the shuttle to the ski valley and back.

With more than 80 galleries, seven museums, and numerous restaurants serving traditional northern New Mexican cuisine and gourmet fare, the nearby town of Taos certainly adds to the skier's overall experience—and gives non-skiers plenty to do. The shops here offer high-quality weaving, furniture, pottery, jewelry, and more. And historic Taos Pueblo just provides guided tours, is just a short drive away.

Adult all-day all-lift tickets cost $45. Half-day tickets, morning or afternoon, are $32. Super seniors, ages 70 and older, ski free; seniors age 65 to 69 pay $31 for all-day, all-lift tickets. Teens (age 13 to 16) ski for $36 all day or $26 for a half-day. For children (age 12 and younger) all-day, all-lift tickets are $27 and half-day tickets are $19. Taos offers lower rates on lift tickets from late November until mid-December and for the last two weeks of the season. It also adds $5 to lift-ticket prices from December 27 through 31.

INSIDERS' TIP

Need a ride to the Santa Fe Ski Area? Check at your hotel—some offer ski shuttles. For shuttle service from the town of Taos to Taos Ski Valley, try The Pride of Taos, (505) 758-8340, or Faust's Transportation, (505) 758-3410.

Equipment rental per day for skis, boots, and poles is $19 to $28 for adults and $11 for children. Junior Elite ski school for ages 3 to 12 costs $73 a day with instruction, lifts, and lunch. Shuttles from town are $5 a person one way.

Cross-Country Skiing, Snowshoeing, and Snowplay

You can snowshoe and cross-country ski on many hiking trails in the Santa Fe area and throughout northern New Mexico. For novice cross-country skiers or families with small children, the Black Canyon Trail in Hyde Park near Santa Fe may provide an enjoyable outing. This 1-mile round-trip route offers nice scenery, gentle to moderate slopes, and picnic tables where you can enjoy lunch. Slightly more experienced skiers head for the Aspen Vista Road, just past Hyde Park on N.M. 475 on the way to the Santa Fe Ski Area. You'll get to practice your uphill technique as you climb from 10,000 to 12,000 feet in about 6 miles. Coming back can be a fast trip!

Due to improvements in equipment and a growing desire to get away from it all in the winter, snowshoeing has become increasingly popular. Snowshoe construction has improved, resulting in lighter shoes with curled toes that don't get buried in the powder. Aluminum and synthetic decking has improved flotation over the snow. Sporting goods stores that sell or rent this equipment—and who may carry state-of-the-art demo models—probably can give you advice on where to go. That technicians or sales person may be a ski fanatic supporting his or her outdoor habit. Don't hesitate to ask them for their suggestions and their favorite runs. You'll also find several guidebooks to cross-country skiing available locally. Santa Fe Community College offers classes that will teach you Nordic skiing and show you some good places to try your new skills.

Enchanted Forest Cross Country Ski Area
106 miles from Santa Fe,
3.5 miles east of Red River on
N.M. Hwy. 38
• (505) 754-2374 (Miller's Crossing ski store)
You'll find 26 kilometers of 12-foot-wide

trails at Enchanted Forest, a five-minute drive from the heart of the village of Red River. New Mexico's largest full-service cross-country ski area, it offers groomed and natural trails through 400 acres of aspen groves in the Carson National Forest. The area usually opens before Thanksgiving and serves skiers into April, depending on the weather.

Skiers can explore trails that wind through the trees. The system is groomed with one side tracked for diagonal stride (the more conventional cross-country skiing) and the other side smooth for snowshoeing and freestyle or skate-skiing. You'll cruise on trails such as Northwest Passage and Jabberwocky. The alpine vistas and the solitude of the Rocky Mountain forest are truly spectacular. Bring your camera. The Enchanted Forest receives an average of 240 inches of snow a year—about two feet more than the Red River Ski Area.

Owners John and Judy Miller opened the area in 1985 with a special-use permit from the Carson National Forest and have been catering to cross-country skiers and their families ever since. They recently added to the warming hut at the base area, and offer a nice menu including pizza and chimicangas in addition to snacks.

For beginners or skiers new to the area, the best place to start is at Miller's Crossing, the in-town headquarters at 212 W. Main Street in Red River. You can rent equipment, make arrangements for instruction, and even line up a ride to the area if you're a beginner, a special service offered to encourage people to try the sport. The shop also offers advice on waxing and will tune your skis. In addition to Nordic skiing, Enchanted Forest has also has snowshoeing, and has added an additional 10 kilometers of trails for showshoers only. Special events at Enchanted Forest include a luminaria tour on Christmas day and moonlight ski tours on the Saturdays closest to the full moon. On the Just Desserts trips you can ski and enjoy a sweet feast.

Passes are $10 for adults, $7 for teens (age 13 to 18) and seniors and $3 for children age 12 and younger. Skiers older than 60 pay $6, and those older than 70 ski free. Rentals are $10.50 for adults and $7 for children 12 and younger. A child's learn-to-ski package is $23.

Ski/Snowboard Shops

In addition to these shops, all in Santa Fe, you can rent equipment at all New Mexico ski areas. You'll also find private ski shops in Taos,

Angelfire, Los Alamos, Albuquerque, and elsewhere.

Alpine Sports
121 Sandoval St.
• **(505) 983-5155**

In business for more than 30 years, Alpine Sports is a full-service sporting goods store. Upstairs you'll discover a fine selection of new, top-of-the-line equipment, ski wear, sportswear, and accessories. Downstairs in the rental department, you'll find all kinds of wintersports equipment—Nordic and alpine skis, snowboards, and snowshoes. Ask about group rates. Alpine's staff includes seasoned skiers who know how to match customers to equipment. The shop has skilled boot fitters at your service. Another benefit—plenty of free parking in the lot right behind the store, or you can walk from any downtown hotel.

Beyond Waves Mountain Surf Shop
333 Montezuma Ave.
• **(505) 988-2240**

This store caters to snowboarders. You can rent or buy Avalanche boards as well as cool outerwear and boots, hats, sunglasses, and other accessories. The shop will also wax, base, tune, and repair your snowboard.

Bike'n Sport
1829 Cerrillos Rd.
• **(505) 820-0809**

This year-round shop spreads its business between winter and summer sports enthusiasts. Snowshoes are a winter specialty here, with many different types available for rent or sale. You'll also find a nice selection of cross-country skis, telemark equipment, and snowboards with the latest in bindings and boots. Bike'n Sport, a full-line mountain bike shop in the summer, also carries clothing and accessories. The staff can offer you plenty of suggestions on where to take your snowshoes for a day of fun.

Cottam's Ski Rentals
Hyde Park Rd.
• **(505) 982-0495**

This business occupies a cozy stone house in Hyde Park—right along the highway to the Santa Fe Ski Area. It specializes in rentals and offers a range of high-performance ski equipment, snowboards, children's equipment, and even some sleds. In addition to downhill skis and snowboards for children and adults, you'll also find waxless cross-country skis for rent. The shop offers complete ski tuning. Forget your jacket? You can also rent clothing here.

The high country in winter is noted for its deep blue sky reflected against the crisp white powder snow.

Photo: Don Strel

Angel Fire Resort provides some chilling steeps as well as beginning and intermediate runs.

Photo: Ben Blankenburg

WINTER SPORTS

Cottam's also has four stores in Taos and a shop in Albuquerque.

Santa Fe Mountain Sports
607 Cerrillos Rd.
• (505) 988-3337

Outdoor sports enthusiasts of all varieties will find something to their liking at Santa Fe Mountain Sports. In addition to a fully stocked retail store, Mountain Sports has rentals galore—downhill ski equipment including high-performance super side-cut skis, snowboards by Volkl, Heelside and Rosignol, snowshoes, and cross-country skis. The shop will even do rentals for children for an entire ski season. You can get binding adjustments, ski repair and tune ups in its full-service shop. If you ask, the staff will give you tips on where to snowshoe or ski. In the summer, look for bike rentals.

Ski Tech Ski Rentals
905 St. Francis Dr.
• (505) 983-5512

This family-owned business specializes in service and has been serving Santa Fe skiers for about 12 years. You can rent all the ski equipment you need as well as adult-size jackets, pants, and bibs. In addition to an assortment of downhill skis, you'll find snowboards and cross-country equipment. The full-service shop offers ski repair, tune ups, binding adjustments, and overnight service. In addition to the St.

Francis Drive store, Ski Tech also offers rentals at the Glorieta Conference Center in Glorieta.

The Skiers Edge
1836 Cerrillos Rd.
• (505) 983-1025

Although mostly known as a rental shop, The Skiers Edge also sells equipment and accessories. You'll discover a selection of K2, Salomon, Niedecker, and Avalanche snowboards here as well as skis to suit all levels and ages including high-performance models and parabolics. The shop gets new equipment annually. You can rent bibs, powder pants, and jackets to keep the cold out. Pickup and delivery are available.

Wild Mountain Outfitters
541 W. Cordova Rd.
• (505) 986-1152

This is one of the biggest ski shops in Santa Fe specializing in cross-country and telemark equipment. You'll find new and rental skis as well as snowshoes. The shop offers a basic touring rental package and new demo skis for customers considering purchasing new equipment. Wild Mountain Outfitters also sells clothing, accessories, and gear of all sorts. You'll find a nice selection of books on cross-country skiing and telemarking here as well as mountain guidebooks about skiing in other states. The management suggests reservations for equipment rental on weekends.

INSIDERS' TIP
Anyone who can prove he or she is president of something skis free on President's Day at Sipapu.

WINTER SPORTS

Real Estate

Let's assume, for a happy moment, that not only have you decided to move to Santa Fe, but that you can also spend as much or as little as you decide on your housing. Among the options:

You can buy a quaint old adobe within walking distance of the Plaza.

You can live in a house with property that gives you access to the Santa Fe River or a historic acequia, or irrigation ditch.

You can settle into a neighborhood with sidewalks, paved streets, and potential friends for your children right next door.

You can buy in an area with hiking trails, parks, and other amenities.

You might purchase a 10-acre lot, hire an architect, and use a custom builder to create the best of Santa Fe style.

You could fall in love with a new, energy-efficient house at the end of a bumpy dirt road with gorgeous views and plenty of privacy.

You could relocate to a condominium development complete with full-time security, a health club, and a dining room.

You might live in a mobile home park or an apartment complex.

Or, you could choose to move to a ranch with horses and maybe even llamas and buffalo.

Like Santa Fe itself, the real estate market here is eclectic, diversified, sophisticated, and, compared to many other places in the country, expensive. Real estate is big business in Santa Fe and—because of Santa Fe's impact as the state capital and a trend-setter—throughout much of northern New Mexico.

Look in the Santa Fe phone book and you'll find 13 pages of advertising listings for real estate agents and companies. The Santa Fe Association of Realtors has some 700 members, all of whom are sincerely interested in making a living in the profession.

The Financial Picture

The early 1990s brought a flood of buyers to Santa Fe's real estate market. Demand was high, and prices skyrocketed. Houses sold quickly, and customers had to act fast, often at full listing price, to get the home they wanted. Then the market slumped in the mid-90s, but enjoyed a strong showing for 1998–1999. The median price in the city was $178,465 in 1998 compared to $187,250 in 1999. Likewise in the county, the median of $222,605 increased to $235,000. The multiple listing service of the Santa Fe Association of Realtors reported 1,148 homes in the county and city combined were sold in 1999.

Home sales and prices in the city continued to rise in the early part of 2000—although prices in the county fell. When all the figures are in, real estate agents expect 2000 to be another strong year unless the volatile stock market causes a recession.

Suzanne Field Kelly, president of the Santa Fe Association of Realtors, noted that Santa Fe real-estate sales in 1999 were the highest ever recorded. And first quarter 2000 sales (the latest available to us) showed a 5 percent increase in the number of homes sold compared to that same period for 1999. The median sales price of city homes rose 13 percent, from $182,000 in the first quarter of 1999 to $205,000 in the same period in 2000. ("Median" means that as many homes sold for more than that amount as sold for less.) The median price of Santa Fe city homes reached a record high of $223,000 in the third quarter of 1999.

In Santa Fe County, meanwhile, the picture was different. The number of homes sold in the first quarter dropped 11 percent. And the county's median sales price also fell, from $259,500 in the first quarter of 1999 to $235,000 in the first three months of 2000, a decrease of 9 percent. In Eldorado, a popular area in the county and east of Santa Fe, the median sales prices dropped about 4 percent in the first quarter of 2000.

Agents dealing with the most expensive properties note that Santa Fe competes for buyers in this million-dollar-plus price range with places such as Aspen and Telluride, Colorado, and Jackson Hole, Wyoming. These communities have become so expensive that some buyers now see Santa Fe's top-end properties as a bargain.

An Overview

Suzanne Field Kelly of the Santa Fe Association of Realtors advises that in Santa Fe, location probably has the single biggest impact on a property's price. Whereas in many communities proximity to downtown is a negative factor, in Santa Fe it's a strong selling point.

"Values in Santa Fe are relative to the distance a home is from the Plaza," Realtor Merrily Pierson added. "The closer to the Plaza, the more a home is worth. For resale appreciation, a buyer is smarter to purchase a house that needs work in a good location rather than a better house farther from the Plaza."

But figuring out a property's value involves more than a home's location and size. Views, open space, lack of highway noise, architectural integrity, landscaping, and "Santa Fe style" — smooth plaster walls, vigas, bancos, tile floors, and other amenities are important factors, Kelly said. (See our close-up in this chapter for more on Santa Fe style.) Santa Fe style isn't just for the wealthy; it can be found in homes of every price range.

For many buyers, the biggest surprise is what their money will buy. The real estate dollar doesn't stretch far here. Most Realtors can tell stories of newcomers who see the east side, one of the city's most prestigious areas, and think they've discovered it. Surely, they think, we'll find a bargain here, a little fixer-upper. And they're more than surprised at the $200 to $300 per square foot price these homes sell for.

Some newcomers are surprised to learn that Santa Fe has no industrial section where they can find a building to remodel into lofts. Still others find it odd to discover homes worth a half-million dollars or more down dusty dirt roads. Some expect that property a few miles out of the city will be available for a huge drop in price. Sorry partners. This is not necessarily the case. Internationally known photographer Herb Ritts put his 160-acre compound just south of Santa Fe on the market in 1999 for a cool $6.8 million.

In recent years, thanks to initiatives involving the City of Santa Fe, Santa Fe County, and private agencies, more housing is available for Santa Fe's working families of average income. Many of these subdivision are on the sprawling south side, where the median price in early 2000 was $157,000—the lowest in the city. In Tierra Contenta, one of the city's newest neighborhoods, three-bedroom, two-bath homes initially sold for between $120,000 and $160,000 in 1997. Builders in this neighborhood use the latest techniques to come up with a high-quality home at lower per-foot cost. Tierra Contenta's first wave of affordable homes— those ranging in price from $80,000 to around $150,000—have been built and sold. Subdivisions off Richards Avenue—Rancho Viejo and Nava Adè—both of which have a variety of homes priced below $200,000—sell new homes quickly. Eldorado is a popular choice for the buyer who wants a house at a moderate price out of town on an acre of land with expansive views.

What are Santa Fe's desirable areas? Well, it depends on what you want and how much you can spend. A buyer for whom money is no object might select a golf course home at Las

INSIDERS' TIP

Because of the requirements of the Fair Housing Act, Realtors can't steer clients to a certain neighborhood. They also have to decline to answer questions about crime and schools. They can suggest that clients look at police records, watch the crime reports in the newspapers, and talk to the public school systems about programs and achievement in different school zones.

Campanas or a historic east side adobe. Buyers looking for homes on larger acreage have begun exploring Galisteo, Lamy, Nambe, and La Cienega.

Some Things to Consider

In her book, Understanding and Buying Santa Fe Real Estate, Realtor Karen Walker offers some advice for potential buyers. Here are a few of her observations:

Before you make a commitment, ask to see and take time to read any restrictive covenants from neighborhood associations. Educate yourself about zoning and building regulations from the city and county that apply to the area you're considering. Don't assume that you can build a guest house, put up outside lights, or paint your window frames green. Get the facts

Examples of city restrictions are the escarpment ordinance, which restricts building on hillsides and ridgetops; terrain management requirements, which govern the building of roads and structures on steep terrain; and historic district requirements that dictate what kinds of changes can be made to the exteriors of vintage buildings. Building code and zoning restraints may require setbacks of construction from lot lines and might limit the percentage of your building site you can cover with "improvements." Both the city and the county have archaeological ordinances that require excavation prior to construction if the property is in an archeological zone.

Santa Fe's City Hall takes its zoning regulations seriously. A few years ago a homeowner was required to remove a third story he'd added because the construction violated the city's escarpment ordinances.

Buyers looking at property should make sure that they'll have access to it. Don't assume that because you drove there, the road will be yours along with the land. Also, ask if the area has plans for any new roads, which could have an impact on your property in terms of noise, dust, or access.

INSIDERS' TIP

Some designers get carried away in their interpretation of Santa Fe style. If you notice vigas protruding from all sides of a building, you can be sure they're fakes—the support beams simply don't work that way. Builders who use real vigas may leave the ends visible on a front-facing wall for a decorative effect.

Views, a strong selling point for some Santa Fe properties, can come with a down side—wind and noise. Often, the same lot placement that gives a home a nice look at the mountains or the lights of the city leaves the place exposed to the wind. With Santa Fe's prevailing westerly winds, the traffic sounds will travel to the east.

If land near the home or lot you're considering is vacant, ask what the owner plans for it and what kind of structure could be built there. Your neighbor could one day be a convenience store!

Find out if the lot has city water and sewer service. Much of the property in the northern quadrants of the city is not connected to city sewer even though it is inside the city limits. Instead, septic systems serve these homes. Some of the land in the eastern and southeastern parts of the city has neither city sewer nor city water; you'll need a well and a septic system here. Speaking of water, you won't find many homes with pools in the Santa Fe area, partly because the climate only allows a few months of outdoor swimming and partly because of the region's concerns about water availability and focus on water conservation.

The higher in elevation your home is, the more snow you'll encounter. Notice the number of four-wheel-drive vehicles on Santa Fe's streets? Many of these aren't just for show—the drivers need them to get home after a storm. If you're looking at property in the summer, be sure to ask what the roads are like in the winter.

Rentals

A few years ago, just finding a place to rent in Santa Fe was a challenge. But recent construction of apartment complexes has made the situation bearable.

According to the Santa Fe Public Housing Authority, which keeps tabs on the situation, renters can find a two-bedroom apartment in an apartment complex for about $620 a month and can locate a three-bedroom place for $730. According to the *Santa Fe Reporter's* Annual Manual for 2000–2001, the "average" rental, a two-bedroom, one bath shelter, goes for about $715.

Santa Fe has roughly 25 apartment complexes with 30 units or more and about 10 complexes with more than 200 rental units. Apartments are scattered around the city, but the largest concentration of apartment complexes can be found in the Zia Road, Airport Road, St. Francis Drive, Rodeo Road, and in the southern part of town. Among the choices are Shadowridge, 941 Calle Mejia; Dos Santos, 2210 San Miguel Chavez Road; Rancho Vizcaya Apartments, 2500 Sawmill Road; Tierra de Zia Apartments, 2600 W. Zia Road; and Zia Vista Apartments at 2501 W. Zia Road; Los Pueblos, 2095 S. Pacheco; and San Mateo of Santa Fe, 610 W. San Mateo Road.

INSIDERS' TIP

Building with straw bale construction is a popular alternative in Santa Fe. It's economical and viable. The plastered bales are secured together with rebar and surrounded by wood or steel for support. For more information call the Straw Bale Builders at (505) 989-4400.

Of course, as with the rest of the real estate market, location is everything. The closer to the Plaza, the better the views and amenities, the nicer the neighborhood, the more square-feet the property has, the more you'll pay for an apartment or a rental home. Places that take pets are harder to find and usually more costly. Low market price for a three-bedroom house is around $850: homes for rent in the $850 to $1,200 price range will go quickly.

The Santa Fe Association of Realtors publishes a list of its members' available rental property each week and includes vacation rentals as well as long-term situations. A recent "Weekly Rental Sheet" illustrated the range of possibilities and prices. Properties listed included "Santa Fe Charmer," a furnished one bedroom casita (that's Spanish for "little house") within walking distance of downtown. The $1,200 rent included utilities and cable TV. Or you could rent a furnished "sunny, two-bedroom adobe in orchard setting" three miles from the plaza for $1,400 a month including utilities and telephone. About a 40-minute drive from Santa Fe in the community of Pecos, you can rent an unfurnished three-bedroom house for $750 a month. In Eldorado, a two-bedroom, two-bath place went for $975 a month. On the south side of town, a two-bedroom home went for $875 a month.

In Santa Fe, incidentally, the market is its own rent control. When there's plenty of property for rent, the owners or their agents may be inclined to lower the cost. If there's more demand than units available, landlords won't be in the mood to dicker on price.

Sometimes people may find that it's difficult to get what they're looking for in the rental market here, but agents say that may be because they're looking for something that isn't realistic in terms of price for the location. If you need a rental, the best plan is to cover all bases, and begin by getting the newspaper early— The New Mexican is best for this—to check the classified ads. Running your own "wanted to rent" ad offers another option. The Santa Fe Association of Realtors (505-982-8385) can give you a list of members who are property managers and can assist you in your search for a place to rent. Don't forget to check the phone book for apartment listings. If you're looking for a home to share, bulletin boards at the natural food stores offer another resource.

And be forewarned: when the Santa Fe Opera and the Chamber Music Festival bring their artists, support crews, and audiences to town in the summer, rents increase and availability drops. If you have a choice, rent in May, with a lease, or wait until the middle of August. Expect to pay first and last month's rent and a damage deposit.

Santa Fe Neighborhoods

Santa Fe was born around the Plaza and along the Santa Fe River, and the city's oldest neighborhoods are downtown. People have been living in the Barrio Analco area, for example, since the city's founding in 1610. Although this area and many of the 12 other neighborhoods included in the City of Santa Fe's Historic Neighborhood Study are now largely commercial,

REAL ESTATE

Santa Fe Style: Simple Beauty

As you look at Santa Fe's neighborhoods or shop for a home or apartment here, you'll notice numerous variations of the phenomenon known as "Santa Fe Style."

Santa Fe style is deceptively simple. Start with a building that blends into its surroundings because it's the same color as the earth around it and because its contours match those of the landscape in which it is built. Typically, Santa Fe style means modified Pueblo or Territorial style—a thick-walled adobe look, with windows to capture the mountains and the sunsets and patios and portals for outdoor living. The doors are likely to be carved wood with a natural finish or perhaps a whimsical painted trim.

In 1918, when an influx of American influences threatened to make Santa Fe look remarkably like Anytown, USA, within a generation, artist Carlos Vierra spearheaded the revival of old styles of building. Vierra, and others who joined him in his work to preserve and contemporize Santa Fe's traditional Pueblo and Territorial look, based Santa Fe style on a combination of the longstanding regional architecture with modifications essential for comfortable contemporary living. Vierra concentrated on the appreciation and development of the great advantages Santa Fe had from it adobe roots. He coined the term "Pueblo Revival" for this updated traditional style. Santa Fe architect John Gaw Meem became one of its finest practitioners.

Santa Fe style homes may look unimposing from the outside—perhaps just a simple adobe wall with an attractive gate—and that's part of their understated charm. Inside you may find a lovely courtyard leading to the house itself. Santa Fe style has evolved in the hands of contemporary builders and designers. It often includes passive solar energy features such as orienting a house to the south with windows to capture the sun's heat in winter and floors and walls to absorb that warmth and hold it into the evening.

The smooth plastered or sand-textured walls tend to be neutral colors—a variation on the adobe plaster used outside—or white or off-white. Exterior doors may be hand-hewn panels of pine, antiques garnered from older homes or even imported from Mexico, or original creations crafted from latillas or hand-adzed planks. Floors are normally of tile—again in earth tones—or natural stone, brick,

Vigas such as these are an important element of Santa Fe Style.

or wood. American Indian rugs are common finishing touches. More color usually comes in the accents, in the art work on the walls, the brightly painted folk art carvings in the nichos, the fresh flowers on the tables, the textiles on the throw pillows.

When tin came to New Mexico in the form of large storage containers used by the United States Army in the mid-19th century, residents quickly adapted this versatile material to a variety of practical and decorative uses. Tin switchplates with cut and stamped designs, mirrors perhaps with fabric or painted decorative touches, and other tincraft are subtle parts of Santa Fe style.

Exterior adobe walls around the house or garden serve many uses. In some cases they shield homes from the noise and closeness of the street; in a different setting they carve a secure enclosure from the vast landscape, frame the views, and offer a haven for plants, pets, and family use.

For definitive information and beautiful pictures, take a look at *Santa Fe Style*, a wonderful book by Christine Mather and Sharon Woods, published by Rizzoni, New York.

Glossary

Adobe: A brick made of mud and straw, dried in the sun and used as a building material. Adobe is the heart of Santa Fe style because of its sculptural quality. Building with this labor-intensive material tends to be expensive unless you can do it yourself. Many Santa Fe homes that have an adobe-like appearance are built of less expensive cinderblock or frame and stuccoed in earth tones to resemble adobe. "Adobe" is also used to mean "earth-colored."

Banco: These plastered built-in benches, often found near a fireplace, are either crafted of adobe or framed of wood and stuccoed over.

Canale: An outlet to allow water to run off flat roofs, canales are a distinctive feature of Santa Fe style. Trouble with canales can lead to leaky roofs.

Casita: This term, meaning a small house, is sometimes used to describe a guesthouse, townhouse, or upscale condo.

Corbel: Usually found atop posts or larger support beams, this decorative feature is usually carved and may also be painted.

Coyote fence: Traditionally crafted from juniper branches wired together vertically, coyote fences are used decoratively, for privacy, and as wind breaks. The posts ought to be so close together that a coyote can't squeeze through.

Horno: An outdoor beehive-shape oven seen extensively on Indian pueblos.

Kiva fireplace: A rounded sculptural fireplace usually crafted from adobe. You'll normally find these in the corner of a room. Kiva fireplaces are often raised from the floor and surrounded with bancos.

Latillas: These small branches (approximately 3 inches in diameter), usually of cedar or aspen, are placed above the vigas to form the ceiling. They can be laid in various patterns such as herringbone or straight rows.

Lintel: A exposed beam placed over a window or door, lintels are sometimes carved or painted.

Nicho: A small niche or indentation in a wall, usually rounded at the top, nichos are designed to display a work of art or family keepsakes. They could be described as traditional built-in shelving.

Portal: A covered porch that is also used as an outdoor walkway, portals can stretch across both the back and the front of a building and may be furnished with benches. In their book Santa Fe Style, Mather and Woods say the portal is the Southwest's most profound contribution to architecture. Santa Fe's best-known portal is the porch in front of the Palace of the Governors, 105 E. Palace Avenue.

(Continued on next page)

REAL ESTATE

> **Pueblo style:** This classic design is typified by the homes of the Pueblo Indians and the early Spanish. People interested in the subtleties may differentiate later construction using this theme as Spanish Pueblo style, Pueblo Revival style, and Spanish Pueblo Revival style. Construction is of adobe or other materials with stucco to resemble the adobe look. Small windows and doorways accent the thick sculptural walls. The oldest of these homes grew organically rather than by floor plan, with more rooms added as the family expanded. Low ceilings, flat roofs, vigas, latillas, bancos, and nichos mark this style, but these features also may be found in Territorial style and in contemporary variations.
>
> **Territorial style:** Stuccoed walls finished with brick coping, decorative trim over windows and door frames, and sharper corners characterize this traditional architecture. With the opening of the Santa Fe Trail and the coming of the railroad, new materials, such as plate glass for windows, flooded into Santa Fe. The result was a happy marriage of sensuous adobe walls with brick and wood trim for a more formal look.
>
> **Saltillo tile:** This fired tile from Mexico, available in a variety of earth tones and usually square, is a popular and practical floor covering.
>
> **Vigas:** Peeled logs used either decoratively or as a ceiling support, vigas are the first part of the ceiling to be installed. These massive timbers may span the house or be found in only a few rooms. In Territorial style, the vigas are often squared-off and finished with a decorated edging.

special zoning encourages residential uses downtown. As you move away from the Plaza in all directions, you'll encounter newer residential areas with their own flavor.

Unlike many communities, Santa Fe generally defines its neighborhoods in terms of geographical locations rather than specific streets, parks, the names of builders, or subway stops. The developers of newer subdivisions name their projects, but these "neighborhoods" are the exception. Because of Santa Fe's long history of Catholicism, many people were more likely to identify themselves in terms of the parish where they went to church rather than the neighborhood, and parish boundaries included many different neighborhoods.

In Santa Fe, more so than in many communities in the country, the housing tends to look similar in many sections of town. This is Santa Fe style in its variations. (Please see our close-up in this chapter.) You will, however, find some differences. Generally, more expensive neighborhoods offer more acreage with your home. But this isn't necessarily true on the east side, where a home worth a half-million dollars or more may have little accompanying land. One of the charming quirks of the city's older neighborhoods, and a part of Santa Fe that is disappearing with its growth, is that a million-dollar home may be next to a less expensive house, built by its owners and their children. This economic mix has been replicated in some of the city's newer developments, which advertise the diversity of single-family homes at a variety of prices, with townhouses and apartments as one of their drawing cards. Both Tierra Contenta, Santa Fe's affordable housing development, and the upper-end Frijoles Village advertise a return to diversity as part of their attraction.

Some of Santa Fe's residential areas have sidewalks, paved streets, parks, and other amenities. Other homes—including million-dollar estates—lie off dirt roads with no curbs or gutters, no parks, and no bus service.

Here's a brief guide to Santa Fe's residential areas:

Downtown/East Side

Unlike many cities, Santa Fe's downtown, which includes the areas closest to the Plaza, is a prestigious place to live. This historic area, surrounded by winding streets, galleries, and towering old trees, is a mixture of historic homes that have been restored and modest houses that haven't been prettied up. The boundaries overlap with the east side, South Capitol area and

Guadalupe Street, but to the north E. Palace Avenue, with its big cottonwoods and Spanish Pueblo- and Territorial-style homes set back from the street, is one of the area's trademarks and boundaries. Guadalupe Street defines the downtown area to the west.

Styles tend to be more eclectic downtown than on the adjoining east side. You'll find stone houses as well as vintage hybrids that blend Santa Fe style and Western ranch design. Because the downtown area is largely commercial, residential property here is at a premium.

If you live downtown, you can take your morning jog along the Santa Fe River, stop in a cafe for coffee and a muffin, and do gourmet grocery shopping at Kaune Food Town, 511 Old Santa Fe Trail. You can walk to the Plaza. You'll have easy access to the Santa Fe River Park along Alameda Street (from Palace Avenue to Agua Fría/Guadalupe Streets), with its picnic tables and walking path, and to quiet Tommy Macaione Park, 301 E. Marcy Street, with its statue of the late Santa Fe artist. If you work at City Hall, the main post office, or for the state in any of its downtown offices, you can stroll home for lunch.

The city keeps a close eye on construction, remodeling, and renovation in this area to preserve Santa Fe's historic feel. Don't buy a home in any of the city's historic neighborhoods and plan on major new construction, demolition, or extensive renovation unless you have the time, money, and inclination to follow all the rules.

The east side is marked by real adobe houses on narrow, twisting streets. It's one of Santa Fe's most expensive areas with prices rising to $200 per square foot or higher. But not everyone who lives here is rich. Families who bought or built them before Santa Fe became chic own many of the homes. The boundaries here are nebulous, but Old Santa Fe Trail to the west and Camino Cabra to the east are the general markers. Camino San Acacio, Camino Don Miguel, Canyon Road, Acequia Madre, Garcia Street, and Camino del Monte Sol are among the neighborhood's defining streets.

You don't get earth-shaking views or huge estates in the heart of the east side, but, as some people see it, you get something better: an old Santa Fe neighborhood and genuine charm. The classic adobe look of the east side has influenced much of contemporary Santa Fe's construction. The city's oldest and best preserved Pueblo and Territorial architecture is within this and the downtown district. Earth-tone walls predominate, although you may find some white walls and decorative murals beneath portals. Buildings here tend to be true adobe with mud-plaster finish. The historic district ordinance requires that the walls be at least 8 inches thick and specifies that "geometrically straight facade lines shall be avoided" to emphasize the plasticity of the adobe look. The characteristic effect is that of long and low. Setbacks, portals, and a second-floor balcony to visually reduce the height and mass of the structure accompany the two-story construction you'll see. Roofs tend to be flat with a slight slope. Wooden lintels and other artistic finishing touches enhance many east side homes.

The lower section of Canyon Road is a mixture of businesses and residential buildings and has become increasingly commercial over the past decade. Canyon Road (see our Attractions chapter) offers galleries, shops and restaurants as well as wonderful ambiance. Garcia Street, Delgado Street, and Camino del Monte Sol also mix businesses and residences. Acequia Madre is residential except for Acequia Madre Elementary School, 700 Acequia Madre. Patrick Smith Park, 1001 Canyon Road, offers a pleasant expanse of grass for soccer and baseball, picnic spots, swings, and basketball courts along the Santa Fe River east of junction of Canyon Road and Acequia Madre.

As you move away from the heart of the east side, the terrain becomes more hilly. Cerro Gordo and Upper Canyon roads are long-established areas where new mansions abut ancient adobe homes. St. John's College, 1160 Camino Cruz Blanca, and Cristo Rey Church, 1120 Canyon Road, are among this area's landmarks. The Wilderness Gate development in the foot-hills behind St. John's College offers exclusive homes, many with exquisite views of Santa Fe, on multi-acre lots secluded amid the ponderosa pines.

Another relatively definable section of the east side is known as the Museum Area because the Wheelwright Museum of the American Indian, the Museum of International Folk Arts, and the Museum of Indian Arts and Culture are all here just off Camino Lejo. (Please see our Attractions chapter.) As late as 1950, much of this rolling, piñon-covered land remained unde-veloped. City planners consider the area "visually important" due to its proximity to the east side neighborhoods—and many buyers like it for the same reason. Some lots here may include ruts created by heavy wagons that traveled the historic Santa Fe Trail.

Heading north along the Old Taos Highway, Bishops Lodge Road, or Hyde Park Road, you get a sense of the countryside. This area, which is also known as the northeast or the near north side, is more sparsely populated. You're likely to see jackrabbits and coyotes along the dirt roads. Many of the homes sit on large lots with fine views of the mountains. Townhouses tend to be hidden among piñon and juniper trees or positioned to capture the views. Some of the property borders on arroyos, or sandy washes, areas that can be great places for walking as long as it isn't during a rainstorm! You won't find many sidewalks in this part of town. The city's Fort Marcy/Mager's Field Sports Complex, 490 Washington Avenue, is the closest place for kids to swim or play baseball or soccer.

Southeast

This area includes the South Capitol neighborhood, one of Santa Fe's most architecturally diverse areas with lots of seasoned homes and some quaint old apartment buildings. Some residents live in California bungalows, a rarity in Santa Fe. You'll also discover brick homes and even a lawn or two.

Old Santa Fe Trail provides the border to the east, and Galisteo Street frames it to the west. Paseo de Peralta and Cordova Road are, roughly, the north and south boundaries.

This predominantly residential area includes the Don Gaspar Historic District, which was subdivided as a residential development during the 1890s. For the first time in Santa Fe's history, people here were able to build with materials other than stone, wood, and adobe, thanks to the railroad. Santa Fe families got to experiment with materials and styles popular in the East, West, and Midwest including Italianate, Mansard, Queen Anne, and Craftsman Bungalow. You'll find gabled and hipped roofs here, gracefully intermixed among small Santa Fe-style, flat-roofed adobes. The city leaders' strong negative reaction to this imported look sparked renewed interest in preserving Santa Fe's historic adobe architecture.

Chinese elms shade the streets here, and the ground is good for gardens. Wood Gormley Elementary School, 141 E. Booth Street, serves the area. You'll find paved streets, concrete driveways, and sidewalks. Continue out Old Santa Fe Trail to the southeast, and you'll come upon homes in a semi-rural area in the piñon and juniper forests of the Sangre de Cristo foothills. Many people who live here have tremendous views of the Sandia and Ortiz Mountains. Much of this land is regulated by strict requirements that limit building on slopes, protect the views of the foothills from town (including limits on glare from windows) and restrict the construction of new roads.

Among the more established residential areas in the southeast section is the Sol y Lomas neighborhood, just across Old Pecos Trail and accessed by Sol y Lomas Road. The neighborhood has a country feeling and expansive homes. Old Santa Fe Trail, St. Francis Drive, Galisteo Street and Cordova Road border the residential area commonly known as the Hospital/E.J. Martinez neighborhood. It includes three- and four-bedroom homes, most surrounded by native landscaping with some sidewalks and some paved streets. Homes here are graciously set back from the road, and neighbors have an easier opportunity to get to know each other. E.J. Martinez School, 401 W. San Mateo Road, St. Vincent Hospital, which borders the neighborhood at 455 St. Michael's Drive, and the lovely Harvey Cornell Rose Garden, 1203 Galisteo Parkway, are among this area's landmarks.

Farther out old Pecos Trail is Quail Run, a gated condominium development of 265 units from studios up to four-bedroom homes, complete with a health club, restaurant, and nine-hole golf course.

Northwest

The oldest of these neighborhoods began as clusters of Hispanic ranches on the outskirts of Santa Fe's more densely developed Plaza area. The land was plotted in long, narrow parcels so

The downtown and capitol areas feature an eclectic mix of housing styles.

Photo: Don Strel

the maximum number of owners could have access to the water in the acequias and from the Santa Fe River for their farms and gardens. The earliest houses were constructed of adobe in the traditional Pueblo style and fronted directly onto the narrow dirt streets.

With the coming of the railroad and construction of its depot and rail yards in the area, the near west side and Guadalupe districts became a core of economic and social activity. As Santa Fe grew during the 20th century, families continued the long-established practice of subdividing their property among descendants. This created the west side's large number of small, oddly shaped lots. You'll notice many owner-built homes here, adding to the eclectic look.

The Guadalupe Street Neighborhood

The Guadalupe area continues as a commercial center with retail shops and restaurants designed to attract both local and visitor business (see our Shopping chapter). It roughly borders both sides of Guadalupe Street from Don Diego Avenue to Agua Fría Street. In addition to old Pueblo-style homes, the Guadalupe area includes bungalows such as those you see in the South Capitol district. The Santuario de Guadalupe, 100 Guadalupe Street, is one of the area's—and Santa Fe's—landmarks.

The Near West Side

About 25 years ago, the construction of St. Francis Drive separated the Guadalupe/near west side district from the west side. Agua Fría Street from Guadalupe Street to St. Francis Drive is the heart of the near west side. The near west side is probably as close as Santa Fe gets to America's perception of "inner city." Because this area contains the least expensive property in what is still considered the downtown area, it has undergone tremendous change in the last decade.

REAL ESTATE

A gentrified adobe, newly replastered and remodeled to include expensive wooden casement windows, may sit next to a home that looks much the same as it did 50 years ago. The Santa Fe Boys and Girls Club, 730 Alto Street, is one of the landmarks of this area.

The West Side

Santa Fe's climate makes interior coutyards, like this one at the Museum of Fine Arts, practical as well as beautiful.

Photo: Don Strel

From St. Francis Drive south, the area between Alameda and Agua Fría streets roughly to Hickox Street is known as the West Side. It's an eclectic, non-glitzy family area, characterized by the remnants of its agricultural days. St. Anne's Church, 511 Alicia Street, and Larragoite Elementary School, 1604 Agua Fría Street, are among its landmarks. There's some commercial development mixed with the residential here.

You'll find mid-priced houses along with a scattering of apartments and rental units. Because of the casual zoning, values don't increase as fast on the west side as they do elsewhere. Many Santa Fe natives who grew up here or on the near west side hold fond memories of these neighborhoods.

Casa Solana/Michelle Drive

Just north of Alameda Street bordered by Solana Drive to the south and St. Francis Drive to the west is Casa Solana, a family area with sidewalks, paved streets and mature landscaping including some beautiful big trees. Here you'll see kids riding their bikes, parents pushing strollers, and gray-haired gardeners hard at work. You'll find a real sense of neighborhood here.

Developer Allen Stamm built these homes in the 1960s, and they're beloved for their vigas, hardwood floors, fireplaces, and solid construction. Gonzales Elementary School, 851 W. Alameda Street, serves this area. For many decades, until the new landfill opened in 1997, Casa Solana did its civic duty by offering a thoroughfare to garbage trucks and people who hauled their own trash up Camino de las Crucitas to the city dump at the intersection of Buckman Road. From the old dump the views soar to 360-degree vistas which encompass the Jemez, Sangre de Cristo, Sandia and Ortiz Mountains.

Barrio de la Canada

This small residential area, just off Camino Alire and West Alameda Street, offers family-size homes and quiet streets because of limited access. The neighborhood's Santa Fe style includes decorative elements such as arches, and many homes are framed with native landscaping or small lawns.

Casa Alegre

Bordered by Agua Fría Street to the west, Cerrillos Road to the east, with a commercial buffer, San Jose Avenue, to the north and Maes Road to the south, Casa Alegre, also an Allen Stamm project, was built in the 1950s. Although the houses are smaller than those in Casa Solana, they have the same nice amenities. After World War II, the area provided homes to GIs and their families, some of whom still live in the same homes today. The Gregory Lopez Park,

1230 San Felipe Road, gives kids a place to play. The area's landmarks are Salazar Elementary School, 1300 Osage Avenue, and St. John the Baptist Catholic Church, 1301 Osage Avenue, just across the street from the school.

Kaune Neighborhood

Another Stamm family area with parks, schools, and churches, Kaune is accessed primarily from Monterey Drive just off Cerrillos Road. The neighborhood is officially known as the Casa Linda neighborhood, but most folks call it the Kaune area because of Kaune Elementary School, 1409 Monterey Drive, which serves the families here. The school, planned by famed Santa Fe architect John Gaw Meem, was named for Alfred Kaune, a past president of the Santa Fe School Board and part of the family that owned Kaune gourmet grocery stores.

The homes here include hardwood floors, vigas, and other Santa Fe-style amenities. Buyers can chose between Spanish Pueblo, Territorial, or California flat roof styles for their homes. The 128 units originally sold for between $9,000 and $14,000—today you'll easily pay 10 times that price.

West Alameda

From Solano Drive south, West Alameda Street serves as an access road to mixed housing areas. You'll find older, small handmade adobes, manufactured housing, and expensive newer construction. As you continue south, you'll discover some designer masterpieces whose very existence bumps the whole area up a notch or two in price. The farther you get from the Plaza, the more rural the area becomes; you'll see horses out here along with some boarding stables. The upscale Puesta del Sol and Piñon Hills developments offer big lots, big views, an openness to variations of Santa Fe style and a country feel.

Southwest

This is the section of Santa Fe where you're most likely to find family-affordable homes and apartments. Most of the construction here is newer, and this part of Santa Fe provides easiest access to Villa Linda Mall, 4250 Cerrillos Road, the Santa Fe Auto Park, 4450 Cerrillos Road, and to Capital High School, 4851 Paseo del Sol. Average home price here was $155,298 in 1999.

La Tierra Contenta

The Tierra Contenta neighborhood, part of the city's fast growing southwest sector, began in 1995, ushering in a hopeful new day for Santa Fe's average working family. Run by a nonprofit group created by the city, Tierra Contenta's prices begin at an unheard of (for Santa Fe) $65,000, with most property in the $100,000 range. Located just off Airport Road west of Cerrillos Road, the neighborhood offers parks and open space and works to cultivate a sense of neighborliness among the homeowners. When complete, Tierra Contenta will feature 5,500 units, of which 3,700 will be single-family residences and the rest multifamily town houses, duplexes, and apartments. The development will also have convenient commercial areas and hundreds of acres of open space with pedestrian walkways and bike trails. Schools and churches are part of the plan. Tierra Contenta was one of the reasons the Ford Foundation awarded the Santa Fe Affordable Housing Roundtable a $100,000 prize in 1996 for success in helping people find affordable housing.

INSIDERS' TIP

The great 20th-century architect Frank Lloyd Wright designed only one adobe house, the Pottery House, which was eventually built on a hillside overlooking Santa Fe. The owner purchased the plans from the Frank Lloyd Wright Foundation and construction began in 1984. The home is shaped like a football.

REAL ESTATE

Graceful arches and simple gates welcome visitors in some of the city's oldest neighborhoods.

Photo: Chris Corrie

REAL ESTATE

Bellamah

Named after builder Dale Bellamah, this neighborhood features houses designed to suit young families. The neighborhood is characterized by square one-story suburban-style homes with touches of Santa Fe-style. These homes are noted for their logical floor plans, garages, and flat or slightly pitched roofs. Bellamah is largely defined by Siringo Road to the north, Richards Avenue to the south, and Yucca Street to the north. The area has several parks, including the city's popular Arroyo Chamiso walking/bike trail that runs from Rodeo Road past the Monica Lucero Park on Avenida de la Campanas, crosses Camino Carlos Rey, and ends at Yucca Street.

General Franklin E. Miles Park, 1027 Camino Carlos Rey, one of the city's largest parks, offers baseball fields, lit basketball courts, playgrounds for the little guys, and grass to roll on for picnics. Francis X. Nava Elementary School, 2655 Siringo Road, sits at the edge of the park. The Herb Martinez/La Resolana Park, 2240 Camino Carlos Rey, has tennis courts and grass, which is often filled with young soccer players.

Rodeo Road Area

Santa Fe residents jokingly refer to this as "the suburbs." Houses are newer and larger than in Bellamah, but the neighborhood feeling is much the same. Your housing dollar goes farther here than in the historic areas, and the number of housing choices is increasing rapidly. You'll find clusters of townhouses and apartments, commercial centers along Rodeo Road and easy access to Interstate 25. The Park Plaza development of townhouses and some single homes is a popular spot because of its walking trails and common-land construction, which consolidates housing to allow for greenbelts and open space. The new city/county biking and hiking trail that will ultimately connect Santa Fe from the Guadalupe Street area to the Eldorado subdivision runs through here, offering a fine place for exercise.

Rancho Viejo

This new development sits on 2,500 acres about a mile south of Interstate 25 off of Richards Avenue. The area's master plan includes a mix of commercial and residential uses. The Village at Rancho Viejo, now under construction, will consist of approximately 334 units on 317 acres. Homesites will focus around a central plaza with shops, delis, small businesses and land set aside for a school. The development sold its first 80 completed homes in four months.

Northwest of Town

U.S. Highway 84/285 serves as the boundary for this area to the east, and Camino La Tierra and Tano Road provide the main access to these properties. The Tano Road neighborhood, La Tierra, La Tierra Nueva and Salva Tierra are among the residential areas here. All are similar—multi-acre lots with expansive views and homes by some of Santa Fe's finest designers and builders. You're likely to find more established homes in the Tano Road area. Dirt roads are the rule, and you won't find any schools, gas stations, churches, or shopping opportunities; they're all in Santa Fe. The trade-off for what some consider inconvenience: plenty of space, the chance to hear coyotes howl at the moon, and breathtaking views.

Las Campanas

This exclusive development includes an 18-hole Jack Nicklaus signature golf course, a beautifully appointed clubhouse with a first-rate restaurant for members and guests, and view lots that range from 1 to 10 acres. All home sites on this 4,700-acre development include gated entries, paved roads, and underground utilities. The development has strict covenants that

REAL ESTATE

Santa Fe style at once incorporates vigas, latillas, flowing adobe lines, corbells, and canales, earthtones predominate.

Photo: Don Strel

dictate construction and style of homes. In 1999 six custom homes sold here at prices over the $1 million mark. Average home price here in 1999 was $880,000.

Frijoles Village

A new development in this section of Santa Fe, Frijoles Village expects to begin construction soon. Described as a "neo-traditional community," the project will be south of Las Campanas and 5 miles northwest of the Santa Fe Plaza. The community will have 433 lots of various sizes, averaging one-third of an acre. The project's homes will range in price from $160,000 to $400,000, with some less-expensive subsidized housing. The community will be designed with narrow, curving roads and a conformity of exterior color, heights, and styles to provide visual unity. Trees will be planted to line the paved streets. An extensive system of foot and bike paths will link the village to a regional trail network. The development will also include parks and a commercial plaza. A school site has been offered to the Santa Fe Public Schools, and the University of New Mexico is considering building a graduate school here. Sixty percent of the development will be open space, and the village will restrict building on its escarpments.

Southeast of Santa Fe

Eldorado and Vicinity

This family-friendly area is Santa Fe's suburbia. When the Eldorado development was first announced, many Santa Fe residents scoffed. Who, they asked, would drive 20 minutes to get to work? Today, Eldorado is nearly a community unto itself, and newer housing developments have sprouted up nearby. Thousands of people live here, enjoying the panorama of mountains and the quiet neighborly feeling. In addition to humans, many kinds of crit-

INSIDERS' TIP

Don't worry if your home doesn't look like Martha Stewart's. Santa Fe is not the place for manicured lawns, prim gardens, or perfectly clean homes. Authentic adobe walls shed authentic brown dust. And dirt roads generate dust with every passing vehicle.

ters, including hawks, coyotes, and rabbits, still call this country home. In 1999, the average home here sold for $220,553.

Unlike much of Santa Fe County, the land here is relatively flat, which makes for easier construction and lower costs. The older homes are arranged in a traditional neighborhood style with several to a block. The newer houses tend to be larger and sit on sprawling lots in this world of sand, sage, and piñon. Amenities include a community clubhouse with meeting rooms and a swimming pool and one of Santa Fe's better elementary schools, El Dorado Elementary, 2 Avenida Torreon. In 1996, residents celebrated the opening of the Agora commercial center, complete with a grocery store, restaurants, and other amenities at 7 Avenida Grande.

Real Estate Agencies

Bear Creek Real Estate Inc.
215 W. San Francisco St., Ste. 200
• **(505) 820-7993**

This six-agent firm has a separate division that deals exclusively with property in Las Campanas, Santa Fe's high-end golf course development. Bear Creek offers property management as well as residential and commercial sales. Owner Nancy Abruzzo also specializes in finding winter rentals for visiting skiers.

Branch Realty
228 S. St. Francis Dr.
• **(505) 984-8100**

The nine agents in this office focus on commercial real estate. They can help with investment property, exchanges, leases, and consultants as well as sales. The firm, established in 1982, prides itself on its "knowledge and effort." Among the company's recent projects are Whole Foods Grocery Store, Home Depot, and Phase II of Plaza Santa Fe, which will include many well-known retail stores.

City Different Realty
130 Grant Ave.
• **(505) 983-1557**

Located in a lovely old brick building—a novelty for adobe-style Santa Fe—this office features six agents, all of whom are brokers with experience from 12 to 20 years in Santa Fe. City Different is by design a small firm, owned and run by four brokers and based on a philosophy of bringing together a select group of experienced, top-producing people who wish to work cooperatively. The office deals mainly

with upper-end properties, but since most business comes through personal referrals it also works in other price ranges.

Coldwell Banker Trails West Realty Ltd.
2000 Old Pecos Tr.
• **(505) 988-7285, (800) 775-5550**

With 46 full-time agents, Coldwell Banker represents both buyers and sellers in residential transactions. In business for 18 years, the firm makes extensive use of the Coldwell Banker national website and national sales programs such as Blue Ribbon & Previews Properties. The office provides ongoing training for its agents.

INSIDERS' TIP

The Santa Fe Association of Realtors reported that Santa Fe real-estate sales in 1999 were the highest ever recorded. Real estate agents expect another strong year in 2000 unless the volatile stock market causes a recession.

Robert Dunn Real Estate Inc./Santa Fe
104 S. Capitol St., Ste. 6
• **(505) 988-2200, (800) 444-9887**
• **www.RobertDunnRealEstate.com**

Owners Robert Dunn and Pam Wickiser have combined 30 years experience in the Santa Fe market. In addition to residences, land, and commercial property, they represent Quail Run luxury resort condominium living. Visit their website for more information and to contact them by e-mail.

French & French Fine Properties
231 Washington Ave.
• **(505) 988-8088, (800) 409-7325**
• **www.french-french.com**

French & French continues to lead the Santa Fe area real estate market in residential sales in all price ranges. In addition to 75 agents, four full-time staff supported offices and an extensive advertising marketing strategy, the agency has a 500-page web site. French & French is the exclusive Santa Fe affiliate of Christie's/Great Estates. The firm has been in business since 1984.

360-degree views are a plus when selecting a site location.

Photo: Chris Corrie

Mares Realty and Accent Property Management
1050 Paseo de Peralta
• **(505) 988-5585, (505) 986-3838**

This five-agent office deals with general real estate and property management. Richard E. Mares, the founding broker, has more than 36 years of experience and is among a select number of brokers who are also licensed appraisers. The office is next to the state PERA building across from the State Capitol, and parking is not a problem.

Santa Fe Properties
1000 Paseo de Peralta
• **(505) 982-4466**

Founded in 1986, this firm has become one of the more successful independently owned brokerages in Santa Fe. Team spirit and a capable staff add to the strength of the company. With an in-depth knowledge of real estate in the Santa Fe area, 64 sales associates provide personal service. More than 60 percent of their sales are from repeat customers. Just a short walk from the downtown plaza, their attractive office is in the historic 100-year-old Jose Alarid adobe.

Sotheby's International Realty
326 Grant Ave.
• **(505) 988-2533**
• **http://santafe.sothebysrealty.com.**

With Sotheby's International Realty's global connections and local expertise, the 17 sales associates specialize in representing buyers and sellers of premiere properties in and around Santa Fe. A full inventory of Sotheby's available property can be seen on the website. The office is open seven days a week.

Town & Ranch Inc.
149 W. Alameda St.
• **(505) 988-3700**

This agency says that its extensive national marketing system, the Better Homes & Gardens Home Buying System and Home Marketing System, sets it apart. Buyers throughout the country can learn about Santa Fe homes before they visit. This full-service brokerage has 40 licensed agents and includes specialists in ranches and commercial property.

Varela Real Estate Inc.
1526 Cerrillos Rd.
• **(505) 982-2525**

Varela Real Estate, previously known as the Frank Gomez Agency, has been in business since 1949. President Susan Varela, Gomez's daughter, has worked in the office since 1973. The office offers residential and commercial sales and management and leasing services for residential and commercial property.

Karen Walker Real Estate
205 Delgado
• **(505) 982-0118, (800) 982-0118**

In business since 1973, this small firm prides itself on its knowledge of land use codes, building regulations, and restrictions. It has an intimate acquaintance with neighborhoods, historic uses and districts. Karen Walker is the author of Understanding and Buying Santa Fe Real Estate, illustrated by professional cartoonist Pat Oliphant.

Resources

ADC Referral
(505) 989-1139

Ready to build or remodel in Santa Fe? Let this free service help you find the architect, design staff, and builders you'll need. The process begins with an in-depth interview to help you understand and define your tastes and vision for your home or office. ADC will then assist you in clarifying design needs, establishing a working budget, and identifying the scope of service you'll need to get the job done. The initials, incidentally, stand for architect, designers, and contractors.

Santa Fe Area Homebuilders Association
411 St. Michael's Dr. 6-A
• (505) 982-1774

The Santa Fe Area Homebuilders Association is a trade organization representing more than 570 firms in the seven-county area in Northern New Mexico. This nonprofit association is dedicated to promoting safe, quality, attractive, cost-effective, and affordable housing. The association sponsors several community-based events each year. The Home and Garden Show, which gives you a look at some of Santa Fe's nicest homes, is held in early spring. Haciendas—A Parade of Homes is a self-guided tour held throughout the Santa Fe area each August. The tour features homes representing many varieties of building products as well as new styles. The builders compete for recognition of their craftsmanship and, as a sidelight, may attract new clients based on the opportunity to see the builder's work first-hand. In 1999, prices of the homes included in the show ranged from $139,000 to $1.6 million. The association also engages in many community service projects.

Neighborhood Housing Services
1570 Pacheco St., Ste. A
• (505) 983-6214, (800) 429-5499

This private, nonprofit organization helps low- and moderate-income families maintain their homes and provides opportunities for new affordable housing. The agency offers below-market mortgages and assistance with down payments. Their home repair program helps families keep property they already own and home-buyer workshops teach potential buyers much of what they need to know to be successful homeowners. The agency also builds new and affordable homes which it makes available to first-time home buyers.

Santa Fe Association of Realtors
510 N. Guadalupe St.
• (505) 982-8385

The Santa Fe Association of Realtors is the local affiliate of the National Association of Realtors. This organization compiles the Multiple Listing Service, provides ongoing education for all licensees and works for legislation to protect property owners. With about 700 local members, the association participates in many community service projects.

Santa Fe Civic Housing Authority
664 Alta Vista St.
• (505) 988-2859

The authority works with the city's low-income families to help them find a decent place to rent. The program includes a low-rent public housing program, rental assistance and other projects to help families become more self-sufficient and eventually purchase their own homes. Funding comes from public and private sources.

Santa Fe County Housing Authority
52 Camino de Jacobo
• (505) 992-3060

The county provides housing services for low-income and elderly people through this program. Included are vouchers that help with the rent and a popular rent-to-buy program in three sites around the county. The elderly, disabled, or families with many dependents may be eligible for help; the waiting list is 6 to 12 months.

Tierra Contenta Corporation
369 Montezuma St., Ste. 220
• (505) 471-4546

Santa Fe has begun to meet its need for housing that working families can afford. This nonprofit group is developing more than 800 acres on the south side of Santa Fe into mixed-income single-family and multi-family homes. The neighborhood uses strict design standards sensitive to the environment and replicates the traditional look of old Santa Fe with narrow, pedestrian-oriented streets. Miles of trails,

Spring lilacs gracefully overhang a carved door in this example of Santa Fe Style.

Photo: Chris Corrie

parks, and open spaces are part of the corporation's plan. When the neighborhood is fully developed, it will include about 5,000 housing units.

Publications

Apartment Guide
7801 Academy Blvd. NE, Ste. 203, Albuquerque
• **(505) 821-5212**
Although Albuquerque captures most of this guide's focus, you'll learn about Santa Fe rentals here too. The digest-sized booklet contains a map that shows some of the major complexes. The guide is available by calling, or pick one up on various free racks throughout the city.

Homes Santa Fe
1229 B St. Francis Dr.
• **(505) 982-2312,**
This full-size, full-color magazine comes complete with an index of the agencies and agents that advertise inside it. It's available free of charge at real estate offices throughout the city and can be found on news racks. For a copy call (800) 753-3643.

The Real Estate Book, Santa Fe and North Central New Mexico
369 Montezuma St., Box 201
• **(505) 989-4411, (800) 841-3401**
This free pocket-size magazine with color photographs is nothing but ads for single-family homes, townhouses, and vacant land. It also includes a classified advertising section. You'll find pictures of houses around the city with prices, descriptions, and the agent to call for more information.

Santa Fe Real Estate Guide
Santa Fe New Mexican, 202 E. Marcy
• **(505) 983-3303**
Published by The Santa Fe New Mexican, this first-rate monthly magazine is jammed with ads and articles. Regular features include a column by the president of the Santa Fe Association of Realtors, a list of building permits recently issued, an update on zoning and annexations that might affect real estate values, a summary of recent home and land sales, a chart of mortgage rates, and a look at the rental market for the previous month. It's distributed free all over town.

Santa Fe Showcase
231 Washington Ave.
• **(505) 988-8088, (800) 409-REAL**
This beautiful magazine features some of the properties listed by French and French, one of Santa Fe's largest real estate firms. The agency has published more than 20 issues of this guide, which rivals many magazines in the quality of its printing and reproduction.

Understanding and Buying Santa Fe Real Estate
Karen Walker Real Estate, 205 Delgado, St.
• **(505) 982-0118, (800) 982-0118**
This paperback delves into some of the quirks of the real estate market in Santa Fe. Walker discusses zoning, private covenants, homeowner associations, site selection, utilities, financing methods and sources and what to do if you buy property that includes an *acequia*, a historic irrigation ditch. Cartoons by Pat Oliphant add to the fun.

Retirement

It's not in the Sun Belt and it's certainly not cheap. So why is Santa Fe rated among the top spots to retire in the United States? For the same reasons it's attractive to so many other segments of the American population. It's beautiful. It has a healthy, highly livable, four-season climate. Its history is as fascinating as its mixture of cultures. And it's got culture—the other kind—in spades: world-class opera, chamber music, symphony and chorale; flamenco and other live dance; theater; repertory cinema; galleries and museums; and dozens of classes and seminars on any number of topics in the city's public and private institutions of higher learning. The food here is superb, with internationally acclaimed restaurants offering creative fare for the discerning palate and dozens of lower priced eateries with good, down-home cookin'. Active seniors can burn off the extra calories skiing, hiking, golfing, kayaking, swimming, or enjoying any number of other outdoor endeavors in an environment that begs to be enjoyed.

But there's something else in Santa Fe, a *je ne sais quoi*, that makes it just a little more attractive for an older population than other cities with similar qualities—the relaxed atmosphere, perhaps, and a cordiality toward older people unmatched in other cities. Indeed, a number of national publications have rated Santa Fe among the top places in the U.S. to retire. It even beats out retirement communities in Arizona, California, Florida, and other states because of the city's lack of congestion. As one local senior citizen succinctly put it, "You can grow old here."

The number of residents age 65 and older in Santa Fe County increased 47.1 percent between 1980 and 1990. The county estimates the number will have tripled between 1990 and 2020, when residents 65 and older will compose 27 percent of the population.

In this chapter, we tell you about the services and housing options available for the growing senior population in the Santa Fe area. For more news and information by, about, and for seniors, pick up a copy of *Prime Time: For New Mexicans 50 Plus* (See our Media chapter), a free, Albuquerque-based monthly tabloid at newsstands throughout Santa Fe.

Santa Fe has a variety of modestly priced retirement homes.

Agencies, Services, and Social/Support Groups:

American Association of Retired Persons (AARP)

Capital City Chapter: P.O. Box 22831, Santa Fe, NM 87502
• **(505) 471-4540**
State offices: 1919 Fifth St., Suite E
• **(505) 473-7606**

AARP is a nonprofit, nonpartisan organization dedicated to helping older Americans live independent, dignified, and useful lives. Its Capital City Chapter, No. 381, fulfills this mission by organizing and joining in many community projects such as the Safe Kids/Safe Seniors Program and Foster Grandparents (see entries under City of Santa Fe Division of Senior Services in this chapter); and Vials for Life program, which alerts emergency medical technicians that an individual is on medication.

Adult Protective Services

2001 Vivican Way
• **(505) 827-7450, 1-800-797-3260**

New Mexico law requires anyone who suspects an adult is being abused, neglected, or exploited to report it. That's where Adult Protective Services steps in. A branch of the New Mexico Children, Youth, and Families Department, the agency investigates allegations of abuse, neglect, or exploitation of people age 18 and older who are unable to protect themselves. The majority of its clients are seniors. In some cases, Adult Protective Services will provide housecleaning, shopping, transportation, and other services to keep an individual from being institutionalized prematurely. Other cases involve family members or acquaintances who are taking advantage of a vulnerable adult, especially

his or her checkbook. The agency has no punitive powers but may refer cases either to other community services or, if it suspects criminal activity, to the police or district attorney.

Alzheimer's Association Support Group

5 Camino Pequeño
• **(505) 982-5906, (800) 777-8155**
(505) 266-4473 Albuquerque chapter),
(800) 272-3900 (national headquarters)

This is a local support group for caregivers of people with Alzheimer's disease. It's affiliated with the Albuquerque Chapter of the Alzheimer's Association, whose national headquarters are in Chicago. The local group meets the second Tuesday of every month at 7:30 PM at La Residencia (505-983-2273), a private nursing home two blocks from the Santa Fe Plaza at 820 Paseo de Peralta.

City of Santa Fe Division of Senior Services

1121 Alto St.
• **(505) 984-6731**

Part of the city's Community Services Department, the Division of Senior Services is a "one-stop shop" for a wide variety of programs and services at minimal cost for adults 60 and over throughout the city and county. The division provides transportation for a suggested donation of 25 cents per trip with 24 hours notice; $1 meals at designated senior centers or delivered to a person's home; preventive health education and services including blood pressure testing, blood sugar and cholesterol screening, hearing and eye tests, breast cancer screening, and flu shots; recreation and activities such as Senior Olympics, dancing, travel, ceramics, sculpture, woodcarving, and weaving; case management; outreach, information, and referrals. The Senior Services Division sponsors numerous volunteer programs including Retired and Senior Volunteer Program (RSVP), where seniors act as Medicare-Medigap counselors, peer counselors, nutrition counselors, ombudsmen, craft

INSIDERS' TIP

Twice each year, volunteers from the Santa Fe–based Living Treasures Program choose three northern New Mexicans age 70 or older to be "Living Treasure Elders" in recognition of their spirit, energy, and community service. Of the 110 men and women named as living treasures since 1984, 93 have been captured in a book of photo essays called Living Treasures: Celebration of the Human Spirit, published in 1997 by Western Edge Press of Santa Fe. The book is widely available in local bookstores and public libraries.

instructors, etc.; Safe Kids/Safe Seniors to prevent accidental injuries; and the USDA Commodities Distribution, which gets food to low-income seniors and disabled clients. It also offers several paying programs for low-income seniors in conjunction with the State Agency on Aging, (see subsequent entry) including Foster Grandparents, which provides a stipend for serving as classroom "grandparents," and Senior Companions, in which individuals 60 and older can supplement their income by providing companionship to frail, homebound elderly clients. The division's Respite Program provides R&R for primary caregivers of people with Alzheimer's Disease and dementia.

The division has eight senior centers within 2,000 square miles, four of them in Santa Fe: Mary Esther Gonzales Center, 1121 Alto St., (505) 984-6731; Pasatiempo Center, 668 Alta Vista St., (505) 984-9859; Luisa Center, 1510 Luisa St., (505) 984-8091; Villa Consuelo Center, 1200 Camino Consuelo, (505) 474-5431

Desert State Life Management Inc.
1500 Fifth St., Ste. 11
• (505) 988-5550

Desert State Life Management is a private, nonprofit organization that provides guardianship services (making healthcare and placement decisions) and conservatorship services (making financial decisions) for mentally incapacitated people. It also manages trusts too small for a bank to handle and can answer questions about durable power of attorney, in which you assign someone to make healthcare decisions for you, and other advanced directives, including living wills. Many of its clients are senior citizens who are unable to make life decisions for themselves. Desert State makes all decisions by team process.

Elderhostel
The College of Santa Fe,
1600 St. Michael's Dr.
• (505) 473-6267, (800) 456-2673

With 90 programs statewide, including 70 in Santa Fe alone, the College of Santa Fe (see listing in "Education") is New Mexico's largest and most active site for Elderhostel, a Boston-based international travel and education program for people older than 55. Elderhostel offers short-term education and adventure. It has programs in all 50 states, Canada and 80 other countries around the world. Northern New Mexico Elderhostel features camping, hiking, climbing, or skiing programs; service programs in which volunteers restore trails in the national forest or adobe structures; theme weeks focusing on the state museums, for example, or perhaps the Santa Fe Opera or the Santa Fe

Ponce de Leon is an independent and assisted living facility.

Photo: Courtesy of Ponce de Leon

Trail; classes on American Indian or Hispanic culture or any number of other offerings. Recent courses have included such topics as "Spanish Colonial Traditions and Customs," "Cultural Encounters: Examining History through Native Eyes," "African Americans in the Southwest," "Legendary Women of the Southwest," "Artistic Traditions in Northern New Mexico: From the Stone Age to the Present;" and "The River of Lost Souls: Aztec, New Mexico, and the San Juan River." Elderhostel courses run in the neighborhood of $75 to $85 a night, including housing, meals, and all field-trip and course fees. Housing ranges from dormitories to hotels. Elderhostel participants may take a companion or spouse of any age older than 21. Other northern New Mexico venues offering Elderhostel programs include Plaza Resolana en Santa Fe (see "Education"), (505) 982-8539, and Ghost Ranch Conference Center, (505) 685-4333, located near Abiquiu in the heart of Georgia O'Keeffe country.

Jubilados
2639 Agua Fría St.
• (505) 438-7383

Jubilados—Spanish for "those who, having shed their careers, are joyous"—is a nonprofit organization dedicated to restoring value to age and to aging through contemplative practice, service, and ecology. Part of the "conscious aging" movement, Jubilados advocates approaching old age and death with dignity and both the recognition and acceptance that most of us will require the care of others toward the end of our lives. In addition to general meditation classes, seminars, and retreats, Jubilados offers special courses designed to "recharge the batteries" of caregivers for the old and chronically ill. It hosts an annual symposium at Ghost Ranch Conference Center to explore the intersection of contemplative practice and community service by and for the aging. Jubilados holds weekly meditation services, open to the public, Sundays at 10 AM. These attract an eclectic mixture of older people whose numbers include Buddhists, Christians, Jews, Vedantists, etc. What they have in common is an unwillingness to age in stereotypical ways—i.e. "retire to Florida and play shuffleboard," as Jubilados' founders put it. Instead, they're searching for, or deepening, their spiritual connection to each other and the world through meditative, political and social activity. To that end, Jubilados is developing a 128-residence, semi-communal, affordable retirement community for aging meditators dedicated to the principles of permaculture—a self-sustaining system of agriculture that relies on and replenishes solely what nature provides. Membership in Jubilados costs $36 a year and is purely optional.

Newcomers Club of Santa Fe
P.O. Box 28933, SF, NM 87592
• (505) 988-7071

Open to people of all ages, the Newcomers Club of Santa Fe seems to attract primarily—though not exclusively—seniors, many of whom have chosen Santa Fe as their retirement or second home. The club is a social group that provides an opportunity to meet people, learn about the Santa Fe area, stimulate the intellect and enjoy good food at fine local restaurants. Club activities include discussion groups on books and movies, study groups, bridge groups, theater-going groups, local travel and monthly Sunday brunches. The club meets once a month for membership luncheons that in the recent past have featured a planetarium show at Santa Fe Community College, history of the Santa Fe Trail, a backstage tour of the Santa Fe Opera, and a slide show of the new Georgia O'Keeffe Museum. Membership runs $10 per year. Call for information and an application form.

Older Adult Outpatient Services
St. Vincent Hospital, 455 St. Michael's Dr.
• (505) 820-5376

This is a specialized program geared toward seniors at risk of becoming—or who already are—severely depressed, isolated, grief stricken, or have difficulties adjusting to changes in their life. Clients go through an intake session before being accepted into the program, which includes art therapy, group therapy, wellness education, and other activities. They usually spend three or four hours per visit, which includes a hot lunch. The hospital will provide or arrange for transportation, if necessary. Medicare, Medicaid, and most supplementary insurance will usually cover the cost. Call for additional information or to make an appointment.

Open Hands
509 Camino de los Marquez
• (505) 982-4258

Established in 1977, Open Hands is a nonprofit agency providing essential services to help elderly, disabled, and poor people live independently and with dignity. The organization offers a wide variety of services such as adult day care for up to 50 people, including those with Alzheimer's or other dementia; group support for caregivers; a home safety program that retrofits homes with wheelchair ramps and grab bars; weatherizing homes by replacing leaky windows and doors, testing for carbon monoxide and radon, and helping clients get funds for necessary renovations; a Youth Services Corps in which student volunteers who do yard work and other chores for elderly and disabled clients; a medical equipment loan bank; emergency financial assistance; and home visits during a crisis or simply for companionship. Open Hands charges for its services based on a client's ability to pay. The agency operates several thrift stores that not only help support its programs, but also employ the disabled. Based in Santa Fe, Open Hands serves 11 counties and 12 pueblos in northern New Mexico.

INSIDERS' TIP

For information about nursing homes in Santa Fe and throughout the state, contact the New Mexico State Agency on Aging for its *Guide to New Mexico's Nursing Homes*, published for the first time in 1997 by the agency's Long Term Care Ombudsman Program. The guide is a good starting point in a search for a nursing home in New Mexico. It gives a brief description of the facility, Medicare/Medicaid reimbursement rates, inspection scores, and a brief rundown of the medical characteristics of its residents.

mandates of the federal Older Americans Act, the agency's mission is to ensure the physical, mental and economic well being of aging New Mexicans. In addition to distributing federal and state funds to senior centers for meals, activities, in-home support, and health education, the agency provides job training and placement for low-income seniors; helps seniors find health and other benefits they've earned; advocates for residents of long-term care facilities; and offers volunteer opportunities for seniors and those who want to work with them. The agency contracts with outside organizations for a variety of other services and activities including free or reduced-cost legal services, Senior Olympics and the Foster Grandparents and Senior Companions programs (see "City of Santa Fe Division of Senior Services" in this chapter).

Seniors Reaching Out
Armory for the Arts Complex, 1050 Old Pecos Tr.
• **(505) 988-5522**

Seniors Reaching Out is a nonprofit group that celebrates aging through literary and performing arts. SRO produces and stages plays, readings, musical numbers and conferences and sponsors oral history and storytelling dialogues among some of Santa Fe's "living treasures" in the arts and humanities. The group performs variety shows and reminiscence theater—called "Elders Entertain Elders"—at nursing and retirement homes and senior centers throughout Santa Fe and northern New Mexico and entertains children with its "Kids and Kin" storytelling performances at Santa Fe public schools, Native American headstart programs, libraries, and summer camps. SRO entertained nearly 2,000 people with more than 50 performances in 1999. That year marked its first "Creativity, Aging & the Arts" conference at Santa Fe Community College with a second scheduled for 2001.

New Mexico State Agency on Aging
La Villa Rivera Building, 228 E. Palace Ave.
• **(505) 827-7640, (800) 432-2080**

The State Agency on Aging oversees the delivery of services for the elderly in New Mexico to help older people and their families achieve a high quality of life. Created to carry out the

Women in Transition
Santa Fe Community College, 6401 Richards Ave.
• **(505) 428-1618**

Women in Transition is a series of free workshops designed to give widows and other women going through major life changes a better self-image. Part of Santa Fe Community College's Institute for Intercultural Community Leadership, the workshops provide education, information, support and referrals in the community.

Tax Aid
Mary Esther Gonzales Senior Center, 1121 Alto St.
• **(505) 984-6731**
Pasatiempo Senior Center, 668 Alta Vista St.
• **(505) 984-9859**

Sponsored by AARP, this is a free, walk-in clinic designed to help low-income seniors filing income tax returns. The clinics are open Monday through Thursday from 9 AM to 2 PM beginning the first Monday in February through April 15. Clinic volunteers are lay people certified by the Internal Revenue Service. Call 983-1750 for more information.

Widowed Persons Program
**1937 Camino Lumbre, Santa Fe, 87505
(Mailing address only)**
• (505) 473-9783

The Widowed Persons Program is a non-profit, AARP-sponsored program that provides one-on-one emotional and practical support to widows and widowers. Trained volunteers attempt to contact people whose spouse recently died. First contact comes through a letter with follow-ups by telephone. The group meets the second Sunday of each month at 1:15 PM for lunch at Ponce de Leon Retirement Community. A monthly newsletter lists the entrées for upcoming lunches.

Home Health Care and Hospice

Kelly Assisted Living
1751 Old Pecos Tr., Ste. P
• (505) 982-9171

A subsidiary of Kelly Services for temporary secretarial help, Kelly Assisted Living is a private, Michigan-based company with offices in Santa Fe, Albuquerque, and elsewhere in the Southwest that provide health care to people who want to live at home but need help with daily activities. Clients include the elderly, people with Alzheimer's disease or other long-term disabilities, and patients recovering from stroke, heart attack, surgery, or other serious illness. Caregivers are available up to 24 hours a day, seven days a week to assist with dressing and bathing, prepare meals, help clients walk and get into and out of bed, monitor medication, provide transportation, run errands, do light housekeeping, and offer companionship. Kelly charges an hourly rate and does not accept Medicare or Medicaid.

The Partners Program
St. Vincent Hospital, Cancer Treatment Education Center, 455 St. Michael's Dr.
• (505) 820-5479

The Partners Program offers pastoral care for people who are terminally ill. This is a well-established program that began at Upaya (see our Worship and Spirituality chapter), a local contemplative retreat and study center and is now under the auspices of the Santa Fe Institute for Medicine and Prayer at St. Vincent Hospital. The program's more than three dozen volunteers teach non-sectarian, contemplative practices based in Zen Buddhism to help bring

Santa Fe's amenities draw retirees from around the country.

peace and acceptance to individuals at any stage of illness or grieving. Partners help nurture a calm, sacred space that emphasizes prayer, deep listening and mindful silence or meditation. The Partners Program offers a series of training sessions twice a year.

Presbyterian Medical Services
1422 Paseo de Peralta
• (505) 982-5565,
(800) 477-7633

Presbyterian Medical Services is a nonprofit corporation that provides medical and dental health care, education, and human services primarily to under-served populations in the Southwest. Its Santa Fe programs include PMS Home Care and The Hospice Center, both based out of the downtown area. The home care program, (505) 988-2211, offers skilled nursing; home health aides for personal hygiene; physical, occupational, and speech therapy; and medical social services. The Hospice Center, (505) 988-2211, provides medicine, medical supplies, and equipment; on-call registered nurses specializing in pain and symptom control; home health aides; physical, occupational, and speech therapists; volunteers to support both patients and caregivers; social workers and pastors for emotional and spiritual counseling and referral; and bereavement services. The Hospice Center also operates a support and counseling service for groups, including schools and businesses, and a thrift store whose revenues support the center. PMS is Medicare/Medicaid-certified.

Professional Home Health Care
10 Calle Medico
• (505) 982-8581

In operation since the 1980s, Professional Home Health Care is a private, nonprofit agency whose mission is to keep individuals—from the elderly, who comprise the majority of its clients, to infants—out of hospitals, nursing homes, and other institutions. The agency provides skilled nursing, home health aides, hospice, and other complementary services in cli-

---

INSIDERS' TIP

Many stores and restaurants in Santa Fe, including some national chains, offer senior discounts. Some establishments set aside a particular day or specified hours for seniors to receive the discount. Others offer a discount every day, including Wild Oats Community Market, a natural foods supermarket that gives a 10 percent discount to seniors; Wild Oats' sister store, Alfalfa's Market, which deducts 5 percent from the total; and the Market Place Natural Grocery, which also takes of 5 percent. While most places advertise their senior discounts prominently, a few prefer to play it low-key. Don't be shy about asking.

---

ents' homes. The agency covers a large territory in New Mexico, from Sandoval County south of Albuquerque to the Colorado border. It accepts Medicare, Medicaid, and private pay clients.

St. Vincent Home Health Services
1601 St. Michael's Dr.
• (505) 989-9331

In 1997, St. Vincent Hospital expanded its home health care division and moved into a separate location, renaming the new facility St. Vincent Home Health Services. Now located a couple of miles from the hospital, HHS still provides the durable medical equipment (beds, wheelchairs, etc.), home infusion (IV), and oxygen it has been supplying homebound clients, most of them seniors, since 1991. It also accommodates travelers, many of them older people suffering from altitude sickness, who can arrange for pickup or delivery. St. Vincent accepts almost all insurance and payer sources, including Medicare and Medicaid.

Retirement Communities

Ponce de Leon Retirement Community
640 Alta Vista St.
• (505) 984-8422

Ponce de Leon is a full-service rental retirement community for independent and assisted living. Its 150 apartments include studios, one- and two-bedroom units, each with an electronic emergency call system. Located just five minutes by car from downtown Santa Fe, Ponce de Leon has a distinct Spanish feel with plenty of wrought iron and a lovely interior courtyard with a reflecting pool, shrubbery, flowers, and trees. Independent living rentals include a continental breakfast and either lunch or dinner; transportation; weekly housekeeping; and flat linen service. These residents enjoy a full activity calendar featuring art exhibits, concerts and other live entertainment, dances, Friday social hours, seminars, art classes, exercise classes, and day trips to Albuquerque, casinos, museums, Indian and Spanish markets, and other events and attractions. Assisted living includes three meals a day, daily housekeeping, help with personal hygiene, dispensing and monitoring medication, regular house checks, and a separate activity calendar with field trips close to home. Ponce de Leon offers on-site banking, a country store and a large city park across the street with an indoor swimming pool, tennis courts and benches and picnic tables.

Kingston Residence of Santa Fe
2400 Legacy Court
• (505) 471-2400, (800) 906-9020

Kingston Residence of Santa Fe is a rental retirement community for the 55 and older set, located on 5½ landscaped acres. It offers 70 large, sunny independent living apartments, each with either a patio or balcony, some overlooking open courtyards, and another 12 rooms each for assisted living and Alzheimer's residents. Independent living rates include breakfast, lunch, and dinner; local transportation in the house Cadillac; all utilities; indoor and outdoor maintenance, including housekeeping every two weeks; social services; and a wide variety of activities from casino excursions, museum visits, and movies to exercise, dancing, and meditation. Assisted care residents enjoy all the services listed above plus 24-hour care by licensed nurses, medication control, physical therapy and personal hygiene care. Independent residents may receive any of these services for an additional cost. Kingston Residence of Santa Fe pro-vides on-site banking, a notary public and free office facilities including copying, faxing, and computer and Internet access. The complex is located a few blocks east of Villa Linda Mall and immediately west of Sam's Club (see our Shopping chapter). The property is adjacent to the City of Santa Fe's Arroyo Chamisa Bike Trail, a 4 ½-mile path for walkers, joggers, skaters, and bicyclists.

El Castillo Retirement Residences
250 E. Alameda St.
• (505) 988-2877

Located just a few blocks east of the Plaza and west of chic Canyon Road, El Castillo Retirement Residences offer what it calls "Life Care" for retirees 62 or older and their spouses of any age. A popular retirement community, El Castillo has a long waiting list for its 150 apartments, each with a private outside entrance. Upon acceptance, residents pay a one-time, partially tax-deductible entrance fee, a significant sum that varies with the size of the apartment and how many will live there. They also pay a monthly service fee that covers one meal a day in the dining room, scheduled transportation, maintenance, security, a library, an outdoor pool, a pool room, and organized activities such as exercise, arts and crafts, and tours. Together, these fees constitute a lifetime contract that assures residents they will have all their needs met—including nursing care and assisted living, should either be necessary. For those in need of temporary assisted living or nursing care, El Castillo has set aside a number of its residences as "rentals."

Education and Child Care

If you want to learn massage therapy or acupuncture, Santa Fe is the right place.

If you're interested in a class in photography, a workshop in flamenco dancing, an intensive experience in cross-cultural awareness, or an afternoon of bird identification, you're in luck.

If you want your child to do well enough in high school to get a scholarship to Harvard, your choices are more limited—but don't despair.

But if you need a Mary Poppins to take care of your toddler, Santa Fe presents a challenge. It's the same story here as in most cities around the United States. Unless Grandma lives close by and delights in caring for the little ones, securing high-quality child care at a reasonable price is as tough as finding a downtown parking place during Indian Market weekend.

In this chapter, we'll take a look at colleges and special post-secondary programs, the Santa Fe Public Schools, private secondary schools, and options for child care and baby-sitters. (You'll find special programs and camps for kids in our Kidstuff chapter.)

Colleges and Universities

The names of Santa Fe's two long-established colleges tend to confuse people. After all, you'd except a college called St. John's to have a religious affiliation. And wouldn't The College of Santa Fe come from secular roots?

In fact, St. John's is a nonsectarian institution, although theology is taught here along with the "great books" curriculum. And The College of Santa Fe began as an outreach of the Christian Brothers, firmly rooted in Catholicism. Once known as St. Michael's College, CSF is New Mexico's oldest institution of higher education (see our close-up in this chapter).

Santa Fe's popular community college and programs through the University of Phoenix and branches of the University of New Mexico and New Mexico Highlands University add to the mixture of higher education opportunities.

The College of Santa Fe
1600 St. Michael's Dr.
- **(505) 473-6011,**
(800) 456-2673
- **www.csf.edu**

Consistently ranked among the top tier of liberal arts colleges in the West by *U.S. News and World Report*, The College of Santa Fe is well known for its programs in the arts. Nationally recognized in visual, performing, and moving-image arts and creative writing, the college draws students to Santa Fe from throughout the country. Professional crews rent the college's sound stages, and the arrangement offers students a chance to work on productions ranging from full-length features to commercials and music videos. In 1998, Santa Fe resident and actress Carol Burnett donated her time to the college as an acting coach. The newest addition to campus is the multimillion-dollar Visual Arts Center housing darkrooms, lecture rooms, and studio space in a structure praised for its architecture. *The Santa Fe Reporter* gave it the "Best New Public Buildings in Santa Fe Since Statehood" award. The article said, "What a relief from the monotony of pueblo architecture and piles of mud bricks." Designed by Ricardo Legoretta, the center uses color, sharp edges, open space, and natural light in unusual ways.

In addition to its arts programs, the college also offers a business curriculum, social science, humanities, science, and teacher education. A CSF collaboration with Alvord Community School, a Santa Fe public elementary school, recently received an award from a program to honor quality education. In 1994, CSF students and faculty began to work at the public school, helping teachers. They organize classes according to a child's development rather than by grade levels.

About 1,600 students attend this private, independent college. Roughly half participate in the traditional residential program and live on campus. Others take evening and weekend courses through the graduate and external programs. CSF also offers programs at campuses in Las Cruces, Albuquerque, and Ignacio, Colorado. The Santa Fe campus also hosts scores of Elderhostel programs each year on topics ranging from Native American literature to New Mexico history. (See our Retirement chapter.)

In addition to the genius and generosity of the Christian Brothers, the college notes its appreciation to the late actress Greer Garson and her husband Buddy Fogelson with campus buildings that bear their names. The Garson Communications Center and Studios, Fogelson Library and Greer Garson Theatre are all campus landmarks. Garson, who lived in nearby Pecos, New Mexico, as well as Dallas, Texas, shared her experience and her fortune with CSF students for many years.

St. John's College
1160 Camino de la Cruz Blanca
• **(505) 984-6000**
• **www.sjcsf.edu**

You won't find any big lecture classes on this campus, and students don't chew their nails over which electives to pick. Most of the course of study for a bachelor's of arts is required and most of the work is done in small seminars.

The student to faculty ratio here is 8 to 1. Instead of textbooks, students read timeless works of Western civilization, the original writing of more than 100 philosophers, scientists, poets, mathematicians, storytellers, and composers. Over their four years of study, students take language and math, three years of laboratory science, a year of music and seminars in philosophy, political science, literature, history, economics, and psychology.

Established in 1964 in a lovely location near the eastern foothills, Santa Fe's St. John's is an extension of the school's historic Maryland campus, founded as King William's School in Annapolis in 1696. Only Harvard and the College of William and Mary have existed in the United States longer.

St. John's ranks in the nation's top 30 colleges for producing graduates who go on to work on higher degrees, with those who earn Ph.D.s evenly split between the sciences and humanities. The campus offers intensive 8-week summer graduate programs in liberal arts and Eastern Studies. That unusual course includes the classical Chinese and Sanskrit languages and uses texts from India, China, and Japan to prompt student discussions. In the summer, St. John's offers its Classics Series, which brings a variety of non-traditional students to Santa Fe to discuss literature, philosophy, and opera.

St. John's invites the public to sample its approach during Community Seminar Day, held twice a year. Tutors, as faculty members are called, lead programs such as "Scientific and Religious Skepticism," which used Shakespeare's *Hamlet* and *Othello* and Descartes' *Meditation* as its texts.

The campus hosts numerous public events and performances, the most popular of which is "Shakespeare in Santa Fe" (See our Arts section.) Readings and book signings, arts shows, lectures, concerts and more bring town and gown together here.

Santa Fe Community College
6401 Richards Ave.
• **(505) 428-1000**
• **www.santa-fe.cc.nm.us.**

Until 1983, Santa Fe had no community college. One of the few things you might get a majority of Santa Fe residents to agree on is that this institution has been of enormous benefit to local families. Some would call it Santa Fe's pride and joy.

Located on 366 acres in southern Santa Fe, the campus consists of a main classroom/administrative center, the 122,000-square-foot

Witter Fitness Center (see our Parks and Recreation chapter) and the Early Childhood Development center. A new Visual Arts Center— 55,800 square feet of classrooms, exhibit space and studios for printmaking, photography, jewelry, drawing, painting, sculpture, and more, opened in the fall of 1999. Facilities for the performing arts and instructional technology are planned in the coming years.

SFCC offers associate's degrees in more than 30 subjects, along with certificates. Some degrees are designed to transfer to four-year colleges and universities, while others are technical/vocational in nature. In spring 1998, SFCC completed a milestone when it conferred a degree on its 1,000th graduate. Enrollment in credit courses usually ranges around 5500. At $21 per credit hour, SFCC's tuition is among the lowest in the state.

SFCC students are typically adults who have jobs and attend college part time. Flexible scheduling—including short-term, evening, and weekend classes and Flex Labs—gives students the options they need. Contract courses can also be customized for area businesses, offered on campus or at their work place.

Through its Adult Basic Education programs, SFCC provides free instruction in reading, writing, math, GED preparation, English as a second language, and job-readiness skills. Literacy Volunteers of Santa Fe is also headquartered at SFCC.

Santa Fe residents also flock to the community college for its extensive Continuing Education program. Each year, more than 8,500 people of all ages enroll in noncredit classes from professional development and leadership skills to sports, Southwest adventures, cooking, and other leisure and cultural activities. Continuing Education also operates the Planetarium at Santa Fe Community College, which offers low-cost shows for the public and free programs for school groups under its skylit dome.

Based on its mission of helping students succeed and serving the community, SFCC truly offers something for everyone. Call the switchboard at (505) 428-1000, or check the 24-hour recorded InfoLine at (505) 428-1777.

University of New Mexico— Santa Fe Campus
Santa Fe Community College campus, 6401 Richards Ave.
• **(505) 428-1234**
• **http://UNM.EDU/~UNMNORTH/ INDEX.HTM**

For more than 20 years, the University of New Mexico, based in Albuquerque, has of-fered graduate and upper-division programs in Santa Fe. UNM began its program at the request of the governor to fill the educational advancement needs of state employees. Until it found a home on the SFCC campus, UNM rented space from various agencies, including the College of Santa Fe. Beginning with 50 students, UNM-Santa Fe enrollment now is near 1,000 annually.

Students at UNM-Santa Fe tend to be working professionals returning to school to complete their bachelor's degree or study toward their master's. For student convenience, most courses are scheduled in the evening. Bachelor's degree programs include nursing, speech and hearing, and University Studies, a nontraditional program in which students design their own course of study. Master's degree programs include counseling, communications, and educational administration. In addition, UNM offers upper-level and graduate classes in multicultural education, Southwestern studies, and more. About half the courses are taught via television from the main campus in Albuquerque. Santa Fe students use the telephone to call in questions or answers.

The UNM office at Santa Fe Community College can provide information to students about main campus programs. They have applications, financial aid information, and UNM's undergraduate catalog and graduate bulletins.

University of Natural Medicine
1519 Canyon Road, Santa Fe
• **(505) 424-7800**

This school, fully licensed by the New Mexico Commission on Higher Education, attempts to bridge the gap between natural and conventional medicine. Students have the opportunity to learn ancient remedies and natural cures along with advanced holistic medical theories, methods, and technologies. Students may select a diploma course in more than 20 areas ranging from aromatherapy to nutritional analysis. The school's international multi-disciplinary faculty works with students to offer independent study degrees and diploma programs as well as a bachelor's degree and eight advanced degrees. Seminars, research opportunities, and clinical training options are part of the program. The university's new Integrative Medicine Clinic was expected to be in full operation by July 2000. Students can work with professional mentors and have an opportunity for clinical practice. Mark Dargan Smith, doctor of naturopathy, is the school's president.

University of Phoenix Santa Fe Learning Center

Holley Office Building
2201 Miguel Chavez Road
- **(505) 821-6079 or 1-800-333-8671**
- **http://www.uophx.edu/newmexico/**

The University of Phoenix offers Bachelor of Science degrees in business administration, accounting, management, and business information systems and a Master of Science in computer information systems. Its program, intended for working adults, has been available in Santa Fe since 1989, and has been housed in the current location since 1996. The Santa Fe programs enroll up to 200 students and are popular for the flexibility and the concentration of academic material they offer their students.

Founded nationally in 1976, University of Phoenix structures its classes to build on the professional experience of working adults. Nationwide, the college enrolls more students than any other private university in the United States and has served more than 400,000 students. In addition to classroom programs, the university offers computer-based education and distance learning, using the Internet and other high-tech tools. In addition to Santa Fe, the university has a main campus in Albuquerque and offers classes in several locations throughout the state. Class enrollment is held in the fall and again in January.

New Mexico Highlands University—Santa Fe

Santa Fe Community College campus,
6401 Richards Ave.
- **(505) 428-1742**

New Mexico Highlands University programs are intended for students who want to earn a bachelor of arts degree in social work, criminal justice, business, or education. Most of the students are working people who have associate's degrees and want to continue their education at a four-year institution. Full-time or adjunct professors do most of the teaching and classes are small. Highlands normally enrolls more than 80 students each semester.

Institute of American Indian Arts

1600 St. Michael's Dr.
- **(505) 424-2300**

Some of America's leading Indian artists—among them Dan Namingha, David Bradley, Estella Loretto, Denise Wallace, Allan Houser, T.C. Cannon, and Darren Vigil-Gray—have taught and/or studied at this unique institution. Established in 1962, the IAIA stands alone as the only two-year fine arts college devoted solely to the study and contemporary practice of the arts and cultures of American Indians and Alaska Natives. The federal government, on which the IAIA depends for most of its support, has reduced the school budget by 77 percent since 1995. However, the IAIA has managed to move forward, raising needed funds for core operations from alumni and supporters throughout the country. Enrollment is expected to reach 225 students for the fall 2000 semester when the long-awaited new campus opens on the south side of Santa Fe, near Santa Fe Community College. In its new home, the school will expand its two-year associate degree program to offer a four-year bachelors degree with a curriculum encompassing visual art and design, creative writing, performing arts, cultural studies, and liberal arts incorporating Native American perspectives. The new programs will also include business courses to help artists become entrepreneurs.

The IAIA Museum houses The National Collection of Contemporary Indian Art, the largest curated by Native Americans in the world. The museum, with a collection of more than 6,500 pieces, is located in downtown Santa Fe and features student and alumni work (see our Attractions chapter).

Special Schools and Programs

In this section, you'll find schools that offer a variety of programs, some unique to Santa Fe. Included here is a selected sampling of education ranging from advanced science to weekend seminars that can teach you how to shoot a great photograph or cook up the *chile verde* (green chili sauce) of your dreams. Santa Fe has a wealth of health care programs to various certifications. The city's two acupuncture schools are among the best in the country. Santa Fe is also home to an educational research center, The Santa Fe Institute, where professors in residence explore the frontier where science meets philosophy.

The Anthropology Film Center

1626 Upper Canyon Rd.
- **(505) 983-4127**

Founded in 1965, The Anthropology Film Center teaches an intensive nine-month course in documentary and ethnographic filmmaking.

The program is structured for those who wish to become visual anthropologists and produce ethnographic films or for social documentary film writers/directors/producers. The center also offers tutorials in the practical uses of computers in visual anthropology and film.

Located in a large adobe studio on 2 acres of wooded foothills in a quiet canyon off one of the city's most historic roads, the center's campus adds to its attraction. Students have access to a production studio, editing and projection facilities, and a specialized library in the fields of visual anthropology, film production, culture, and communication.

Art and Clay Studio
851 W. San Mateo Rd., Ste. 4
• (505) 989-4278

This program offers classes for children and adults. Instruction may run for weeks or be offered as weekend workshops. Teachers are often college-level educators as well as first-rate artists and craftspeople. The school welcomes students from beginners to advanced and may include classes in porcelain, wood firing, raku, figure sculpture, using the potter's wheel, and more. The studio also offers regular free public slide lectures and demonstrations with guest faculty. Although clay is the focus, the studio also offers classes in writing, watercolors, drawing, and other arts. (See our Kidstuff chapter for information on children's classes.)

Hypnotherapy
Academy of America
509 Camino de los Marquez, Suite 1
• (505) 983-1515 or
(877) 983-1515 toll free
• www.hypnosisacademy.com

This school, state approved and nationally certified by the American Council of Hypnotist Examiners, offers classes for hypnotism certification and continuing education programs. Among the classes are fundamentals of hypnotism, healing and pain management, preparation for childbirth with hypnotherapy, and how to cure insomnia with hypnotherapy. Classes

are offered from beginning levels to master classes. The school, established in 1988, hosts free introductory seminars for people who are curious about hypnosis or interested in hypnotism as a career. Marriage and family therapists, counselors, and others may receive continuing education credits for classes in hypnosis and related areas.

International Institute of Chinese Medicine
4884 La Junta del Alamo (Off Lopez Lane.)
• (505) 473-5233

Students interested in learning acupuncture and other aspects of Chinese medicine get a taste of China with their studies here. More than half of the institute's teachers received their primary training in China, and more than a third of the 40-some faculty members are Chinese. Michael Zeng, a Chinese M.D. and a Doctor of Oriental Medicine, is the institute's president, director, and academic dean. In addition to an extensive medical practice, Zeng has been a senior medical consultant and guest lecturer at colleges across China, the United States, and Canada.

The institute offers a four-year Master of Oriental Medicine degree program, a certificate program in Oriental bodywork, and a continuing education certificate program for licensed acupuncturists and other healing arts practitioners. Students can also learn to speak and read Chinese. A herbal pharmacy, low-cost clinic (505-474-9330), library, and student bookstore are part of the institute. Students receive free healthcare at the student clinic. The campus sits on 1.2 acres of land at the foot of the Sangre de Cristo Mountains off Airport Road (see our Healthcare and Wellness chapter).

New Mexico Academy
of Healing Arts
501 Franklin Ave.
• (505) 982-6271

Students can become certified massage

INSIDERS' TIP

To enroll your child in the Santa Fe Public Schools you must provide a current record of immunization, a birth certificate and proof that your family lives within the district boundaries—a document with your address such as a utility bill or driver's license. If possible, provide a copy of your child's last report card or a school transcript and his or her social security number. If your child in going into first grade, he or she must be 5 years old by September 1 of the current school year. For more information, call the district's central office, (505) 982-2631. They can also tell you which school your children should attend.

EDUCATION AND CHILD CARE

therapists and learn polarity therapy at this school, which has operated in Santa Fe since 1981. The academy takes a holistic approach to education and uses meditation as a foundation. About 70 percent of the enrollment comes from outside New Mexico. For their massage therapy certification, students choose programs up to nine months in length, learning anatomy and physiology, aromatherapy, and communication skills and ethics. Polarity therapy, a comprehensive healthcare system created by Randolph Stone, draws upon Ayurvedic and Chinese traditions as well as modern physics. Students study to become Registered Polarity Practitioners or Associated Polarity Practitioners and can enroll in dual certification programs. A public clinic offers those enrolled here an opportunity to practice their skills. (See our Healthcare and Wellness chapter.)

Santa Fe Art Institute
1600 St. Michael's Drive
• **(505) 424-5050**
• **www.sfai.org**

Santa Fe Art Institute's elegant new home on the College of Santa Fe campus turned Santa Fe style on its head. Vivid use of reds, blues, and yellows and angular edges characterize SFAI's award winning building, designed by internationally acclaimed architect Ricardo Legorreta. The 16,774-square-foot facility includes skylit studios, gallery space, living areas for the students, meeting areas, and office space. SFAI moved to its new home in 1999.

An independent, non-profit art center, SFAI is dedicated to the creative development of the emerging artist. Each year artists come from around the world to SFAI to work with the program's internationally acclaimed Visiting Artists. The institute invites up to 12 critically acclaimed Visiting Artists to Santa Fe annually. Their classes provide an opportunity for a small group of participants—no more than a dozen—to work in a studio situation with a major mentor. Through critiques, lectures, studio sessions, and informal discussions, the Visiting Artist encourages students to define and hone their individual artistic vision and their life-long commitment to art. Through the program hundreds of students—selected for their merit— have had the opportunity to work with highly respected professional artists in a variety of media. The Visiting Artists have included such luminaries Larry Bell, Richard Diebenkorn, Helen Frankenthaler, Donald Lipski, Roberto Marquez, Susan Rothenberg, Fritz Scholder, Wayne Thiebaud, and Henrietta Wyeth-Hurd.

Established as an independent educational non-profit organization in 1985, the Institute also offers the Artists and Writers Residency Program and the Interactive Media Arts Program. The summer design program provides an introduction to architecture and advanced architectural design studies. Since moving to its new home, the Institute has begun a program with the Santa Fe Public Schools' Academy for teens at risk and has expanded its public lecture series and other public programs. The donation of a print by the program's first Visiting Artist, Richard Diebenkorn, led to the establishment of a scholarship fund for deserving students. That original donation has been joined by The Anne and John L. Marion Endowed Scholarship Fund, which allows SFAI draw top-level students regardless of their ability to pay.

Santa Fe Institute
1399 Hyde Park Road
• **(505) 984-8800**
• **www.santafe.edu/index.html**

The Santa Fe Institute is a private, non-profit, multidisciplinary research and education center, founded in Santa Fe 1984. The mission of the Santa Fe Institute is to conduct and foster scientific research that has four dominant traits: transdiciplinary, excellent, fresh, and catalytic.

SFI has devoted itself to creating a new kind of scientific research community pursuing emerging science. SFI supports scientific research by providing an environment for multidisciplinary collaborations among visiting and resident scientists from the physical, biological, computational, and social science fields. Over the course of a year, SFI houses more than 100 scientists with about 35 in residence at any one time. Researchers-in-residence could stay for weeks, months, or years. They might be postdoctoral fellows, graduate students, or scientists predominantly from universities in the U.S. and Europe.

The Institute's research agenda is overseen by a Science Advisory Board that includes Nobel Laureates, MacArthur Foundation Fellows, members of the National Academy of Sciences, and several dozen distinguished scientists from leading universities. They come from a wide variety of fields to guide the general direction, integration, and quality of the Institute's work.

Students are important at SFI. Although it does not grant degrees, the Santa Fe Institute has a strong commitment to training the next generation of scientists. SFI programs include a highly competitive Postdoctoral Fellows program, long and short-term interdisciplinary research opportunities for graduate students and undergraduates, the Complex Systems Summer School, and the Graduate Workshop for Computational Economics. In 2000, the institute began its advanced physics program, supported by the physics division of the National Science Foundation. For high school students in the Santa Fe area, SFI offers a program in simulations of complex systems. SFI also presents a monthly free public lecture series.

Santa Fe Photography and Digital Workshops
P.O. Box 9916, Santa Fe 87504
• **(505) 983-1400**
• **www.santafeworkshops.com**

This prestigious program teams amateur and professional photographers with nationally and internationally known photographers who share their insights both technically and artistically. The weeklong workshops, which run virtually year-round, attract more than 1,000 photographers to Santa Fe and guide them to appropriate sites for shooting assignments. Classes for beginners include aesthetics, technique, and an overview of equipment. Professionals can choose from portraits, lighting techniques, fashion and beauty, hand-colored photos, landscape, color work, and more. The school also features a free summer lecture series, open to anyone interested, which gives the instructors an opportunity to discuss and show their work.

School of American Research
660 Garcia St.
• **(505) 954-7200**

If Santa Fe gave an award for the most beautiful and historic campus, the School of American Research would win, hands down. The shaded, beautifully landscaped grounds and historic adobe headquarters speak of Santa Fe's early days as a magnet for the great minds in archaeology. This nonprofit center has supported innovative scholarship and American Indian artists since its founding in 1905.

The SAR presents six fellowships to outstanding scholars, giving them nine-month residencies devoted to writing projects related to anthropology, the humanities, and the arts. The school shares their work as part of its publication division. The SAR press also publishes books designed for a popular audience on topics such as the peoples and cultures of the American Southwest. Three times a year, the School

of American Research invites 10 scholars to campus for a week of discussion and debate on issues on the frontier of anthropological research. (These meetings are closed to the public and the media.)

As another part of its educational mission, the SAR produces periodic newsletters, hosts traveling seminars to notable sites in the Southwest and around the world and offers illustrated lectures. The Indian Arts Research Center with its extensive collection of art and artifacts is open to the public through special tours (see our Attractions chapter).

Santa Fe School of Cooking
116 W. San Francisco St.
• **(505) 983-4511**

That great green chile enchilada doesn't have to become just a Santa Fe memory. At Santa Fe School of Cooking, you can learn the secrets of Santa Fe cuisine in programs that only take a morning or an afternoon. During the summer, the school offers classes as often as six days a week. Conveniently located downtown in the Plaza Mercado building, the teachers/chefs use indigenous Southwestern ingredients to prepare both traditional and contemporary meals. Afterward, the students eat their creations and take home the recipes. Classes range from two to five hours.

Santa Fe School of Cooking also offers extended programs that include field trips to explore the farms and food of northern New Mexican villages and exciting dinners that take you behind adobe walls for meals in charming private homes. The school happily arranges classes and food tours for groups on request.

Southwest Acupuncture College
2960 Rodeo Park Drive West, Santa Fe,
• **(505) 438-8884**
• **www.swacupuncture.com**

Operating from Santa Fe, Albuquerque, and Boulder, Colorado, campuses, Southwest Acupuncture College offers a Master's of Science in Oriental Medicine with extensive national accreditation. Enrollment is open to students age 20 and older who have successfully completed two years of general education at the college level. According to the school's guidelines, they must also possess the "personal credentials and intellectual skills" to obtain admission. The academic program consists of more than 2,800 hours of training in the five branches of classical Oriental medicine: acupuncture, herbal medicine, physical therapy, nutrition, and exercise/breathing therapy.

St. John's College, founded in Santa Fe in 1964, is the sister college of St. John's in Annapolis, Maryland, which was founded in 1696. It uses the great books as a basis for seminars.

Photo: Courtesy of St. John's College

Since its inception in 1980, the for-profit college reports that its graduates have achieved an unsurpassed passage rate on all state and national exams. The preponderance of the curriculum takes a hands-on and clinical approach. Students locate acupuncture points, practice techniques, develop diagnoses and treatment plans, prepare herbal formulas, and observe and treat patients. To help students become proficient, the school operates an active teaching clinic (see our Healthcare and Wellness chapter).

In addition to the master's program, the college offers continuing education classes in specialty topics, seminars with international experts and externships in China.

Southwest Learning Centers Inc.
P.O. Box 8627, Santa Fe 87504
• **(505) 989-8898**

Southwest Learning Centers was established in 1972 as an educational resource to serve the multicultural population of the Southwest. The nonprofit organization presents interdisciplinary classes, research projects, conferences, workshops, apprenticeship programs, community service projects, and special events. SWLC cultural programs promote a deeper understanding of native traditions. Current programs include the Center for Indigenous Arts & Cultures, Mountain Light Center/Adopt a Grandparent Program, the Sustainable Native Agriculture Center, Native Roots & Rhythms, and Xochimoki. Programs are funded by tuition for classes, foundation grants, and corporate and private contributions.

Southwestern College
Rt. 20, Box 29D
• **(505) 471-5756,**
Toll Free: 1-877-471-5756
• **www.swc.edu**

Class offerings in counseling and art therapy bring students here. The college has an accredited two-year residential program as well as other options for full-time, part-time, evening, and weekend study. In its literature the college describes its "transformational approach" to education and a style of teaching that is person-centered, holistic, experiential, reflective, and ecological. The school traces the roots of

the transformational approach to Ralph Waldo Emerson, John Dewey, and Carl Jung. The college was dedicated in 1976 and began its programs in 1979.

Certificate programs are offered in grief counseling, school counseling, action methods, and art therapy.

Plaza Resolana en Santa Fe
401 Old Taos Hwy.
• **(505) 982-8539**
• **www.plazaresolana.com**

Subtitled "Santa Fe Study and Conference Center," Plaza Resolana presents a variety of workshops with an emphasis on spirituality, local arts, and regional culture. Classes attract both area residents and visitors who stay at the center. Course offerings include "Celtic Spirituality and the Image of God," "Spirit of Clay," "*Tres Culturas* and the Visual Language of Art," "Fly Fishing in an Enchanted Land," and "Media, Politics, and Religion," with Jim Wall, editor of *Christian Century Magazine*. Plaza Resolana also offers a popular new performing arts course, "Santa Fe Voices," which treats students to the sounds of the Desert Chorale, the Santa Fe Symphony and the Santa Fe Opera. In addition to its own classes, the center hosts international Elderhostel programs (see our Retirement chapter), and Recursos de Santa Fe uses the center for its writing programs. Plaza Resolana has begun to focus on partnerships with college and universities, seminaries, churches and other nonprofit groups to arrange specially tailored programs. The center is affiliated with the Ghost Ranch Foundation in Abiquiu.

INSIDERS' TIP
The College of Santa Fe is one of only a few private U.S. schools offering an undergraduate creative writing degree. CSF is the fifth largest college in the state of New Mexico and New Mexico's largest private college.

Public Schools

Santa Fe Public Schools
610 Alta Vista St.
• **(505) 982-2631**
• **www.sfps.k12.nm.us**

For its first public schoolhouse, which served the community beginning in 1891, Santa Fe paid rent on a home at 352 Palace Avenue. The little one-room school, which sat on the edge of an empty field, welcomed students from first grade through high school.

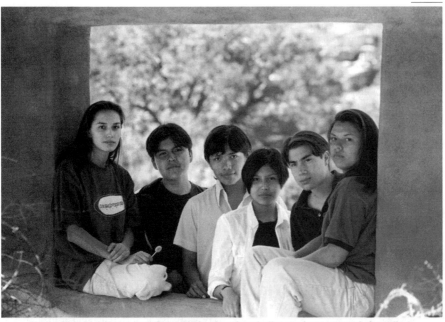

Native American Preparatory School helps American Indian students get ready for college.

Photo: Courtesy of Native American Preparatory School

Today, Santa Fe Public Schools serve the City of Santa Fe and much of Santa Fe County—1,016 square miles—with a wide assortment of buildings, programs, and opportunities. The district includes a bilingual early childhood center, 20 elementary schools, three middle schools, two high schools, and an alternative high school. The district also planned to open two new secondary "charter schools" for the 2000–2001 school year. The school system enrolls approximately 13,700 students. SFPS also provides educational services to registered home school students and to students at the New Mexico School for the Deaf, the Santa Fe County Juvenile Detention Center and the New Mexico Girls Ranch.

Of the students in the public schools, some 60 percent are Hispanic, 36 percent Caucasian, 3 percent Native American, and 1 percent each African American and Asian. Santa Fe High, with about 2,000 students, is the largest school in the system. Next to state government, the schools are the biggest employer in Santa Fe County, with about 1,900 employees on the payroll. The district operates on an annual budget of some $90 million, and about 96 percent of that comes from the State of New Mexico.

The public schools have traveled a rocky road in recent years. In 1998, the district overspent its budget by $2.6 million, borrowing money from the state to make a summer payroll. The budget crisis brought in the State Department of Education to manage the district's finances beginning in June 1999.

But the problem concerned more than money. Santa Fe ranked 79th of the 88 districts in the state in 1999 for graduation rates—and New Mexico tends to place in the bottom quartile when it come to the percentage of students who graduate from high school. The reasons for the Santa Fe public schools' poor performance and high dropout rate depend on who's doing the talking, but inadequate funding, children's lack of preparation for school, family stress, and teacher salaries lower than the national average are usually mentioned.

Community anxiety about the district's budget as well as sagging teacher morale, student test-scores below national average, low parent involvement, and the steady dropout rate led to the commissioning of an outside audit. PricewaterhouseCoopers analyzed the district's organizational structure and governance, the budgetary process, use of technology, personnel practices, and more. The resulting 250-page report, paid for by private foundations and the business community, made 48 recommendations for improvements. Suggestions included privatizing the personnel office because of concerns about nepotism and conflicts of interest and improving salaries for teachers, secretaries, and custodians. The school board vows to do all it can to make the schools better. Superintendent Veronica C. Garcia, appointed in 1999, was able to balance the budget and has a plan to bring the district back to fiscal responsibility.

One of the strongest hopes for improving the public schools lies with school-community partnerships. Through an emphasis on volunteers as mentors, tutors and guests in the classroom, the district wants to give the children in its care more opportunities for success. The nonprofit Santa Fe Partners in Education (505-474-0240), builds links between the community and the public schools to help teachers do their work better. The group underwrites those things beyond the district budget: field trips, special programs in the classroom, and supplies beyond the normal allotment. Partners also honors innovative teachers. In cooperation with the public schools, Partners hosts the Partners in Education Ball in the spring to raise money for teacher grants and student scholarships and to increase rapport between the schools and the community. Teenage students work as volunteer servers, decorators, and greeters. Those in the black-tie crowd dance to music provided by a topnotch high school jazz band and enjoy other entertainment from the secondary schools' theater departments.

The Santa Fe Public Schools do some things well. In addition to the state-approved curriculum, the Santa Fe Public Schools offer a wide variety of special programs including art immersion, bilingual education, culinary arts, peer mediation and after-school care. A Foster Grandparents program matches elementary school children who need extra attention with senior citizens for tutoring and conversation. The district has plans to build new schools, repair old schools, and begin to replace the antiquated Santa Fe High School campus.

The two new charter secondary schools, set to open beginning with the 2000–2001 school year, are other signs of optimism. The Academy for Technology and Classics, housed at the Glorieta Conference Center, will have room for almost 300 students in grades 7 through 12. Every student will be pre-tested, with tutoring and remediation not only available if necessary, but built into his or her schedule. The school also plans to coordinate with area colleges to allow students to begin to work on associate or bachelor's degrees while still in high school. Monte del Sol, which planned to use portable buildings near downtown Santa Fe as its head-

quarters, will begin with students in the seventh and eighth grades and eventually serve up to grade 12. Both are schools that have been granted more autonomy to create their own rules and programs. Santa Fe's Turquoise Trail Elementary, on N.M.Highway14, was one of the state's first charter schools.

Each public school in the system has exceptional teachers among its faculty and students who work hard and gain notable success. Individual students win national awards, and high school graduates are accepted to major universities and offered scholarships. In any given school year, it's not unusual for more than half of the teachers to have a master's degree or better. The public school system offers diversity among its schools in terms of programs. The Academy, the alternative high school within the public system, works with students who are pregnant, have dropped out and want to return to school, or who need attention not available at the other two public high schools. And, of course, we have sports: students can try close to 30 different sports in grades 7 through 12.

On the elementary and middle school levels, some schools offer intensive arts programs or focus on science and the environment. You'll find conflict-mediation programs, multi-age classes, collaboration with senior citizens, opera, theater, and chamber music enrichment, peer counseling, buddy-to-buddy tutoring, and literary magazines. Depending on the teachers and principals, classes may help with the AIDS walk, sponsor holiday food drives or coat and mitten collections, or work with the Santa Fe Animal Shelter.

In 1999, a collaborative program between the University of New Mexico and the Santa Fe Public Schools received a national award for its good work. The project enables liberal arts graduates to obtain a New Mexico teaching license in 14 months. The interns work in pairs with supervision from public school teachers and their UNM professors.

Other Publicly Funded Schools

Santa Fe also is home to the state-funded New Mexico School for the Deaf, 1060 Cerrillos Road, (505) 827-6744, which serves deaf and hard-of-hearing children from throughout New Mexico. NMSD offers preschool through 12th-grade education to about 135 students. The residential Santa Fe campus is home to the James A. Little Theater, a popular venue for lectures and performances. (See our Arts chapter.) NMSD has outreach programs in Albuquerque, Las Cruces, and Shiprock. Students pay no fees or tuition

Another publicly funded school, Santa Fe Indian School, 1501 Cerrillos Road, (505) 989-6300, is a boarding school for Native American children that enrolls about 500 students in grades 7 through 12. To attend, students must be at least one-quarter Indian. Many students come from the nearby Pueblos, but 25 other tribes also fill the roster. The Bureau of Indian Affairs established the school in 1890. The All-Indian Pueblo Council, made up of governors from all 19 New Mexico Pueblos, now runs it. The school recently received approval from Congress and the U.S. Interior Department and an authorization of $20 million to begin construction of a new campus. Despite the on-going struggle for funding, the school received an Excellence in Education Award in 1987. Some 90 percent of seniors plan on attending college.

Private Schools

Almost 25 percent of the city's middle and high school students attend private schools, according to statistics compiled by the New Mexico Department of Education. (The national average is around 14 percent.) Santa Fe has an abundance of private schools from preschool through secondary. For younger students, choices include church-affiliated elementaries, Waldorf and Montessori schools, informal schools, and those with a structured academic focus. High school students have several interesting options.

Not all of Santa Fe's private schools are accredited. The State Department of Education, 300 Don Gaspar, (505) 827-6555, can give you a list of all private schools in the Santa Fe area. We have listed some of our secondary schools to give you an idea of the range of options available in Santa Fe.

Desert Academy
242 Los Pinos Road
• **(505) 474-7800**
With its inception in 1994, Desert Academy filled a niche in Santa Fe's private school galaxy. The school welcomes children with learning differences among its 130-student enrollment and offers unique elective choices in-

cluding honors and advanced placement classes. On a beautiful site south of Santa Fe in an area known as La Cienega, Desert Academy offers a college preparatory program combined with classes designed to encourage both creativity and critical thinking. School culture fosters genuine civility, appreciation for learning, and a commitment to character. Student-teacher ratio is 7 to 1, with a maximum class size of 15. The school is fully accredited. Scholarships and financial aid are available.

Native American Preparatory School
P.O. Box 260, Rowe
• **(505) 474-6801**
• **www.naprep.org/**
Native American Preparatory School holds a place of distinction in U.S. education; it was the first private college-prep academy in the country with an Indian-only enrollment. Students from about two dozen tribes around the nation come for a four-year program that stresses character and cultural development. The curriculum encompasses academics, community service, the arts, and athletics. Full-time enrollment is about 60 students. NAPS began in 1988 as a summer program for Navajo teens, received recognition on *Good Morning America*, and expanded by acquiring as its campus the former home of the Pecos River Learning Center, 35 miles northeast of Santa Fe.

New Mexico Academy for Sciences and Mathematics
7300 Old Santa Fe Trail
• **(505) 954-4000**
• **www.newmexacad.org**
Founded by Brazilian educator Fernando Multedo, this preparatory school offers programs normally associated with community colleges or East Coast prep schools. Opened in 1998, the 32-acre facility serves its students with an indoor swimming pool and an academic smorgasbord that includes applied and social sciences, visual and performing arts, and foreign languages including German and Portuguese. The school admits candidates based on test scores, personal interviews, and academic standings. The first high school class will graduate in May 2002. The academy's website describes the school as the only six-year secondary school in the United States specializing math and sciences.

Although academic challenges are plentiful, the Academy also stresses extra-curricular activities by making them mandatory. Students are required to belong to at least two school clubs and participate in summer internship programs or community organizations. Parents and students who would like to learn more should make arrangements to attend an open house, meet the teachers—who come from Europe, Latin America, and the United States—and tour the campus.

The Santa Fe–style administration and classroom building have large windows that let in the light and stunning view. The master site plan provides for additional facilities on the campus as enrollment grows. Scholarships and financial aid are available.

Nizhoni School for Global Consciousness
HC75, Box 72, Galisteo, N.M.
• (505) 466-4336
• www.nizhonischool.com

As you'd guess from the name, this isn't your little red school house. Founded by spiritual teacher and author Chris Griscom, Nizhoni's "soul-centered" education focuses on what is described as "the integration of the student's spiritual essence." The class list includes cosmology, herbology, astrology, exercises in consciousness, and global communication, as well as traditional courses like English, math, social studies, and science. The high school accepts both boarders and day students and recruits internationally. It promotes itself as "a school without violence, fear, or drugs." Nizhoni also teaches younger children and adults, who can sign up for intensives and short courses including "Spirituality and Life."

Santa Fe Girls' School
331 E. Buena Vista, Santa Fe
• (505) 820-3188

The only junior high in New Mexico just for girls, Santa Fe Girls' School opened in September 1999 with its first seventh grade class. The school will add eighth grade for the 2000–2001 school year, when it expects to reach its full enrollment for the current location of 24 students.

The school grew from the philosophy that during early adolescence girls thrive in an all-girl environment where they feel safe to balance personal, academic, and social concerns.

The school's mission is to foster intellectual growth and emotional strength in adolescent girls, preparing them for the demands of high school and beyond. In terms of curriculum, the school focuses on building and refining skills needed for success in high school, with an emphasis on multicultural social studies that includes Spanish as a second language. Scholarships are available.

Santa Fe Preparatory School
1101 Camino de la Cruz Blanca
• (505) 982-1829
• www.santafe.edu/sfp

Santa Fe Prep is an independent, non-profit, coeducational college preparatory day school. It serves roughly 300 students in grades 7 through 12. Established in 1961, the school's 13-acre campus is located in the eastside historic district in the foothills of the Sangre de Cristo Mountains. The campus was donated by famed architect John Gaw Meem, and what was once his atelier is now the school's outstanding arts facility. Prep offers a rigorous academic program that emphasizes critical reading and writing, while seeking to inspire in students a love of learning. The school offers further opportunities for growth through athletics (including soccer and lacrosse), the arts, and an award-winning community service program. With a faculty-student ration of 1 to 9, students get personalized attention from the faculty, 70 percent of whom hold advanced degrees. An active financial aid program makes this school an increasingly accessible to children from all economic levels. Prep has a full-time college counselor who helps students choose the right school for them. In the 1998, 34 percent of graduating seniors were accepted to the top 2 percent of colleges in the country.

INSIDERS' TIP

The donation of a print by the Santa Fe Art Institute's first Visiting Artist, Richard Diebenkorn, led to the establishment of a scholarship fund for deserving students. That original donation has been joined by The Anne and John L. Marion Endowed Scholarship Fund, which allows SFAI draw top-level students from throughout the country regardless of their ability to pay.

Santa Fe Secondary
230 St. Francis Dr., Ste. 5&6
• (505) 982-2240

This small school (40 students) works with teens in a multi-graded classroom. In addition to traditional academic subjects, including Latin and Spanish, students study Aikido twice a week and have the opportunity for internships, community service, or employment.

Another interesting program is "PeaceJam," where students have the opportunity to meet with a Nobel Peace Prize Laureate for a weekend. Peace-Jam takes an in-depth look at violence and its origins and the qualities of peace. The teens study the Nobel Laureate's life and his or her country of origin in preparation for their weekend with the Laureate. Then they select a service project that addresses the violence they have identified in their community.

St. Michael's High School
100 Siringo Rd.
• (505) 983-7353

This Catholic school offers a traditional college preparatory program and attracts students with an interest in athletics—more than 40 teams compete in 15 separate sports. St. Mike's regularly wins district sports titles and often takes its teams to the state championships. The school also promotes and encourages service projects, a tradition of the LaSallian Brothers of Christian Schools. (Please see our close-up in this chapter for more information.) The high school enrolls about 725 students. St. Mike's also offers grades 7 and 8. There's usually a waiting list to attend, especially for seventh graders.

The Tutorial School
400 Brunn Rd.
• (505) 988-1859

With an enrollment that varies between 20 and 50 students, this school is based on a belief that the pursuit of knowledge thrives in an environment "that is free of fear and authority and whatever else interferes with creativity." That means the school also steers away from coercion, reward and punishments, competition, comparison, and unsolicited criticism or evaluation. The school has no hierarchical structures and students and staff members run the school together. Students are not required to attend formal classes or follow a set curriculum. The school advises parents only to send their children here "if you have absolute trust in the ability of children to take charge of their lives and make their own decisions or if you are at least willing to learn to develop that trust."

INSIDERS' TIP

Santa Fe has a large network of private schools. At last count, according to the Santa Fe Chamber of Commerce, there were 36 private elementaries, six junior highs, and four high schools. Private school enrollment in Santa Fe, and New Mexico, outdistances the national average in terms of percentage of children who attend these schools instead of public schools.

Zia Middle School
310 West Zia Road
• (505) 982-5255

Under founder and headmaster Michael Mayer-Feldberg, Zia serves 25 students in grades 5 through 8, operating under the theory that a small school can supply extraordinary educational and social benefits to children in the middle school years. In addition to a strong academic program, Zia offers extensive travel opportunities. Each fall, the school year starts with a one-week trip to Catalina Island, where students attend the California Marine Institute. This experience is a major component of the school's science curriculum. Spring field trips complement the social studies theme, which influences many activities in other curriculum areas throughout the year. These trips have included visits to San Francisco, New York, Washington, D.C., Montreal, Quebec City, Vancouver, Galveston Island and the Gulf of Mexico, and socially important sites.

Child Care

When it comes to child care, Santa Fe isn't much different from the rest of the country. Especially for infants and the 3-and-younger crowd, finding high quality, affordable childcare can be harder than finding opening-night seats to the opera. Of course, some families hire nannies to stay with children in their own homes. Some have relatives who care for their kids. But most moms and dads have to look for outside help.

Santa Fe has a wonderful resource, the Division of Early Childhood, Family Studies, and Teacher Education at Santa Fe Community College, which make parents' plight easier. You can reach them at 6401 Richards Avenue, (505) 428-1354. The center offers a variety of services and programs including information and referrals, fact sheets to help parents select good child care and training programs for people who wish to go into the child-care field (call 505-428-1344 for information).

Another resource worth checking, the non-profit Santa Fe Home Child Care Niños Program, (505) 473-1109, has information about home day care throughout the city. Call to learn about registered and licensed home day care providers in your area. The Early Childhood Center at Santa Fe Community College and the Home Child Care help line will not recommend one center or one provider over another, but they give parents a place to start.

The regulations for licensing are complex and confusing. Still, licensing offers parents some assurance of quality care. The average rate per child in Santa Fe is roughly $95 a week for an infant and $85 for an older child for eight hours of care. Many home day care providers have waiting lists and do not accept infants.

Besides in-home day care, most parents have two other basic options: commercial child-care centers and preschools. There are a few excellent facilities here, several good ones, and many that are adequate. The Santa Fe Public Schools have a preschool for children with special needs that enrolls a limited number of other children. Some tribal governments offer their own programs, as well. The Santa Fe telephone book lists 14 child-care centers and 21 preschools. Many programs have waiting lists. Fees range from $70 to $120 a week per child.

The National Association for the Education of Young Children accredits high-quality child-care centers and preschools throughout the country. Here's a list of accredited centers in Santa Fe and a few others Santa Fe parents have recommended. Unless otherwise noted, these facilities are open from 7:30 AM to 5:30 PM five days a week.

Day Care and Preschools

Garcia Street Club
569 Garcia St.
• **(505) 983-9512**

The Garcia Street Club offers child care, preschool, and kindergarten for ages 3 to 6 and has served Santa Fe families for more than 50 years. The former residence that houses the school is on the National Register of Historic Places. The year-round operation appeals to parents who work downtown, but also attracts children from around the city. The nationally accredited program offers appropriate activities designed to help the child develop as a whole person. Unlike many preschools, Garcia Street Club does not follow the public schools schedule and does not cancel when the Santa Fe Public Schools declare a snow day. The school is only closed 10 days a year.

Head Start
1150 Canyon Rd. (next to Cristo Rey Church) and other locations
• **(505) 982-4484**

The federal government specifically designed this long-established program to give kids a boost before they start first grade. Families who meet low-income requirements can enroll their 3, 4, and 5 year-olds, and there is no fee. Ten percent of the children served are kids with special needs.

In addition to the programs' educational and developmental activities, children receive a meal and a snack and medical and dental screening. Besides the Canyon Road school, Head Start offers several other centers in Santa Fe County, including the newest in the Tierra Contenta neighborhood. The program encourages family involvement, and at least half the Head Start staff are parents of former Head Start children. The staff holds Child Development Associate credentials.

Santa Fe Community College Childcare Center and Preschool
6401 Richards Ave.
• **(505) 438-1344**

The college offers infant/toddler care beginning with infants 8 weeks old, a program for two-year-olds, and a preschool program, all designed to suit a child's level of development. Each group has its own bright spacious room and access to its own area in a large outdoor play yard. Preference in enrollment goes to SFCC students, and the college reserves about 75 percent of the slots for these kids. The other places are roughly divided between staff/faculty and the general public. There's always a waiting list for infant care. Kindergartners and preschoolers thrive at this clean, sunny center on the south side of the campus. Adult-to-child ratio is high here, and the staff is well trained and professional.

Temple Beth Shalom
205 E. Barcelona Rd.
• **(505) 982-6888**

This well-regarded, now nationally accredited Santa Fe school serves up to 42 children from age 3 to kindergarten. The schedule offers a balance of activities—indoor and outdoor, group and solitary play, quiet and energetic. One of the program's main goals is to stimulate lifelong learning in children. The ratio of adults to children is 1 to 7.

Pre-reading and writing are offered to the 3- and 4-year-olds. Children are introduced to

Hebrew and Spanish. Kindergartners have a more structured program designed around hands-on academics and creativity. As part of the Temple Beth Shalom's larger community, the school integrates teachings about Jewish life and values into the curriculum.

La Casa Feliz
1060 Cerrillos Rd.
• (505) 982-4896

Santa Fe's weekly newspaper, Santa Fe Reporter, voted this as Santa Fe's best child care based on comments from its readers. The school also received the Piñon Award for its work from the nonprofit Santa Fe Community Foundation.

Operated on the grounds of the New Mexico School for the Deaf, La Casa Feliz serves an enrollment of 75, toddlers through age 6, with a staff-to-child ratio of 1 to 7. The school caters to children by observing what each child needs to learn at his or her own pace. The school's organization gives children choices while also offering consistency. Students have an opportunity to learn sign language and Spanish. Special needs students are integrated into the classrooms. La Casa Feliz is closed for a week during the Christmas holidays and only a week during the summer. Otherwise, the school follows the Santa Fe Public School schedule.

La Comunidad de los Niños
1121 Alto St.
• (505) 820-1604

A collaboration between the City of Santa Fe and Presbyterian Medical Services, this center accepts children ages 2 to 5. With a maximum enrollment of 87, the center offers a 1-to-4 adult-to-child ratio in its 2-year-old program and a 1-to-6 ratio in the preschool. Besides enjoying a clean new building specifically designed for the child care, La Comunidad offers access to the play yard from each classroom and gives kids a choice of indoor or outdoor activities throughout the day. Some spaces are reserved for the children of city employees and for low-income families; fees are on a sliding scale. The play-based program incorporates sound early-childhood theory.

Wee Wonders Learning Center
Agora Shopping Center, 7 Avenida Vista Grande, Ste. B2, Eldorado
• (505) 466-4610

This bright new center accepts children from ages 2 to 6 years old and is the only commercial child-care operation that serves the popular and populous Eldorado area southeast of the city. Wee Wonders operates from 7 AM to 6 PM and accepts school-age children during the summer. In addition to playing in a large outdoor play area, children can learn art, music, and Spanish, spend time in the library, and go on field trips. Adult-to-child ratios are 1 to 8 for children 2 to 3 years old, and 1 to 13 for 4 to 6 year olds.

La Casita Preschool and Kindergarten
438 Alamo Dr.
• (505) 983-2803
• www.lacasita.edu

A nonprofit parent co-op school, based on the philosophy of Reggio Emilia in Italy, La Casita caters to children between the ages of 3 and 6. Parents commit time as well as tuition here. They make up the school's board of directors, serve on committees and get together twice a year to give the building a thorough cleaning. Once a month, parents work in the school along with teachers and bring a snack for the class.

For kids, play is essential here and a wide range of opportunities is available. Established in 1971, La Casita serves about 30 children with two teachers and two parents assigned to the morning preschool class and one parent and one teacher in the accredited afternoon kindergarten class. Preschool enrollment is limited to 21, and a maximum of 9 children in the kindergarten. Morning and afternoon programs are available; some children are eligible for all-day school, but La Casita is not a day-care center.

Special Child-Care Services

New Vistas Early Childhood Services
1121 Alto St.
• (505) 988-3803

This long-established nonprofit agency provides a full scope of services for children from birth to age 3 who have, or are at risk for, developmental delays. In addition to direct work with some fragile little ones, the program helps their parents, teaching them how to work with children to promote optimal development. Services include parental support; speech, physical, occupational and family therapy; home-based assistance; therapeutic programs for toddlers; a lending library; and consultation and coordination of other professional services.

A Legacy of Learning

If a sense of astonishment goes with you to Heaven, the Christian Brothers who established St. Michael's High School and College must be amazed and delighted.

What they started in 1859 has undergone some remarkable changes. But the schools they began, the oldest educational institutions in New Mexico, continue to thrive after more than 100 years.

Archbishop Jean Baptiste Lamy, the energetic French cleric who supervised the construction of St. Francis Cathedral, Loretto Chapel, and Santa Fe's first hospital and orphanage, sent for Brothers of the Christian Schools to help bring Catholic education to the territory. Four Brothers, chosen because they were skilled teachers, left for their American adventure from Clermont, France, on an old steamer. They traveled across the ocean for 14 days, then went by train from New York to St. Louis. They continued by wagon to Kansas City, where they set out for the plains and mountains beyond. They arrived in Santa Fe on October 27, 1859, after 71 days of travel.

Only two weeks later, the hard-working Brothers opened St. Michael's, named in honor of St. Michael the Archangel. Boarding students began to arrive on November 9, 1859, and the school has served Santa Fe families continually ever since. For many years, it was the only source of education beyond an elementary level in the territory. Lamy and the Brothers shared a dream that their school for boys would develop into a college, helping to train the leaders New Mexico needed to move toward statehood and to prepare those who wished to study for the priesthood.

The city's newspaper welcomed the Brothers' work and praised the boys in language one seldom hears today. One writer complimented "the cleanly, joyous little fellows, going and coming from the place." The school quickly had 30 boarders and more than 150 day scholars. By the time the Territory of New Mexico granted a charter to the College of the Christian Brothers of New Mexico in 1874, St. Michael's curriculum had expanded to include college courses.

When New Mexico achieved statehood in 1912, St. Michael's was a well-respected religious and academic institution. As the Brothers and Lamy hoped, many of their graduates had contributed to the territory's achievement.

Under Brother Botulph Schneider's 36 years of leadership, the original school gave way to an impressive two-story building with a third story incorporated in a mansard roof. A tall central cupola rose at the center, distinguishing the school as the first building of its type in Santa Fe. The walls were adobe, and the college quickly became famous as the Southwest's tallest adobe structure.

A Good Idea Reborn

The Brothers discontinued the college program after World War I to focus on the high school but didn't let the dream die. Brother Benildus of Mary began the arduous work of raising the money needed to re-establish the college. In 1947, the Brothers bought land that had been used as an Army hospital and re-opened St. Michael's College with a campus of 51 barracks. Scoffers said the venture was doomed because the college sat too far from the center of town. Today, the college touts its convenient central location.

In 1966, St. Michael's College became The College of Santa Fe to more closely reflect its long ties with the community. That same year, the college admitted women for the first time. While the influence of the Christian Brothers is still felt at the College of Santa Fe, 80 percent of the board members are lay people and only a handful of Brothers remain on the faculty.

The Christian Brothers' presence continues strongly at St. Michael's High School, the oldest high school in New Mexico. The high school moved from its downtown location to a large modern campus just off St. Michael's Drive in December 1967. In the fall of 1968, the first girls were admitted as students. (Loretto Academy, an all-girls school operated by the Sisters of Loretto, had just closed.) A Christian Brother still serves as principal at St. Mike's, and several of the current board members are Christian Brothers.

Nosotros Program,
housed at the Early Childhood Development Center, Santa Fe Community College 6401 Richards Ave.
• (505) 428-1697

Nosotros helps strengthen the bonds between moms and dads and children from birth to age 5 by teaching the adults skills they need to parent successfully. Using play as a tool for learning, child development specialists work with families individually or in small groups to help parents learn how to better care for their children physically, psychologically and emotionally. A licensed therapist may consult with the parents and children if necessary. The city of Santa Fe provides some of the program's funding; Santa Fe Community College offers the space and staff. Participation is free.

Emergency Child Care
6401 Richards Ave.
• (505) 428-1610

Families with children ages 12 and younger can receive temporary, short-term help of up to 100 hours of child care, in some cases 24 hours a day, through this program. It also offers consultations with child-care specialists and referrals to other agencies to help families dealing with hospitalization, financial crises and other types of stress.

Early Childhood Resource Center and Toy Lending Center
6401 Richards Ave.
• (505) 428-1612

You'll find a wealth of goodies here! The Toy Lending Center, affectionately known as TLC, has more than 2,000 toys and playthings for infants and children up to kindergarten age and a small selection of toys for school-age children. Families, teachers, and child-care workers may borrow from the collection for free. The resource center offers books, videotapes, films, and slide/tape presentations for teachers

and caregivers who work with children. The phone number above will also connect you to the Warm Line, where child development specialists will answer questions about children's behaviors and attitudes and suggest ways to solve problems. All these services are free. The center is open each Wednesday 1 to 5 PM. It's also open the second Wednesday of each month 1 to 8 pm and the second Saturday, 9 AM to 1 PM.

Babysitters and Babysitting Services

For a come-to-the-house teen to watch your little ones, the informal parent-sitter referral network may be your ticket to freedom. Your 6-year-old's best friend's oldest sister might be the babysitter of your dreams. Nieces and nephews might know classmates who baby-sit. Your child's teacher may have some ideas. If your favorite sitter can't come when you need her, ask if she or he has any friends who might be interested. Some parents trade kids with families of friends so Mom and Dad get an occasional break and then return the favor. Ask, ask, and ask again. Take names and phone numbers. Keep notes. Be generous with your help to other parents.

If you run out of leads, consider the youth group at your church as a resource. They might have a list of recommended sitters. Or call Girls Inc., (505) 982-2042, the YMCA, (505) 983-8821, or Santa Fe Community College, (505) 471-8200, and ask if they've done any babysitter training lately. (YMCA memberships are valid from other cities; although the Santa Fe program has no facility of its own it offers year-round programs and may have drop-in space for children.) Employment services at the local colleges can sometimes give you the names and numbers of college kids who like to baby-sit.

If you're in Santa Fe on a family trip and need a vacation from the kids, there are re-

St. Michael's High School emphasizes sports as well as academics
In this photo a St. Mikes "Horseman" is in the air.

Photo: Don Strel

sources to help. And don't feel guilty. After all, it's your vacation too!

Santa Fe has three commercial services that provide babysitters so Mom and Dad can take a break. (Locals can use this service, too.)

Santa Fe Kid Connection Inc.
2422 Cerrillos Rd., Ste. 322
• (505) 954-4849

Founded in 1983, Kid Connection offers care for infants and children of all ages. It screens and requires references from all employees and provides sitters for days, evenings, weekends, holidays and overnight. Advance reservations are strongly recommended. Kid Connection charges for a required minimum number of hours and increases the rate depending on the number of children. They offer an annual $75 membership for residents or frequent visitors, which lowers the hourly rate. Among their clientele are many return visitors who appreciate being able to request a sitter their child knows.

Tender Care Learning
1004 Santa Clara Drive
• (505) 471-0508

Focusing exclusively on Santa Fe visitors, this service offers mature sitters with formal training and experience in early childhood education. The people sent to care for your child will also know CPR and have passed a criminal record check and TB screening. While reservations aren't required, they are a good idea. Most referrals come from concierges. Rates are $16/hour for one child or $19/hour for two with additional fees for special needs children "requiring exceptional physical or emotional fortitude." Tender Care Learning also operates a home daycare program that sometimes has space for drop-ins. The day care serves a maximum of three babies at a time, ages two months to two years. Children may attend morning or afternoon sessions or stay at the center all day.

Magical Happenings Babysitting Service and Children's Tours
1124 Don Juan • (505) 982-9327,
(505) 982-1570

This special babysitting service, which has been in business since 1990, provides childcare for guests in hotels or vacation units and to Santa Fe residents. In the summer months, they happily arrange daytrips and explorations for its young clients and will put together a custom tour for your children. Sometimes you can find a sitter with this agency on short notice, but it's best to make reservations.

Healthcare and Wellness

Long before the term "alternative medicine" came into vogue—and we're talking about centuries, not merely decades—New Mexicans were using herbs, potions, massage, and incantations to cure what ailed them. They came not from acupuncturists, aromatherapists, or biofeedback, but from Hispanic *curanderas*, medicine men, and other native healers who have long been an integral part of New Mexican society.

Some of their therapies—echinacea and goldenseal for colds, for example, or St. John's Wort for depression—have been "discovered" in recent years by traditional Western medicine, much as Columbus "discovered" an America that had been home to Indians for centuries. Those particular remedies are so common these days that you can usually find them in your local Walgreen's.

LOOK FOR:
- **Alternative Healthcare**
- **Student Clinics**
- **AIDS/HIV Care**
- **Traditional Western Medicine**

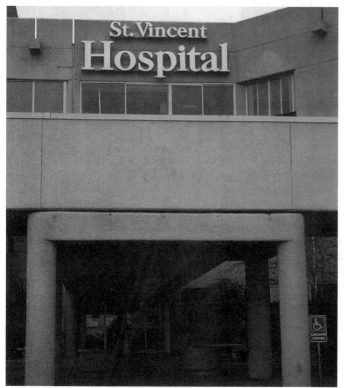

St. Vincent Hospital is the region's major medical center and Santa Fe's largest private employer.

Photo: Don Strel

At last count, Santa Fe was home to eight licensed schools of alternative/natural/holistic healing and massage, many of them with international reputations. Northern New Mexicans seem comfortable to forego the customary white coat, black bag, and medical degree of European medicine for less institutionalized healing methods such as acupuncture, Ayurvedics, and herbs—no doubt because non-Western doctoring has a formidable history here. Of course, Santa Fe has always been a beacon for alternative lifestyles and ideologies; hence, it's nickname, "The City Different." But long before some smart marketing person came up with that sound bite, both the ailing and the healers have made northern New Mexico a destination to fulfill their medical destinies.

For some, fulfillment may come in more conventional settings such as hospitals and doctors offices. While Santa Fe has only one hospital—St. Vincent (see entry below)—there are a number of medical centers and clinics in town as well as a healthy list of MDs from which to choose whether you're looking for a general practitioner or a specialist. And choice is certainly the operative word. St. Vincent has a number of publications that rate New Mexico physicians, including one put out by Ralph Nader's Public Citizen called Questionable Doctors: State Listing for New Mexico and The Best Doctors in America: Central Region, by Steven W. Naifeh. (For more information about St. Vincent's medical library, see the entry for St. Vincent Hospital.) Or, you can pick your doctor the old-fashioned way—by word-of-mouth. If you can't wait for an appointment, you can get same-day medical care at a number of locations including St. Vincent Hospital, Lovelace Health Systems, and La Familia Medical Center; see the write-ups in this chapter for more information. In the meantime, here are a few places to start:

Alternative Healthcare

Acupuncture Associates of America
1505 Llano St.
• (505) 984-3034

In business since 1987, Acupuncture Associates of America is a well-established healthcare provider in Santa Fe with a sister clinic in Albuquerque. They receive numerous referrals from New Mexico's major health plans and insurers, including Lovelace (see entry below) and BlueCross/BlueShield. The Santa Fe clinic has three doctors of Oriental medicine on staff, all of whom specialize in acupuncture, herbology, and "injection therapy"—introducing herbal or homeopathic formulas into acupuncture points for pain that doesn't respond to needles. Clinic director Gurusant Khalsa, D.O.M., is past president of the American Association of Acupuncture and Oriental Medicine and a former chairman of the board of Southwest Acupuncture College (see entry below). He is currently president of Preferred Providers of New Mexico, a private nonprofit organization that sets standards for integrating alternative and traditional medicine. The Santa Fe clinic is open Monday through Friday from 9 AM to 6 PM.

GRD Health Clinic
1505 Llano St.
• (505) 984-0934

GRD is a holistic healing clinic, which means it considers the whole system rather than just the part that hurts. Primarily a chiropractic clinic, GRD also offers therapeutic massage and colonics. All practitioners are licensed or board-certified. The clinic refers many patients next door to Acupuncture Associates of America, (505) 984-3034, (see entry above). GRD is open Monday, Tuesday, Wednesday, and Friday, 9 AM to 6 PM, and Saturday from 9 AM to noon.

Ojo Caliente Mineral Springs
50 Los Baños Rd. (N.M. Hwy 285)
• (505) 583-2233, (800) 222-9162

Though located about 50 miles north of Santa Fe, where it straddles the Rio Arriba and Taos County lines, Ojo Caliente Mineral Springs are close enough—and special enough—to warrant a mention in this chapter.

Named by 16th Century explorer Cabeza de Vaca, Ojo Caliente ("Hot Eye") Mineral Springs is the only spa in the world with its particular combination of five naturally hot, bubbling waters that flow from geothermal wells deep beneath the earth. Many people "take the waters" for their purported therapeutic value, others for the sheer pleasure and relaxation.

Ojo Caliente's 113-degree arsenic spring is thought to be the only one outside of Baden-Baden, Germany. In trace amounts, arsenic is supposed to relieve arthritis, rheumatism, stomach ulcers, burns, eczema, and a host of other complaints. The spa also has an iron spring, which comes out of the ground at 109 degrees Fahrenheit into a large pool used for a hot plunge that reportedly rejuvenates the blood. The lithia, soda, and sodium springs are primarily for drinking to heal a variety of symptoms, from depression and sluggish kidneys to excess gas.

One of the oldest health spas in North America, Ojo Caliente was once considered a sacred spot by ancient Tewa Pueblo Indians who lived on a mesa above the present village. Today, the spa is spread out over approximately 1,000 hilly, river-lined acres in the Española Valley. The waters are piped into various pools and tubs, public and private. The spa offers other services such as therapeutic massage, herbal wraps, facials, and salt rubs. The grounds support a quaint old adobe hotel whose rooms have no showers; guests use the public bathhouse.

Ojo Caliente is open year round, seven days a week—from 8 AM to 9 PM Sunday through Thursday and to 10 PM on Fridays and Saturdays. The spa closes only on Christmas. The public tubs on weekends cost $12.50 for 90 minutes, $25 all day. Weekdays are less expensive: $9.50 for 90 minutes, $18 all day Private tubs run $17 for 25 minutes on weekends, including mineral baths; $13 per person during the week.

Parcells Center
P.O. Box 2120
• (505) 986-1441

Parcells Center is named for Hazel Parcells, a pioneer in the fields of nutrition and energy healing who died in 1996 near her home near Las Vegas, N.M. She was 106 years old. Dr. Parcells—she was a doctor of naturopathy and of chiropractic and held Ph.D.s in nutrition and world religion—founded the center in 1995 to ensure that her work in natural self-healing would continue after her death.

A staff of dedicated professionals operates the Santa Fe center in conjunction with a wide network of experienced health specialists, many of whom are students and followers of Dr. Parcells. The center promotes the Parcells Method—a regimen that includes food cleansing and combining, therapeutic bathing, and herbal remedies—and offers classes in its Santa Fe headquarters as well as day-long and week-

end workshops in cities around the country. Parcells Center also conducts in-depth courses in natural and nutritional self-healing for health professionals and others seeking certification in the Parcells Method. The center publishes a monthly electronic newsletter that provides nutrition and health news, including discoveries from the Parcells lab. You can find Parcells Newsletter at www.parcellscenter.com. The center also sells products Dr. Parcells developed herself, from food supplements and homeopathic remedies to bath aids and home appliances.

Ten Thousand Waves Japanese Health Spa
3451 Hyde Park Rd.
• (505) 982-9304

Ten Thousand Waves is not just a spa, it's an experience that literally and figuratively bathes your every sense from the moment you enter the premises. To get to the tubs, you pass rock sculptures and copious hanging plants and climb a few steps that form a bridge over an indoor stream where you might catch sight of a large orange koi or two. In the lobby, you collect your kimono and keys and head to the dressing rooms, pleasantly fragrant with the citrus scent of Yuzu, a vegetable-based lotion the spa puts out for clients to use after a soak, a massage, or both. Beforehand, however, you're expected to be clean and lotion free. Be sure to grab one of the towels you'll find stacked neatly next to a bin of rubber zori on your way to the shower. Freshly showered and kimono-clad, you'll make your way to one of nine chlorine free tubs. For $15, you can spend the entire day in the outdoor, co-ed public tub, which is clothing optional until 8:15 PM, or the women's tub, which is fenced but open to the skies. The spa's luxurious private tubs cost between $19 and $26 an hour per person). Some are outfitted with a sauna, others with a steam room, and one even has a waterfall.

If it's a therapeutic massage you're after, Ten Thousand Waves has more than 100 bodyworkers on its roster, all of them trained in Swedish and deep tissue massage. Many

INSIDERS' TIP

Travelers with physical disabilities take note: New Mexico provides truly usable information about destinations and businesses with wheelchair ramps, electronic doors, handicapped-friendly bathrooms, etc. in its "Access Santa Fe" and "Access New Mexico" guides. For a copy of either or both, write to the Governor's Committee on Concerns for the Handicapped, 491 Old Santa Fe Trail, Lamy Building, Suite 117, Santa Fe, NM 87501 or call (505) 827-6465.

are also skilled in shiatsu, reflexology, acupressure, Trager, Reiki, Alexander Technique, watsu . . . the list goes on. Or you might want to indulge in a "spa treatment" such as an herbal wrap, salt glow, aromatherapy massage, or Japanese hot stone massage. A standard massage runs $65 to $75 for 55 minutes an hour and $40 for 25 minutes, while a masters massage start at $85 for 55 minutes. It's best to schedule weekday massages a couple of days in advance. Call at least a week ahead if you want your massage on the weekend. Ten Thousand Waves opens at 10 AM every day except Thursday, when it doesn't open 'til 4:30 PM. In the summer, it closes at 11 PM during the week and at midnight on Fridays and Saturdays. In winter the spa closes an hour earlier. Except during the peak season from mid-July to mid-September, locals get an across-the-board discount of 20 percent. They must present a New Mexico driver's license or other state identification.

Student Clinics

International Institute of Chinese Medicine
4884 La Junta del Alamo Rd.
• (505) 474-9330 (clinic), (505) 473-5233 (school), (888) 937-4426

IICM is a world-renowned graduate school of Chinese medicine that teaches and practices acupuncture, herbology, and movement. An important component of the school's curriculum is its advanced student clinic in which third and fourth year students—and occasionally last-semester, second-year students—see patients under the supervision of a D.O.M. (Doctor of Oriental Medicine). Visits include a consultation, acupuncture treatment, and often an herbal prescription—either a patent medicine or bag of herbs to be brewed into tea. Prescriptions are available at the clinic—patents generally for less than $10, herbs for $20 to $30—and may include an ingredient as exotic as silkworm feces or as common as ginger. All IICM students memorize the names of each of the 300 herbs used at the school.

IICM opened in 1984 with about 20 students. Today, it boasts close to 300 students divided between its Santa Fe and Albuquerque campuses. Founders Nancy and Michael Zeng are both M.D.s as well as D.O.M.s and personally oversee both schools, including the student clinics. Patients usually spend an hour at the clinic and return on a weekly basis for six or

seven weeks. Sometimes, however, one treatment will do the trick—especially for allergies or pain relief. Visits cost $18 each for the general public, $10 for seniors. The clinic also offers a sliding fee scale for people in financial need. Clinic hours are Monday through Friday from 8:30 AM to 5:30 PM and Thursday evenings from 7 to 9 PM.

New Mexico Academy of Healing Arts
501 Franklin Ave.
• (505) 982-6271 (office);
(505) 982-1001 (clinic)

Founded in 1981, the New Mexico Academy of Healing Arts offers certification programs in both massage and polarity, a therapy that utilizes bodywork, nutrition, and counseling in conjunction with the body's magnetic energy. The academy's foundation is Swedish massage, though it also teaches other forms of bodywork, including sports massage; cranial-sacral therapy, which aids circulation along the spinal pathway; and orthobionomy, which relies on movement to re-align the body for relief of acute or chronic pain. The academy is also developing a certification program for Oriental bodywork. The public may sample the school's "wares" at a student clinic open Thursday evenings from 6 to 9 PM and Friday through Sunday during the day. Hours will vary depending on the time of year. Student massages start at $15 an hour. Call ahead for an appointment.

The Scherer Institute of Natural Healing
935 Alto St.
• (505) 982-8398

The world-famous Scherer Institute of Natural Healing opened in 1979 as Dr. Jay Scherer's Academy of Natural Healing. In addition to Swedish massage, the school incorporates aromatherapy, herbology, homeopathy, and shiatsu (Japanese pressure point massage) into its curriculum. Founder Jay Scherer was a naturopathic doctor who died at age 83 in 1990, six years after being named one of Santa Fe's "Living Treasures."

The Scherer Institute holds a couple of two-month student clinics a year where the public can get an hour-long nurturing Swedish massage—the school's specialty—for $15 to $25. The massage clinic is part of institute's internship program, which requires students halfway through the six-month program to perform 30 massages under supervision. The clinics generally operate January to April and June to December. They're open for business two evenings

Santa Fe Stands Out in AIDS/HIV Care

For a city of only 68,000 people, Santa Fe has an extensive network of AIDS/HIV health services and support groups. That's largely due to efforts by, and in response to, the city's sizable gay population—a segment of the community that in Santa Fe, as elsewhere, has been hit particularly hard by the AIDS epidemic.

Many gays and lesbians move to Santa Fe because of its reputation for welcoming people who, whatever their orientation, might not be welcome elsewhere. This isn't a new phenomenon; homosexuals have been coming here since the 1920s, during the city's heyday as an art colony. Indeed, Santa Fe is a gay-friendly town. Its city council has an openly gay member; its mayors have offered a supportive voice for the city's homosexual population, many of them speaking at the annual Santa Fe Lesbian, Gay & Bi Pride Parade; and the general population has traditionally been non-judgmental and accepting.

Starting in the 1980s, however, gay men began coming to Santa Fe in droves for another reason—to die. They made the pilgrimage so that they could succumb to AIDS in a beautiful, mystical place that didn't condemn them for who they were or for the illness they contracted. In a small town like Santa Fe, AIDS touches everybody—with horror, at first, then fear, and finally compassion, especially for those who've died alone because no support systems existed.

Even before people understood that AIDS was an equal-opportunity killer—when the disease appeared to be uniquely the scourge of gay men, who have been a significant and visible presence in Santa Fe—both the city and state rallied with aggressive treatment and substantial public funding to provide a host of public services. As AIDS widened its net, so did Santa Fe's health community, creating an enviable network of publicly funded support and cutting edge AIDS treatment, which has turned Santa Fe into a Lourdes for those afflicted with AIDS or HIV-related illnesses. Lots of support comes from Santa Fe's private sector, too—particularly from the arts community, which has lost so much talent and friendship to AIDS.

Much of the private funding comes from Santa Fe's numerous fund-raisers throughout the year including AID and Comfort Gala (see the entry in this Close-up), which puts on an annual party at the elegant Eldorado hotel with proceeds helping to cover HIV-related bills; the yearly Santa Fe AIDS Walk, which brings out more than 1,200 participants; and Santa Fe Cares' annual "Live at the Lensic," a stage revue which has featured such international celebrities as Lauren Bacall, British actor Michael York, and Grammy-nominated musician Michael Feinstein, as well as famous local talent including comedienne Carol Burnett, world-famous flamenco dancer Maria Benitez, and jazz vocalist Chris Calloway, who carries on the legacy of her father, Cab Calloway. Anyone even remotely connected to AIDS/HIV work in Santa Fe will necessarily interact with Southwest C.A.R.E. (Comprehensive AIDS Treatment, Research and Education) Center, specialty AIDS/HIV clinic providing some of the most comprehensive care in New Mexico. Located near downtown Santa Fe at 230 W. Manhattan St., Suite 300, the clinic offers under one roof virtually every service someone with AIDS or an HIV-related illness might need. In addition to state-of-the-art medical care, including access to clinical trials, Southwest C.A.R.E. works with the state to provide a full range of practical and emotional support services for its clients. That might

(Continued on next page)

HEALTHCARE
AND WELLNESS

include finding a dentist who will treat an HIV-infected person; making referrals for alternative medical treatment; coordinating home or hospice care; finding insurance or emergency funding for patients in need; or matching up trained volunteers to visit isolated AIDS patients. Southwest C.A.R.E. offers medical treatment on a sliding scale. The nonprofit center is open Monday through Friday from 8 AM to 5 PM but there are staffers on call 24 hours a day, seven days a week for emergencies. Locally, call (505) 989-8200. For out-of-town callers, Southwest C.A.R.E. also has a toll free line at (888) 320-8200.

It's precisely these sorts of comprehensive and compassionate services that draw people with AIDS or the HIV infection to Santa Fe. But unlike in the recent past, they're arriving with some hope. Combination therapy, used aggressively in Santa Fe long before it became de rigeur throughout the nation, has prolonged the lives of many an AIDS sufferer, some of whom are returning to the large urban areas they fled a few years earlier.

For more information about AIDS/HIV resources in Santa Fe, contact any of the following organizations:

AID & Comfort of New Mexico
418 Cerrillos Rd, Ste. 20
• (505) 989-3399
Founded in 1989, AID & Comfort is a volunteer organization that raises funds to help those with HIV or AIDS pay medical bills after they've exhausted all other resources. Its main fundraising event is an annual Thanksgiving weekend party and silent auction at the Eldorado Hotel.

People of Color AIDS Foundation
1217 Parkway Drive, Ste. A
• (505) 474-7602
People of Color AIDS Foundation (POCAF) is a non-profit organization offers HIV/AIDS education, prevention, referrals, advocacy, and care to New Mexicans of all races and colors.

Santa Fe Cares
117 N. Guadalupe St., Suite B
• (505) 986-3820
Santa Fe Cares is a non-profit community fundraising and grant-making organization that funds treatment, care, education, and prevention of HIV/AIDS. Since its founding in 1991, Santa Fe Cares has raised more than $4 million from such events as its annual AIDS Walk and "Live at the Lensic," a musical and comedy revue that brings international celebrities to Santa Fe's beautiful old Lensic movie theater.

HEALTHCARE AND WELNESS

a week—they vary, so call in advance—from 6 to 9 PM and Fridays from 9 AM to 5 PM. The school is open 9 AM to 5 PM Monday through Friday.

Southwest Acupuncture College and Chinese Medical Clinic
2960 Rodeo Park Drive West
• (505) 438-8884
Established in 1980, Southwest Acupuncture College and Chinese Medical Clinic is an accredited four-year masters degree program that teaches the five branches of classical Oriental medicine: acupuncture; herbology; physical therapy; nutrition; and exercise and breathing therapy. Built into the program is clinical experience which, unlike at other colleges, starts in the students' first year and continues throughout the entire program, culminating in more than 1,000 hours of practical experience. In addition, the college operates a student clinic, open Monday through Thursday from 9 AM to 9 PM. and Fridays from 9 AM to 5 PM. The first treatment can take up to an hour and a half and costs a maximum of $9, while subsequent treatments cost up to $18 and usually last an

hour. The clinic charges according to a patient's ability to pay. The elderly, handicapped, battered women, substance abusers, and patients with AIDS or cancer may be eligible for reduced-cost or free treatments.

Southwestern Counseling Center at Southwestern College
Rte. 20 (San Felipe Rd.), Box 29D
• **(505) 471-5756 (college),**
(505) 471-8575 (clinic)

Southwestern Counseling Center is a student clinic under the auspices of Southwestern College, Founded in 1976, the college is an accredited institution that offers masters degrees in spiritually-oriented counseling and art therapy. The clinic, located near Airport Road on Santa Fe's south side, has served the community here for more than 10 years with low-cost and free counseling services for individuals, couples, families, and groups. Clinicians are second-year students working under the supervision of licensed professionals. The clinic charges on a sliding fee scale up to $15 per person, $20 for couples. Call ahead for an appointment.

Traditional Western Medicine

La Familia Medical Center
1035 Alto St.
• **(505) 982-4425 2145**
Caja del Oro Grant Rd.
• **(505) 438-3195**

With a recently opened second clinic on Santa Fe's south side, La Familia truly is a community health center. The clinics provide primary medical care from obstetrics to geriatrics. The nonprofit medical center is the primary deliverer of babies in the community. Its obstetricians introduced 412 babies to the world in 1999. Both locations have dental clinics that take Medicaid patients. Between them, the two clinics employ 10 board-certified family physicians; four residents from University of New Mexico Medical School; five family nurse practitioners; an RN who is also a certified diabetes educator; three full-time dentists; and two dental hygienists. La Familia's health providers recognize the validity of alternative medicine and respect its cultural importance, particularly to Hispanic and Native American patients. They

often incorporate alternative therapies into patients' healthcare plans, referring them outside if La Familia doesn't offer a particular treatment.

La Familia started in 1972 as a little neighborhood clinic in a building it shared with a daycare center on Santa Fe's west side. Today, it operates two full-time, stand-alone medical centers. It leases each building from the City of Santa Fe for $1 a year. At last count, the center had more than 9,000 registered patients and expects to serve another 3,000 at its new clinic. The majority—54 percent—is uninsured, relying either on the county indigent fund or La Familia's sliding fee scale. A number of patients who can afford to go elsewhere choose La Familia for its quality comprehensive health care. The clinics ask for a minimum payment of $12, though they will provide services to anyone who walks in their doors, regardless of ability to pay. They accept all forms of insurance and contract with HMOs to provide medical care for their patients. La Familia also operates a number of outstanding community outreach programs including "Prometoras," which promotes community health education through lay advisors. Prometoras provide information on such topics as pre-natal care, diabetes, child immunization, asthma, and breast feeding, including teaching working mothers how to pump their breast milk to leave with their children's caregiver.

Both clinics are open from 8 AM to 5 PM Monday, Tuesday, Thursday, and Friday and from 9 AM to 8 PM on Wednesday. The centers accept walk-in patients but ask that you try to call ahead so the staff can fit you into the best available appointment slot or, if one isn't available, send you to St. Vincent Hospital. La Familia sees an average of 44 walk-ins per day.

Lovelace Health Systems
440 St. Michael's Dr.
• **(505) 995-2400,**
(800) 877-7526, ext. 2400,

A subsidiary of CIGNA HealthCare, Lovelace is New Mexico's oldest and largest health maintenance organization with headquarters in Albuquerque at 5400 Gibson Blvd. SE, (505) 262-7000, (800) 877-7526. HMOs have earned a reputation as being a frustrating maze of referrals and counter-referrals. But in Santa Fe, at least, many staffers—from doctors and nurses to pharmacists and receptionists—seem to sympathize with patients' frustration and try to help them work within the system. Perhaps that's why *U.S. News and World Report* named Lovelace Health Plan the top-ranked

HMO in New Mexico in 1997 and 1998 and among the nation's leading HMOs by *Newsweek* in 1998. *Modern Healthcare* magazine ranked Lovelace 11th among the 100 best integrated health care networks in the country

Lovelace offers a full range of primary care services including family practice, internal medicine, pediatrics, women's health, rehabilitation and fitness, diabetes education, X-rays, laboratory work, and a pharmacy. It also provides a number of specialty services on site such as gastroenterology, endocrinology, allergy, urology, and nephrology. For other specialties, it contracts with local practitioners—even acupuncturists and other non-traditional healers, if a patient meets Lovelace's criteria—or may send a patient to Albuquerque where its medical centers and contract physicians cover up to 43 medical specialties, including cardiology, cosmetic surgery, occupational medicine, and orthopedics. Lovelace's Gibson Boulevard hospital also operates a Level II trauma center, an accredited sleep disorders clinic, and the state's largest birthing center.

Lovelace opened its first Santa Fe clinic in 1985 at the DeVargas Center near downtown Santa Fe. In 1989 it moved to brand-new quarters on nearby Alameda Avenue and, three years later, opened a second branch on St. Michael's Drive, close to St. Vincent Hospital. Today, all Santa Fe operations have been consolidated in the St. Michael's Drive clinic, which offers same-day care seven days a week—from 8 AM to 7 PM Monday through Thursday, 8 AM to 5 PM on Friday, and 8 AM to 3 PM on Saturday. The clinic accepts walk-ins but encourages people to call ahead.

Presbyterian Medical Services
1422 Paseo de Peralta
• **(505) 982-5565, (800) 477-7633**

Presbyterian Medical Services is the primary provider of mental health and counseling services in Santa Fe County. A non-profit corpora-

INSIDERS' TIP

Though more of a grocery store than a bona fide member of the healing community, Wild Oats Community Market carries a wide range of dietary supplements, herbs and homeopathic products and tries to hire employees who are knowledgeable about what they sell. You can even get a quickie massage at Wild Oats in an ergonomically correct massage chair complete with a padded, donut-shaped face rest. Massages cost $7 for 15 minutes and are available from 8 AM to 8 PM, seven days a week. Both Wild Oats and its sister store, Alfalfa's (located just a few blocks away), offer informative symposia on natural healing and living. Check their bulletin boards or their monthly calendars, available at the customer service counters.

tion, its mission is to furnish high-quality, affordable medical, dental, mental health, hospice, retirement, and other human services throughout the Southwest, particularly to Hispanic and Native American communities. PMS is the successor to the Presbyterian Church's medical mission to the Southwest, which began in 1901. When the church could no longer provide financial support, PMS incorporated in 1969 to carry on the work. Although it's an independent organization, it maintains its ties to the church through a covenant with the Presbytery of Santa Fe and the Synod of the Southwest.

PMS employs about 1,100 people in 54 programs including primary healthcare centers and agencies; comprehensive mental health care programs; home health care and hospice programs; nursing homes; developmental disabilities programs for children and adults; substance abuse treatment; Head Start programs; AIDS and other health education and counseling; and a pharmacy consulting service. PMS also offers the following services:

Brain Injury Community Services, 820 Paseo de Peralta, (505) 986-9633, part of the Santa Fe Community Guidance Center (see subsequent entry), service provides case management for individuals with traumatic brain injury by assisting clients and their families in reintegrating into the community.

Crisis Response of Santa Fe, 1422 Paseo de Peralta, Building 2, (505) 820-1440 (office), (505) 820-6333 (hotline) is a suicide prevention program with a telephone hotline and mobile crisis team, both available 24-hours a day, seven days a week in Santa Fe County. Volunteers trained in short-term telephone crisis intervention operate the hotline to offer immediate suicide counseling as well as information and referrals. The mobile crisis team comprises professionals who respond to suicide, drug/alcohol abuse and psychiatric emergencies.

The Hospice Center, 1400 Chama Street, (505) 988-1477, (800) 880-8001, established in

1991, The Hospice Center provides at-home care for people with terminal illnesses and their families. Its registered nurses are specialists in pain and symptom control and are on call 24 hours a day. The center offers regularly scheduled nursing visits; volunteer support services for patients and their families; home health aide services for personal care; social work visits for counseling; pastoral counseling and referral; physical, occupational, and speech therapy; bereavement services; medication; medical treatment, equipment, and supplies. The center also operates The Hospice Center, which offers support for individuals and groups, including schools or businesses, facing life-threatening illness or experiencing grief or loss.

Ortiz Mountain Health Center, 08A Main Street, Cerrillos, (505) 471-6266, open since 1995, is a three-day-a-week primary healthcare clinic located in Cerrillos, N.M., about 20 miles southwest of Santa Fe. The center provides diagnostic and treatment services, limited pharmacy and laboratory services, prenatal and perinatal care and treatment of minor emergencies. It coordinates with healthcare providers in Santa Fe for referral and specialty care.

PMS Home Care, 1400 Chama Street, (505) 988-4156, (800) 880-8001, provides comprehensive home care services to residents of Santa Fe County with an emphasis on rehabilitation. Licensed by both Medicaid and Medicare, it provides skilled nursing, home health aides, physical therapy, occupational therapy, speech pathology, and medical social services. The staff works with physicians, hospitals, rehabilitation centers, nursing homes, and medical equipment suppliers to make a smooth transition to home health care.

Santa Fe Community Guidance Center, 820 Paseo de Peralta, (505) 986-9633, is a mental health outpatient facility for day treatment; case management; and supported living and employment. The program provides rehabilitation for the long-term mentally ill through its Spirit Club, 1505 Fifth Street, (505) 986-8827, which focuses on social, recreational and vocational skills.

Santa Fe Community Partnership, 1604 Berry Avenue, (505) 982-8899, founded as a community coalition of organizations and individuals, is primarily an educational organization that aims to increase community awareness about substance abuse and prevention and ensure the existence of treatment and recovery options. Among the programs it has initiated are life skills training, including parenting; special training for clergy; and a free/low-cost small business employee assistance program to help workers cope with marriage and family issues, alcohol and drug abuse, gambling, depression, or financial troubles.

St. Vincent Hospital
St. Michael's Dr.
• (505) 983-3361

St. Vincent is the regional medical center for northern New Mexico and the largest medical facility between Albuquerque and Pueblo, Colorado. It's a non-profit, non-sectarian hospital with 268 beds, around 250 staff physicians representing 22 medical specialties and a nursing staff of more than 400. With close to 1,300 employees, the hospital is also Santa Fe's largest private employer.

Established in 1865 by Sisters of Charity out of Cincinnati, Ohio, St. Vincent was New Mexico's first hospital. It began its days in an old adobe building next to St. Francis Cathedral in downtown Santa Fe. The sisters ran the hospital for more than a century, moving it three times before turning it over to a community-based board of trustees in 1973. In 1977, it moved to its current location on St. Michael's Drive. Today, St. Vincent remains the only hospital in Santa Fe and while four smaller local hospitals also serve this region, many residents and physicians from those areas come to St. Vincent for more specialized care. In addition to the usual departments, St. Vincent has a pain clinic, a sleep disorders clinic, comprehensive cancer services, and the second busiest a Level III trauma center in the state.

St. Vincent admits more than 12,000 patients a year and treats an additional 5,500 in outpatient surgery. The emergency room and adjacent FirstCARE unit treat more than 60,0000 patients annually, making it the second busiest acute care facility in New Mexico after University Hospital in Albuquerque. FirstCARE is open for walk-ins from 9 AM to 9 PM. The emergency room is open 24 hours.

St. Vincent periodically offers free medical services throughout the year, including flu shots and breast cancer screenings. It also opens its medical library to the public weekdays from

INSIDERS' TIP
The suicide rate in Santa Fe from 1993 through 1995 was nearly double the national average—22 suicides per 100,000 Santa Feans compared to 12 per 100,000 nationwide.

8 AM until at least 2 PM and sometimes later. In addition to the professional collection, the library has a pretty good consumer health section including reference books listing physicians' background and training. It also maintains special collections on such topics as altitude and wilderness medicine, herbal medicine, and complementary therapies. Although the public may not check out books, they can photocopy library materials for 25 cents a page, 10 cents for students and the disabled. Call (505) 820-5218 for more information.

Women's Health Services Family Care and Counseling Center
901 W. Alameda
• (505) 988-8869

Located in Solana Center just west of St. Francis Drive, Women's Health Services is a primary care health facility with an extensive family practice that includes obstetric, gynecological, and family planning services; mental health care; therapeutic massage; acupuncture; and limited laboratory work. Its staff includes physicians, nurse practitioners, and masters level mental health practitioners, all of whom provide services on a sliding fee scale. The center also has several grant programs to lessen the financial burden on low-income and uninsured patients. Although Women's Health Services has no pediatricians on staff, a good many of its patients are children, while 10 to 15 percent are men, the center's name notwithstanding. Women's Health Services opened in 1973 as a self-health education resource center for women. A progeny of the feminist self-help movement, the clinic's initial raison d'être was to give women more information to take better care of themselves. Within a couple of years, it began to provide services and, by the late 1970s, became a full-fledged medical clinic staffed by volunteers. It's only in the last decade that staff doctors, nurses, and therapists have been on full salary. Although the clinic is geared toward low-income and uninsured patients, its waiting room is a true cross-section of Santa Fe. Many women who could afford to go elsewhere choose Women's Health Services because of its reputation for excellent healthcare and for providing patients with information and suggestions about complementary therapies, including such alternatives as acupuncture, herbology, and homeopathy. Open Monday through Friday from 8 AM to 5:30 PM, the center operates by appointment only. Walk-ins will be sent to St. Vincent or Lovelace.

Emergency Numbers

Local:
AIDS Hotline: .... (800) 545-AIDS (2437)
Domestic Violence 24-Hour Hotline: .... (800) 773-3645
Environmental Emergency (after hours): .... (505) 827-9329
Esperanza Shelter for Battered Families: .... (505) 473-5200 or (505) 474-5536
Hantavirus Hotline .... (800) 879-3421
Lovelace Health Care Systems Hotline: .... (800) 877-7526
Police, Fire, Ambulance: 911
Rape Crisis Center Hotline: .... (505) 986-9111
St. Vincent Hospital: .... (505) 820-5250
Suicide Intervention Project: .... (505) 820-1066
Teen Suicide & Crisis Hotline: .... (505) 820-0024

National:
Alcohol and Drug Abuse Hotline: .... (800) 962-8963
Depression and Anxiety Hotline: .... (800) 234-0038
Missing Children Hotline: .... (800) 587-4357
National Runaway Switchboard: .... (800) 621-4000
National Youth Crisis Hotline: .... (800) 448-4663
Poison control: .... (800) 432-6866
Suicide Intervention Project: .... (800) 274-2995

Media

Santa Fe might be small in population, but it's huge in diversity. One need only spend a few hours nursing a latte at Downtown Subscription, 376 Garcia Street, (505) 983-3085 (see our chapter on restaurants and shopping) to witness first-hand the fascinating mix of residents—and visitors, too—that makes Santa Fe "The City Different."

It's not just what the habitués are drinking or wearing that gives them away; it's also whatever magazine or newspaper they happen to be thumbing through—and there are plenty to choose from at Downtown Subscription. The newsstand/café offers up to 1,000 periodical titles from around the world and around the corner.

It's what comes from around the corner that interests us here. For such a small metropolis—remember, only 68,000 people call this city home—Santa Fe offers a surprisingly wide variety of home-grown publications to suit almost any taste, lifestyle, or political persuasion. Also included in this chapter are a number of Albuquerque publications that have enough of a following in Santa Fe to merit mention.

LOOK FOR:
• **Dailies**
• **Weeklies**
• **Monthlies**
• **Quarterlies**
• **Irregular Circulation**
• **Magazines**
• **Radio**
• **Television**

Dailies

Albuquerque Journal
7777 Jefferson St. NE, Albuquerque
• **(800) 641-3451**

The 120-year-old *Albuquerque Journal* takes great pride in being part of an ever-shrinking pool of independently owned American dailies. The front page proclaims in bold white-on-blue that the paper is "home-owned and home-operated." Home is Journal Center, an industrial park owned by Journal publisher Thompson H. Lang. Lang rose to the helm of the family-owned Journal in 1971 with the death of his father, C. Thompson Lang. Along with the title of owner/publisher, he inherited a 40-year-old "joint operating agreement" (JOA) with the Journal's nearest competitor, The Albuquerque Tribune.

Despite sharing business operations, the Journal and Tribune remain separate and competing entities with obvious differences in style and content. As a seven-day-a-week morning paper with statewide circulation, the *Journal* considers itself New Mexico's newspaper of record and concentrates heavily on state and local government. While stories are generally accurate and balanced, they tend to be rather dry and heavily edited. In contrast, the afternoon-only Tribune takes itself far less seriously, focusing on news features and issue stories written with a light, bright touch. The *Albuquerque Journal* is unquestionably the dominant news voice in its hometown and throughout the state with a daily circulation of 111,743 and 158,616 on Sundays.

For $11.25 a month, *Journal* subscribers get a variety of special sections throughout the week including "Business Outlook" on Mondays and Thursday's "Go!" for outdoors and recreation; a Friday entertainment section called "Venue;" "Wheels" on Saturday; and a Sunday paper fat with ads.

Journal North
328 Galisteo St.
• **(505) 988-8881**

The upstart *Journal North*—a

17-year-old zoned edition of New Mexico's largest and most widely read newspaper, the *Albuquerque Journal*—is the primary competitor for daily news coverage in Santa Fe and northern New Mexico against the hometown paper, *The Santa Fe New Mexican*. While parochial Santa Feans will always consider it "the other paper," *Journal North* certainly gives *The New Mexican* a run for its money with even-handed, tightly edited, if somewhat dry coverage of local government and breaking news.

In contrast to *The New Mexican* and especially to the heretofore unapologetically liberal weekly, the *Santa Fe Reporter* (see the entry under our Weeklies section), *Journal North* tends to be conservative in its editorial policy as well as its style, though somewhat less so on both counts than its parent publication, the *Albuquerque Journal*.

Journal North appears seven days a week wrapped around the *Albuquerque Journal*. Its northern New Mexico circulation hovers around 16,000 during the week and 18,000 on Sunday. The Santa Fe circulation rate falls in the 9,000 range. Just six to eight pages long, *Journal North* often prompts readers to wonder why they seem to get so much news from such a small section. It's because *Journal North* is wall-to-wall news stories with only a smattering of display ads in between. Santa Fe classified ads appear in the main paper. Despite being a fixture in Santa Fe for nearly 20 years, *Journal North* can't shake its reputation as an interloper. That's due, in part, to the section's relative youth compared to the 151-year-old *New Mexican*. But it's primarily *Journal North's* umbilicus to Albuquerque that irks xenophobic Santa Feans. While local reporters write the section, *Journal North* is edited and printed in Albuquerque. This is a double whammy for *Journal North*. Not only can't it claim to be a hometown paper, but its deadlines are far earlier than the *New Mexican's*—sometimes by as much as two-and-a-half hours. This puts *Journal North* at a distinct disadvantage in the Santa Fe news war. It loses nearly every time to *The New Mexican* on late-breaking stories. As a relative newcomer, *Journal North* is also often left in the dust on insider news. For local political gossip, the inside scoop, the "Hey, Martha" stories, most Santa Feans will tell you they rely on *The New Mexican*.

The Albuquerque Tribune
7777 Jefferson St. NE, Albuquerque
• (800) 665-8742

As a result of a 67-year-old agreement with its primary competitor, the *Albuquerque Journal*, this Scripps-Howard publication will always be the No. 2 newspaper in its hometown. So, like Avis, it has to try harder. And it does.

The *Albuquerque Tribune* long ago gave up trying to compete head-to-head on daily news coverage with its business partner and roommate. (The *Tribune* lives in a separate wing of *Albuquerque Journal* headquarters in Journal Center, an industrial park owned by *Journal* publisher Thompson H. Lang.) Instead, it focuses on issue stories and news features, doing both remarkably well. And it still manages to scoop the *Journal* from time to time on daily news.

With a daily circulation of 23,022, The *Albuquerque Tribune* is about one-fifth the size of the *Journal*. Its Santa Fe circulation is almost nil. But readers can find the *Tribune* at newsstands and in boxes located in key parts of the city, particularly around the state capitol and the Plaza. The *Tribune* publishes Monday though Saturday and costs 50 cents for a single copy, $6 a month to subscribe.

The Santa Fe New Mexican
202 E. Marcy St.
• (505) 983-3303

Founded in 1849, Santa Fe's only local daily boasts on its masthead that it's "The West's Oldest Newspaper." But *The New Mexican*, as Santa Feans call it, stands out for another reason: it's one of a steadily declining number of American newspapers that have remained independently owned and operated—though only by the skin of its journalistic teeth.

In 1975, publisher Robert McKinney sold *The Santa Fe New Mexican* to Gannett, the largest newspaper chain in the United States. Less than three years later, however, McKinney sued Gannett for breach of contract. McKinney, a Virginia resident who maintains a hacienda in northern Santa Fe County, claimed Gannett reneged on its agreement to let him retain editorial and operational control of *The New Mexican*. A jury agreed and, in July 1980, a federal judge ordered Gannett to return the newspaper to McKinney, a one-time assistant secretary of the interior and a former ambassador to Switzerland.

Although it took several years for *The New Mexican* to gain back readership it lost during Gannett's brief reign, the newspaper has once again become a staple—and a favorite target— of locals. Indeed, Santa Feans have a love-hate relationship with *The New Mexican*. Readers, especially local politicians, love to hate the newspaper for its "gotcha" articles, its no-holds-barred editorials and its frequent editing errors. But—and its a big "but"—*The New Mexican* is widely read in Santa Fe, whose slightly left-of-center politics and ideology jibe with the newspaper's editorial leaning.

The proof is in the numbers and *The New Mexican* has them; its household penetration rate in the city is nearly 58.69 percent during the week and close to 61.83 percent on Sunday. That translates to a daily circulation rate— which includes paid subscriptions and street sales—of 24,235 and 26,626 on Sunday.

Many *New Mexican* readers—up to 40 percent, according to some sources—also subscribe to *Journal North*, a zoned edition of the *Albuquerque Journal*. While *The New Mexican* covers the heck out of Santa Fe as both a municipality and the state capital, it tends to ignore the rest of New Mexico and often relegates major national and international news to inside stories or briefs.

Still, more than 16,000 subscribers pay from $42.25 for 13 weeks to $152.10 per year for the privilege of getting *The New Mexican* on their doorstep every morning. Many will tell you that "Pasatiempo," the newspaper's Friday arts and entertainment section, alone is worth the subscription price. "Pasatiempo" (pastime in Spanish) contains comprehensive, informative, and entertaining sections on movies, music, theater, art, dance, and all other manner of diversion in and around Santa Fe for the upcoming week. It features primarily local reviewers who are knowledgeable in their fields and give the skinny on what's good and what's not.

Other weekly sections include Monday's "El Nuevo Mexicano," an all-Spanish news feature page; "Taste," the Wednesday food section;

"Outdoors" on Thursday; Saturday's "Teen Page;" and "¿Que Pasa?," a day-by-day calendar of free and non-profit events and meetings that accompanies the usual array of Sunday sections. The Sunday *New Mexican* is a must-have for jobs and rentals in the Santa Fe area.

Weeklies

Crosswinds
3701 San Mateo Blvd. NE, Ste. J, Albuquerque
• **(505) 883-4750**

Originally based out of Santa Fe, *Crosswinds* started out 11 years ago as a progressive alternative monthly that focused on the environment and what then-publisher Stephen Kress called the "cutting edge of consciousness." Despite dogged attempts, Kress couldn't shake the community's perception of *Crosswinds* as a new-age newspaper.

Kress sold *Crosswinds* in 1996 to publisher Steve Lawrence, a former editor at Forbes and the *Financial Times of Canada*, who moved the paper to Albuquerque. While it remains a progressive, alternative newspaper, *Crosswinds* has taken a distinct turn in the direction of investigative journalism.

Crosswinds distributes 25,000 copies a week throughout Albuquerque and northern New Mexico, including 6,000 in Santa Fe alone. The paper is free at newsstands. Subscriptions cost $80 per year.

Santa Fe Reporter
132 E. Marcy St.
• **(505) 988-5541**

No doubt, the first issue of the *Santa Fe Reporter* on June 26, 1974, gave the local hometown daily, *The Santa Fe New Mexican*, the willies. Grown fat and lazy from lack of any real competition—the *Reporter's* predecessor, the *Santa Fe News*, was primarily a "shopper" and didn't pose much of a threat—*The New Mexican* now had to deal with the new kid on the block, who was lean and hungry. Founding publishers Dick McCord, a former *Newsday* reporter, and Laurel Knowles, a writer for *Women's Wear Daily*, were ready to kick butt. And kick butt they did in the very first issue with a scoop on commercial flights between Santa Fe and Denver. A mere weekly, and a free one at that, the *Reporter* would beat *The New Mexican* on other occasions over the next two decades on local news and investigative stories.

Under its second publisher—Rockefeller

heiress Hope Aldrich, a former *Newsday* reporter and a staff writer for the *Reporter* who bought the paper in 1988—the alternative weekly focused on issue reporting, publishing the occasional investigative pieces. It tended, however, to be a mite bit obsequious to a City Hall swimming in controversy.

In 1997, Aldrich sold the newspaper to the owners of an alternative weekly in Willamette, Oregon. For the first time in its 24-year history, the *Reporter* was in the hands of absentee owners. The new publishers lived up to their promise to put greater emphasis on art coverage. However, the quality and breadth of its news stories have suffered. The *Reporter* distributes about 23,000 papers a week and has an estimated readership of 55,000 to 60,000 a week.

Thrifty Nickel
1722 St. Michael's Drive, Suite D
• **(505) 473-4111, (800) 382-6330**
This free weekly is a favorite among Santa Fe's workday lunch crowd, especially lone diners who thumb through it while downing green chile cheeseburgers or chicken enchiladas with red chile. The *Thrifty Nickel* is a hefty little tabloid with 24 to 32 pages chock full of mostly local ads trying to sell everything from cockateels to used equipment from nearby Los Alamos National Laboratory (the folks who brought you "The Bomb.") Every once in a while, you'll happen across an ad praising St. Jude or one of the other saints—just another reminder of Santa Fe's Catholic roots.

In addition to merchandise and garage sales, the *Thrifty Nickel* advertises real estate, both sales and rentals; local and national jobs; and, of course, vehicles—lots of them. It also contains a one-page listing of local businesses and services.

Thrifty Nickel distributes 20,000 copies a week to racks throughout Santa Fe County and parts of neighboring Rio Arriba and San Miguel counties. Classifieds run $5 for 10 words at the counter, $6 by phone, and 20 cents for each additional word; display ads start at $8.50 per column inch.

Weekly Alibi
205 Suite A Wellesley Dr. SE, Albuquerque
• **(505) 346-0660**
The *Weekly Alibi*, formerly *NuCity*, is a free alternative weekly that emphasizes Albuquerque politics, culture, and entertainment but isn't afraid to venture into Santa Fe, too. The seven-year-old tabloid appeals to Santa Feans because of its irreverence and strong counterculture voice as well as its in-depth coverage of art and mu-

sic. It also contains an extensive "personals" section toward the back with some truly off-the-wall ads that make for great reading even if you're not in the market. Although it's free, some 500 subscribers pay $80 a year to have the *Alibi* delivered to their door every Wednesday. The remaining 49,500 papers go to newsstands, news racks, coffee shops, bookstores, and other locations throughout metro Albuquerque and Santa Fe.

Monthlies

Prime Time
5015 Prospect Ave. NE, Albuquerque
• **(505) 880-0470**
Calling itself "The Monthly For New Mexicans 50 Plus," *Prime Time* focuses on issues, entertainment and history by, for, and about senior citizens. The free tabloid features nostalgia pieces as well as up-to-the-minute items of particular interest to older people, including AARP news and updates on pertinent state and federal legislation. Prime Time contains regular departments on money; sports and fitness; "Body & Soul," which explores the physical and psychological aspects of aging; plants; pets; personal ads for the senior set; and the arts, including music and books.

Quarterlies

New Mexico Kids! Magazine
6392 Entrada de Milagro
• **(505) 473-5189, (888) 466-5189**
With both children and parents in mind, this free quarterly "magaloid" is geared toward local and visiting families in search of children's activities from Tijeras to Taos—an area that includes Santa Fe, Los Alamos, Albuquerque and points in between. *New Mexico Kids!* got its start in 1992 when publisher Alexis Sabin of Santa Fe discovered that her 4-year-old was one of 25,000 children, including babies and high-schoolers, growing up in a town perceived primarily as an adult playground. It's not that kid stuff doesn't exist here. On the contrary, says Sabin, there's plenty for kids to do in Santa Fe. At that time, however, there wasn't a whole lot of information about what was available and where. So Sabin decided to fill in the void. She compiled what turned out to be a tremendous number of youth activities and published it in a newspaper she called *Santa Fe Kids!* The concept met with so much enthusiasm that she expanded to Albuquerque the fol-

Outside Magazine found a cozy niche for itself near the railyards in downtown Santa Fe.

Photo: Don Strel

lowing year with a sister publication called, you guessed it, *Albuquerque Kids!* The two papers merged in 1997 to become *New Mexico Kids!* with separate Albuquerque and Santa Fe events calendars.

Each issue usually contains at least two feature stories about seasonal events or activities such as fairs and festivals, hiking or camping, or family day trips. It also includes a seasonal calendar of events as well as seasonal directories of camps in the summer issue, schools in the fall, and winter's "It's Party Time!" with places to throw a child's party, buy party supplies or locate storytellers, puppeteers, magicians, photographers, etc. A collection of short articles and announcements called "KIDBITS" appears regularly as do book reviews, community resources, and non-profit organizations.

New Mexico Kids! claims 35,000 readers in Santa Fe and Albuquerque, including a small list of out-of-state subscribers who pay $15 a year.

Tumbleweeds
369 Montezuma Ave. #191
• (505) 984-3171

Tumbleweeds started out in 1991 as a four-page photocopied newsletter called Tot's Hot News. In the intervening nine years, it has matured to a full-grown tabloid of 30 or more pages offering support, information, and resources for parents with kids in their low teens or younger and professionals who work with children. Its advisory board includes an impressive assemblage of child welfare specialists from health, education, legal, and other relevant arenas.

Tumbleweeds includes news and feature articles

written by and for children and includes a comprehensive calendar of child- and parent-oriented events. You can pick up Tumbleweeds free throughout Santa Fe and nearby Española and Los Alamos. Paid subscriptions run $10 a year.

Irregular Circulation

Puntos de Vista
702 Felipe Place
• (505) 982-4083

Puntos de Vista—Spanish for "Points of View"—is a free, grassroots publication which describes itself as a "community-advocacy newsletter that carries important information hard to find elsewhere." It first appeared in 1989 when editor and publisher Joan Chernock churned out 300 copies of a one-page flyer alerting her neighbors about a contaminated public well in their west side neighborhood. Since that time, the bilingual newsletter has grown—to 24 pages at times, many of them written by readers—with a regional distribution of up to 25,000 copies. *Puntos de Vista* appears erratically—"whenever we have enough money," says Chernock, who has put out as many as four issues a year and, in leaner times, as few as one.

Magazines

Countermeasures: A Magazine of Poetry and Ideas
College of Santa Fe
1600 St. Michael's Dr.
• (505) 473-6205

Countermeasures is the literary magazine of the College of Santa Fe's creative writing program, As its subtitle implies, the biannual periodical focuses on poetry. But it's not simply a magazine of poems. It's a magazine about poems as well as poets, both new and established. A critical journal, *Countermeasures* happily takes on such issues as postmodernism, deconstruction, the juncture of science and poetry, and other esoteric topics. Nor is it afraid to knock off the pedestal the likes of William Carlos Williams, Frank O'Hara, and other icons of poetry. *Countermeasures* costs $2.50 per issue, $5 for an annual subscription.

DESIGNER/builder
2405 Maclovia Lane
• (505) 471-4549

Officially subtitled "A Journal of the Human Environment"—and, unofficially, "Architecture's More Than a Pretty Face"—*DESIGNER/builder* started locally in 1994 with an emphasis on Santa Fe. It has since gone international, raising design and building issues around the globe, from the Third World to the First World, and describing all manner of architecture, from mud floors to high-rise buildings. Among the topics *DESIGNER/builder* discusses are cultural issues affecting architecture (and vice versa); urban landscapes; social spaces(i.e., malls, parks, streets, and other places where people congregate); alternative building materials and technologies; affordable housing; architectural history; and criticism.

Never shy of controversy, *DESIGNER/builder* has run stories deconstructing Nazi architecture, including concentration camps; describing a "vertical village" in Manhattan of Senegalese nationals trying to preserve their culture in a completely foreign landscape by taking over a high-rise and living in it as they would in their villages back home; and discussing a program in which prison convicts create city gardens in San Francisco that supply produce to local restaurants.

Many of the articles featured in *DESIGNER/builder* come from other magazines à lá Utne Reader. The husband and wife team of Kingsley and Jerilou Hammett, publisher and managing editor, respectively, write the rest. *DESIGNER/builder* costs $2.50 at newsstands; $28 for a 12-month subscription.

El Palacio
113 Lincoln Ave.
• (505) 476-5055

El Palacio: The Museum of New Mexico Magazine, is the oldest museum publication in the United States. What started out 87 years ago as a weekly pamphlet about the size of one's hand is today a four-color glossy showpiece for the state's museum system: the Palace of the Governors, Museum of Indian Arts & Culture, Laboratory of Anthropology, Museum of International Folk Art, Museum of Fine Arts—all in Santa Fe—and five state monuments. Taking its lead from the museums it represents, *El Palacio* (The Palace) covers New Mexico history, culture, art, and anthropology with lively articles accompanied by striking photos and graphics. It's also a darned good substitute, both visually and textually, for those who can't attend museum exhibits or events in person.

An oddly shaped magazine—10¾" by 8¾"—printed on beautiful stock, *El Palacio* practically jumps out at you on the newsstand. Only 12 years ago, it was a staid, black and white

KUNM-FM

Go into anyone's home or car in Santa Fe and check the pre-tuned stations on their stereo. Chances are pretty good they'll have their first or second button set to 89.9 FM. That's the home in Santa Fe for KUNM, the state's largest volunteer-operated public radio station and certainly the most diverse.

Broadcasting day and night from the campus of the University of New Mexico in Albuquerque, KUNM provides news, talk, and every kind of music imaginable. Its goal is to satisfy a broad spectrum of listeners in a state that's home to New Agers and rednecks, liberals and reactionaries, sophisticates and simple folk, and everything in between.

For that very reason, you'll hear griping from all corners about how KUNM is too progressive or not progressive enough, that it has to much talk or too little, that it plays too much classical music and not enough rock, jazz, folk—pick a genre—or vice versa. What no one complains about, however, is the absence—almost—of commercials. But there's a price to pay for that, too: membership.

Twice a year, KUNM holds a weeklong on-the-air fundraising drive to raise enough money to keep up its eclectic programming. An annual membership

costs a minimum of $40 a year for the general public, $20 a year for students, seniors, and low-income listeners, though it will happily take whatever listeners can afford, be it $10 or $1,000. Members get KUNM's monthly program guide, "Zounds," which includes a day-by-day listing of on-air events as well as a detailed description of its regularly scheduled programs and times.

Even a cursory glance at the program listings makes it clear that KUNM offers something for everyone:

News hounds can tune in Monday through Friday from 5, to 8:30 AM, to hear in-depth news and features on "Morning Edition" and again from 5:30, to 7 PM, for "All Things Considered"—both award winning news magazines from National Public Radio. For local news, tune in at 5 PM, Monday through Friday for the 30-minute "KUNM Evening Report." The station also gives news junkies a weekend fix with NPR's "Weekend Edition," airing 6 AM on Saturday and Sundays at 9 AM.

There's even news on the news Tuesdays at 8:30 AM, with "Counterspin," a critique on the week's stories hosted by Fairness and Accuracy in Reporting (FAIR), a national media watch group.

Musically, KUNM has the widest offering of any station in New Mexico. Its repertoire includes blues, bluegrass, Cajun, classical, country music, folk, gospel, heavy metal, hip-hop, jazz,

Jim Bailey and Joan LaBabara are among KUNM's staff.

Photo: Courtesy of KUNM

(Continued on next page)

MEDIA

Native American music, new rock, oldies, reggae, salsa, Tejano, and world beat—whew!—to give just a partial list. You can tune in 24 hours a day, seven days a week and rarely, if ever, hear the same thing twice—except, of course, the news.

DJs for the local music programs—which includes all but NPR's weekday classical music show, "Performance Today"—are volunteers who truly know and love the music they play. As non-professionals, few affect the classic, suavecito radio voice that commercial stations require, though the local newscasters, most of them UNM students, could do with a little more of that polish.

KUNM features a variety of Hispanic programs including "Latino USA," a half-hour English-language radio journal of Hispanic news and culture Mondays at 8:30 AM. A Latin-American "free-form" show called "Raices," plays all genres of Hispanic music at 2 PM on Saturdays and 7 PM on Mondays; and Friday night's "Salsa Sabrosa," three hours of Afro-Caribbean music from Puerto Rico, Cuba, the Dominican Republic, etc. starting at 7 PM.

The station also airs a number of programs for and about Native Americans such as "National Native News" weekdays at 5:25 PM, five minutes of news and issues affecting American Indians; "Native America Calling," a live call-in show weekdays at 11 AM; and "Singing Wire," a Sunday afternoon program featuring Native American music from the traditional to country and western, rock and roll to folk.

The programs mentioned here are only a partial listing of KUNM's offerings. For more information, call the business office at (505) 277-4806. After hours, call the request line at (505) 277-5615 for information about whatever program is airing at that time.

MEDIA

scholarly journal read almost exclusively by museum members and a few hundred academics and professionals. After suspending publication for about eight months, the magazine re-appeared in the spring of 1991 with a cleaner, slightly more colorful format. By the very next issue—the first in its history to incorporate outside advertising—*El Palacio* had metamorphosed into a full color magazine on the art and culture, history and lore of the Southwest, winning an honorary mention for design from the American Association of Museums. Since that time, the magazine has once again narrowed its focus to New Mexico rather than the entire southwestern region, garnering a 1995 AAM honorary mention in the process.

El Palacio publishes twice each year with an average run of 10,000 issues. Subscriptions are free for the Museum of New Mexico's approximately 6,100 members. Others pay $8.95 for a year's subscription or $5.95 per issue at any of the state museums and select newsstands and bookstores.

La Herencia
P.O. Box 22576, Santa Fe, NM 87504
• (505) 474-2800

Dedicated to the preservation of Hispanic culture, *La Herencia*—"Heritage"—will turn seven in spring 2001. In that short time it has carved out a niche for itself, primarily among middle class, highly assimilated Hispanics. "We speak perfect English but have a real affinity to our culture and language," explains founding editor and publisher Ana Pacheco. The oversized, black-and-white quarterly describes itself as "documenting history on the Camino Real." Indeed, many of its articles are by historians from New Mexico and elsewhere in the Southwest. *La Herencia* also highlights current issues and trends that directly affect Hispanics in New Mexico, though newcomers and visitors would do well to read *La Herencia* to learn more about the history and culture of the region, home to the oldest continuous Spanish population in the United States. The magazine features oral history, literature, book reviews, recipes, poetry, myths, and folklore accompanied by documentary photographs and illustrations.

La Herencia distributes 40,000 copies each quarter throughout northern New Mexico and Albuquerque. You can get it free at newsstands or, for $19.99, mailed to your door.

localflavor
223 N. Guadalupe St., No. 442
• (505) 988-7560

In a town as obsessed with food as Santa Fe, it's appropriate that there be a magazine here devoted to New Mexican fare and other types of cuisine. localflavor fills that niche, "explor(ing) the world of food and wine from ground to plate."

The oversized black and white magazine comes out six times a year filled with articles and photos profiling chefs throughout New Mexico, though it tends to focus on its home base of Santa Fe. localflavor also features first -person prose on food and cooking, recipes, cooking techniques, a wine section and dispatches from around the state. localflavor is free at newsstands and street boxes; subscriptions run $24 a year.

Mothering
649 Harkle Rd., Ste. F
• (505) 984-8116, (800) 984-8116

Read in more than 65 countries, this 24-year-old bi-monthly is a progressive parenting magazine that addresses contemporary health, personal, environmental, medical, and lifestyle issues affecting today's families. Articles range in tone from practical to philosophical on such topics as circumcision, midwifery, home birth, and home schooling, organic food, alternative and traditional health care, and home businesses, to name just a few. It also features reviews of books, music, films, and videos. Subscriptions run $18.95 in the United States. Single issues cost $5.95 at the newsstand.

New Mexico Business Journal
420 Central Ave. SW, Albuquerque
• (505) 243-3444

New Mexico Business Journal, founded in 1976, is a good-looking monthly that covers business news in and around New Mexico. It counts more than 78,000 readers in New Mexico, West Texas and throughout the Southwest. In addition to business-oriented features stories, each issue of *New Mexico Business Journal* contains one or more annual community profiles—in-depth looks with an eye toward business at cities and counties throughout the state—as well as observations from the publisher; a small business section and business news briefs under "The Beat: Whispers and Tidbits."

New Mexico Business Journal prints about 22,000 magazines a month; 20,000 go to subscribers, including 4,000 in Santa Fe. Subscriptions cost $24 a year, $42 for two years, $60 for three years. The cover price for a single issue is $3.50.

New Mexico Magazine
Lew Wallace Bldg., 495 Old Santa Fe Tr.
• (505) 827-7447

First published in 1923 as the *Highway Journal, New Mexico Magazine* started out as a high quality, internal newsletter of the state Highway Department to promote "interest in good roads through the state" and "advertise to the people of the United States the attractions of New Mexico as a playground, and its possibilities as a place of location and business."

Little did editor Ray W. Bennett realize to what extent New Mexico would indeed turn into a playground, nor could he have imagined at the time the beautiful and highly popular magazine his little newsletter would become. The first metamorphosis occurred in 1931, when *Highway Journal* merged with the Game and Fish Department's magazine, *The Conservationist* to become *New Mexico: The Sunshine State's Recreational and Highway Magazine*. Six years later, the publication took on its current name and style, becoming the first official state magazine in the nation with a format that would be emulated many times over.

New Mexico Magazine specializes in travel and historical features with regular sections on regional cuisine, literature, art, and culture and high quality color photographs and illustrations. The magazine's list of contributing authors, photographers, and illustrators reads like a "Who's Who" of major New Mexican writers and artists.

New Mexico Magazine has a paid circulation of more than 118,000 with an estimated readership of 500,000. Subscribers pay $23.95 for 12 issues. The newsstand price is $3.95.

Outside
400 Market St.
• (505) 989-7100, (505) 678-1131

When *Outside* magazine decided to move its headquarters from Chicago to Santa Fe in 1994, it received less than an open-armed welcome. First, the magazine met with loud opposition to locating its offices on the road leading to the Santa Fe Ski Area. So publisher Larry Burke built a showcase office building near downtown's upscale Sanbusco Center. Then he caught flack for not hiring enough locals. And just last year, an ex-employee sued the magazine for civil rights violations. *Outside* prevailed in the lawsuit, but at the cost of more negative publicity, not to mention legal fees.

Still, none of this seems to have hurt *Outside's* circulation which, at 575,000, is up by 75,000 since the magazine came to Santa Fe in 1994. It has an estimated readership of 1.7 million. *Outside* is the largest publication based out of "The City Different."

As its name implies, *Outside* covers active outdoor sports such as hiking, climbing, kayaking, and cycling (to name just a few) as well as travel, people, politics, art, and outdoors-y literature. In addition to its regular monthly magazine, *Outside* publishes two special issues a year—a buying guide for outdoor gear and a travel guide. A 12-month subscription runs $18; special issues are extra. The newsstand price is $3.95.

Focus/Santa Fe
Box 251, Glorieta
• (505) 757-6661

Subtitled "A Select Look at Santa Fe Arts, Crafts, Tastes and Styles," *Focus/Santa Fe* is a five-times-a-year glossy showcasing the local art scene. Each issue is chock full of beautifully photographed artwork and crafts on display at some of Santa Fe's finer galleries. A dozen or so brightly written, four-page profiles of the featured artists and their work—or sometimes a featured gallery and its owner(s)—accompany the photos. Not coincidentally, every article corresponds to a full-page color ad located either toward the front or back of the magazine. *Focus/Santa Fe* is based out of Glorieta—a small, historic village 18 miles southeast of Santa Fe where Anne and Hal Mayer started the magazine in 1986. You can find *Focus/Santa Fe* in most downtown hotels and galleries. Subcriptions cost $20 a year. Single issues cost $3.

Santa Fean
444 Galisteo St.
• (505) 983-1444

After a brief hiatus covering politics and local personalities, the 28-year-old *Santa Fean* has returned to its roots as a lifestyle magazine "celebrating the best of the west," as its subtitle proclaims. The magazine focuses on art, first and foremost, as well as entertainment, home design, fashion, dining, and always some of Santa Fe's fascinating history. The *Santa Fean* also features a day-by-day calendar of events every month and regular columns such as "Tales of the City Different"—tidbits on "personalities, oddities, and hit and run news," as the magazine describes it. Ubiquitous in hotel rooms in northern New Mexico and art galleries throughout the state, the glossy monthly has attracted a sizable out-of-state readership with 80 percent of its subscriptions outside New Mexico. The cover price is $3.95, but hotel guests can pick them up for free in their rooms. A one-year subscription costs $19.97. The Santa Fean's total circulation runs close to 40,000.

THE magazine
1208-A Mercantile Rd.
• (505) 424-7641

When Judith Wolf and Guy Cross moved to Santa Fe in 1988, they were amazed to discover that what is reputedly the third largest art market in the country had no local magazine dedicated to the arts. Sure, there was good old "Pasatiempo," a Friday insert in the *Santa Fe New Mexican* that serves as Santa Fe's what's-happening bible. But they considered "Pasatiempo" primarily a preview vehicle. What Santa Fe needed, they felt, was a critical voice.

As Cross puts it, "We saw a niche and we sold it." That was six years ago. Since then, *THE magazine* has taken off like a rocket with readership all over the United States. It even has a handful of international subscribers in places as far flung as Thailand, Japan, South America, Australia, and London. Total circulation runs 20,000 a month.

Unlike most art magazines, *THE* is neither glossy nor color. Yet its matte black and white format lends it an air of simple sophistication – not unlike a basic black dress with pearls. At 10 ¾ X 13 ¼, it's also a large magazine—one that stands out on a coffee table. But *THE* is more than just a pretty face. It covers the Santa Fe art scene with articles, reviews, and a listing of exhibits and openings.

Free for the taking in Santa Fe, *THE* costs $40 for a yearlong subscription, $75 for two years.

3D Artist
P.O. Box 4787
• (505) 424-8945

3D Artist is a locally produced glossy magazine "dedicated to all whose artful occupations and avocations make use of affordable desktop 3D graphics," as its web site proclaims. Written by its readers, *3D's* target audience is freelance artists who make—or aspire to make—a living with computer graphics. The magazine describes itself as "the original 3D how-to publication" and takes credit for inventing the term "3D Artist" as well as "desktop cinematography." Founded in 1991, *3D Artist* began life as a newsletter, upgrading two years later to magazine format and, in 1994, to full color. *3D Artist* puts out five issues a year. Annual subscriptions cost $25 by first class mail, $19 for bulk mail. The newsstand price is $6.

Radio

For a state with only 1.8 million residents and a radio market ranked 235 out of a possible 276, New Mexico's airwaves carry a surprisingly eclectic collection of sounds that come to Santa Fe via 30 or so radio stations, depending on the area, most of them from Albuquerque.

On the music front, listeners can tune in to anything from rap to rock, jazz to Jewish Klezmer music, oldies to opera, classical to Christian music—the list goes on and on. If news/talk is your preference, you can choose between left-leaning National Public Radio and conservative poster boy Rush Limbaugh.

Like elsewhere in the country, however, New Mexico's radio options are becoming increasingly limited as chains buy out independent stations and homogenize the musical mix. Still, many stations have managed to avoid the Top 40 abyss that seems to be sucking in the larger markets.

Oh, sure, you'll hear the occasional complaint among country music fans about the notable—and surprising—absence of classic country music stations in the Santa Fe/Albuquerque area; you have to tune into KANW's (89.1 FM) Saturday night classic country show from 10 PM to 2 AM to catch such old-timers as Johnny Cash, Patsy Cline, Loretta Lynn, or Hank Williams, for example. Still, it's the rare Santa Fean who doesn't appreciate the wide range of radio choices for such a small market.

Adult Nostalgic

KTRC 1400 AM, music of the '40s, '50s, and '60s. (Santa Fe)

KIVA 1310 AM, big band, crooners. (Albuquerque)

Christian

KFLQ 91.5 FM, music, news/talk. (Albuquerque)

KKIM 1000 AM, news/talk. (Albuquerque)

KLYT 88.3 FM, Christian hit radio—all rock, some news. (Albuquerque)

Classical

KANW 89.1 FM, variable programming includes classical. (Albuquerque)

KHFM 96.3/96.7FM, all music. (Albuquerque)

KSFR 90.7 FM, variable programming includes classical. (Santa Fe)

KUNM 89.9 FM, variable programming includes classical. (Albuquerque) (See our close-up in this chapter).

Community

KRSN 1490 AM, 23 hours of news/talk/information, one hour daily jazz and/or classical from 5 to 6 PM. (Los Alamos)

KSFR 90.7 FM, local community radio, alternative programming includes blues, classical, jazz, opera, Spanish music, news, talk, and information. (Santa Fe)

KUNM 89.9 FM, public radio includes community programming. (Albuquerque)

Country

KRST 92.3 FM, new country, morning and evening drive-time news, weather, traffic. (Albuquerque)

KTBL 103.3 FM, country favorites. (Albuquerque)

KYBR 92.9 FM, new country, news. (Española)

Jazz

KANW 89.1 FM, variable programming includes jazz. (Albuquerque)

M,- KSFR 90.7 FM, variable programming includes jazz. (Santa Fe)

KUNM 89.9 FM, variable programming includes jazz. (Albuquerque)

News/Talk

KANW 89.1 FM, variable programming includes Public Radio International and National Public Radio. (Albuquerque)

KKOB 770 AM, news/talk—local and syndicated programs. (Albuquerque)

KRSN 1490 AM, news/talk, one hour daily of light jazz. (Los Alamos)

KUNM 89.9-FM, variable programming includes National Public Radio, Pacifica News, and Public Radio International. (Albuquerque)

KVSF 1260 AM, morning news/talk, sports. (Santa Fe)

KSVA 610 AM, personal achievement and motivational programming. (Albuquerque)

Public Radio

KANW 89.1 FM, Public Radio International, National Public Radio, variable programming includes classical music, jazz, New Mexico music, Native American programming, news, and talk shows. (Albuquerque)

KSFR 90.7 FM, local public radio, alternative format includesg blues, classical, jazz, opera, Spanish music, and news/talk/information. (Santa Fe)

KUNM 89.9.FM, National Public Radio, alternative programming. (Albuquerque)

Rock

KABG 98.5 FM, oldies—'60s and '70s. (Albuquerque)

KBAC 98.1 FM, progressive music format includes alternative rock, reggae, world

MEDIA

beat, local music and live studio appearances by visiting musicians. (Santa Fe)

KBOM 106.7 FM, oldies—'50s, '60s, '70s. (Santa Fe)

KIOT 102.5 FM, classic rock—'60s, '70s, and '80s. (Albuquerque)

KKOB 93.3 FM, pop adult contemporary. (Albuquerque)

KKSS 97.3 FM, contemporary hits, urban. (Albuquerque)

KLSK 104.1/100.9 FM, classic rock—'60s, '70s, and '80s. (Albuquerque)

KMGA 99.5 FM, light rock. (Albuquerque)

KPEK 100.3 FM, adult contemporary. (Albuquerque)

KSFQ 101.1 FM, oldies—'70s, '80s. (Los Alamos)

KTEG 107.9 FM, alternative rock. (Albuquerque)

KUNM 89.9.FM, alternative programming includes rock. (Albuquerque)

KZKL 101.7 FM, oldies—'50s, '60s. (Albuquerque)

KZRR 94.1 FM, classic rock. (Albuquerque)

Spanish

KANW 89.1 FM, bilingual, alternative programming includes New Mexico music, classical, jazz, Native American programming, news/talk. (Albuquerque)

KARS 860 AM, country/Spanish music, bilingual news/talk. (Albuquerque)

KDCE 950 AM, Spanish language, music, news, talk. (Española)

KEXT 104.7 FM, Spanish language, music. (Albuquerque)

KLVO 97.7 FM, Spanish language, music. (Albuquerque)

KRZY 1450 AM, Spanish language, music, news, traffic. (Albuquerque)

KSWV 810 AM, bilingual, music, news, weather, sports. (Santa Fe)

KXKS 1190 AM, all Spanish, regional music, hourly news. (Albuquerque)

KZRY 105.9/106.3 FM, Spanish language. (Albuquerque)

Sports

KNML 1050 AM, 24-hour sports. (Albuquerque)

KVSF 1260 AM, sports, morning news/talk. (Santa Fe)

Television

As with radio, Santa Fe has few television stations of its own; the majority of network stations come from Albuquerque, the state's largest city. Combining network television with cable, Santa Fe has an enviable choice of stations—50 in all including premium and Pay-Per-View stations. TCI Cablevision of Santa Fe, 2534 Camino Entrada, (505) 438-2600, is the primary cable provider for Santa Fe County. Surrounding areas—Eldorado, Tesuque and South Santa Fe, for example—have their own cable systems with different channels. Check The Santa Fe New Mexican for details.

Network channels:

Ch. 2 – KASA-TV (Fox)
Ch. 4 – KOB (NBC)
Ch. 5 – KNME (PBS)
Ch. 7 – KOAT (ABC)
Ch. 8 – KLUZ (Univision - Spanish variety)
Ch. 11 – KCHF (Christian)
Ch. 13 – KRQE (CBS)
Ch. 32 – KAZQ (Independent)
Ch. 50 – KASY (UPN)

Worship and Spirituality

"I am always most religious upon a sunshiny day . . . "

Lord Byron wrote those words just a few years before he died in 1824 at age 36. He might have been less glib (and perhaps have lived longer) had he experienced Santa Fe, where for 300 days out of the year the sun shines gloriously down across the brooding, protective Sangre de Cristo—"Blood of Christ"—mountain range and the Rio Grande Valley below.

Indeed, it's no accident that this high desert land of magnificent natural beauty, crystal clean air and spectacular sunshine has for centuries drawn spiritual seekers and inspired religious awe among followers of all faiths. From the ancient Anasazi and Athapascan—respective forebears of the region's Pueblo Indians and Navajo and Apache tribes, for whom the land they call "ground of the dancing sun" remains sacred— to today's New Age adherents, who combine ancient mysticism with modern thought, northern New Mexico beckons. For what is religion if not the spiritual cement that binds humankind to nature and supernature—what some call "God" and others call "Yahweh," "Allah," "Krishna" or simply "higher power."

The late Fray Angélico Chávez—a Franciscan priest, poet, and author from northern New Mexico who wrote some two dozen books about his homeland and the *anima hispanica* (Hispanic soul)—understood this clearly when he likened New Mexico to Palestine in both topography and climate. "New Mexican landscape . . . is the holy land," Chávez wrote in his compelling 1974 book, My Penitente Land. He called the Rio Grande New Mexico's Jordan River and Santa Fe its Jerusalem. He similarly compared Palestine to Spain, the land from which the first European settlers in what would become New Mexico arrived nearly 450 years ago. "Grazing lands all and most alike in their physical aspects," Chávez wrote, adding that they "share a distinctive underlying human mystique born of that very type of arid landscape." Thus both the *pobladores* (settlers) sanctioned by the Spanish crown, whose Catholicism was as much a part of their *anima hispanica* as their Spanish roots, and the Jews who fled the Spanish Inquisition to the New World in search of religious freedom, sensed a comfortable familiarity in this strange new land they called "Nuevomejico," whose appearance and clime approximated not only the home they recently left, but also the ancient biblical soil of their common ancestors.

An ocean and a continent away from the watchful eyes of the inquisitorial Spanish government, the colonists and the *conversos*—those Spanish Jews who converted to Catholicism rather than face exile, many of whom continued practicing Judaism in secret—lived in relative peace with each other and the natives they found in New Mexico. They had more imminent worries than religious differences, namely survival in the wilderness and a common enemy in the Plains Indians.

This atmosphere of religious tolerance extended to Jews, but not necessarily to the pueblos. Indians occasionally fell victim to fanatical friars and fearful colonists who suspected witchcraft in such things as fetishes and nature-bound rituals. Despite orders from the homeland to convert the Indians by peaceful means (Spain didn't want to repeat in New Mexico the atrocities Pizarro and Cortés respectively visited upon the Incas in Peru and the Aztecs in Mexico), overzealous missionaries and their followers destroyed Indian kivas (sacred underground ceremonial rooms), persecuted medicine men, and forced the natives into indentured servitude in exchange for teaching them Christianity.

Tired of their spiritual and virtual subordination to the Spaniards' Catholic chauvinism, the Indians made a number of unsuccessful attempts to expel the intruders. It wasn't until the Pueblo Revolt of 1680 that they succeeded. They overthrew their colonizers, burned churches, killed priests, and forced the Spanish colonial government to flee.

Twelve years later Spain returned for the "reconquest." This time, however, the monarchy resolved to colonize the area without conflict and to live in peaceful co-existence with the natives and their religion. Thus began a new era of tolerance that, for the better part of the past 300 years, has remained a constant in Santa Fe and northern New Mexico.

That's not to say tensions didn't exist. The Catholic Church, firmly entrenched in New Mexico, vigorously opposed the Protestant incursion that arrived in the form of missionaries from points east on the Santa Fe Trail after the U.S. invasion and conquest of 1846. While hostilities rarely erupted in violence, they came out in other ways. It was not unheard of for Catholic clergymen to drown out Protestant sermons by ringing their church bells as loudly as possible.

Relations between Catholics and Protestants became still more strained with the arrival in 1850 of Jean Baptiste Lamy, a French priest whom the pope named as Santa Fe's first bishop. Lamy attempted to suppress the Protestant movement by subtle means, including wedding local government to the Catholic Church; replacing Hispanic clergy with less tolerant French and Italian priests; sheltering the local Hispanic and Indian population from the Protestant influence of Americans, who were arriving in wagonloads on the Santa Fe Trail; and by making outcasts of Protestant preachers and their converts.

INSIDERS' TIP

President Lyndon Baines Johnson married Claudia "Lady Bird" Taylor at St. John's United Methodist Church in Santa Fe, where Lady Bird's brother was a member.

New Mexico's first Protestant missionary, a Northern Baptist preacher named Hiram Walter Read, arrived in 1849—three years after the U.S. conquered New Mexico during the Mexican-American War (see history chapter) and one year before it became an American territory. Methodist, Presbyterian, and Episcopalian missionaries arrived on the heels of the Baptists. Meanwhile American Jews, many of them German immigrants, predated the Baptists by six years. Documents place Albert Speyers, a Jewish trader from New York, on the Santa Fe Trail as early as 1843. Unlike the Protestants, however, the Jews came not on a religious mission, but an economic one. In fact, Santa Fe had no synagogue until 1952—76 years after New Mexico's first recorded bar mitzvah.

It wasn't until early in the 20th century that the next wave of pilgrims came to northern New Mexico. But they differed dramatically from their predecessors in that they came not to spread religion, but to find it. These were the artists, writers and thinkers of the East Coast who left the decadence and materialism of their own culture for what they felt was the purity and mysticism of New Mexico. It's largely the legacy of this generation—one that included the likes of Georgia O'Keeffe, D. H. Lawrence, and Mabel Dodge Luhan—which lends Santa Fe a mystique that has since achieved mythological proportions. However patronizing, they idealized the place, inadvertently advertising it through their artwork and their prose and luring others—artists and free thinkers in the early part of the century, hippies and New Age practitioners in recent generations.

Today, Santa Fe is home to more than 50 active Christian churches; two synagogues, and five Jewish congregations; two Buddhist temples and several meditation centers; and dozens of other non-denominational and unaffiliated spiritual centers of every bent.

There's no doubt, however, that Santa Fe is first and foremost a Catholic town, an identity so profound that it is an unconscious part of daily life here. Public prayers open government meetings at City Hall, the County Courthouse, and the state Legislature. Prayers even preceded sporting events at public schools until a 1997 legal challenge put an end to the practice, causing an uproar among students and parents. You'll still hear religion taught in some classrooms, though it's not an official part of the curriculum. It might be, however, were it left up to the state Board of Education, which in 1996 attracted national attention after voting to remove evolution as a school requirement to make way for teaching creationism as described in the Bible. But none of this is to the exclusion of other belief systems. Just open the Yellow Pages to "religion" and you'll find a mind-boggling array of choices. Or look in the religion page of Saturday's "The New Mexican" for a large listing of spiritual groups along with addresses and phone numbers.

What follows is a small sampling of what Santa Fe has to offer in the spiritual realm. Please note that entries in this chapter are for practicing groups only. For church museums and relics, please look under "Churches" in the Attractions chapter.

Alaya

Alaya is a Santa Fe-based spiritual organization founded in 1987 by a Missouri-born man now called Ishvara. Raised as a fundamentalist Christian, Ishvara professes experiencing a profound transcendental metamorphosis in Lincoln, Oregon, where he had been operating a metaphysical bookstore for 10 years. That's when he founded "Shambhala," Alaya's original name. The group changed its name in 1997 to avoid confusion with other organizations of the same name. Alaya honors many of the doctrines of conventional religions while remaining free of their structures. The group describes itself as "dedicated to the ongoing awakening of the highest consciousness, as brought forth by Ishvara." Ishvara moved to Santa Fe in 1995, bringing a number of his followers with him. The core group consists of about 15 members.

Baha'i Faith

The local Baha'i community consists of about 80 people throughout Santa Fe County who follow the teachings of the religion's founder, Baha'u'llah (Glory of God). They believe in the spiritual unity of humankind; that while the religions of the world are many, their god is one. They advocate simplicity and clarity, world peace, equality of men and women, universal education, and an international language and government. They also strive to eliminate extreme wealth and poverty as well as prejudice of all kinds. In company with fellow believers around the world, Santa Fe Baha'is hold feasts every 19 days—the length of the Baha'i "month"—as well as celebrations or special observances on holy days and informal "firesides"—informational meetings open to the public—in private homes several times a month, often followed by a meal.

Buddhist

Santa Fe Buddhists are numerous and varied, some following Japanese lineage, others Vietnamese, and still others Tibetan Buddhism. The county is home to a number of beautiful Buddhist centers, each as unique as the individuals they attract. Upaya campus, located on Santa Fe's rustically fashionable—and fashionably expensive—east side, offers a magnificent view of the Sangre de Cristo Mountains and five traditional adobe buildings that reflect both its Southwestern and Asian roots. Among them is Cerro Gordo ("Fat Hill") Temple, once the site of the first Tibetan stupa (temple) in the United States. The temple hosts several Buddhist groups who use the simple and beautiful premises for regularly scheduled meditation practice and special events with visiting teachers. The largest and most well established group is Upaya— Sanskrit for "skillful means" or "the craft of compassion." Founded in 1990 by renowned Soto priest, teacher, and author Joan Halifax Roshi, Upaya, (505) 986-8518,offers Zen training and meditation retreats. It also gives courses and retreats on "engaged spirituality" and contemplative care of the dying (see "The Partners Program" in the Retirement chapter—a subject on which the Roshi has written extensively. The temple is on the south side of Cerro Gordo Road— a steep, winding, and extremely narrow street named for the turtle-shaped mountain to the north. Below the temple runs the Santa Fe River—a streamlet, really, except in spring when it gushes with mountain runoff. On Santa Fe's south side, the 69-foot-tall stupa of Kagyu Shenpen Kunchab (KSK) Dharma Center, and especially its 12-foot bronzed spire, provide a stunning contrast to Santa Fe's primarily single-story adobe or adobe-colored architecture. Founded in 1975 by the late meditation master Kalu Rinpoche, KSK is a Tibetan Buddhist center under the guidance of resident Lama (teacher) Karma Dorje, who oversees a similar center in nearby Taos. Begun in 1982 and completed four years later, KSK's temple was built in the classic style of stupas throughout Tibet. Its form is that of an ancient architectural structure called a "caitya," which dates back to 1000 B.C. These shrines often held relics of "enlightened" beings. The blessing post in the Santa Fe spire contains a pearl-like crystal said to have been recovered from the Buddha's cremation. The center regularly sponsors visits by Tibetan Buddhist teachers of all lineages and offers classes in Tibetan art, music and language. Behind the center is Noble Truth Bookstore, which sells literature and other items related to primarily Tibetan Buddhism.

Mountain Cloud Zen Center is a beautiful, remote Buddhist retreat tucked away on 43 acres in the foothills of the Sangre de Cristo Mountains. Its members follow a combination of the Rinzai and Soto schools of Zen Buddhism as practiced by their teacher, Robert Aitken Roshi, who founded the Diamond Sangha in Hawaii. The Santa Fe sangha holds formal sittings several times a week and periodic four- to seven-day "sesshins" (silent retreats) throughout the year in a lovely wooden building that does justice to its stunning, rustic setting. Its large, sunny zendo (meditation room) has windows on three sides and raised wooden platforms upon which sit 24 flat cushions topped by plump round meditation cushions. The indoor corbels supporting the huge wooden ceiling beams (vigas) are carved into lotus flowers; the outdoor corbels into cloud designs inspired by Japanese and Tibetan temples. Beneath the building rests a mandala—a ritualistic geometric design symbolic of the universe—that a member created in the shape of a turtle to signify the Native American concept of "Turtle Island"—the Earth. Vipassana students, who practice a form of Thervada Buddhism found primarily in Southeast Asia, rent space at Mountain Cloud for regularly scheduled meditation sessions.

The newest addition to Santa Fe's growing Buddhist community, Hidden Mountain Center Prajna Zendo, holds weekly meditation sessions in the evening in Eldorado, a sprawling suburb located about 20 miles southeast of Santa Fe. The sangha is a satellite of Hidden Mountain Zen Center in Albuquerque.

Catholic

Independent

The Church of Antioch at Santa Fe is a metaphysically orientated Catholic church whose parent organization was founded in 1959 as part of the centuries-old independent Catholic movement. Named for the city in which followers of Jesus were first called Christians, the Church of Antioch is not part of the Roman Catholic Church, though it looks and sounds much like the Roman Catholic church and honors many of the same traditions. It celebrates the Holy Eucharist, practices the sacraments, and its priests wear vestments and burn incense. But the churches have different apostolic successions—i.e., the true successors of the apostles. The Church of Antioch believes individuals create their own reality and should remain in control of their own lives rather than turn authority over to a religious authority. It teaches that individuals are responsible for saving themselves. The church supports freedom of choice in all aspects of an individual's life, from sexual orientation to abortion. Its leader is a woman, the Most Reverend Meri Louise Spruit.

The 12-year-old Church of Antioch at Santa Fe is the seat of the Diocese of the Southwest, which includes six churches and 14 priests throughout New Mexico, Nevada, Colorado, and Arizona. The local church has been celebrating mass since 1992 in the Loretto Chapel, famous for its "miraculous" spiral staircase (see the Churches

INSIDERS' TIP
Catholicism arrived in New Mexico in 1598 with Don Juan de Oñate, who colonized the region for Spain, making it the first European settlement west of the Mississippi River.

section in our Attractions chapter). About half the church's 100 or so members attend mass on a regular basis at the chapel, which the Roman Catholic Church stopped using as a place of worship because it's no longer consecrated with the blessed Sacraments.

Orthodox

Holy Trinity Orthodox Church is an Eastern Rite church whose diocese was founded in Antioch, the birthplace of Paul and the place where Christians were first called by that name. Orthodox Catholic churches broke from the Roman Catholic church in the 11th Century, when the Roman church insisted on the infallibility of the pope and maintained the supremacy in the Trinity of the Father and Son over the Holy Spirit—in other words, that Jesus is purely divine. Orthodox churches believe what's called the Holy Paradox—that Jesus is both human and divine. This translates to a heavy dose of mysticism in Holy Trinity and other orthodox churches, which commonly are filled with icons and the scent of burning incense. Holy Trinity parish formed in 1996 when its priest, Father John Bethancourt, defected from a local Episcopalian church, taking a quarter of the congregation with him. At first, the new parish comprised only 22 people, but their numbers quickly grew to 35 households. They eventually bought a ranch-style house in Santa Fe's South Capital neighborhood, near a number of other houses of worship, and converted it into a church with a couple of bell towers and an interior richly decorated with the ubiquitous icons of orthodox Catholicism. Mass at Holy Trinity is very ornate and sung and chanted from start to finish.

St. Elias the Prophet Greek Orthodox Church is a beautiful white Byzantine structure so unusual for Santa Fe that it seems to stand out for miles. It was built in 1992 in the Dos Griegos (Two Greeks) development located in Santa Fe County some 15 miles southeast of downtown Santa Fe. The "Two Greeks" for whom the subdivision is named—Alex Constantaras and Frank Carras—donated the land for the church as well as much of the 4,000-square-foot building. Completed in 1992, St. Elias is in the shape of a cruciform and, typical of Byzantine structures, has a dome in the center with a large icon of Christ called the "Pantocrator." As you enter the church, you're faced with a remarkable wall of icons, called an "iconostasti," that divides the main sanctuary from the altar. Services are sung in a mixture of Greek and English. The priest wears ornate vestments and incense burns constantly. About 70 families belong to the parish, which worshipped at churches in town before building its own church. At 7,200 feet altitude, St. Elias is reputedly the highest Greek Orthodox church in the nation—at least according to a Santa Fe mayor, who made a proclamation to that effect.

Roman

At the junction of Canyon Road and Upper Canyon Roads, where the art galleries and fashionable restaurants make way for homes old and new, of varying sizes and values, beautiful Cristo Rey Church provides a haven for those seeking spiritual solace or simply a peaceful break from shopping and gallery hopping. Designed by internationally acclaimed New Mexico architect John Gaw Meem, the church was built in 1939 in traditional New Mexico mission style. Parishioners provided the land and helped make and lay the more than 150,000 adobe bricks—each weighing between 20 and 40 pounds—it took to complete the church. In 1940, only 14 months after construction commenced, the church was dedicated to commemorate the 400th anniversary of Spain's initial foray into New Mexico by explorer Francisco Vasquez de Coronado. Although only 60 years old, Cristo Rey (Christ the King) is considered a historic church primarily because of its architecture and decor rather than its age. It contains a spectacular 238-year-old "reredos" or altar screen, composed of three large pieces of white stone believed to have been quarried some 25 miles northeast of Santa Fe. Unknown artists carved detailed depictions of saints, angels, flowers, human heads, and other decorative and religious motifs in a style similar to that found in Mexican churches. The artists worked for then-Governor Francisco Antonio Marin del Valle, who commissioned the piece for a military chapel in Santa Fe Plaza. Meem chose Cristo Rey's dimensions—the nave alone occupies 5,000 square feet and has 33-foot tall ceilings—and clerestory windows—to create a rarefied atmosphere that would do justice to the

La Conquistadora, who is also known as Our Lady of Reconciliation, is Catholic Santa Fe's best-loved image of the Virgin.

Photo: Russ Young

impressive "reredos." He succeeded. The same motivation inspired the love and dedication parishioners put into its construction. The church's adobe walls range in depth from two to nine feet. Its "vigas" (wooden ceiling beams) and "latillas" (split cedar poles laid between the vigas) come from New Mexico forests, while the carved braces (corbels) supporting the vigas were hand-carved on site. Students from the diocesan Lourdes Trade School in Albuquerque crafted the doors, pews, confessionals, vestment cases and wrought iron light fixtures. Today, Cristo Rey serves the growing population of Santa Fe's east side. Its congregation of about 750 families is primarily a mixture of Hispanics and Anglos—the former mostly long-time residents whose families have been here for generations; the latter relatively recent, and affluent, arrivals—who share a desire for traditional Catholic worship and social values.

In the heart of downtown Santa Fe, just one block east of the Plaza, stands Santa Fe's most recognized landmark —the majestic, Romanesque-style St. Francis Cathedral. Named for the city's patron saint, St. Francis is without a doubt Santa Fe's most imposing church—and certainly its largest with an active parish of 1,700 families. As a cathedral church, St. Francis is the "mother church" for the Archdiocese of Santa Fe, which covers half of New Mexico, from Socorro County north to the Colorado border and east to Oklahoma. All major celebrations, including ordinations to the priesthood, take place at St. Francis Cathedral. Indeed, the cathedral is impressive with its vaulted ceilings and a seating capacity of 1,200, including the Conquistadora and Blessed Sacrament chapels. Construction of the church began in 1869 under the watchful eye of Bishop—later Archbishop—Jean Baptiste Lamy, an influential, aristocratic Jesuit clergyman who presided over New Mexico's Catholic community for 38 years. He made it his personal mission to build a grand cathedral for his diocese, one that would rival the churches he left behind in his native France. Sadly, Lamy never got to see the outcome of his pet project. He died in 1888, seven years before the cathedral's completion. As the seat of the Archdiocese, and the place to which other churches in the diocese look for direction, St. Francis Cathedral is traditional and conservative. It also tends to be a little less personal than other churches in town—and its staff a little crustier—both because of it's size and the revolving door of tourists, sometimes busloads at a time, who drop in on a daily basis. Unfortunately, tourists sometimes forget that the church is a place of meditation and prayer even when it's not being used for services.

Located on the original "Camino Real"—the 2,000-mile "Royal Road" or "King's Highway" from Mexico City to Santa Fe, whose heyday spanned two centuries—"La Iglesia de San Isidro" is truly a parish that serves its community—a low-income, largely Hispanic section of Santa Fe County called the Village of Agua Fría. Young families, many whose kin go back several centuries in Santa Fe, compose a good portion of the congregation. Founded in 1836, La Iglesia de San

Penitentes

Driving along the back roads of northern New Mexico, you're likely to pass many a simple, one room adobe structure with no windows and little external evidence of life. What you're looking at is probably a "morada"—a house of worship used by "penitentes" and that, despite appearances, is teeming with life, but of a spiritual nature.

"Penitentes" are members of the centuries-old "Hermandad de Nuestro Padre Jesus Nazareno"— Brotherhood of Our Father Jesus of Nazarene—a religious fraternity that traces its roots back to a 16th Century nobleman from Seville who was so moved to see pilgrims in Jerusalem carrying heavy crosses along the Via Dolorosa—the route Jesus walked to his crucifixion—that he founded a society to carry on the tradition in Spain.

Present day New Mexican "penitentes" keep the tradition alive while keeping a low profile, as evidenced by their humble "moradas." While not precisely a secret society, they are certainly a reserved one. Their reasons are both reverent and pragmatic. The practice of the "penitente" is one of humility; of subservience to, and demonstrative empathy for, a suffering Christ expressed in prayer, meditation, and physical penance; of community service, whether by feeding the hungry or comforting the dying; of preserving their culture. They wish also to avoid the prurient gaze of the curious and the sensation-seekers, the voyeurs who want to witness the rituals of self-flagellation and the rigors of Holy Week, when "penitentes" re-enact Christ's march to Calvary. Better to rent *The Penitent*, a 1988 movie starring Raul Julia and Armand Assante, which provides an admittedly melodramatic glimpse of the "penitente" society.

This morada, on the grounds of El Rancho de las Golondrinas, is a copy of a morada in Abiquiú. While real moradas are closed to the public, this one is open for touring.

Photo: Russ Young

Isidro was originally built as a chapel. The adobe church is small and humble, seating 175 people as comfortably as can be expected in its 162-year-old pews. With up to 250 people regularly coming to mass, services wind up being "standing room only," with parishioners spilling into the aisles and out the doors. They come out of devotion to their faith and a love for their pastor, Father Franklin Pretto. Father Pretto is also known as the "Salsa Priest" because his salsa band, Pretto & Parranda, regularly performs at nightclubs around town (See our "Nightlife section). To be sure, mass at San Isidro is a wholly different experience than at St. Francis Cathedral. While Father Pretto follows the rubrics, he's very informal, often inviting members of the congregation to participate in the mass, which they do willingly. San Isidro has no formal choir; instead, church members bring guitars and sing. If no one is so inclined during a particular service, Father Pretto will sit at the piano and lead the congregation in song. The only post-Vatican II Catholic congregation in Santa Fe, Santa María de la Paz is without doubt the most progressive of the area's Catholic communities. Though very traditional in its devotion to the Eucharist (Holy Communion), Santa María de la Paz celebrates mass in many non-traditional ways that embrace its multicultural congregation. Every year in October, for example, the church performs a Native American liturgy, inviting representative of New Mexico pueblos to participate in the mass with traditional Indian blessings, drumming, and gifts. It has also celebrated the feast of Our Lady of Guadalupe with a mariachi mass followed by tamales; invited a gospel choir from Albuquerque to sing on Martin Luther King Jr.'s birthday; and honored St. Patrick with Irish jigs and soda bread. Santa María de la Paz takes pride in its outreach programs, which include support groups for divorced and remarried Catholics and for people with AIDS as well as their loved ones and caregivers. The church shares an ecumenical "sister" relationship with two equally progressive houses of worship: St. Bede's Episcopal Church and United Church of the World (see entries below). Its founding pastor, Father Jerome Martinez y Alire, once described the parish as "catholic in the best sense of the word"—i.e., liberal and universal in scope. A relatively new parish—the congregation formed in 1990 and finished building its remarkable church four years later—Santa María de la Paz has grown 10-fold from some 200 families that met in the gymnasium of nearby Piñon Elementary School for Sunday to more than 2,200 registered households from Santa Fe's fast-growing, suburban southside. Today, Santa María de la Paz's parishioners—a mixture of natives and newcomers of many races, languages and ways of life—meet in a church they designed and built themselves and of which they're rightfully proud. With a gently sloping floor that leads to a center altar surrounded by pews in a horseshoe formation, the church's topography looks as if it emerged from the very earth upon which it was built. And in many ways, it has. Everything about and in the structure— its "santos" (religious images), whether carved into sculptures called "bultos" or painted on panels called "retablos;" altar; pews; tinwork baptismal font—were crafted from native materials by New Mexican artists. Santa María de la Paz is a veritable "Who's Who" of New Mexico folk art. Works by some of the finest santeros in the world—among them Charles Carrillo, Marie Romero Cash, Victor Goler, Felix Lopez, David Nabor Lucero—as well as a bronze by renowned Native American sculptor Allan Houser have found a home in the church. Each of the corbels—curlicue supports for the hefty vigas (wooden ceiling beams)—is a unique work of art carved by a parishioner.

Charismatic Christian

Calvary Chapel de Santa Fe is only 14 years old, but already it has grown to 1,800 local members, including children, making it the largest non-denominational congregation in Santa Fe. The church describes itself as "conservative charismatic"—a fundamentalist, evangelical congregation that takes the word of the Bible literally, but with a minimum of display, such as speaking in tongues or the laying on of hands.

At the other end of the charismatic spectrum is the Potter's House Christian Center, an evangelical Pentecostal church that does indeed practice spontaneous displays of faith. Services at Potter House are exuberant affairs during which people sing, clap, shout, weep, speak in tongues and perform the "laying on of hands." The church also conducts adult baptisms from time to time at either of two municipal swimming pools. One of 995 Potter's Houses throughout the United States, the Santa Fe chapter began in 1979 with 15 people. It has since grown to

Bishop Jean Lamy's chapel, now part of the Bishop's Lodge Resort, is open to the public free of charge.

Photo: courtesy of The Bishop's Lodge

a regular congregation of more than 400 members who take "spreading the gospel" to heart. The congregation is a mix of all ages and ethnicities. They attend services in a simple, prefabricated metal building with rows of padded metal chairs in front of a raised platform from which Pastor Henry Houghton preaches in English while someone simultaneously translates in Spanish and musicians play gospel songs.

Templo Betel is a Spanish Assembly of God church that attracts native Spanish speakers, many of them from Mexico and Central America. This is a fundamentalist Pentecostal church that believes in the "manifestation of the Holy Spirit" whether it arrives in the form of speaking in tongues or divine healing. Located on a busy residential street on Santa Fe's west side, Templo Betel has been in existence since the late 1930s. Pastor Facundo Benavidez has been its preacher since 1976. Membership fluctuates but averages about 65 individuals—a good thing because the church is small and humble. It only holds about 125, and then only if they're packed in tightly. Services are joyful with lots of music and singing that reflect the various Latino cultures the congregation represents.

Eckankar

Santa Fe claims about 35 members of ECKANKAR, Religion of the Light and Sound of God. They meet twice a month to read from the sacred writings of Eckankar (pronounced ECK-in-car) and to sing HU (pronounced HEW)—an ancient name for God that serves as a mantra to assist them in finding a conscious connection with ECK, or Holy Spirit. Founded in 1965 by Paul Twitchell, a Kentuckian who died in 1971, Eckankar believes in karma, reincarnation, dreams, and soul travel. Its current spiritual leader is Sri Harold Klemp, who is known as the Mahanta, or Living ECK Master.

Jewish

When Chabad Jewish Center, (505) 983-2000, set up shop in 1996 in the home of its rabbi, it brought for the first time a Chasidic Jewish presence to Santa Fe where previously only re-formed, conservative, and orthodox congregations coexisted, sharing a single synagogue—Temple Beth Shalom. While Chabad wasn't the first to alter that mold—a breakaway reform congrega-tion called Beit Tikva (see entry below) began holding services in a separate location in 1995 and the Orthodox group, Pardes Yisroel, moved out two years later—it's certainly the first local Jewish group with a highly active outreach program. Chabad, an acronym that stands for Chachma Bina Das—"wisdom," "understanding," and "knowledge"—is part of the ultratraditional Lubavitcher movement, an orthodox Jewish sect founded in 1772 in Lubavitch, Russia that studies Kabbala (the Jewish book of mysticism) and strictly adheres to Jewish law in daily life and religious practice. Chabad's goal for Santa Fe is to bring awareness, pride, and continuity to the Jewish community here and to bring spirituality and joy into their everyday practice.

Congregation Beit Tikva began in April 1995 with just a dozen families who met for services in a private home. In five months time, the congregation had more than quadrupled and started holding services at Lutheran Church of the Servant. Today, 170 families belong to this "tradi-tional reform" congregation whose services include regular Friday night readings from the Torah in English and Hebrew. Beit Tikva's founding is a natural outgrowth of Santa Fe's expanding Jewish population, which numbers between 3,000 and 4,000. Its members are largely conserva-tive Jews who had been practicing Reformed Judaism. Many came to Santa Fe in the 1960s in search of alternative spiritual paths and now want to return to their roots in a more traditional way.

Pardes Yisroel is a small Orthodox Jewish congregation that started in 1984 when a handful of families from the Reformed synagogue, Temple Beth Shalom, decided they wanted a more traditional approach to Judaism. With the help of Beth Shalom's rabbi, the group organized a minion, hired a young rabbi to be its schoolteacher, and officially declared itself Orthodox. At its height, the congregation consisted of 10 Orthodox families who, in highly unorthodox fashion, worshipped in the Reformed synagogue. While such a situation would create shock waves in other cities, it seemed perfectly natural in "The City Different." The departure of its rabbi in 1991 fractured the congregation, leaving it with just a few members. Despite the upheaval, Pardes Yisroel has regrouped and grown to about three dozen core families who bought a house on Don Diego Street in 1997 and converted it into a synagogue and school. The congregation, which describes itself as "centrist," is lay-led except during the High Holy Days and other special occasions, when visiting rabbis lead the services.

Until just a few years ago, Temple Beth Shalom was the only central place of worship for Jews in Santa Fe and was almost certainly the only synagogue in the country shared by reform, conservative, and orthodox Jews. Today, a Reformed and a lay-led conservative congregation share the temple, which is located in a largely residential area shared by a number of houses of worship as well as two museums and a repertory cinema. An orthodox minion still meets in what was the original sanctuary. Although practicing Jews have been in Santa Fe at least since the mid-19th Century, they didn't build a synagogue until 1953. During World War II, laymen conducted Sabbath services in the chapel of Bruns General Hospital, a military facility that stood where the College of Santa Fe stands today. (No one's quite sure where Jews met for Sabbath services before that time.) After the war, however, the Santa Fe Jewish Temple and Community Center collected $100 from 18 families toward the purchase of land. It hired nationally re-nowned local architect John Gaw Meem, whose signature is on a number of Santa Fe churches, to design a synagogue. The temple was dedicated in 1953, but there was no money left to furnish it. The congregation of 40 families sold raffle tickets for $100 each to pay for seats, carpeting, drapes and paving. By 1980, the congregation—now called Temple Beth Shalom— was well established with a full-time rabbi and a congregation that had quintupled in size from

27 years earlier to 200 families. It commissioned a new sanctuary from solar architect Ed Mazria, completed 12 years ago. Judging by the temple's growth—its membership currently numbers more than 350 families—another expansion is likely.

New Thought

Because of the iconoclastic nature of so many Santa Feans, it's not surprising that New Thought religions have flourished here; at least half a dozen exist in this small city. While they come in a variety of wrappings, most New Thought religions emphasize spiritual healing, the individual and the creative power of positive thought. Followers believe that constructive use of the mind will enable them to achieve freedom, power, health and prosperity. The New Thought movement began in the late 19th century on the heels of New England Transcendentalism—a literary and philosophical movement popularized by Ralph Waldo Emerson, Margaret Fuller, Henry David Thoreau, and others who believed that God is inherent in humans and in nature and that individual intuition is the highest source of knowledge. New Thought encourages individuals to have a personal relationship with God instead of one whose parameters are defined by a particular organization. Many New Thought religions have strong overtones of mysticism and/or the occult and might be considered a bridge between traditional and new age religions.

Among the New Thought groups in Santa Fe is the Church of Religious Science, an alternative religion serving those who strive for a personal relationship with God. Founded in the early 20th century by Ernest Holmes, the religion has a strong existential and humanistic base while touching on the metaphysical. Its core belief is that God is alive through an individual's thoughts

Loretto Chapel is a popular place for weddings and concerts.

Photo: Don Strel

and beliefs; that the spirit moves in each person's mind and heart. The church is a teaching and healing denomination that, like its distant cousin Christian Science, believes in healing the body through prayer. Unlike its cousin, however, it does not eschew doctors, medicine or science. The Church of Religious Science has a worldwide following, including 300 members in Santa Fe whose minister, the Rev. Bernardo Monserrat, leads Sunday services at 9:30 AM and 11 AM. Unity Church of Santa Fe is part of the Unity School of Christianity, founded in 1889 by Charles and Myrtle Fillmore of Kansas City, Missouri. Unity, whose roots lie in the New Thought movement, believes in Christian principles, spiritual values, and the healing power of prayer, though not to the exclusion of medical care. Its message is a little untraditional in that it focuses on the teachings of Jesus, not on the man himself. Members believe that if they follow the teachings of Christ, they will experience peace and joy and love right here on earth. About 150 members belong to the Santa Fe church, whose Sunday services attract up to 120 people. Services focus on applying spiritual principles to daily life. About an hour long, they are filled with song and a few minutes of silent meditation.

Symphony of Love is a tiny, evolving Santa Fe-based New Thought group founded in 1995. It describes itself as a "non-religious spiritual fellowship" that rejects institutionalism and dogma. The interfaith group has no formal membership, no board of trustees, no dues or tithes, and no church. Its main ministry is a public access cable television show called "Tao of Now" on Channel 6. Symphony of Love began in 1993 as an informal weekly study group loosely affiliated with Brooks Divinity School, part of the First Divine Science Church in Denver. They have continued meeting for in-depth discussions of spiritual literature, spending several months at a time on a portion of the Bible, for example, or the "Tao Te Ching" of ancient China. The group also offers T'ai Chi and other movement classes for a nominal fee and performs weddings, spiritual coaching, and counseling.

Protestant

Episcopalian

Episcopalians made their first official appearance in Santa Fe in 1863 with the arrival from the American northwest of the Right Rev. Josiah C. Talbot. On July 5th of that year, he administered to seven people the Holy Communion according to the Anglican rite—the first ever in the Spanish speaking Roman Catholic town. Four years later, Good Shepherd Mission was born. It became a parish in 1868 and 10 years later, at the urging of then Gov. Bradford Prince, it changed its name to Church of the Holy Faith—the literal translation for "Santa Fe."

Just as New Mexico's Spanish history is inseparable from the Catholic Church, so is its history as a territory—and eventually a state—closely linked to the Episcopal Church. Governor Bradford Prince, a chief justice of the New Mexico Supreme Court whom U.S. Pres. Rutherford B. Hayes appointed territorial governor in 1889, was chancellor of the diocese for 42 years. Governor William T. Thornton, who became governor in 1893, belonged to the church's original building committee. Thornton's law partner, T. B. Catron, elected U.S. senator in 1912, belonged to Holy Faith as did U.S. Sen. Bronson Cutting, (he served from 1927 until his death in a plane crash in 1935), who bought The Santa Fe New Mexican newspaper in 1912. It was another famous parishioner, architect John Gaw Meem, who in 1927 designed Palen Hall, named for the daughter of Episcopalian Rufus J. Palen, a territorial treasurer who became president of First National Bank in 1894. A cloister attaches the hall to the east side of the folk-Gothic stone church, built in 1882. Meem also designed a chancel and a

Roadside shrines are common in Northern New Mexico, often marking the place where a person has died in a traffic accident.

Photo: Don Strel

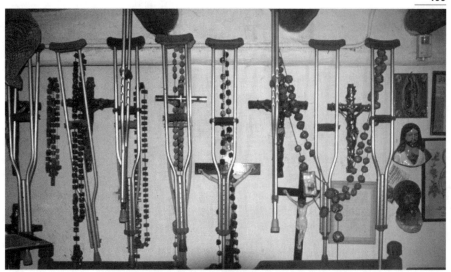

Crutches left by pilgrims at the Santuario de Chimayó.

Photo: Don Strel

sanctuary at the back of the main church in 1954. Its centerpiece is a carved "reredos" (altar screen), completed in 1945 by world-renowned Santa Fe artist Gustave Baumann, one of many east coast artists who emigrated to New Mexico in the early part of this century. Over the church's main doors is a small window with a Star of David in recognition of the Jewish merchants who donated generously to the church's building fund in 1879. Holy Faith has experienced a number of other alterations since that time, including Conkey House, completed in 1966. Conkey House contains Chapel of the Good Shepherd and Holy Faith Library, which holds more than 5,000 books and tapes, many by the current bishop, Terence Kelshaw. The collection is estimated to be worth close to $300,000. Holy Faith is a wealthy church and historically rather conservative, though women recently have begun serving at the altar. As a "medium-high" church, Holy Faith follows Rite I, a relatively austere service used by the Anglican Church when it formed in the 16th Century. Its ceremonies and liturgies are extremely formal with much ritual and spectacular vestments. Among the newest and most liberal of Santa Fe's churches, St. Bede's, was founded in 1962 as a mission of the Church of the Holy Faith (see entry above). A few dozen families composed the congregation, which met in a rented building on Cerrillos Road for two years before moving into its own newly built church on San Mateo Road. At that time, San Mateo was a dusty dirt road on the outskirts of town. Today, it's a bustling residential commuter street that meets with St. Francis Drive directly in front of St. Bede's to create one of the busiest intersections of the city. The city's growth is clearly reflected at St. Bede's, a thriving church with 210 households and a 10,000 square foot building on four-and-a-half acres. Worship centers on the Eucharist, Rite II, a less formal ritual than the older, more traditional Rite I. The atmosphere at St. Bede's tends to be informal, or what one parishioner describes as "relaxed spirituality."

Lutheran

Among the last of the mainstream Protestant faiths to send missionaries to Santa Fe were the Lutherans, who arrived in 1914 when Pastor Carl F. Schmid of Albuquerque began coming to the state capital for monthly services. That lasted about two years followed by a 12-year dormant period when Santa Fe had little, if any, Lutheran activity. But in the late 1920s, Santa Fe enjoyed a period of growth that brought more Lutherans to the small city. Services resumed irregularly but with increased frequency until 1938, when the church inaugurated regular Sunday services and officially became Immanuel Lutheran Church. With 240 baptized members,

Immanuel Lutheran (Lutheran Church-Missouri Synod) is the largest Lutheran church in Santa Fe as well as being its oldest and most conservative. It worships in a simple, Spanish-style adobe structure that architect John Gaw Meem designed in 1948. Once past the open portal and inside the church, visitors are greeted with a beautiful collection of banners depicting biblical themes hand-made by members. The altarware—candlesticks, offering plates, missal stand, etc.—are all Nambéware, a special silver-colored metal manufactured near Nambé Pueblo, about 20 minutes north of Santa Fe.

Methodist

With about 1,000 members, St. John's United Methodist Church is the largest Protestant congregation in Santa Fe. Its beginnings go back to 1850, when the Rev. E.G. Nicholson set out from his home in Independence, Missouri—not coincidentally the beginning of the Santa Fe Trail—to establish the first Methodist church in the frontier territory of New Mexico. Nicholson managed to achieve his goal in 1853, but not without vigorous opposition by the Catholic Church. Still, the congregation grew and the church flourished until 1866, when the U.S. Army withdrew from the territory, taking much of the area's Methodists with it. Those who remained persevered, slowly building up their congregation once again until, in 1881—the year after the first railroad steamed into northern New Mexico—they built their first church on West San Francisco Street. They moved twice more before 1954, when they settled into their present location on Old Pecos Trail.

Presbyterian

Presbyterians weren't the first Protestants in New Mexico—Baptists and Methodists preceded them by a number of years—but theirs was the first Protestant congregation to survive the 1866 departure of the U.S. Army, whose members accounted for the majority of the area's Protestants. It was in November 1866—more than a year after the Civil War ended—that the Rev. David McFarland of Mattoon, Illinois, held the first Presbyterian service in Santa Fe at the Palace of the Governors. Within a few months, he established the First Presbyterian Church. Shortly thereafter, the new congregation bought the ruins of an adobe chapel built in 1853-54 by Baptists, who had abandoned their mission in Santa Fe. The First Presbyterian Church restored the building—located at what is now the corner of Grant Avenue and Griffin Street—to a useful, if not terribly comfortable, condition and held its first service there in 1867. First Presbyterian would rebuild its church twice more on the same site, consecrating its present structure—a grand Pueblo-style church whose sanctuary was designed by renowned architect John Gaw Meem—in 1939.

Southern Baptist:

Baptists not only established New Mexico's first Protestant congregation, they also built the territory's first Protestant house of worship. It was a little adobe chapel at the corner of Grant Avenue and Griffin Street, completed in 1954 and purchased 13 years later by the Presbyterian Church (see entry above). The chapel followed by five years the arrival of the area's first Protestant missionary, a Northern Baptist named Hiram Walter Read who stayed in the territory for two years before taking his mission to other parts. Baptists survived Read's departure, maintaining an official presence in Santa Fe until 1866 when the American Baptist Home Mission Society—the governing board for Northern Baptists—thought its money and time would be better spent back East, where newly freed slaves were trying to make a life for themselves and their families. The Baptists that remained, most of whom were Hispanic, turned to the Presbyterian and Methodist missionaries just arriving in the territory to spread their style of Christianity. It would be another 13 years before the American Baptist Home Mission Society would resume its work in Santa Fe. In 1912, it turned its mission over to the Southern Baptist convention which, five years later, established the First Baptist Church of Santa Fe. First Baptist originally operated out of a small adobe chapel at the corner of Manhattan and Don Gaspar avenues, very close to what is now downtown Santa Fe. Later it moved to its present location on Old Pecos Trail to accommodate a growing congregation. Today, First Baptist is the largest Southern Baptist church in Santa Fe with more than 600 members.

Quakers (Religious Society of Friends)

The Santa Fe Monthly Meeting of Friends gathers every Sunday at 630 Canyon Road in what was once the home and studio of the late Olive Rush (see Attractions). A Quaker reputed to be the first female artist to move to Santa Fe, Rush left her beautiful, earthy 150-year-old house to the Friends when she died in the mid-60s. The group had only formed some 10 years earlier when a handful of people met in different homes. Today, about 75 people belong to the Santa Fe Monthly Meeting of Friends.

Established in 1647 as a reaction to the extreme Puritan formalism of the Presbyterian Church, the Religious Society of Friends places a high value on conscience, self-examination and social responsibility, embracing pacifism and left-leaning political activism. In Santa Fe, that translates into such affiliations as Concerned Citizens for Nuclear Safety, which opposes the opening of the Waste Isolation Pilot Plant—an underground nuclear waste dump near Carlsbad, New Mexico; Los Alamos Study Group, a grassroots watchdog organization that keeps tabs on Los Alamos National Laboratory and the U.S. Department of Energy; and other progressive organizations and causes.

United Church of Christ

The United Church of Santa Fe is part of the United Church of Christ (U.C.C.), a denomination that dates back to the Protestant Reformation and the pilgrims of New England. Like its parent organization, United Church of Santa Fe believes spirituality is inextricably tied to social justice. It's an activist church that has been involved in community projects such as Habitat for Humanity, Esperanza Shelter for Battered Women, the hospitality center at the Penitentiary of New Mexico, St. Elizabeth's Shelter for the needy and the Inter-Faith Council (see entry below). United Church of Santa Fe's liberal bent hearkens back to the United Church of Christ, the first Protestant church to allow women clergy and to ordain an openly gay man.

From the outside, there's nothing particularly remarkable about United Church of Santa Fe. The interior, however, is quite remarkable. Built into the "gathering room" (sanctuary) is an indoor acequia (irrigation channel), there to irrigate not the soil but the soul. It wraps like the letter "J" around the entire south wall to form a complete set of elements—earth, wind, fire and water—within and around the church. While its presence is primarily symbolic, the acequia also serves a practical function: it's part of the solar gain system that heats the building. The church's music program is very popular, featuring everything from classical to gospel to South African freedom songs.

Sikh

Some 25 miles north of Santa Fe, off the main drag that goes through Española— a small, but bustling village nestled between the Jemez Mountains and Truchas Peaks—a large golden dome marks the entrance to Hacienda de Guru Ram Dass, the "gudwara" where the Sikh community attends services Sundays at 11AM. Inside, worshippers sit with bare feet and covered heads on the floor, singing and chanting and praising God to music. After the service, which usually lasts a couple of hours, they share a free vegetarian meal. Visitors are welcome at both the service and the meal.

Española, a small city that sits both in Santa Fe and Rio Arriba counties, is headquarters for the Sikh Dharma of the Western Hemisphere. The Sikh presence in northern New Mexico began in the early 1970s, when Yogi Bhajan, the chief religious authority for Sikhs in the western hemisphere, moved to Santa Fe from Los Angeles, bought land in Española and began teaching Kundalini yoga. He soon attracted a following of converts that over the past 25 years has evolved into a community of 300 people.

Members of the Sikh community have a high profile in northern New Mexico not only because of their distinctive white garb and turbans, but also because of their involvement in such arenas as politics, business and especially health. Following the tenets of health, happy, holy organizations (3HO), Sikh Dharma in the west places holistic health high up on its list of religious virtues and some of its members operate a number of alternative healthcare clinics and yoga centers in northern New Mexico.

Other tenets of the Sikh religion, which began in India, include belief in one god who created all humans equally; eating no flesh—meat, fish, fowl, or eggs; abstinence from alcohol and drugs; not cutting or removing any body hair, hence the turbans; and wearing white as a sign to each other and the rest of the world that they are of service.

Unitarian/Universalist

The Unitarian Church of Santa Fe on West Barcelona Rd. got started in 1952 as a lay-led fellowship of about two dozen liberal-minded families from Santa Fe and Los Alamos. They were attracted to the church's doctrine of no doctrine. Rather, the Unitarian/Universalist Church, once part of the Congregationalist movement, functions by a consensus that is constantly in flux because its "eternal truths' are still emerging.

For two years after its founding, the Santa Fe Fellowship met at a private club on Garcia Street near downtown Santa Fe. In 1954, they began meeting at Temple Beth Shalom—Santa Fe's first synagogue, completed only a year earlier. There they conducted an active Sunday school which attracted so many children that the youngsters reportedly outnumbered the adults—perhaps because they learned "social graces" in addition to the usual Sunday school subjects.

This forced another move—and another and another, including one to the local Mormon church whose rules against coffee, tea, and smoking, even outside, proved difficult. Finally, in 1968, the 35-member fellowship bought a house it could barely afford, one that allegedly came with a ghost. None except a live-in caretaker family ever heard or saw him, however.

By 1979, the congregation once again outgrew its quarters and bought the Mormon Church it had rented two decades earlier, its current base of operations. It hired a full-time minister in 1981 and has since renovated and enlarged its church, located in Santa Fe's upscale South Capital area. Today, the Unitarian Church of Santa Fe, has 300 members from a variety of religious backgrounds. They're a relatively well educated and well-heeled group whose members, like their church, tend to be activists with politics that lie somewhere left of center.

Other Religious Groups

New Mexico Faith Communities Against Hate Crimes began four years ago as a coalition of about a dozen Santa Fe spiritual communities following an incident in which two gay men were harassed and beaten after a shopping trip to a local supermarket. The beating received a lot of press because of its rarity in Santa Fe, long known for its tolerance of live-and-let-live lifestyles. Gay and lesbians are welcome. Members of the Aryan Brotherhood are not. The organization, originally called Santa Fe Faith Communities Against Hate Crimes, has expanded to include 65 churches and other spiritual communities throughout the state, including 17 in Santa Fe alone. It meets 7 PM on the third Tuesday of every month at the First Presbyterian Church, which founded the organization. Members of the public are welcome to attend. In addition to operating a hate crimes hotline at (505) 992-7199. It's also working with the public schools to develop educational programs about diversity and inclusiveness.

Index

INDEX

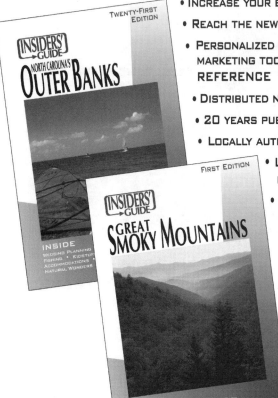